Democracy AND THE American Party System

Democracy AND THE

American Party System

AUSTIN RANNEY
University of Illinois

WILLMOORE KENDALL
Yale University

Under the General Editorship of
EARL LATHAM
Amherst College

HARCOURT, BRACE AND COMPANY · NEW YORK

To CHARLES S. HYNEMAN—
our teacher, gadfly, and friend.

Contents

Preface

This book has three main objectives: to describe the present structure and operation of the American party system; to portray its role in our total governing process; and to suggest a set of intellectual tools for appraising its value as an agency of democratic government. We have selected these objectives because our major concern is for the future of democracy in this country, because we believe that most Americans share this concern, and because we are convinced that the parties play a critical role in determining the character of our political system.

Our objectives have largely determined what we have included in the book and what we have left out, what we have emphasized and what we have mentioned only in passing. We have, for example, omitted any detailed description of various specific pressure groups; but we have described at some length the general nature of such groups, and have depicted their relations with each other, with the parties, and with public officials as an aspect of the present policy-making process in the United States. Again, we have omitted a special history of the platforms, policies, candidates, and electoral success of the major American parties, although we have referred to such matters wherever it seemed necessary to do so in order to explain why our present system operates as it does. But we have included a general account of the institutional and intellectual history of party systems in the various Western democracies, including the United States, in order to show the relationships between the development of political parties and the development of democratic government. And we have devoted two chapters to a brief history of American "third" parties, since their story is essential to an understanding of our governing parties. Moreover, we have included four chapters on the nature, problems, and institutional requirements of democracy as our basic framework for both describing and appraising the American party system as an agency of democratic government.

Our objectives have influenced not only the content of the book, but our general approach to the problems we have dealt with. In particular, they have required us to give political theory a more prominent and explicit role than it usually plays in books on the American party system.

It is impossible to write about present-day political parties without dealing with a large number of controversial political issues and personalities. In a book such as this there is always the danger of portraying—or appearing to portray—one party more favorably than the other. As a guarantee against such partisanship and favoritism, we have relied mainly on the fact that one of us is a liberal

Democrat and a Democratic precinct committeeman, while the other is a conservative Republican and an editor of a conservative journal. We believe that the fact that we have been able to agree upon what this book says about democracy and the American party system shows that it is possible for persons of very different political, economic, and social views to agree upon a description of the actual nature of the party system and its role in forming public policy without necessarily agreeing upon what that policy should be.

Like the authors of any general survey, we are deeply indebted to the many writers cited in the text from whose works we have drawn both information and insights. We also wish to express our special gratitude to Professor Earl Latham of Amherst College, who read the entire manuscript and made many helpful suggestions; to Professors Jack W. Peltason, Charles B. Hagan, Alvin W. Gouldner, and Charles M. Kneier of the University of Illinois, Charles S. Hyneman of Northwestern University, and Robert A. Dahl of Yale University, each of whom read parts of the manuscript and suggested ways of improving it; to Mrs. Lena Frances Carter, who converted our maze of bad typing and illegible handwriting into a readable typescript; and to Mrs. Frank A. Ranney, whose generous hospitality enabled us to finish the manuscript on schedule. One of the authors (W. K.) is grateful to the Foundation for Foreign Affairs for a grant that made it possible for him to undertake the research needed for his contribution to the present volume.

For whatever errors of fact and interpretation may appear in the following pages, however, the authors are solely responsible.

A. R.
W. K.

February 1, 1956

Editor's Foreword

In 1889, James Bryce said in the first edition of *The American Commonwealth* that "no native American has yet essayed the task of describing the party system of his country." Some sixty-five or so years later, Maurice Duverger could say of American writing about political parties that "studies of political parties abound." Within the short space of six and a half decades, what once did not exist now abounds; and American studies of political parties and their operations have come to occupy that central place in political science once held by legal and institutional treatments of the organs and agencies of the public government. Indeed, some will say that the study of political parties and of electoral behavior is the growing point of political science; and that it is through such study that political science can make easiest and most effective concourse with sister disciplines.

But Duverger went beyond the simple assertion that studies abound. In *Political Parties,* he said that "not one" of the American works threw any light upon such problems as the evolution of party structures, and the role they play in the State, because "all these studies are conceived within the framework of America alone, they deal with problems that are specifically American and do not refer to general questions." He then proceeded to make the desert of American provincialism bloom with cacti plucked from the deserts of European provincialism.

In liturgies, the preface is an exhortation to thanksgiving, said or sung responsively. It is enough here to point out that Ranney and Kendall have written a book that not only talks about American parties, but does so within a context of questions quite as "general" as those Duverger proposes, and indeed well beyond the marks he sets; for they are concerned with the ultimate issues of party and democracy, and not merely with the illustration of dictum by extended reference. Far from having only a local application, their conclusions are operative for democracy everywhere. If Duverger was right at the time he wrote that "not one" American work on parties considered "general questions," there is one now.

Both Bryce and Duverger noted that as late as 1850 no country in the world except the United States knew political parties in the modern sense. The development of this party system, like that of any social institution, was the product of invention working in a context of circumstances and interacting events. In our culture, the achievements of technology are afforded prestige and value superior to that of social invention; but social critics and humanists are much too modest about those whom they study. The invention of the political party in its modern sense is at least as praiseworthy as the invention of the wheel. Representative government, federalism, majority rule—all of these social and political devices are at least as consequential as the discovery of the cantilever principle, the internal-combustion engine, or the torque converter. The study of political parties is as important an aspect of a political science as the study of mechanics is of physical science; and the study of this subject is of particular interest to Americans because the modern political party first appeared here.

The genius of the American party system lies in two elements which may be characterized as *plurality* and *access*. The national parties are associations of constituent structures, with power tending to drain from the centers to the roots. Plurality, not singularity; multifarious, not unifarious—these are words that express the extent to which local diversity has been able to thrive within the narrowest consensus needed to mount and operate a vast nationally unified effort every four years. The parties exhibit in less undeviating rigor the federal principle which balances the imperatives of national unity and local diversity in the formal system of the public government. They are not massive concentrations of centralized authority. Power does not trickle down from the top but bubbles up from the bottom. A defeated presidential candidate is referred to only as the "titular" leader of the party, moving Adlai Stevenson to remark after the election of 1952 that there was no one more titular than he.

Connected with the characteristic called "plurality" is the characteristic called "access." Parties are a device for providing access to the controls of government to the groups that support them. Ranney and Kendall make the point that there is no single party system in the United States, by which they mean that there are several degrees of extent to which any given local party organization can count on success in state and congressional elections. But there is a more substantive and substantial sense in which it can be said that there are different parties. American parties are not parties of commitment but of access. They may be distinguished from each other in some considerable degree by the differential access to the controls of government they afford to some groups as against others. Thus, in the northern states, urban dwellers, factory workers, and Catholics exercise more influence upon legislation and administration through the Democratic party than they do generally through the Republican party. Rural dwellers, businessmen, and farm and Protestant organizations find access easier through the Republican party. Generalizations as broad as this may of course be refuted in many particulars: both major parties attempt to appeal to the same social and economic groups, and both parties provide representation to incompatible and even hostile groups. But in the main, the Republican party is more self-consciously based upon the business community than is the Democratic party.

A useful way of looking at parties, then, is to consider them as one of the levels of compromise and conciliation among groups that seek access to the controls of the public government. The process of adaptation is continuous. The parties help to make it viable. They make social change possible without risking the need to shoot up the opposition. The national conventions which M. Ostrogorski once thought were a "colossal travesty of popular institutions" may be more correctly understood as the place where the politicos, those brokers of the public interest (honest brokers if they do not trade on their own account), come together to mediate group concessions for purposes of the campaign. The parties, in short, are the agencies through which are made "the political decisions in which individuals acquire the power to decide [i.e., access to the governmental controls] by means of a competitive struggle for the people's vote"—to borrow language from Schumpeter.

All of this and more is explained by the authors. They do not overlook the group basis of party politics by any means, but their attention is primarily fixed upon the role of parties in a democratic system, and the compatibility of parties with the theory of democracy. All of the standard materials are covered—nominations, elections, campaign expenses, the composition of the conventions, the party machinery, voting behavior, reform of the ballot; it is all here, but there is more besides. There is the context within which all of this is relevant—the roots, trunk, branches, and twigs which show the leaves of detail to be part of a single intellectual complex. This book is not a basket but a bell; not a container of miscellanies but a single piece of intellectual workmanship, cast in a piece, and needing only the clapper of the reader's mind to call forth its harmony. The authors have amply fulfilled the implied prescription of Duverger that good books on parties "refer to general questions."

Such a work as this is its own justification. As a synthesis of research and speculation, it tells much about parties and so increases our knowledge of this important area of politics. For those who think that knowledge is good for its own sake, to know about parties is enough, no matter what one does with the knowledge. But some years ago, Robert Lynd wrote a book titled *Knowledge for What?* which spoke in critical tone about those who separate learning from doing, especially in the field of the social sciences. Now, a book about parties is not a "How to Do It" book. Readers will probably never learn how to carry a precinct by going from door to door with book in hand. But a book about parties may happily yield its readers an extra dividend—what might be called a civic dividend—if it encourages them to take an active part in party affairs.

This is not to suggest that all readers should put aside their affairs and run for public office. Politics is not a form of social security. To use the memorable phrase of a student who left his contribution if not his name, candidates run the risk of getting "diselected." But even if the reader does not take the politician's vows of poverty, probity, and patience, there is much that can and should be done. The reader may not want to run for office, but he can join a party and identify himself with it. Although the number of people who call themselves "independents" is large, some may do so out of timidity or a feeling that the label "Independent" has more prestige than "Republican" or "Democrat." There are even some like the southerner who calls himself an

Independent but who in the exercise of his independence has never found it necessary to vote Republican.

Political participation beyond voting is a form of activity that has at least two principal justifications, one personal and the other social. First, it is fun. It is a form of personal enterprise more strenuous than golf and more meaningful than bridge. It is a way of joining others in common activities. It is a way of learning and keeping fresh intellectually. It is not a game, however, despite the frequent reference to it in this fashion; it is a discipline more fateful than any game. There is also a distinction in doing politics successfully. And successful political leadership is one of the highest distinctions. The well-known magazine advertisements that show the Man of Distinction with a glass in his hand might better show him with a ballot in his hand.

The second reason for active participation in politics is less personal and more social. The Book of Job mentions two giant creatures—Behemoth, whose bones were like bars of iron and who moved his tail like a cedar; and Leviathan, who made the deep to boil like a pot. We live in an age of behemoths and leviathans, for this is a time of big business, big labor, big government, and big explosions. The management of this bigness requires organizations correspondingly large, and it is a characteristic of big organizations that they tend to fall into the hands of the few who run everything for the many who don't.

It has been a long time since we could decide issues of public policy by standing under an oak tree clashing our swords on our shields. In a society of giant organizations, the individual is easily lost. Power has a way of passing from his hands into those of others who have no mandate from him. Surely it is important to get a little closer to the controls that govern us. How do we do this? Through political activity, because politics organizes and distributes the political power in the society according to the dominant ethical and moral values by which the society lives. Each one can help to influence the distribution.

It is much better to be on the back of a behemoth than under his foot.

Earl Latham

Democracy AND THE American Party System

PART ONE

Democracy and Popular Consultation

Chapter 1

"DEMOCRACY": CONFUSION AND AGREEMENT [1]

Our primary concern throughout this book will be with the question, Is the American party system *a valuable agency of democratic government?*

There are, of course, many other questions one might use as a point of departure for describing and appraising our party system, each involving a different criterion or combination of criteria. One might ask, for example, to what extent the party system helps the government produce maximum services for minimum costs; to what extent it fosters swift, purposive, coherent, and positive governmental action; to what extent it acts as a barrier against sudden and drastic social change and rapid turnover in governmental personnel; or to what extent it contributes a dignified and statesmanlike tone to our national public life and politics.

Each of the criteria just mentioned has been used by one writer or another in appraising the American party system. Nor is there any valid objection to any of them, or any reason why each of them should not prove useful, provided we remember that the appraisal we arrive at is binding only to the extent that we actually value the quality being tested for, and that a system can merit a high mark under one criterion and a low mark under another.

In the present book we shall base our appraisal of the American party system upon a single criterion: *democracy*. We have chosen it rather than some other for the following reasons. Like most Americans, we value highly the ideal of self-government. We regard the question, "To what extent does our

[1] Parts of this chapter were published in the *Western Political Quarterly,* Vol. IV (September, 1951), pp. 430-39, and are reprinted here by permission of the editor.

total governing system provide self-government?" as the most crucial question that can be asked about it. And—but this brings us to the threshold of a
whole series of difficulties—we understand the terms "democracy" and "self-
government" to mean *exactly* the same thing.

"Democracy" Today

What difficulties are created by equating democracy and self-government?
First and foremost, the difficulty that Americans, though as we have said they
value self-government, rarely speak of it nowadays, while they speak often of
"democracy," which they also value, but do not necessarily equate with "self-
government"—or, for that matter, with *any* clearly understood and generally
accepted concrete idea. As Albert Jay Nock puts it:

> There must be as many different kinds of democracy in this country as there
> are of Baptists, or even more. . . . Press-agencies must keep half a hundred assorted
> encomiums on democracy in standing type, like Western Union's canned messages
> for Mother's Day. . . . Every time one of our first-string publicists opens his mouth,
> a "democracy" falls out; and every time he shuts it, he bites one in two that was
> trying to *get* out.[2]

Most of us, then, "believe in" democracy. We can pay a social institution
we like no higher compliment than to call it "democratic." We can cast no
greater slur upon an attitude or an institution we dislike than to brand it "undemocratic." This is not, however, a sign of democracy's triumph in the United
States; for—let us face it—Americans do *not* have any clearly understood and
generally accepted notion of what democracy *is*. Our apparent agreement upon
the desirability of "democracy" masks considerable *dis*agreement about what
the word means.

Let us take just one example: Almost everyone who writes about our
economic system seems to agree that it should be "democratic." But for an
Eric Johnston or an Edwin G. Nourse a "democratic" economic system is one
in which there is a minimum of government planning or government interference with private enterprise. For an Upton Sinclair or a Frederick L.
Schuman, on the other hand, "democracy" in the economy is large-scale government ownership and operation of the basic industries.[3] All four say (and
we have no reason to doubt their sincerity) they believe in a "democratic"

---

[2] Albert Jay Nock, "What Is Democracy?" *American Mercury,* Vol. XLI (January, 1939), p. 85.
Cf. Carl Becker's statement that democracy is a word "which connotes different things to different
people, a kind of conceptual Gladstone bag which, with a little manipulation, can be made to
accommodate almost any collection of social facts we may wish to carry about in it": *Modern Democracy* (New Haven: Yale University Press, 1941), p. 4.

[3] See Eric Johnston, "America Unlimited," *Vital Speeches,* Vol. IX (June 15, 1943), pp.
521-25; Edwin G. Nourse, "Democracy as a Principle of Business," *Yale Review,* new series,
Vol. XXXI (March, 1942), pp. 454-75; Upton Sinclair, "America's False Democracy," *American
Mercury,* Vol. XLIV (June, 1938), pp. 208-10; and Frederick L. Schuman, "Designs for Democracy," *Current History,* new series, Vol. IX (December, 1945), pp. 497-502.

economic system, but hold sharply divergent positions about just what kind of economic system we ought to have. And we could easily find countless examples of this same kind of semantic confusion about "democracy" in current discussions of all sorts of issues.

Using "democracy" to cover mutually antagonistic ends and institutions is a bad habit by no means peculiar to Americans. The spokesmen of the Soviet Union and its satellites, for example, describe their one-party elite regimes as "people's democracies"; and twenty years ago Signor Mussolini hailed his version of the corporate state as "the realization of true democracy." And Dr. Goebbels, not long after, proclaimed the Third Reich "the most ennobled form of a modern democratic state." [4]

The fact is that "democracy" the world over has become what Richard Weaver calls a "god-word." Like "truth," "justice," and "decency," it arouses such pleasant associations in the breasts of most of us that we wish to associate ourselves and our ideas with it. Only the extreme eccentric has the temerity to declare himself "against" democracy. [5]

The latter-day universal popularity of "democracy," since it ends us up equating "democratic" with "good" or "desirable," has not been an unmixed blessing. Among other things, it complicates the task of trying to decide just what democracy is—in part by tricking us into such circular reasoning as the following: "I believe in democracy (translation: when I hear the word I feel all warm inside, and wish to associate myself and my ideas with it); I favor institution X (anything from the New England town meeting to the Nazi or Soviet one-party state); *therefore,* institution X must be democratic!" We should, evidently, understand each other (and ourselves!) better if we contented ourselves with saying: "I believe in the Good; I favor institution X; therefore, institution X is good." Not that it is better for us to be confused about the "Good" than about "democracy." The point is, rather, that when we mean "good" we should say "good," not "democratic."

Another harmful consequence of our habit of equating "democracy" with "the Good" is that any attempt to give a more specific content to the term "democracy" encounters considerable resistance. Not only do a surprisingly large number of people object to the results of any particular attempt; many resent the attempt's being made at all. The present writers know from their experience in the classroom that any conception of democracy they may propose

---

[4] John D. Lewis, "The Elements of Democracy," *American Political Science Review,* Vol. XXXIV (June, 1940), p. 467. See also John R. Beery, *Current Conceptions of Democracy* (New York: Teachers College, Columbia University, 1943).

[5] It is interesting to note that the term has only very recently achieved its present respectability. Many people, even as recently as fifty years ago, regarded it as roughly synonymous with "mob rule," and thought that to label a man a "democrat" was to insult him. As we shall see below, even Thomas Paine and Thomas Jefferson, whom most of us would surely describe as "democrats," rarely used the word, and described themselves instead as believers in "republican" government. According to Charles A. Beard, the current vogue of "democracy" dates only from the 1914-1918 war: Cf. his discussion of the history of the word in the United States, in *The Republic* (New York: The Viking Press, 1946), pp. 27-33.

will be greeted by some readers with some such comment as this: "All right, that's what *you* say democracy is; but *I* say it is something else, and what right have you to say I am wrong?" They also realize that any effort to argue the relative merits of differing ideas of democracy will elicit from some readers the protest, "But you're trying to impose your definition of democracy on me, and that's undemocratic!" Nor is this belief—that it is somehow good (that is, "democratic") for democracy to mean different things to different persons—by any means confined to students. So influential and august a body as, for example, the Educational Policies Commission of the National Education Association of the United States declares:

Democracy prizes diversity. The complexity, the richness, and, to a degree, even the vagueness of the democratic tradition are counted in ordinary times as among its glories. That these qualities lead to a certain measure of disagreement is not regarded as a liability but rather as an opportunity for forging a progressive and wholesome social order.[6]

And, in the same vein, the New York *Times* editorializes: ". . . What is this democracy? . . . The essence of the answer is in the fact that the question may be freely asked and that we may disagree as to the definition."[7]

At this point it becomes necessary to ask ourselves just what function any word is supposed to perform, and whether, if we accept the attitude involved in the foregoing statements, the word "democracy" can still perform a useful function. Now, we may assume that the function of language is to enable us to communicate with each other, and that the function of particular words is to enable us to call up in the minds of listeners or readers pictures of the things about which we wish to communicate without actually producing the things themselves and dumbly pointing to them. Our ability to communicate is thus strictly dependent upon the measure of our agreement about the connection between the words we use and the things we wish them to represent.

Let us take a simple physical object as an illustration of the foregoing point: We can meaningfully communicate with each other about a "pencil" only so long as we are generally agreed that the word denotes a "slender cylinder or strip of black lead, colored chalk, etc., usually encased in wood, for writing or drawing." Suppose, however, that we are talking to A and B, and that to A a "pencil" is a four-legged animal that eats grass, moos, and gives milk for consumers other than its own offspring, while to B a "pencil" is an inflated oblate leather spheroid employed in athletic contests between two teams of eleven men each. If we say to A and B respectively, "Please bring us a pencil," the results are likely to be interesting, but not what we had hoped to produce by making the request. Nor will the resulting confusion be lessened if A, for example, indignantly responds to our objections to what he

---

[6] *The Education of Free Men in American Democracy*, Educational Policies Commission, National Education Association (Washington, 1941), pp. 25-26.

[7] Editorial, "What We Defend," New York *Times*, August 26, 1940, p. 14.

has brought, "All right, *you* call this thing I have brought you a 'cow,' but *I* call it a 'pencil,' and I have as much right to call it a pencil as you have to call it a cow!"

Of course the language problem becomes much more complicated and difficult when words are called upon to do service for other than simple physical objects. The principle involved in the use of such words, however, is exactly the same as in the simple illustration above: if we cannot agree upon what a word represents—upon, in the language of the semanticists, its "referent"—meaningful communication employing that word becomes impossible, and its continued use cannot avoid producing trouble.[8] We have only to remember, as just one illustration of this point, that at the Yalta Conference in 1945 the "big three" agreed that "democratic elections" should be held in Poland. The elections that subsequently took place seemed to Marshal Stalin to fit that description perfectly, but Mr. Churchill and the Americans regarded them as distinctly *un*democratic. The disagreement was far less over what had actually happened in Poland than over title to the adjective "democratic." The mildest of the charges that flew back and forth in consequence were those of insincerity and bad faith.

For better or worse, however, the prevailing ambiguity about the meaning of "democracy" is not likely to result in the word's being less widely used. Since that is so, it becomes incumbent upon anyone who wishes to talk seriously about "democracy" to try to assign to the word a somewhat more definite meaning than it has at present. Nor does the fact that this is hard to do—especially if we are students of politics—exempt us from the necessity of trying. For the issues that must be faced in an attempt to define democracy are precisely the issues that any community must face when it seeks to determine what kind of government it wants and tries to answer the question of fact as to whether or not its existing institutions are appropriate to such a government. That is why we turn now to consider the nature and requirements of democracy.

Exploring the Nature of Democracy

Assigning a definite and unequivocal meaning to a word as widely and loosely used as "democracy" is, we repeat, no easy task. Before making the attempt, therefore, a word is in order about the process by which we propose to set about the job.

Since "democracy" has been in use for about twenty-five hundred years, our first and most obvious task is to inquire whether there has ever been any more general agreement about its meaning than there is today. If so, what was

[8] One observer, indeed, argues that "there is a real danger that, for want of definition, for want of direction in principle and practice, the idea of democracy, and with it the idea of liberty, may become confused, and eventually subverted, in men's minds": James Hogan, *Election and Representation* (Cork, Eire: Cork University Press, 1945), p. xxxvii.

the agreed-upon definition? Having answered these questions, we must, however, remind ourselves that words grow and change through usage and that the original meaning may have altered, or even completely disappeared, in the intervening centuries. We must therefore also examine the way the term is used today, taking special account of areas of disagreement and agreement as to its proper meaning.

The final and most difficult part of the job (which will be reserved for the succeeding chapter) will take its departure from such areas of agreement as we may have found. We shall examine carefully the nature and requirements of those elements that are generally agreed to be essential to democracy, in order to determine whether other "democratic" ideas and institutions may be deduced from them. The result of such an inquiry may not be a conception of democracy which every reader will accept; but even the reader who does not accept it may feel that we have at least isolated the fundamental issues that must be faced by anyone who seeks to formulate his own definition.

"Democracy"—Its Origins and Historical Usage

Although we do not know precisely who was the first person in all history to talk about "democracy," we do know that the word first began to appear in the works of Greek writers on politics about the fifth century before Christ. It was compounded from two Greek words: *demos,* meaning "the people"; and *kratos,* meaning "authority," or *kratein,* meaning "to rule." Thus the original meaning of democracy was "rule by (or authority in) the people." It was conceived in the context of the Athenian city-state of the Age of Pericles—a community which most Greeks of the period regarded as popularly governed. While it is unnecessary for our purposes to discuss the structure of Athenian government in any detail, we may note that the basic governing body of the city was the ecclesia, an assembly of all male citizens over twenty years of age.[9] All other governing bodies—the "Council of Five Hundred" and the *heliaia,* or courts—were selected by and responsible to the ecclesia, so that Greek democracy was, in effect, direct government by an assembly of the whole body of citizens.[10]

It was this kind of government that Plato observed and condemned, and to the criticism of which a sizable portion of his most famous work was devoted. In *The Republic* he discussed five forms of government, the next-to-worst of which was democracy, or government in which the poor, as the most numerous class of society, wield power *in their own interests* (Plato believed such government automatically degenerates into a tyranny of the most per-

[9] It should also be pointed out, however, that a considerable portion of the total adult population of Athens was excluded from the class of "citizens" and therefore from any share in the city's decision-making power; neither women, slaves, nor *metics* (resident foreigners) could attend the ecclesia.

[10] A. N. Hattersley, *A Short History of Democracy* (Cambridge: Cambridge University Press, 1930), Ch. III.

suasive demagogue).[11] Plato's pupil, Aristotle, inherited his definition of—and animus against—democracy, but toyed speculatively with the idea of a democracy founded on respect for law, and put it down as a better form of government than tyranny or oligarchy.[12]

In general, traditional political theory, under the influence of Plato's and Aristotle's terminology, has used a threefold classification of the possible forms of government: *monarchy,* in which ultimate governmental power resides in one person; *aristocracy,* in which power resides in a small group of persons; and *democracy,* in which power resides in all the members of the community. And, again following the Greeks, traditional political theory has always associated the third of these forms with majority rule, and in doing so has appealed to roughly the following logic: Democracy vests ruling power in all the members of the community; often, however, issues arise that divide the community into a majority and a minority; and when this happens the democratic rule is for the majority's view to prevail over that of the minority.[13]

Through the two thousand years after the Greeks, "democracy" received, in general, much less attention from political theorists than the former had given it; but when the word was used at all it seems, by and large, to have retained its original meaning. One at a time, however, a number of tributary ideas joined the general stream of democratic thought, and each deserves at least passing notice here. The Stoic philosophers contributed the idea of the basic equality of human beings and of their right to decent treatment (note, however, that they did *not* elaborate this notion into an assertion of the desirability of government *controlled* by the people). The Roman Republic developed the beginnings of representative institutions, and the citizens of Rome had at least the nominal right to override resolutions of the Senate.[14]

During the Middle Ages there arose such quasi-representative bodies as the Anglo-Saxon Witenagemot and the later Norman-English "High Court of Parliament"; but they represented the "great estates of the realm" rather than the people, and were, therefore, very remote from the Greek conception of democracy. There were, to be sure, some self-governing towns which approximated the Athenian town-meeting model, but the predominant form of government in medieval Europe was the feudal contractual monarchy. Such a document as the Magna Carta (1215) thus resulted from an effort on the part of the nobility to hold the king to the feudal contract rather than from an intent to establish popular sovereignty;[15] and the characteristically feudal and

---

[11] Plato, *The Republic,* translated by Benjamin Jowett (New York: The Modern Library, 1937), Bk. VIII, especially pp. 308-12. See also Ernest Barker, *The Political Thought of Plato and Aristotle* (London: Methuen and Company, 1906), pp. 182-83.

[12] Aristotle, *Politics,* translated by Benjamin Jowett (Oxford: Clarendon Press, 1908), Bk. IV, Chs. 3-8. See also Barker, *op. cit.,* pp. 308, 314, 446-59.

[13] Cf. Willmoore Kendall, *John Locke and the Doctrine of Majority-Rule* (Urbana: University of Illinois Press, 1941), pp. 11-13.

[14] Cf. Hattersley, *op. cit.,* Ch. IV.

[15] Cf. *ibid.,* Ch. V.

medieval idea that the monarch has only limited power, though finally expanded by such writers as Marsiglio of Padua (c. 1270-1343) and Nicholas of Cusa (1401-1464) into the assertion of the right of the subjects to overthrow an unworthy prince, had little in common with either Greek or modern notions of self-government.[16]

The Renaissance and Reformation witnessed the breakdown of the universal spiritual authority of the Roman Catholic Church and the destruction of the system of decentralized and fragmented public power known as feudalism. A new form of political community made its appearance—the nation-state, which claimed and exercised unlimited power over all the persons within its geographical and political boundaries. Jean Bodin in 1576 provided a name for this unlimited power—*sovereignty;* and he declared that the presence somewhere in a community of such a final power to make decisions is what makes that community a "state" and sets it apart from all other social groups [17] —an idea that has become central to most subsequent political thought, democratic or otherwise. The early leaders of the Reformation, Martin Luther and John Calvin, both supported absolute monarchy as the proper location of this sovereign power; but their notion of "every man his own priest" was extended by some of their Protestant successors into doctrines of religious freedom—*and* popular control of government. In fact, as will be pointed out in the next chapter, one of the greatest germinators of modern democracy was the congregational organization of certain Protestant churches. But in the Reformation and Renaissance, as during the Middle Ages, the word "democracy" was rarely used, and when it was, it retained its classical meaning.

The milieu from which modern ideas of democracy emerged was the pivotal struggle in seventeenth-century England between king and Parliament. When the century opened, the dominant political ideal in England was that of the "divine right of kings," as expounded by, among others, James I in his *Trew Law of Free Monarchies* (1598). At its close, the supremacy of Parliament had been established, and the first great classic of modern democratic thought had emerged: John Locke's *Second Treatise on Civil Government* (1690). Not all the groups opposed to the Stuarts held democratic ideas, but some of them, particularly James Lilburne and the "Levelers," adopted positions which, while they had little impact on current events, later deeply affected the development of the democratic ideal.

Most students of democratic thought agree that the foundations of the modern conception of and case for democracy were laid in the writings of John Locke, Jean Jacques Rousseau, Thomas Paine, and Thomas Jefferson. It therefore seems particularly important to see how they used the word and what they meant by it. Locke, for one, carried on the familiar monarchy-

---

[16] Cf. Otto von Gierke, *Political Theories of the Middle Age,* translated by F. W. Maitland (Cambridge: Cambridge University Press, 1900).

[17] In his *Six livres de la république.*

aristocracy-democracy classification of the forms of government and identified democracy with popular sovereignty and majority rule:

> The majority having, as has been showed, upon men's first uniting into society, the whole power of the community naturally in them, may employ all that power in making laws for the community from time to time, and executing those laws by officers of their own appointing, and then the form of the government is a perfect *democracy.* . . .[18]

Unlike some of his successors, therefore, Locke did not restrict democracy to direct government in a face-to-face assembly of all the people; he believed rather that so long as governmental power ultimately resides in all the people, and all decisions are made by officers responsible to the majority, such a government is a democracy.[19]

Rousseau turned the traditional classification of forms of government to his own purposes, and made of "democracy," not a form of government in the usual sense of the term, but a way of organizing administration. A democracy was, for him, an administration in which all or most of the citizens are "magistrates," i.e., officeholders. Thus:

> No real democracy—taking this term in its most rigorous sense—ever existed, and none ever will exist. . . . A people constantly assembled to dispatch public business is impossible to imagine. . . .[20]

The kind of political constitution Locke had talked about Rousseau called, contemptuously, "representation." [21]

Paine, like Rousseau, thought of democracy as direct popular rule, but did not equate rule with mere administration. He distinguished between democracy and representative government; but, unlike Rousseau, he had no quarrel with representation, and believed that a representative republic retains all the essential characteristics of democracy, enabling them to be extended over a considerable area and among a large population:

> Simple democracy was society governing itself without the use of secondary means. By ingrafting representation upon democracy, we arrive at a system capable

---

[18] John Locke, *Second Treatise on Civil Government* (London: Everyman's Library), Ch. X, p. 182. Italics added. Montesquieu also took Locke's view of the nature of democracy: "When the body of the people is possessed of the supreme power, it is called a democracy. When the supreme power is lodged in the hands of a part of the people, it is then an aristocracy": *The Spirit of the Laws,* translated by Thomas Nugent (New York: The Colonial Press, 1900), Bk. II, Ch. 2, p. 8.

[19] We remind our readers that here, as throughout this brief history of the usage of "democracy," we are not concerned with the *total* position of Locke or of any of the other "classical" democratic thinkers about what is desirable in government. Our sole concern is with their definition and use of the term "democracy." In the next chapter we shall consult their writings as they bear upon the problem of what is involved in a government in which "all" rule.

[20] Jean Jacques Rousseau, *The Social Contract,* translated by Willmoore Kendall (Chicago: Henry Regnery Co., 1954), Bk. III, Ch. IV, p. 73.

[21] *Ibid.,* Bk. III, Ch. V, pp. 60-61.

of embracing and confederating all the various interests and every extent of territory and population. . . .[22]

The term both Paine and Jefferson usually employed to describe the kind of government they favored was "republican." To Paine this seems to have meant a *res-publica*—a government which settles the affairs of the public in their best interests:

> Republican government is no other than government established and conducted for the interest of the public, as well individually as collectively. It is not necessarily connected with any particular form, but it most naturally associates with the representative form. . . .[23]

Jefferson, though he used the term "republican" in this sense, seems to have thought of it as inseparable from representative government. He almost never used the term "democracy"; when he did do so, however, he too equated it with direct government by the people:

> [The Greeks] knew no medium between a democracy (the only pure republic) and an abandonment of themselves to an aristocracy or a tyranny independent of the people. . . . The full experiment of government democratical, but representative, was and still is reserved for us.[24]

In the nineteenth century, debate over the merits of democracy engaged the attention of political theorists in most Western nations beyond any other political problem, and in all of these nations there arose movements whose avowed objective was the rapid democratization of existing governmental institutions.[25] Yet the avowed advocates of democracy, such as John Stuart Mill, and its opponents, such as Thomas Carlyle, John Ruskin, and Sir Henry Sumner Maine, all agreed with the classical definition of democracy as a form of government which, in contrast with monarchy and aristocracy, involves rule by *all* the people.[26]

[22] Thomas Paine, *The Rights of Man*, Part II, Ch. III, in *The Life and Works of Thomas Paine,* edited by M. M. Van der Weyde (New Rochelle, N. Y.: Thomas Paine Historical Association, 1925), Vol. VI, pp. 272, 266-67, 271.

[23] *Ibid.,* Vol. VI, p. 268.

[24] Letter to Isaac H. Tiffany, August 26, 1816, in *The Writings of Thomas Jefferson,* edited by H. A. Washington (Washington, D. C.: Taylor and Maury, 1854), Vol. VII, p. 32. John Taylor of Caroline defined democracy as "a nation exercising personally the function of government," and concluded that "election" (i.e., representation) "filtered [it] of its evil moral qualities": *An Inquiry into the Principles and Policy of the Government of the United States* (Fredericksburg: Green and Cady, 1814), p. 79. The *Federalist* papers also took this view of democracy; thus Madison wrote in the Tenth Paper: ". . . a pure democracy [is] a society consisting of a small number of citizens, who assemble and administer the government in person . . .": *The Federalist,* edited by Max Beloff (New York: The Macmillan Company, 1948), p. 45. For John Adams' similar view, see Correa M. Walsh, *The Political Science of John Adams* (New York: G. P. Putnam's Sons, 1915), pp. 23-25.

[25] Examples are Jacksonian Democracy in the United States, the Chartist movement in England, and the various revolutionary movements of 1848 in continental Europe.

[26] John Stuart Mill, *Representative Government* (London: Everyman's Library), p. 256; Henry Sumner Maine, *Popular Government* (London, 1886). For Carlyle's and Ruskin's con-

We conclude this brief survey of the history of the term "democracy" by noting that the present-day confusion and disagreement about its meaning is almost entirely a product of the period following the 1914-1918 war. Since this period has also seen "democracy" achieve the well-nigh universal popularity referred to above, the conclusion seems justified that one of these developments is related to the other. So long, that is to say, as it was at least as respectable to be "anti-democratic" as to be "pro-democratic" (as it certainly was before this century), the term could and did retain a considerable degree of precision; but now that everyone apparently feels that he must "believe in" democracy, the word is called upon (in the fashion noted at the beginning of this chapter) to do service for all manner of dissimilar ideas and institutions. "Democracy's" present vagueness would therefore appear to be the product of its popularity.

Thus during most of its history "democracy" possessed a reasonably precise and generally adhered-to definition; and it is only in our own time that it has come to mean many different things. Just what vagueness it has acquired and what precision it still retains is the subject of our next inquiry.

Areas of Disagreement

Simply to list each of the apparently conflicting current definitions of democracy would be the task of a lifetime. Happily, however, its performance is unnecessary, since these definitions are for the most part variations upon a few fundamental themes. Most of them, that is to say, are capable of being distributed into one or another of a few basic categories, each of which will bring together writers who, for all their differences in emphasis, agree on some one of the issues involved. The most important of these issues are: (1) that between those who regard democracy as merely a form of government, and those for whom it is also a social system, an economic system, or a "way of life" as well; and (2) that between those who identify democracy with majority rule, and those who refuse to do so. Without exhaustively going into all the issues involved, there follow brief summaries of the various positions taken on these questions.

ceptions of democracy, see the relevant chapters in Benjamin E. Lippincott, *Victorian Critics of Democracy* (Minneapolis: University of Minnesota Press, 1938). Of the prominent nineteenth-century writers on democracy, only Alexis de Tocqueville seems to have strayed very far from the classical definition. In his famous *Democracy in America* he never presents a clear and definite picture of what he means by the term, but he seems to identify it with equality—social and economic as well as political—plus rule by popular majorities. Thus, in the preface, he writes that when there is general equality of rank, property, and power, "society becomes democratic, and the empire of democracy is slowly and peaceably introduced into institutions and customs": *Democracy in America,* translated by Henry Reeve, edited by Phillips Bradley (New York: Alfred A. Knopf, 1945), Vol. I, p. 9; see also p. 14.

DEMOCRACY AS A WAY OF LIFE

The basic question at stake in the first issue identified above is whether democracy should be regarded as a purely *political* concept. Is democracy simply a way of making governmental decisions? Does the claim of any given governmental decision to the label "democratic" depend solely upon the nature of the process by which it was arrived at, or does it also depend upon its content? A very large and eminent group of contemporary writers say that democracy necessarily involves more than just universal suffrage and elected representatives; it also requires that the voters and their representatives adopt certain kinds of social and economic policies. Probably the greatest spokesman of this point of view is the philosopher John Dewey, who regards democracy as "a name for a life of free and enriching communion," and who declares:

> The idea of democracy is a wider and fuller idea than can be exemplified in the state even at its best. To be realized it must affect all modes of human association, the family, the school, industry, religion.[27]

Since Professor Dewey is also the intellectual father of the dominant school of contemporary American educational philosophy, it is not surprising that his disciples in that field also follow (and even enlarge upon) his conception. Thus the Educational Policies Commission of the National Education Association says of democracy:

> It is a form of government; it is a kind of economy; it is an order of society; it is a way of life; it is all of these things together. But it is more. . . . Democracy . . . is a great social faith which, in response to the yearnings and struggles of many races and peoples, has been developing through the centuries.[28]

Some who take this view argue that, although democracy admittedly was once thought of as a purely political concept, it has grown and expanded so that today it includes social, economic, and ethical ideas, and thus is, in Professor C. E. Merriam's words, "a spirit, an attitude toward our fellow-men."[29] Or, as Professor T. V. Smith puts it, "the tendency of the noun 'democracy' to pass into the adjective 'democratic,' as descriptive of the kind of person easy to live with, well illustrates this ethical potential of a term historically political."[30]

[27] John Dewey, *The Public and Its Problems* (New York: Henry Holt and Company, 1927), p. 143.

[28] *Op. cit.,* pp. 32-33. See also Carrol D. Champlin, "Democracy—Another Definition," *School and Society,* Vol. LIV (September 20, 1941), pp. 220-22.

[29] C. E. Merriam, *What Is Democracy?* (Chicago: University of Chicago Press, 1941), p. 92.

[30] T. V. Smith, *The Democratic Way of Life,* rev. ed. (Chicago: University of Chicago Press, 1939), p. 12. For other American expositions of this point of view, see George S. Counts, *The Prospects of American Democracy* (New York: The John Day Company, 1938); F. L. Bacon, *American Democracy* (Chicago: Denoyer-Geppert Co., 1950); Charles A. Beard, "Essentials of Democracy," *School and Society,* Vol. L (August 19, 1939), pp. 228-35; and Dorothy Thompson, *Dorothy Thompson's Political Guide* (New York: Stackpole Sons, 1938), pp. 31-32. For an eloquent statement of this position by an Eastern philosopher-statesman, see Pandit Jawaharlal

It is this view of the nature of democracy that evidently induces Julian Huxley, for example, to argue that, despite the fact that Great Britain's social system is admittedly less "democratic" than that of the United States, she is more "democratic" than America in other respects. For one thing, he says, "our Civil Service is appointed by the democratic system of examination [and] the undemocratic 'spoils system' has never played the part it has in the United States." And for another, Britain's labor relations are more "democratic" than those in America, since Britain's strikes are less violent, and she has plenty of unions, collective bargaining in abundance, and no vigilante strike-breaking organizations.[31] And Professor Schuman adopts a similar view when he compares America's "political democracy" with the Soviet Union's "economic democracy," and concludes that each nation should try to achieve a combination of the two kinds of democracy.[32]

DEMOCRACY AS A FORM OF GOVERNMENT

The disciples of Professor Dewey recognize that, in the words of one of them, there are still a few "conservatives who treat with a certain aristocratic superciliousness any attempt to broaden the meaning of democracy by giving it the wider significance of a social program and a humane ideal." [33] Among the more prominent of these "conservatives" are Lord Bryce, Ernest Barker, Carl Becker, J. A. Corry, E. M. Sait, R. M. MacIver, and Sidney Hook. Ernest Barker put the position of this group very succinctly when he wrote:

Democracy does not mean the well-being or prosperity of the people, but a method of the *government* of the people; and a democratic measure is one which originates from, or tends to promote, such a method of government—not a measure which tends to increase the amount, or rectify the distribution, of prosperity or well-being.[34]

Hence this group believes that the claim of any decision to be labeled "democratic"—whether in economic, social, or other matters—depends upon *how it was made,* not upon its *content.*

Nehru's definition of democracy as "not only political, not only economic, but something of the mind . . . a mental approach applied to our political and economic problems": *Saturday Review of Literature,* Vol. XXXIV (April 14, 1951), pp. 14-15.

[31] Julian Huxley, "Two Versions of Democracy," *Living Age,* Vol. CCCLX (March, 1941), pp. 48-52. For a comparison of British and American "democracies" in almost these same terms, see David McCord Wright, *Democracy and Progress* (New York: The Macmillan Company, 1949), pp. 25-26.

[32] *Op. cit.,* pp. 497-502.

[33] I. B. Berkson, *Preface to an Educational Philosophy* (New York: Columbia University Press, 1940), p. 57.

[34] Ernest Barker, *Reflections on Government* (London: Oxford University Press, 1942), p. 314, n. 1. See also James Bryce, *Modern Democracies* (New York: The Macmillan Company, 1924), Vol. I, pp. 20, 23; Becker, *op. cit.,* pp. 6-7; J. A. Corry, *Elements of Democratic Government* (New York: Oxford University Press, 1947), pp. 14-15; Edward M. Sait, *Political Institutions: A Preface* (New York: D. Appleton-Century Co., 1938), p. 424; Robert M. MacIver, *The Web of Government* (New York: The Macmillan Company, 1947), pp. 206-08; and Sidney Hook, *New York Times Sunday Magazine,* March 16, 1947, pp. 10, 48-49.

This brings us to the second major area of disagreement we have to consider: that which relates to the question, Does democracy demand that bare popular majorities be able to take any action they see fit? Or must the right of the majority to rule be "limited" in some fashion?

DEMOCRACY AS "UNLIMITED" MAJORITY RULE

Since so much of the debate about the nature of democracy revolves about the question of the status of "majority rule," it seems desirable at this point to define with some care just what that term means. Anyone who reads carefully the current literature about "majority rule" soon discovers that the term is frequently used to denote three quite different things, among which most of us fail to distinguish. These are:

(1) What we shall henceforth call the *"majority principle."* This is a *rule of action,* which any organized body may adopt, whereby all the body's decisions will be made by, at the very least, 50 per cent plus one of its members. One example of the majority principle is the rule under which the United States Supreme Court permits any five of its nine members to lay down an authoritative and binding decision for the whole Court, in the teeth of objections from the remaining four.

(2) What we shall call the *"doctrine of majority rule."* It holds that the *ideal* government of any political society is one in which all political decisions represent the wishes of at least 50 per cent plus one of all its members.

(3) What we shall call *"majority-rule democracy."* This is the *form of government* which exists in any community where the "doctrine of majority rule" is accepted and in full operation.

In these terms the position of the "absolute majoritarians" is easy to state. They hold that only a "majority-rule democracy," in the above sense, has any legitimate claim to the term "democracy." Some leading exponents of this point of view are Lord Bryce, Hugo Krabbe, and Hans Kelsen; and the authors of this book have from time to time written in its defense.[35]

DEMOCRACY AS "LIMITED" MAJORITY RULE

Against the advocates of "unlimited" majority rule are arrayed a group of writers who hold that an essential characteristic of true democracy is the possession by all its citizens of certain "rights," which *no* governmental agency may violate, even in response to the wishes of a popular majority. There are, of course, many listings of such rights. For many years the first eight amendments to the Constitution of the United States contained the most generally agreed-upon catalog, but the most recent (and most complete, to say the least) recital is the Universal Declaration of Human Rights issued by the United

[35] Cf. Bryce, *op. cit.,* Vol. I, pp. 57-58; Hugo Krabbe, *The Modern Idea of the State,* translated by George H. Sabine and Walter J. Shepard (New York: D. Appleton and Co., 1922), pp. 72 ff.; Hans Kelsen, *Vom Wesen und Wert der Demokratie* (Tübingen, 1928); and Willmoore Kendall, "Prolegomena to Any Future Work on Majority Rule," *Journal of Politics,* Vol. XII (November, 1950), pp. 694-713.

Nations.[36] To some members of this group of writers these individual rights are so essential that they define democracy solely in terms of such rights, without any reference at all to majority rule or even to popular control of government. Thus General George C. Marshall, when called upon at the Moscow Conference of 1947 to contrast the American conception of democracy with that talked about by the Soviet leaders, said:

> I realize that the word "democracy" is given many interpretations. To the American Government and citizens it has a basic meaning. We believe that human beings have certain inalienable rights—that is, rights which may not be given or taken away. They include the right of every individual to develop his mind and soul in the ways of his own choice, free of fear and coercion—provided only that he does not interfere with the rights of others.[37]

Most members of this school, however, hold that democracy means both majority rule *and* individual (or minority) rights. As they argue it, in a true democracy certain areas of individual freedom—such as those listed in our national Bill of Rights—are set aside and removed from the power of *any* kind of government, popularly controlled or otherwise. In all *other* areas, however, the government of a democracy should do anything 50 per cent plus one of the people want it to do.[38] Thus, they declare, *limited* majority rule is the essence of democracy: "limited" by the inalienable rights of the citizen against abridgment by any governmental agency—"limited," if you will, by the fact that the majority may not destroy the conditions of political freedom by which it became a majority in order to prevent some present minority from becoming a future majority. Some writers describe this kind of government as "constitutionalism" or "constitutional democracy"; [39] but most of them are content to call it simply "democracy," prefaced by no qualifying adjective.

This is perhaps the most significant area of disagreement in the current discussion of the nature of democracy, and we intend to explore the whole problem thoroughly in the next chapter.

Areas of Agreement

Despite the present confusion and disagreement about the nature of democracy indicated by the foregoing, we need not abandon all hope of achiev-

[36] Universal Declaration of Human Rights, approved by the General Assembly of the United Nations on December 10, 1948; U.N. Document A/811, December 16, 1948.

[37] New York *Times,* March 15, 1947, p. 1.

[38] Cf. Laurence Stapleton, *The Design of Democracy* (New York: Oxford University Press, 1949), p. 67; Carl J. Friedrich, *Constitutional Government and Politics* (New York: Harper and Brothers, 1937); J. Roland Pennock, *Liberal Democracy: Its Merits and Prospects* (New York: Rinehart and Company, Inc., 1950); Robert M. MacIver, *op. cit.,* pp. 197-205; and Herbert McClosky, "The Fallacy of Absolute Majority Rule," *Journal of Politics,* Vol. XI (November, 1949), pp. 637-54.

[39] Cf. Beard, "Essentials of Democracy," *School and Society,* pp. 233-34; Roscoe Pound, "Law and Federal Government," in *Federalism as a Democratic Process* (New Brunswick, N. J.: Rutgers University Press, 1942), pp. 7-9, 27-28.

ing some more definite understanding of what it involves. Amid the jumble of the current discussions of the problem there stand out certain propositions that command general assent. If we can identify these propositions, it will at least then be possible to discover the extent of these areas of agreement and to learn what minimum common ground exists as a starting point for any future exploration of the problem. In this light, therefore, we now consider three observations upon the nature of democracy that seem to be agreed upon by almost all who talk or write about it.

POLITICAL EQUALITY

One characteristic that most persons regard as essential to democracy is political equality. A familiar way of describing this trait is "one man, one vote," which we take to mean that in a democracy political power must be equally shared by all its citizens, and no man should have any larger a share than any other man. To be sure, such a reputedly democratic thinker as John Stuart Mill advocated plural voting, with extra votes for those citizens with a high degree of formal education; [40] but most of us today feel that (entirely aside from the separate question of whether such a system would be *good*) plural voting would create a politically privileged class, a kind of elite of the (formally) educated—and that this would smack of what men have always called "aristocracy" or "oligarchy," and therefore not be consonant with what most of us agree democracy requires.

"Political equality" in this sense does not, of course, mean equality of income or social prestige or formal education. It means only the right of each citizen to count as one in the decision-making process of the community. Most people agree that, thus defined, it is an essential characteristic of any genuine democracy.

GOVERNMENTAL RESPONSE TO THE POPULAR WILL

Most of us also agree that in a democracy the popular will should be faithfully translated into governmental action. Or, to put the same idea in other words, a democratic government should do whatever the people want it to do and should not do anything they object to. The Communists (taking them at their word) apparently regard democracy as doing whatever is best for the people, and believe that an elite, the Communist Party, is better qualified than the people themselves to decide what *is* best for the people. They seem to believe, that is to say, that democracy is government *for* the people, but not government *by* the people. In the West, on the other hand, most of us believe that the people should themselves decide what is best for them, and that democracy necessarily is government *by* the people. We subscribe to what Jefferson wrote to his aristocratic friend, Dupont de Nemours:

[40] Mill, *op. cit.*, Ch. VIII.

We of the United States, you know, are constitutionally and conscientiously democrats. . . . [We believe that society is one of man's] acquisitions which he has a right to regulate and control, jointly indeed with all those who have concurred in the procurement, whom he cannot exclude from its use or direction more than they him. . . . We both consider the people as our children, and love them with parental affection. But you love them as infants whom you are afraid to trust without nurses; and I as adults whom I freely leave to self-government.[41]

RULE BY THE MAJORITY INSTEAD OF THE MINORITY

In one sense at least, most people agree that majority rule is an essential characteristic of democracy. The writers we have previously discussed, who object to "unlimited" majority rule, certainly do not think of themselves as advocating *minority* rule as more democratic. Their position is rather that in a true democracy *no* governmental agency may have the power to abridge certain minority rights. It is thus an assertion of the necessary limitation of the power of government itself in a democracy; they do not regard it as an assertion as to how the decisions of a democratic government should be made. Most of them would heartily agree with the proposition that in a democracy, *if* the government has the legitimate power in any given matter to act *at all* (which, they say, it has in all matters where the rights of individuals and minorities are not abridged by such action), it should do whatever the majority of the members of the community want it to do. In short, all we are saying here is that no one argues that *minority* rule is essential to or even consonant with democracy.

All this, however, tells us nothing about the kind of governing institutions that would satisfy those who agree to majority rule in the restricted sense just explained. The same thing is true of the two other areas of agreement: we are left in the dark as to the details of what democracy involves. Without at least this much agreement, however—that democracy must include political equality, a government responsive to the popular will, and majority rule rather than minority rule—the word "democracy" would be worse than useless, and our only recourse would be to discard it and to use in its stead a series of new words, invented *ad hoc* for the purposes of our discussion. Fortunately no such drastic procedure is needed, and "democracy" may yet be converted into a term that refers to something reasonably definite instead of serving, as at present, merely to mask confusion and disagreement. These areas of agreement offer, at the very least, a promising foundation and starting point for the toilsome but imperative task of searching for a more meaningful conception of democracy than we now have.

[41] Letter to Pierre Dupont de Nemours, April 24, 1816, in *Correspondence between Thomas Jefferson and Pierre Samuel Dupont de Nemours,* edited by Dumas Malone (Boston: Houghton Mifflin Company, 1930), pp. 181-84.

Chapter 2

BASIC PRINCIPLES
FOR A MODEL
OF DEMOCRACY

The preceding chapter reveals some of the obstacles that confront our effort in this book to appraise the American party system as an agency of *democratic* government. Prominent among them is the widespread disagreement among Americans about just what democratic government is—a disagreement stemming largely from the powerful emotional appeal of the word "democracy" to most Americans and their consequent desire to identify "democratic" government with their varying conceptions of *good* government.[1]

In the present chapter, nevertheless, the authors will offer their own conception of the basic principles of democracy; and in Chapter 3 they will present the outlines of a "model" or "ideal" democratic government which, in their opinion, most fully realizes those principles in the context of the modern nation-state. They undertake these tasks because of their conviction that one can appraise the American party system—or any other institution—as an agency of democratic government only in the light of some kind of model.

Let us therefore begin our inquiry by asking what a "model" is, and how it can and cannot be usefully employed in social and political analysis.

The Nature of Models

EXISTING GOVERNMENTS AND "FORMS" OF GOVERNMENT

When we reflect upon the nature of the governments that actually exist in the world today and upon the way in which men customarily think and talk about them, one of the first things we notice is that all existing govern-

---

[1] Cf. this judgment by a distinguished pair of logicians: ". . . The emotional associations and overtones of words may often prevent a clear apprehension of the issues at stake. This is particularly true in the social sciences. Words like 'democracy,' 'liberty,' 'duty,' have a powerful emotive function; they are frequently used as battle cries, as appeals to emotions, and as substitutes for thought. Many of the disputes . . . which undoubtedly arise from a conflict of emotional attitudes, would assuredly disappear if the precisely defined equivalents were substituted for these words": Morris R. Cohen and Ernest Nagel, *Introduction to Logic and Scientific Method* (New York: Harcourt, Brace and Company, 1934), p. 232.

ments are alike in some respects. For example, they all make rules for the conduct of their peoples, and they all use force to punish persons who disobey the rules. On the other hand, no two governments are exactly alike in *every* respect; each one, in fact, differs considerably from all the others. Yet despite the fact that all governments are somewhat alike but each government differs materially from all others, most men believe (and have long believed) that governments can usefully be classified as to their *form*—that they can legitimately be described, for example, either as "monarchies," "aristocracies," and "democracies," or as "democracies" and "dictatorships."

Now just what do we mean when we talk about the "form" of governments—when, for example, we call the United States and Great Britain "democracies," and the Soviet Union and Red China "dictatorships"? Surely we do not mean thereby that the first two are exactly alike; nor do we mean that they are completely unlike the latter two. We mean rather that *in certain respects* the first two are alike, and that in those particular respects they are unlike the latter two. In other words, in deciding whether an existing government is a democracy, we are not concerned with *all* its characteristics; we look at only *part* of them—the part which, in our opinion, determines whether or not any government is a democracy. But how do we decide which of its many parts to base our judgment on? There is only one possible answer: We decide in terms of a mental picture of the *essential* nature of democracy—in terms of a model of democracy.

MODEL GOVERNMENTS AND ACTUAL GOVERNMENTS

What is a "model of democracy" in this context, and how does it differ from the actual governments men generally call "democratic"? A *model* of democracy, as we shall henceforth use the term, is a mental picture of a *type* or *kind* of government stripped of all its nonessential and irrelevant characteristics—a government reduced to its differentiae, i.e., to the *principles of organization* that make it different from a "monarchy" or an "aristocracy," each of which in turn has its basic principles of organization and its model.

As a means of grasping the difference between a model of a government and an actual government, let us look for a moment at how models are used in economics. In speaking of the model "market economy," Wilhelm Röpke warns that

we must make a sharp distinction between the *principle* of a market economy as such—bound as it is to no historical period but representing rather one of the permanent elements out of which an historical economic order can be put together—and the *actual development* which during the nineteenth and twentieth centuries has led to the historical form of market economy. One is a philosophical category [in our terminology, a "model" economy], the other an historical individuality; one is a simple structural element [i.e., a carefully worked-out principle of organization], the other an historical and therefore unique, a non-recurrent *compound* of economic, social, legal, political, moral and cultural elements, a compound which, in this highly complicated mixture of ingredients, never occurred before and will never recur hereafter.[2]

Our point is that anyone who talks about the "form" or "type" of existing governments—and this includes most of us—is speaking, consciously or unconsciously, in terms of models. Anyone who applies the label "democratic" to an actual government or institution must in doing so appeal to a mental picture of an ideal or model democracy, which is there whether he recognizes its presence or not.

If this is true, the only choice open to the writer on democracy is this: he can leave his model implicit in his comments on existing institutions and have his readers dig it out for themselves; or he can present his model, explicitly and in as clear and straightforward a manner as possible, before he starts talking about existing institutions. The latter procedure is likely to make for better communication between writer and reader; and the purpose of the present chapter is to make clear the model we have in mind when we use the term "democracy." [3]

The Function of Models

Throughout this book we shall be examining various American institutions, and particularly those of our party system, with a view to answering two fundamental questions: What kind of government do these institutions add up to? And to what extent is this the kind of government the American people appear to want? In the course of this inquiry we shall doubtless discover that some of these institutions serve the purposes of democracy less well than others, and that the total governing system of the United States does not, therefore, correspond exactly to our model of democracy. Such a procedure

---

[2] Wilhelm Röpke, *Civitas Humana*, translated by C. S. Fox (London: William Hodge and Company, Ltd., 1948), pp. 6-7. Emphasis added. See also Röpke, pp. 7-10. Max Weber offers these illustrations of models or "ideal types": "A panic on the stock exchange can be most conveniently analysed by attempting to determine first what the course of action would have been if it had not been influenced by irrational affects; it is then possible to introduce the irrational components as accounting for the observed deviations from this hypothetical course. Similarly, in analysing a political or military campaign it is convenient to determine in the first place what would have been a rational course, given the ends of the participants and adequate knowledge of all the circumstances. Only in this way is it possible to assess the causal significance of irrational factors as accounting for the deviations from this type. The construction of a purely rational course of action in such cases serves the sociologist as a type ('ideal type') which has the merit of clear understandability and lack of ambiguity. By comparison with this it is possible to understand the ways in which actual action is influenced by irrational deviation from the line of conduct which would be expected on the hypothesis that the action were purely rational": *The Theory of Social and Economic Organization*, translated by A. R. Henderson and Talcott Parsons, revised and edited by Talcott Parsons (London: William Hodge and Company, Ltd., 1947), pp. 83-84.

[3] On the desirability of frankly and didactically presenting models in social science analysis, see Robert M. MacIver, *The Web of Government* (New York: The Macmillan Company, 1947), pp. 8, 403-04; and M. A. Girshick and Daniel Lerner, "Model Construction in the Social Sciences," *Public Opinion Quarterly*, Vol. XIV (Winter, 1950-1951), pp. 710-23.

may well disturb many of our readers—some of them to the point that they will ask in dismay, "Aren't you really saying that America is not a democracy?"

Stated in such terms, this question involves a misconception as to the sort of inquiry we are attempting, and cannot be answered Yes or No. Certainly we do not propose to compare all existing governments with our model of democracy and then label "democratic" all those governments that measure up to it in every respect, and lump together all those that do not as "undemocratic." If this were our purpose, we should have great difficulty in finding an acceptable candidate for the "democratic" category, and even some difficulty in discovering a completely eligible candidate for the "undemocratic" category.

Our model of democracy will serve rather to fix one end of a spectrum or scale, along which we can place various existing institutions and governments. The notion of the spectrum is, in fact, so basic to our whole project that we must pause to explain in some detail its nature and its relation to our model of democracy. Let us take the common word "bald" as an illustration. We could take any number of men with varying amounts of hair, some of whom we could all agree are "bald," count the number of hairs on each, and range them along a scale in the order of the number of hairs each possesses. At this point we should have a great deal of difficulty deciding just where "baldness" begins. Would we, for example, select a certain number of hairs and say that a man with only one less hair than that is "bald"? Clearly not. Or do we call "bald" only the man who has no hair at all? This certainly is not the way most of us use the word. Yet we still feel justified—and properly so—in calling the men at one end of the scale "bald" even though each one has some hair and even though the variations from man to man as we ascend the scale are minute.

We now have an example of a spectrum. We have set up a "model"—the complete absence of hair—and we have established a scale of increasing distance from the model. Along this scale any particular man can be placed according to the number of hairs he has on his head. But the scale, the measuring, and indeed any use of the term "bald" makes sense only in terms of the model that fixes one end of the spectrum. What purposes does this spectrum serve? It enables us to measure and compare individual men as to their *degrees* of baldness, and it permits us to make sense of the statement about a man, "He is getting bald"—i.e., it enables us to determine the direction of change.

So it is with our model of democracy. It will serve to fix one end of a spectrum, which, in turn, will enable us to measure the degrees of democracy of existing governments and institutions and to compare them with each other. In terms of such a spectrum—but only in terms of it—it is perfectly legitimate to call some existing governments "democracies." Thus, to return to the hypothetical question that touched off the present discussion, although the United States can hardly be placed at the democratic extreme of our spectrum, and may even be less near to our model than, say, Switzerland or Great Britain, it is nevertheless so much nearer to it than, say, the Soviet Union or Red China that we are justified in saying that *compared to* the Communist nations the United States *is* a democracy.[4]

The kind of spectrum we have been talking about, we repeat, can perform its functions only if one end of the scale has been clearly and unequivocally fixed by the construction of a model. And that model, in turn, can perform its functions only if we bear in mind at least two considerations. First, the model is a conception of the *most democratic* government possible, and not necessarily a conception of the *best* government possible. In other words, the fact that a particular person does not "believe in" such a government (that is, does not wish the actual community in which he lives to be governed in exactly that fashion) need not keep him from using the model as a purely *analytical* device in the manner described above. And second, a model of democracy is not identical with the "historic compound" of traits found in any of the existing governments that are generally called "democracies."

Constructing a Model of Democracy

In the remainder of the present chapter the authors of this book will present the basic principles on which, in their opinion, a model of democracy for the modern nation-state should be built. They believe that a fairly strong case can be made out on common-sense grounds for reserving the term "democracy" for these principles and the resulting model. But having presented the broad outlines of that case in the ensuing pages, they will press no quarrel with the reader who refuses to go along with it—provided he remembers that this is what "democracy" means wherever it is used in the rest of *this* book.

The authors urge the reader to accompany them in adopting the following point of view: The most important tasks for any student of forms of government are (a) to "isolate the alternatives" (i.e., to answer the question, What kinds of government are there, in fact or in theory, from which a people or group may choose in establishing a system for making its political decisions?); (b) to make sure we understand their differentiae (i.e., the essential, bedrock differences between them); (c) to try to bring about a situation in which we can refer first to one alternative and then to another without any danger of misunderstanding each other; and (d) to shed what light we can on what results a people may expect when it chooses one of them and passes up the others.

In other words, what matters to the United States or to any nation is the kind of government it *has*. The important thing is that each of us should have a clear idea of the kind of governing institutions we want—whether they are called "democracy" or "numbersocracy" or whatever—and that he

[4] Cf. James Bryce, *Modern Democracies* (New York: The Macmillan Company, 1924), Vol. I, pp. 47-50.

should have an accurate picture of the extent to which the institutions we actually have do or do not provide us with what he wants. And the kind of inquiry we shall make in the present chapter may help the reader to raise and answer these questions for himself.

Our point of departure for explaining our conception of "democracy" is provided by the areas of agreement about what the word means that we outlined at the end of Chapter 1.

Principles of Democracy

Most writers on democracy, whatever else they may insist must be present in order for a government to be called a "democracy," are, as we noted in the preceding chapter, committed to the view that it must exhibit the following minimum characteristics: (1) Those who hold office in it must stand ready, *in some sense,* to do whatever the people want them to do, and to refrain from doing anything the people oppose; (2) each member of the "community" for which it acts should have, *in some sense,* as good a chance as his fellows to participate in the community's decision making—no better and no worse; and (3) it must operate in terms of an understanding that when the enfranchised members of the community disagree as to what ought to be done, the last word lies, *in some sense,* with the larger number and never the smaller—i.e., the majority of the electorate and not the minority should carry the day. So much, we repeat, seems to be pretty well agreed on all sides.

One of the basic contentions of this chapter is that once one has committed himself to that much, he has committed himself to at least the broad outline of a highly meaningful conception of democratic government. Another is that this conception of democratic government, despite the presence of the words "in some sense" in the foregoing statements, leaves less room to move around in, and be "different," than is commonly supposed.

Anyone who carefully analyzes the above three minima will find that the conception as a whole breaks down into four, not three, principles. These are (a) popular sovereignty, (b) political equality, (c) popular consultation, and (d) majority rule. In the ensuing subsections we shall inquire what logically is involved in each of these principles.

POPULAR SOVEREIGNTY

In Chapter 1 we observed that the word "democracy," through most of its history and to most people, has meant "government ruled by all"—as opposed to "government ruled by a few" ("aristocracy") and "government ruled by one" ("monarchy"). "Popular sovereignty," if we mean by it sovereignty of the entire people, is undoubtedly therefore the *oldest* of the ideas associated with democracy. As Lord Bryce put it:

The word Democracy has been used ever since the time of Herodotus to denote that form of government in which the ruling power of a State is legally vested, not in any particular class or classes, but *in the members of the community as a whole.*[5]

For a full understanding of what is involved in popular sovereignty (and thus in one major element of democracy), we might now look closely at each of the key phrases in Bryce's statement in order to understand all that it has to say:

(1) "The ruling power of a State." To speak of "popular sovereignty" is to take for granted something called "sovereignty," which can be either "popular" or "non-popular." "Sovereignty," as the term is ordinarily used in traditional political science, denotes *the* definite source of *final* decisions, the power to make and enforce laws (Bryce's "ruling power of a State") above which there is no law. It is, traditional political science holds, present as a matter of course in every genuine "political community"—and so much as a matter of course that where it is not present the "political community" either has not yet been born or has already died. A decision of the "sovereign," so defined, can be revised only by another act of that same "sovereign"; its power to make decisions, furthermore, is subject to no limitations except those it sees fit to impose on *itself* (and even these it can remove at will). No group whose power is limited by some *other* group can, therefore, be called "sovereign." In the political community, power is embodied and institutionalized in the machinery of "the State"; and it is the possession of such sovereign power that sets the State apart from all other social groupings.

The doctrine of "popular sovereignty," then, is that according to which power vests in *all* the members of the community rather than in any part of them or in any one of them. Just as sovereign power is what makes a State a State, sovereign power vested in all the community's members is what makes the State "democratic." Democracy, in other words, is one among several *ways of organizing the State,* one among several answers a community can make to the question as to where within it sovereign power is to be lodged. It is *not* an answer to the question whether such power ought to exist at all, for where it does not (as, for example, in the United Nations Organization) there is no State to organize. In a word, the doctrine of popular sovereignty means it when it says "sovereignty" every bit as much as when it says "popular."

We must notice at once, however, that the notion that popular sovereignty is fundamental to democracy is highly unpalatable to certain present-day writers.[6] Of special importance in this connection are the writers, mentioned

---

[5] *Op. cit.,* Vol. I, p. 20. Italics added.

[6] The so-called "pluralists" of the 1920's denied the desirability (and some even denied the possibility) of creating a "sovereign State" in this sense; and thus, from the point of view set forth in the text, classified themselves as opponents of the very idea of government, and therefore were neither critics nor supporters of democracy. It is unnecessary for our purposes to go into the rather rarefied academic argument about the idea of sovereignty; but those who would like to pursue the subject further will find a convenient starting place in the summary and evaluation of the pluralist attack on sovereignty in Francis W. Coker, *Recent Political Thought*

in the preceding chapter, who proclaim that in a true democracy there can be *no* unlimited power—that a State is democratic only so long as certain individual rights are entirely removed from the power of *any* governmental agency, whether popularly controlled or not. To them "limited government" or "constitutional government" is an essential attribute of democracy. Such a position, of course, is difficult to square with the assertion that popular sovereignty is a basic element of democracy; but the whole question is so inextricably interwoven with the problem of majority rule and minority rights that we will reserve further discussion of it for our exposition below of the doctrine of majority rule.

(2) "Is legally vested." When we say that in a democracy sovereignty is "legally" vested in the people, we do not mean to imply that it may "actually" reside elsewhere. Democracy, that is to say, surely does not mean a government whose formal constitution "legally" vests all power in the people, but where the power is "actually"—behind the legal formalisms—wielded by a dictator. But neither does democracy mean a government in which the sovereign power is "legally" vested in the dictator, but in which the people start a violent revolution and depose the dictator every time he does something they dislike. The phrase means merely that the legal-formal governing institutions of a democracy are such that the government's actions are always made in response to an orderly and nonviolent expression of the popular will. It means, in short, that both the "legal" and the "actual" ruling power reside in the people.

(3) "In the members of the community." Who are "the people"? Are they *all* the individuals who at any point in time happen to be physically present within the geographical boundaries of the democratic community? The answer, it seems to us, is clear: Membership in any community, democratic or otherwise, means something more than mere physical presence among a haphazard agglomeration of individuals tossed together by chance in a given geographic area. The term "community" suggests something *common* among those individuals, something binding them together, some overlap or commonality of interests and feelings—it surely is something more than just an arithmetical term denoting "the total number of any collection of persons."

We do not suggest that a genuine community exists only where each individual completely ignores his own selfish interest and cares only for the welfare of others. Such a suggestion would indeed be naïve. Almost everything we know about the process of politics indicates that dissension and disagreement and "selfishness" are always present—that politics consists to a considerable degree of the struggle for power and satisfaction of their varying desires

(New York: D. Appleton-Century Co., Inc., 1934), Chs. XVIII, XIX. The pluralist point of view, as just defined, appears to have no contemporary exponents, and must be carefully distinguished from contemporary American pluralism, which is a defense of the pluralistic *exercise* of sovereignty—that is, has no quarrel with the idea of sovereignty as such.

among numberless antagonistic interest groups.[7] Yet in most countries this struggle for power does not produce the perpetual civil war that we would expect to be its inevitable result; it operates rather within a number of sharp limitations. The various interest groups do not as a rule maintain private armies and use tanks, machine guns, and atomic bombs against one another; their political game is played according to certain rules, and the rules are for the most part obeyed even when obeying them prevents the full victory of one or another of the groups. Why? Rousseau gave us the answer two hundred years ago:

What made the establishment of societies necessary was . . . the fact that the interests of individuals clashed. But what made their establishment possible was the fact that these same interests *also* coincided. *In other words,* it is the overlap among different interests that creates the social bond, so that no society can possibly exist save as there is some point at which all the interests *concerned* are in harmony.[8]

In other words, the "popular sovereignty" of a democratic State is possible only if its members' desire to continue to live together as a community is at least as strong as their desire to satisfy their separate and antagonistic interests. Mary Parker Follett put it this way:

Real authority inheres in a genuine whole. The individual is sovereign over himself as far as he unifies the heterogeneous elements of his nature. Two people are sovereign over themselves as far as they are capable of creating one out of two. A group is sovereign over itself as far as it is capable of creating one out of several or many. A state is sovereign only as it has the power of creating one in which all are. Sovereignty is the power engendered by a complete interdependence becoming conscious of itself.[9]

In the pages to come we shall have frequent occasion to talk further of the nature of community and its importance for democracy. But for present purposes it is clear that *any* community, democratic or otherwise, must decide what qualifications should be required as the condition of admittance to full membership (and, in a democratic society, the right to participate in making the community's political decisions). And the decision upon such qualifications

[7] The classic statement of this view of the nature of politics is presented in Arthur F. Bentley's *The Process of Government* (Chicago: The University of Chicago Press, 1908). This work has since been reprinted by the Principia Press of Bloomington, Indiana. For an illuminating discussion of Bentley's critics and a restatement of his position, see Richard W. Taylor, "Arthur F. Bentley's Political Science," *Western Political Quarterly*, V (June, 1952), pp. 214-30. A leading present-day application of Bentley's attitude toward politics is David B. Truman, *The Governmental Process* (New York: Alfred A. Knopf, 1951).

[8] Jean Jacques Rousseau, *The Social Contract*, translated by Willmoore Kendall (Chicago: Henry Regnery Co., 1954), Bk. II, Ch. I, p. 24.

[9] Mary Parker Follett, *The New State* (New York: Longmans, Green and Co., 1918), p. 271. On the nature and necessity of community for democratic government, see also Robert M. MacIver, *Community* (London: Macmillan and Company, Ltd., 1917), pp. 128-29, and *The Web of Government* (New York: The Macmillan Company, 1947), pp. 4 ff.; and A. D. Lindsay, *The Essentials of Democracy*, 2nd ed. (London: Oxford University Press, 1935), p. 4.

is made in a democracy by the same process by which other political decisions are made, and is revisable by the same process.

(4) "Not in any particular class or classes, but in the members of the community as a whole." Little comment is required upon this dictum—for if the community's ruling power *is* vested in a particular class, then such a government would, by definition, be what men have generally called "aristocracy" or "oligarchy."

POLITICAL EQUALITY

The second basic principle of democracy is that of political equality. Each member of the community must have the same chance as his fellows to participate in its total decision-making process. Only thus can there be genuine popular sovereignty; for if any individual or group of individuals has *more* power (through such devices as plural voting or special officeholding requirements) than the other members of the community, that group becomes a politically privileged class or elite, and popular sovereignty, as we have defined it above, cannot exist. It is for these reasons that political equality is, as we observed in Chapter 1, generally regarded as an essential element of democracy.

It is necessary to point out, however, that political equality involves far more than the classical slogan of "one man, one vote." If equality in voting rights were synonymous with political equality, then—on this score at least—the Communist nations' claim that they are more democratic than their Western opponents would be hard to dispute. After all, they hold elections frequently, and it is probable that a higher percentage of the population holds the suffrage than in any Western nation; and a larger proportion of the eligible voters actually go to the polls. But does this mean that therefore the Communist nations really *do* have a higher degree of political equality than the West?

The answer, we believe, can be found by analyzing the nature of the decision-making process and the part that voting plays therein. What do we do when we make decisions? "Policy-making," says Professor MacIver, "depends upon the *assessing of alternatives* with a view to translating one of them into action." [10] In other words, the essence of making a decision is the *choice among alternatives*. And in order to make a genuine choice, each of these three conditions must obtain for the policy maker: (1) the presence of genuine alternatives before him; (2) the opportunity to find out about the nature and probable consequences of each alternative; and (3) full freedom to choose whichever of the alternatives seems to him—for whatever reasons he deems sufficient—the most desirable. In the absence of any one of these conditions he can hardly be said to be making a genuine choice. Where, then, does voting come in? At most it is a kind of machinery whereby each policy maker registers the choice he has made. In other words, voting is just one part—

[10] *The Web of Government*, p. 9. Italics added.

albeit a necessary one—of the total decision-making process, and its significance depends upon the degree to which the other parts of the process have
operated *before* voting takes place. In the Communist countries the voter has
only the candidates of the Communist party to choose—there are no opposition candidates. In the same manner, in Hitler's Germany the voter was asked
in periodic plebiscites if he approved of what his Führer was doing, but on
his ballot there was only a *ja* for him to mark. In such "elections" the voters
have no choice; and the fact that such impressive percentages of the population mark ballots is no indication at all that the principle of political equality is
being observed.

Thus political equality means not only "one man, one vote," but also an
equal chance for each member of the community to participate in the total
decision-making process of the community.

POPULAR CONSULTATION

In Chapter 1 we noted the general agreement upon the proposition that
a democratic government should do what the people want it to do and
should not do anything they don't want it to do. And in this chapter we
have said that this must mean something more than a state of affairs in which
the people, playing the role Locke claims for them in the *Second Treatise,*
violently and successfully rebel against the holders of public office whenever
these ignore or flout the popular will. In democratic government, that is to
say, the people must be "consulted" about the policy they wish those in
power to pursue in a given matter—and the holders of office, having learned
the popular desire, should proceed to do whatever the people want them to
do. Thus "popular consultation" in this sense requires at least these three
attributes: (1) on matters of public policy there must *be* a genuine popular
will; (2) the officeholders must be aware of what that will requires; and (3)
having ascertained the nature of the popular will, they must then faithfully
and invariably translate it into action.

A considerable portion of the discussion of democracy rests, as we will
show in the next chapter, upon the assumption that once most members of
the community are agreed that these things *should* happen they automatically
do take place—that when democracy is generally regarded as desirable, it
springs into being. This book proceeds upon quite a different assumption:
that there is nothing at all "automatic" about popular consultation, that some
kind of institutional machinery must be set up to accomplish the job, and that
the search for such machinery is at once the most difficult and the most
urgent job facing anyone who wants to see democracy more fully realized in
any particular nation. The purpose of this book, we again remind our readers,
is to examine the institutions—particularly those of our party system—which
now purport to carry on the process of popular consultation, in order to see
how well or how badly they do the job. That the full and effective operation
of popular consultation is vital to democracy, however, is undeniable.

MAJORITY RULE

Up to this point in our analysis we have said little that any contemporary theorist of democracy would dispute, though many of them might say (and we should agree) that as yet we have not by any means told the whole story. Actually, all we are asserting up to this point is that no one thinks of democracy as requiring the location of the ruling power in a special elite or ruling class, or necessitating political *in*equality, or making governmental decisions *contrary* to what the people desire.

Our fourth principle of democracy, however, is considerably more controversial than the other three. For we believe that a model democratic government must always be able to justify its actions on the grounds that they accord with the wishes of a majority of the enfranchised members of the community. Or, to put it another way, we believe that when there are two opinions among the members of a democratic community as to whether the government should perform any given action, the opinion of the larger group, which for most purposes we can usefully think of as one-half of the enfranchised members plus at least one, ought to prevail.

This affirmation, of course, plunges us into the middle of the greatest single theoretical controversy about the nature of democracy: "absolute" majority rule versus "limited" majority rule, a dispute which we briefly noted in Chapter 1. An understanding of the issues on which this quarrel turns is essential to the case for our conception of democracy. We will therefore explore them as carefully as we can, attempting to state fully and fairly the position contrary to our own, and then showing why we are convinced that "absolute" majority rule is an inescapable attribute of any model of *perfectly* democratic government—that it is, in short, the only decision-making principle that is consistent with the other three principles of democracy we have previously presented.

The "Absolute" Majority Rule Position. Much of the opposition to absolute majority rule results, we believe, from misunderstandings as to what it involves—or, to put this a little differently, from a tendency to attribute to "majoritarian" democratic theorists certain ideas that are not necessary to the position as we have stated it, and that, so far as the present writers have been able to discover, no majoritarian has ever asserted. Before going further, then, let us deal with some of these misunderstandings.

(1) Some critics charge that "the majority," in whom the majoritarians wish to vest the community's decision-making power, really does not exist and is only a convenient fiction invented by the majoritarians to shore up their case. The majoritarian, however, is *not* called upon to show that "the majority" exists, or that he views with favor the continuous exercise of power in the democratic society by one identifiable *and permanent* group of the enfranchised citizens at the expense of all other such groups. Power in the democratic state belongs to the *whole* people; ideally, power in the democratic state is

exercised by the *whole* people; and if the people in such a state could be counted upon to reach unanimous decisions on all governmental problems, the issue on which the controversy over majority rule turns could be ignored. For that issue is this: What happens in the democratic state when the people are *divided*—when, as we put it above, there are *two* opinions as to the course to be followed? The majoritarian is saying, above all, that no doctrine of the democratic state is complete that does not deal with that issue. His way of dealing with it is to say, Let the opinion that has the greater number of sup- porters prevail. But as a democrat he naturally prefers unanimous decisions to nearly unanimous ones, and nearly unanimous ones to decisions opposed by a considerable minority, and decisions opposed by a considerable minority to decisions opposed by a minority accounting for nearly half the popula- tion. And, far from being required by his position to demonstrate that *the* majority exists, he knows that a society in which it is possible to point to such a majority—a society, in other words, permanently divided between *a* perma- nent majority and *a* permanent minority, so that all issues become issues be- tween those two groups—is a society in which democracy is about to become impossible to operate. In short, the majoritarian wishes to locate the decision- making power in popular majorities, not in *"the"* majority" conceived as one never-changing group of persons.

(2) Other critics argue that it is impossible for each and every one of the myriad day-to-day decisions a modern government must make to be based upon a specific majority mandate. When the majoritarian says that the gov- ernment of a democratic state must be able to point to the "wishes of a ma- jority" as justification for any action it takes, however, he is not saying that it must be able to point to a *specific majority mandate* for that specific action (though, admittedly, majoritarians have sometimes talked as though that were the case). For democracy—like aristocracy and monarchy—is a matter of who exercises the *ultimate* ruling power, and the processes by which day-to-day decisions are made become important only when they immediately affect the location and exercise of that ultimate ruling power. To illustrate the point we are making, let us draw an analogy with another form of government. If an absolute monarch called in one of his courtiers and said to him, "I'm tired of figuring out each of my subjects' tax bills, so you take over the job," surely no one would say, "But he can't do that—he's an absolute monarch and must make *all* the decisions." The monarch's absoluteness consists in his ability to take back the tax-fixing power any time and in any case he wants to even if the courtier wants to keep it. And so it is with popular majorities in a democracy: if a majority wishes to entrust such-and-such a type of decision to, say, a supreme court, and thus give that court a "blanket" mandate for all such decisions, it certainly can do so without violating any of the principles of democracy. So long as any future majority can take the power away from the court (even if the court wants to retain it) by the same process by which it initially awarded the power, the majority, and not the court, exercises ultimate

power. And to deny the majority the power to "delegate" part of its power or to cancel the "delegation" when it wishes to is to say that in a democracy the whole people has less power than the monarch in an absolute monarchy.

There is also another reason why majoritarian democracy does not demand specific majority mandates on each and every governmental decision. To demand such mandates is to ask of the people what is obviously impossible, and even if it were not impossible something they would be unlikely to do, namely, to give to public affairs an unlimited amount of time and attention (since if they gave less than that some of the necessary mandates would not get formulated). Absolute monarchy does not require that the monarch actually *make* each and every governmental decision, but only that he have the *power* to make whatever decisions he *wishes* to make. And, by the same token, democracy does not require that popular majorities actually *make* each and every governmental decision, but only that they have the *power* to make whatever decisions they *wish* to make.

In short, majoritarian democracy demands only that popular majorities have the *final* word on whatever matters they wish to have the final word on, whether these have to do with the *procedures* by which decisions are made or the *content* of decisions. If on a given matter they are more desirous of preserving a certain procedure (e.g., the Supreme Court's power of judicial review) than of having a particular course of action followed (e.g., preserving racial segregation in the public schools), they can, without any diminution of their ultimate power, decide to let an unpopular decision made by a popular procedure stand. But if the content of the decision is more important to them than preserving the procedure, they should have full power to alter the procedure or set it aside in order to get the particular course of action they wish. So long as it is a majority, and not a minority, that decides whether preserving the procedure or getting the course of action is more important, the requirements of majority-rule democracy are satisfied.

(3) Some critics charge that the case for majority rule rests upon an alleged connection between the rightness or wisdom of a procedure or a policy and the number of people who support it. The majoritarian replies that the difference between a majority and a minority is, to be sure, a difference in numbers; and the technique by which we discover which procedure or policy represents the wishes of the majority is indeed what is called "holding an election" by those who think it a good technique and "counting noses" by those who think it a bad one. But the difference between a people risen unanimously against a dictator on the one hand, and that dictator on the other hand, is also a difference in numbers—as is also the difference between five Supreme Court justices and four, or the difference between two-thirds of the senators present and voting, and two-thirds-minus-one of the senators present and voting, both of which are differences made much of by the anti-majoritarians. In other words, the special fascination with numbers of which majoritarians are frequently accused is characteristic not of majority-rule

democracy in particular but of democracy itself. For all who value freedom, a state of affairs where two human beings are subordinated to the
arbitrary will of a third is twice as bad as a state of affairs where only one is
so subordinated. And the connection upon which the majoritarian insists is not
the connection between numbers and rightness but that between numbers
and human freedom. A policy or procedure, obviously, does not gain in rightness by picking up enough support to justify the claim that it represents the
wishes of the majority, or lose in rightness by losing support. But that is not
the point at issue, since what the majoritarian asserts is not the superior intelligence or wisdom or even morality of popular majorities, but the wrong-
ness, from the democratic point of view, of a state of affairs where the few
are in position to have their way over the wishes of the many.

   The "Limited" Majority Rule Position. The first thing to note about
those who oppose "absolute" majority rule is that they do not argue that democracy requires lodging the ultimate decision-making power in the hands of
minorities. These writers are above all concerned to deny that the alternatives
majority-rule-versus-minority-rule are exhaustive—since, they say, there is a
third alternative, which is the principle a genuine democracy must adopt.
Among the proponents of "limited" majority rule, or, as some call it, *"constitutional* democracy," this third alternative appears in one of two versions. The
first of these, which is advanced by relatively few present-day theorists, holds
that in a genuine democracy there must be certain things that the government
may not do *at all,* even if the whole people wishes it to. The question is not,
say these writers, whether majorities *or* minorities should rule; in a true democracy *both* majorities *and* minorities should be subordinate to and controlled by a third force—The Law, which, in an American context, we may
take to be equivalent to the Constitution. In Dean Roscoe Pound's formulation
of this point of view:

   An idea of a covenant of people not to do certain things and only to do certain
other things in a certain way was well known in the formative era of our polity.
. . . Shall we say then that the foundations of modern democracy were undemocratic, or shall we say that *Demos, no less than Rex, may . . . rule under God and
the Law?* [11]

   The more often-encountered version of this "third alternative" position
holds, not that there are certain things a democratic government may *never* do,
but rather that it may do those things only when a "more substantial" popular
majority than just 50 per cent plus one wants them done. Such "extraordinary
majorities" as two-thirds or three-fourths of the people should, in this view,
be required before such action may properly be taken in a democracy.

   Although in some disagreement as to *how* to protect certain things from
action by bare popular majorities, the opponents of "absolute" majority rule

[11] Roscoe Pound, "Law and Federal Government," in *Federalism as a Democratic Process*
(New Brunswick, N. J.: Rutgers University Press, 1942), pp. 8-9. Italics added.

generally agree that such things as free speech, free press, free worship, and
"due process" guarantees to persons accused of crime should be protected. A
recent variation upon this third-alternative theme is provided by those who
argue that certain limitations on majorities are inherent in the principle of
majority rule itself—no majority, they say, may rightfully change the conditions (presumably of political freedom) by which it became a majority, because to do so would be to destroy majority rule itself.[12]

Let us summarize the "limited" majority rule position by representing it
diagrammatically:

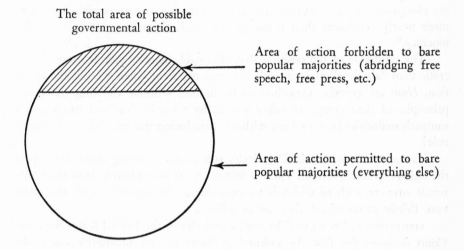

The total area of possible
governmental action

Area of action forbidden to bare
popular majorities (abridging free
speech, free press, etc.)

Area of action permitted to bare
popular majorities (everything else)

The circle represents everything any government could possibly do, from setting up speed limits for automobiles to forcing everyone to have at least three
wives. The shaded portion of the circle represents such actions as the latter,
which in a democracy bare popular majorities must not be allowed to do.
The remainder of the circle represents all the possible governmental actions
remaining, which may be taken whenever a popular majority of *any* size
wishes them to be taken. As these writers view their own position, therefore,
they are not asserting that minority rule is more democratic than majority
rule. So long as bare popular majorities do not invade the areas which true
democracy forbids them to enter, say these writers, such majorities should have
full power to rule. So their conclusion is that democracy involves *both* majority rule *and* the protection of individual and minority rights against invasion by bare popular majorities.

[12] Cf. Laurence Stapleton, *The Design of Democracy* (New York: Oxford University Press,
1949), pp. 67-68, 74-76; Herbert McClosky, "The Fallacy of Absolute Majority Rule," *The
Journal of Politics*, XI (Nov., 1949), pp. 637-54; and J. Roland Pennock, "Responsiveness, Responsibility, and Majority Rule," *American Political Science Review*, XLVI (Sept., 1952), pp.
791-96.

A Critique of the "Limited" Majority Rule Position. Before criticizing the "limited" majority rule position, let us recall that in the present chapter we are not drawing up detailed blueprints for the government of any *actual* community; rather we are attempting to reason out a set of principles to guide us in the construction of a *model of democracy.* For the reasons noted in the first section of this chapter, the essential characteristic of such a model must be logical consistency among its various principles. And our basic objection to the "limited" majority rule position is therefore that its "third alternative" to majority rule and minority rule is logically invalid. There is, we believe, no logical alternative to majority rule except minority rule; and of the two, majority rule must be chosen as a principle of democracy, since it is more nearly consistent than minority rule with the other principles of democracy.[13]

The weakness of the position that "limited" majority rule is more democratic than "absolute" majority rule becomes apparent when we ask the question, *How* are popular majorities to be limited without violating the other principles of democracy? In other words, by what institutional mechanisms can such majorities be restrained without introducing the principle of *minority* rule?

The advocates of "limited" majority rule disagree among themselves upon the answer to this question. Their writings appear to contain at least three different answers, each of which is to some degree incompatible with the other two. Briefly summarized, they are as follows.

LIMITATION BY "THE LAW." In 1936, a majority of the United States Supreme Court declared the first Agricultural Adjustment Act unconstitutional. Mr. Justice Owen J. Roberts took the occasion to explain his conception of the role of the court and of the Constitution in determining what the people's elected representatives in Congress may and may not do. As he put it:

> There should be no misunderstanding as to the function of this court in such a case. It is sometimes said that the court assumes a power to overrule or control the action of the people's representatives. This is a misconception. The Constitution is the supreme law of the land ordained and established by the people. All legislation must conform to the principles it lays down. When an act of Congress is appropriately challenged in the courts as not conforming to the constitutional mandate the judicial branch of the government has only one duty,—to lay the article of the Constitution which is invoked beside the statute which is challenged and to decide whether the latter squares with the former.[14]

Relatively few advocates of "limited" majority rule, however, rely upon Mr. Justice Roberts' fiction of "The Constitution" and "The Law" as some-

---

[13] Some readers may agree that the principle of "absolute" majority rule is logically consistent with democracy, but feel that they do not wish to live in an America in which popular majorities exercise their absolute powers in an absolute way. To such readers we shall have something to say in the section of Chapter 3 on "Majority 'Tyranny' and Minority Acquiescence."

[14] *United States v. Butler* 297 U.S. 1 (1936).

thing that exists entirely apart from what fallible human beings think it is. Most observers recognize that professors of political science, law-school professors, constitutional lawyers, congressmen, and even Supreme Court judges do not agree among themselves about what many crucial parts of the Constitution mean when applied to specific policy-making situations. And this has inclined most of them to conclude that every time a government tries to decide whether or not it should adopt a certain policy, there will be no absolutely "right" answer—that is, there will be available no divine revelation or "scientific" law to indicate *the* proper decision. If there were, goverment would be a simple matter indeed. But instead there will be only a decision which the members of the community will have to make the best way they can—on the basis of the evidence available and according to their own differing values and differing interpretations of the evidence. If all of them agree about what should be done, then no problem about who should rule arises, for neither a majority nor a minority will exist.

Unanimity on matters of governmental policy is, however, difficult to achieve and rarely present. Consequently, on all yes-or-no issues (which all public issues ultimately become: Shall we or shall we not adopt this specific policy, or elect this candidate instead of that?), all members of the community will fall into either the yes-group or the no-group. Except in cases of a flat tie, one group will be larger than the other. One, in other words, will be the majority and the other the minority.

Seen from this point of view, the issue over the status of majority rule can be put thus: If a majority wishes, for example, to adopt a policy that a minority regards as intolerably destructive of human rights, how can the majority be restrained?

LIMITATION BY FORMAL MINORITY VETO. A second group of writers argue that a true democracy must provide formal institutional devices by which the minority can, in the situation just described, prevent the majority from having its way. Among the devices proposed for this purpose are such familiar American practices as the requirement of extraordinary majorities for such matters as amending the Constitution and ratifying treaties; and, most important of all, the institution of judicial review, which gives a body of judges beyond the control of bare popular majorities the power to nullify any act of such majorities that the judges deem to be an invasion of minority rights.

To limit the power of the majority in this fashion is, we believe, to give the minority an absolute veto over change, and thus to invite the minority, insofar as such a veto makes this possible, to rule whenever it pleases. When, for example, a two-thirds majority is required before some governmental action can be taken, a "no" vote is made to count for just twice as much as a "yes" vote. Not only is this a clear violation of the principle of political equality—which, as we have previously noted, is generally regarded as essential to democracy—but it also means that when 60 per cent of the people want something and 40 per cent don't want it, the smaller and not the larger group gets its way. And the ability to get one's way is nothing other than the power to *rule*. So wherever a two-thirds majority is required for action, it is always possible that a minority, if it is large enough, can carry the day.[15]

"But wait a minute," it might be objected, "the minority doesn't *rule* in such a case—it only keeps the majority from ruling. It, like judicial review, is a *veto* power, not a power to rule." Such an objection, however, ignores the nature of the decision-making process. In any policy-making situation there are always a number of alternatives to choose among, and one of those alternatives is always the retention of the status quo. A veto, to be sure, always chooses the status quo in preference to any of the other alternatives. But to choose the status quo does not mean that no policy at all is chosen; on the contrary, a very definite policy is chosen, for the government is thereby committed to a certain course of action just as much as it would have been committed to another course of action had some alternative other than the status quo been chosen instead. And to give a minority the power to veto any act of a majority is to give it the power to *rule*.

But, it might be further objected to our position on majority rule, suppose a watchdog like the Supreme Court has been given its veto power *by the majority itself*? What if the majority *wants* to give some minority agency the task of keeping the majority on its toes and warning it when it is going too far? Such a situation, it seems to us, is perfectly consonant with democracy so long as everyone knows the watchdog is the agent of and responsible to the majority, and acts accordingly. Those who defend judicial review on the ground that the majority has willed it, however, are simply postponing the day of reckoning with the basic question. For when the watchdog tells the majority that they must give up a certain piece of legislation, and the majority replies that they must have it and let the heavens fall, who wins in such a situation—the majority or their agent-watchdog? This, of course, is another way of asking the familiar question: When the majority wants above all else to do a certain thing and a minority believes that that thing should not be done, which group gets its way? And our answer to the question remains: In any government which can legitimately be called "democratic," the majority and not the minority must carry the day.

LIMITATION BY MAJORITY SELF-RESTRAINT. Some writers who advocate "limited" majority rule do not propose any *formal* limitations upon the power of popular majorities. They hold, instead, that in a true democracy majorities will not *be* restrained but rather will *restrain themselves* from violating human rights. Now if "limited" majority rule means nothing more than this, then the authors of this book have no quarrel with it; for such a "limitation" is no limitation at all upon the *power* of the majority, and therefore cannot be-

15 Cf. Hugo Krabbe, *The Modern Idea of the State*, translated by G. H. Sabine and W. J. Shepard (New York: D. Appleton and Company, 1922), p. 76.

come, strictly speaking, minority *rule*. At most it is no more than a way of saying that if the majority chooses to destroy any of the elements of democracy, then democracy will no longer exist—that democracies which have committed suicide are democracies no longer. Since the propositions just stated are undeniable, there are no significant logical differences between this third version of the "limited" majority rule position and the "absolute" majority rule position outlined previously.

Why "Absolute" Majority Rule? For the reasons given in the foregoing pages, any attempt to place *formal* institutional limitations upon the "absolute" power of popular majorities logically results in the establishment of *minority* rule. And from the standpoint of strict logic, "absolute" majority rule must be chosen over minority rule as a principle of ideally *democratic* government, not because there is any magical virtue or omniscience in popular majorities, but because majority rule is more nearly in accord than minority rule with the other principles of democracy that we have previously discussed. It is the only principle of decision making that men have yet discovered which "grants a perpetual privilege to none and permits an equal share of power to all." [16]

For the prevention of majority "tyranny" and the protection of human rights in our model of democracy, therefore, we must depend upon factors other than formal limitations upon the power of popular majorities. In Chapter 3 we shall consider what "other factors" are logically consistent with the principles of democracy and can therefore be written into the model; and in the final three chapters of the book we shall consider some of the "other factors" that actually operate in the United States today.

The Principles Considered

It is for the reasons given above that we believe that a model of democracy must be constructed according to the principles of popular sovereignty, political equality, popular consultation, and majority rule. Let us conclude our statement of these principles by pointing out two consequences of the position we have taken.

In the first place, it is important to remember that *all four* of these elements must be present, and that each one considered by itself makes democratic sense only as the presence of the other three is assumed. If, for example, we are told that the Supreme Court—or, for that matter, the Politburo—is committed to decisions made by bare majorities of its members and is therefore a "majority-rule institution," we are hardly justified in concluding that the government of which it is a part must be fully democratic. Why not? Because in the total governing system within which each of these institu-

[16] Ladislas Konopczynski, "Majority Rule," *Encyclopedia of the Social Sciences* (New York: The Macmillan Company, 1937), Vol. IX, pp. 55-60.

tions operates, the elements of popular sovereignty, political equality, and popular consultation are, in varying degrees, lacking.[17]

Second, we have urged a purely *political* conception of democracy—one according to which democracy is simply and solely a way of making decisions, and the *content* of any particular decision (except insofar as it may affect the nature of the decision-making *process*) is irrelevant to the question of the presence or absence of democracy. We have taken this position partly because, as we observed in Chapter 1, the word "democracy" throughout most of its history has denoted a certain form of government only.[18] But, it might be objected, since other words have grown and taken on new meanings, why not "democracy"? The answer is that words acquire new meanings only when those new meanings are generally agreed upon and the words are made more useful thereby—and surely neither of these conditions has resulted from the attempts to add to the original purely political meaning of "democracy."

In any case, even if one does introduce social and economic principles into his conception of democracy, he still must assign priorities. Let us assume, by way of illustrating this point, that we decide that democracy means not only the four principles listed above but also requires a publicly guaranteed minimum standard of living for all. Suppose that in a given community 70 per cent of the people want to end all government aid to the poor, and only 30 per cent want to retain it. What, in such a situation, would be the "democratic" solution? Which is the more fundamental to democracy—that the people get what they want even if it isn't "democratic," or that they be forced to have "democracy" even if they don't want it? To argue the latter position is to give democracy a very peculiar meaning indeed; but the only alternative is to admit that a certain *way* of making decisions is more fundamental to democracy than any particular *kind* of decision—and that is in effect to admit that democracy is basically a political matter. As Sidney Hook puts it:

What do those who contrast economic democracy with political democracy mean by the phrase "economic democracy"? If we examine the social systems which they regard as exemplifications of it, we find that by "economic democracy" they really mean economic security. This is a radically different concept. That it cannot legitimately be regarded as a species of democracy is apparent when we realize that

[17] The easiest way to avoid the obvious error of calling something like the Politburo a "majority-rule" body is to use the term "majority principle" to denote the rule by which *any* decision-making body, however removed from and set over the bulk of the populace, may make its own decisions. The term "majority rule" is most usefully reserved to denote that principle in a total governing system by which all political decisions are ultimately subject to control by at least 50 per cent plus one of the enfranchised citizens: Cf. Willmoore Kendall, *John Locke and the Doctrine of Majority-Rule* (Urbana: University of Illinois Press, 1941), pp. 24-27.

[18] Cf. Carl Becker, ". . . as a historian, I am naturally disposed to be satisfied with the meaning which, in the history of politics, men have commonly attributed to the word—a meaning, needless to say, which derives partly from experience and partly from the aspirations of mankind. So regarded, the term democracy refers primarily to a form of government, and it has always meant government by the many as opposed to government by the one . . .": *Modern Democracy* (New Haven: Yale University Press, 1941), pp. 6-7.

one may be secure without having any control over the conditions of security. . . .
Soldiers have economic security, but not democracy.[19]

This, of course, is not to say that it is unimportant to ask what kind of
social and economic systems provide the most favorable soil for democracy to
flourish in. Clearly this is a highly important question for anyone who wishes
to see democracy achieved in his community. We are saying only that the
question of what *helps* democracy is entirely different from the question of
what *is* democracy. And it is the latter question alone with which we are
here concerned.

[19] *New York Times Sunday Magazine,* March 16, 1947, pp. 48-49. For another exposition
of this position, see Krabbe, *op. cit.,* pp. 6-7.

Chapter 3

A MODEL OF
DEMOCRACY FOR
THE NATION-STATE

In the preceding chapter we presented a statement of the basic principles that should guide the construction of a "model" or "ideal" of democratic government for the modern nation-state. In the present chapter we shall attempt to complete the construction of the model by asking the question, What is involved—*besides* our four principles of popular sovereignty, political equality, popular consultation, and majority rule—in a model of democracy that will not be open to the charge of being logically inconsistent with generally accepted democratic principles, or with the traditional meaning of the term "democracy"? And one thing that might be involved, we may note to begin with, is one or another refinement of the four principles themselves.

The Town-Meeting Model

THE NEW ENGLAND TOWN MEETING AS "IDEAL" DEMOCRACY

Anyone who discusses the "ideal" democracy can be sure that someone early in the discussion will bring up the New England town meeting, and that one proposition everyone present will agree to is this: "Whatever democracy may or may not be, the New England town meeting was democratic. That was *genuine* self-government."

So it was; or, to put it a little differently, the kind of democratic doctrine that readily identifies the New England town meeting as the real thing reflects, *as far as it goes,* both sound scholarship and clear thinking. If, therefore, it were possible to take the town meeting as our model for the purposes of this book, we could do so with complete confidence that we were on the right track. But it is not possible, first for the reason that prompted the italicizing of "as far as it goes" in the sentence above, and second because, though everyone agrees that the town meeting was democratic, people differ as to what were the essential characteristics that made it democratic.

LEADING CHARACTERISTICS OF THE TOWN MEETING

Let us begin our description of the town-meeting model by getting down in black and white as complete a picture of the general conception of the town meeting as we can manage without venturing into the controversial.

(1) The town meeting brought together all the grown-up citizens who cared to attend; no citizen was, to use Rousseau's phrase, "flatly excluded."

(2) The citizen, once in his seat at the town meeting, was, *formally speaking,* the political equal of every other citizen present, with the same "right" to be heard in any discussion, the same right to call attention to his interests and preferences as something to be taken into account in any of the town's decisions, and the same right to be counted as one for or against any proposal that the meeting might vote on.

Because of (1) and (2), therefore, we can safely speak of "political equality" as one of the characteristics of any faithful model of the town meeting. The purpose of the words "formally speaking" in (2) is merely to remind us that any *actual* town meeting was merely a greater or lesser approximation to the model we are piecing together.[1] If Citizen A at an actual meeting did not speak English well, for example, his actual as opposed to his formal right to be heard might fall away nearly to zero. If Citizen B was known to his fellow townsmen as a "hothead" or a "screwball," his formal right to be heard might well be reduced, not by his being denied the floor, but by the others' refusal to listen attentively to him once he got it. And Citizen C might be known to the others as a man of great knowledge and wise counsel, and thus be encouraged to do a very large percentage of the talking.

(3) The town meeting was understood by all concerned to be the final authority on any problem of town policy or procedure that might arise in the course of the meeting, in at least the sense that no individual or minority among its members was formally in position to declare a proposal *ultra vires* (i.e., beyond the town's proper sphere of power). A more or less remote colonial or state government might subsequently declare its action *ultra vires,* or discipline it for violation of some law or principle laid down by higher authority; but the decision whether to go ahead and invite such corrective or disciplinary action from outside was one that the people of the town made for themselves.

Thus a further characteristic of our model town meeting is popular sovereignty.

(4) The town meeting met periodically; between meetings, elected officials exercised such authority as the most recent meeting had vested in them, but always in the context of a clear understanding that they would be held accountable at the next scheduled meeting for the use they had made of that authority. And in any case, it was understood that *all* authority reverted to the meeting itself when it was again assembled.

[1] See pp. 58-61 for a description of actual town meetings past and present.

Thus the town meeting had, so to speak, built-in machinery for popular consultation; and the latter becomes a further characteristic of our town-meeting model.

(5) The power of a *majority* of the town meeting to exercise the full power of the meeting—of one-half plus one to do whatever the whole people might do—was formally unlimited.

Unlimited majority rule, then, goes down as a further characteristic of our model.

(6) The town meeting dealt with *local* problems, of which as a matter of course the citizens had firsthand experience. Some persons present might know more about those problems, or understand them better, than others present; and an "expert" brought in—or admitted—from outside might understand them better by a wide margin than any citizen present; but no citizen found himself called upon to discuss or vote on problems concerning which he was ignorant in the way that the average citizen of the United States is ignorant about, say, United States–Soviet relations or the basing-point system of pricing industrial commodities.

Another characteristic of the model town meeting, then, is its *small size:* the town is not so populous that its citizens cannot meet face to face, or so large in area as to pose problems that the citizens have merely read or heard about.

DIFFICULTIES IN APPLYING THE TOWN-MEETING MODEL TO THE NATION-STATE

All the foregoing points about the town meeting appear, we repeat, to be generally accepted, and thus noncontroversial; and one possibility would be to take the town-meeting model, as it has emerged from the preceding discussion, as one end of our spectrum, and agree that systems of government are democratic or undemocratic according as they prove, upon examination, to be more or less like the model town meeting. But any such suggestion brings us hard up against two difficulties: (1) The party system we are attempting to evaluate in this book operates in the governments of a huge and populous nation-state, which *ipso facto* lacks the *smallness* called for by the model; and (2) the town-meeting model itself, as we have developed it thus far, leaves unanswered a number of questions that are of fundamental importance from the standpoint of self-government.

Primary among these questions is this: What, given the tremendous difference in scale, must we do to make the institutions of a huge and populous nation-state resemble those of the town meeting? In other words, what happens to the town-meeting model when, in photographers' language, we "blow it up" to many hundred times its original size in an attempt to make an equivalent model for the democratic nation-state?

Problems in "Blowing Up" the Town-Meeting Model

POPULAR SOVEREIGNTY

Some of the town meeting's characteristics we can reproduce in a "blown-up" model readily enough. To reproduce its characteristic of popular sovereignty, for instance, we need only specify that the whole people of the nation must have the same full power over the nation's government and affairs that the whole people of the town have over the town's government and affairs.

POLITICAL EQUALITY

There is also no problem in reproducing the town-meeting model's characteristic of political equality in our nation-state model; for we can require that each of the latter's citizens, however numerous they may be, are all to enjoy the same political rights (to be heard, to have their interests and preferences taken into account, to vote when there is voting to be done) that the members of the model town meeting enjoy.

POPULAR CONSULTATION

It is otherwise with popular consultation, however. The citizens of the nation-state not only cannot meet periodically to resume their full powers, bring their elected officials to heel, etc.; they cannot meet at all. Our blown-up model, then, has to provide machinery of popular consultation that enables the model's citizens to stand in the same relation to the model's policies and procedures as the members of the model town meeting to the town's policies and procedures. And the question at once arises, Can we, even on the level of pure theory—which is the level appropriate to model building—visualize such machinery?

The question just asked is the central problem with which the theorists of the democratic state have been wrestling through the past two or three centuries. Some of them, like the framers of our own Constitution, have tried to solve it, so to speak, in reverse—that is, out of a wish to *avoid* complete democracy in building the actual institutions of the nation-state rather than to *realize* it. But, paradoxical though it may seem, one needs the nation-state equivalent of the town-meeting model just as badly in order to *limit* popular control over government as to *establish* it.

The Problem of the Citizens' Inability to Assemble. The citizens of the large and populous nation-state cannot assemble together in a particular place to discuss public problems; they can, however, discuss these problems informally with one another; and they can choose representatives, one per constituency of so many thousands of citizens, who can assemble in a particular place to discuss them formally. The citizens cannot—as the members of the town meeting can—personally participate in the elaboration of proposals and then proceed at once to cast votes for or against them; but the act of choosing representatives calls for *elections,* and the latter, if organized and handled in a certain way, can give them direct if not continuous control over some decisions (questions can be submitted to them, as in a referendum, to be answered Yes or No), and can give them indirect if not continuous control over most questions (since they can choose representatives who can be counted on to vote as their constituents would have voted if actually present).[2] They cannot call their executive and administrative officials before them for an accounting; but their representatives can be empowered to "ride herd" on such officials, and, to the extent that the representatives truly reflect the wishes of their constituents, produce a kind of control of the officials in question not unlike that accomplished by the town meeting.

The solution of the popular-consultation problem which the theory of the democratic state has increasingly put forth in recent decades requires the elections for the representative assembly to be primarily a series of choices, in each constituency over the land, between two candidates, each representing a political party bent on controlling the personnel and policies of government, and each, therefore, sure to put maximum effort into its attempt to anticipate and fully represent the electorate's wishes. This kind of electoral solution further calls for keeping the two parties on their toes by leaving the voters free to organize a third or a fourth party. This theory holds, in other words, that the *important* decisions will in such a situation be made *directly* by the electorate, which in giving a majority to Party A rather than Party B, determines the "issues" between the two, and gives Party A a "mandate" that it must carry out. It also holds that, insofar as decisions need to be made on problems that were not discussed at election time, Party A, having been chosen by the electorate because of the latter's adherence to its "principles" and the "representativeness" of its leaders, can be counted on to make them as the electorate would have made them. Such a solution appears to meet the popular-consultation test very well *in theory,* but should not necessarily be regarded as part of our model—since to regard it as such would close the door to other solutions that might also meet the test.

In short, theorists have seen in representative assemblies chosen in nation-wide elections a more or less satisfactory near approach to popular consultation in the town meeting; and a near approach may well be the best we can hope for. In any case, the problem of popular consultation is not an insuperable barrier to the building of a model for a nation-state democracy if we are clear that the less near the approach the less claim our model has to be regarded as fully democratic. For the reasons mentioned above, we can now say that the model must include (a) a representative assembly that exercises the full powers of the people, and (b) electoral arrangements for choosing the members of the assembly which keep it subordinated to the citizens to the extent

---

[2] For more detailed discussions of the theory of representation and the theory of direct legislation, see pp. 61-65, 76-77, 79-80.

that they wish it subordinated, and which create a presumption that the representatives' decisions will be the same as the citizens would decree if they were all present and voting. This gives us an adequate criterion for evaluating the actual institutions of a nation-state from the standpoint of popular consultation. For to the extent that the full powers of the people in any actual nation-state are *not* concentrated in a single elected representative assembly, and to the extent that the electoral arrangements do *not* maximize correspondence between the will of the representative assembly and the wishes of the electorate, we can call that nation's government *un*democratic.

The Problem of Acquainting the Citizens with the Facts. The theory of the democratic state has in general sidestepped another aspect of the problem of popular consultation. The town meeting discusses and makes decisions about problems that fall within the firsthand experience of its members, and that do not make intellectual demands upon the members that the latter are incapable of meeting. The nation-state, by contrast, poses problems of both foreign and domestic policy that far transcend the individual citizen's firsthand experience. Because of their scale and complexity, these problems call for intellectual operations of the highest order of difficulty—operations some of which are clearly beyond the intellectual capacity even of those citizens who have had the benefit of the best training the democratic state—or any other—has to offer. A completely faithful blown-up model of the town meeting would, therefore, include arrangements for giving the citizens, before election time, the kind of factual knowledge about and understanding of each "issue" that the town-meeting members brought to the making of decisions about their issues. This, in modern conditions, means *communicating* to them—not merely making available to them—at least the essentials of what proved experts on each problem have to say about it.

It is not easy to say what arrangements would have to be built into the nation-state equivalent of the town-meeting model in order to achieve even a near approach to the resolution of this difficulty. Rousseau attempted to solve this problem, in the only book he addressed to the problem of the nation-state (*Considerations on the Government of Poland*), by urging the Poles (a) to see to it that every Polish boy, in the process of growing up, became familiar with every highway and byway in all Poland, (b) to keep their economic and social organization simple, and (c) to pursue an isolationist policy in foreign affairs, and so avoid the necessity of making decisions about matters external to the nation's territory. Walter Lippmann, who has shown deep penetration into this aspect of the problem of popular consultation, sought to resolve the difficulty by means of a huge public corporation which would do for the electorate what the intelligence branch of an army does for the commanding general—that is, tell it what the facts are and what they mean.[3] Here again, however, we would be wise not to try to write a detailed solution into our

[3] Walter Lippmann, *Public Opinion* (New York: Harcourt, Brace and Company, 1922), Ch. XXVI.

blown-up model, and to say only that the model must include arrangements for gathering and communicating to the citizens the fullest and most expert information available about the problems they are to deal with at election time. And this enables us to add: To the extent that the institutions of an actual nation-state fail to provide such arrangements, we must regard them as undemocratic.

The Problem of Consent or Participation. "Any body of men," writes A. Lawrence Lowell, "be it a board of directors, a legislative assembly, a mass meeting, or the electorate as a whole, can express itself intelligently only by answering 'Yes' or 'No' to a question submitted to it." [4] In the present writers' opinion, however, this depends on what *kind* of men the "body of men" is made up of. If it consists of men with a strong determination to govern themselves, they will not acquiesce in any such limitation of their functions, but will rather insist upon active participation in their affairs at a much earlier moment than that for voting Yes or No. No government can be fully democratic if its citizens play only the role Lowell describes; for if the community is to be truly self-governing, proposals must well up out of the citizens' own knowledge and understanding of their problems; and this will not happen if, as a matter of course, they look elsewhere for the proposals.

Our town-meeting model, then, presupposes members who conceive their function as involving creative participation in the shaping of the proposals brought forward as well as giving or withholding consent to them. It may well be more difficult for the citizens of a nation-state than for the members of a town meeting to participate in this fashion; [5] but to the extent that the nation's citizens do not so participate, we must regard it as less democratic than one whose citizens *do* so participate.

MAJORITY RULE

The Problem of Majority "Tyranny" and Minority Acquiescence. In any government based upon the principle of unlimited majority rule, whether at the town-meeting level or the nation-state level, what reason is there to think that minorities can be counted on to acquiesce in all the majorities' decisions? Since the citizens in such a community are "sovereign" as regards the government's powers, *no* proposals, however controversial, however disagreeable to some, are *formally* forbidden to majorities. It is therefore entirely possible that sooner or later some majority will adopt a proposal so repugnant to some minority that the latter will feel it has no alternative but to say to the majority: "This we cannot accept and continue to regard ourselves as free." And

[4] A. Lawrence Lowell, *Public Opinion and Popular Government* (New York: Longmans, Green and Co., 1913), p. 69.

[5] Cf. E. E. Schattschneider's statement that "the people are a sovereign whose vocabulary is limited to two words, 'Yes' and 'No.' This sovereign, moreover, can speak only when spoken to. . . . *This characteristic . . . is due to numbers, not to want of intelligence.* An electorate of sixty million Aristotles would be equally restricted": *Party Government* (New York: Rinehart & Company, Inc., 1942), p. 52. Italics added.

this question becomes more urgent to the extent that we assume, along with many of the great political theorists, that there is something in the very nature of political power that pushes its holders along toward the abuse of it—toward self-aggrandizement, toward using one's neighbors as means to one's own ends, toward what the Greeks called *hubris*.

These are not easy questions to answer, and there is nothing magical in the combination of popular sovereignty, political equality, popular consultation, and majority rule that offers any automatic answers to them. On the contrary, there is, theoretically speaking *and other things being equal,* real danger of majority tyranny and even, in situations of extreme majority-minority tension, arbitrament of some issue by *force*—that is, by civil war. Unlimited majority rule, in other words, *is* an invitation to the majority to abuse its power in such a fashion.

Must we say, then—along with the defenders of limited majority rule—that unlimited majority rule is a recipe for tyranny in the short run and for civil war in the long run? Must we construct *both* our town-meeting and nation-state models so as to place formal limitations upon the majority's powers? The present writers think not, and for two reasons. First, as a matter of history, the actual town meetings, which are a fairly close approximation to our model, have operated, some of them for hundreds of years, *without* producing either majority tyranny or civil war; and so, on the nation-state level, has the parliamentary system in Great Britain, which, beyond any other national system, is based on the idea of unlimited majority rule. Empirical reality, in other words, does not appear to confirm the results of the theory. Either, therefore, the theorizing we have just considered is faulty, or "other things," as they exist in empirical reality, have not been "equal." And second, it is easy to show that "limited majority rule," with the *un*limited veto power it gives minorities, has the same theoretical danger as "unlimited majority rule" of leading to arbitraments by force.

There has evidently been something in the *character* of town-meeting members, or something about their *relatedness* to one another, or something about both, that has either caused majorities to stop short of the point where they are about to drive minorities into rebellion, or has caused minorities to be very slow about concluding that they are being tyrannized over, or has caused both to act with a certain forbearance when arbitrament by force is visible on the horizon.

Relatively few political theorists have addressed themselves directly to the question, What characteristics, or what kind of relatedness, would the members of a model town meeting with an unlimited majority-rule system have to possess in order for majorities and minorities to act with the forbearance needed in order to avoid civil war? Rousseau, however, posed the question in terms at least similar to ours; and many theorists have said things that bear upon it at least tangentially, so that we have several possibilities, not all mutually exclusive, to choose from in our attempt to answer it.

Possible Sources of Majority and Minority Forbearance. The first possible source of majority and minority forbearance, as some theorists have advanced it, is the recognition by minorities that they have to accept majority decisions because, realistically speaking, they cannot do anything else. The minority, the argument runs, is smaller and weaker than the majority and knows it; so if the former rebels, it does so knowing it will be beaten. Thus both the minority and the community have everything to gain by accepting the verdict of the *ballots,* rather than appealing to the *bullets* that would fly in a civil war. Where unlimited majority rule functions without arbitrament by force, accordingly, it does so because minorities recognize that the majority will get its way in any case.

This view of the matter has, in the opinion of the present writers, two fatal shortcomings. In the first place, while it explains the "easy" cases of minority acquiescence—that is, those cases where the minority is so small that it obviously would lose any fight it might start—it does not explain the cases in which the majority and the minority are so nearly the same size that the presence of one Sergeant York on the minority's side and two gun-shy pacifists on the majority's might make the difference between victory and defeat, and where, therefore, the minority might well be tempted to chance it. The second shortcoming of this explanation is the fact that it overlooks that crucial aspect of the political behavior of human beings that is caught up in General Zapata's memorable phrase, "It is better to die on your feet than to live on your knees." It assumes, that is to say, that people never fight except when they think they are sure to win, which is demonstrably not true, and is especially apt not to be true in the case of people who think their neighbors are tyrannizing over them.[6]

A second possible source of majority-minority forbearance is that suggested by those writers, Locke and Rousseau for example, who argue that such forbearance obtains in a situation where *all* the citizens are bound, and think of themselves as bound, by the very fact of belonging to the community —that is, by a "social contract," which includes a *promise* to obey when they find themselves in the minority.[7] As Rousseau puts it, in order for the minority to obey majority decisions, the citizens of the community must on some prior occasion have agreed *unanimously* (not, be it noted, by majority vote) to adopt the majority principle as their rule for decision making.

This line of argument, in the present writers' view, explains more than

[6] We may note, incidentally, that this line of argument explains forbearance only on the part of *minorities,* and that recognition by *majorities* that they will have their way no matter what might well dispose them toward greater rather than lesser abuses of power. It is perhaps not surprising, therefore, that it is a great favorite with anti-majoritarian writers, who use it as a basis for identifying majority rule with government by force—as opposed to, say, "law" or "right reason."

[7] Opinions differ among experts on political theory as to whether Locke and Rousseau thought that a "social contract" embodying such a promise is actually negotiated and subscribed to in each community as it originates, or that it is implicit in the facts of community life. Both spoke sometimes as if the contract were a historical fact.

the the-majority-will-gets-its-way-anyhow line of argument. It directs attention to at least one good reason a minority might have for *wanting* to acquiesce in a majority decision that it dislikes, and suggests a stipulation that we might well feel tempted to write into both our town-meeting and our nation-state models: the citizens must feel *obligated* to accept majority decisions, whether because they think of themselves as having promised to do so, or because they think that the notion of majority rule is implicit in the very notion of community. Rousseau's explanation of minority forbearance is, however, open to some grave objections. For one thing, it, like the first explanation, accounts for minority forbearance where the minority in fact forbears, but does not explain why the *majority* forbears. It therefore offers no grounds for expecting the majority to forbear—as forbear it must sometimes if it is to keep the minority from deciding that keeping its promise to acquiesce will sacrifice larger moral interests. And for another thing, Rousseau's explanation overlooks the fact that each citizen, before agreeing to accept an obligation to the community to go along with majority decisions, must have some good reason for doing so; and the crucial question is, *What* reasons might prompt a reasonable man to accept such an obligation?

Let us, then, include in our model the provision that the citizens must feel *obligated* to accept majority decisions. But let us also seek a further provision that will give us reason to expect them to live up to the obligation.

Rousseau had a good deal to say about this aspect of the problem. He speaks repeatedly of a "bond" or "tie" among the members of the community, and regards it as logically prior to the contract by which they commit themselves to majority rule. This bond or tie he explains in terms of the members' mutual *need* for one another's resources, and thus for the resources of the entire community. Concretely, the citizens subscribe to the contract because if they tried to go it alone they would be unable to cope with the problems they face, and so would perish. Each citizen needs all the others, in other words, because only by retaining their cooperation for the common purposes of the community can he realize his own purposes.

Rousseau does not say that the bond or tie in question obtains among the members of all *actual* communities. Since the *Social Contract* is itself a venture in model building, his point is that the *genuine* community (what we would call one end of the community spectrum) is one in which the bond is universal and powerful, that actual communities can be ranked according to the incidence and strength of the bond, and that the chances of a given community's doing its business by majority-rule procedures depend on the bond's incidence and strength.[8]

Rousseau does not go into detail about the character of the reciprocal needs that constitute the community bond—wisely, in the present writers' opinion, because they are capable of infinite variation from situation to situa-

[8] Jean Jacques Rousseau, *The Social Contract,* translated by Willmoore Kendall (Chicago: Henry Regnery Co., 1954), Bk. IV, Ch. II, pp. 121-23.

tion and from time to time within one and the same situation. People may need each other, particularly within the small local community for which he was primarily constructing a model, because they are so fond of one another that the thought of living away from each other is unbearable.[9] People may need each other, again, for reasons having to do with sheer survival—because, for example, they face a common enemy bent upon destroying them.[10] People may need each other, still again, out of a wish (which we may distinguish from the wish to survive as such) to maintain a particular standard of living; their mutual needs may, that is to say, be "economic." Or they may need each other because they share what is commonly called a "common belief-system" embodied in a common "way of life," whose perpetuation they regard as supremely important, and see as dependent upon the continued cooperation of fellow believers. Nor is it necessary for all the members of a given community to feel a need for each other for the *same* reasons. A's need for B and C may rest on different grounds from B's and C's need for him (A may be the town's only cobbler, and he may be remaining in the community merely out of a determination to convert B and C to his brand of atheism; B and C may abhor his atheism, which places him outside the common belief-system, but feel a great need for him on standard-of-living grounds). And a given individual's need for the other members of the community may rest on *several* of the grounds we have noted.

Rousseau, then, was confident that the members of a community whose members *need* each other in this fashion can make their political decisions by majority vote without danger of majorities' abusing their power and so driving minorities into rebellion or withdrawal. Such is their need for each other, such the value they put upon each member's continuing within the bosom of the community and contributing his resources to the achievement of the community's purposes, such their sense of what *all* would suffer in danger or heartache or impoverishment or loss of accustomed satisfactions, that equally when they are with the majority and when they are with the minority, they want nothing done that might do real hurt to the other members. Thus those who find themselves in the majority on a given proposal that the minority clearly regards as obnoxious know they have the *power* to disregard the minority's wishes; but they also have the best of good reasons for not doing so, namely, that their *own* needs are such that they would end up doing *themselves* the kind of hurt they deeply wish to avoid. They use their power, accordingly, with forbearance. So too with those who find themselves in the

[9] Anyone who finds this difficult to imagine should read the last paragraphs of Plato's *Crito*, in which the condemned Socrates, having refused an opportunity to flee Athens, explains to his friend Crito why he would rather die than live away from Athens: *Crito* in *The Dialogues of Plato*, translated by B. Jowett (New York: Charles Scribner's Sons, 1908), Vol. I, pp. 356-59.

[10] Albert Camus' novel *The Plague* will richly reward anyone interested in this point. It traces, almost as if it were intended to illustrate Rousseau's point, the process by which the citizens of a great city develop reciprocal needs, and *become* a community, in the presence of a threat to their lives, then rapidly cease to be a community as the danger recedes: *The Plague*, translated by Stuart Gilbert (New York: Alfred A. Knopf, 1948).

minority. The latter know that by threatening active resistance or withdrawal, or that lesser form of withdrawal known as "irredentism" (where the dissident minority remains within the community but only to frustrate and obstruct until a previous majority determination is reversed) they can either blackmail the majority into giving them their way, or cause it to strike back in a way that, at the extreme, will make the community ungovernable. But like the majority, they have, in the hurt they would do *themselves* by such action, the best of good reasons for not going too far. Thus they also forbear, and both the majority and the minority seek a determination of the issue in hand that, though it may pass only by a bare majority vote, gives the majority a great deal less of its way than it has the *power* to get, and the minority a great deal more of its way than it can get by its voting power alone.

We must, then, write into our model the provision that the members of the community must feel for one another at least that minimum of mutual need that makes for forbearance on the part of majorities and minorities alike. And having done so, we may reasonably adjourn most of the understandable anxieties that underlie the limited-majority-rule position we summarized in Chapter 2.

The Problem of Majority Miscalculation of Minority Feelings. Suppose the members of the community *do* approach all decisions in the spirit just described, so that we may confidently predict that all of them will try to put the maintenance of the community first, and will therefore act with forbearance in order to prevent majority-minority hostilities. In such a situation majorities will certainly *try* to take into account the interests, preferences, and opinions of minorities, and make a genuine effort to strike a fair balance between those interests, preferences, and opinions and their own. But this still does not *guarantee* the prevention of majority tyranny, irredentism, or civil war. For what is to prevent the majority on a given issue from misjudging the minority's interests, preferences, and opinions, and so, with the best intentions in the world, decreeing a solution that looks fair to it but strikes the minority as outrageous?

Several political theorists have answered this question by saying that both in the democratic town meeting and in the democratic nation-state there must be "full and free discussion" of all problems that the community considers; and if votes are always preceded by such discussion, the minority can hardly fail to "get its point of view across." The essence of democracy, from this point of view, is the kind of discussion process that gets the minority's point of view brought out into the open.

Shall we, then, write into our model a requirement that the character and relatedness of the citizens be such as to guarantee "full and free discussion," and let that suffice? The present writers would reply No, on the ground that the phrase "full and free discussion" raises more problems than it solves, and the conception of the discussion process held by many who use this phrase is not, in our opinion, appropriate to a democracy.

The whole problem, as we see it, turns upon whether one thinks of discussion—as many highly informed and thoughtful people do—as essentially *competitive* and *combative,* or whether one thinks of it as essentially *cooperative* and *heuristic* (that is, serving to advance knowledge and discover truth). Those who think of it as competitive and combative apparently conceive of democratic discussion as a process in which all problems turn promptly into issues, in which all issues promptly divide the members into a "pro" faction and a "con" faction, in which all divisions into factions promptly produce the phenomenon known as "debate," with the pros marshaling all the arguments they can think of for a certain course of action, and the cons all they can think of against it, and in which all debates are as a matter of course nothing more than attempts on the part of each "side" to convince any persons present who are still undecided, and, *per impossibile,* each other. Many discussions, of course, *are* of such a nature, because the participants themselves conceive of discussion in these terms; and where this is the case there is indeed a serious danger that the larger of the two factions will use its power to choke off discussion before the smaller has had what it regards as a "fair hearing." And those who hold this conception of discussion believe that the way to guard against the danger is to set up guarantees that the discussion shall be sufficiently "full and free" to assure the minority a "hearing"—the best of all guarantees being, of course, a citizenry that believes in full and free discussion in this sense.

Those who think of discussion as essentially cooperative and heuristic, on the other hand, have had their case well stated by A. D. Lindsay in *The Essentials of Democracy.* The first modern attempt to make decisions by a process of genuine *democratic* discussion, Lindsay believes, was made by such self-governing religious congregations of the seventeenth century as the Anabaptists, the Independents, and the Quakers. These congregations, he argues, used discussion not as a means of ventilating opposed positions, but rather as a means of *finding out something*—not as a debate but as a process of collective thinking, the purpose of which was to discover what the Quakers call "the sense of the meeting." In such a discussion the participants attempt to *avoid* tests of strength, whether in forensics or in voting, between competing groups each concerned only with getting what it wants. In Lindsay's words:

The creativeness of discussion assumes a common purpose animating those who take part in it. They are trying to find out something. They are asking what the purpose of their community requires. . . . The moment that those discussing begin to play for their own hands, or try to enforce their own personal will, the purpose of the discussion is lost. The sense of the meeting, when it is effective, ensures that the discussion shall serve and be controlled by the common purpose. To that end every one contributes and the contribution of all is necessary.[11]

[11] A. D. Lindsay, *The Essentials of Democracy,* 2nd ed. (London: Oxford University Press, 1942), pp. 45-46. Alfred Bingham points out that this kind of creative discussion is also characteristic of the best examples of the "conference method" in private industry: *Techniques of Democracy* (New York: Duell, Sloan and Pearce, 1942), pp. 120-21.

The idea that animates such a group, Lindsay continues, is "the priesthood of all believers"—the faith that each individual has some unique quality all his own that he can contribute to the group, and from which the group can benefit. Its discussion process, therefore, is calculated to elicit from each member his unique contribution, and out of all such contributions to form a group decision that reflects a complete canvass of all available alternatives with a view to the members' *learning* which one is best for the group as a whole. Thus voting takes place only when each of them has gained a kind of knowledge and understanding of the problem in hand that he could not possibly have had when the discussion began. Ideally, therefore, voting plays a relatively minor role in the group's deliberations.

What each person present wants in such a group is a unanimous decision, embodying the best wisdom of the entire group about all the interests involved; and, this being the case, each member regards the vote as merely a makeshift for getting action when action is needed in a hurry and there is no time to let the discussion take its full course. "Equal counting of heads and agreement to abide by the majority vote are rough and ready means of getting a second-best decision." [12]

On Lindsay's showing, then, the prerequisites of democratic discussion are: first, a readiness on the part of the participants to treat the discussion as a means of gaining information and insights and *not* as a means of converting others to their own point of view; second, a disposition on the part of the participants to treat voting and majority rule as merely second-best ways of getting decisions when the community cannot remain assembled long enough to achieve unanimity. The latter prerequisite explains why discussion comes up properly, for model-building purposes, in connection with majority rule as well as popular consultation. For, as Ernest Barker points out, the *context* in which a majority will is arrived at makes all the difference about its acceptability to a minority:

Discussion is not only like a war; it is also like love. It is not only a battle of ideas; it is also a marriage of minds. If a majority engages in discussion with a minority, and if that discussion is conducted in a spirit of giving and taking, the result will be that the ideas of the majority are widened to include some of the ideas of the minority which have established their truth in the give and take of debate. When this happens, the will of the majority will not be the abstract or isolated will of a mere majority, considered in itself and as standing by itself in opposition to the similar will of a mere minority. Some fusion will have taken place: some accommodation will have been attained.[13]

[12] Lindsay, *op. cit.*, p. 47. See also the discussion of the place of voting and majority rule in Quaker meetings in Laurence Stapleton, *The Design of Democracy* (New York: Oxford University Press, 1949), pp. 70-72.

[13] *Reflections on Government* (London: Oxford University Press, 1942), p. 67. Many opponents of "unlimited" majority rule conceive of the discussion that precedes voting in terms that we have described as competitive—which explains the challenge some of them make to the majoritarian, "Do you mean that if 51 per cent of the people want to make slaves out of the rest, they should have the power to do so?" The only possible reply to such a question is

The Nature and Role of Consensus. The question that perpetually concerns each member of the community in which genuine cooperative discussion takes place is, then, What is best for the *community?* and never merely, What is best for *me?*—and never mind the community! He believes *and acts,* in other words, in accordance with Thomas Jefferson's faith that man is a social and political animal, that his only real happiness can come through being part of a healthy and happy community, and that it is therefore impossible for him ever to be really happy and well off individually if the community of which he is a member is unhappy and badly off.[14] He needs the community, needs the continued participation of all its members, and therefore has good "selfish" reasons to regard them with respect and treat them well. In short, in the religious congregation as Lindsay pictures it there is a high degree of what in this book we shall henceforth call *consensus.* "Consensus," as we shall use the term, refers to the kind of fundamental agreement among the members of the community that exists when they feel for each other that minimum of mutual need that disposes them to conduct their discussion in the manner just described, and to act with forbearance when divisive issues arise. Disagreement aplenty there may be among them on all other matters, but *not* about the prime importance of their continuing to live together as a community. Both our town-meeting and nation-state models must, accordingly, include the provision that the character and relatedness of the citizens must be of such nature as to guarantee cooperative and mutually instructive discussion.

The Nation-State Model

We have now completed our canvass of the main problems that arise when we attempt to construct a model of democracy for the modern nation-state by "blowing up" the town-meeting model. Let us, then, present in summary form a list of the leading characteristics of our nation-state model of democracy as they have emerged from the foregoing discussion.

(1) *Popular sovereignty.* The whole power of government resides in the whole people—that is, in *all* the members of the community, and not in any special ruling class or in any single individual.

(2) *Political equality.* Each member of the community has the same formal right as all the other members to participate in the community's total decision-making process.

(3) *Popular consultation.* (a) The community's laws are made by a representative assembly.

that *no* version of democratic government, majoritarian or otherwise, could be made to work among a people so divided.

[14] Cf. Jefferson's opinion that among the primary motivations in men to do good and eschew evil are "the love, or the hatred and rejection of those among whom he lives, and whose society is necessary to his happiness and even existence": Letter to Thomas Law, June 13, 1814, in *The Works of Thomas Jefferson,* edited by H. A. Washington (New York: Townsend MacCoun, 1884), Vol. VI, p. 350.

(b) The electoral arrangements for selecting members of the representative assembly are such that the assembly will be as subordinate to the people as the latter wish it to be.

(c) Failing (b), the members of the assembly make decisions as the whole people would make them if the latter were present and voting.

(d) The assembly supervises, holds accountable, and has full control over all other public officials.

(e) There are arrangements for communicating to the people full factual knowledge and understanding of all public problems they wish to do something about.

(f) The citizens participate in the *development* of proposals for public policy as well as give or withhold consent to such proposals.

(4) *Majority rule.* (a) No decision as to public policy or procedure is deemed valid if opposed by more than half of the members of the community.

(b) A majority of the representative assembly has the same power over the assembly's decisions as a majority of the town meeting has over the latter's decisions.

(c) Majorities forbear from tyranny and minorities from irredentism and civil war because of a sense of *obligation* to do so on the part of *all* the members of the community (and of their elected representatives) based on the feeling of each that he needs to keep all the others loyal to the community if he is to realize his own values.

(d) Decisions are made after a process of creative discussion in which all the members of the community are trying to find out what is best for the *community*.

(e) Voting and majority rule are regarded merely as makeshifts for getting action when action is needed in a hurry and there is not sufficient time for a full "sense of the community" to emerge from the discussion on the issue in hand.

Putting the Model to Work

POSSIBLE USES FOR THE MODEL

The model of democracy we have constructed in the foregoing pages will be put to work repeatedly in the remainder of this book. But it can also serve purposes other than that for which we shall be using it, especially for anyone who is troubled about the kind of government he would like to see his country adopt, or at least move in the direction of. Such a person will find in the model a means of at least clarifying, if not deciding, most of the issues he needs to face. The model provides him a picture of one alternative stripped of its usual identification with "the good" and reduced to its differentiae—i.e., those essential properties that distinguish it from other forms of government. By visualizing his country's government as it would be if brought into conformity with the model—which the present writers call democratic, but do not insist that others do—he can see what he would have to give up in order to make it conform, and so prepare himself for the central question: Are the gains promised by the advocates of democracy thus defined likely to be forthcoming, and, once they are achieved, are they likely to be worth the price? For the logic of political reality, like that of economic reality, involves costs— stiff ones sometimes—that we should not commit ourselves to meet without first making sure that the probable gains are worth that much to us.

Such issues are not, however, germane to the purposes of this book. It is not our task to inquire whether democracy as we define it is a *better* form of government for the United States than monarchy or aristocracy (though the present writers do argue that the American people apparently want something closely approximate to our model). Our task, rather, is to try to answer such questions as these: To what extent does our party system conform to the model of democracy as it now lies before us? And what changes, if any, in the party system seem best calculated to make it conform better?

EVALUATING THE AMERICAN PARTY SYSTEM

We shall evaluate the American party system's claim to be regarded as a useful instrument of democratic government mainly in terms of its performance as an agency for *popular consultation* and as an agency for *majority rule*. Concretely, we shall ask questions of this sort: Does the party system assist in keeping the decisions of our elected officials in accord with the people's desires? Does it help to provide the people with the factual knowledge and understanding they need to decide governmental problems? Does it aid them in participating in the development of proposals for public action? Does it foster the kind of consensus and creative discussion that prevents majority tyranny and minority irredentism and rebellion? And we shall summarize our answers to these questions in Chapter 22.

The reader should realize that the party system, like any of our other governing institutions, may score well on some of these points, less well on others, and badly on still others. It may even be that the very characteristics that enable it to score well on one point keep it from scoring well on another. For this reason we shall avoid any *summary* judgment as to whether the party system is, on balance, "democratic" or "undemocratic."

We are likely to achieve a fuller understanding of the party system's operations, successes, and failures if we precede our description of it with a brief examination of the operations, successes, and failures of the institutions that the United States—and the other Western democracies—traditionally have used in addition to political parties as means for achieving popular consultation and majority rule. Those institutions—the town meeting, representation, and direct legislation—we shall describe in the next chapter.

Chapter 4

POPULAR CONSULTATION: TRADITIONAL INSTITUTIONS

For at least four hundred years the nation-state has received far more attention from political theorists than any other form of political organization among Western peoples. For three centuries or more, moreover, political theorists have tended increasingly to argue—and with an ever-increasing show of reason—that the democratically organized nation-state, as variously defined by them, is the form of government most likely to bring about and maintain the type of political situation that is most satisfactory from the standpoint of the values of Western civilization. And for some one hundred and seventy-five years now a considerable number of Western nation-states have actually attempted to realize democracy in their governing institutions.

We have attempted above to explain what popular consultation is and involves, and have pointed out that the story of man's successes and failures in his efforts to establish democratic government is best told in terms of the institutions he has created in the attempt to "solve" the problem of popular consultation. Numerous methods of discovering and implementing the popular will have been proposed, debated, adopted with or without modification, tested, perhaps altered in the light of developing experience, and then retained or abandoned completely.

To examine all the details of each institution in each nation where it has been employed is a task far too vast to undertake in this book. It can be argued, however, that all the attempts men have made to achieve genuine popular consultation turn out to be variants, more or less different in detail, of one or another of three traditional institutions: the town meeting, representation, and direct legislation. And the present chapter is devoted to a detailed examination of the rationale, organization, and comparative strengths and shortcomings of each of these three traditional institutions as revealed in actual practice.

The Town Meeting

As we noted in Chapter 3, most persons agree that the most purely democratic method of popular consultation is direct government via assemblies. in which *all* the members of the community participate; and we adopted these assemblies as the foundation for our model of democratic government. The older writers who took this view (the Levelers and Rousseau, for example) apparently had been led to this belief by meditating on the government of ancient Athens or of republican Rome. Present-day writers are more likely to cite the town meetings by which the people of New England have traditionally consulted themselves on matters of public policy.

From their earliest existence as English colonies to the present day the New England states have used the town as the basic unit of local government. (Counties, sanitary districts, park districts, incorporated municipalities, etc., have thus never had the importance there they have assumed elsewhere.) Even at the present time, with the system in relative decline, there are some 1,400 towns in the six states of Maine, Vermont, New Hampshire, Massachusetts, Rhode Island, and Connecticut.

The typical New England town as often as not includes both rural and built-up areas. The towns vary greatly in size, but are, for the most part, small in point of population: fully a third have less than 500 citizens, only a very few are as large as 25,000, and the average is around two to three thousand.[1]

Almost all these 1,400 towns are governed by town meetings, a little different, as far as organization is concerned, from state to state, but enough alike for a single general description to serve for all of them.[2]

ORGANIZATION AND PROCEDURES

It is state law that vests the governing power of the town in its town meeting, though of course many of the towns and town meetings were going concerns long before the state in which they are situated came into existence. All qualified voters residing within the town limits are *ipso facto* members

[1] Lane W. Lancaster, *Government in Rural America* (New York: D. Van Nostrand Company, Inc., 1937), pp. 42-43; Clyde F. Snider, *American State and Local Government* (New York: Appleton-Century-Crofts, Inc., 1950), pp. 294-95.

[2] For an account of the sevententh-century origins of the New England town meetings, see Anne B. MacLear, *Early New England Towns*, doctoral dissertation in political science, Columbia University, published by the author in 1908. For descriptions of their present-day organization and procedures, see Lancaster, *op. cit.*, pp. 43 ff.; Snider, *op. cit.*, pp. 349-56; John A. Fairlie and Charles M. Kneier, *County Government and Administration* (New York: The Century Co., 1930), pp. 430 ff.; Theodore B. Manny, *Rural Municipalities* (New York: The Century Co., 1930), Ch. IV; John Gould, *New England Town Meeting, Safeguard of Democracy* (Brattleboro, Vt.: Stephen Daye Press, 1940); John F. Sly, *Town Government in Massachusetts* (Cambridge, Mass.: Harvard University Press, 1930), Chs. VI-VIII; G. F. Palmer, ed., *Town Government in New Hampshire* (Manchester, N. H.: The New Hampshire Historical Records Survey Project, 1940); and M. R. White, *The Connecticut Town Meeting: A Handbook for Moderators and Other Town Meeting Officials* (Storrs, Conn.: Institute of Public Service, University of Connecticut, 1949).

of the meeting, which convenes once each year, usually in the early spring or "mud season" (except in Connecticut, where meetings are held in October). Special meetings can be called to deal with unusual problems or situations that arise, but this rarely happens, and most town business is transacted annually at the regular town meeting. The official call for the meeting is drawn up and issued by the town's board of selectmen. It takes the form of a "warrant," posted in various prominent places about the town well in advance of the meeting, so that everybody will know when and where the meeting will occur and what matters it will consider.

The morning of meeting day is devoted to balloting for various town officials, such as the moderator, board of selectmen, town clerk, tax assessor, tax collector, treasurer, library trustees, constable, etc. Voting is normally by secret ballot, although in general secrecy is neither so highly valued nor so rigidly enforced as in most American elections outside New England.[3] After lunch, the citizens assemble in the town hall and, with the "moderator" presiding, transact other business specified in the warrant. They discuss the "town report," which is in fact a series of individual reports from the several town officials covering their activities through the previous year (it is compiled and printed by the selectmen, then circulated among the citizens before the meeting). They make appropriations, fix tax rates, enact town laws, and draw up such special instructions as seem to be needed for the town officials. Finally the meeting is adjourned, to be followed, in most towns, by a community dinner and dance.

Between annual town meetings, a board of selectmen, three to five in number, is the chief administrative authority of the town. It grants licenses, lays out highways, pays town bills, prepares the agenda and issues the warrant for the next town meeting, and, as noted above, compiles the town report.

All the New England states except Rhode Island permit their towns, under certain conditions, to adopt the "town manager" plan, under which the board of selectmen appoints a qualified manager to supervise the town's administrative functions—much as a city manager would do in a state outside New England. As of 1949, however, only about 100 towns had adopted the town-manager plan, so that it has not yet greatly changed the face of New England's local government.[4]

THE "LIMITED" TOWN MEETING

In the past half-century the inhabitants of a number of New England towns with populations above five or six thousand have come to feel that the pure form of the traditional town meeting serves their needs less well than it

---

[3] Gould, *op. cit.*, p. 41. This book contains a colorful description of meeting-day proceedings, liberally illustrated with photographs of some Maine town meetings, and gives the reader the flavor of the town meeting better than any other available work.

[4] Snider, *op. cit.*, pp. 355-56.

did those of their parents and grandparents. As their towns have grown, they have found it increasingly difficult, for one thing, to get all the town's citizens into a single hall, and, for another, to persuade all of them to turn up. Increasing size has, moreover, brought with it increasingly complicated administrative and policy problems that a large popular assembly cannot—in the view of many people—deal with very successfully. On the other hand, there has been a great reluctance to junk the town meeting altogether and replace it with a mayor-council or commission form of government. Many communities have found a suitable compromise in the form of organization known as the "limited town meeting." Here the town is divided into precincts, of approximately equal population, each of which elects from among its residents a number of delegates or "town-meeting members" (usually thirty to forty). Only the latter can actually cast votes at such town meetings as may occur during their incumbency. The meetings themselves are called and organized in the traditional fashion, still exercise the town's governing powers, and still (curiously, some might say) admit to the floor and permit to speak any citizen who wishes to attend and make known his views. The only difference between the traditional and limited form, in short, is that the number of citizens who are entitled to be counted when votes are taken is "limited." [5]

THE TOWN MEETING TODAY

In the opinion of most observers, the town meeting remains a vital and dynamic form of local government, with great current achievements to its credit—to which those who live under it are the first to call attention. In any case, its successful operation in New England over three centuries provides democratic theory with actual, functioning governments that are very close indeed to the model of democracy outlined in the third chapter of this book, and has proved to the satisfaction of many that government along purely democratic lines can be "good" government. The town meeting's claim to attention and analysis by theorists of democracy everywhere appears to be indisputable.

Experience with the town meeting does indicate, however, that this way of dealing with popular consultation runs into genuine difficulties when either or both of two things happen to a community in which it is used—two things, moreover, which are happening to many of the communities of which we have been speaking. For one thing, as we have already indicated, the town meeting tends to develop stresses and strains when the town's population goes above, say, five thousand, for then either not everyone can be present or, worse still, not everyone even tries to be present, so that the meeting loses its traditional meaning as a gathering of *all* the citizenry. Some have concluded from this, in effect, that towns must either see to it that they remain small, or give up the town meeting in favor of a local-government form not quite so

[5] Sly, *op. cit.*, Ch. VII, has the best description of the "limited" town meeting. See also Manny, *op. cit.*, Ch. IV.

close to our model. Others, as will be clear from the above, believe that you can have it both ways, i.e., let the town grow and keep the town meeting, *provided* you content yourself with having something less than all the citizens present but do not leave to chance (e.g., who gets there first) the question of who gets left out. It is this second group who have invented and launched on its career the limited town meeting, about whose merits, admittedly, much less is known (or knowable, given the brief and spotty character of New England's experience with it) than about those of the meeting in its original form. For another thing, the town meeting appears to go halt and lame when a community using it develops within itself groups so conscious of their "special" interests (as opposed to the interests of the whole town) that they tend to vote together as blocs on most public questions. This problem has become particularly troublesome in northern New England, which, since the turn of the century, has received substantial numbers of French Canadian immigrants from Quebec.[6] The reader will remember that just such a difficulty was cited in Chapter 3 as a danger inherent in the public meeting as a model of democracy. The actual experience of the New England towns where this problem has arisen appears to bear out our contention that the public meeting is a viable model of democratic government only if it is animated by a certain nuance of spirit and outlook among its members, and if its decisions are made as the result of a certain kind of discussion. It would also seem to reinforce the suggestion that such a spirit and such a mode of discussion are essential to democracy, while any particular form of machinery is not.

Representation

THE MEANING OF REPRESENTATION

Etymologically, "to represent" means "to present again" and, by extension, "to present again by standing in the place of another." Thus a "representative" is a person who, for certain purposes and in certain situations, stands in the place of another person or persons not physically there, and presents on their behalf what they would present if they were there.[7] These are the terms in which John Stuart Mill, for example, formulated his well-known definition of representative government: it is government in which "the whole people, or some numerous portion of them, exercise through deputies [i.e., *representatives*] periodically elected by themselves the ultimate controlling power. . . ."[8]

[6] Cf. Gould, *op. cit.*, p. 60. See also Snider, *op. cit.*, p. 350.

[7] Cf. John A. Fairlie, "The Nature of Political Representation," *American Political Science Review*, Vol. XXXIV (April, June, 1940), pp. 236-48, 456-66; and Alfred de Grazia, *Public and Republic* (New York: Alfred A. Knopf, 1951), pp. 3-6.

[8] John Stuart Mill, *Utilitarianism, Liberty, and Representative Government*, Everyman's edition (London: J. M. Dent and Sons, Ltd., 1944), p. 228.

PRE-DEMOCRATIC REPRESENTATION

Representation, as defined above, is an ancient institution, which antedates democracy and the modern nation-state as well. Scholars are not entirely agreed as to when representative institutions first appeared in the Western world, but there seems no doubt that representation was a familiar political device in the early Middle Ages—that is, for centuries before the emergence of anything like the modern nation-state and even more centuries before men began to demand that the ruling power be lodged in the hands of all its citizens.[9]

Such pre-democratic representative bodies as the Anglo-Saxon Witenage-mot, the Norman-Angevin Curia Regis, and the various French *parlements* were, to be sure, organized upon a different *principle* of representation than that which underlies modern democratic legislatures; for they were based on representation of *estates,* not individuals. According to the political theory characteristic of the medieval-feudal period, the community was made up of three great interests or "estates" (the rulers of the Church, or Lords Spiritual; the feudal nobility, or Lords Temporal; and the knights and burgesses of the towns, or Commons), each of which was to be regarded as, so to speak, a monolithic whole—the irreducible and basic political unit of the community. Logically enough, therefore (since the concept just stated was generally accepted), each *whole* "estate" became a "constituency" for purposes of representation, and named particular representatives who were to present themselves before the monarch and speak for it.[10] There was no room, in the medieval approach to representation, for the idea that the individual human being is the irreducible basic unit of the community, and that it is he, not this or that corporate group or "estate," who should be represented. That idea, when it was first brought forward by the democrats of seventeenth-century England, was viewed as a major political heresy.

THE ORIGINAL DEMOCRATIC THEORY OF REPRESENTATION

We observed in the preceding chapters that most political theorists in the seventeenth and eighteenth centuries thought of democracy—or at least of "pure" democracy—as rule by the direct action of a face-to-face assembly of all the members of the community (i.e., in straight town-meeting terms). The communities with whose form of government they were preoccupied, how-

---

[9] Edward M. Sait agreed with Duguit and Barker that ancient Greece and Rome had representative institutions of a sort, and that the idea migrated to England from the Mediterranean areas: *Political Institutions: A Preface* (New York: D. Appleton-Century Co., Inc., 1938), Ch. XX. Henry Jones Ford, on the other hand, concluded that English representative institutions, like the Anglo-Saxon Witenagemot and the Norman-Angevin Curia Regis, modeled as they were on the representative system used by the Dominican Order of the Church, were the first instance of genuine *political* representation: *Representative Government* (New York: Henry Holt and Company, 1924), Part I. See also Robert M. MacIver, *The Web of Government* (New York: The Macmillan Company, 1947), pp. 184-85.

[10] Cf. MacIver, *op. cit.,* p. 210.

ever, were the *nation-states* in which they happened to live, and all of them took it for granted that such communities were simply too large—both in territory and in population—to organize themselves in terms of face-to-face assemblies. One of the questions they had to answer, therefore, was whether the typical modern nation-state must as a matter of course be governed undemocratically. Most of them found the solution to that question in the answer to another, quite different question: Is satisfactory representation possible? If properly conceived and organized, they argued, representative assemblies like the English Parliament can be made to express the popular will. And the theory of representation upon which they rested that contention was to dominate democratic thinking for at least the next two centuries. It is, indeed, the theory most democrats appear to hold even today.

Briefly stated, the original democratic theory of representation runs as follows. The basic units of the community are *not* its corporate interests or "estates," but its individual members. It is, accordingly, the latter who should be represented—and represented equally—in the lawmaking body. Each representative in the legislative assembly should express the will of a determinate "constituency" of those individual members, and the *whole* assembly should express the will of *all* the people. Consequently the representative assembly should be, in Mirabeau's famous metaphor, a *carte réduite*—a "map to scale." The various opinions expressed in the assembly and their relative influence upon policy should, that is to say, correspond to the opinions held and their relative strength among the members of the community generally. To go on with the metaphor, the representative assembly should be to the popular will what a map is to the territory it represents—"an exact working model of the mass of the people in action." [11]

Such, then, is the prevailing democratic theory of representation. It is based, as A. Lawrence Lowell pointed out, upon these assumptions:

. . . that an election is a more or less trustworthy expression of public opinion; that while the persons chosen may not hold precisely the same views as their constituents on all the questions that arise, yet they will reflect the general tone of thought of the electorate and its party complexion with some approach to accuracy.[12]

And, as our summary shows, its authors, far from attributing to representation any peculiar virtue or advantage, *accepted* it (whether uncritically or not we shall inquire later) as a more or less satisfactory make-do for the desirable but clearly impossible face-to-face assembly of the whole body of citizens. William Paterson put the point succinctly at the American Constitutional Convention in 1787: "What is the principle of representation? It is an expedience

[11] De Grazia, *op. cit.*, pp. 242-43. See also Herman Finer, *Theory and Practice of Modern Government*, rev. ed. (New York: Henry Holt and Company, 1949), p. 225.

[12] A. Lawrence Lowell, *Public Opinion and Popular Government*, rev. ed. (New York: Longmans, Green and Co., 1914), p. 113.

by which an assembly of certain individuals chosen by the people is substituted in place of the inconvenient meeting of the people themselves." [13]

The early democrats, as just indicated, were not in complete agreement as to whether representation is as "good" as the face-to-face assembly, or about as good, or only a second-best way of discovering the popular will. For example, James Wilson of Pennsylvania, one of the few democrats at the Constitutional Convention, had no doubts about representation's being *as* good as that for which it substitutes:

> . . . As [the people] cannot . . . act by themselves, they must act by their representatives. And, indeed, in point of right, there is no difference between that which is done by the people in their own persons, and that which is done by their deputies, acting agreeably to the powers received from them. In point of utility, there is as little difference; for there is no advantage, which may not be obtained from a free and adequate representation, in as effectual a manner, as if every citizen were to deliberate and vote in person.[14]

Rousseau, by contrast, held representation to be basically incompatible with his model of a healthy constitution, for he doubted whether any man can really express the thoughts and desires of any other man or group of men.[15] He did, to be sure, build some representative arrangements into his scheme for the government of Poland. But his contention was merely that in a nation of the size and character of Poland, representation was what one had to accept in lieu of genuine self-government, and he did not suggest that Poland, by adopting the kind of representative system he proposed (in which, as we shall see below, the representatives were to be their constituents' rubber stamps) would enjoy the kind of freedom under law that he sketched in the *Social Contract* (where each citizen willed the general will).[16]

Thomas Jefferson took the middle position that representation, while not as democratic (or, as he said, "republican") as an assembly of all the citizens, was an approximation to the ideal and, in a nation-state, a sufficiently close approximation to be well worth fighting for. What the proponent of self-government must do, according to Jefferson, is to make sure his nation's representative system expresses the popular will as accurately and fully as possible.[17] On this minimum statement, indeed, most of the early democrats could have

[13] Quoted in William S. Carpenter, *Democracy and Representation* (Princeton: Princeton University Press, 1925), pp. 39-40. See also James Hogan, *Election and Representation* (Cork, Eire: Cork University Press, 1945), p. 108.

[14] *The Works of James Wilson*, edited by James D. Andrews (Chicago: Callaghan and Company, 1896), Vol. II, p. 14. See also Finer, *op. cit.*, p. 220.

[15] Jean Jacques Rousseau, *The Social Contract*, anonymous eighteenth-century translation, rev. and ed. by Charles Frankel (New York: Hafner Publishing Company, 1947), Bk. II, Ch. I; and Bk. III, Ch. XV.

[16] A. D. Lindsay argues that this anti-representation strain in Rousseau has had more influence on democratic thought than most commentators allow it: *The Essentials of Democracy*, 2nd ed. (London: Oxford University Press, 1935), pp. 25-26.

[17] Cf. Jefferson's statement that a republic is "a government by its citizens in mass, acting directly and personally, according to rules established by the majority; and . . . every other gov-

agreed, as they could also on the proposition that the representative assembly expresses the popular will better than any other known device for eliciting it, and should therefore be the fundamental organ of government—it should make the laws, supervise and hold responsible those who are charged with carrying out the laws, and, in general, do whatever the people it represents wish it to do.[18]

SYSTEMS OF REPRESENTATION

Territorial Representation—The Single-Member Constituency. There was agreement, then, on the desirability of a representative assembly, which would represent the individual members of the community in such fashion that the assembly would present a *carte réduite* of public opinion. The obvious next question was, What method of naming representatives is best calculated to produce such an assembly?

The first answer produced by the democratic theorists was that of *territorial* representation: divide the nation into territorial areas ("constituencies"), each containing approximately the same number of citizens, and have each, at specified and not-too-infrequent intervals, elect a specified number of representatives to the assembly.[19]

The most common form of territorial representation has always been the single-member constituency, in which, as the name suggests, each constituency returns one representative to the assembly. This is the system actually employed, for example, in the selection of members for the United States House of Representatives, in slightly more than half of American state legislative houses, in the municipal councils of many American and British cities, in the British House of Commons, and in the lower houses of the parliaments of most of the British dominions. Most (though not all) of the assemblies just mentioned are, moreover, made up of representatives who are required to win only a "plurality" or "relative majority" of the constituency's votes in order to win the relevant "mandate." Whatever the number of candidates, that is to say, the one who wins the highest number or "plurality" of the votes, even if this be less than half of the votes cast, stands elected.

ernment is more or less republican, in proportion as it has in its composition more or less of this ingredient of the direct action of the citizens. Such a government is evidently restrained to very narrow limits of space and population. I doubt if it would be practicable beyond the extent of a New England township. . . . The first shade from this pure element, which, like that of pure vital air, cannot sustain life of itself, would be where the powers of the government, being divided, should be exercised each by representatives chosen either *pro hac vice,* or for such short terms as should render secure the duty of expressing the will of their constituents. This I should consider as the nearest approach to a pure republic, which is practicable on a large scale of country or population. . . . The further the departure from direct and constant control by the citizens, the less has the government of the ingredient of republicanism . . .": Letter to John Taylor, 1816, quoted in de Grazia, *op. cit.,* pp. 105-06.

[18] Cf. Mill, *op. cit.,* pp. 231-33; Finer, *op. cit.,* p. 111; de Grazia, *op. cit.,* pp. 8-9; and Ernest Barker, *Reflections on Government* (London: Oxford University Press, 1942), p. 42.

[19] Finer, *op. cit.,* p. 221; Wilson, *op. cit.,* Vol. II, pp. 14-15.

Ever since the middle of the nineteenth century the single-member, plurality-vote constituency has been sharply criticized on the grounds that it does not measure up to the clear requirements for a genuinely democratic system of representation. Some of the critics have confined their objections to the plurality vote, and have no quarrel either with the territorial basis of the single-member constituency or with the fact that it elects only one member. The system, they contend, invites a situation where the representative of each constituency can claim the electoral support of less than half of his constituents, and where, accordingly, a majority of the whole assembly can hardly be said to represent a majority of the whole people.[20] Some of the British dominions (and, at one time, some of the American states) attempted to meet this criticism by adopting a device known as the "preferential ballot." Where it is used, the voter indicates not only his first but also his second (or even his third, fourth, etc.) choice, and if no candidate receives a majority of all first choices, the second choices are brought into play by dropping all but the two highest candidates and adding to their totals the second choices cast for them on the ballots of all the dropped candidates—or, in some cases, the second choices on all ballots.

A somewhat more popular device for ending plurality victories, however, is the "second ballot" or "runoff," which is now used in some British dominions and in primary elections in a number of southern American states. It works as follows. If the constituency gives one of its candidates a majority of all votes cast, he is declared elected (as he would be in a straight plurality-vote election). But if it does *not* give one candidate an absolute majority of the votes case, a second election is held in which only the two top candidates at the first election are on the ballot, so that one of them is bound to get a majority.

The basic purpose of both the "preferential ballot" and "runoff" systems, then, is to make sure that no representative shall be sent to the assembly with the approval of less than 50 per cent of those of his constituents who vote.[21]

In the eyes of some critics, however, to adopt either the preferential ballot or the runoff is to accept and perpetuate the single-member constituency system's shortcomings, or at most merely to scratch the surface of them. What is needed, they say, is to get rid of the system itself, and replace it with something entirely different—namely, *proportional* representation.

Proportional Representation. The advocates of proportional representation argue that no variant of the single-member constituency system can satisfy the

[20] Finer, *op. cit.*, p. 552, presents a table showing how, in Great Britain, three-cornered races for parliamentary seats have had their results distorted by the system of single-member constituencies with plurality elections.

[21] *Ibid.*, pp. 552-53. See also Snider, *op. cit.*, pp. 136-37; and Howard R. Penniman, *Sait's American Parties and Elections*, 4th ed. (New York: Appleton-Century-Crofts, Inc., 1948), pp. 435-38. Eleven American states have, at one time or another, adopted the preferential ballot; but all eleven have subsequently abandoned it.

requirements for democratic representation, so that if the latter is what we really want we shall be driven to one form or another of the *multiple*-member constituency system. And if persistence and patience were all that were needed to accomplish a major political reform, we should have such a system today; for, beginning in 1844, when the American publicist Thomas Gilpin published his pamphlet, "The Representation of Minorities of Electors to Act with the Majority in Elected Assemblies," there has been a flood of didactic pamphlets and books arguing the case for "PR." After Gilpin, the big turning point in the development of this literature came in 1859, with the publication in England of Thomas Hare's book, *On the Election of Representatives, Parliamentary and Municipal,* which made a convert of John Stuart Mill and thus got the case for PR written into one of the greatest and most widely read political treatises ever written in England, Mill's *Representative Government.*

By the 1870's, a number of American states had adopted PR for electing legislators, judges, municipal officials, and county administrators. In 1893, an organization devoted exclusively to spreading the PR gospel, the American Proportional Representation League, came into existence, and is in large part responsible not only for the numerous subsequent adoptions in this country, but also for the widespread impression, among people of the type we may loosely call "political reformers," that any move in the direction of PR is, *ipso facto,* a good thing.[22]

The case for PR, as it appears in the various broadsides of its partisans (who, more than most defenders of proposals in the general field of political gadgetry, tend to develop an almost religious fervor) can be reduced to these basic propositions: (1) Each vote cast in a democracy should, so far as is technically possible, command an equal share of representation in the assembly. (Each voter, that is to say, should have a representative whom he can regard as speaking for *him*.) (2) The single-member constituency system, no matter what twist it is given, inevitably results in a considerable number of individuals going unrepresented. The representative from any individual constituency speaks only for those who voted for him; thus there is no one to speak for those who voted against him. And it is no answer to this to say that there are similarly unrepresented people, on the other side of the fence politically, in other constituencies, so that the inequities cancel each other out. The majority party almost always has a larger percentage of the seats than it has of the popular votes, for one thing, and, in any case, the answer is question-begging. If someone's being unrepresented is the evil, that evil is increased and not lessened by the fact that others are unrepresented. (3) The single-member constituency system consequently produces two inevitable results, either of which is enough to disqualify it as an appropriate system of representation for a democracy: the majority and the minority (or minorities) are not represented in the assembly in proportion to their actual strength throughout the

[22] For a brief history of the PR movement, see de Grazia, *op. cit.,* pp. 186-90.

country, and small minorities are not represented at all. Hence, the *carte réduite* provided by this system is a false, or at least highly distorted, picture of the public opinion it is supposed to portray.[23]

The remedy, say the advocates of PR, is clear: Abolish the single-member constituency system and put in its place a system that will make the representative assembly *a mathematically exact representation of the various segments of opinion among the electorate.* A considerable number of systems have been devised with this end in view, all, however, involving *multiple-member constituencies,* and balloting arrangements calculated to give each "coherent well-knit group of voters with a faith sufficiently different from that of the others" representation in proportion to its actual electoral strength from constituency to constituency.[24]

There are two basic types of PR systems: (1) the "single transferable vote" system, which we find in use in a number of American municipalities and in scattered localities in the British Commonwealth and the Scandinavian countries; and (2) the "party list" system, which was used in the Weimar Republic of pre-Hitler Germany and which the Fourth French Republic uses for its parliamentary elections today.[25]

PR, then, has been tried out in actual practice over a considerable period and in a wide variety of political environments. Its merits and demerits are, therefore, no longer matters for theoretical determination, and we already have a considerable body of literature dealing with its results.[26] This literature is fairly evenly divided as to whether the results are desirable or undesirable, but is fairly unanimous on one point: that PR, wherever it has been adopted, has produced or intensified a trend toward something known as the "multiple-party system." And any judgment of PR's claim to be *the* system of representation for a democracy must, therefore, rest for the most part upon the claim of the multiple-party system to be *the* party system for a democracy.

Functional Representation. Though they disagree profoundly on questions of democratic technique and organization, the advocates and opponents of PR do share two premises: first, that in a democracy the individual human being must be regarded as the basic political unit, and second, that the goal of any

---

[23] For statements of the PR case against the single-member constituency system, see Mill, *op. cit.,* pp. 256-63; Hogan, *op. cit.,* pp. 125 ff.; and C. G. Hoag and G. H. Hallett, *Proportional Representation* (New York: The Macmillan Company, 1926), Ch. II.

[24] Finer, *op. cit.,* pp. 554-55.

[25] Readers interested in a more detailed treatment of these systems may consult any of a number of accounts. The most complete description of the various PR systems is to be found in Hoag and Hallett, *op. cit.* For briefer but still fairly exhaustive treatments see Finer, *op. cit.,* pp. 555-60; and De Grazia, *op. cit.,* pp. 166-68.

[26] The main statements in defense of PR's results are provided by Hoag and Hallett, *op. cit.;* and J. H. Humphreys, *Proportional Representation* (London: Methuen and Co., Ltd., 1911). The most extensive attack on PR is that by F. A. Hermens, *Democracy or Anarchy?* (Notre Dame, Ind.: The Review of Politics, 1941). Generally unfavorable assessments of PR have also been made by Finer, *op. cit.,* pp. 556-58; Barker, *op. cit.,* pp. 78-81; Hogan, *op. cit.,* pp. 16 ff.; and J. A. Corry, *Elements of Democratic Government,* new ed. (New York: Oxford University Press, 1951), pp. 238-45.

democratic system of representation should be the most accurate reflection possible of the views of all the individual members of the community on public policy. Some democratic theorists repudiate both these propositions, and insist that the whole idea of representing individuals, whether "proportionally" or not, be abandoned in favor of "functional" or "occupational" representation. The most famous exponent of this point of view (or rather ex-exponent, since he long ago abandoned it) is the British political theorist, G. D. H. Cole.[27]

Cole's attack on traditional democratic theories of representation, reduced to its simplest terms, runs as follows. Modern social psychology and political science have taught us that the functional group, not the individual human being, is the basic unit of politics. No citizen acts in politics entirely by himself, that is, outside a context of relatedness with other persons. The individual acts, rather, as *a member of a group* of persons with a common objective, which is what we mean by the term "functional group" or "interest group." [28] And we cannot, all this being the case, expect the representative assembly to represent the "views" of isolated individuals. The individual as such, the individual regarded as a unit, has no "views." Take, for example, an "individual" legislator who makes his living as a lawyer, is a Baptist by religion, has a game leg because of which he is a "non-veteran," and belongs to the upper-income-group segment of the population. How can he be expected to "represent" businessmen, workers, farmers, Catholics, Quakers, veterans, and people with low incomes? The only possible answer, given our present system, is that all the latter, so long as he is speaking for them, will feel that they are not represented in the legislative assembly. They will, therefore, seek to influence policy formation by exerting "pressure" on agencies of government other than the lawmaking body. "The essentials of democratic representation," Cole wrote,

. . . are, first, that the represented shall have free choice of, constant contact with, and considerable control over, his representative. The second is that he should be called upon, not to choose someone to represent him as a man or as a citizen in all the aspects of citizenship, but only to choose someone to represent his point of view in relation to some particular purpose or group of purposes, in other words, some particular *function*. All true and democratic representation is therefore *functional* representation.[29]

[27] Cole stated the case for functional representation in his *Social Theory* (New York: Frederick A. Stokes Co., 1920) and *Guild Socialism Re-stated* (London: L. Parsons, 1920). Later, however, he recorded his abandonment of this position in *The Next Ten Years in British Social and Economic Policy* (London: Macmillan and Co., Ltd., 1929). Somewhat shorter statements of the FR position can be found in G. C. Field, *Guild Socialism; A Critical Examination* (London: W. Gardner, Darton and Co., Ltd., 1920), Ch. VI; and Sidney and Beatrice Webb, *A Constitution for the Socialist Commonwealth of Great Britain* (New York: Longmans, Green and Co., 1920), pp. xiii ff. A recent revival of this point of view is Fritz Nova, *Functional Representation* (Dubuque, Ia.: Wm. C. Brown Co., 1950).

[28] For a recent statement of this view of the nature of politics—but one that does not advance from it to the advocacy of FR—see David B. Truman, *The Governmental Process* (New York: Alfred A. Knopf, 1951), especially Chs. II and III.

[29] Cole, *Guild Socialism Re-stated*, pp. 32-33. See also Nova, *op. cit.*, pp. 2-6; and Fairlie, *op. cit.*, p. 460.

In a word, the indicated remedy for the unrepresentativeness of our present institutions, according to Cole, is to reconstitute our legislative assemblies so that they represent *directly* the great functional groups of society, not its isolated individual members.

A number of modern nations have made gestures in the direction of functional representation. Some, like Weimar Germany and the French Third and Fourth Republics, have set up "economic councils"—bodies representing the leading economic interests of their respective nations, with power only to advise and recommend. Certain non-democratic nations, Mussolini's Italy and Dr. Salazar's Portugal in particular, have declared themselves to be "corporate states," in which one house of the legislature is composed of representatives from the great corporate interests of the nation.[30]

Of the nations presumably committed to realizing democracy, only one has ever experimented with a legislative assembly organized on the principle of functional representation and endowed it with real power. The 1922 Constitution of Eire (the Irish Free State) provided that the upper house (Senate) of its Parliament should be "composed of citizens who shall be proposed on the grounds that they have done honour to the nation . . . or that, because of special qualifications or attainments, they represent important aspects of the nation's life." [31] One-fourth of the Senate was to be renewed at each triennial election, in which the voters were to choose from a panel of candidates, two-thirds of the members of which were to be nominated by the lower house of Parliament and one-third by the Senate, both houses to make their nominations "with special reference to the necessity for arranging for the representation of important interests and institutions in the country." [32] The lower house of Parliament, however, was organized along traditional lines.

The Irish Senate had only the power to delay action on proposed legislation. But the De Valera government, by the middle 1930's, had come to regard it as a nuisance. In 1936, therefore, it got through a constitutional amendment abolishing the Senate and making the Parliament a unicameral body, organized along traditional democratic lines. Thus the only attempt made thus far to fit functional representation into democratic government suggests that Cole and its other proponents rather overestimated its potential usefulness.

Many commentators argue that the "failure" of the Irish Senate was unavoidable because of a basic incompatibility between formal functional representation and democracy, and the present writers would agree at least with the

[30] For more complete descriptions of these economic councils, see Finer, *op. cit.*, pp. 545-51; and Edward G. Lewis, "The Operation of the French Economic Council," *American Political Science Review*, Vol. XLIX (March, 1955), pp. 161-72. For descriptions of the corporate states, see G. L. Field, *The Syndical and Corporative Institutions of Italian Fascism* (New York: Columbia University Press, 1938), Part III; and S. G. West, *The New Corporative State of Portugal* (London: The New Temple Press, 1937).

[31] Article 30, quoted in Donal O'Sullivan, *The Irish Free State and Its Senate* (London: Faber and Faber, Ltd., 1940). This work presents the fullest account available of the Irish Senate's early organization, later difficulties, and eventual demise.

[32] Article 33 of the 1922 Irish Constitution.

point about the incompatibility of the two. Functional representation cannot solve the problems of integration and consensus which, as we saw in the earlier chapters of this book, are capital problems in any democracy. On the contrary, it actually emphasizes and deepens existing divisions among the members of a community.[33] Nor is it any coincidence—or mystery—that no way has ever been found for apportioning the available seats among the numerous functional groups that are sure to demand representation under such a system, or at least no way that is not demonstrably repugnant to democratic principles. The allegedly successful ventures in FR have been carried out exactly where, on this showing, we should have expected them, that is, in states (e.g., Mussolini's Italy and Salazar's Portugal) where the apportionment could be accomplished by the fiat of a dictator, and did not have to justify itself in the eyes of democratic theory.[34] In any case, the few writers who feel that functional representation in democratic government has something to be said for it, claim only advisory powers for the proposed functional legislative chambers. We have found no theorist or publicist belonging to the democratic camp who believes that *the* lawmaking body in a democracy should be organized on functional-representation lines.

THE PROPER RELATIONSHIP BETWEEN REPRESENTATIVES AND THEIR CONSTITUENTS

We come now to what many writers on democracy consider the key problem in the theory of representation, that of the reciprocal rights and duties of representatives and their constituents. This problem has been broken down into a great number of subordinate issues, the most widely discussed of which revolves, curiously, around the question, Insofar as we must rely on an analogy in coming to grips with the relation between representatives and constituents, is the correct analogy that of the legal relation between agent and principal? We turn our attention first to the writers who have answered this question in the negative, and who, in general, seem to have been the more persuasive of those who have attempted answers to this question.

The Representative as Delegate. Many writers hold that the voters in any constituency, once they have elected a representative, should think of themselves as having *delegated* to him, for the duration of his term of office, their own shares of the total lawmaking power. They should, that is to say, leave it up to him to vote, speak, and act, in the legislative body to which they send him, as *he* sees fit. Moreover, when at the end of his term they are considering whether or not to re-elect him, they should ask themselves not whether he has done exactly what they would have done had they been actually present in the legislature, but whether, on the whole, he has used the power they have given him wisely or unwisely. *During* his term, finally, they must not

[33] Cf. Corry, *op. cit.,* pp. 252-54; Finer, *op. cit.,* pp. 543-45; and Lowell, *op. cit.,* pp. 121-22.
[34] Cf. Finer, *op. cit.,* pp. 545-46.

expect him, where his opinions differ from theirs on any given issue, to sacrifice his judgment to theirs. For he is not, say these writers, a mere spokesman they dispatch to the assembly to communicate to it their wills, a mere mouthpiece; he is, rather, a maker of decisions—decisions on which he brings to bear, and is expected to bring to bear, his own knowledge, his own wits, and his own instructed judgment. And only if he proves unworthy of being trusted should they return him to private life.

The ablest and most famous exposition of this "delegate" theory was offered by the British politician and political theorist Edmund Burke in 1774. Having just been elected by the voters of Bristol as their representative in the House of Commons, Burke addressed a pamphlet to them in which he told them what relative weight they could expect him to assign to their views and his:

> [The constituents'] wishes ought to have great weight with [the representative]; their opinions high respect, their business unremitted attention. It is his duty to sacrifice his repose, his pleasure, his satisfaction, to theirs—and above all, ever, and in all cases, to prefer their interest to his own. But his unbiased opinion, his mature judgment, his enlightened conscience, he ought not to sacrifice to you, to any man, or to any set of men living. . . . Your representative owes you, not his industry only, but his judgment; and he betrays, instead of serving you, if he sacrifices it to your opinion.[35]

Burke justified his position in this manner: If making governmental decisions were merely a matter of registering conflicting wills and determining their relative strength, of course the constituents' wills would count for everything and the representatives' views for nothing. But the process of forming public policy, where it is properly thought out and properly organized, is a matter of settling public problems by enlightened discussion and reasoned judgments *and* in the light of the available evidence. The representative is in a much better position than his constituents to settle them in that way—not because he is necessarily wiser or more public-spirited than they, but because, armed with the wisdom and public spirit that led his constituents to select him, he is present at the central spot, where opinions, ideas, and facts from all over the nation are marshaled, and because he can spend all his time thinking about public questions while his constituents must necessarily spend most of their time thinking about how to make a living and raise a family. Thus, Burke concluded, if on any given issue before the assembly the representative's views should differ from his constituents' views, it is right and proper that he should vote as *he* thinks best; and at the end of his term his constituents should pass general judgment on whether or not he has used wisely the lawmaking power they have delegated to him.

In the present writers' opinion, the argument just summarized constitutes

---

35 Edmund Burke, "Address to the Electors of Bristol, November 3, 1774," in *Works* (Boston: Little, Brown and Company, 1871), Vol. II, p. 95.

a complicated and hesitant No to the question, Is the correct analogy for the constituent-representative relation that of principal and agent? Burke certainly *appears* to be offering an unambiguously negative answer, but this, demonstrably, depends on how far you press him. The representative, to be sure, is supposed, according to Burke, to make his own decision as to how to cast his vote on the issues that arise in the assembly. He is *not* supposed to ask himself, How would my constituents wish me to vote? And if we were to leave it at that, the representative-as-delegate approach would indeed be, as it appears to be at first glance, an open challenge to what we may call the *plebiscitary* concept of self-government—according to which the citizens, acting by majority vote, should themselves make the final decision on such matters of public policy as *they* wish to make final decisions about.

Actually, however, no such challenge is present. In the first place, Burke is perfectly clear that the representative ought to be guided by his constituents' interests, which presumably means that he is to put his knowledge, wits, and judgment to work on behalf of their interests. Secondly, Burke does not, either expressly or by implication, question that the last word lies with the constituents, who have a right to remove him not so much if he *has* in fact used bad judgment in, say, casting his votes in the assembly, as if they happen to *think* he has used bad judgment. On Burke's own showing, in short, the constituents' will and judgment is supreme, and the representative's freedom to use his own judgment is merely a short-term (i.e., between elections) freedom. It seems improbable, moreover, that Burke intended to drive any such wedge between the constituents' interests on the one hand and their wishes and opinions on the other as some writers have read into the passage quoted above (writers who forget that it is, after all, self-government that Burke is talking about). In short, over the long period, election-in election-out, the representative-as-delegate conception of the constituent-representative relation is a good deal closer to the representative-as-agent conception we are about to examine than is commonly supposed. For Burke does not question the constituents' right, in the long pull, to bring their representative's votes into line with their wishes.

The Representative as Agent. Some writers, as noted above, have held that the representative in a democracy is or should be the mere *agent* of his constituents. They elect him, that is to say, solely for the purpose of registering *their* beliefs, opinions, values, etc., in the national assembly, and if they want something he feels is wrong, he should either treat his own views as unimportant and vote for it or resign in favor of someone who will. And, finally, if an issue comes before him on which he has received no instructions from his constituents, he ought to go home, talk it over with them, and get instructions before casting his vote. In brief, the representative in a democracy should simply be a communications-device, selected with an eye to the accuracy with which it will transmit to the national assembly decisions arrived at by the constituents.

Among the democrats who have held this view we must mention at least the following: the Levelers, James Wilson, the Jacksonian Democrats,[36] and, certainly the most insistent of them all, Rousseau. In the *Social Contract,* as we noted above, Rousseau argued that *any* kind of representation is incompatible with democracy. But when he came to propose a scheme of self-government for Poland, he reluctantly adopted the premise that *some* form of representation is unavoidable in the modern nation-state, and contented himself with making sure that the representatives would be mere rubber stamps for their constituents. He proposed, to this end, that the representative system of Poland be organized as follows. The nation was to remain divided into constituencies, each with its own "dietene," i.e., its own face-to-face assembly of citizens. Each dietene was to elect a representative to the national assembly, and its members, after discussing among themselves the various issues before the assembly, were to give him complete and detailed instructions as to how to vote and what to say on those problems. Then, when the time for his re-election or retirement came around, he would be judged not on how wisely he had voted or how brilliantly he had spoken, but on how faithfully he had carried out the letter of his instructions.[37]

There seems little doubt that it is Rousseau's position, not Burke's (and certainly not Burke's as it is usually understood) at which the ordinary voter is likely to arrive if he attempts to think the constituent-representative relation out for himself. Certainly it is a near-axiom of American politics that the representative who goes against his constituents' known wishes, or fails to guess correctly those that are not known, has "asked for it," and ought to be replaced at the first opportunity. The voting record of the incumbent is almost invariably the main point of attack used by his opponents during a typical congressional campaign, and the discussion does *not* go forward in terms of the question, "Did he do his best for you as he saw it?" but rather the question, "Did he do his best for you as *you,* his constituents, see it?"

On the other hand, legislators themselves tend to lean toward Burke's position rather than Rousseau's, or at least do not regard their constituents' wishes as binding upon them when they are deciding how to vote on legislative questions. There is, indeed, evidence that American legislators regard their constituents' wishes as merely one of several considerations that they must take into account. For example, in September, 1939, during a special session of Congress called to consider repeal of the arms-embargo provisions of the Neutrality Act, ninety-six congressmen were interviewed in the hope of determining the relative weight they actually gave to the following factors that might have influenced them: their own independent judgment, party consid-

---

[36] For the Levelers' views, see *Remonstrance of Many Thousand Citizens* (1646) in D. M. Wolfe, ed., *Leveller Manifestoes of the Puritan Revolution* (New York: Thomas Nelson and Sons, 1944), p. 113. For the others, see Fairlie, *op. cit.,* p. 459.

[37] Jean Jacques Rousseau, *Considerations on the Government of Poland,* translated by Willmoore Kendall (Minneapolis: Minnesota Book Store, 1947), pp. 21-23.

erations, their constituents' views, presidential leadership, congressional debates, newspaper editorials, their colleagues' views, the views of pressure groups, and public opinion polls. "Independent judgment" won, as Burke presumably would have wished it to, hands down; "constituents' wishes" did not even come in second, as witness the tabulation of the results in Table 1.

*TABLE 1   Congressmen's Estimates of the Factors Influencing
Their Votes* [38]

Factor	1st	2nd	3rd	Percentage of First Choices
Independent judgment	50	15	3	52
Party considerations	29	13	4	30
Constituents' views	13	20	3	14
Presidential leadership	2	3	0	2
Congressional debates	1	1	3	1
Newspaper editorials	1	0	0	1
Colleagues' views	0	1	3	0
Pressure groups' views	0	1	2	0
Public opinion polls	0	1	2	0

Burke, of course, had in mind the representative to a *national* assembly in a *unitary* state, and it is, of course, to our "federal" assembly in our *federal* state that the above statistics relate. But the situation, in the United States at least, does not appear to be very different at the state-assembly level. In 1942, a researcher named George W. Hartmann put to fifty-eight members of the New York State legislature the question, "Do you consider it your public duty as a 'representative' to reflect in official voting whatever preponderant sentiment your district displays on every issue, even if this is contrary to your personal conception of community welfare?" Thirty-nine per cent replied "Yes," 57 per cent replied "No," and 4 per cent replied "Both"! [39]

These two studies, then, suggest (though they hardly prove conclusively) that most American congressmen and state legislators, unlike most ordinary

[38] L. E. Gleeck, "96 Congressmen Make Up Their Minds," *Public Opinion Quarterly*, Vol. IV (1940), pp. 3-24.

[39] George W. Hartmann, "Judgments of State Legislators Concerning Public Opinion," *Journal of Social Psychology*, Vol. XXI (February, 1945), pp. 105-14. If, on the other hand, we assume that the best evidence of a legislator's conception of his relation to his constituents is what he *does*, not what he *says*, the behavior of actual legislators seems to be other than that reported by Gleeck and Hartmann. Julius Turner's study of voting behavior by members of the U.S. House of Representatives indicates that most of them, despite any claims of "independence," tend to vote in response to the pressure that on a given issue seems most likely to unseat them if they fail to vote in the desired way. Sometimes this pressure is party and sometimes constituency; but there is little evidence of the unresponsive "independence" envisioned in the Gleeck and Hartmann studies: *Party and Constituency: Pressures on Congress* (Baltimore: The Johns Hopkins Press, 1951).

Americans and many professional political theorists,[40] hold Burke's rather than Rousseau's position about the proper relation between the representative and his constituents in a democracy.

The Recall. Various devices have been developed for making sure that representatives *shall* act as their constituents wish—petitions, letters, postcards, and telegrams from the constituents to their representatives, and, most fundamental of all, periodic elections at which the constituents can retire a representative who they feel is not speaking for them faithfully. Many democrats have felt, however, that the fact that elections are held only at certain specified intervals limits their effectiveness, since it means that a representative who has lost the confidence of his constituents can remain in office until his term runs out—sometimes a matter of years. And the institutional device known as the "recall" has been developed precisely with a view to keeping public officials (executive and judicial as well as legislative) *continuously* responsible to their constituents.

"Recall" laws usually provide that when a specified number of voters (usually a certain percentage of those who voted for the office in question at the last election) so petition, a special election shall be held to determine whether a particular officer shall remain in office or immediately vacate it. During the "progressive era" of the early 1900's, the "recall" was regarded by many publicists and some political scientists as a panacea not only for the evil, if such it be, of official irresponsibility, but also for such evils as corruption and nepotism; and the campaign put on in its behalf assumed tremendous proportions (the only recent parallel is perhaps the campaign for the council-manager plan). At present twelve American states have the recall for state offices (four of these exempt judges), and over three-fourths of the states provide for some form of recall procedure for municipal officials. But for some twenty years now, no state has adopted it, so that while it seems to be holding its own where it has been tried, it does not seem to be gaining any ground. It is of interest for our purposes mainly as one attempt to institutionalize and make more secure the agency relationship between representatives and their constituents.[41]

Direct Legislation

Most writers on democracy, as we have seen, have regarded representation as a second-best method of accomplishing popular consultation—a half-loaf that we must make do with because it is impossible to bring the whole citizenry of any populous community together in face-to-face meetings. Many of these writers, however, have continued to hunger for the whole loaf, or at least to

[40] Cf. de Grazia, *op. cit.*, pp. 114-28, 252, for documentation of this point.

[41] Snider, *op. cit.*, pp. 145-48. Despite its limitation to the experience of a single state, F. L. Bird and F. M. Ryan, *The Recall of Public Officers: A Study of the Operation of the Recall in California* (New York: The Macmillan Company, 1930), is the most complete study of the recall in operation.

grumble because their half-loaf is so small, so that there is a notable anti-representation emphasis in much of the literature about the machinery of democratic government.[42] One major result of this dissatisfaction has been the elaboration of such devices as PR and FR that, as noted above, might enable us to have representation and still express the popular will in all its shadings and divisions more accurately than we manage to do through the single-member constituency. Another group of proposals, however, have taken a quite different tack. Some writers have argued that *no* system of representation *by itself* can give accurate expression to the popular will; representation must, accordingly, be supplemented by another method or methods of popular consultation. Actually, however, only two devices have been proposed that fall, properly speaking, under the heading "other methods": the *initiative,* which permits rank-and-file citizens to originate and bring to popular vote legislative and constitutional measures the representative body is unwilling to pass; and the *referendum,* which puts in the hands of the electorate the power to veto measures passed by the representative assembly. Political science textbooks usually lump the two devices together under the topic "direct legislation."

ORIGINS AND PRESENT STATUS

The earliest precedents for modern direct legislation appeared in France in 1793, when a new constitution was submitted to the people for their direct approval or rejection (they approved it, by a vote of 1,602,000 to 11,600), and in Switzerland in 1802, when a proposed new constitution was submitted to the people and rejected (92,400 to 72,400). Various Swiss cantons (which are to the Swiss federal system approximately what the states are to the American federal system) adopted the initiative and referendum for ordinary legislative measures as well as for constitutional proposals between 1831 and 1890; and in 1891 both devices were added to the Swiss federal constitution.[43]

Several nations today use—or at least have available for use when needed—one form or another of direct legislation. In Australia, constitutional amendments must be referred to the people for their direct approval, but direct-legislation processes are not used for any other type of legal enactment. The Weimar Constitution of Germany permitted the initiative and referendum for both constitutional amendments and ordinary legislation. By far the most extensive experience with direct legislation, however, has been that of Switzerland and certain American states.[44]

Direct legislation in the Swiss Federal Constitution involves three devices: (1) *The compulsory constitutional referendum.* Any constitutional amendment which is approved by the Swiss Federal Assembly must be submitted

---

[42] Cf. Lindsay, *The Essentials of Democracy,* pp. 25-26.

[43] Felix Bonjour, *Real Democracy in Operation* (New York: Frederick A. Stokes Company, 1920), pp. 30-39.

[44] See Finer, *op. cit.,* pp. 561-62, for a survey of the present status of direct legislation in the various democratic nations.

to the people and must, in order to become a part of the federal constitution, be approved both by a majority of the voters over the whole federation and by the voters in a majority of the cantons. (2) *The constitutional initiative.* Upon petition by 50,000 voters either for a general revision of the federal constitution or a specific amendment to it, a proposal for such revision or the projected amendment (whichever the petition has specified) must be submitted at the next federal election; and here too a double majority is required in order for the proposal or amendment to succeed. (3) *The optional legislative referendum.* Upon petition by 30,000 voters, any act of the Federal Assembly can be submitted to a vote at the next federal election, and simple majorities of all the voters over the whole federation carry the day here (i.e., the double majority required for [1] and [2] does not apply). Why, the reader may ask, have the Swiss, having gone this far with direct-legislation devices, not provided for initiation of ordinary legislative measures as well as constitutional amendments? The answer is that the constitutional-initiative provision in the Swiss constitution is so worded that such measures can be initiated by the simple procedure of calling them amendments, and have been so initiated on several occasions. Most of the individual Swiss cantons, we may note in conclusion, maintain arrangements for direct legislation on strictly cantonal matters.[45]

In the United States the initiative and referendum for ordinary legislation were first adopted in South Dakota in 1898. At the present time that state and eighteen others use both devices, while two states have the referendum only. And all the states except Indiana, Rhode Island, and Delaware permit municipalities to use one or another form of direct legislation.[46]

Thirteen states now permit popular initiation of proposals for specific amendments to their constitutions. All states except Delaware, moreover, require that constitutional amendments, however proposed, be ratified by the voters before they become effective, and most but not all the states have a direct-legislation step in their procedure for general revision of their constitutions (the legislature submits to the voters the question whether they wish a constitutional convention called). All states except Virginia and Louisiana require any constitutional changes proposed by a constitutional convention to be submitted to the people for ratification.[47]

There are numerous variations in detail among the several states' systems of direct legislation, but the basic procedures differ little from state to state. The essential steps are as follows.

Initiative Procedures. Those who wish to start a legislative or constitutional proposal prepare a draft of it, secure petition blanks, attach copies of their proposal to the blanks, and then attempt to mobilize the required num-

[45] William E. Rappard, *The Government of Switzerland* (New York: D. Van Nostrand Co., Inc., 1936), pp. 67-70, has a useful description of the Swiss machinery for direct legislation.
[46] Snider, *op. cit.,* pp. 149-50.
[47] *Ibid.,* pp. 17-26.

ber of signers. In most states this is a stipulated percentage (usually 5 to 10 per cent) of the votes cast in the last preceding state election (in a few it is a stipulated round number of voters). When enough signatures have been obtained, the proposal is placed on the ballot, to be approved or rejected at the next general election.

Referendum Procedures. As we have already observed, popular referenda are held as a matter of course for certain kinds of measures, notably constitutional amendments. The special "petition referendum," which concerns us here, usually operates as follows. Acts of the representative assembly do not become effective until a certain period of time (usually sixty to ninety days) after their passage. If before that period expires a petition—drawn up in the same general manner as an initiative petition, but requiring fewer signatures— is filed requesting a referendum on the particular act, the latter does not go into operation until after the next election, and then only if it meets with popular approval (in most states this means a simple majority of the votes cast).[48]

RATIONALE

None of the advocates of direct legislation put it forward as a *substitute* for representation, or argue that the initiative and referendum are all the law-making machinery that is needed. The usual contention is, rather, that direct legislation usefully supplements the work of representative assemblies, and provides a sorely needed corrective for some of the latter's native vices. As one of its early advocates put it:

Representative government, or some legislation by means of chosen agents, is necessary, but it need not be exclusive and displace all legislative action by the people. The former will always remain as a great achievement of modern politics, and a necessary convenience for the government of a modern nation, but it may be best to combine it with a modified form of that ancient, primitive direct government, which is at once the earliest, the most natural to freemen, and the most interesting form of government in the world.[49]

Let us note, in conclusion, one further point urged by the advocates of direct legislation—a point that is of especial interest in connection with our general inquiry in this book: The reason why representative assemblies *need* supplementing, the argument runs, is that representative assemblies invariably generate political parties; and, having generated them and allowed them to become adept at maneuver and machination within the legislative process, the assemblies come to act as if party considerations and party loyalties were more important than the public weal. Representative government, in a word,

---

[48] *Ibid.,* pp. 150-52.

[49] Nathan Cree, *Direct Legislation by the People* (Chicago: A. C. McClurg and Co., 1892), pp. 26-27. For other statements of this position, see various articles in William B. Munro, ed., *The Initiative, Referendum, and Recall* (New York: D. Appleton and Co., 1912), pp. 87-88; and Bonjour, *op. cit.,* p. 113.

"degenerates" ineluctably into "party government"; and the public weal will suffer unless direct legislation is called in as a guarantee that at least some measures will be considered "upon their merits as schemes of public policy instead of as mere party proposals." [50]

RESULTS AND EVALUATION

We now have at our disposal a substantial body of literature summarizing the actual operation and results of direct legislation, both in Switzerland and in the United States.[51] The evidence shows, among other things, that strictly initiative and referendum elections tend to draw substantially smaller numbers of voters than those drawn by elections at which government officials are being chosen; that the voters generally vote against measures designed to increase taxes or regulate public expenditures, but generally favor bond issues and measures regulating public debts; and that initiative measures for the most part originate with organized interest groups rather than individual citizens.[52]

There is, however, little agreement as regards the value of direct legislation as a device for popular consultation. A few writers contend that the initiative and referendum are "the first practical application of Rousseau's theories of popular sovereignty," and have proved themselves to be *the* basic solution to the problem of establishing genuine democracy in large-scale communities.[53] But the supporting evidence here is both scanty and difficult to interpret, though two American writers have recently shown that the disasters which the original opponents of direct legislation in this country believed it would usher in have not, in fact, occurred. These writers do not, unfortunately, attempt a similar treatment of the extravagances put forward by the other side in the debate, which predicted that it would bring great blessings: better laws on the statute books, either put there by direct legislation itself or, by the law of anticipated reactions, put there by legislators acting under the threat of direct legislation; heightened political consciousness and knowledgeability on the part of the electorate; and so on. But we suspect these would be, if anything, easier to explode than the predictions of disaster.[54]

In the United States, at least, the major political trends and events do not appear to be much affected one way or the other by direct popular action via

[50] Cree, *op. cit.,* p. 16. See Cree, pp. 54-58, for the anti-party bias of the case against representation unsupplemented by direct legislation. See also Finer, *op. cit.,* p. 560, for a summary of the case for direct legislation.

[51] For a convenient bibliography on the operation and results of direct legislation in the United States, see Snider, *op. cit.,* p. 149, note 5.

[52] See H. F. Gosnell and M. J. Schmidt, "Popular Law-Making in the United States, 1924-1936," *New York State Constitutional Convention, 1938,* Vol. VII, pp. 314-35, for the most complete general survey of American experience with direct legislation. See Finer, *op. cit.,* pp. 562-67, for a summary of American, German, and Swiss experience with the initiative and referendum.

[53] Bonjour, *op. cit.,* pp. 29-30.

[54] Joseph G. LaPalombara and Charles B. Hagan, "Direct Legislation: An Appraisal and a Suggestion," *American Political Science Review,* Vol. XLV (June, 1951), pp. 400-21.

the initiative and referendum; the big and interesting issues continue to be handled via *in*direct processes, and there appears, for the moment anyhow, to be little likelihood of further inroads upon these processes by the initiative and referendum. In Switzerland, by contrast, interesting and important problems often fall within the scope of direct legislation, and some at least would argue both that the Swiss political process produces better results than the political process in other countries, and that this is due to direct legislation. But the first point is, in the nature of the case, a matter of opinion, and the central idea of the second (that direct-legislation devices are responsible for the quality of Swiss politics) remains to be demonstrated.

Political Parties

The traditional institutions of representation and direct legislation are, as we have seen, attempts to write into the laws of the modern nation-state *formal* institutional machinery which will provide a community of many millions of citizens with something close to the kind of popular consultation that the town meeting provides in the small community.

In addition to these two formal (i.e., legally provided-for) institutions, however, a third institution—namely, *a system of political parties*—has, as we know, emerged in every modern nation-state that has attempted to achieve democracy in its governing system, and has greatly influenced the character and operation of the nation's formal institutions for popular consultation.[55] Many modern scholars, indeed, would fully agree with the following statement by Professor MacIver:

> Although party is often "extraconstitutional" it is an essential organ of every large-scale democracy. . . . The organization of opinion by parties inevitably followed the rise of large-scale democracy. The principle of representation had to be vitalized by the conflict of parties. When parties flourish we have in effect passed from a pre-democratic mode of representative government to a genuinely democratic one.[56]

In the next chapter we shall examine the circumstances in which political parties emerged in the Western democratic nations, with a view to determining what social needs called them into being and what role they played in the formative years of democracy in those nations.

---

[55] Cf. Alfred M. Bingham, *The Techniques of Democracy* (New York: Duell, Sloan and Pearce, 1942), p. 33; Maurice Duverger, *Political Parties: Their Organization and Activity in the Modern State,* translated by Barbara and Robert North (New York: John Wiley and Sons, Inc., 1954); Barker, *op. cit.,* pp. 38-39; and Finer, *op. cit.,* pp. 220-21, 227.

[56] MacIver, *op. cit.,* pp. 209-10. Reprinted by permission of The Macmillan Company.

PART TWO

A Short History of Political Parties

Chapter 5

AN INSTITUTIONAL HISTORY OF POLITICAL PARTIES

We concluded the preceding chapter by noting that political parties have arisen in all modern nation-states whose peoples have undertaken to democratize their governing institutions. The purpose of the present chapter is to scrutinize more closely some of the forces that have produced parties in the Western democracies and have shaped their development. We propose to accomplish this by examining in some detail the *institutional* history of parties. Our primary concern, that is to say, is to grasp the developmental pattern, if any, of parties *as institutions*—the pattern of their organization and of their relation to one another and to the other institutions of government. In this our purpose differs sharply from that of most party histories, whose primary concern is with the positions adopted on certain issues by the various parties and with the alignment of groups in the electorate behind the several parties.[1]

Our approach will not be a history-for-history's-sake approach. We assume

---

[1] Most party histories concern themselves largely with elections, not with parties as institutions. They offer useful accounts of the positions parties have adopted on past issues, and the alignments of groups in the electorate on those issues; but they throw little light on the origins and development of parties as democratic institutional machinery. Leading examples dealing with the United States and England are: Wilfred E. Binkley, *American Political Parties: Their Natural History* (New York: Alfred A. Knopf, 1944); Charles A. Beard, *The American Party Battle* (New York: The Macmillan Company, 1938); Frank R. Kent, *The Democratic Party, A History* (New York: The Century Co., 1928); William S. Myers, *The Republican Party, A History* (New York: The Century Co., 1928); Keith G. Feiling, *A History of the Tory Party, 1640-1714* (Oxford: Clarendon Press, 1924), and *The Second Tory Party, 1714-1832* (London: Macmillan and Company, Ltd., 1938); Henry H. Slesser, *A History of the Liberal Party* (London: Hutchinson and Co., Ltd., 1944); and G. D. H. Cole, *A History of the Labour Party from 1914* (London: Routledge and Kegan Paul, Ltd., 1948).

merely that a correct understanding of the historical circumstances in which parties first arose, and of their relationship to other emergent democratic institutions, will shed useful light upon the role parties have performed. This approach should also help us to check our American experience against the pattern of development of parties in the other democracies, and will help us determine the respects in which it has been like that of parties elsewhere, and those in which it has been unique.

Our hope, in short, is that the kind of historical analysis we shall undertake in the present chapter will serve to increase our understanding of the nature and role of political parties wherever men have sought after democracy, but especially in the United States.

What Is a "Political Party"?

The question arises at once, what kinds of political groups shall we include in our survey, and what kinds shall we ignore? What kind of group, in other words, do we have in mind when we speak of a "political party"?—a question that has, necessarily, received attention from almost everyone who has written on parties.

One of the oldest and most-quoted definitions of a political party is that of Edmund Burke. "Party," he wrote, "is a body of men united, for promoting by their joint endeavors the national interest, upon some particular principle in which they are all agreed." [2] The contemporary scholar, however, is apt to say that Burke's formula does not square with the observed facts, that it passes off as a definition of party a statement as to what a political party *ought* to be, and that it treats as a characteristic of *all* parties a trait that belongs only to some.

A contemporary definition that is less open to such criticism is that according to which a party is merely "an organized group that seeks to control the personnel and policy of government." [3] But just as Burke's definition excludes groups that we are in the habit of calling "parties," the second definition includes groups that most of us are not in the habit of calling by that name. In the remote past, for instance, long before the advent of modern democracy, there were numerous more or less organized groups seeking to control the personnel and policy of government: for example, the Papalists

---

[2] Edmund Burke, "Thoughts on the Cause of Present Discontents," in *Works* (Boston: Little, Brown and Company, 1871), Vol. I, p. 151.

[3] Howard R. Penniman, *Sait's American Parties and Elections*, 4th ed. (New York: Appleton-Century-Crofts, Inc., 1948), p. 161. For other definitions of "political parties" by leading present-day scholars, see Peter H. Odegard and E. Allen Helms, *American Politics*, 2nd ed. (New York: Harper and Brothers, 1947), pp. 1-2; Dayton D. McKean, *Party and Pressure Politics* (Boston: Houghton Mifflin Company, 1949), pp. 15-16; Charles E. Merriam and Harold F. Gosnell, *The American Party System*, 3rd ed. (New York: The Macmillan Company, 1947), p. 8; Hugh A. Bone, *American Politics and the Party System* (New York: McGraw-Hill Book Company, Inc., 1949), p. 354; V. O. Key, Jr., *Politics, Parties, and Pressure Groups*, 3rd ed. (New York: Thomas Y. Crowell Company, 1952), pp. 215-24.

and Imperialists of medieval Europe, generally known as the "Guelphs" and the "Ghibellines," and the Yorkists and Lancastrians of fifteenth-century England. In the days of absolute monarchy, similarly, there were always and everywhere groups of courtiers contending for the monarch's favor and for positions in his ministry. But in neither case do we feel any temptation to speak of a contest between "political parties." The word "factions" or "cabals" or "juntas" seems more in line with good usage.

Why does the term "parties" sound all right when applied to Republicans and Democrats but absurd when applied to Guelphs and Ghibellines? The answer, as far as usage is concerned, lies in the term's history—in the fact that it established itself in our language and other modern languages at a time when the modern democratic state was abuilding, and has normally been employed in connection with its politics. The result has been that any definition that relates it, even potentially, to pre-democratic, pre–nation-state politics falls peculiarly on our ears.

Even if that were not true, the term "political party" could not be of much use to us, for the purposes of this book, if defined too broadly. If, that is to say, no term existed for the kind of organized group that seeks to control the personnel and policies of the modern democratic state, we should have had to invent one. For, as the reader already knows, our concern is with the competition for power in a democratic, nation-state context. We shall, then, apply the term "political parties" to organizations that compete, and have competed in the past, for control over public personnel and policy in the democratic state—which is to say, in the Western democracies. And we shall offer as our definition of "political parties" the following statement: *Political parties are autonomous organized groups that make nominations and contest elections in the hope of eventually gaining and exercising control of the personnel and policies of government.*[4] And it is the major characteristics of these organizations that we now propose to isolate and describe.

CHARACTERISTICS OF POLITICAL PARTIES

Competitiveness. Political parties are essentially competitors—*genuine* competitors—for the community's stakes of political power. There must, therefore, be at least two of them in any given nation-state.

Organization. A "party" is not merely the sum of individuals who tend to adopt the same attitude toward issues of public policy. The term implies a certain degree of "organization" on the part of such individuals—in the sense that they consciously band together, pool their strength, consult on matters of policy and strategy, and take conscious collective action on behalf of their goals.[5] Each party's organization normally has two aspects: (1) *intragovern-*

[4] For further discussion of the differences between political parties and other types of social and political groups, see pp. 198-99. For a discussion of whether the Communist parties of the United States and elsewhere should be called "political parties," see Chapter 19.

[5] For a more detailed discussion of the concept of "organization," particularly as it applies to political parties, see pp. 213-17.

mental organization, which is the organization, in the above sense, of such party members as hold public office; and (2) *extragovernmental organization,* the organization of party members as such, regardless of whether or not they hold public office.

To distinguish between these two aspects of party organization is to suggest a number of problems that we must keep in mind. What, for example, is or should be the relationship between them? What is or should be the proper dividing line between *members* of the extragovernmental organization and supporters or partisans of (but not workers in) the party? (These questions will come up for further notice both in the present chapter and in later chapters.)

Preoccupation with Naming and Control of Governmental Personnel. Democratic parties attempt to influence the selection of official governmental personnel, primarily through such electoral activities (carried on mainly by their extragovernmental organizations) as making nominations and winning electoral support for their nominees. And, characteristically, they "follow through" in this matter by seeking to control such personnel, once it is in office, by setting party standards of behavior which the officeholders are expected to observe on pain of removal or repudiation, and by demanding that it maintain relations of a certain kind with the party organization.

Preoccupation with Formation and Execution of Governmental Policy. Democratic parties also attempt to influence the formation and execution of governmental policy, both through their intragovernmental organizations and through pressures that, in the very nature of the case, only the extragovernmental organizations can exert.

Which of the two preoccupations, personnel selection or policy formation, is that to which a political party characteristically assigns the higher priority, is a question that we may profitably postpone, although no party of which we have knowledge has been *exclusively* concerned with the one and *totally* unconcerned with the other. Any adequate account of parties must fix attention now on the one, now on the other.

Preoccupation with the Maintenance of Democratic Consensus. Political parties use *peaceful* methods to gain their ends—caucuses, speeches, campaign leaflets, and such other devices and procedures as are generally sanctioned by the community.[6] After an election, the losing parties peacefully accept the electorate's verdict; they do not, for example, attempt to reverse it by resorting to violent revolution, sabotage, or even civil disobedience. By the same token, the winning party or parties do not set out to exterminate the losers

[6] The point is an important one. One democratic system may view with indulgence the acquisition of a radio station by a candidate for the senate who is determined to get his case before the voters (e.g., Oklahoma), but put beyond the pale the plying of prospective voters with alcoholic drinks (Oklahoma is a dry state). Another (e.g., Great Britain) would square off to this dilemma the other way around. The mysterious process by which a community's mores are determined fixes, in large part, the limits a political party must respect in choosing the means it will use in forwarding its ends (see Chapter 21).

or even to reduce them to political impotence. In short, all democratic parties, winners and losers alike, are committed to the maintenance of the kind of consensus on which any democracy must rest, and strive only for such objectives and employ only such methods as are consistent with that commitment.

THE FIVE CHARACTERISTICS AS CRITERIA OF RELEVANCE

Contemporary political scientists are in the habit of classifying existing governments as "democracies" or "dictatorships" or "oligarchies." For the reasons indicated in Chapter 2, this is a perfectly legitimate and useful intellectual procedure—*provided* it is grounded in clear thinking about the model that gives these judgments what meaning they have, and provided it employs the concept of a spectrum rather than a black-and-white distinction between governments that are democracies and governments that are not democracies.[7] Few of us would quarrel with the notion that certain nations may usefully and accurately be called "democracies"; and most contemporary political scientists include in this category at the present time *at least* the United States, Great Britain, Ireland, Canada, Australia, New Zealand, Switzerland, France, Belgium, Holland, Norway, Sweden, Denmark, Finland, Italy, West Germany, Austria, Turkey, Uruguay, India, Pakistan, and Japan—though they do not, of course, feel that all these countries are *equally* democratic. Other countries are believed to lie somewhere in between the democracies and such obvious dictatorships as the Soviet Union and its satellites; and some of us may feel that certain nations should be moved from this middle category into the "democracies."[8] But few of us would question the claim of any of the nations listed above to be regarded as "democratic."

Each of these democracies has its own party system, which differs in greater or lesser degree from every other party system. All the systems in question, however, seem to have in common, though again in greater or lesser degree, each of the five characteristics listed above. It seems safe to say, therefore, that these are the characteristics of modern political parties—as distinct from the political organizations we find in, say, the Soviet Union, Spain, or Saudi Arabia. And since the purpose of the present chapter is to understand the circumstances in which the modern democracies developed such parties, the sequence in which the latter took on these essential qualities, and the factors that produced them, there should be no objection to our using these five characteristics as our criteria of relevance throughout this stage of our inquiry—that is, to our using them, as we go along, to determine what out of the endless detail of the general history of the modern democracies is significant for *party* history.

[7] See pp. 20-22.

[8] The reader will note that this list does not include such nations as Chile, Brazil, Mexico, Argentina, and South Africa. All manner of interesting questions, both factual and theoretical, would have to be raised and answered in order to adjudicate the claims of these and other borderline cases; but deciding such questions is well beyond the scope and purposes of this book.

The political groups that exhibit in high degree all of the above characteristics did not suddenly spring into full-blown existence at some particular
moment in history; our task therefore becomes one of discovering where and
in what circumstances political groups have arisen which displayed *any* of
these characteristics in some degree, and of observing the circumstances in
which these groups acquired, and in what order, the other characteristics of
modern democratic parties.

In this brief historical survey, we can hardly examine the total experience
of *all* the present-day democracies. Rather we shall confine our attention to
those nations which have had a relatively long and continuous history as independent sovereign nations developing in the direction of democracy. Thus
we pass up such nations as the British dominions (except Canada), Norway,
and Finland, all of which have become *independent* nations only during this
century, and such nations as Czechoslovakia, Italy, Germany, and Japan, which
in their recent political history have had both democratic and authoritarian
regimes, and thus cannot point to a record of continuous development toward
democracy.

This means confining our survey to the development of political parties in
the United States, Great Britain, Canada, France, Belgium, Holland, Switzerland, Sweden, and Denmark.

Origins of Modern Democratic Parties

WHIGS AND TORIES IN RESTORATION ENGLAND

Long before anything resembling modern democracy existed in the world,
there were, as noted above, more or less organized political groups contending
for power. These groups did not, however, possess any of the characteristics
we ascribe to political parties. Ultimate decision-making power—insofar as it
existed at all—resided in the monarch, and, this being the case, the only stake
of power for which groups *could* compete was the monarch's favor. In saying
this, we do not ignore the existence of representative bodies such as the English Parliament, the French *parlements,* and the Spanish *cortes,* or forget that
some of their members were chosen by a kind of elective procedure. But the
nearest these bodies ever came to power over personnel and policy was to
exercise, at rare intervals, a limited and ill-understood veto power over the
king's proposals—and most of them did not even have this much power. In
short, such competing groups as existed within these bodies so little resembled the kind of institutions we have described above that modern scholars
shy away from calling them political parties and speak of them, rather, as
"factions" and "cabals." [9]

[9] Cf. S. B. Chrimes, "The Evolution of Parties and the Party System before 1600," in Sidney
D. Bailey, ed., *Political Parties and the Party System in Great Britain* (New York: Frederick A.
Praeger, 1952), pp. 1-12.

Most authorities agree that the first political groups that in any important respect resembled the organizations we are concerned with arose during the period in English history immediately following Charles II's restoration to the throne in 1660. The Restoration, to be sure, seemed to contemporary observers to constitute a complete victory for the idea of the divine right of kings and royal absolutism. But this does not dispose of the fact that Parliament had won, in the course of the events taking place from 1640 to 1660, the right to be regarded as a significant decision-making agency in English government. It had not estalished itself, of course, as *the* decision-making agency, since the royal prerogative remained an important center of power. But never again in England would the monarch's favor be the *sole* (or even necessarily the principal) stake of power. From 1660 on—for the first time in any modern nation—control of a partially elected legislative body was a necessary and important goal for any group that wished to win power; and again for the first time in any modern nation, the power to be won was a power to affect public policy.[10]

Shortly after their return to power, for instance, Charles II and his ministers, led by Lord Chancellor Clarendon, secretly took steps to line up support in Parliament for their policies, thus breaking with the traditional practice of announcing their desires and commanding the members of Parliament to fall in line. Word of what they were doing quickly got around, and the ministerial group's opponents were soon speaking of it as "the cabal." [11] Before long, moreover, an issue arose in Parliament that drew a sharp line between the king's supporters and his opponents, and gave each of the resulting "parties" a name—another "first" in the history of parties. For the adherence of the heir apparent (later to become James II) to the Roman Catholic faith posed the highly explosive issue of whether Parliament had the rightful power to regulate the succession to the throne and thus prevent a Catholic from occupying it. One group insisted on Parliament's right to regulate the succession, and the other insisted it was none of Parliament's business. And the two suddenly found themselves standing over against each other in the normal posture of modern partisan conflict. Even their names, one of which still figures prominently in our political vocabulary, are familiar. For the first group were the "Whigs" and the second the "Tories." [12]

---

[10] Cf. George B. Adams, *Constitutional History of England* (New York: Henry Holt and Company, 1934), pp. 334-37.

[11] Cf. A. Browning, "Parties and Party Organization in the Reign of Charles II," *Transactions of the Royal Historical Society,* Fourth Series, Vol. XXX (1948), pp. 21-23. See also G. M. Trevelyan, *The Two-Party System in English Political History* (Oxford: Clarendon Press, 1926), p. 11.

[12] The names were, originally, epithets applied to the groups by their opponents. The name "Whig" was first applied to the Scottish Presbyterian zealots who, unwilling to let themselves be regulated in religious matters by the Anglican king and his bishops, became outlaws. It was supposedly derived from "whey"—the refuse-milk which, because of their poverty, they had to get along on. The name "Tory" was first applied to the Irish Catholic outlaws who, from the

Although these rather unflattering names were applied to individual members of Parliament solely on the basis of their views on regulating the succession, each group soon developed a certain amount of rudimentary organization. During the elections of 1679 and 1681, the members of each met together from time to time and planned strategy for operations both inside Parliament and out in the constituencies. And each had its more or less generally recognized leaders.[13]

On the other hand, the original "Whigs" and "Tories" conspicuously lacked some characteristics of their modern descendants. Most of all they lacked any preoccupation with the maintenance of consensus. They were engaged in a bitter-end struggle over the nature of the regime—as is clearly shown by the fact that their contest ended in 1688 in a revolution that, however bloodless, was an all-out struggle over fundamental issues. They did not, then, provide England with a full-fledged party system, but only with its beginnings—"A myth and a martyrology and the names of two gangs of ruffians."[14]

WHIGS AND TORIES IN EIGHTEENTH- AND EARLY-NINETEENTH-CENTURY BRITAIN

Despite the hands-down Whig victory in the "glorious revolution" of 1688, "Whig" and "Tory" remained key words in British politics until well into the nineteenth century (even today, as noted above, the latter term is widely used as synonymous with "Conservative"). To say, however, that British politics between 1688 and 1832 was a contest between two well-organized, easily identifiable political parties labeled "Whig" and "Tory" would be grossly inaccurate. There were indeed Whigs and Tories throughout the period; but only in the loosest possible sense were they political parties.

One reason for this is that while Parliament in the course of the eighteenth century displaced the king as the basic decision-making agency, it was, even at the end of the century, still very far from having become a representative assembly of the type we associate with modern democracy. The House of Lords, at that time the full equal in power of the House of Commons, laid no claim whatever to representativeness in the democratic sense of that term; and the House of Commons—with its unrepresentative "rotten boroughs," its for-sale "pocket boroughs," and the extremely limited franchise on which its members were elected—was representative in only the rather dubiously democratic sense that we associate with Burke's phrase "virtual representa-

bogs of Ireland, defied Anglican regulation of *their* religion. The terms were thus roughly equivalent to "sour-milk eaters" and "bogtrotters": cf. James A. Woodburn, *Political Parties and Party Problems in the United States* (New York: G. P. Putnam's Sons, 1903), pp. 6-7.

[13] Cecil S. Emden, *The People and the Constitution* (Oxford: Clarendon Press, 1933), pp. 128-31. See also H. R. Williamson, "The Evolution of Parties and the Party System in the Seventeenth Century," in Bailey, *op. cit.,* pp. 13-18.

[14] Williamson, *op. cit.,* p. 18. See also Emden, *op. cit.,* pp. 99-100.

tion." [15] What we call "public opinion" had little or no direct influence on the course of political events.

Politics in eighteenth- and early-nineteenth-century Britain should be thought of as a contest, not between two great parties called "Whig" and "Tory," but among several nuclei of political power built largely around *family* interests, ties, and loyalties (often cemented together by the trading of parliamentary seats in return for favors), of which there are perhaps no contemporary equivalents.[16] Thus contemporary accounts of parliamentary struggles of the time refer to the contestants as "the Bedford interest," "the Rutland interest," etc.[17] Inside Parliament these nuclei coalesced behind various prominent parliamentary leaders and went under such titles as "Pittites," "Grenvillites," and "Addingtonites," and control of Parliament was determined by the shifting alliances among them. There was very little conscious political organization of any sort, and such as there was was strictly intragovernmental in nature.[18]

In eighteenth-century Britain, the term "Whig" was generally applied to those politicians who enthusiastically supported the Hanoverian succession and viewed the 1688 revolution with approval. The name "Tory" was generally applied to those who had been originally opposed to or at least unenthusiastic about the Hanoverian succession (only a few of them, however, were accused of actively attempting to overthrow it). This had become, practically speaking, a dead issue by well before 1750; even so, and despite the fact that there were no organized political groups for them to refer to, the names continued to hang on and to affect political careers. Until the accession to power of William Pitt the Younger in 1783, for example, no politician not generally regarded as a "Whig" could hope to hold important ministerial office.[19]

In the first decades of the nineteenth century, however, the terms "Whig" and "Tory" began to take on new meanings. Each began to denote a group of politicians known to have associated together with a view to acting, for certain purposes anyhow, in concert; and known also to be actively opposed to the other group on a new issue, the product of the social and economic

[15] Cf. E. Porritt, *The Unreformed House of Commons,* 2 volumes (Cambridge: Cambridge University Press, 1903).

[16] Perhaps the nearest approach to such an interest in contemporary American politics is the Rockefellers and the members of what might be called the Rockefeller bureaucracy, some of whom are now in official positions in Washington, now back at their posts in the Rockefeller empire. They are a genuine nucleus of power in contemporary America. They are as likely to turn up in Washington under a Democratic administration as under a Republican. And they can hardly be expected, when in office, to divest themselves of their concern with Rockefeller family interests any more than a Bedford man divested himself, in his performance of official functions, of concern with Bedford family interests.

[17] Cf. M. I. Ostrogorski, *Democracy and the Organization of Political Parties,* translated by Frederick Clarke (New York: The Macmillan Company, 1902), Vol. I, pp. 135, 138-39.

[18] *Ibid.,* Vol. I, p. 136. See also Browning, *op. cit.,* pp. 28-36; Trevelyan, *op. cit.,* pp. 8-10; and Emden, *op. cit.,* pp. 101-19.

[19] Trevelyan, *op. cit.,* pp. 14-27. See also W. L. Burn, "The Evolution of Parties and the Party System in the Eighteenth Century," in Bailey, *op. cit.,* pp. 18-25.

ferment that followed the Napoleonic wars, which seemed to overshadow all other issues: Should British political institutions be reformed along more democratic lines, or should they be left pretty much as they were? The term "Whig" came to denote the group in favor of reform, the term "Tory" that which wished to cling to the heritage from the past. The power of the Crown to call the political tricks had, by this time, declined almost to the vanishing point: certainly it was in no position to say No to Parliament, which was being subjected to insistent and increasing public pressure, largely expressed by demonstrations and riots, on behalf of reform. Britain was on the verge of taking the next step toward developing genuine political parties. It was finally taken in the years following 1832.[20]

WHIG-PATRIOTS AND TORY-LOYALISTS IN COLONIAL AMERICA

From the time of their establishment, Britain's American colonies offered, in addition to the local equivalent of the favor of the king (i.e., the favor of the royal governors), stakes of power for which a considerable element of the population were eligible—and invariably willing—to compete. All the colonies, for example, had legislative assemblies, whose membership was here partly, there entirely, elected; and these assemblies had some little influence on the course of events, despite the fact that their actions were for the most part subject to the governor's absolute veto. There were also local government units, whose officials, like the members of the assemblies, owed their tenure to popular election—"popular" at least as it was then conceived in the colonies as in Britain, which meant election on a franchise based on ownership of considerable property.[21]

Each of the assemblies early developed its party-like groupings, and these varied little from colony to colony. There was always a "court party," made up of members whose values and interests disposed them to play along with the governor, and who could thus be counted upon to resist any attempt to decrease his power in favor of the assembly. And there was always a "country party," made up of members who opposed the governor and sought to maximize the power of the assembly. The supporters of the governor were generally known as "Tories" or "Loyalists," and his opponents as "Whigs" or "Patriots." [22]

Inside the assemblies the two groups were far more sharply defined than their counterparts in the British Parliament—since, unlike the latter, they were divided upon a single, highly controversial issue of *contemporary* significance. But the constituent elements, that is, the lesser groupings out of which

[20] Burn, *op. cit.*, pp. 24-25.

[21] For the conditions under which colonial politics operated, see Cortlandt F. Bishop, *History of Elections in the American Colonies* (New York: Columbia University Press, 1893), Ch. II; George D. Luetscher, *Early Political Machinery in the United States* (Philadelphia: University of Pennsylvania, 1903), p. 1; and Edgar E. Robinson, *The Evolution of American Political Parties* (New York: Harcourt, Brace and Company, 1924), pp. 16-20.

[22] Carl L. Becker, *The History of Political Parties in New York, 1760-1776* (Madison, Wis.: Bulletin of the University of Wisconsin, 1909), pp. 7-8.

the wider ones were built, were much the same as in Britain; nuclei of political power clustered mainly around family interests, ties, and loyalties—
which, however, tended to form alliances of a more permanent character than
those known to British politics.[23] There was, on the other hand, only a little
more conscious organization, intragovernmental or extragovernmental, among
American "Whigs" and "Tories" than among British Whigs and Tories.
Nominations for elective offices, for example, were not made via organized
"party" procedures: candidates either put themselves forward, or were designated by "parlor caucuses" in which a few prominent families participated.[24]
And inside the assemblies, cooperation within each "party" was more the
product of spontaneous agreement among the members on questions relating
to the relative power of the governor and the assembly than of conscious organization.[25]

In short, the Whig and Tory "parties" in colonial America exhibited the
characteristics of modern democratic parties on about the same scale as their
eighteenth-century British counterparts. The labels denoted somewhat more
definite political groupings in America than in Britain; but there was far less
consensus between them—as witness the telltale fact that in 1775 the American
colonial party contest broke out into a violent revolution.

"HATS" AND "CAPS" IN PARLIAMENTARY SWEDEN

Besides Britain and colonial America, the only eighteenth-century nation
in which elected officials had any significant share of governmental power was
Sweden, though only during its so-called "parliamentary period," which began
in 1719, following the assassination of Charles XII (1718), and lasted until
1772. Charles' successor was forced by the riksdag, which was a sort of parliament, to accept a new constitution, one of the earliest European departures
from absolute monarchy. It made the king responsible to a riksradet (Council
of the Realm) of seventeen members, and provided for the latter's election
by and responsibility to the riksdag in such fashion that it soon began to function not unlike a parliamentary cabinet. The riksdag itself consisted of four
houses, or "estates": the nobility, the clergy, the bourgeoisie, and the peas-
antry. Members of the latter three houses were elected, in each case on a franchise limited to the social class they were to represent. The riksdag, in other
words, was by no means a model democratic representative assembly even
under the new constitution. On the other hand, it was not, from the standpoint
of our models, markedly inferior to the eighteenth-century British Parliament.[26]

[23] *Ibid.,* pp. 1-16.
[24] Frederick W. Dallinger, *Nominations for Elective Office in the United States* (New York:
Longmans, Green and Company, 1897), pp. 5-7; Bishop, *op. cit.,* pp. 120-27; Luetscher, *op. cit.,*
pp. 63-67; Woodburn, *op. cit.,* pp. 165-67.
[25] Robinson, *op. cit.,* pp. 21-24; Woodburn, *op. cit.,* pp. 4, 8, 11-12.
[26] B. J. Hovde, *The Scandinavian Countries, 1720-1865* (Boston: Chapman and Grimes, Inc.,
1943), Vol. I, pp. 180-83; A. A. Stomberg, *A History of Sweden* (New York: The Macmillan
Company, 1931), pp. 515-16; Ben A. Arneson, *The Democratic Monarchies of Scandinavia* (New
York: D. Van Nostrand Company, Inc., 1939), pp. 33-34.

Through the first decade after 1719, the riksradet and riksdag were led, with little opposition of any sort, by Count Arvid Horn, whose role came to be rather similar to that of a modern prime minister. In the early 1730's, however, an unprecedented development occurred: a considerable group in the riksdag became actively displeased with Horn's allegedly moderate and conciliatory foreign policy toward Russia, which they denounced as sheer cowardice, "fit only for old women in nightcaps." Before long, therefore, they had saddled Horn and his supporters with an uncomplimentary name—"Caps"— of the kind that has figured so prominently in party history. They styled themselves the party of the "Hats," hats being *men's* garb, and thus the appropriate symbol for a virile policy of determined and uncompromising resistance to the Russian Czar.[27]

The "Hats" and "Caps" rapidly became sharply defined groups in the riksdag and riksradet, each with views of its own on domestic issues as well as foreign policy. And before long each had moved a long way, by eighteenth-century standards at least, toward intragovernmental organization as we understand it today, and was even attempting, according to some of the evidence, to influence the election of members to the three lower estates.[28] From the 1730's to the 1760's, Swedish politics was in large part a continuing contest for power between these two parties, with the "Hats" in control most of the time.

By the 1760's, the "Hats" had developed into a party that spoke primarily for the nobility, and the "Caps" into a party of commoners. Before long, moreover, this state of affairs began to be reflected in their contest for power, which took on the overtones of class warfare, and undermined *pari passu* what consensus (in the sense of this term we have previously explained) there had been between them in previous decades. Worse still, from the standpoint of consensus, certain foreign nations that were interested in the outcome of the contest began to contribute heavily to the parties' war chests—the French helping the "Hats" and the Russians the "Caps." The breaking point came with the election of 1769, which took on some of the characteristics of a civil war and brought into play scandalous sums of French and Russian money. For such was the public reaction that by 1771, when Gustavus III came to the throne resolved to end the bitter and corrupt party strife and become a true "patriot king," he quickly got his way. His 1772 *coup d'état* broke the power of the riksradet and riksdag, and restored absolute monarchy.

Most historians agree that the principal cause for the failure of this early Swedish experiment with parliamentary government—a failure with few parallels in modern history, which has seen only a handful of nations achieve parliamentary government and then abandon it for absolutism—was popular dis-

---

[27] Hovde, *op. cit.,* Vol. I, p. 185; Arneson, *op. cit.,* p. 36; Jon Stefansson, *Denmark and Sweden* (London: T. Fisher Unwin, Ltd., 1916), p. 309.

[28] Stomberg, *op. cit.,* pp. 535 ff.

approval of the violent partisanship and corruption of the "Hats" and the "Caps." [29]

Development of Intragovernmental Party Organization

IN GREAT BRITAIN

We have seen that the first step in the evolution of modern parties was the formation of a certain type of more or less well-defined political groups *inside* the government. The next step was the development of these groups in the direction of conscious *organization,* and the creation of political machinery by which their members could pool their strength and more effectively pursue their collective goals. At first only the holders of public office took part in these organizational activities, which, accordingly, were well advanced in most countries before they began anywhere to embrace party supporters and sympathizers *outside* official circles.

We have already observed the beginnings of this second step in Britain, where by about 1815 the "Whigs" and "Tories" were clearly divided on the matter of institutional reform and were taking the first conscious steps toward developing machinery that would enable them to press their demands more effectively. The "whip," for example, one of the most notable components of the machinery that was to be created, was well established in both parties by the 1820's, and, working under the direction of the party leaders, was doing pretty much what a party whip does today: rounding up party members whenever an important vote was to be taken in Parliament; attempting to persuade the "backbenchers" to vote as their leaders wished them to; sounding out opinion among the rank and file in Parliament and transmitting it to the leaders; and even exercising a certain influence upon the making of party nominations in the various constituencies.[30] Party discipline and unity, to be sure, were still much less strong than in the parties of our day, so that the whips could rarely deliver anything like the full party vote on any issue. The beginnings of party organization and machinery were there, however, and they developed rapidly in vigor and effectiveness throughout the rest of the century.[31]

IN THE UNITED STATES

Some precedents for intragovernmental party organization were established by "patriot" groups in certain colonial assemblies in the 1760's and early 1770's. The best-organized and most powerful was the "Boston Junto" in the Massachusetts assembly. Its leaders, the Boston delegation to the House of Representatives under the captainship of Samuel Adams, early in the period

[29] Hovde, *op. cit.,* Vol. I, pp. 188-91; Stomberg, *op. cit.,* p. 541.
[30] Ostrogorski, *op. cit.,* Vol. I, pp. 137-38.
[31] Emden, *op. cit.,* pp. 113-15; J. A. Hawgood, "The Evolution of Parties and the Party System in the Nineteenth Century," in Bailey, *op. cit.,* pp. 26-28.

mentioned, began to bring together all the "patriots" in the assembly for periodic consultations on strategy. Before long, moreover, they were stirring up agitation outside the assembly against such things as the Stamp Act, and each type of activity tended to give them a stronger hand for the other, so that by a moment well before the Revolution they had welded the anti-imperial forces into a powerful opposition group.[32] Much the same sort of organization was attempted, although with less success, by the "patriot" elements in the assemblies of New York and North Carolina.[33] These groups were, to be sure, essentially revolutionary (as we have already noted), so that the organizations they developed can hardly—on our showing—be called *party* organizations. They did serve, however, as precedents, although they disappeared with the outbreak of the Revolution, and the legislatures in the period from 1775 to 1789 produced nothing really comparable to them.

During the period of the Revolution and of the Articles of Confederation —a period, of course, of intense political controversy both among the citizens of the emergent nation and within its several governments—a considerable number of more or less ephemeral groupings took shape in the various legislative assemblies. None of them, however, appears to have developed anything like real party organization. Even during the fight over the ratification of the new federal Constitution (1788-1789), the contestants never built anything properly describable as organization. The "federalists" and "antifederalists," in other words, were simply two sets of individuals holding different opinions about adopting the Constitution; they were not, in our sense of the term, parties, because they lacked the necessary organizational structure.[34]

The first real intragovernmental party organizations in the United States were not created until the early 1790's, when the contest over Alexander Hamilton's financial program finally called them into existence. Hamilton, once he had drawn up his program, appears to have decided that he could not take any chances with the opposition it might run up against in Congress, and that there was nothing for it but to bring together a group of senators and representatives whose continued support he could count on. This he proceeded to do, and he had soon provided himself with (though it was not called that) a *caucus*. The group's members consulted together regularly on matters of policy and strategy, and made a concerted and sustained drive to persuade other congressmen to support Hamilton's program. It was, however, a purely intragovernmental organization, which made no attempt whatever to influence public opinion outside official circles.[35]

Shortly after the formation of the Hamiltonian party, the opponents of its program, recognizing its existence and its potential impact on events, con-

[32] Ralph V. Harlow, *The History of Legislative Methods in the Period Before 1825* (New Haven: Yale University Press, 1917), Ch. II.

[33] *Ibid.*, Ch. III.

[34] Henry Jones Ford, *The Rise and Growth of American Politics* (New York: The Macmillan Company, 1898), pp. 101-02; Robinson, *op. cit.*, pp. 51-53.

[35] Robinson, *op. cit.*, pp. 60-75.

vinced themselves (as many a politician has had occasion to do since—though often only after getting roundly beaten) that the only effective answer to organization is counterorganization, and began to hold conferences of their own. The formation and structuring of both groups were considerably speeded up, and the issues between them notably sharpened, by the submission to the Senate of the pro-British and highly controversial Jay's Treaty. But by the middle 1790's there existed in the new national government two quite definite groups of officeholders, each with a definite program, an appetite for control over policy and personnel, and a rapidly developing organization. The group that formed behind Hamilton called itself the "Federalists," thus reminding people that they were the true defenders of the Constitution against the radical "Jacobins," who wanted to decentralize government and give the propertyless mob control over governmental policy. Hamilton's opponents, who soon mobilized behind Jefferson's leadership, feared that among the many intolerable objectives the Federalists had set themselves was that of restoring royalty, nobility, and a monarchical form of government in the United States. This they were determined at all costs to prevent, and they accordingly called themselves "Republicans." [36]

By the middle 1790's, therefore, American parties were already characterized, inside the government, by a high degree of organization. Over the next two decades, moreover, they developed many new devices for solidifying their organizations and making them more effective. As early as 1800, for instance, each party had its congressional caucus, had built it up into a well-established institution for making legislative policy and strategy, and was using it to nominate candidates for the presidency and vice-presidency. During an initial period, caucus meetings were secret in the twofold sense that (a) outsiders were excluded from their deliberations, and (b) members kept to themselves the fact of their being held. Soon, however, the results of the caucuses' functioning became so obvious that no attempt was made to maintain secrecy of the latter type. And soon too there were legislative caucuses serving the same purposes and acting much the same way in the developing party organizations in most of the state legislatures.[37]

In the late 1790's, the Republicans took a further step toward modern party organization by creating the institution of the "floor leader," whose task it was to lead the party's forces in the House of Representatives. The first incumbent of this office, Albert Gallatin, became Secretary of the Treasury in 1801. But he was promptly succeeded as floor leader by William B. Giles, with the clear implication that the office was now regarded as a permanent party institution.

By the end of Jefferson's second administration in 1809, the speakership of the House and the membership of congressional committees had come to be

---

[36] William A. Robinson, *Jeffersonian Democracy in New England* (New Haven: Yale University Press, 1916), Ch. I; Ford, *op. cit.*, p. 105; Woodburn, *op. cit.*, pp. 13-20.

[37] Ostrogorski, *op. cit.*, Vol. II, pp. 10-17.

controlled by the majority party's caucus, and intragovernmental party organization had become one of the central facts of the nation's political life.[38]

IN CANADA

Canada's experience with political parties in many respects parallels that of the United States more closely than that of Great Britain. In 1791 the British Parliament created two new colonial units, Upper Canada (Ontario) and Lower Canada (Quebec). Each thenceforth had its legislative assembly, elected on a franchise sharply restricted by high property qualifications. Each also had an Executive Council and a Legislative Council, however, and these bodies rather than the respective assemblies held and exercised the real power. Since both councils in both provinces were appointed by the royal governor and were responsible to him rather than to the assemblies, no real opposition to the governor developed in any of them. Opposition to the governor did develop in the assemblies, however, much as it did in the colonial legislatures in the United States before the revolution, and with, for our purposes, much the same results. Soon in each assembly two distinct groups of assemblymen emerged: a "country party," which demanded a larger share of power for the assembly, and a "court party," which supported the governor and wished the assembly to remain powerless. The contest between the two was sharper in Quebec than in Ontario because the court party there was largely British and the country party French-Canadian. And in Canada as in the United States of earlier days, each was merely a loose set of like-minded individuals, and cooperation among the latter was more a matter of spontaneous agreement than of conscious organization and consultation.[39]

Both provinces achieved full parliamentary government when, in 1847, the councils were made responsible to the assemblies. The issue between the country party and the court party was thus resolved in favor of the former, with the result that the old grouping of the assemblymen lost most of its significance, and the two "parties" disappeared—in favor of little clusterings of assemblymen formed about a few prominent parliamentary leaders, much in the fashion of British politics in the eighteenth century. (Even today the position of the party leader is perhaps more important in Canada than in any other democratic party system.) [40]

After 1847, some of the small groups just mentioned formed, under the leadership of Sir John A. Macdonald, a coalition whose main purpose was to press for the federation of the several Canadian provinces into one nation. Under the name "Liberal-Conservative Party" it won its primary objective— and lost its original *raison d'être*—when the British Parliament passed the

---

[38] Harlow, *op. cit.,* Chs. IX, X, and XII; E. E. Robinson, *op. cit.,* pp. 79-85.

[39] D. A. McArthur in the *Cambridge History of the British Empire* (New York: The Macmillan Company, 1930), Vol. VI, pp. 207-10.

[40] F. H. Underhill, "The Development of National Political Parties in Canada," *Canadian Historical Review,* Vol. XVI (December, 1935), pp. 367-87; Hugh McD. Clokie, *Canadian Government and Politics* (Toronto: Longmans, Green and Company, 1944), pp. 90-92.

British North America Act in 1867. But it continued to be the dominant party of the new federation over several decades, in the course of which it developed a certain amount of machinery for forming and carrying out its program. For the most part, however, both the Liberal-Conservatives and their opponents, the Liberals, lagged far behind American and British parties in this regard, so that, up to a moment well into the twentieth century, their organization at the center was extremely meager. Even today the major Canadian parties have even less effective permanent central organizations than we have in this country, and are essentially alliances of provincial parties. In short, national intra-governmental party organization was a long time coming in Canada, and still has not assumed the proportions there that it has assumed in most modern democracies.[41]

IN WESTERN EUROPE AND SCANDINAVIA

The generalizations we are about to offer concerning the development of parties in France, Belgium, the Netherlands, Switzerland, Sweden, and Denmark admittedly do less than full justice to that which is unique in the party history of each country. We have attempted merely to draw from the data the *pattern* of development from country to country, to show that we can properly speak of a pattern, and, finally, to call attention to major departures from the pattern in each country. To do more would run the present chapter to intolerable lengths, while to do less would be to pass up materials of great interest for our present inquiry.[42]

Parliamentary government—with real power lodged in an elected legislative assembly, thus no longer the monopoly of an absolute monarch—was achieved in western Europe and Scandinavia around the middle of the nineteenth century (in several countries, indeed, the turning point came in one

---

[41] E. N. Reid, "The Rise of National Parties in Canada," *Proceedings of the Canadian Political Science Association*, Vol. IV (1932), pp. 187-200; Alexander Brady, *Democracy in the Dominions* (Toronto: The University of Toronto Press, 1947), pp. 90-105; Clokie, *op. cit.*, pp. 76-78, 94-95.

[42] The major sources upon which the present writers have drawn for this discussion of party development in western Europe and Scandinavia are as follows: For French parties, A. Lawrence Lowell, *Governments and Parties in Continental Europe*, 2 volumes (Boston: Houghton Mifflin Company, 1896); R. K. Gooch, "The Government and Politics of France," in James T. Shotwell, ed., *Governments of Continental Europe*, rev. ed. (New York: The Macmillan Company, 1952), pp. 35-213; Walter R. Sharp, *The Government of the French Republic* (New York: D. Van Nostrand Company, Inc., 1938); and Roger H. Soltau, *French Parties and Politics* (London: Oxford University Press, 1922). For Belgian parties, Thomas H. Reed, *Government and Politics of Belgium* (Yonkers, N. Y.: World Book Company, 1924). For Dutch parties, B. H. M. Vlekke, *Evolution of the Dutch Nation* (New York: Roy Publishers, 1945). For Swiss parties, William E. Rappard, *The Government of Switzerland* (New York: D. Van Nostrand Company, Inc., 1936); Robert C. Brooks, *Government and Politics of Switzerland* (Yonkers, N. Y.: World Book Company, 1918); and Arnold D. Zurcher, "The Political System of Switzerland," in Shotwell, *op. cit.*, pp. 331-86. For Swedish parties, Nils Herlitz, *Sweden: A Modern Democracy on Ancient Foundations* (Minneapolis: University of Minnesota Press, 1939); Bjarne Braatoy, *The New Sweden* (London: Thomas Nelson and Sons, Ltd., 1939); and Arneson, *op. cit.* For Danish parties, Arneson, *op. cit.*

and the same year, 1848).[43] And in each nation it soon produced the result the foregoing section of the present chapter would lead us to expect, namely the crystallization within the assembly of two more or less definite groups: a "liberal" group, determined to expand the suffrage (which in each country was limited to those who could meet certain property qualifications) and to force all other agencies of government to knuckle under to the parliament; and a "conservative" group, similarly determined to prevent forward movement on either of these two fronts. In some of the countries, indeed, the chasm between these two groups was so wide and deep that we cannot properly speak of any real consensus between them with respect to basic constitutional issues. And in two of the countries, Belgium and the Netherlands, bitter conflict between Protestants and Catholics, most particularly over the problem of whether and how to secularize education,[44] long stood in the way of any *rapprochement* of the kind that might make the building—or emergence—of consensus possible.

In most western European and Scandinavian countries, the parties developed, some sooner, some later, a certain measure of intragovernmental organization, although nothing so elaborate and effective as the machinery developed by American parties in the early 1800's. Mostly it was a matter of adopting procedures for intra-"group"[45] consultation on parliamentary policy and strategy and nothing more. This was possible, it seems, because the groups were made up of men so agreed—or assumed to be so agreed—about matters of common interest that no problem could arise as to what to do about dissidents. In actual practice it did not, of course, always work that way, and what happened was that the member who took exception to a group decision simply got out and either joined another group or became a "lone wolf."

Such intragovernmental party organization as these nations developed was, in all cases, highly centralized—in part because the only discernible parties were those inside the national legislature. Switzerland is the one exception: the parties that grew up there after the Confederation of 1848 were cantonal parties, and until a very late date in the nineteenth century the history of party or-

[43] The exact dates are: for France, from 1830 to 1849, and from 1875 on; for Belgium, 1830; for Holland, 1848; for Switzerland, a parliamentary *federal* constitution in 1848, although many of the cantons had had parliamentary government before 1848; for Sweden, 1866; for Denmark, 1848.

[44] Reed, *op. cit.*, pp. 141-58; Vlekke, *op. cit.*, Ch. XII.

[45] In some European countries, notably France, the word "group" has a technical meaning that indicates a considerably sharper distinction between intragovernmental and extragovernmental party organization than exists in the English-speaking nations. A French *groupe*, strictly speaking, is a formally organized collection of like-minded members of the legislative assembly. It is thus roughly equivalent to the British "parliamentary party" and the American "legislative caucus." A French *parti*, on the other hand, like the parties in the United States and England, is a political organization that cultivates the electorate out over the country (not necessarily the entire country) at election time, but with this difference: it lapses into inactivity *after* the election. Most *groupes* have, to be sure, corresponding *partis*. But there are some *groupes* without *partis* and some *partis* without *groupes*: cf. R. K. Gooch, "The Government and Politics of France," in James T. Shotwell, ed., *Governments of Continental Europe*, rev. ed. (New York: The Macmillan Company, 1952), pp. 172, 181.

ganization in Switzerland is merely the history of these parties. The latter did, to be sure, form national alliances, which had their points of similarity with the national parties of other countries, but did not and could not become genuine parties because the last word always lay with the cantonal organizations, where it lies today.[46] The Social Democratic Party, founded in the late nintenth century and, like all Marxist parties, highly centralized, is the only Swiss party whose national organization is more powerful than its cantonal organizations.

Development of Extragovernmental Party Organization

IN THE UNITED STATES

In some respects, the "patriotic societies" of prerevolutionary America were forerunners of the large-scale extragovernmental party organizations that emerged in the nineteenth century. These groups were formed in most of the colonies in the 1760's to oppose more effectively the new "get tough" policy of the British colonial office. Such opposition meant, first of all, seeing to it that "Patriots," not "Tories," were elected to the colonial legislatures, which in turn meant seeing to it that promising patriot candidates were nominated and then conducting vigorous campaigns on their behalf. Both activities, be it noted, called in the very nature of the case for participation by *non-officeholders,* and many such persons were in fact brought into the extremely "hush-hush" local "caucuses," or "clubs," that were early recognized as the most appropriate organizational devices for achieving their objectives.[47] Perhaps the most powerful and certainly the most famous of these societies was the Boston "Caucus Club," whose activities as of 1763 John Adams described for us in this often-quoted passage:

> This day learned that the Caucus club meets at certain times in the garret of Tom Dawes, the Adjutant of the Boston regiment. He has a large house, and he has a movable partition in his garret which he takes down, and the whole club meets in one room. There they smoke tobacco till you cannot see from one end of the garret to the other. There they drink flip, I suppose, and they choose a moderator who puts questions to the vote regularly; and selectmen, assessors, collectors, firewards, *and representatives are regularly chosen before they are chosen in the town.*[48]

Here again, however, we must speak of forerunners, not of early examples, for the caucuses' objectives were revolutionary and thus directed not at the control of policy and personnel within a self-governing circumscription, but at the achievement of self-government by overthrowing a regime. Or perhaps it

[46] Rappard, *op. cit.,* pp. 104-05; Zurcher, *op. cit.,* pp. 365-66; Lowell, *op. cit.,* Vol. II, pp. 318-33; Brooks, *op. cit.,* pp. 305-09.

[47] For more detailed descriptions of these groups, see Dallinger, *op. cit.,* pp. 7-12, 44; Becker, *op. cit.,* p. 17; Ostrogorski, *op. cit.,* Vol. II, pp. 3-7; E. E. Robinson, *op. cit.,* pp. 28-30; and Binkley, *op. cit.,* pp. 67-68.

[48] Entry in John Adams' journal, February, 1763, quoted in Ostrogorski, *op. cit.,* Vol. II, p. 4. Italics added.

would be more accurate to say by initiating the overthrow of a regime, for their activities and importance sharply declined during the Revolution, and they had little impact on events during the revolutionary aftermath.

For the unmistakable early examples of modern American extragovernmental party organization we must look to the "Democratic Societies" of the early 1790's—the major weapons used by the pro-Jefferson, pro-French elements of the population in the struggle that eventually led to the downfall of the Federalists. Two events—Washington's Proclamation of Neutrality (in the Anglo-French War) and the American tour of the French Ambassador, "Citizen" Genêt—appear to have provided the turning point that first (1793) brought them into existence; for before these events were a year old, certainly, twenty-four of these societies were doing business (some of them, we might note in passing, by petitioning for admission to the Jacobin Order in Paris). But their characteristic feature was their crystal-clear conception of their own function, which they saw as that of launching and keeping going, each in its own county, activities likely to result in the election of Republicans and the defeat of Federalists at all levels of government. This meant, on one side, directing a steady flow of resolutions at the Congress; but mostly it meant *making nominations* for elective offices, and seeing to it that no Republican candidate should be beaten by a Federalist because his supporters had failed to organize a campaign of tireless and systematic electioneering on his behalf. Almost overnight, in other words, they found themselves engaged in most of the activities that extragovernmental party organizations engage in today— and under comparable auspices.[49] For Jefferson's intragovernmental organization soon established liaison with and supervision over the local committees. No one questions that they accounted for a vast number of Republican votes in the election of 1800 and taught the Federalists what was to become an axiom of American politics: that there is no answer to organized local electioneering except organized local electioneering. No American major party would ever again go into a national election having failed to act upon it.

During the period from 1800 to the 1830's, the trend toward extragovernmental organization was accentuated by a number of developments. New states were admitted to the Union, and constitutions and basic laws were revised in the older states, with the result that both the number of voters and the number of elective offices rapidly increased. More elective offices meant more rewards for successful organization, and more votes meant larger organizations (in order to be sure of reaching everyone) and greater penalties for failure to organize. (If the opposition reached everyone, and you didn't, you would be swamped at the polls.) Making nominations and contesting elections became big business, and the tight, secret, closed-corporation type of party organization that had dominated politics heretofore could no longer turn the trick. By the end of the period mentioned, in consequence, extragovernmental party organization both spread geographically and increased in depth and complexity.

[49] Luetscher, *op. cit.,* Ch. II.

The New England Republicans, for example, within a few years after 1800, had state party committees, which appointed county committees, which in turn appointed town committees; and all of them, on all three levels, were conducting campaigns, carrying voters to the polls, publishing and circulating party newspapers and pamphlets, and holding political rallies. Before long, moreover, party committees were even taking over the organization and control of many town meetings.[50] Appeals to party supporters to stand loyally behind the decisions of the committees were of much the same nature as, though perhaps more florid than, such appeals today—as witness the following public appeal made in 1803 by the Bucks County (Pa.) Republican Committee in response to a rumor that there was dissatisfaction with and potential rebellion against the committee's nominees:

Would you merit the character of Republicans? Bow to the will of the majority, and support the ticket formed by your representatives. Would you aspire to the name of patriots? Would you promote the cause of liberty and extend its blessings to the generations unborn? Cleave to the system of Republican union, as to the horns of freedom's altar. Would you merit the appellation of wise men and good politicians? Take the obvious means to extend your power and influence, and do not madly pull down with your own hands the fabric you erected with so much care. In fine, would you disappoint the hopes of your enemies, and avoid the ridicule which awaits your fall? Make your Committees a just representation of the Republican interest—support by your votes the ticket they recommend—and take for your pole star that political maxim, United We Stand, Divided We Fall![51]

General replacement of the legislative caucus with the representative party convention as *the* method for making nominations at all levels of government, which came soon after the close of the period mentioned, set the character of the extragovernmental organization of American parties in a mold that was not materially altered until the advent of the direct primary in the early twentieth century (see Chapter 14).[52]

IN GREAT BRITAIN

Extragovernmental party organization did not develop in Great Britain until after 1832. Members of the House of Commons were elected, until that time, on a highly restrictive "40-shilling freeholder" franchise that dated back to 1420, and seats were quite unevenly distributed, both geographically and numerically speaking, even among this small electorate. Few candidates for Parliament, in consequence, found themselves obliged to make any sort of generalized appeal to "the people," so that there was scant pressure on the parties to organize for the purpose of disseminating such appeals. An Edmund Burke

---

[50] W. A. Robinson, *op. cit.*, Ch. IV.

[51] Quoted in Luetscher, *op. cit.*, pp. 80-81. For a useful description of the nature and activities of the early Federalists, see Manning J. Dauer, *The Adams Federalists* (Baltimore: The Johns Hopkins Press, 1954).

[52] Ford, *op. cit.*, pp. 167-68; Ostrogorski, *op. cit.*, Vol. II, pp. 54-59; E. E. Robinson, *op. cit.*, pp. 101-09.

might, to be sure, find it advisable to "address" the electors of Bristol, but when he did so it was in highly *personal* terms, and what he talked of was his own qualifications, not his "stand" on the issues of the day. The prevailing attitude among both candidates and voters was: Elect virtuous men and let *them* decide public questions.[53] The only channel open to "public opinion" for influencing parliamentary decision was the mass meetings (sometimes they turned into riots) that assembled, passed resolutions to be dispatched to Parliament, paraded, and demonstrated. (One of the most famous of such demonstrations in the eighteenth century was that over the Wilkes case, in which the ministers were attempting to prevent a popular member and political leader from taking his seat.) In short, the presuppositions for extragovernmental party *organization* of the kind that had already developed in the United States were simply not present in pre-1832 Britain.[54]

The year 1832 was the turning point because it brought the passage of the Reform Act, which both redistributed parliamentary seats and added some quarter of a million new voters to the electorate—that is, gave both parties new territory to penetrate, and good reason for penetrating it rapidly. Both, in consequence, promptly established local "registration associations" to get the new voters on the rolls and invite their adherence, and these associations have been the heart and core of extragovernmental party organization in Britain ever since. From the very first most of their members were—as they are today— *voters,* not officeholders or even aspirants to public office, who helped to pay party expenses by putting themselves down for subscriptions.

After the first post–Reform Act election, the associations found themselves, as we should expect, less and less in the business of registering voters and more and more in the business of making nominations and conducting campaigns. By the early 1840's, it was clearly understood in many constituencies that anyone who wished to be the party's candidate first had to apply to the local association. If rejected he could, at first anyhow, go ahead and run under the party's label; but gradually nomination by the local association came to carry with it the sole right to use the party's label.

Liaison between the old intragovernmental party organizations and the new local associations grew up in the first instance around London's Carlton Club, founded in 1831 as a place where Conservatives—inside and outside Parliament—could meet and discuss party matters, and its Reform Club, which the Liberals established (curiously enough, right next door) in 1836. From the 1830's through the 1850's, these clubs served as headquarters for informal but often effective collaboration between the party whips and their respective local associations. The first step in the direction of formal liaison was not taken until 1861, when the Liberals created the Liberal Registration Association, and assigned it the task of coordinating the local associations' activities—both vis-à-vis one another and vis-à-vis the party's intragovernmental organs. The Conserva-

53 Cf. Emden, *op. cit.,* Ch. VIII.
54 Ostrogorski, *op. cit.,* Vol. I, pp. 117-24.

tives set up a similar organization, the National Union of Conservative and Constitutional Associations, in 1867.[55]

Subsequent developments in British extragovernmental party organization have all come as direct results of further (post-1832) extensions of the suffrage. The Reform Act of 1867, which enfranchised the bulk of the urban working class, increased the electorate by approximately a million votes and thus posed again the registration problem that had first called the associations into existence, but in a form which, in and of itself, would not have required any modification of existing party structure. But it turned out quite otherwise with one of the more or less incidental provisions of the act, which sought, in certain constituencies that elected three M.P.'s, to keep all three from going to a single party by having each voter vote for only two. One such borough was Birmingham, where the Liberals, who knew they had a substantial majority of the voters over the whole city, determined to organize their forces along American lines and, act or no act, capture all three seats. They proceeded, under Joseph Chamberlain's leadership, to organize the "Birmingham Caucus," [56] and used it to such good effect that it was soon imitated in most other localities—by *both* parties. In the course of the 1870's, in consequence, local extragovernmental organization became a matter of caucus and convention based on full party membership, and ceased to confine itself to the small, rather exclusive local registration association. The extent to which these local "caucuses" had, by the 1880's, arrogated to themselves the capacity to make binding nominations may be clearly seen from two well-known incidents, the Forster case and the Cowen case. In each instance the issue at stake was whether a local Liberal caucus could "instruct" its M.P. to either support the national party leadership more faithfully or refrain from calling himself a Liberal at the next election. Both Forster and Cowen attempted to resist such "dictation" from the constituency level, and both failed. The local caucuses, it was agreed, had as a matter of course the last word as to the use of the party label.[57]

Through the 1880's, relations between the extragovernmental and intragovernmental organizations became more and more intimate—and, at the same time, more and more a matter of the intragovernmental organizations' exercising effective control over the policies and activities of the extragovernmental. By 1890, in any case, British party organization had developed into its present-day pattern, which we may now speak of as so firmly established that

[55] *Ibid.*, Vol. I, pp. 143-53, and Vol. I, Part 2, Chs. VII and VIII.

[56] All the party workers in each of the city's wards met in a ward caucus and chose a ward committee. Each of these committees, in turn, chose delegates to a city central committee; and the central committee, working through the ward organizations, created and carried through a strategy of distributing Liberal votes among their three candidates. The Liberals indeed carried all three seats in the general election of 1868.

[57] One of these cases involved the disciplining of W. E. Forster, Minister of Education in the Liberal Government of 1868-1874, by the Bradford Liberal Caucus. The other involved the retirement of Joseph Cowen by the Newcastle Liberal Caucus. For detailed accounts of these cases, see Ostrogorski, *op. cit.*, Vol. I, pp. 194-201, 230-39.

it has been able, without essential modification, to absorb even a major political event like the eclipse of the Liberal Party by the Labor Party.[58]

IN CANADA

Canadian extragovernmental party organization has sprung up for the most part in the present century—by American or British standards, at a surprisingly late moment in the history of the country's political parties. For no readily apparent reason, it has patterned itself upon American rather than British models, so that, for example, we find the Canadians picking their party leaders at national representative party conventions. (From 1878 to 1919, Canadian party leaders were named—as they still are in Great Britain—by caucuses of each party's members in Parliament.) The Liberal party, the first to adopt the present system, did so with the avowed purpose of "democratizing" the nomination procedure—that is, of turning it over to representatives of the party's provincial organizations, which presumably could have been done without imitating such other features of the typical American convention as the keynote speech, the written platform, and nominating and seconding speeches. But the first Liberal convention (1919) imitated these features also, and departed from American precedent only by using the secret rather than the open ballot in the nominating process. The Conservatives began holding similar conventions in 1927, and there seems no immediate likelihood of either party's returning to the earlier nominating procedures.[59]

IN WESTERN EUROPE AND SCANDINAVIA

In most of the western European and Scandinavian nations, as in Canada, extragovernmental party organization on any considerable scale emerged as recently as the early years of the present century. For the most part, it was the creation, in the first instance, of the local equivalent of the Social Democratic party, and spread to other parties only as the former's electoral successes drove them to create counterorganizations.

In general in these countries, extragovernmental party organization came late because the suffrage remained highly restricted for a relatively long time. Belgium, for example, adopted manhood suffrage as recently as 1894, Sweden as recently as 1909, and the Netherlands as recently as 1917. France, by contrast, had adopted it as long ago as 1848—long before it adopted parliamentary government, which it did finally only in 1875 (in the other Western democracies parliamentary government came first, then manhood suffrage). But, and in part for the reason just mentioned, genuine parties—as opposed to parliamentary "groups"—did not appear in France until the early 1900's.[60]

[58] Hawgood, *op. cit.,* pp. 26-34; D. C. Somervell, "The Evolution of Parties and the Party System in the Twentieth Century," in Bailey, *op. cit.,* pp. 35-41; Ostrogorski, *op. cit.,* Vol. I, Part 3, Chs. I-III, V.

[59] William B. Munro, *American Influences on Canadian Government* (Toronto: The Macmillan Company of Canada, Ltd., 1929), pp. 63-67; Clokie, *op. cit.,* pp. 92-93.

[60] Lowell, *op. cit.,* Vol. I, pp. 91-94, 133-34; Sharp, *op. cit.,* pp. 50-53.

In general, the Anglo-American pattern of development has repeated itself in western Europe and Scandinavia. The moment comes when some degree of power is lodged in the hands of elected officials; soon afterward, extra-governmental party organization appears upon the scene, most probably in connection with a drive for extending the suffrage; and it develops apace after manhood suffrage has been achieved, i.e., when the parties can achieve their objectives only by attracting and delivering to the polls large numbers of voters.

Development of the Idea of the Loyal Opposition

In certain political quarters—among Communists and their fellow-travelers, for instance—the notion of a "loyal opposition" is regarded as self-contradictory. Either—so runs the political logic in these quarters—one is loyal to one's government, or one opposes it; so that if one opposes it, one is by that very token disloyal to it. The notion of a "loyal opposition," and institutions appropriate to the emergence and maintenance of a loyal opposition, are nevertheless presuppositions of the basic consensus on which democratic government necessarily rests, and without which it cannot lead a healthy existence.

The notion of loyal opposition presupposes, first of all, a sharp distinction between the *government-of-the-day* on the one hand, and the *regime* on the other hand—i.e., between those *persons* who as of a given moment hold public office, and so make decisions about current policy, and the decision-making *process* in the context of which those persons perform their functions.[61] For only if this distinction is clearly grasped and generally accepted by the members of any community can the notion of a loyal opposition so much as begin to take root in that community. In its absence, being "against" those in power and the policies they are pursuing is—or if not necessarily is, will certainly be regarded as—treasonable. In other words, the central characteristic of loyal opposition is that it wishes the government-of-the-day replaced, and its policies set aside, but has no quarrel with the regime, and no intention other than to perpetuate it. Loyal opposition *opposes* the government-of-the-day, but is *loyal* to the regime.

The notion of *"the* loyal opposition" is this concept applied to a situation where there are two major parties, or two major coalitions of parties, competing regularly for power. We speak of the loyal opposition, in other words, when (a) the government-of-the-day, itself an organized party group, faces a second organized party group sufficiently larger, more powerful, or more influential than any third or fourth organized party group to get itself recognized as *the* opposition, and (b) this opposition is a "shadow government," in

---

[61] "In the context of" in at least two senses: (1) the regime was "there" before they became the government-of-the-day, and will be there after they have yielded to the subsequent government-of-the-day; and (2) the regime is the framework of rules, understandings, precedents, etc., in which the government-of-the-day makes and executes its decisions.

the sense that, in addition to criticizing the personnel and policies of the government-of-the-day, it stands ready to assume decision-making responsibility itself whenever a majority of the members of the community (or, in a parliamentary government, a majority of the legislature) decide it's time for a change. In short, *the* loyal opposition is *organized party* opposition; and it provides the community with a continuing alternative to—as well as a source of criticism of—the government-of-the-day.

Let us, in the light of this conception, now ask ourselves this question: What conditions would have to obtain in a given community in order for it to institutionalize these notions—that is, in order for it to operate its political system on a government-of-the-day-versus-*the*-loyal-opposition basis? The following, at least, suggest themselves at once: (1) The members of the community and the competing political parties must, in general, be content with the existing regime. (2) The parties must be sufficiently well organized to retain their identity, so that they can readily be recognized as either the government-of-the-day or the loyal opposition. (3) There must be consensus—as we have explained it earlier—between the parties. And (4) not merely the parties but the voters also must be familiar—and have no quarrel—with the idea of loyal *party* opposition.

As a matter of history, countries in which the loyal opposition is today an established institution do appear to have developed it as they have met the conditions we have just named: general popular satisfaction with the political regime; full development of both intragovernmental and extragovernmental party organization; development on the part of each of the major parties, in a context of general popular acceptance, of a disposition to tolerate the existence and activities of the other; and general popular acceptance of party organizations as legitimate agencies of democratic government. Let us look briefly at the record in the several democracies we have been speaking of.

IN GREAT BRITAIN AND CANADA

The notion that *individual members of Parliament* could oppose a particular set of ministers—i.e., express the wish to see them out of office—and yet view with approval the existing regime, seems to have been generally accepted in Britain at least as long ago as the younger Pitt's accession to power (1783). So much seems clear from the fact that before his peaceful succession to the post of prime minister he had not only been an avowed "Tory," but had actually led the opposition to the various "Whig" ministers whom he and his colleagues succeeded. His opposition to the Whigs, in other words, had not been construed as opposition to the ruling house, or as proof that he could not safely be trusted with high public office. Only a short time before, let us recall, i.e., in the early years of the eighteenth century, large numbers of Englishmen had regarded "Tories" as *ipso facto* subversive.[62]

[62] Francis Lieber placed the origins of "this great institution" even earlier than 1783. It was first perfected, he believed, in England in the middle of the eighteenth century during the

We must be careful, however, not to read too much into the events of 1783. Practically no one thought of these events as meaning that a Tory party had assumed power, if by "party" we mean a united, consciously organized group of individuals with a common program and strategy. Large numbers of Englishmen still thought of any organized *party* opposition to the ministry in power (as opposed to temporary and shifting alliances among individuals opposed to the ministry) as a "cabal" or a "junta"—in the ancient, highly pejorative sense of those terms.[63] Not until the 1830's and 1840's, the period of the more or less open struggle for power waged by Sir Robert Peel and his organization, did the idea of loyal *party* opposition begin to win acceptance; and not until the 1870's did it cease to evoke sharp and often bitter criticism, now from politicians, now from laymen.[64] Today, in any case, it is familiar British constitutional doctrine, as witness the fact that since 1937 the Leader of Her Majesty's Loyal Opposition has been legally recognized as such and has received a salary from the Crown.

In Canada, the Leader of the Opposition has since 1905 enjoyed the status now accorded his counterpart in Britain. Thus the idea of loyal party opposition was established in Canada not long after the solidification of party organization in the 1880's.

IN THE UNITED STATES

We have already noted that in the early days of the Republic the Federalists believed they were fighting to keep the Republicans from destroying the new Constitution and nation. The Republicans, similarly, regarded themselves as resisting Federalist attempts to establish a monarchy. Opposed leaders like John Adams and Jefferson could, to be sure, be tied to one another by bonds of close personal friendship; but the parties as such did not look upon each other with mutual tolerance, or with a conscious common loyalty to an established regime. And if from their defeat in 1800 to their dissolution after 1816 the Federalists were too weak electorally to put up much opposition of any kind, they were still so vigorously opposed to the party in power as to take under advisement, at their secret Hartford convention in 1814, possible secession of the New England states from the Union—and this at a moment when the nation was at war! In short, the idea of loyal party opposition was unlikely to gain much ground until the feelings aroused by the bitter election of 1800, and by the events that preceded them, had had time to die out. It did not, in

reign of George II, at which time the Jacobites had given up the idea of restoring the Stuarts, and a continuing opposition to Walpole's ministry, led by the Earl of Bath, was tolerated all around. The first use of the term "the Leader of His Majesty's Loyal Opposition," Lieber believed, was that by an observer named Ellice in 1838 to describe Sir Robert Peel: *Manual of Political Ethics,* 2nd ed. (Philadelphia: J. B. Lippincott and Co., 1876), Vol. II, pp. 270-71.

[63] In the next chapter we shall explain in greater detail the nature of this eighteenth-century attitude toward organized *party* opposition.

[64] Hawgood, *op. cit.,* pp. 26-29.

fact, win general acceptance, or come to be clearly understood by large numbers of Americans, until the 1840's.

From 1816 until well into the 1830's, most Americans believed that "there could be but one political party—the Republicans—and that all of them belonged to it. There might be factions, but Adams and Clay men no less than Jackson men insisted they were the true Jeffersonians." [65] Hence the opposing parties that began to emerge in the 1830's were known at first as "National Republicans" and "Democratic Republicans." Only in the 1840's were the labels "Whigs" and "Democrats" generally adopted; and only then, we repeat, did the idea of loyal party opposition receive acceptance and approval from most Americans.[66]

IN WESTERN EUROPE AND SCANDINAVIA

The idea of the loyal opposition is even now less well established in most western European and Scandinavian countries than in the United States, Great Britain, and Canada. And even where it has won a fair measure of acceptance, it has done so much later than in the English-speaking nations— as we should expect, because one or more of the conditions on which we are fixing attention was fulfilled at a relatively tardy date.

In contemporary France, for example, not only is our condition concerning democratic consensus among the parties unfulfilled, but the prevailing trends seem to be undermining such consensus as does exist. The Communist "party" is, and seems likely to remain, one of the three leading parties, and while for tactical purposes of the moment it may be willing to confine itself to "peaceful electoral methods," everyone knows it looks ultimately to the complete overthrow of the present democratic regime.[67] The long-run intentions of such parties of the right as the *Poujadistes* are less clear; but many observers believe that they include elements that, like the Communists, seek power in order to work their will not with the statute book but with the Fourth Republic itself. The parties of the center, the moderate left, and the moderate right, whose kaleidoscopic coalitions are just strong enough to control the government, apparently maintain *among themselves* a degree of consensus not notably inferior to that which we associate with the other leading Western democracies. But there is no readily identifiable alternative coalition both strong enough and sufficiently devoted to the regime to be regarded as the loyal opposition, and, we repeat, none seems likely to appear within the foreseeable future.

This, be it noted, is merely France living up to a witty French turn of phrase: "The more it changes, the more it becomes itself." As A. Lawrence Lowell observed in the last century, there has been no general consensus among Frenchmen about their form of government since well before the

---

[65] Binkley, *op. cit.*, p. 152.

[66] *Ibid.*, p. 181; Woodburn, *op. cit.*, pp. 32-34.

[67] Cf. A. Rossi, *A Communist Party in Action*, translated and edited by Willmoore Kendall (New Haven: Yale University Press, 1949).

French Revolution. France has, moreover, tried out several forms, and each form it has tried, and each of a great many that it may try in the future, today has its corps of defenders, which if not yet organized as a political party, may organize as one tomorrow—and so postpone still further the day when France can work out the consensus she would need in order to meet our conditions.[68]

A similar state of affairs has obtained to a greater or lesser degree in all the other western European democracies except Switzerland, and in the Scandinavian democracies as well, until a fairly recent date. In Belgium and Holland, for example, there was an acrimonious struggle between the Catholic parties and the Liberal and Socialist parties over secularization of the educational system right down to the turn of the century; only in the last decades, therefore, have the major parties in those countries begun to show each other the toleration that characterizes consensus situations, and that might dispose the general populace to accept the idea of loyal party opposition.[69] In the Scandinavian countries, similarly, issues concerning the regime remained alive until the late nineteenth and early twentieth centuries; and only gradually, as those issues were disposed of, did the contest for governmental power narrow down to a continuing test of strength between an "in" party and a loyal opposition.[70]

Only Switzerland, of all the countries mentioned in this section, had achieved a loyal party opposition as early as the mid-nineteenth century.

Conclusions

The purpose of the present chapter, we remind our readers, has been to summarize the institutional history of political parties in certain Western democracies, and so shed light upon two questions: (1) Has there been some kind of general pattern in the development of modern democratic parties? (2) If so, what, if anything, does that pattern tell us about the role parties have played in the Western democracies? Let us now address ourselves directly to those questions, and try to decide what answers to them are warranted by the facts presented in the foregoing pages.

THE GENERAL PATTERN OF PARTY DEVELOPMENT

In the first place, the institutional history of political parties does seem to run to one and the same general developmental pattern in the nations we have studied. There are marked differences from nation to nation in organizational forms and in the rate at which the developmental pattern has unfolded; but

[68] Cf. Lowell, *op. cit.,* Vol. I, pp. 101-05, 138.
[69] See Reed, *op. cit.,* pp. 141-58, for the story of the struggle in Belgium over the educational system. In 1955 this struggle again flared into street fighting and riots. In addition, the Belgian parties are sharply divided over the position of the monarchy.
[70] Cf. Arneson, *op. cit.,* pp. 45-46, 50-65; and Herlitz, *op. cit.,* pp. 37-38, 46-47.

the modern democratic party systems we have studied all appear to have grown up via the following stages, taken in the following order:

(1) *The emergence of identifiable intragovernmental party organization.* So long as the sole or even the major power stake in Western communities was the "favor" of the ruling monarch, group organization in politics—and *some* form of group organization seems to be characteristic of politics under all forms of government—took the form of "cabals" and "juntas." These were small, secret, conspiratorial bands of courtiers seeking either to ingratiate themselves with the current occupant of the throne, or to replace him with someone whose favor could, for whatever reasons, be counted upon. They should not, however, be thought of as resembling modern political parties in any significant respect.

A time came in the countries of which we are speaking, however, when *elected* government officials (for the most part members of representative legislative assemblies) had taken over some at least of the power formerly monopolized by the monarch, so that *their* approval and good will had to be courted by those who wished to influence the decision-making process. And it was always a short step, at least in point of time, until a controversial issue arose among the elected officials themselves and divided them into two or more (but usually only two) rival groups, each with a "stand" on the issue that it was determined to see prevail. Each group, therefore, needed to swing a majority of the legislative assembly behind its stand, and each, in consequence, had good reason to *organize* to that end. Accordingly, they made prior arrangements for pooling their voting and forensic strength when and where it might be needed, and for continuous mutual consultation on matters of policy or means for winning new supporters.

These new political groups were strictly *intra*governmental organizations. Because of the extremely limited franchise characteristic of the age, the "opinion" of the "general public" had little impact on the governmental decision-making process, and did not, therefore, have to be courted or appealed to, so that conditions were not yet ripe for the emergence of *extra*governmental organization. But the new groups differed profoundly from the secret and conspiratorial "cabals" of earlier days: for example, almost all of them promptly found themselves saddled with party labels usually not of their own (or their friends') invention, and helped make the labels stick by adopting them. In a word, the new intragovernmental organizations are—as the older "cabals" are not—rightly regarded as the true ancestors of modern political parties.

(2) *The development of extragovernmental party organization.* For a time —longer in one country, shorter in another—the initial development of intragovernmental party organization, politics, and party contests remained the exclusive concern of holders of public office. In eighteenth-century Britain, for example, where the issue that first divided the parties was settled and no new issue arose to divide them anew, the bonds of party organization notably

weakened; and while the old party labels hung on, the real political struggles took place between shifting alliances of power nuclei formed mainly about family ties and interests. In all the other countries considered, the parties either continued to oppose each other on the issue that had brought them into existence, or found themselves in the presence of a new issue on which they could not see eye to eye, with the result that intragovernmental party organization not only persisted but grew in strength. Equally in those countries and in England, however, the struggles involved no one outside the formal government; the "people" were not in a position to affect them, and in general took little interest in them.

So it went until that turn of events in each country that called into being a movement for further democratization of government and politics, particularly via progressive extension of the suffrage. In none of our countries did such a movement fail to appear in due course, and in none of them did one of the existing intragovernmental parties fail to adopt the movement, when it came, as its own, and, having adopted it, to develop auxiliary *extra*governmental organizations reaching down into the populace at large. With each successive demand for expansion of the suffrage, moreover, the need for such organizations, and the reason for making them ever larger and more complex, became more urgent. Winning votes became, increasingly, *the* means of gaining and holding political power—equally, of course, for the party that opposed the successive expansions of the suffrage and for that which favored them. In a word, extragovernmental party organizations increasingly vast and elaborate established closer and closer liaison with the older intragovernmental party organizations, and had greater and greater impact on the latter's policies. And the end result in each country was that extragovernmental party organizations had, by the time the suffrage had expanded to include all adult males ("universal manhood suffrage"), become *the* agency that conducted elections and determined the selection of key governmental personnel.

(3) *The growth of the idea of the loyal opposition.* Institutionalization of the idea of *the* loyal opposition is posterior, both logically and in point of time, to the emergence of extragovernmental party organization (as the latter is posterior to that of intragovernmental party organization). Some of the Western democracies, indeed, are still very far from having institutionalized it, and the evidence suggests that in at least one of them the very idea is little understood and tends to be regarded with suspicion. A number of prior conditions, we have seen, must be fulfilled in any country before it can run its party system on a government-of-the-day-versus-the-loyal-opposition basis: general acceptance of the regime, full development of party organizations, both intragovernmental and extragovernmental, and popular understanding and approval of the role those organizations are playing.

THE SIGNIFICANCE OF THE PATTERN

The general pattern of party development just outlined suggests certain tentative conclusions about the role of parties in the political systems of the Western democracies. First of all, party activity (as described in the early pages of this chapter) appears to be a characteristic feature of *democratic* government. Theoretically, a democratic system might dispense with parties; but in practice, as we have observed, the first rudiments of modern party organization appeared in each Western nation shortly after the first significant step was taken toward democracy and away from absolutism—i.e., the lodging of power in the hands of *elected* officials. And each subsequent step toward democracy—the transfer of *all* power to elected officials, the extension of the suffrage, and the achievement of consensus on the nature of the regime—resulted in (or was in part produced by) party activity, and in a corresponding change in party organization. The state of the party system at any given moment in any given country, in other words, appears to be a reliable index of the progress of that country toward self-government; so that if we wish to determine the extent to which an existing government approximates our democratic model, the indicated starting point is an inquiry into the state of development of its party system.

Secondly, the state of the party system at any given moment seems to determine in large part the manner in which the formal institutions for popular consultation work, especially if the latter are evaluated from the standpoint of their *representativeness.* As we have pointed out above, most pro-democratic writers, both during the "classical" period and since, have seen *the* solution to the problem of popular consultation in the ancient pre-democratic institution of representation, though with the proviso that the representative must faithfully register not his own views on public policy, but the views of his constituents; and our guess is that insofar as this kind of representation has been achieved in the Western democracies, *party* activities have been one of the primary means of achieving it. For it was the development of extragovernmental party organizations that finally put the *selection* of governmental personnel in hands outside the government, and produced a state of affairs in which the members of the community possess, by virtue of the power they exercise as *the electorate,* a means of seeing to it that their views, not those of their representatives, prevail—concretely, by retiring from office the representative who flouts their wishes, and putting in his place a representative who reflects them. The voters do this, however, in elections that are organized and carried through largely by extragovernmental party organizations; so that their judgment as to whether a given representative is or is not representing them is, in actual practice, a judgment as to which of two party organizations more accurately reflects their views. Thus Professor Herman Finer's aphorism, "representative government is party government," [71] appears, wherever we look at democratic systems in operation, to be borne out by the facts.

The next question that arises is this: What have our writers on politics and democracy to say about political parties as agencies for popular consultation? That question we shall attempt to answer in the next chapter.

[71] This is the title of Ch. XIII of *Theory and Practice of Modern Government*, rev. ed. (New York: Henry Holt and Company, 1949). Finer's thought about parties has profoundly influenced both the present writers.

Chapter 6

AN INTELLECTUAL HISTORY OF POLITICAL PARTIES

The Growth of Concern with Parties

The intellectual history of political parties can be said to fall into two well-defined periods: an early period, initiated by events in England in the late seventeenth century and lasting well into the nineteenth century; and a recent period, ushered in by events in the United States following the Civil War and continuing to our own time.

The early period roughly coincides with the time when, as we observed in the preceding chapter, political parties were ceasing to be secret, conspiratorial groupings inside legislative assemblies and were developing into the complex intra- and extragovernmental organizations that we know today. These impressive institutional developments, however, were little noticed by writers on democracy or, for that matter, by students of politics in general during the period. Most writers on politics mentioned parties, some merely acknowledging their existence but letting it go at that; a very few went further, and ventured an opinion as to whether their existence was to be welcomed or deplored; but an astonishing number failed to speak of them at all.

The fact that parties were more or less ignored for so long a time has been commented upon and puzzled over by a number of present-day political analysts.[1] Any extended explanation of the phenomenon would clearly be

---

[1] Cf. E. E. Schattschneider, *Party Government* (New York: Rinehart & Company, Inc., 1942), pp. 4-16; Francis G. Wilson, *Elements of Modern Politics* (New York: McGraw-Hill Book Company, Inc., 1936), pp. 330-31; Charles E. Merriam and Harold F. Gosnell, *The American Party System*, rev. ed. (New York: The Macmillan Company, 1933), pp. 409-14. James Bryce, in the first edition of *The American Commonwealth,* complained that in preparing its chapters describing and analyzing American parties, he had been seriously handicapped by not having had "the advantage of being able to cite any previous treatise on the subject; for though the books and articles dealing with the public life of the United States may be counted by the hundreds, I know of no author who has set himself to describe impartially the actual daily working of [American political parties]": *The American Commonwealth* (London: Macmillan and Co., 1889), Vol. I, pp. 636-37.

beyond the scope of the present work.[2] It is enough to say there were only two kinds of writers on government who had any reason to regard parties as worth describing and evaluating, and that even they conceived their task in terms that disposed them to dismiss parties as of little or no importance. There were, first, the writers whose primary concern was to debate the merits of democracy—that is, to put forward an answer to the question, *Should* the people rule or should they not? These writers tended not to get around to the question, *How* are the people to rule? Whether organizations like the Whigs and Tories showed promise as agencies for popular consultation thus seemed to most of them, naturally enough, an issue so remote from the main one that they simply never raised it.

Thus the Levelers, Locke, and Rousseau never mentioned parties at all. Paine disposed of the entire subject with a single warning against the evil effects that the "intoxicating spirit" of party might have upon popular government.[3] Jefferson—himself an active and successful party leader—had little more to say about parties, although on balance he did approve of them.

There was, second, a group of writers—among them William Blackstone, Chancellor James Kent, Justice Joseph Story, and William Rawle—who regarded it as their task not to debate the merits of democracy, but to describe the actual workings of government in their own day and age. Political parties, as we have seen, were in fact performing important roles in the governments they observed, so that writers with this more "descriptionist" orientation might well have been expected to study them and face up to the questions they posed. They did not do so, however; if anything, they paid even less attention to parties than the debaters on democracy. The reason is clear: They proceeded on the assumption that *legal* institutions and processes constitute the essence of government, or, to put it a little differently, that nothing outside the legal-constitutional structure and its formal elaboration by the courts needs or deserves to be described and analyzed by the political scientist. Political parties in this period were, as we know, entirely *extra*legal institutions; and these writers, insofar as they showed themselves aware of parties at all, merely noted them in passing and out of a corner of the eye as unfortunate but probably momentary aberrations from the constitutional-legal norm.[4]

[2] For one attempt to account for the early neglect in America of the subject of parties, see Austin Ranney, "The Reception of Political Parties into American Political Science," *Southwestern Social Science Quarterly,* Vol. XXXII (Dec., 1951), pp. 183-91. Some of the material for the present chapter is drawn from this article.

[3] Thomas Paine, *Writings,* edited by P. S. Foner (New York: The Citadel Press, 1945), Vol. II, pp. 430, 692.

[4] See, for example, the following writers' brief and disapproving comments on the influence of parties on the constitutional order in America: James Kent, *Commentaries on American Law,* 5th ed. (New York: O. Halsted, 1826-1830), Vol. I, p. 279; Joseph Story, *Commentaries on the Constitution of the United States* (Boston: Hilliard, Gray and Company, 1833), Vol. II, p. 365; and William Rawle, *A View of the Constitution of the United States of America,* 2nd ed. (Philadelphia: P. H. Nicklin, 1829), pp. 50, 57-58, 162.

Not until the late 1870's in the United States did writers on government begin to treat political parties as fit subjects for extended description and analysis. President Theodore Dwight Woolsey of Yale helped to initiate the trend in 1877 by devoting an entire chapter of his general survey of political science to an analysis of parties.[5] Before the end of the decade, two well-known publicists, Charles C. P. Clark and Albert Stickney, went further still, each by publishing an entire book expounding a thesis about parties (concretely, the thesis that the very existence of parties is fatal to genuine democracy) and advancing a number of proposals for controlling or abolishing them.[6] By the early 1880's there were even some textbooks in secondary-school civics that included fairly lengthy discussions of party structure and operations.[7] And since then, of course (as a glance at the footnotes in the present volume will convince the reader), the literature on parties has grown by geometric progression, and the study of political parties has come to be regarded as one of the major "fields" of political science.

Such, in brief, is the story of the growth of interest in political parties on the part of writers on democracy. In the remainder of this chapter we shall, first, summarize in some detail the ideas about party put forward by those few early writers who did consider the subject at some length, and, second, identify the major schools of thought about party that have arisen in the recent period, mentioning some of the prominent names associated with each.

Early Appraisals of Party

The few extended statements on party by writers in the early period noted above all reduce themselves to one or another of three fairly distinct positions, namely: (1) that parties in any guise are inherently destructive of good government and should therefore be discouraged as much as possible; (2) that parties are unavoidable in a free society, and should be not discouraged but controlled; and (3) that parties are vitally necessary instruments of popular government, and should be kept live and healthy. Let us pause to note how the leading exponents of these positions articulated them.

PARTY AS THE ENEMY OF GOOD GOVERNMENT

Halifax (1633-1695). The first extended commentary on political parties appears to have been that of George Savile, First Marquis of Halifax. Halifax was a Privy Councillor and minister during much of the Restoration period from 1660 to 1688, and most of his active political career was devoted to the

---

[5] *Political Science, or the State Theoretically and Practically Considered* (New York: Charles Scribner's Sons, 1877), Vol. II, pp. 542-67.

[6] Charles C. P. Clark, *The Commonwealth Reconstructed* (New York: A. S. Barnes and Co., 1878); and Albert Stickney, *A True Republic* (New York: Harper and Brothers, 1879).

[7] W. C. Ford, *The American Citizen's Manual*, 2 volumes (New York: G. P. Putnam's Sons, 1882-1883); and Charles Nordhoff, *Politics for Young Americans* (New York: Harper and Brothers, 1882).

attempt to compromise the struggle between the Whigs and the Tories over the succession. He himself was, in the language of the time, a "trimmer," i.e., not a party man,[8] and his experience of party conflict seems to have confirmed the low opinion of parties implicit in his refusal to join one. For after his retirement from active politics in 1692, he wrote a series of pamphlets in which he attacked the whole idea of parties.

Halifax' objections to parties were several. The party man, he believed, necessarily sacrifices all personal freedom of thought and action, and becomes his party's slave. Indeed, no man of any spirit or ability will risk such a fate; that being the case, able men refuse to participate in government when the latter falls under party control. The field is left, accordingly, to "low and insignificant men"; for

. . . most Men enter into a Party rashly, and retreat from it shamefully. . . . Party is little less than an Inquisition, where Men are under such a Discipline in carrying on the common Cause, as leaves no Liberty of private Opinion. . . . Ignorance maketh most Men go into a Party, and Shame keepeth them from getting out of it.[9]

Secondly, Halifax detested the alleged hypocrisy of parties, most particularly their pretended concern for the public good, which, he thought, ill conceals their members' determination to line their own pockets. Thus one of his "Maxims of State" was that

Parties in a State generally, like Freebooters, hang out False Colours; the pretence is the Publick Good; the real Business is, to catch Prizes; like the Tartars, wherever they succeed, instead of Improving their Victory, they presently fall upon the Baggage.[10]

His most serious indictment of parties, however, was that they divide the nation into two hostile camps, replace public spirit with party spirit, and make it impossible for citizens to communicate with each other. Thus "the best Party is but a kind of a Conspiracy against the rest of the Nation" that "cutteth off one half of the World from the other, so that the mutual Improvement of Men's Understanding by conversing, &c., is lost." [11]

Thus where parties are strong we know without looking further that

. . . the Good of the Nation hath been sacrificed to the Animosities of the several Contending Parties; and without entering into the dispute which of them are more or less in the right, it is pretty sure, that whilst these Opposite Sets of Angry

---

[8] For Halifax' defense of his refusal to join a party, see his pamphlet, "The Character of a Trimmer," in *The Complete Works of George Savile, First Marquess of Halifax,* edited by Walter Raleigh (Oxford: Clarendon Press, 1912), pp. 48-103.

[9] Halifax, "Political Thoughts and Reflections," in *Works,* p. 227. See also "Some Cautions Offered," op. cit., pp. 157-60.

[10] Halifax, "Maxims of State," op. cit., p. 182.

[11] Halifax, "Political Thoughts and Reflections," op. cit., p. 225.

Men are playing at Foot-ball, they will break all the Windows, and do more hurt than their pretended Zeal for the Nation will ever make amends for.[12]

Bolingbroke (1678-1751). Henry St. John, Viscount Bolingbroke, wrote the eighteenth century's most famous and influential diatribe against political parties: *The Patriot King* (1738). One of the most colorful and controversial figures of his age, Bolingbroke was successively a strong and active leader of the Tory party (1701-1715), an exile in France, a leader of the Jacobite resistance to the Hanoverian succession (1715-1716), a first convicted and later pardoned traitor and advocate of an anti-Whig, multifactional coalition (1716-1735), and, finally, from 1735 to his death, a professional publicist, who refused to participate in active politics and contented himself with writing detached and philosophical commentaries on public affairs. It was in this latter period— when, as G. M. Trevelyan puts it, he "found the party grapes sour" [13]—that Bolingbroke wrote *The Patriot King*.

The inherent vice of parties, Bolingbroke declared, is that they concentrate upon private interests and utterly neglect the general interest. This, he recognized, is not what their members intend. Just as churches are brought into existence so that their members may practice and promote their religion, so party organizations are, for the most part anyway, created out of the determination of their members to advance the general interest more effectively. In both, however, the organization itself somehow always becomes more important than the purposes for which it was created—in parties especially, where "the interest of the state becomes . . . a remote consideration, is never pursued for its own sake, and is often sacrificed to the other." [14]

Bolingbroke felt strongly that, because of his long association with parties, he was better qualified than most men to know just how bad they are:

A man who has not seen the inside of parties, nor had opportunities to examine nearly their secret motives, can hardly conceive how little a share principle of any sort, tho principle of some sort or other be always pretended, has in the determination of their conduct. Reason has small effect on numbers: a turn of imagination, often as violent and as sudden as a gust of wind, determines their conduct; and passion is taken by others, and by themselves too, when it grows into habit especially, for principle.[15]

Good government, Bolingbroke believed, is possible only in a *unified* nation. *Any* kind of division among the citizens, therefore, makes good government impossible; and the worst of all divisions, of course, are party divisions.[16]

[12] Halifax, "Some Cautions Offered," *op. cit.*, pp. 159-60.

[13] G. M. Trevelyan, *The Two-Party System in English Political History* (Oxford: Clarendon Press: 1926), p. 13.

[14] Henry St. John, Viscount Bolingbroke, *Letters on the Spirit of Patriotism, on the Idea of a Patriot King, and on the State of Parties at the Accession of King George the First* (London: printed for A. Millar, 1749), pp. 150-51.

[15] *Ibid.*, pp. 172-73.

[16] *Ibid.*, pp. 151-52, 176-77.

The England of his day, he insisted, torn as it was by virulent party divisions, was accordingly in a most perilous condition, and its only hope for salvation lay in the accession of such a "patriot king" as the first Elizabeth had been. Such a king would concern himself only with the welfare of the whole kingdom. He would serve as both a creator and a symbol of national unity. And, most important of all, besides ruling above party, he would, by his very presence, discourage and eventually prevent altogether the survival of party. Thus and only thus would England be rescued from the doom to which her party strife would unavoidably lead.[17]

George Washington (1732-1799). Probably the most famous denunciation of political parties ever made by an American is to be found in George Washington's Farewell Address, delivered on September 17, 1796, shortly before he left the presidency. During his eight years in office, Washington had tried valiantly to be a "patriot president." He was, therefore, deeply disturbed at the developing split between the Hamiltonians and the Jeffersonians, and annoyed and hurt because, in the later years of his presidency, the Jeffersonians had more and more regarded him as a front man for the Hamiltonian party rather than as the "patriot president" that he had wished, and that some people believed him, to be. And when he came to bid his countrymen an official farewell and point out to them the dangers he saw threatening the infant republic, he had a good deal to say about the rising spirit of party, which seemed to him the most threatening danger of all.

Let me warn you [he said] in the most solemn manner against the baneful effects of the spirit of party generally. This spirit, unfortunately, is inseparable from our nature, having its root in the strongest passions of the human mind. It exists under different shapes in all governments, more or less stifled, controlled, or repressed; but in those of the popular form it is seen in its greatest rankness and is truly their worst enemy.[18]

Carried to its extreme, party strife can lead to despotism, for

. . . the disorders and miseries which result gradually incline the minds of men to seek security and repose in the absolute power of an individual, and sooner or later the chief of some prevailing faction, more able or more fortunate than his competitors, turns this disposition to the purpose of his own elevation on the ruins of public liberty.[19]

Even if such a drastic result of party strife can be avoided in the United States, party will still make good government impossible:

It serves always to distract the public councils and enfeeble the public administration. It agitates the community with ill-founded jealousies and false alarms; kindles the animosity of one part against another; foments occasionally riot and

---

[17] *Ibid.*, pp. 148-60, 183, 212-14.

[18] In J. D. Richardson, ed., *Messages and Papers of the Presidents, 1789-1897* (Washington, D. C.: Government Printing Office, 1896), Vol. I, p. 218.

[19] *Ibid.*, Vol. I, p. 219.

insurrection. It opens the door to foreign influence and corruption, which find a facilitated access to the government itself through the channels of party passion.[20]

Party, Washington concluded, may possibly have some justification in a monarchical government, but it has no function whatever in a popular goverment:

> There is an opinion that parties in free countries are useful checks upon the administration of the government, and serve to keep alive the spirit of liberty. This within certain limits is probably true; and in governments of a monarchical cast patriotism may look with indulgence, if not with favor, upon the spirit of party. But in those of the popular character, in governments purely elective, it is a spirit not to be encouraged. From their natural tendency it is certain there will always be enough of that spirit for every salutary purpose; and there being constant danger of excess, the effort ought to be by force of public opinion to mitigate and assuage it. A fire not to be quenched, it demands a uniform vigilance to prevent its bursting into a flame, lest, instead of warming, it should consume.[21]

John Taylor of Caroline (1753-1824). John Taylor was a Jeffersonian Republican who served for two years in the Virginia House of Delegates and for six years in the United States Senate. Most of his life he spent on his farm in Caroline County, Virginia, where he devoted himself to agricultural experiments and reforms and wrote several books on politics in which he attacked the Federalist position and upheld the Jeffersonian. His most famous book, *An Inquiry into the Principles and Policy of the Government of the United States,* has been called by Charles A. Beard "among the two or three really historic contributions to political science which have been produced in the United States." [22] It is, certainly, the clearest statement we have of the political ideas of the non-party or one-party "era of good feeling" from the early 1800's to the late 1820's.

Taylor's attack on political parties was based upon one value-charged premise and one allegation of fact. He assumed that in the United States the general interest was identical with the agricultural interest, and he maintained that that interest was adequately represented by only one party—the Jeffersonian Republicans. The latter was the party of the majority, he held, and opposition to it from any quarter must be regarded as an attempt by a mere faction, representing the aristocrats and industrial interests, to subvert the general interest.

Where there is conflict among parties, Taylor argued—or, more accurately, where such conflict presides over the selection of public officials—truly representative institutions are impossible; for representation, limited to the alterna-

---

[20] *Ibid.*

[21] *Ibid.*

[22] Charles A. Beard, *Economic Origins of Jeffersonian Democracy* (New York: The Macmillan Company, 1915), p. 323. For a brief summary of Taylor's life and reputation, see the biographical note in Eugene T. Mudge, *The Social Philosophy of John Taylor of Caroline* (New York: Columbia University Press, 1939), pp. 1-5.

tive of enlisting under one of these parties, ceases to be an instrument of national self-government, and dwindles into an instrument of oppression for the prime minister or his antagonist.[23] And again:

> [Party] converts representation into vassalage to the leaders of parties, disciplined, not by the comparatively honourable infliction of the lash, but by the base and wicked sophism, that it is honourable to stick to a party, and treacherous to adhere to conscience. The disciples of this infamous doctrine are forged into tools for ambition and tyranny by praises and rewards, whilst honesty is discouraged by base epithets, as a foil to the varnish with which the decoys are painted, designed to deceive and enslave the multitude.[24]

Nor did Taylor agree for a moment with Madison's view (see page 133) that parties can be restrained and kept within safe bounds by legal and constitutional devices. All such notions rest on misapprehensions regarding parties' secretive and extralegal—i.e., their real—character, which places them beyond such regulation:

> The danger of parties to free governments arises from the impossibility of controlling them by the restraints of political law. . . . No division of power, no responsibility, no periodical change of leaders, no limitation of "thus far you may go and no farther," stops their career. . . . No numerical checks or balances can reach this dreadful party tyranny. It is even able to suspend or destroy those solemnly established by nations, and to make the people themselves the authors of their own ruin.[25]

The only effective barrier against parties and their (in his view) ruinous consequences, Taylor believed, is to be found in a deep commitment on the part of all the citizens *and* their public officials to moral principles as contrasted to party principles—to the *general* (i.e., agricultural) interest as contrasted with party interests.[26]

The virtual eclipse of the Federalist party around the time Taylor wrote the *Inquiry,* and the ensuing "era of good feeling," largely satisfied Taylor that party spirit had been brought to heel in the United States, which he saw as more fortunate in this regard than England. But it could not, he insisted, be counted on to remain at heel; rather its reassertion could be taken for granted save as there might be eternal vigilance on the part of all good Americans, born of a determination to prevent it and of a recognition that the continuation of good government in the United States could be assured in no other way.[27]

[23] John Taylor, *An Inquiry into the Principles and Policy of the Government of the United States* (Fredericksburg: Green and Cady, 1914), p. 196.

[24] *Ibid.,* pp. 198-99.

[25] *Ibid.,* pp. 654-55.

[26] *Ibid.,* pp. 655-56. Note that Taylor, in a manner highly congenial to the argument of this book, regards the ideas and preferences of individuals as the determining factor in the problem.

[27] For a summary of Taylor's views on parties and what to do about them, see Mudge, *op. cit.,* pp. 146-50.

John C. Calhoun (1782-1850). The most impressive attack on political parties during this early period—though not the best known—came from the pen of John C. Calhoun, whose fame as an active participant in public life has tended, except among specialists in the history of American political ideas, to obscure his eminence as a political theorist.

Calhoun's indictment of the doctrine of the "numerical majority" (which term he used to describe the body of ideas that the present writers call "the doctrine of majority rule") has, along with his advocacy of the doctrine of the "concurrent majority," come in for a good deal of attention by scholars in the fields of history and political science. Not so, however, the anti-party emphasis of his writings, despite the fact that it is a natural, not to say unavoidable, corollary of his general position. Calhoun regarded party combat as the inescapable fate of any society founded upon the principle of the "numerical majority"; and, believing as he did that such combat is socially disastrous, he uncompromisingly rejected that principle. His argument may be briefly summarized as follows:

In any community where the suffrage is free, there will arise, as a matter of course, a rich variety of conflicting interests. Each of these, moreover, will seek to control the government and thus impose its will upon the others. Nor is that all: If no one interest is strong enough to capture governmental power by itself, "a combination will be formed between those whose interests are most alike;—each conceding something to the others, until a sufficient number is obtained to make a majority," with the result that

. . . the community will be divided into two great parties,—a major and minor, between which there will be incessant struggles on the one side to retain, and on the other to obtain the majority,—and, thereby, the control of the government and the advantages it confers.[28]

In a government based upon the principle of the "numerical majority," Calhoun is saying, a bare majority of all the popular votes and of all the public offices is enough to give the majority party control of the entire power of the government; and once the majority party has that power, he goes on to say, it will not hesitate to use it to promote its own selfish interests. The minority party will be helpless to stop it; nor will any of the constitutional devices created by the Founding Fathers be of any avail against it.[29]

The main objections to party warfare in a "numerical majority" context, in Calhoun's view, are that the stakes are so high, and being so high, cause everything other than how to win power to be forgotten. Party unity, discipline, spoils, corruption—all these (for him) evil things that parties find helpful in winning elections unavoidably become standard practices in political life.

[28] John C. Calhoun, *A Disquisition on Government* (New York: Political Science Classics, 1947), p. 16. This work was first published in 1853.
[29] *Ibid.,* pp. 31-34.

The power to control the party organization falls into the hands of a few leaders, whose power is not unlike that of the high command of any army engaged in a desperate battle, and the government is actually run not so much by the majority party as by a small group within it. They—"a minority, usually, and under the most favorable circumstances, [one] of not much more than one-fourth of the whole community" [30]—are the real rulers.

The consequences of party battles, Calhoun insists, speedily prove to be absolutely ruinous to the community. For one thing, the latter ceases to be united (or, as the present writers would put it, consensus disappears), and the common goal is subordinated to this or that interest of some far-from-inclusive group:

> . . . the numerical majority will divide the community, let it be ever so homogeneous, into two great parties, which will be engaged in perpetual struggles to obtain the control of the government. . . . It is not then wonderful, that a form of government, which periodically stakes all its honors and emoluments, as prizes to be contended for, should divide the community into two great hostile parties; or that party attachments, in the progress of the strife, should become so strong among the members of each respectively, as to absorb every feeling of our nature, both social and individual. . . . It is thus that, in such governments, devotion to party becomes stronger than devotion to country;—the promotion of the interests of the party more important than the promotion of the common good of the whole, and its triumph and ascendancy, objects of far greater solicitude, than the safety and prosperity of the community.[31]

All this, moreover, can have but one result: Party combat will grow more and more virulent, and the methods used by the combatants more and more destructive. Finally, "confusion, corruption, disorder and anarchy [will] lead to an appeal to force;—to be followed by a revolution in the form of the government," which in turn will lead to what we would today term some kind of authoritarianism: "the elevation to supreme power of the general of the successful party." [32]

On Calhoun's showing, then, "numerical" majority rule is a self-defeating principle *precisely because it produces party government*. Party government—so runs the argument—produces party warfare; party warfare ends in dictatorship; and dictatorship means the destruction of all free government. The only way for a free people to avoid this disaster is to abandon the whole idea of the "numerical majority" and adhere instead to the principle of the "concurrent majority." This latter principle

regards interests as well as numbers, considering the community as made up of different and conflicting interests, as far as the action of the government is con-

[30] *Ibid.*, p. 41.
[31] *Ibid.*, pp. 47-48.
[32] *Ibid.*, pp. 42, 82-83.

cerned; and takes the sense of each, *through its majority or appropriate organ,* and the united sense of all as the sense of the entire community.[33]

And since in the United States the most important interests are those of class and section, each of these should have its special voice—regardless of the number of individuals who compose it. Ideally, Calhoun believed, *all* interests should be consulted and their unanimous consent required before any national governmental action can be taken. Short of this, requiring approval by three-quarters of all the states for an amendment to the Constitution seemed to him an excellent approach to the ideal; and this rule, he felt, should be applied not only to constitutional amendments but to other matters as well: slavery, the tariff, the bank, and internal improvements. In the absence of a concurrent majority requirement, however, the numerically more powerful interests will try to impose their will upon the numerically less powerful interests on all such matters, and nothing can prevent tyranny by the majority party or, in the long run, the destruction of the community.[34]

The Early Anti-Party Writers Summarized. In order fully to understand the early anti-party writers whose views we have just examined, we must first grasp what they meant by "party." Actually, the meaning of the term changed as the period progressed. In most seventeenth- and eighteenth-century writing on political organization, the terms "party" and "faction" were used interchangeably—as, for example, in James Madison's statement that a free society "involves the spirit of party and faction in the necessary and ordinary operations of government."[35] In our own time, the terms have quite distinct meanings: "party" now generally refers to a large-scale organization whose purpose is to control the personnel and policies *of the government;* and "faction" refers to an element inside a party whose purpose is to control the personnel and policies *of the party.*[36] When we read the denunciations of "party" by these early writers, therefore, we must ask ourselves at every moment whether they are talking about what we call "parties," or rather about what we call "factions" or "pressure groups."

We must bear in mind, in this connection, the changing nature of political organization from the late seventeenth to the late nineteenth century. During most of the seventeenth and eighteenth centuries, as we observed in the preceding chapter, the characteristic form of political organization in Britain and America was the "nucleus of political power," made up entirely of persons inside the government and held together by ties of personal and family loyalties and interests—e.g., the "Rockingham Whigs" and the "Pittite Tories."

---

[33] Quoted in August O. Spain, *The Political Theory of John C. Calhoun* (New York: Bookman Associates, 1951), p. 129. Italics added. Note that Calhoun has no necessary quarrel with majority rule within the "interests."

[34] For a convenient summary of Calhoun's ideas on "the concurrent majority," see Spain, *op. cit.,* Ch. V.

[35] *The Federalist,* Number Ten.

[36] Cf. Dayton D. McKean, *Party and Pressure Politics* (Boston: Houghton Mifflin Company, 1949), pp. 15-17.

These groups—as well as the amorphous and largely meaningless "Whigs" and "Tories"—were generally referred to as "parties" or "factions," the two terms being regarded as interchangeable. And it was such groups that Halifax, Bolingbroke, Hume, and other publicists of the period had in mind as they wrote.

Beginning with the 1790's in the United States, on the other hand, political organization began to take the form that we today associate with "party." George Washington saw the beginnings of this development, for the clash between the "Republicans" and the "Federalists" that he observed and deplored was a clash between "parties" that were, though still immature, recognizably of the new type. Half a century later, the "parties" had not only taken on most of their present-day characteristics, but had related themselves to one another in such fashion as to constitute what we know today as the American party system, upon which Calhoun poured the acids of his logic and eloquence. In short, any reader who wishes to know just what "party" means, as used in any of the positions summarized in the foregoing pages, will be well advised to bear in mind the institutional state of parties (as shown in Chapter 5) at and immediately preceding the time at which the position was expounded.

Does this mean that no *general* statements can be made about anti-party doctrine? Not at all. They must, indeed, be phrased—and read—with caution, lest we get into the habit of thinking that political reality and political language were less complex than we know them to have been. But at least four broad statements seem warranted. First, the view that political parties in any guise are by nature the implacable enemies of good government appears to have been held by most respectable and well-informed non-politicians until well into the nineteenth century. Party was regarded as "a gangrene, a cancer, which patriotic citizens should combine to eradicate" [37] and as "almost tantamount to treasonable conspiracy." Halifax, Bolingbroke, Washington, and the other prominent detractors of party were not, therefore, saying anything that was likely to strike their contemporaries as novel, daring, or even controversial. They were only repeating a commonplace.[38]

Second, many active politicians thought as poorly of parties as did the non-politicals. The elder William Pitt, for example, held aloof from the Rockingham Whigs, and so helped postpone the date at which a stable party government was to emerge in England. And Pitt defended his action precisely on the ground that no change would do which "did not comprehend or annihilate every party in the kingdom." One of his followers, indeed, quotes him as having said in effect that "this country ought not to be governed by any party

[37] Henry Jones Ford, *The Rise and Growth of American Politics* (New York: The Macmillan Company, 1898), p. 90.

[38] Cf. W. L. Burn, "The Evolution of Parties and the Party System in the Eighteenth Century," in Sidney D. Bailey, ed., *Political Parties and the Party System in Britain* (New York: Frederick A. Praeger, 1952), p. 20; George H. Sabine, *A History of Political Theory*, rev. ed. (New York, Henry Holt and Company, 1950), p. 522; and Cecil S. Emden, *The People and the Constitution* (Oxford: Clarendon Press, 1933), p. 109.

or faction, and . . . if it were to be so governed the constitution must necessarily expire." [39]

So too with the Federalists in America. They regarded any kind of extra-governmental party activity as a kind of mob conspiracy against the nation, and did not hesitate to describe the Jeffersonian organizations in New England as "insurgents." One Federalist partisan wrote, for example, as follows:

> While abusing Great Britain, [the Jeffersonians] copy [British] abuses of the true freedom of election. Until recently elections in New England were free beyond any example to be found elsewhere. . . . Unhappily our democrats have already had some influence in changing this truly republican state of things [and] the detestable practice of electioneering is coming in.[40]

And few good Federalists would have questioned John Marshall's judgment that "nothing . . . more debases or pollutes the human mind than faction." [41] When, therefore, the Federalists found themselves compelled either to counter Jeffersonian electioneering organization with similar organization of their own or perish, they did what was necessary but tried to be as secretive about it as possible. Their national convention of 1808, for example, was kept completely secret.[42]

Party organization developed much later in Europe than it did in England and America, and European discussion of parties in this early period accordingly got off to a slow start. Such comment as there was, however, was largely anti-party, that of the European liberals especially so. The latter were enthusiastic, for example, in their applause for Napoleon III's book praising the Bolingbrokian idea of a "patriot king" and holding up Napoleon I (and, by implication, himself) as the perfect example of such a king.[43]

Third, the early anti-party writers—and the intellectuals and statesmen who shared their views—had no good word to say for the kind of majority-rule democracy outlined in Chapters 2 and 3. They all believed that democracy of that kind produces, in the very nature of the case, *bad* government—since unbridled popular majorities cannot be other than tyrannical, oppressive of the better elements of society, and destructive of society's true values. Many of the arguments they nominally directed against political parties, in consequence, are really arguments against majority-rule democracy. Only Calhoun,

[39] Quoted in Ford, *op. cit.*, p. 92.

[40] Quoted in William A. Robinson, *Jeffersonian Democracy in New England* (New Haven: Yale University Press, 1916), pp. 54-55.

[41] Quoted in Albert J. Beveridge, *The Life of John Marshall* (Boston: Houghton Mifflin Company, 1916), Vol. II, p. 410. Marshall delivered this pronouncement in the course of a letter to his brother complaining about the unfair (and effective!) methods the Jeffersonians were using to defeat him in an election.

[42] Cf. Wilfred E. Binkley, *American Political Parties: Their Natural History* (New York: Alfred A. Knopf, 1944), pp. 50-51.

[43] For Napoleon III's ideas, see his *Napoleonic Ideas*, translated by J. A. Dorr (New York: D. Appleton and Company, 1859), p. 47. For the general anti-party bias of most nineteenth-century European liberals, see Guido de Ruggiero, *The History of European Liberalism*, translated by R. G. Collingwood (London: Oxford University Press, 1927), pp. 162-63.

of all the writers we have mentioned, insisted in so many words on the close connection between majority rule and political parties. But it can be shown that the others, in denouncing party, spoke out of an animus that was for the most part anti-majoritarian.

Fourth, all the writers we have cited placed a high value upon national unity. The idea of a "loyal opposition" of any kind was incomprehensible to them, and that of a loyal *party* opposition would, necessarily, have struck them as an outrageous contradiction in terms. Hence the recurrent theme in their writings that the contest between parties is civil war, and that only the suppression of party strife—whether by a "patriot king," a "patriot president," or a "concurrent majority"—can prevent ultimate disaster.

More recently in the history of party analysis, as we shall note below, there have been instances of writers starting from majoritarian-democratic premises and yet arriving at strong anti-party conclusions. To the anti-party writers of the early period, however, "good government" and "majority-rule democracy" were antithetical rather than synonymous terms; and their rejection of parties was founded upon unambiguously anti-democratic grounds.

PARTY AS AN UNAVOIDABLE EVIL IN FREE GOVERNMENTS

A second group of writers in the early period adopted the general position that political parties inevitably arise in free governments and, as a matter of course, do more harm than good in such governments.[44] Unlike the anti-party group, however, they believed that the worst effects of parties could be controlled and that it was not necessary either to abolish parties completely or to condemn "free government" because it always produces political parties. The most prominent spokesmen of this second point of view were David Hume, James Madison, John Adams, and Alexis de Tocqueville.

David Hume (1711-1776). David Hume, whose major interest in philosophy was epistemology, not political theory, nevertheless wrote three essays on the nature and effects of political parties. And one of the three, "Of Parties in General," [45] directly addresses itself to questions highly relevant to our present inquiry.

Moving from the premise that parties, though they may arise under any form of government, spring up most readily and develop most fully where government is free, Hume proceeds to draw a curious distinction between "personal" parties—i.e., those founded on personal friendship for or personal

[44] The idea of a "free government," which is the now explicit, now tacit context in which this second group of writers elected to discuss parties, seems to have called, above all, for a maximum amount of freedom for the individual citizen from regulation by the state. They tended to assume that freedom of expression and of association would logically result in the formation of political parties, and, at the same time, that any attempt at outright suppression of parties would automatically entail the abridgment and even total destruction of civil liberties. This, for all their dislike of parties, they were unwilling to contemplate.

[45] In David Hume, *Essays, Moral, Political, and Literary*, edited by T. H. Green and T. H. Grose (London: Longmans, Green, and Co., 1875), Vol. I, pp. 127-33. The other essays on party are entitled "Of the Parties of Great Britain," and "Of the Coalition of Parties."

animosity against a particular political leader—and "real" parties, whose members are drawn together either by a particular "interest" or by a particular principle, or by "affection." Parties founded on a particular principle, he goes on to say, are a recent development, and are stronger and more combative than those founded on interest or affection. This is because men who have a principle or opinion and who have banded together to protect it do not like to see that principle or opinion challenged:

. . . the human mind . . . always lays hold on every mind that approaches it; and as it is wonderfully fortified by an unanimity of sentiments, so it is shocked and disturbed by any contrariety. Hence the eagerness, which most people discover in a dispute; and hence their impatience of opposition, even in the most speculate and indifferent opinions.[46]

In other words, a party founded on principle generates intolerance, and, along with it, a momentum (mutual "fortification" via "unanimity of sentiments" on the part of party members) of its own. But Hume drops the point just where it becomes most interesting, leaves unexplored such questions as that of the relation between principle on the one hand and interest and affection on the other and that of the extent to which parties founded on interest or affection "discover" this same characteristic, and turns once again to parties "in general."

One of the latter's most striking characteristics, according to Hume, is their tendency to become permanent.[47] As he puts it:

Nothing is more usual than to see parties, which have begun upon a real difference, continue even after that difference is lost. When men are once inlisted on opposite sides, they contract an affection to the persons with whom they are united, and an animosity against their antagonists: And these passions they often transmit to their posterity.[48]

It is, then, not only parties that become "permanent," but the conflict between them, that is, "party strife," as well. And in the nature of the case, party strife, in establishing itself as a permanent characteristic of a political society, becomes both more intense and more noxious in its results:

As much as legislators and founders of states ought to be honoured and respected among men, as much ought the founders of sects and factions to be de-

---

[46] *Ibid.*, Vol. I, p. 131.

[47] Hume was one of the first commentators to note this characteristic of parties. Some of his nineteenth-century successors, notably Lord Brougham and M. I. Ostrogorski, seized upon it as the central characteristic of parties. Having assumed that there is no justification whatever for party organizations that persist after the disappearance of the reason for their formation, both arrived unavoidably at this conclusion: Parties are admissible instruments of democratic government only when they dissolve immediately upon resolution of the issues that call them into existence. For Brougham's views, see his *Political Philosophy* (London: Chapman and Hall, 1843), Vol. II, pp. 37-47. Ostrogorski's views will be noted in greater detail later in this chapter.

[48] Hume, *op. cit.*, Vol. I, p. 129. Here, be it noted, Hume suggests an interplay between "affection" and "principle," from which notion it would have been a brief step to that of an interplay between "affection," "principle," and "interest" which, despite differences in terminology, would be very close to the conception underlying the present book.

tested and hated; because the influence of faction is directly contrary to that of laws. Factions subvert government, render laws impotent, and beget the fiercest animosities among men of the same nation, who ought to give mutual assistance and protection to each other. And what should render the founders of parties more odious is, the difficulty of extirpating these weeds, when once they have taken root in any state. They naturally propagate themselves for many centuries, and seldom end but by the total dissolution of that government, in which they are sown. . . .[49]

Hume was not, however, prepared to follow his logic to the apparently inescapable conclusion that parties should be prohibited altogether, perhaps because he assumed that the prohibition could not be enforced, perhaps because he feared that an attempt to enforce it would gravely threaten free government itself. The best way to control the worst effects of party, he believed, is to encourage and support the formation of coalitions among the various parties, *and thus keep the party contest from involving such fundamental issues as the succession of the crown or the basic structure of the constitution. So long as parties are divided only on lesser questions than these,* he concluded, *they cannot destroy the community.*[50]

John Adams (1735-1826). If John Adams had ever set forth his views on party in a single pamphlet, he might well have entitled it, "The Patriot President." He believed, with Hume, that parties inevitably arise in any free government and, again with Hume, that in the long run they split the community into warring camps. Unlike Hume, and in a vein more reminiscent of Bolingbroke, he argued that destruction of the nation as a result of party strife can conceivably be avoided if some officer of the government—in the United States, for example, the President—is situated "above" parties—to mediate between them and "moderate" their struggle.

"All countries under the sun," he wrote, "must have parties. The great secret is to control them." [51] Where a nation has a "simple" government (i.e., one founded upon a single governing principle—pure monarchy, pure aristocracy, or pure democracy), there will be three parties: one advocating monarchy, one advocating aristocracy, and one advocating democracy. After the constitution is finally settled—even if it provides for a "mixed government" incorporating all three principles—there will still be two parties, the aristocrats and the democrats, and the part of wisdom is to see to it that neither gets its foot into the door of *both* houses of the legislature. One party, that is to say, should be confined to one of the houses, and the other to the other. And the task of the executive is to bridge the gap and moderate the clash between the houses.[52]

---

[49] *Ibid.,* Vol. I, pp. 127-28.
[50] The argument is made in "Of the Coalition of Parties," in Hume, *op. cit.,* Vol. I, p. 464.
[51] Quoted in Correa M. Walsh, *The Political Science of John Adams* (New York: G. P. Putnam's Sons, 1915), p. 152.
[52] Cf. *ibid.,* pp. 55-57.

In the United States, on Adams' showing, the Senate is the house of the "aristocratic" party, the House of Representatives that of the "democratic" party, and unless the president keeps the strife between them from getting out of hand, "they will oppose each other in all things, and go to war until one subjugates the other. The executive authority is the only mediator that can maintain peace between them." [53]

James Madison (1751-1836). One of the best-known and most influential of the early analyses of the causes and effects of parties and the means of controlling them is that presented in the Tenth Paper of *The Federalist* by James Madison.[54] His argument, briefly summarized, is as follows:

The worst trait of popular governments is to be found in their tendency to develop *factions*, which introduce "instability, injustice, and confusion" into their public councils and ultimately lead to their destruction. This tendency might, to be sure, be counteracted by abolishing the liberty which is indispensable to its existence; but since such a cure would be worse than the disease, we must seek rather to control its effects. This calls for a clear understanding of, first, what a faction is, and, second, what causes factions to come into existence. Faction is "a number of citizens, *whether amounting to a majority or a minority of the whole,* who are united and actuated by some common impulse of passion, or of interest, adverse to the rights of other citizens, or to the permanent and aggregate interests of the community." And the causes of faction lie in the very nature of man—in his "propensity . . . to fall into mutual animosities" on matters of religion, government, leadership, and myriad other issues. Especially important has been the "various and unequal distribution of property," which has been "the most common and durable source of factions. . . . A landed interest, a manufacturing interest, a mercantile interest, a moneyed interest, with many lesser interests, grow up of necessity in civilized nations, and divide them into different classes, activated by different sentiments and views. The regulation of these various and interfering interests forms the principal task of modern legislation, and involves the spirit of party and faction in the necessary and ordinary operations of government."

So long as any single faction commands less than a majority of votes, the argument continues, it is easily controlled by the "republican principle of majority rule." But when a single faction wins over a majority of the population and has only a minority to say it nay, "the form of popular government . . . enables it to sacrifice to its ruling passion or interest, both the public good and the rights of other citizens." The problem, then, is this: How to save the community from such majority-faction tyranny *without* sacrificing the essentials of popular government?

[53] Quoted in *ibid.,* pp. 152-53.
[54] There are many editions of *The Federalist*. We have used that edited by Max Beloff, published by The Macmillan Company in 1948. In this edition, the Tenth Paper is at pp. 41-48. The present writers have added the italics in the quotations in the text.

There are, Madison argues, only two possible ways of solving this problem: "Either the existence of the same passion or interest in a majority, at the same time must be prevented; or the majority, having such coexistence of passion or interest, must be rendered, by their number and local situation, unable to concert and carry into effect schemes of oppression." Both are out of the question in a pure democracy ("by which I mean a society consisting of a small number of citizens, who assemble and administer the government in person"), where majority factions readily arise, and there is nothing to check the tyrannical use of governmental power. In a republic ("by which I mean a government in which the scheme of representation takes place"), on the other hand, particularly in a republic spread over an extensive territory and with a large population, the chances of preventing tyranny by majority factions are pretty good. Interests are likely to be more numerous and varied, making it less likely that any one interest or party can command the support of a majority of the citizens; and, even if there be—or should arise—a common motive for party action among a popular majority, "it will be more difficult for all who feel it to discover their own strength, and to act in unison with each other." In a federal republic, indeed, the fragmentation of power among the various units of government makes it difficult for any particular faction, even if it seizes power in a particular unit of government, to dominate all the units—especially that unit which governs the whole republic. Hence the new Constitution is a most promising device for eliminating the worst effects of party without abolishing popular government itself.[55]

In order to understand the views Madison expressed in this famous paper —and grasp their implications, if any, with respect to the political problems of our own time—we must be quite clear as to what kind of political group or organization he had in mind when he spoke of a "party" or "faction." (The same statement, as we have noted above, can be made about all the writers here under consideration; but it is especially applicable to Madison.) And three points seem worth making in this connection: (1) He appears to have used the terms "party" and "faction" as virtually synonymous, that is, as denoting slightly different facets of one and the same political phenomenon. (2) His own first-hand knowledge of politics was derived from observation of colonial and state legislatures and of the Congress under the Articles of Confederation, and the interests-factions-parties that he cites as examples are the propertied and the propertyless, the creditors and the debtors, the landed interests, the manufacturing interests, etc.—that is, the kind of groups at work in American legislatures from the Revolution to the emergence of the Federalist and Republican parties in the 1790's. And since, as we pointed out in Chapter 5, these groups had little in common with modern parties (they were entirely *intra*governmental affairs; they had no real organization of any kind; above all, there was

[55] See also Madison's article on "Parties" in the *National Gazette,* January 23, 1792, in *The Writings of James Madison,* edited by Gaillard Hunt (New York: G. P. Putnam's Sons, 1906), Vol. VI, p. 86.

little consensus among them about the form of government that should be established in America), no one can say with any assurance what Madison would have thought of the nationwide parties we have today. Each of the latter is a coalition including most of the major interest groups in the whole population; each appeals for support by offering a moderate program that attempts to reconcile, via "compromise," the demands of the various groups, and thus neither *completely* satisfies nor *completely* dissatisfies any single major interest. Each of them, moreover, draws its support, more or less uniformly, from a republic spread over a territory vastly more extensive, and with a population enormously larger, than he envisaged. Thus we cannot, from his strictures on the narrow groupings with which *he* was familiar, infer any views whatever on the broad party groupings with which *we* are familiar.

Alexis de Tocqueville (1805-1859). De Tocqueville's views on party are of interest to the present-day student for two reasons. First, he was one of the first analysts of party whose comments were based upon extensive observation of a party system closely resembling that of our own day. The year (1831-1832) which he spent traveling in the United States and gathering his material for *Democracy in America* fell in the period in which, as we saw in Chapter 5, the American party system was acquiring what we now regard as its essential characteristics. And, secondly, de Tocqueville was, in general, deeply committed to—and an eloquent spokesman for—nineteenth-century European liberalism. Consequently, his views on party may, in the absence of evidence to the contrary, be fairly regarded as reflecting those of many European liberals of his day.[56]

"Parties," de Tocqueville wrote, "are a necessary evil in free governments"—"necessary" because "the most natural privilege of man, next to the right of acting for himself, is that of combining his exertions with those of his fellow creatures and of acting in common with them."[57] In any government where that right is guaranteed, therefore, men will avail themselves of it, and parties will be formed.

There are, however, two different kinds of parties: "great" parties and "minor" parties.[58] "Great" parties are parties whose members think of themselves as primarily concerned with principles, and only secondarily with winning power: "In them private interest, which always plays the chief part in political passions, is more studiously veiled under the pretext of the public good; and it may even be sometimes concealed from the eyes of the very persons whom it excites and impels." "Minor" parties, on the other hand, are those whose members have no illusions about lofty purposes; they are out for selfish gain only, and know it. "They glow with a factitious zeal; their language is

---

[56] Cf. de Ruggiero, *op. cit.,* pp. 162-63.

[57] Alexis de Tocqueville, *Democracy in America,* translated by Henry Reeve, edited by Phillips Bradley (New York: Alfred A. Knopf, 1945), Vol. I, pp. 174, 197.

[58] De Tocqueville, be it noted, used the terms "great" and "minor" in a *moral* sense. They are not equivalent to our present-day categories of "major" and "minor" parties.

vehement, but their conduct is timid and irresolute. The means which they employ are as wretched as the end at which they aim."

We have, then, great parties and minor ones, and a nation's politics may be dominated either by the one or by the other. Both are noxious, but each does its characteristic kind of damage to society:

> Society is convulsed by great parties, it is only agitated by minor ones; it is torn by the former, by the latter it is degraded; and if the first sometimes save it by a salutary perturbation, the last invariably disturb it to no good end.

When de Tocqueville asked himself which kind of party has dominated national politics in America, he found the answer to be: Both, but at different times. "America has had great parties,[59] but has them no longer; and if her happiness is thereby considerably increased, her morality has suffered." [60] Once the Federalist-Jeffersonian issue was settled, that is to say, America became a country in which there was no disagreement about any fundamental question, but only "a thousand minute shades of difference upon questions of detail."

Parties, to be sure, continue to grow up and influence the course of events. But they are parties whose *raison d'être* lies in the fact that those who do not hold office desire it and know that they can get it only through party organization; and we must not be put off, as regards their central character, by the fact that they adopt some kind of "principle" as a slogan. They *must* do the latter, for the simple reason that "it is difficult to eject a person from authority upon the mere ground that his place is coveted by others." What happens is this:

> A political aspirant in the United States begins by discerning his own interest, and discovering those other interests which may be collected around and amalgamated with it. He then contrives to find out some doctrine or principle that may suit the purposes of this new association, which he adopts in order to bring forward his party and secure its popularity. . . . This being done, the new party is ushered into the political world.[61]

And America is fortunate in this regard. Its "minor" parties are less dangerous to the community than the "major" parties of Europe, and are so *precisely because they are not divided upon fundamental questions:*

> In Europe there are parties which differ so much from the majority that they can never hope to acquire its support, and yet they think they are strong enough in themselves to contend against it. When a party of this kind forms an association, its object is not to convince but to fight. . . . In a country like the United States, in which the differences of opinion are mere differences of hue, the right of association may remain unrestrained without evil consequences.[62]

[59] De Tocqueville here was referring to the old contest between the Federalists and the Jeffersonian Republicans.

[60] This quotation, and the three preceding it, are from de Tocqueville, *op. cit.*, Vol. I, p. 175.

[61] *Ibid.*, Vol. I, pp. 177-78.

[62] *Ibid.*, Vol. I, pp. 196-97.

For de Tocqueville, as for many liberals, unrestrained majority rule is a menace both to liberty and to a stable community. He invariably referred to it as the "omnipotence of the majority," and missed no opportunity to remind his readers that such "omnipotence" was "full of perils" for "the American Republic." *Democracy in America,* indeed, is first and foremost an attempt to clarify the dimensions of the danger, and to identify every possible step that might be taken to reduce it. But he differed sharply from most of his fellow-liberals on one point. They regarded parties as perfect instruments for making majority rule effective. De Tocqueville, by contrast, believed that the American party system was, potentially at least, a barrier *against* effective majority rule; and we find him, in a passage that he never took time to develop, thinking along such lines as these:

> In the United States, as soon as a party has become dominant, all public authority passes into its hands; its private supporters occupy all the offices and have all the force of the administration at their disposal. As the most distinguished members of the opposite party cannot surmount the barrier that excludes them from power, they must establish themselves outside of it, and oppose the whole moral authority of the minority to the physical power that domineers over it. Thus a dangerous expedient is used to obviate a still more formidable danger.[63]

As we shall see below, the notion that the kind of parties we have in America may be checks upon—rather than instruments of—rule by popular majorities was revived and developed by several writers in the second of our two periods.

George Cornewall Lewis (1806-1863). One of the best-known and most influential nineteenth-century works on government is George Cornewall Lewis's *Essay on the Influence of Authority in Matters of Opinion* (1849). In it Lewis registers his conviction that the worst aspect of democracy is to be found in the practice of deciding matters of public policy purely on the basis of the number of persons who favor a given course of action rather than on the basis of what is *right.* Decision-making power, he recognized, on the other hand, is unlikely to be lodged exclusively in persons who know what is right, and the problem (to which he devoted the rest of his book) becomes that of seeking out every possible method or device whereby "authority" (the opinions of persons who *know*) can be made a source of guidance for popular majorities, thus maximizing the chances of their making the right decisions. And one of these methods or devices is the political party.

"The system of party," he writes, "is one of the most potent means by which the principle of authority is rendered predominant over numbers, and the votes of the majority are brought under the control of a few persons." [64] Parties have been formed in the legislative assemblies of all free states; and this makes

---

[63] *Ibid.,* Vol. I, pp. 194-95.

[64] George Cornewall Lewis, *An Essay on the Influence of Authority in Matters of Opinion* (London: John W. Parker, 1849), p. 263. Note that he does not explain why the "few" thus placed in control will be persons distinguished by their knowledge rather than by their ignorance.

such assemblies susceptible to the influence of authority in a way that the mass assemblies of the ancient republics never were:

> The system of parties in a legislative body leads to preliminary and separate discussions among its members, out of the chamber, upon the questions to be discussed within it, and to a prior settlement of the course which each party is to take. This renders the assembled body less accessible to the influence of speeches delivered in its debates, and prevents it from being carried away by the sudden and vehement impulse of an impassioned appeal to its feelings. A greater ascendancy is thus secured to calm and prudent counsels than in the ancient republics—where the citizens generally came together without any fixed opinion, and were convinced by the speech of the most eloquent demagogue.[65]

Lewis is not, to be sure, blind to the alleged dangers of party. Party members, he observes, do sometimes forget the end for which the party was formed, and do regard party success as an end in itself.[66] Party zeal, moreover, may run away with itself, so that "the two rival parties are like hostile armies, each contending for victory, and regardless of the cause for which they are fighting."[67] Authority is then stripped of its capacity to influence majority decisions, and the whole community, in consequence, sustains serious injury. But all that is the exception, not the rule, and in normal conditions party can be counted on to help the principle of authority prevail over that of numbers in "matters of opinion."

The Second Group of Early Writers Summarized. Hume, Madison, Adams, de Tocqueville, and Lewis shared many convictions with the first group of writers we examined. Like the anti-party writers, they regarded majority-rule democracy as a dangerous and disruptive form of government. Most of them were convinced, moreover, that political parties, if unchecked and unregulated, must transform themselves into instruments for majority oppression of minorities, and that, insofar as this is true, no further indictment of parties is needed. Their bill of particulars against party, in other words, like that of the writers in our first group, is for the most part a bill of particulars against majority-rule democracy rather than against party as such. One cannot help wondering, as one reads them, why they did not see this, and have at the enemy rather than the shadow.

The major difference between the two groups of writers can be stated as follows: For Halifax, Bolingbroke, Washington, and the other anti-party writers, the essence of "good government" is order, tranquillity, and patriotic unity among all the citizens of the nation. An institution like the political party, therefore, which *ipso facto* sets one group of the populace against another, cannot be other than subversive of good government. Hume, Madison, Adams, de Tocqueville, and Lewis, on the other hand, equated "good govern-

[65] *Ibid.*, p. 218.
[66] *Ibid.*, pp. 385-86.
[67] *Ibid.*, p. 390.

ment" and *"free* government," that is, government in which the citizen's rights to free speech, free press, freedom of assembly, and political organization are not abridged by official action. And they were prepared to accept political parties as one component of the price a nation must pay for such government.

No writer in either of these first two groups could be accurately described as a democrat; and none of them, in consequence, had any reason to raise what is for us the central question in this area, that of the efficacy of parties as agencies for popular consultation. Popular consultation was not one of the ends to which they addressed themselves, and the search for the means of achieving it could, for that reason, be left to others to conduct.

PARTY AS A NECESSARY INSTRUMENT OF POPULAR GOVERNMENT

During the early period we have been discussing, some writers did favor majority-rule democracy, were deeply concerned with the problem of popular consultation, and did pay attention to the possible usefulness of political parties as agencies for forming, expressing, and implementing the popular will. Almost without exception, moreover, these writers took the position that no popular government can function without parties. We shall attempt to summarize the views of the three most prominent writers in this group.

Edmund Burke (*1729-1797*). In the late 1760's, King George III of England, supported by a group of sympathetic M.P.'s known as the "King's Friends," sought to expand his personal influence over government to such a point that he, rather than the dominant party group of the moment, would "rule" (and not, as the British phrase goes, merely "reign"). There is, indeed, reason to believe that he had steeped himself in the ideas of Bolingbroke, and was attempting to become the long-dreamed-of "patriot king." Edmund Burke, who entered Parliament in 1765 and soon became a leading spokesman of a group—the so-called "Rockingham Whigs"—opposed to the King's Friends, became convinced that the king's bid for personal power was contrary to all the principles of popular government. Toward the end of the decade, accordingly, Burke decided to put his already-famous pen to work in an attempt to point up, for a wider audience than he could have in the House of Commons, the errors and dangers of the king's course of action. And by 1770 he was ready to publish his extraordinary pamphlet, "Thoughts on the Cause of the Present Discontents," which was the first, and for a long while the only, full-dress attempt to state the case for political parties. Even today this pamphlet remains a major classic of pro-party literature.[68]

The "cause" referred to in the title is the attempt of the king and his friends to substitute personal rule by the monarch for party rule by the representatives of the nation; and Burke's way of getting into his problem is to develop—and insist upon—a sharp distinction between the "cabal" or "faction"

[68] See R. H. Murray, *Edmund Burke: A Biography* (London: Oxford University Press, 1931), pp. 176-77, for an account of the circumstances in which this pamphlet was written and published.

and the "party," and to take exception to the practice of lumping together, for blanket condemnation, *all* forms of political organization. "Cabals," he explains, are groups of men "who have got together, avowedly without any public principle, in order to sell their conjunct iniquity at the higher rate"; they are "universally odious," "ought never to be suffered to domineer in the state," and are, in any case, useless as agencies of popular government because "they have *no connection with the sentiments and opinions of the people.*" [69] The "party" is a different kind of organization altogether. It is, according to Burke's now-famous definition, "a body of men united, for promoting by their joint endeavors the national interest, upon some particular principle in which they are all agreed." [70]

As to why men "unite" to promote the national interest, Burke assumes that endeavors that are *not* "joint" get nowhere and, worse still, abandon the national interest to those who *do* unite. "Single, unsupported, desultory, unsystematic" action by individuals, he insists, is in the very nature of the case ineffective in politics, so that the citizen who wishes to do more than merely talk about his political principles, and has his mind made up to affect the course of political events in a direction congenial to those principles, *must* identify—and team up with—other individuals who believe in them. Only associated, organized action—*party* action—is effective. To refuse to engage in it is to surrender to other men, whose principles may be different and may even be downright bad. It is, indeed, above all when "bad men combine" that "the good must associate; else they will fall, one by one, an unpitied sacrifice in a contemptible struggle." [71]

Burke did not deny that "the behavior of many parties should have made persons of tender and scrupulous virtue somewhat out of humor with all sorts of connection in politics." The fact that some parties have behaved badly, however, does not justify us in condemning the whole idea of parties. Every profession, even that of the soldier and that of the priest, is liable to its own peculiar vices; but the latter "form no argument against those ways of life; nor are the vices themselves inevitable to every individual in those professions." Similarly, parties are not always all that they should be; but we must remember, when confronted with evidence of their deficiencies, that

. . . where duty renders a critical situation a necessary one, it is our business to keep free from the evils attendant upon it; and not to fly from the situation itself.[72]

Burke concluded, then, that in any situation where the parties are "bad," the proper course is not to abolish them but to reform them. The real enemies

[69] "Thoughts on the Cause of the Present Discontents," in *The Works of Edmund Burke* (London: Henry G. Bohn, 1861), Vol. I, p. 474. Italics in the original.
[70] *Ibid.,* Vol. I, p. 530.
[71] *Ibid.,* Vol. I, pp. 525-26.
[72] *Ibid.,* Vol. I, p. 527.

of the nation are its factions—the King's Friends, for example—which seek always to destroy parties and rule without them:

. . . whoever becomes a party to an administration, composed of insulated individuals, without faith plighted, tie, or common principle; an administration constitutionally impotent, because supported by no party in the nation; he who contributes to destroy the connections of men and their trust in one another, or in any sort to throw the dependence of public counsels upon private will and favor . . . abets a faction that is driving hard to the ruin of the country.[73]

For a long time after it was written, Burke's defense of parties was little heeded by writers and intellectuals in the English-speaking world, and still less by those in Europe. Burke himself, to be sure, did not lack for admirers and disciples among them; but it was Burke the author of the *Reflections,* Burke the castigator of Warren Hastings, and Burke the protagonist of a new colonial policy for Britain who excited admiration and won followers. The Burke who actively and proudly associated himself with a political party, gave it his loyalty, and on occasion ran errands for it, either was not mentioned or was sent on his way with a word of reproof (in somewhat the same manner that the Winston Churchill who once boasted that he had in his lifetime consumed a railway-carful of brandy is, in our day, "de-emphasized" in favor of Winston Churchill the Architect of Victory over the Nazis). And as for Burke's open—some intellectuals would have said shameless—defense of parties, it was normally written off as a yet-to-be-explained aberration on the part of an otherwise first-rate mind. Burke's good friend, Oliver Goldsmith, undoubtedly spoke for most Burke admirers when he wrote:

> Here lies our good Edmund, whose genius was such,
> We scarcely can praise it, or blame it too much;
> Who, born for the Universe, narrow'd his mind,
> And to party gave up what was meant for mankind.[74]

Francis Lieber (1800-1872). Sixty-eight years after the publication of "Thoughts on the Cause of the Present Discontents," there appeared the second sustained defense of political parties that has come to the attention of the present writers: Francis Lieber's *Manual of Political Ethics* (1838). Lieber, German-born and -educated, had come to the United States in 1827, and had become a professor at Columbia College in New York City by the time he wrote this work. Like Burke, he set himself against the prevailing tendency to use the terms "party" and "faction" interchangeably, and began his analysis by drawing a distinction between them:

By a party we understand a number of citizens who, for some period and not momentarily, act in unison respecting some principles, interest, or measure, by lawful means, keeping therefore within the bounds of the fundamental law and for

[73] *Ibid.,* Vol. I, pp. 468-69.
[74] "Retaliation, a Poem," in *The Poems and Plays of Oliver Goldsmith,* Everyman's Library edition (London: J. M. Dent and Sons, 1910), p. 38.

the real or sincerely supposed common good of the whole commonwealth. If either of these latter requisites be wanting; if that body of citizens act by unlawful means or for sordid, selfish ends, or strive, secretly or openly, beyond the fundamental law—that is, if they no longer strive for a change of administration or of some laws, but for a change of the government itself—they are called a faction.[75]

Factions, Lieber believed, arise under all forms of government; parties, by contrast, are characteristic of free governments:

. . . as far as my knowledge goes, I know of no instance of a free state without parties. . . . Where there is free action of whatever sort . . . , and especially where men thus situated strive to obtain some common end, to establish some principle or to act out some idea, those who hold to the same principles will naturally and must necessarily unite in some degree and combine their endeavors, strength and energy. . . . We may lay it down, then, as a principle, that in the same degree as there is room for combined and self-directing action in any sphere, so likewise must parties exist.[76]

Lieber's explanation of the genesis of parties, in other words, is much the same as Burke's. Men (where, Lieber is more careful than Burke to add, they are free) form parties as a matter of course because only by doing so can they produce desired political results. But he goes much further than Burke in insisting that "upon many grounds it is desirable that parties should exist," and thus forces his way into a good deal of new territory which the reader will recognize as reminiscent of, though not identical with, that opened up by de Tocqueville. He argues, for example, that "without parties there could be no loyal, steady, lasting, and effective opposition," and that effective opposition, in turn, is "one of the surest safeguards of public peace." [77] And he supports these propositions with such logic as the following: Where there are no parties, opposition to the government-of-the-day necessarily takes the form of secret conspiracy and rebellion. Where there are parties, opposition becomes *party* opposition, and the parties, far from being instruments for oppressing minorities, are the best guarantors of the rights of minorities.[78] And, again for example, we find this startling new emphasis in Lieber: Where no parties exist, there is little effective machinery for compromise; most new proposals for public action remain "harsh, unmodified, absolute," and many of them never get carried out. Where parties do exist, by contrast, society has a built-in meeting ground for new proposals: the party councils, where they are thrashed out, compromised, formed into a program, and duly submitted for electoral approval or disapproval. In short, the parties help translate opinion, once it has become public, into appropriate governmental action.[79]

[75] Francis Lieber, *Manual of Political Ethics,* 2nd ed. (Philadelphia: J. B. Lippincott and Co., 1876), Vol. II, p. 253. The first edition of this work was published in 1838.
[76] *Ibid.,* Vol. II, pp. 253-54.
[77] *Ibid.,* Vol. II, p. 254.
[78] *Ibid.,* Vol. II, pp. 268-69.
[79] *Ibid.,* Vol. II, pp. 254-55.

Lieber was not, we must note in conclusion, so remote from the other writers here under consideration as to be blind to the possibility that parties will do—if not more harm than good—a great deal of harm; rather he enjoins constant vigilance upon us in this regard, and a determination to prevent the harm from being done. Party members may confuse their party with the whole community and regard its success as an end in itself, forgetting that party is only a means, and that it and its interests are never identical with the whole community and its interests. Again, party action and animosity may pass over into private life in the form of party badges, party schools, etc., and party spirit may finally cut so deep that certain words will come to mean one thing to members of one party and another thing to members of another, so that the citizens can no longer communicate with one another.[80] This too must be guarded against. Once it is on guard against these perils, however, the free nation can, according to Lieber, see to it that they do not assume major proportions—and, having done so, count its political parties among its most valuable institutions.

Philip C. Friese. Philip C. Friese's *Essay on Party,* published in 1856,[81] was little noticed by his contemporaries, and has continued to be overlooked by the present-day analysts of party who have made it their business to canvass the party literature of the past. But it is much the sturdiest pro-party work we have from the early students of party. Friese had a clear grasp of the central issue, which is whether political parties are useful agencies of democratic government, handled it with great theoretical skill, and showed his insight into the processes of free government by anticipating point after point about parties that many believe to have been made for the first time in our own day.

Friese addressed his book to those "many good men and lovers of their country [who] think that they see in the action of political parties a rising tide of evil, which threatens to overwhelm the land in a fearful flood of appalling wickedness." [82] And what he had to say to them was in effect this: Consider well what parties actually are and what they actually do; above all, let us be clear about the kind of government we want in the United States, and the role the parties must play in it, before we speak ill of them.

Even Friese's definition of party reveals a kind of sophistication about the democratic process that one looks for in vain among the other writers we have been discussing, not excluding even Lieber. A party, he writes, is a

union of citizens agreed in opinion and design concerning government, and organized for the double purpose of propagating those opinions and designs by discussion, and of personifying them *by the election and appointment of persons strongly entertaining them* to fill the leading positions of the state.[83]

[80] *Ibid.,* Vol. II, pp. 259-64.
[81] Philip C. Friese, *An Essay on Party, Showing Its Uses, Its Abuses, and Natural Dissolution* (New York: Fowler and Wells, 1856).
[82] *Ibid.,* p. v.
[83] *Ibid.,* p. 7. Italics added.

Thus parties, according to Friese, have two great and characteristic functions.

The first is that of creating public opinion, which they accomplish by spreading their views throughout the land, thus giving the citizens definite policies and principles to discuss and to choose among (not necessarily, be it noted, by standing over against each other with *different* principles). Friese pressed the point vigorously, conceding, among other things, that the discussion process he is describing is certain to generate the phenomenon known as "party spirit," and meeting head-on the view, which as we have seen was then highly fashionable, that party spirit is *ipso facto* divisive and disgusting. This phenomenon, he insisted, is neither unique to parties nor necessarily a bad thing:

> This feeling is the spring of action in every joint enterprise. It is called by various names. When it springs from the relation to a common country, it is called patriotic zeal. When it arises from common religious convictions, it is called religious zeal. When it grows out of opinions held in common concerning politics, it is called party spirit.
>
> Party spirit, in a moderate degree, is beneficial. It inspires to vigorous, concerted action. It seems to be the means appointed by Providence to simplify and make practical the political action of a free people, by attracting them, through the influence of general political principles, to act together in large masses. *In this manner it diminishes the number of issues which would otherwise be pending before the people at one time. Without party spirit there would be almost innumerable diversities of political opinion, feebly entertained, and producing no effect on government.* The warmth of party spirit leads to an energetic and clear statement of opinion, and to bold discussion; non-essential differences become neglected, and the masses entertaining virtually the same opinions become fixed into one.[84]

The second is that of "personifying" party members' opinions "by the election and appointment of persons strongly entertaining them to fill the leading positions of the state." This party accomplishes, he thought, through its representative organization and nominating processes, and so meets a need that no thickly populated community can leave unsatisfied if its citizens are to have a manageable number of alternatives to choose among. Here also Friese challenges accepted political opinions. The American party nominating system—operating as it does by means of conventions of the elected representatives of the party members—is *the democratic* way of satisfying the need,[85] if for no other reason than because it is based on majority rule, which he deems the basic principle of American government:

> . . . the practice in every assembly of solving every question by vote, and declaring the majority of votes to prevail, *a practice repeated perhaps in millions of instances every year, in many of which almost every man must participate,* begets so habitual a deference to the decision of the majority, that *when the will of the majority of the people is once ascertained, even in the most exciting political question, there is at once a universal acquiescence in its determination.*

[84] *Ibid.*, pp. 10-11. Italics added.
[85] *Ibid.*, pp. 11-19.

This absolute deference to the decision of the majority is the true keystone of the arch of our liberties. . . .[86]

Friese, like Lieber, recognizes that we cannot enjoy the advantages of party without letting ourselves in for its disadvantages and its untoward consequences, which he proceeds to list—more exhaustively, perhaps, than any anti-party writer of the age: the excesses of party spirit; the violations of the principle of equality of representation in party conventions, where delegations from certain areas have more votes than the number of party members they speak for entitles them to; the extension of party nominations to minor offices—justice of the peace, sheriff, constable—in which party principles are evidently not involved; corrupt practices on the part of candidates seeking nominations; the spoils system; the levies on the salaries of public officials to support party treasuries.[87] Like Burke, however, Friese felt that such abuses do not justify us in condemning the whole institution—especially since an efficacious remedy is always at hand, namely, for all good citizens to withdraw their support from any party which engages in any of these practices.[88]

The true virtue and excellence of normal American parties, Friese argues further, becomes clear when we project them against the background of current attempts to substitute secret political associations for public ones. The reference here, of course, is to the "Know-Nothing Party," which was in its heyday at the time he wrote the *Essay*. It was an anti-Catholic, anti-immigrant, nativist movement, which sought to check what its partisans regarded as the growing influence of the foreign-born in American affairs. Its technique was indeed that of secret, conspiratorial organization—to such an extent that its members, when queried about it, professed ignorance of its very existence (whence the name "Know-Nothings").[89] Friese, writing many decades before the invention of the straw-vote and sample-survey polls that have since documented his views, argued brilliantly that neither Catholics nor immigrants vote as blocs, and that papal authority does not and, moreover, could not extend to political matters. But his major contention is that secret and conspiratorial political organization *ipso facto* undermines the very foundations of the American system.[90]

Party action, Friese concluded, is the most honorable and effective channel through which a citizen may exercise his sovereignty over his government and make sure that public officials act as the people want them to act:

Citizens acting as members of a party are, both in dignity and in power, true sovereigns. Public officers, even the highest, are public servants. Members of a party exercise original power, public officers that only which is delegated. As members of a party, the citizens originate political measures and principles. As public

[86] *Ibid.*, pp. 20-21. Italics added.
[87] *Ibid.*, pp. 24-39.
[88] *Ibid.*, pp. 40-45, 95.
[89] See pp. 446-47.
[90] Friese, *op. cit.*, pp. 58-69.

officers they merely execute them, supply their forms, and add some of their details. The power and glory of citizens acting as members of a party, and elaborating wholesome political measures, and demonstrating great political principles, are the highest aspirations of earthly ambition, and they may be felt and admired through all time and over the whole world.[91]

Even the adherents of the defeated party, if they rightly understand democratic government and the function of a minority party therein, can play an important role in the whole process:

They may be proved by the result to have been in error; still their efforts, coming from a pure source, gave strength to the cause of truth, though directed against it, as the rushing blasts of heaven, roaring through the swaying branches, but increase the firmness of the solid oak. So the masses of a defeated party have an opportunity to display *one of the highest of republican virtues—a prompt and cheerful acquiescence in the decision of the majority.*[92]

Thus in Philip Friese's view, American government is and ought to be democratic government; democratic government is in the very nature of the case a matter of rule by popular majorities; and popular majorities can—in a thickly populated nation like the United States—rule only through the agency of political parties.

Walter Bagehot (1826-1877). Walter Bagehot's *The English Constitution,* published in 1867, was an attempt to explain the actual operating principles of British government—as opposed to what he called the "literary theory" of its operation. He put political parties high on his list of aspects of the constitution that, in his opinion, most of the "literary" theorists had failed to take into account.

The House of Commons, Bagehot wrote, is no longer primarily a deliberative-legislative assembly, but rather an *electoral* body, whose major function is to select a prime minister. And parties, which he regarded as essential to the sound functioning of any electoral process, are caught up in that of the House to an extent hardly hinted at in contemporary books on British government and politics: "Party is inherent in it, is bone of its bone, and breath of its breath."[93] And, for that matter, "party organization is the vital principle of representative government" anywhere.[94]

To those who admit the facts about the role of parties but deplore them, who fear the division of England into warring parties, and are perturbed by the violence of party oratory, Bagehot replies as follows:

The body is eager, but the atoms are cool. If it were otherwise, parliamentary government would become the worst of all governments—a sectarian government.

[91] *Ibid.,* pp. 98-99.
[92] *Ibid.,* p. 56. Italics added.
[93] Walter Bagehot, *The English Constitution* (London: Oxford University Press, 1928), p. 125. This work was first published in 1867, and a second edition with an additional chapter appeared in 1872.
[94] *Ibid.,* p. 126.

The party in power would go to all the lengths their orators proposed—all that their formulae enjoined, as far as they had ever said they would go. But the partisans of the English Parliament are not of such a temper. They are Whigs, or Radicals, or Tories, but they are much else too. They are common Englishmen, and, as Father Newman complains, "hard to be worked up to the dogmatic level." [95]

The quality of being "hard to be worked up to the dogmatic level" is what Bagehot calls "moderation," and moderation, he insists, is the characteristic mood of the kind of political parties that is appropriate and essential to the success of representative government. Bagehot thus implies a distinction between moderate parties and immoderate ones, and goes on to relate the former to situations in which the people are of a certain temper and the community is drawn together on such and such terms (which Bagehot thought it the task of students of politics to identify). Given such parties, he thinks, representative government will work well—as, on his showing, it does in England.[96]

The Early Pro-Party Writers Summarized. In the period before 1870, then, the literature on politics had little to offer in the way of sustained defense of party. Here and there, to be sure, one finds a sympathetic passing reference to parties—a comment by Thomas Jefferson, for example, to the effect that parties are inevitable in a free society, and that "perhaps this party division is necessary to induce each to watch and delate to the people the proceedings of the other," [97] or some brief comments by two Italian liberals, Alfieri writing in 1777 and Foscola writing in 1815, who think well of parties as agencies for forming and expressing the popular will.[98] But the only writers between the late seventeenth and the late nineteenth century who defended parties at any length were Burke, Lieber, Friese, and Bagehot.

Each of these four writers was committed, in some degree, to majority-rule democracy as it is defined and explicated in this book—one of them (Burke) much less committed and one of them (Friese) much more committed to it than the other two. Burke was the least majoritarian of the four, but even so he was far closer to a majority-rule position than any of the anti-party writers of the period. The latter, as we have seen, valued order and tranquillity above all other political goods, while Burke, like the other three pro-party writers, put individual liberties at the top of the political-values hierarchy. All of them, moreover, were preoccupied with the problem of popular consultation and treated parties as, above all, instrumental agencies indispensable to the conduct of popular government.

Let us note, in concluding this section, three developments that occurred in the period from the late seventeenth to the late nineteenth century: (1) The idea of democracy won more and more adherents, both among intellectuals

---

[95] *Ibid.*

[96] *Ibid.*, p. 128.

[97] *The Writings of Thomas Jefferson,* edited by H. A. Washington (Washington, D. C.: Taylor and Maury, 1854), Vol. IV, pp. 246, 562; Vol. VI, p. 143.

[98] De Ruggiero, *op. cit.,* pp. 283, 295.

and among the people at large. (2) Political parties transformed themselves from the secret, conspiratorial, strictly intragovernmental organizations of Restoration England into the large-scale extragovernmental organizations of nineteenth-century England and America. (3) Thought about political parties, as expressed in the professional literature of the subject, underwent rapid and kaleidoscopic changes. Blanket condemnation of parties dominated the early part of the period; the disposition to extend them a sort of *de facto* recognition as regrettable but unavoidable ruled the scene in its middle years; and attempts to defend parties began to appear with any frequency only well toward its end. One is tempted, while recognizing that not all democrats at all times have approved of parties, to suggest that as democracy won a larger and larger place in popular affection, political parties did likewise. Not until the late nineteenth century did the discussion of parties take on something of the tone that characterizes it today; and only then did parties acquire their present status—which we may perhaps define as somewhere between quasi-respectability and wholehearted acceptance.

Recent Appraisals of Party

Since the late 1870's the literature on political parties—especially that written by Americans on American parties, which today accounts for the greater part of it—has grown enormously. Little or none of it can be dismissed as irrelevant to the purposes of the present book—not even on grounds of obsolescence. In fact, one of the first impressions that force themselves on the present-day reader of the party literature of fifty or sixty years ago is that much of it sounds as if it had been written only yesterday. For the questions asked about parties were about the same at the beginning of the recent period as those we are asking at the present time. The answers given to those questions have, similarly, varied only in minute detail. And the factual descriptions of parties that have come down to us from as long ago as the 1880's and 1890's differ little from those written in the 1940's and 1950's.

To call attention to this peculiarity of the recent literature on American parties is not, be it noted, to suggest that all is not as it should be, or to imply that the literature has not "made any progress" since the 1870's. For it may be that the American party system became "stabilized" in the 1870's and has since undergone a bare and hardly perceptible minimum of evolutionary change. Our point, for the moment, is merely that the post-1870 works on American parties cannot profitably be grouped according to the date of publication, because the date at which a given work was published tells us little or nothing about it.

Limitations of space preclude any summary of all the questions raised and all the answers given by each of these writers. For our present purposes perhaps the most useful way of grouping their works is to classify them according to the way in which their authors *approach* the study of parties—that is, according to the kinds of questions they are *most* concerned with and the kinds of data they are *most* interested in. The following pages, accordingly, attempt to identify the various approaches to the study of political parties and to familiarize the reader with the names of some of the leading practitioners of each; they do not attempt to present a complete summary of the ideas of each writer mentioned.[99]

THE MAIN APPROACHES TO THE STUDY OF PARTIES

Party as an American Institution. A number of writers have made it their major task to describe, without evaluating, the structure and operations of American parties, treating the latter, for this purpose, as one of the several important institutions that go to make up the American governmental and political system. They have concentrated their attention upon such matters as the legal regulation of parties, the formal organization and selection of leaders and candidates, party finance, party conventions, party campaign techniques, etc. Only incidentally have they touched upon the theoretical and more or less value-laden questions that the data seem (to other writers anyhow) to suggest—e.g., the question whether American parties promote or hinder the development of democracy in the United States. This point of view might be called the "textbook" approach, since most of the leading college textbooks, old and new alike, have adopted it. And much of the present empirical knowledge we possess about American parties has been accumulated by these writers, who have, accordingly, made a rich contribution to the development of our knowledge and understanding of American parties. Some of the leading writers who recognizably identify themselves with this approach are Jesse Macy, Anson D. Morse, P. Orman Ray, James A. Woodburn, Robert C. Brooks, and Edward M. Sait.[100]

The Pathology of American Parties. Particularly during the earlier years of the recent period, a number of writers got at the study of parties by fixing attention upon bosses, machines, spoils, and corruption. They assumed these phenomena to be the very essence of the American party problem, and would certainly have taken exception to the implication (in our subtitle) that they were losing sight of the otherwise healthy organ by overemphasizing its diseased area. If one understands all about bosses and machines—so runs their tacit premise—one has learned most of what is needed in order to understand what American parties are *really* like; one will not, for example, be

[99] For a somewhat different identification of the various approaches to the study of political parties by American writers, see Merriam and Gosnell, *op. cit.*, pp. 414-15.

[100] See such works as Jesse Macy, *Party Organization and Machinery* (New York: The Century Co., 1904); Anson D. Morse, *Parties and Party Leaders* (Boston: Marshall Jones Co., 1923); P. Orman Ray, *An Introduction to Political Parties and Practical Politics* (New York: Charles Scribner's Sons, 1913); James A. Woodburn, *Political Parties and Party Problems in the United States* (New York: G. P. Putnam's Sons, 1903); Robert C. Brooks, *Political Parties and Electoral Problems* (New York: Harper and Brothers, 1923); and Edward M. Sait, *American Parties and Elections* (New York: The Century Co., 1927).

taken in by any ill-informed talk about the importance of platforms or "principles."

Most of the party pathologists, like the textbook writers previously mentioned, conceived their task in terms of *describing* American parties, and did not feel called upon to talk much about whether or not parties are of value to the body politic. They had, therefore, no reason to address themselves to the question of whether American parties pay their way as agencies of democratic government, although the clear implication of their conclusions is that they do not. Among the writers who have adopted this approach are L. G. Tyler, Lincoln Steffens, Samuel P. Orth, and Frank R. Kent.[101]

Party as a Group Among Groups. A third body of writers move from the premise that society is made up of groups (economic, religious, racial, political, etc.), political parties being simply one of several kinds of group, all of which lend themselves to the familiar techniques of group analysis. Like the textbook writers and the students of bossism and corruption, they think of themselves as empirical observers of the nature and operations of parties, not only entitled but obligated to leave to one side such matters as the nature of democracy and the utility of parties as agencies of democratic government. Among the leading exponents of this approach have been Albion W. Small, Arthur F. Bentley, and David B. Truman.[102]

Parties as Reflections of Voting-Group Alignments. A fourth group of writers have been primarily concerned with the shifting tides of public opinion over the broad sweep of American history, and fix their attention on available data concerning the election-by-election alignment of identifiable groups of voters. For these writers, parties, as of any given moment, are merely reflections of the continuing process that determines what groups line up together. It is, therefore, the electoral support the particular parties command in successive elections, not party organization and party activity *between* elections, that engages their attention. Among those who have adopted this approach to parties are Arthur N. Holcombe, Edgar E. Robinson, Wilfred E. Binkley, Samuel Lubell, and Louis Harris.[103]

[101] See such works as L. G. Tyler, *Parties and Patronage in the United States* (New York: G. P. Putnam's Sons, 1891); Lincoln Steffens, *The Struggle for Self-Government* (New York: McClure, Phillips and Co., 1906) and *Autobiography* (New York: Harcourt, Brace and Company, 1931); Samuel P. Orth, *The Boss and the Machine* (New Haven: Yale University Press, 1919); and Frank R. Kent, *The Great Game of Politics* (Garden City, N. Y.: Doubleday, Page and Company, 1923).

[102] See such works as Albion W. Small, *General Sociology* (Chicago: The University of Chicago Press, 1905); Arthur F. Bentley, *The Process of Government* (Chicago: The University of Chicago Press, 1908); and David B. Truman, *The Governmental Process* (New York: Alfred A. Knopf, 1951).

[103] See such works as Arthur N. Holcombe, *The Political Parties of Today* (New York: Harper and Brothers, 1924) and *The New Party Politics* (New York: W. W. Norton and Co., Inc., 1933); Edgar E. Robinson, *The Evolution of American Political Parties* (New York: Harcourt, Brace and Company, 1924); Wilfred E. Binkley, *op. cit.;* Samuel Lubell, *The Future of American Politics* (New York: Harper and Brothers, 1952); and Louis Harris, *Is There a Republican Majority?* (New York: Harper and Brothers, 1954).

AMERICAN PARTIES AS AGENCIES OF DEMOCRATIC GOVERNMENT

As we have pointed out repeatedly, none of the writers we have discussed in the foregoing section is more than incidentally interested in the question whether existing American parties are or can be useful agencies of democratic government. They all proceed on the assumption that their job ends with the *description* of American parties and does not commit them to trying to decide whether American parties—much less parties in other countries or parties in general—are political institutions appropriate to a democratic form of government. They differ—at the margin, differ sharply—as to *how* to describe American parties; but they are agreed in setting aside as irrelevant (or *ultra vires*) all speculation as to the nature of democracy and the role parties *should* perform therein.

The silence on these latter questions has not, however, been complete; some writers have treated them as the central problem of parties research, and have thought of factual description of parties as valuable only insofar as it sheds light upon them. The fact that these writers have reached widely varying conclusions about the nature of democracy and the utility of parties has tended to obscure, in the eyes of certain critics, the extent to which they share certain premises concerning values and methodology. Yet the common ground is considerable. Most of them think of themselves as democrats, and feel obliged to face certain speculative questions concerning the nature of democracy. All of them raise the question whether *any* kind of party system can be fitted into a democratic government. And all of them evaluate existing American parties with an eye not to the alleged facts alone, but to "theoretical" considerations as well.

In short, these writers seek to piece together an accurate and illuminating description of the existing American party system, not for its own sake, but because it will help them determine whether American parties are helping or hindering the growth of democracy in the United States.

Among the writers employing this approach, three relatively distinct positions seem to have emerged. Let us briefly summarize each.

The Anti-Party Writers. A number of writers in the late 1800's and early 1900's took the position that political parties in any form—and particularly as they exist in the United States—are incompatible with genuine democratic government. And they did not hesitate to draw the indicated conclusion: that the outlawing, suppression, or abolition of parties is an indispensable prerequisite to the attainment of true democracy in America. The leading exponents of this point of view are Charles C. P. Clark, Albert Stickney, Samuel E. Moffett, James S. Brown, M. I. Ostrogorski, and Herbert Croly.[104]

---

[104] See such works as Charles C. P. Clark, *The "Machine" Abolished and the People Restored to Power* (New York: G. P. Putnam's Sons, 1900); Albert Stickney, *A True Republic* (New York: Harper and Brothers, 1879) and *Democratic Government* (New York: Harper and Brothers, 1885); Samuel E. Moffett, *Suggestions on Government* (New York: Rand, McNally and Company, 1894); James S. Brown, *Partisan Politics: The Evil and Remedy* (Philadelphia: J. B.

In general terms, their indictment runs as follows:[105] Democracy requires, among other things, the widest possible *direct* popular participation in government, and the latter becomes impossible just to the extent that parties interpose themselves between the sovereign citizen and his government. Secondly, parties, in the very nature of the case, confuse popular discussion of public issus and distort the expression of the popular will beyond all recognition. Thirdly, they tend to destroy consensus, corrupt public officers, and lower civic morality generally. They may, indeed, have served in the past to counterbalance the most flagrant antidemocratic aspects of our constitutional system and may, in that sense, have been of some small use to American democracy. But in the truly democratic America of the future, political parties, *however* organized, can have no place. Therefore, the first step to take toward its achievement is to draw the parties' teeth and thus destroy their power and influence.

The writers in question are, let us note in conclusion, ready—each in his own way—for the objection that the parties' power and influence *cannot* be destroyed. All of them, that is to say, assume that given the will to uproot political parties we can—on the level of practical statecraft—find the means. Some of them, indeed, have concrete measures to propose in this area. Clark and Stickney, for example, would have us govern ourselves by means of a pyramidal series of "town meetings." And Brown would have us declare legally ineligible any candidate for public office nominated by a political party.

The Advocates of Responsible Party Government. Among professional political scientists today, the most widely held position on political parties is that which looks, for the solution of the parties' problems, to the "doctrine of responsible party government," that is, the doctrine according to which a thickly populated modern community that wants genuine popular consultation must first develop for itself—as the United States, they say, is still very far from having done—a *responsible party system.*

The doctrine in question was first advanced in the late nineteenth and early twentieth centuries by Woodrow Wilson, A. Lawrence Lowell, Henry Jones Ford, and Frank J. Goodnow.[106] It was revived and modernized in the 1940's by E. E. Schattschneider.[107] And it achieved its present eminence in

Lippincott Company, 1897); M. I. Ostrogorski, *Democracy and the Organization of Political Parties,* 2 volumes, translated by Frederick Clarke (New York: The Macmillan Company, 1902); and Herbert Croly, *The Promise of American Life* (New York: The Macmillan Company, 1909) and *Progressive Democracy* (New York: The Macmillan Company, 1914).

[105] Cf. Austin Ranney, *The Doctrine of Responsible Party Government* (Urbana: The University of Illinois Press, 1954), Chs. VII and VIII.

[106] See such works as Woodrow Wilson, *Congressional Government* (Boston: Houghton Mifflin Company, 1885) and *Constitutional Government in the United States* (New York: Columbia University Press, 1908); A. Lawrence Lowell, *Public Opinion and Popular Government* (New York: Longmans, Green and Company, 1913); Henry Jones Ford, *op. cit.;* and Frank J. Goodnow, *Politics and Administration* (New York: The Macmillan Company, 1900).

[107] See E. E. Schattschneider, *Party Government* (New York: Rinehart & Company, Inc., 1942) and *The Struggle for Party Government* (College Park, Md.: Program in American Civilization, University of Maryland, 1948).

1950 with the publication of the report of the Committee on Political Parties of the American Political Science Association.[108]

Briefly summarized, the literature of responsible party government addresses itself to three main issues: (1) the function of parties in a democracy; (2) the kind of parties necessary to perform this function; and (3) the adequacy of existing American parties.[109]

(1) As to the function of parties, these writers take the position that democracy, in any thickly populated modern community, must be conceived of as popular *control* over government, not popular *participation* in its day-to-day activities. The function of the people in a democracy, that is to say, must be that of choosing the decision makers, and not—except in a very broad and general sense—that of making decisions themselves. And popular control, at its best, is a matter of popular choice between competing *responsible* political parties, which alone can provide coherent, unified sets of rulers who will be both strong enough to run the government and sufficiently identifiable to be genuinely answerable for the way it is run.

(2) With respect to the second of the three issues, exponents of this doctrine hold that in order to have responsible party government a community must have at least—and preferably *only*—two main parties, and that these must be *unified* and *disciplined* so that their members in public office will vote and act together, that is, *as a party,* on matters of public policy. Only where these conditions are fulfilled can the majority *party*—as contrasted with its individual officeholders—be held responsible for how the government is run. (The British party system, they contend, is a close approximation to responsible party government.)

(3) American parties as we know them are, according to this doctrine's exponents, utterly incapable of providing responsible party government. They are decentralized, loosely organized, and, worst of all, *un*disciplined—and thus unable, save in rare instances, to hold their lines on matters of public policy. *Every* public policy in the United States, therefore, can properly be called a "*bi*partisan"—or, if not that, a "*non*partisan"—policy. And, that being the case, there is no meaningful sense in which the voters can hold the majority party responsible for what the government has done or has not done. Nor shall we ever achieve democracy in the United States until we teach our parties the language and logic of unity and discipline, and so render them capable of taking part in a political system based on the idea of responsibility. Like the abolish-the-parties-forthwith writers, the responsible-parties school—especially the authors of the Parties Committee report—propose a number of specific party reforms, to which we shall direct the reader's attention at a later point in our argument.

108 "Toward a More Responsible Two-Party System," *American Political Science Review,* Vol. XLIV (September, 1950), Supplement. This report was also published in 1950 by Rinehart and Company.

109 For a detailed summary and critical evaluation of this position, see Ranney, *op. cit.;* and Chapter 22 of this book.

The Defenders of the Existing American Party System. A third group of writers have defended the existing American party system against the attacks of both the anti-party writers and the advocates of making the parties more centralized and disciplined, but have directed their fire mainly at the latter. The most prominent exposition of this point of view is Pendleton Herring's *The Politics of Democracy* (1940); [110] but it has been echoed by such critics of the Parties Committee report as Julius Turner, T. William Goodman, Murray S. Stedman, Jr., and Herbert Sonthoff. [111]

Their case for the existing American party system runs along the following general lines: British parties are appropriate to the relatively homogeneous and high-consensus British community, but not to the heterogeneous, diversified, and lower-consensus American community. American parties, as now organized, are excellent instrumentalities for moderating and compromising the profound conflicts, actual and potential, among various kinds of interest groups, sectional, economic, racial, religious, etc., that are peculiar to American politics. The process of forming and expressing the popular will is far more complicated than the advocates of centralized parties realize; and the persistence of American parties in their present form is evidence of popular satisfaction with their performance. Only when and as the nature of the American community has undergone drastic change, they conclude, will increased centralization of American parties be possible or make any sense.

Conclusion

The present chapter completes our preliminary canvass of the basic theoretical questions that, in our judgment, must be taken into account in any attempt to evaluate the American party system as an agency of democratic government. It is our hope, concretely, that these chapters will have helped the reader to identify some of the problems that are implicit in such questions as the following: What is democracy? Is it the kind of government we want in the United States? What kind of institutional requirements does it impose? Along what lines have communities in the past actually attempted to satisfy those requirements? Where have political parties fitted into the picture? What have men said about political parties?

This book rests upon the assumption that any careful appraisal of the desirability of the present American party system as an agency for popular consultation must begin with an attempt to answer these questions. Where predominantly factual answers have been called for, we have attempted to

---

[110] E. Pendleton Herring, *The Politics of Democracy* (New York: Rinehart & Company, Inc., 1940).

[111] Julius Turner, "Responsible Parties; A Dissent from the Floor," *American Political Science Review,* Vol. XLV (March, 1951), pp. 143-52; T. William Goodman, "How Much Political Party Centralization Do We Want?" *Journal of Politics,* Vol. XIII (November, 1951), pp. 536-61; and Murray S. Stedman, Jr., and Herbert Sonthoff, "Party Responsibility—A Critical Inquiry," *Western Political Quarterly,* Vol. IV (September, 1951), pp. 454-86.

provide them. Where the questions have been of such character that persons with differing values will answer them differently, we have sought to indicate what alternative answers are available, and, we trust, have encouraged the reader to choose that which is most nearly in accord with his own values.

Our next task is that of trying to find out what the existing American party system is actually like—the nature of its constituent elements, their relation to each other, to the total governing system, and to the community, and the role they perform in American government.

When we have completed this survey of the existing party system, however, we shall return to the theoretical questions we have raised in these first six chapters—and, in the light of what we have learned about the nature of the party system, attempt to deal with them.

PART THREE

The Structure of the American Party System

Chapter 7

TYPES OF AMERICAN PARTY SYSTEMS [1]

Why and How Party Systems Are Classified

WHAT IS A "PARTY SYSTEM"?

When we look at the facts of political party life in any governmental area, we find certain recurrent patterns of individual and group behavior reaching well back into the past and likely, by the same token, to persist in the future. These patterns lend themselves to being described as if the individuals involved were engaged in a game, with fairly definite and clearly understood rules, that goes on from election to election—although for the most part nobody is in position to *force* the individuals concerned to behave in accordance with those rules. The observer can, as he comes to understand the pattern better and better, get the relevant rules down in black and white, grasp the interrelations between them, and, provided he realizes that his "system" is merely an expository device and does not exist apart from the actual behavior of individuals and groups, safely call them a "system." "Party system," then, is the term which political scientists customarily apply to the rules of a community's party "game."

---

[1] Parts of this chapter were published in the *American Political Science Review*, Vol. XLVIII (June, 1954), pp. 477-85, under the title, "The American Party Systems," and are reprinted here by permission of E. M. Kirkpatrick, Executive Director of the American Political Science Association.

In Illinois, for example, the voters normally express their preferences as to governmental personnel and policy by shifting their votes back and forth between the Republican and Democratic parties; and so we say that Illinois has a "two-party system." The voters of the Netherlands, on the other hand, do not limit themselves in this fashion, and shift their votes back and forth among four or five or more parties; and so we say that the Dutch have a "multiple-party system."

The number of parties that receive the bulk of the votes and public offices, however, is by no means the only variable involved in the concept of "party systems." For example, the national "two-party system" of the United States, as we shall observe repeatedly in subsequent chapters, has the effect of blurring and suppressing basically divisive political issues, and thus helps to unite the community. The national "two-party system" of the Union of South Africa, on the other hand, has the effect of clearly posing basically divisive political issues, and thus helps to divide the community into two hostile camps.[2] And, again for example, the parties in the American national "two-party system" are financed in a manner quite different from that in which the parties in the British national "two-party system" are financed.

The variable which receives the most attention in the literature on political parties, however, is the number of parties that receive the bulk of the votes and public offices. By far the most commonly employed set of "types" of party systems[3] is that according to which party systems are "one-party," "two-party," or "multiple-party." Most discussions of particular party systems begin by assigning the system under investigation to one of these categories; and in the present chapter we shall confine our discussion to this one variable.

THE BASES FOR CLASSIFICATION

The question that serves as the basis for the table of categories just mentioned appears to be this: *How many* parties in the system being classified have been winning or are likely to win in the foreseeable future a significant share of the popular vote and thus of the elective public offices? The classifier answers this question in terms of the past behavior of the voters. Have most of them voted for a single party? If not, which of two alternative courses have they followed—divided their votes between two parties, or divided them among several parties? For the tacit premise of this table of categories is that the voters will behave in tomorrow's election pretty much as they behaved in yesterday's. The statement that a particular system is a two-party system, that is to say, rests upon a statement about the past and a rough prediction

---

[2] For descriptions of the party situation in South Africa in recent years, see Alexander Brady, *Democracy in the Dominions,* 2nd ed. (Toronto: University of Toronto Press, 1952), pp. 385-99; Arthur Keppel-Jones, "The Dilemma of South Africa," *Behind the Headlines,* Vol. V (November, 1950); and Austin F. Macdonald, "Politics in the Union of South Africa," *Annals of the American Academy of Political and Social Science,* Vol. CCLXXXVIII (July, 1953), pp. 140-52.

[3] Party systems of a certain "type" are those which, despite their differences in other respects, share a certain trait or set of traits in common.

about the future: the statement that voters' behavior in the past—or at least in the fairly recent past—has been such that neither of two parties could have been said, before any fairly recent election, to be assured of winning, and the prediction that either party therefore has a reasonably good chance of winning in any future election. The classifier's estimate of the future prospects of any party in any system, in other words, is and must be simply an extrapolation based on the statistics of its successes and failures in past elections.

On this showing, however, there appear to be not three but at least five possible types of party systems:

(1) *The multiple-party type.* To this type belongs any system in which at most elections in the fairly recent past (a) three or more parties have shared the bulk of the votes and public offices, and (b) no single party has won a majority of either votes or offices. The classic example of such a party system is the French, where, under both the Third and Fourth Republics, no single party has ever obtained a majority of the votes or offices; where from eight to fifteen parties normally hold seats in the national legislature; and where all governments have been coalitions of several parties.[4]

(2) *The two-party type.* To this type belongs any system in which at most elections in the fairly recent past (a) two parties have shared the bulk of the votes and public offices between them, (b) the winning party has gained a majority of the votes or offices or both, and (c) *each* of the two dominant parties has won majorities in a substantial number of elections. The American *national* party system,[5] as we shall see below, is an example of such a system.

(3) *The modified one-party type.* To this type belongs any system in which at most elections in the fairly recent past (a) one party has won all or nearly all the offices, but (b) the second party, though it has seldom won any offices, has normally received a substantial percentage of the votes and thus constitutes a significant center of organized party opposition. The party system of New Hampshire is a good example of this type. Since 1914, the Democrats there have won only six out of forty-three elections for president, United States senator, and governor—a mere 14 per cent of the total. However, the Democrats have never polled less than 30 per cent of the vote, and in 86 per cent of the elections they have polled over 40 per cent of the vote. Consequently, the Republican party in New Hampshire, while usually victorious in elections, normally faces strong opposition from the Democrats and therefore cannot afford to act as though it faced no significant opposition whatever.

(4) *The one-party type.* To this type belongs any system in which at most

[4] Multiple-party systems are not unknown to American politics. In New York City, for example, it is not uncommon for as many as five parties to make serious bids for the various city offices. Fiorello H. La Guardia ran for public office in New York, at one time or another, under no less than nine different party labels! In fact, he apparently became so unimpressed by party labels and tickets that he once boasted, "Listen, I could run on a laundry ticket and be elected!": Cf. Hugh A. Bone, "Political Parties in New York City," *American Political Science Review,* Vol. XL (April, 1946), pp. 272-82.

[5] Not, for reasons that will be explained below, the *entire* American party system.

elections in the fairly recent past (a) one party has won all or nearly all of the offices, and (b) the second party has usually received only a small percentage of the popular votes. The party system in Georgia is a good example of this type. Since 1914, the Georgia Republicans have won not a single contest for presidential electors, United States senator, or governor. In the forty-four most recent elections for those offices, moreover, they have won over 30 per cent of the vote in only two elections, and over 40 per cent in only one. The Republican party in Georgia, in other words, is not a serious organized opposition to the Democrats. And the difference between party systems like Georgia's and party systems like New Hampshire's seems sufficiently sharp and clear to justify distinguishing between the third and fourth types.

(5) *The totalitarian one-party type.* To this type belongs any system in which either (a) only one party has been permitted to participate in elections in the fairly recent past, or (b) any so-called parties other than the dominant single party that have participated are clearly fronts for the dominant party. The party systems of the Communist "people's democracies" are all examples of this type. The classic example here, however, is the party system of the U.S.S.R., whose Communist party is legally and actually the only party permitted to exist. Non-party persons, to be sure, are sometimes nominated for and elected to office. But their candidacies are possible only because *the* Party views them with approval; and normally there is only one candidate on the ballot for any office. Hence, in this kind of party system, an election is merely a "periodic public endorsement of the leadership." [6] The differences between this system and Georgia's are fundamental: In Georgia opposition parties *can* (and sometimes do) run candidates, and in any case such parties do not have to obtain the dominant party's permission to do so. In short, Georgia's one-party system operates in a context that permits (even if it does not encourage) organized party opposition; the Soviet Union's does not. And this seems to warrant the distinction between the "one-party type" of which Georgia's party system is an example, and the "totalitarian one-party type" of which Soviet Russia's is an example.

A METHOD OF CLASSIFICATION

We have thus far stated the criteria for each of our types only in very general and rough terms. We have not attempted to say, for example, *how many times* power must have changed hands between the parties in the recent past for us to be able to say that both parties have won from time to time (i.e., have "alternated" in power), or *how long* a period constitutes "the fairly recent past," or *how large a percentage* of the popular votes may fairly be regarded as "substantial." Yet these are questions that have to be answered, even if arbitrarily, before the classifier can begin to assign particular party

---

[6] Julian Towster, *Political Power in the U.S.S.R., 1917-1947* (New York: Oxford University Press, 1948), pp. 192-96.

systems to the various categories. And answering them requires the investigator to take at least the following steps:

First, he must determine for what period he is going to compile election statistics. This determination, unless he proposes to compile statistics for the entire electoral history of the system in question, must be to some extent arbitrary. But that will do no harm if those who are to use and criticize his results are given reason to believe that the period is long enough for the purposes of the classification he is attempting—which is a matter of giving them a critical date, since which time the system has apparently functioned in a fairly uniform manner.

Second, he must determine what offices are regarded by the parties and the voters as among the more desirable prizes. Among the relevant questions here are: The contests for what offices call out the largest votes? And in what contests do we find the parties campaigning, election by election, most energetically, most expensively, and on the largest scale? If, for example, the popular vote is usually twice as heavy for president of the United States as it is for the state auditor of public accounts in a particular state, and if the contending parties expend much more energy, money, and man-hours on the contests for the former office than for the latter, the former is evidently the more pertinent for the classifier's purpose.

Third, he must compile election statistics for as many of the more significant offices as the time and resources at his disposal permit. At the very least he must learn how many of the relevant contests each of the contending parties has won and what percentage of the vote it has polled in each.

Fourth, if he is simultaneously studying two or more party systems, he must tabulate his data in such fashion as to show how the percentages of victories and percentages of popular votes received by the contending parties vary from system to system. What he is looking for here is telltale "clusters" in the data, which will help to determine the dividing lines between his types.

Fifth, if no telltale clusters appear, or if the classifier is concerned with a single party system, he should compare his data with parallel data from party systems whose classification is already generally agreed upon, and use the generally accepted dividing lines.

In short, he must give such specific content to the general criteria of party-system types as seem practicable to him in the circumstances, and must make clear to himself and others his reasons for proceeding thus far and no further. The last word as to the adequacy of his reasons lies, operationally speaking, with those of his colleagues who are called upon to read and criticize his work —that is, with other workers in his part of the scholarly community. If his reasons fail to pass muster with them, there is nothing for it but for him to revise his dividing lines and classifications in the light of their criticism.[7]

[7] On the whole question of the last word in such matters, see the brilliant analysis of the workings of the scholarly community in Michael Polanyi, *The Logic of Liberty* (Chicago: University of Chicago Press, 1951).

Types of American Party Systems

WHY "SYSTEMS"?

By far the most common classification used in analyzing American party conflict is that which takes as its point of departure the concept "the American two-party system." This usage rests upon the assumption that there *is* a single over-all party system in this country, and the further assumption that that system is a *two-party* system.[8] All this, clearly, wants some thinking about, since we all know that there is no two-party system in, for example, Georgia or Mississippi or South Carolina. We also know that there are many areas of party conflict in the United States—states, counties, cities, wards, precincts— where, now for this reason, now for that, the party system does not fit the two-party pattern. In other words, we have not one but many party systems (as we have defined that term above) in the United States, and by no means all of them are two-party systems. The familiar statement that "America has a two-party system" is, therefore, incorrect on the face of it.

Probably most of those who make this statement mean to say that the American *national* party system—that in which parties contest elections for national offices—is a two-party system. But to use the phrase "the American two-party system" as synonymous with "the American national two-party system" is inaccurate and can be highly misleading. This usage implies one of two things, neither of which is true: (a) that party conflict in all parts of America is essentially like that which takes place at the national level, which is to attribute a far greater degree of homogeneity and uniformity to American party conflict than the facts warrant; or (b) that the national party system is so much more important than the state and local party systems that, for all practical purposes, we can ignore the latter. But this is the reverse of true. For one thing, party conflict over national offices is fought out in elections that are held in *local* constituencies (the states and the congressional districts). No national official is elected by a homogeneous national constituency. The president, more than any other national official, might seem to be elected by national plebiscite; but even he owes his office to having won a series of contests in *state* constituencies. And certainly not all nor even nearly all the state and congressional-district constituencies have two-party systems. For another thing, there is perhaps no point on which writers on American politics are so generally agreed as that our state and local party organizations, taken collectively, are far more powerful than our national party organizations. As Professor Macmahon puts it, "Considered nationally political parties in the United States

---

[8] Cf. the statement by the Committee on Political Parties of the American Political Science Association that "the two-party system is so strongly rooted in the political traditions of this country, and public preference for it so well established that consideration of other possibilities seems entirely academic": "Toward a More Responsible Two-Party System," *American Political Science Review*, Vol. XLIV (September, 1950), Supplement, p. 18.

may be described as loose alliances [alliances, that is, of state and local party organizations] to win the stakes of power embodied in the presidency." [9] This usage, then, cannot be justified on the ground that the national party system overshadows the other American party systems as far as influencing the course of events is concerned.

In short, we must abandon the concept *"the* American two-party system," or at least begin to use it far more cautiously than we have been doing. No such system exists. And the only meaning that can sensibly be assigned to the phrase *"the* American party system" is that of a shorthand expression for the totality of party conflict in the United States. That is what it is intended to convey wherever it is used throughout this book. Using the term in this fashion will keep us reminded that there are party systems of at least three types operating in various parts of this country, and that "the American party system," insofar as we can properly speak of such a thing, is what you get when you lump them all together.

It is not necessary, for our purposes, to identify the type of party system operating in each precinct, ward, city, and county in the United States. The rest of this chapter will be devoted, however, to classifying the party systems that operate in forty-nine important governmental areas—in each of the forty-eight states and in the forty-eight taken together, that is, the nation as a whole.

THE STATE PARTY SYSTEMS

The Classifying Procedure. The forty-eight state party systems were classified by the following procedure. First, the period from 1914 to 1954 was selected because it eliminates most of the effects of the 1912 split in the Republican party—an abnormal and short-lived situation—and because it provides a period of four decades, which seems long enough to overcome the effects of any aberration from the state's "norm." Second, the results of all elections for three offices—president, United States senator, and governor—were compiled from figures published in the *World Almanac* and in the *Congressional Quarterly*. These offices were chosen because they are generally regarded as the most important and because they are the only offices voted upon by *statewide* constituencies in each of the forty-eight states. Third, when the resulting data were tabulated according to percentages of victories for each of the contending parties in all elections in each state, two clusters appeared: states in which the second party had won more than 25 per cent of all elections, and states in which it had won 25 per cent or less. The former were, without further investigation, classified as two-party states. Fourth, the remaining twenty-two states were classified as modified one-party or one-party in the following man-

<hr/>

[9] *Encyclopaedia of the Social Sciences* (New York: The Macmillan Company, 1937), Vol. XI, p. 596. See also E. E. Schattschneider, *Party Government* (New York: Rinehart & Company, Inc., 1942), pp. 66-67; and V. O. Key, Jr., *Politics, Parties, and Pressure Groups*, 3rd ed. (New York: Thomas Y. Crowell Company, 1952), Ch. 11.

ner: the percentages of the popular vote cast for the second party in each election in each state were tabulated and the results compared. Two sets of clusters were apparent: (1) states in which the second party had won over 30 per cent of the vote in over 70 per cent of all elections, and states in which the second party had done less well; and (2) states in which the second party had won over 40 per cent of the vote in over 30 per cent of all elections, and states in which the second party had done less well. Each state in which the second party's share of the popular vote was included in the higher of each of the two clusters was classified as a modified one-party state. All other states were classified as one-party.[10]

The Classifications. According to the criteria just outlined, the forty-eight state party systems in the United States fall into one or another of three types: two-party, modified one-party, and one-party. The particular states in each of the three categories are listed in Tables 2, 3, and 4 below. Figure 1 is a map of the state party systems as classified above.

TABLE 2   The Two-Party States

State	TOTAL OF ALL ELECTIONS Rep. Wins	Dem. Wins	3-P Wins	Per Cent of Second-Party Wins	State	TOTAL OF ALL ELECTIONS Rep. Wins	Dem. Wins	3-P Wins	Per Cent of Second-Party Wins
Arizona	12	33	0	26.7	Montana	9	25	0	26.5
California	24	11	1	33.3 *	Nebraska	33	13	1	29.8 *
Colorado	23	22	0	48.9	Nevada	12	26	0	31.6
Connecticut	31	16	0	34.0	New Jersey	25	14	0	35.9
Delaware	22	12	0	35.3	New Mexico	14	31	0	31.8
Idaho	28	18	0	39.1	New York	17	24	0	41.5
Illinois	21	15	0	41.7	Ohio	24	23	0	48.9
Indiana	21	13	0	38.2	Rhode Island	17	28	0	37.8
Maryland	12	23	0	34.3	Utah	13	21	0	38.2
Massachusetts	26	19	0	42.2	Washington	15	19	0	44.1
Michigan	30	15	0	33.3	West Virginia	12	22	0	35.3
Minnesota	28	9	4	37.8 *	Wisconsin	32	7	6	28.9 *
Missouri	13	22	0	37.1	Wyoming	16	21	0	43.2

* Second-party and thirty-party victories combined to make a total-opposition percentage.

[10] Admittedly, this method cannot show *trends*, but can only produce classifications on the basis of the percentages as of a given moment. According to it, for example, Pennsylvania and Oregon must be classified as modified one-party Republican states, and Virginia must be classified as a one-party Democratic state. In recent elections in each of these three states, however, the second party has won some notable electoral triumphs, and its position seems likely to improve even more in the years to come. For a criticism of the present writers' classifying procedures and a suggestion for improving upon them, see Joseph A. Schlesinger, "A Two-Dimensional Scheme for Classifying the States According to Degree of Inter-Party Competition," *American Political Science Review*, Vol. XLIX (December, 1955), pp. 1120-28.

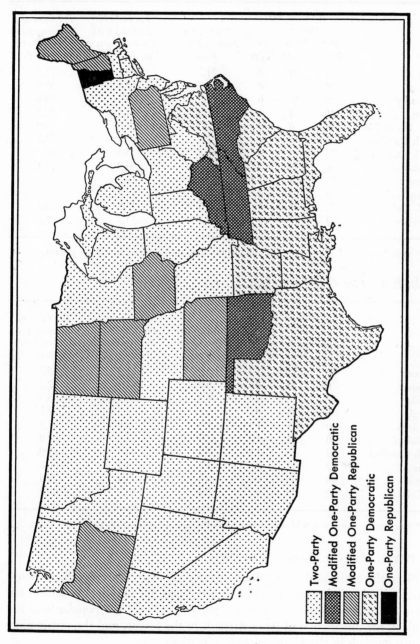

Figure 1. Political map of the state party systems.

TABLE 3 The Modified One-Party States

State	Rep. Wins	Dem. Wins	3-P Wins	Per Cent of Second-Party Wins	Per Cent of Elections with Second-Party Vote over 30%	Per Cent of Elections with Second-Party Vote over 40%
Iowa	36	10	0	21.7	89.1	71.7
Kansas	38	7	0	15.5	97.8	68.9
Kentucky	8	28	0	22.2	100.0	94.4
Maine	41	4	0	8.9	91.1	55.5
New Hampshire	40	6	0	13.0	100.0	86.9
North Carolina	1	35	0	2.8	77.8	30.7
North Dakota	37	8	0	17.8	75.5	57.8
Oklahoma	6	29	0	17.1	94.3	77.1
Oregon	27	8	1 *	25.0	89.1	56.8
Pennsylvania	28	8	0	22.2	91.7	66.7
South Dakota	36	9	0	20.0	97.8	73.3
Tennessee	4	42	0	8.7	71.7	32.6

* Second-party and thirty-party victories combined to make a total-opposition percentage.

TABLE 4 The One-Party States

State	Rep. Wins	Dem. Wins	3-P Wins	Per Cent of Second-Party Wins	Per Cent of Elections with Second-Party Vote over 30%	Per Cent of Elections with Second-Party Vote over 40%
Alabama	0	34	1 *	2.8	11.4	5.7
Arkansas	0	45	0	0.0	13.3	2.2
Florida	2	33	1	8.3	13.9	5.5
Georgia	0	45	0	0.0	2.2	2.2
Louisiana	0	33	1 *	2.9	8.8	5.9
Mississippi	0	33	1 *	2.9	2.9	2.9
South Carolina	0	33	1 *	2.9	5.9	5.9
Texas	2	43	0	4.4	15.5	6.7
Vermont	45	0	0	0.0	55.5	20.0
Virginia	2	35	0	5.4	40.5	10.8

* Third-party victories considered as second-party (i.e., opposition) victories.

THE NATIONAL PARTY SYSTEM

Since three kinds of national officials are popularly elected (all, as noted above, in local constituencies) in the United States, the appropriate indices for determining the nature of our national party system are the popular vote for president, the distribution of party strength in the Senate, and the distribution of party strength in the House of Representatives.

In the twenty-two presidential elections since the Civil War, the Republicans have won thirteen times (or 59 per cent of the time), the Democrats nine

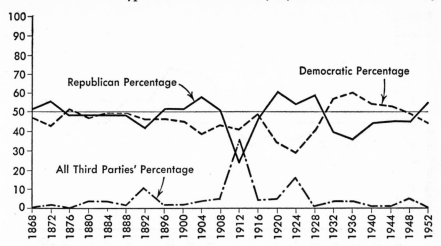

FIGURE 2. Distribution of popular vote for president, 1868-1952.

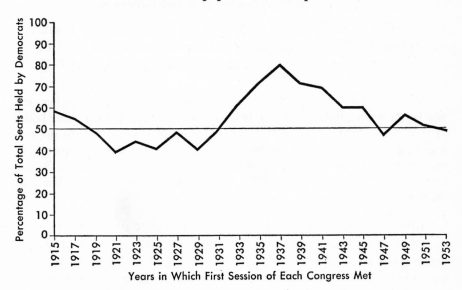

FIGURE 3. Distribution of party strength in the Senate, 1915-1953. *Highest percentage of total seats held by third-party members was 4 per cent, in sessions beginning in 1937 and 1939.*

times (or 41 per cent), and third parties never. If we study the popular vote, as shown in Figure 2, we find that third parties have won over 10 per cent of the vote in only three elections (those of 1892, 1912, and 1924). And in only four elections [11] have third parties won any votes in the electoral college.

[11] 1892—Weaver (Populist), 22; 1912—Roosevelt (Progressive), 88; 1924—LaFollette (Progressive), 13; 1948—Thurmond (States' Rights), 39.

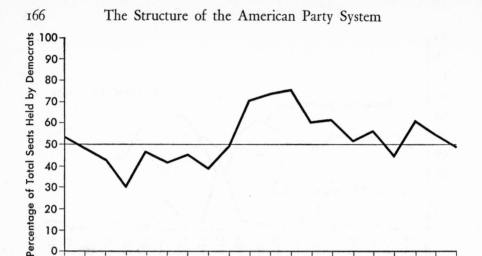

FIGURE 4. Distribution of party strength in the House of Representatives, 1915-1953. *Highest percentage of total seats held by
third-party members was 4 per cent, in session beginning in 1937.*

We further find that in the twenty Congresses since that whose first session began in 1915, the highest percentage of total seats ever held in either house
by third parties was 4 per cent.[12] The distribution of seats as between the two
major parties, as shown in Figures 3 and 4, indicates the same two-party pattern suggested by the distribution of popular votes for the presidency. On the
showing of these three indices, then, our national party system is clearly of
the two-party type.

INCIDENCE OF TYPES AMONG THE AMERICAN PARTY SYSTEMS

Of the forty-nine American party systems we have attempted to classify,
twenty-seven are of the two-party type, twelve are of the modified one-party
type, and ten are of the one-party type. Or, to put this in another way, twenty-
seven of these party systems are of the two-party variety, and twenty-two are
not.

On the basis of this evidence, then, we are perhaps justified in saying that
the American party system as a whole has more two-party systems than it has
systems of any other type. But our objections to the statement "The United
States has a two-party system," as set forth above, still stand.

[12] In the Senate, third parties held 4 per cent of the seats in the Congresses whose first sessions began in 1937 and 1939. In the House of Representatives, third parties held 4 per cent of the
seats in the Congress whose first session began in 1937.

Chapter 8

THE ONE-PARTY

SYSTEMS

The American complex of party systems, as we have seen, includes twenty-two that are not two-party systems. Nine southern states—Alabama, Arkansas, Florida, Georgia, Louisiana, Mississippi, South Carolina, Texas, and Virginia—which are Democratic, and the northern state of Vermont, which is Republican, all have one-party systems. Kentucky, North Carolina, Oklahoma, and Tennessee, all Democratic, and Iowa, Kansas, Maine, New Hampshire, North Dakota, Oregon, Pennsylvania, and South Dakota, all Republican, have modified one-party systems.[1]

For a number of reasons, no study of American political parties would be complete that did not give careful consideration to the workings, the special problems, and the significance of these systems. Some commentators, to be sure, regard them as anachronistic and doomed; some regard them as blots on the escutcheon of American democracy, and look forward to the day when educational processes, with perhaps an assist from time to time by the United States Supreme Court and liberal majorities in Congress, shall have eradicated the conditions that produce them. Meantime, however, for millions of Americans they are the only machinery for self-government at hand; moreover, some of the spokesmen of these millions think that the two-party systems provide less and poorer democracy, not more and better; and in any case the very existence of the one-party enclaves and one-party coastal regions in a two-party continent creates problems for the latter that can be understood only by grasping the character of the former. In the present chapter, therefore, we shall summarize what is known about the one-party and modified one-party systems —which, because they are regarded as atypical and under sentence of death, is not much—so that we may have it in mind as we undertake our canvass, throughout the rest of the book, of the two-party systems—about which, by the same token, more is known.[2]

[1] See Chapter 7 for the procedures by which these states have been classified.

[2] The current literature on parties, concentrating as it does upon "the" American party system, until recently had relatively little to offer on the one-party areas and even less on the

The Nature and Role of the "Solid South"

THE MEANING OF THE TERM

As it is normally used, the term "Solid South" refers to the Democratic party's nearly complete monopoly of popular votes and public offices—national, state, and local—in the eleven southern states that made up the Confederacy.[3] The monopoly dates back to the period just following the disappearance of the Reconstruction governments in these states, and seems likely to perpetuate itself for some time to come.

The story of one-party politics in America is, for the most part, the story of the Solid South, which has furnished most of the relevant data and all of the classic examples.

ITS PURPOSE

Although the "Negro problem" is by no means the sole explanation for and basis of the Solid South, it has been, in recent decades, the area in which the values, interests, and purposes of the southern whites have been most resolutely challenged from outside, and thus the area around which southern politics *had* to revolve if the southern whites were to defend their institutions against this challenge.[4] Consequently they have channeled large amounts of political energy into the attempt to maintain traditional Negro-white relations —mainly segregation and white supremacy—and have shaped their political institutions with this end mainly in view.

The Solid South is most strongly adhered to and supported by white persons living in the southern "black belts"—the areas with the heaviest concen-

modified one-party areas. V. O. Key, Jr., offers some discussion of one-party politics in his *Politics, Parties, and Pressure Groups,* 3rd ed. (New York: Thomas Y. Crowell Company, 1952), pp. 261-68, 425-28. Ch. III of Howard R. Penniman, *Sait's American Parties and Elections,* 4th ed. (New York: Appleton-Century-Crofts, 1948), is devoted to "Negro Suffrage and the Solid South." And Dayton D. McKean has some comments on southern politics in his *Party and Pressure Politics* (Boston: Houghton Mifflin Company, 1949), in Ch. IV, "The Sectional, Traditional, and Class Basis of Party." Fortunately, however, two detailed works on southern politics have recently been published: V. O. Key, Jr., *Southern Politics in State and Nation* (New York: Alfred A. Knopf, 1949); and Alexander Heard, *A Two-Party South?* (Chapel Hill, N. C.: University of North Carolina Press, 1952). Our analysis of the southern one-party and modified one-party · systems is largely drawn from these two works, with a special reliance upon Professor Key's impressive body of empirical data.

[3] There is some disagreement among modern scholars as to what states make up the "Solid South." Key holds that the term should include the eleven states that seceded from the Union to form the Confederacy: Alabama, Arkansas, Florida, Georgia, Louisiana, Mississippi, North Carolina, South Carolina, Tennessee, Texas, and Virginia: *Southern Politics in State and Nation,* p. 10. Penniman feels that Tennessee should be excluded from the list: *op. cit.,* p. 32. Others maintain that such "border states" as Kentucky, Oklahoma, Maryland, and Delaware should be added to the Confederate states. For purposes of the discussion in the text, however, the present writers will use the term "Solid South" in Key's sense—with the reminder to our readers that, according to our analysis in Chapter 8, North Carolina and Tennessee are considerably less "solid" than the other southern states.

[4] Cf. Key, *Southern Politics in State and Nation,* p. 5.

tration of Negroes, where the threat to white supremacy is most acutely felt. Although relatively few southern whites live in counties with over 40 per cent Negro population, the tone of southern politics seems to have been set in large part by the whites who do live in such areas.[5]

There are, as we have already indicated, other reasons than the race problem for the persistence of the Solid South. It tends to favor the dominance of certain white groups over other white groups, and is especially convenient for what one southern scholar calls the "banker-merchant-farmer-lawyer-doctor governing class."[6] But students of southern politics generally agree that the Solid South exists primarily to prevent any outside interference with southern Negro-white relationships, and that its main support comes from southern whites who are willing, at the margin, to subordinate all other political objectives to that one overriding purpose.[7]

ITS METHODS

In General. The basic strategy of the southern whites has developed along two main lines: excluding Negroes from any effective participation in politics at home, and maintaining a solid front in national politics against any intervention by the national government in southern race relations.

The first of these lines of strategy has been pursued by such tactics as (1) preventing Negroes from voting in general elections, through such devices as poll taxes, literacy and "understanding" tests, and terrorism, and (2) maintaining the "white primary," which has meant winning the adherence of all whites to the Democratic party, keeping all political conflict among whites *inside* the Democratic party, assuring complete control of that party by whites, and thus guaranteeing that decisions of the Democratic party—decisions made exclusively by whites—as to officeholders and public policies shall be the *final* decisions. And this has meant reducing the general elections to mere formalities, in which the nominees of the white-controlled Democratic party win as a matter of course.

The second line has been carried out in Congress, by solidly opposing all proposals for national intervention in southern race relations, and in Democratic national conventions, by opposing candidates and platform planks urging such intervention.

Let us examine each of these devices in somewhat greater detail:

In Elections. Here, as suggested above, we may usefully distinguish between devices calculated to keep Negroes from voting at all and measures aimed at excluding them from primaries.

[5] *Ibid.*, pp. 5-6. Cf. Penniman, *op. cit.*, pp. 32-33.

[6] Jasper B. Shannon, quoted in Heard, *op. cit.*, p. 145. See also Marian D. Irish, "The Southern One-Party System and National Politics," *Journal of Politics*, Vol. IV (February, 1942), pp. 80-81; and Key, *Politics, Parties, and Pressure Groups*, pp. 261-62.

[7] Cf. Key, *Southern Politics in State and Nation, passim;* Heard, *op. cit.*, pp. 20-29; and Irish, *op. cit.*, pp. 80-84.

MEASURES TO KEEP NEGROES FROM VOTING.[8] The Fifteenth Amendment to the
Constitution of the United States, adopted in 1870, provides that "the right of
citizens of the United States to vote shall not be denied or abridged by the
United States or by any State on account of race, color, or previous condition
of servitude" and that "the Congress shall have power to enforce this article
by appropriate legislation." In that same year, Congress passed the Enforcement Act, which prohibited all forms of racial discrimination in elections and
all kinds of violence, threats, or bribery calculated to discourage citizens from
exercising their voting rights. For a brief time Negroes did vote and hold
office on a large scale throughout the South, and the southern whites thereupon
became convinced that "white supremacy" must be regained at all costs.

Despite the Enforcement Act, the first method employed was *terrorism*. The
major device was the secret and thus nominally anonymous band of "activists"
called the Ku Klux Klan, which used now force and now the threat of force to
keep the Negroes away from the polls—and with such success that by the late
1870's white control had been restored in all the southern states. The Enforcement Act, which seems to have accomplished no purpose other than that of
angering the southern whites, was repealed in 1894.

Terroristic methods, however, never won the approval of most southern
whites. Well before the end of the nineteenth century, therefore, the dominant
groups in the South were seeking devices for getting around the Fifteenth
Amendment peacefully, legally, and, above all, constitutionally. That is, they
were seeking devices which, whether consistent with the letter and spirit of the
Constitution or not, at least would not be declared unconstitutional by the
courts. Considerable ingenuity went into the elaboration of stratagems of this
type. Their detailed pattern was by no means uniform from state to state, and
we shall attempt here only a broad outline of the tactics the southerners employed to keep Negroes from voting without openly violating the Fifteenth
and Fourteenth [9] Amendments and without at the same time excluding poor
whites as well.

Among the more popular devices was the *literacy test,* that is, the practice of requiring the prospective voter to prove his ability to read and write
before admitting him to the suffrage. At first this seemed a very effective barrier to Negro voting, since few Negroes knew how to read and write. But the

---

[8] One of the most complete summaries of the past history and present status of the various
southern techniques for keeping. Negroes from voting is offered in Key, *Southern Politics in State
and Nation*, Chs. 25-30. A useful short summary is presented in Penniman, *op. cit.*, Ch. III. The
discussion in the text is largely drawn from these two sources.

[9] The first section of the Fourteenth Amendment provides, among other things, that "no
State shall make or enforce any law which shall abridge the privileges or immunities of citizens
of the United States [in which class the Amendment placed all persons—including Negroes—
born or naturalized in the United States]; nor shall any State deprive any person of life, liberty,
or property, without due process of law; nor deny to any person within its jurisdiction the equal
protection of the laws." Both the "privileges or immunities" and "equal protection of the laws"
clauses were regarded as additional barriers against discriminatory treatment of Negroes in the
voting process.

inventors of the device had overlooked the fact that few poor whites knew how to read and write either, and that the literacy test could not be waived for the poor whites without running afoul of the courts on the point of discrimination. The problem, accordingly, became that of discovering an alternative test that poor whites could meet and that Negroes could not meet. For a time, the problem appeared to have been solved by the so-called "grandfather clauses"—stipulations in suffrage laws that all persons who had voted before the adoption of the Fifteenth Amendment, and also *the descendants of such persons,* could register without having to pass literacy tests. In 1915, however, the Supreme Court held Oklahoma's version of this loophole enactment unconstitutional.[10] Another device was the property-ownership test, that is, the rule permitting any citizen owning a certain amount of property to register without proving that he could read and write. Another was the "good character" provision, under which a citizen could register without passing a literacy test if he could convince the registrar of his "good character" and his grasp of the "duties and obligations of citizenship under a republican form of government." Still another was the "understanding" test, which made it possible even for the man unable to read the constitution of his state to register if he could satisfy the registrar of his ability to "understand and interpret" it.

As Key quite aptly points out, however, in discussing the present status of these stratagems, "a solemn recapitulation of the formal literacy and understanding requirements verges on the ridiculous. In practice literacy and understanding have little to do with the acquisition of the right to vote. Whether a person can register to vote depends on what the man down at the courthouse says, and he usually has the final say. It is how the tests are administered that matters."[11] His conclusion is that "the constitutionally prescribed test of ability to read and write a section of the constitution is rarely administered to whites. It is applied chiefly to Negroes, and not always to them."[12]

Another device used to disfranchise Negroes has been the *poll tax* requirement, under which payment of a capitation tax—ranging from $1.00 to $2.00 per year—is a prerequisite for admission to the suffrage. In Key's view, this device has received a great deal more publicity than it deserves: "Unquestionably," he writes, "the poll tax contributes to a reduction of popular participation in primaries and elections. Originally designed chiefly to discourage Negro participation, it became obsolete for that purpose, with the invention of the white primary. It became simply a tax on voting by whites and nothing more."[13] This conclusion is borne out by the fact that four southern states (Florida, Georgia, Louisiana, and North Carolina) have abolished the poll tax, and that others appear to be on the point of following their example.

[10] *Guinn v. United States,* 238 U.S. 347 (1915).
[11] *Southern Politics in State and Nation,* p. 560.
[12] *Ibid.,* p. 576.
[13] *Ibid.,* p. 579.

THE WHITE PRIMARY. In the eyes of the southern white who is determined to exclude the Negro from participation in politics, both the devices mentioned above have two great shortcomings. They tend, as we have noted already, to exclude poor whites as well as Negroes; and they are formal-legal devices, and thus vulnerable to attack before the national Supreme Court as violations of the Fourteenth and Fifteenth Amendments. The device on which he has mainly relied for ensuring white supremacy, therefore, is the white primary, which can fairly be described as the foundation upon which the Solid South finally rests.

The theory behind the white primary, briefly stated, is this: While the legal voting requirements for final elections are formal governmental matters, and thus subject to review by the courts, political parties are *private*, non-governmental associations, whose rules are *not* subject to review by the courts. The safest (that is, the most unassailable) way to exclude Negroes from effective political participation, therefore, is to organize a political party that will exclude Negroes from its deliberations, and to get all the whites to support that party in the general elections, so that its candidates will always win. And the indicated party, from the white southerner's point of view, was of course the Democratic—the Republicans having disqualified themselves by identifying themselves with Abraham Lincoln, emancipation, reconstruction, and the cause of the Negro in general. Many southerners still regard the Grand Old Party as "the agent of an occupying power."

The most powerful sanction the Solid South has at its command for seeing that all southern whites stick to the Democratic party in the general election lies in the punitive social pressures that can be—and are—exerted on those who bolt. As Key says, "Voting a Republican ticket in the general election came to be regarded not as the erraticism of a mugwump, but as a desecration of the memory of Robert E. Lee, disrespect for one's gallant forebears who fought at Gettysburg, and an open invitation to boycott one's grocery business." [14] In addition to this social pressure, however, the Democrats have adopted certain legal guarantees of loyalty as well. They attempt to ensure *voter* loyalty by closed-primary laws that exclude voters from the primary election unless they declare their adherence to party principles and formally commit themselves to supporting the party's candidates in the final election. To ensure loyalty on the part of *candidates,* all the southern states except Tennessee confront the potential bolter with a flat legal provision to the effect that a candidate defeated in the primary cannot run in the general election as an independent, and that all candidates in the primary must take a pledge not to oppose the winner of the primary in the general election. Although the candidate oaths are sometimes violated with legal impunity (for reasons to be noted in detail in Chapter 11), they appear to be taken far more seriously than the voters' oaths, and are, in general (evidently because of the *extra*legal sanctions

[14] *Ibid.,* pp. 424-25.

that can be visited upon the bolter) quite effective for ensuring the finality of the Democratic primary.[15]

The white primary appears to have sprung up in the southern states simultaneously with the direct primary, and, with occasional local exceptions, it has been employed over the entire South ever since. For several decades, it was assumed to be beyond attack constitutionally, because, as noted above, the southerners considered the Democratic party in the South a purely private association, not subject to regulation even by the state governments. Until 1944, moreover, the Supreme Court accepted that view of the matter, with only the proviso that the state statutes remain silent on the subject of the eligibility of Negroes to vote in Democratic primaries. For example, in 1923, when the Texas legislature passed a law excluding Negroes from participating in Democratic primaries, the Court ruled that the law violated the "equal protection" clause of the Fourteenth Amendment.[16] The Texas legislature promptly passed a further law, authorizing the Democratic party authorities to exclude Negroes from the party's primaries—which the State Executive Committee of the party proceeded at once to do. But this statute was also declared unconstitutional, on the ground that the party committee, in acting under authority specifically granted by the state, had become an organ of the state, and that its exclusion rule accordingly violated the Fourteenth Amendment.[17] The Texas legislature then repealed all its laws on such matters, and the initiative passed to the state convention of the party, which forthwith adopted a Negro-exclusion rule. In the case of *Grovey v. Townsend* (1935), the Supreme Court made the decision the southern whites had their hearts set on: Since the Democratic party was at last acting purely as a private association, its rule, the Court held, could not violate the Fourteenth Amendment.[18] The private-association theory—and the white primary—had apparently been incorporated in the law of the land.

In 1941, however, the Supreme Court upset the apple cart again. In a case involving fraud in a New Orleans Democratic primary, the Court took the novel position that where the primary is in effect the final election, the national government is empowered to regulate it.[19] And finally, in 1944, in the case of *Smith v. Allwright,* the Court specifically overruled the decision in *Grovey v. Townsend.* Since the Democratic primary is an integral part of the machinery of elections in the state of Texas, it declared, and since the primary is in some respects regulated by the state of Texas, the executive committee of the Democratic party is acting as an agent of the state when it discriminates against Negroes; the Committee's discriminatory rules are, there-

---

[15] *Ibid.,* Ch. 20.
[16] *Nixon v. Herndon,* 273 U.S. 536 (1927).
[17] *Nixon v. Condon,* 286 U.S. 73 (1932).
[18] *Grovey v. Townsend,* 295 U.S. 45 (1935).
[19] *United States v. Classic,* 313 U.S. 299 (1941).

fore, no less unconstitutional than they would be if adopted by the state legislature.[20]

The decision in *Smith v. Allwright* destroyed the whole private-association theory on which the white primary was based, and left the southern states no choice but to admit Negroes to their Democratic primaries. They reacted to the new legal bombshell in various ways. The states in which the incidence of Negroes is smallest (Florida, Texas, Tennessee, North Carolina, and Virginia) and a few others (Arkansas and Louisiana) did not even try to circumvent the Court's ruling. The "black-belt" states—South Carolina, Alabama, Georgia, and Mississippi—made some attempt, by statute or constitutional amendment, to keep their Democratic primaries closed against Negroes. But to no avail, since each new dodge either proved ineffective or was struck down by the courts.[21] The warranted conclusion seems to be that the white primary is legally and constitutionally dead, and that Negroes are going to participate in Democratic primaries in the South in ever-increasing numbers.[22]

In Congress. The Solid South relies on maintaining a united front in national politics against any intervention by the national government in southern race relations. Its major operations in this connection are conducted in Congress, where southern representatives and senators hold the line against Yankee interference year after year by making the most of three main tactical weapons, used either singly or in combination. These are bloc voting, the filibuster, and the exploitation of committee chairmanships.

BLOC VOTING. Key has studied the voting records of southern senators and representatives on major roll calls in seven sessions in the Senate and four sessions in the House between 1933 and 1945.[23] His conclusions are as follows: The votes of southern congressmen show a higher degree of "cohesion" than those of Republicans and nonsouthern Democrats. While the southern congressmen do not by any means vote together on all issues, where any question involving national intervention in race relations is at stake—anti-lynch bills, for example, or proposals to add antisegregation clauses to bills for federal aid to state schools, or proposed appropriations for a national Committee on Fair Employment Practices—all the southern senators and over 90 per cent of the southern representatives consistently vote in what amounts to a bloc. Because of the higher level of discipline in the House than in the Senate, southern representatives also vote quite solidly on certain other issues, although, says Key, "the inference to be drawn from House behavior is similar to that deducible from Senate voting: southern attitude toward the Negro provides the bedrock of southern sectionalism." [24]

[20] *Smith v. Allwright*, 321 U.S. 649 (1944).
[21] See Key, *Southern Politics in State and Nation*, pp. 625-43, for a summary of southern attempts to get around the decision in *Smith v. Allwright*.
[22] Cf. *ibid.*, pp. 642-43.
[23] *Ibid.*, Chs. 16 and 17.
[24] *Ibid.*, p. 372.

Since there are currently twenty-two southern senators out of a total of ninety-six in the Senate (21.8 per cent), and 106 southern representatives out of a total of 435 in the House (24.3 per cent), nothing short of determined and united action by the Republicans and nonsouthern Democrats can put across a measure involving interference in race relations—even if it can be brought to a vote. This, as we shall observe in detail below, the southerners can usually prevent in the Senate if not in the House.

SENATE FILIBUSTERS. In 1890, a group of Republican senators introduced the "Force Bill," which if passed would have empowered the federal government to supervise southern elections in order to protect Negroes against disfranchisement. The bill clearly had enough Republican and nonsouthern Democratic support to assure its passage; but despite that fact it never came to a vote. Why? Because for twenty-nine long and weary days, a succession of southern senators spoke against it, and kept everyone on notice that they would continue to speak against it until it was dropped. And since the Senate rules provided no form of cloture—no procedural device for shutting off debate so that a vote could be taken—when the pressure of other business became so great that it could no longer be ignored, the proponents of the Force Bill finally admitted defeat, dropped the bill, and thus freed the Senate to turn its attention to other matters.

This episode constituted the first major "filibuster," that is, the first instance of continuous talking by a Senate minority to prevent the taking of a vote. There have been others as and when the Solid South has been sorely pressed. And even today the filibuster, though not quite the "absolute" weapon it was in 1890, is still the defensive weapon the southern (and also every other regional or "special-interest") minority reaches for when all else has failed. This is still possible because of the extreme difficulty of obtaining cloture under the Senate rules.

The story of past attempts to obtain an effective cloture rule in the Senate tells us a great deal not only about the techniques and purposes of the Solid South, but also about one of the most important minoritarian aspects of our governmental structure. The first successful attempt to obtain some kind of cloture rule was made in 1917, during the administration of Woodrow Wilson. After a filibuster by what Wilson called "a little band of willful men" against a bill for arming merchant ships, the Senate adopted Rule XXII, the purpose of which was to make possible the "limitation" of debate. It provided that two days after the presentation of a petition for the close of debate signed by at least sixteen senators, the presiding officer must put the question, itself nondebatable, whether debate should now cease. If two-thirds of the senators present and voting vote Yes on this question, the presiding officer must then apply cloture, and the substantive measure must be voted upon forthwith.

In point of fact, Rule XXII has not proved an effective check against filibusters. Even when—as rarely happens—all the senators are present and voting, only thirty-three votes are needed to block a cloture motion; in a typical Senate session the number needed is considerably less than that, and hence not many more than the southern senators themselves can muster. In the period from 1917 to 1946, nineteen cloture motions were presented, but only four were passed. And among the measures on which cloture was rejected were, as we would expect from the foregoing discussion, two anti-lynch bills, three anti–poll tax bills, and two F.E.P.C. bills.

The two-thirds requirement, then, always made cloture hard to invoke. And in due course it was made even harder by two unprecedented rulings from the chair as to the kind of measures to which it could be applied: (1) In 1946, when cloture was being sought against an anti-F.E.P.C. filibuster, President pro tem Kenneth McKellar (D.—Tenn.) ruled that Rule XXII applies only to bills, and is not applicable to debate on proposed amendments to the Journal, the latter being what the southern filibusterers were nominally talking about. (2) In 1948, when cloture was attempted against a filibuster on an anti–poll tax bill, President pro tem Arthur Vandenberg (R.—Mich.) ruled that *motions to consider* a particular piece of legislation are "procedural" matters and thus outside the scope of Rule XXII, which, he said, applies only to debate on "substantive" matters, such as, for example, the *content* of a bill. His ruling was appealed—i.e., put to a vote of the Senate membership. But it was sustained, and the day on which the Senate would turn its back on the filibuster, and on the minority veto that it involves, indefinitely postponed.

The most recent major attempt to strengthen Rule XXII and discourage filibustering occurred in 1949; but it also, in the end, discouraged cloture and strengthened the filibuster. The Truman Democrats, unambiguously committed to a program of national civil rights legislation on behalf of Negroes, had just chalked up their surprising victory in the 1948 elections, and had come into the first session of the Senate in 1949 determined to reverse the McKellar and Vandenberg rulings—that is, to make cloture at least as easy to invoke as it had been before 1946. On February 28, 1949, accordingly, the Senate began to debate the Wherry-Hayden resolution, whose purpose was to seal off the "escape hatches" in the old rule. The southerners responded by launching a typical filibuster; on March 9, thirty-three senators—sixteen Republicans and seventeen Democrats—presented a cloture petition. Vice-President Barkley (D.—Ky.), specifically reversing Vandenberg, ruled that the cloture motion was in order, on the ground that Rule XXII *is* applicable to matters such as a proposed change in Senate rules. His ruling also was appealed to the Senate membership, which *reversed* it by a vote of 46 to 41.[25] Nor was that all. The Senate soon after adopted a substitute amendment to Rule XXII which (a) *specifically exempts* from cloture motions to revise the rules, e.g. motions to revise the cloture rule itself, and (b) requires a two-thirds vote *of the entire Senate membership* to invoke cloture on all other motions. At present, therefore, "debate" can be choked off—and filibusters ended—only if sixty-four

[25] Of the twenty-two senators from the Solid South, nineteen voted to overrule, two (Kefauver of Tennessee and Pepper of Florida) voted to sustain, and one was absent.

senators can be persuaded to vote Yes on the relevant motion. Since eighty to eighty-five senators present and voting is a larger-than-normal number, and since the southern and border senators can normally be counted on to turn up in full force when cloture is being attempted on a civil-rights issue, the new version of Rule XXII strengthens rather than weakens the filibuster as an absolute veto weapon in the hands of any substantial Senate minority. The effect has been to shore up, for the Solid South, a traditional "situation of strength" that many observers had expected to go to pieces long ago.[26]

The reader must not, however, get the impression that only the Solid South is opposed to the adoption of an effective cloture rule. The vote on the Barkley ruling in March, 1949, was, as we have noted, 46 to 41. That vote indicated that when the chips were down, a considerable number of *non-*southern senators voted in favor of the filibuster. Moreover, the character of the 1949 Senate debate on changing Rule XXII bears out the same point. Nearly every speaker in that debate was content to discuss the problem in majority-rule-versus-minority-rights terms, and no senator's voice was heard arguing that these terms were inappropriate. And the Senate divided, from this point of view, into three rather distinct groups, each taking a distinct position: (1) *The southerners* argued in favor of "freedom of speech" in the Senate, opposed *any* kind of "gag rule" (their term for *any* form of cloture), and, in effect, asked for an absolute veto power not only for the South but for *any* minority, though they made no secret of the fact that they themselves value the filibuster as a weapon for protecting the southern white minority against northern majorities. Senator Russell Long of Louisiana stated this position with crystal clarity:

Today the United States Senate stands as the last great protector of the rights of the minority. Why is that true? It is because of the right of unlimited debate in these halls. A mere handful of men, armed with sincere conviction, can hold off the majority for days on end. The minority, through the right of unlimited debate, may test the determination and the conscience as well as the endurance of the majority. . . . Today we of the South are in the minority, Mr. President. We insist that the rules designed to protect the minority remain unchanged. Would not any minority do the same? [27]

(2) *The northern liberals* of both parties were accused by the other two groups of aiming at cloture by simple majorities of those present and voting, although in their statements on the floor the liberals' position appeared to be that of settling for a restoration of cloture to its pre-1946 status by a reversal of the McKellar and Vandenberg rulings. This group, which had little to say in the

[26] See Bertram M. Gross, *The Legislative Struggle* (New York: McGraw-Hill Book Company, Inc., 1953), pp. 375-79, for a useful short summary of the history, recent developments concerning, and present status of the filibuster. For a more extended discussion of the earlier history of the filibuster, see Franklin L. Burdette, *Filibustering in the Senate* (Princeton, N. J.: Princeton University Press, 1940).

[27] *Congressional Record*, Vol. 95, Part 2, p. 1719 (March 2, 1949).

debate, apparently looked for leadership to such senators as Humphrey (D.—Minn.), Douglas (D.—Ill.), Lehman (D.—N. Y.), and Ives (R.—N. Y.). (3) *The corn-belt Republicans* criticized the two positions just noted as too extreme, and argued that the cloture rule should be neither so easy to invoke as to threaten free discussion nor so difficult to invoke as to transform the right to discuss into an absolute power to veto. Senator Wherry (R.—Neb.), the main spokesman for this group, argued that while "the minority has rights that are just as inviolable as those of the majority," still "an *overwhelming* majority of the Senate, such as *two-thirds,* also have rights, and so do the people whom they represent." [28]

The present version of Rule XXII, which locates a highly effective though not necessarily final veto power in any fairly substantial Senate minority, evidently represents the third group's notion of compromise between the two extremes. The filibuster, in consequence, remains an established and significant part of our governmental machinery. Moreover, despite the fact that actual, full-fledged filibusters are staged relatively infrequently, the *threat*—the ever-present *possibility*—of a filibuster is a major influence upon the way the Senate goes about its business. This point was made clear in a recent statement by Senator Clinton Anderson (D.—N. Mex.), a member of the liberal anti-filibuster group:

> I am not suggesting that the filibuster is the regular order of the day on this floor. It does not have to be. However infrequently the hammer on the filibuster gun is drawn back and cocked, this veto power of the minority over the will of the majority is, as all of us well know, a factor never overlooked in legislative drafting, appropriations, strategy, and tactics in the Senate of the United States. It affects and conditions every piece of legislation from the time it is a twinkle in the eye of its parent through every stage of gestation and birth. Considering the fact that, under rule XXII, the majority at all times functions by the consent of the minority, it is surprising that we accomplish as much as we do. . . .[29]

Not only is there no immediate prospect of anyone's mobilizing against the filibuster the kind of determined opposition that would be needed in order to abolish it; it clearly has, for the moment at least, a kind of majority support that makes it, properly speaking, incorrect to speak of the issue involved as one between majority rule and minority rights. Since the majority of one house of our popularly elected national legislature wills its continuance, the majoritarian is on doubtful ground when he demands its immediate abolition. And, in acquiescing in its continuance, the majority of the senators consciously agree to the continuance of the Solid South as a part of our political machinery.

---

[28] *Ibid.,* p. 1589. Italics added. Note that both the Republican senators from each of several states (Indiana, North Dakota, South Dakota, Kansas, and Nebraska) voted to overrule Barkley; while both Republican senators from Vermont, Maine, New Jersey, Massachusetts, and Wisconsin voted to sustain him: *ibid.,* p. 2274.

[29] *Congressional Record,* Vol. 100, Part 1, p. 330 (January 18, 1954).

Two points are worth emphasizing here. First, while the Solid South needs the filibuster to accomplish its purposes, and can be counted on to fight sturdily any attempt to abolish it, it is not itself sufficiently powerful to perpetuate the filibuster. Secondly, to the extent that the filibuster *is* indispensable to the Solid South's survival, it owes its present existence to the support given it, willingly or not, from other parts of the country by persons and groups with axes of their own to grind. We shall return to this general problem in Chapter 20.

WINNING AND EXPLOITING COMMITTEE CHAIRMANSHIPS. The chairman of a congressional committee does not have the *last* word on any important aspect of his committee's business. His position, nevertheless, is a highly strategic one, which gives him powers that are much sought after under our system of government. He arranges hearings, calls meetings, assumes the primary responsibility for getting any bill his committee reports considered on the floor, and serves on conference committees if the two houses disagree on a bill his committee has been concerned with. And while his decision on any matter *can* be overridden by a majority of his committee, he is in practice left free to act on many matters as he sees fit.[30]

In both Houses of Congress the committee chairmen are picked according to the "seniority rule," which provides that the chairman of a given standing committee shall be that member of the majority party with the longest continuous service on the committee. Since they face no real Republican opposition in their home constituencies, it is easier for southern Democrats than for northern Democrats to pile up seniority; for the latter not only for the most part face such opposition but, at best, get beaten by it from time to time, and have to begin the weary trudge up the mountain of seniority all over again if and when they recapture their seats. Thus when the Democrats control Congress, southern Democrats get, as a matter of course, a higher percentage of committee chairmanships than their share of total Democratic representation warrants.

Table 5 shows the disparity between the number of Democratic seats held by southerners in thirteen recent Congresses and the number of committee chairmanships they enjoyed during the same period.

What we find here is that in most (but not all) Democratically controlled Congresses the southern Democrats have held a higher percentage of the committee chairmanships than their share of Democratic representation in the two houses would, seniority apart, entitle them to. And, although we have not attempted to weight the above figures for the importance of the particular chairmanships held, the southern Democrats naturally make it their business to seek berths on key committees.

Thus, while it is not accurate to say that the southern Democrats "overwhelmingly dominate" committee chairmanships in Congress when the Demo-

[30] Joseph P. Chamberlain, *Legislative Processes, National and State* (New York: D. Appleton-Century Company, 1936), pp. 80-82.

TABLE 5   *Percentage Ratio of Committee Chairmanships Held by Southern Democrats* [31]

| | SENATE | | HOUSE OF REPRESENTATIVES | |
| | | | | |
Congress	Percentage Ratio of Southern Dems. to All Dems.	Per Cent of All Chairman-ships Held by Southern Dems.	Percentage Ratio of Southern Dems. to All Dems.	Per Cent of All Chairman-ships Held by Southern Dems.
63rd (1913)	43.1	42.5	34.8	51.7
64th (1915)	39.4	41.3	44.1	50.0
65th (1917)	40.7	44.0	47.6	47.5
72nd (1931)	Republican control		46.3	57.3
73rd (1933)	36.6	39.4	32.6	57.3
74th (1935)	31.8	36.3	31.0	46.8
75th (1937)	29.3	36.3	30.0	44.6
76th (1939)	31.8	39.4	38.3	38.2
77th (1941)	33.8	48.4	37.7	34.0
78th (1943)	38.6	42.4	46.8	48.9
79th (1945)	40.0	42.4	43.1	51.0
81st (1949)	40.7	40.0	39.5	47.3
82nd (1951)	44.9	53.3	44.4	47.3

crats are in power, they do fare better in this regard, man for man, than the northern Democrats. And, while it is a considerably less potent weapon than their bloc voting or the filibuster, their possession of committee chairmanships does enhance their veto power over unwelcome legislative proposals.

In Democratic National Conventions. The final device of southern strategy is that of maintaining a solid front in Democratic national conventions against candidates and platform resolutions favoring national intervention in southern race relations. Southern voting power in recent conventions is shown in Table 6.

As Table 6 demonstrates, the Solid South's voting strength in Democratic conventions since 1920 has varied little: it has never risen above 24.1 per cent or fallen below 22.5 per cent. Here as elsewhere the South is distinctly a minority; but, in this as in other areas, it has maximized its influence over events by keeping its rank and file in line and voting them *en bloc.*

The bargaining power of the southern Democrats has traditionally been enhanced by their claim that they constitute the "hard core" of Democratic strength, in Congress and in presidential elections alike. The South, as they are always able to remind their northern confreres, contributes the permanent and irreducible base of electoral votes on which national Democratic victory must be built. Table 7 shows the extent to which this claim is based on solid fact.

[31] These figures are drawn from the *Congressional Directory* (Washington, D. C.: U.S. Government Printing Office), various issues from 1913 to 1951.

TABLE 6   *Southern Voting Power in Democratic National Conventions* [32]

Convention Year	Total Votes	Southern Votes	Southern Per Cent of Total Votes
1920	1083	252	23.2
1924	1098	252	22.9
1928	1100	252	22.8
1932	1154	262	22.7
1936	1100	248	22.5
1940	1100	248	22.5
1944	1176	276	23.4
1948	1234	298	24.1
1952	1230	290	23.5

The figures in Table 7 indicate that in each of the Democratic *losing* years since 1900, the Solid South has furnished over 70 per cent of the Democrats' total electoral votes. But an equally important question is this: How necessary have the southern electoral votes been to the Democrats in victorious years?

TABLE 7   *Southern Share of Democratic Votes in the Electoral College, 1900-1952* [33]

Election	Total Democratic Votes	Southern Democratic Votes	Per Cent of Total Democratic Votes Cast by Southern Electors
1900	155	112	72.2
1904	140	120	85.7
1908	162	120	74.0
1912	435	126	28.9
1916	277	126	45.4
1920	127	114	89.7
1924	136	126	92.6
1928	87	64	73.5
1932	472	124	26.2
1936	523	124	23.7
1940	449	124	27.6
1944	432	127	29.6
1948	303	88	29.0
1952	89	71	79.7

[32] The figures for the conventions from 1920 to 1948 are drawn from the various Official Proceedings for each of the conventions, published by the Democratic National Committee. The figures for the 1952 convention are drawn from the New York *Times*.

[33] These figures are drawn from the *World Almanac*, published by the New York *World-Telegram and Sun*.

Table 8 shows what the results would have been if, in each of these years, all southern electoral votes had gone to the Republicans instead of to the Democrats.

TABLE 8   Importance of Southern Electoral Votes to Democratic Victories

Election Year	Actual Results		Results if All Southern Votes Had Gone to GOP	
	REP.	DEM.	REP.	DEM.
1912	96 *	435	222	309
1916	254	277	380	151
1932	59	472	183	348
1936	8	523	132	399
1940	82	449	206	325
1944	99	432	226	305
1948	228 *	303	316	215

* Third-party vote added to Republican total.

In two of the seven victorious Democratic years (1916 and 1948), the Democrats indeed could not have won without *some* southern votes. In the other five winning years, they could have. The role of southern electoral votes in Democratic presidential campaigns, then, seems to be this: If the Democrats carry most of the big northern industrial states plus either the mountain states or the border states, they do not need the southern electoral votes at all. If, however, the Republicans cut heavily into Democratic strength in the industrial, border, or mountain states, the Democratic candidate cannot win without the southern votes. And finally, if the Republicans generally sweep the nation, as they did in the 1920's and in 1952, southern votes are about all that keep the Democratic party from being completely swamped.

It would seem, therefore, that the northern Democrats still have something to gain by placating the Solid South. Their main prospects for capturing the presidency, on the other hand, are seldom much better than their prospects of carrying the industrial, border, and mountain states. And this helps to explain why, from the 1930's to the present, they have been increasingly reluctant to abandon—or even to soft-pedal—ideas and proposals, such as federal civil-rights programs, that presumably are attractive to voters in the nonsouthern states but anathema to southerners.

It also explains why the South does not today enjoy the kind of veto power in Democratic conventions that it exercised as a matter of course before the Roosevelt era. One of the earliest manifestations of this change was the abandonment, in 1936, of the "two-thirds rule" in the national conventions. From the very beginning of their history, Democratic conventions kept in force a rule requiring a two-thirds majority of all votes to nominate presidential and vice-presidential candidates. In practice, the rule meant that successful candidates for these nominations needed either to land the southern delegations *en bloc,* to split them, or to mobilize almost all the nonsouthern votes. The result was that the southerners, so long as they stuck together, could eliminate pretty much any candidate unacceptable to them.

In the 1932 convention, an attempt by the Roosevelt forces to substitute a simple majority for the two-thirds rule met with determined southern opposition, and was not brought to a vote. In the 1936 convention, however, the Roosevelt forces were in complete command, and the rules committee's recommendation for abolition of the rule was presented to the convention by its chairman, Bennett Champ Clark of Missouri, whose father had lost the presidential nomination in 1912 because he could not turn a simple majority into the required two-thirds majority.[34] In his presentation speech Clark made many laudatory references to the "Jeffersonian principle of the rule of the majority," and concluded that abolishing the two-thirds rule posed no "sectional issue, because no section of the United States could be injured or affronted by being subjected to the will of the majority of the Democratic National Convention. And, thank God, Mr. President, the Democratic Party is no longer a sectional party; it has become a great national party! (Applause and cheers)."[35] The two-thirds rule was duly abrogated, and the southerners' veto-power in Democratic national conventions, at least in its traditional form, went by the board.[36]

The Southern Democratic Parties

With the above facts in mind as to the general nature, purposes, and techniques of the Solid South, let us turn to a consideration of the kind of parties and politics the one-party systems have produced in the South.

THE ROLE OF PARTY MACHINERY

In every southern state the Democratic party maintains the full organizational apparatus of major parties in the two-party states—conventions, primaries, committees, officers—and, on paper at least, appears to be pretty much the same kind of organization, performing pretty much the same functions as the Democratic parties in states outside the South. But, writes Key, "in the performance of these functions the party operates in a different context than does a party in a dual-party system, and party organization or party nomina-

[34] See James A. Farley's account of this fight in *Behind the Ballots* (New York: Harcourt, Brace and Company, 1938), pp. 118, 123-24, 293, 307. See also Key, *Politics, Parties, and Pressure Groups,* pp. 469-70; and Penniman, *op. cit.,* pp. 496-98.

[35] *Official Proceedings of the Democratic National Convention of 1936* (published by the Democratic National Committee), p. 191.

[36] Tension between the northern and southern Democrats has increased markedly in recent national conventions. In 1948 it resulted in the "Dixiecrat" bolt (see pp. 427-31), and in 1952 it resulted in the bitter "loyalty-pledge" fight (see pp. 312-13).

tions are usually quite different in reality though in name they may be the same." [37]

For one thing, most southern Democratic party organizations do little or no electioneering against the Republicans. After all, why bother? The Democrats will win hands down in the general election, and everyone, including the Republicans, knows they will. The only exceptions to this generalization are found, as might be expected, in the two *modified* one-party states, North Carolina and Tennessee, and in Virginia, which alone among the Democratic one-party states (as we have classified them) has an organized Republican opposition that cannot be completely ignored without incurring some risks.

In the other southern states, the Democratic party machinery performs only two major functions: (1) It selects delegates to the national conventions and endorses slates of presidential electors; and (2) it acts as a neutral framework for *intraparty* factional and personal competition in state and local politics.[38] The second of these functions, though little understood outside the South, is part and parcel of the pattern—and mores—of southern politics. The 1948 election furnishes an illuminating example. The Dixiecrat rebels against the national Democratic ticket in 1948 aimed not at setting themselves up as a third party inside the South, but rather at making their nominees the nominees of the *regular* Democratic party in each southern state. And the Dixiecrat nominees, Thurmond and Wright, did carry each of the four states (Alabama, Louisiana, Mississippi, and South Carolina) in which they captured the official Democratic name and party machinery, while the other seven states, where Truman and Barkley were the regular Democratic candidates and Thurmond and Wright ran under the "States' Rights" banner, went strongly against the latter. Indeed, in six of these states, the Dixiecrats ran behind the Republicans.[39]

FACTIONALISM

In most southern states, then, most political conflict takes place entirely *inside* the Democratic party machinery. The kind of politics involved is best described as *factionalism*—a series of contests among what Key describes as "transient, squabbling factions, most of which fail by far to meet the standards of permanence, cohesiveness, and responsibility that characterize the political party." [40]

We can for our purposes define a "faction" as any combination, clique, or grouping of voters and political leaders bearing a particular party label who unite at a particular time in support of a candidate against other groups and candidates under the same party label.[41] And, following Key, we may distinguish three main varieties of southern factionalism.

[37] Key, *Southern Politics in State and Nation*, p. 385.
[38] *Ibid.*, Ch. 18.
[39] *Ibid.*, pp. 336-37; Heard, *op. cit.*, pp. 20-28.
[40] Key, *Southern Politics in State and Nation*, p. 16.
[41] Cf. *ibid.*, p. 16 n. See also McKean, *op. cit.*, p. 17.

Bifactionalism. In some states there is a relatively well-organized, cohesive, enduring, and clearly identifiable majority faction, like that led by Senator Harry F. Byrd in Virginia. Where such a faction exists, opposition groups tend to coalesce into a single opposition faction, for the simple reason that to fail to do so is to acquiesce in permanent futility. This kind of factionalism prevails in states where Republican opposition is so strong that the Democrats find it necessary to maintain a fairly tight organization, namely, North Carolina, Tennessee, and Virginia.[42]

Personalism. In some southern states there have been long periods during which a single dominant personality, such as Eugene Talmadge in Georgia or Huey Long in Louisiana, has so overshadowed the political scene that voters and politicians divide automatically into "pro" and "anti" factions. Sometimes, as in Louisiana, the lines have become so sharp that each faction runs its own complete "slate" of candidates in the primary. In each of the instances mentioned, moreover, the factions have persisted since the death of the original controversial leader.[43]

Multifactionalism. In the remaining states, "cleavages among voters form and reform from campaign to campaign depending on the issues and candidates involved. In extreme situations only the most shadowy continuity of faction prevails, either in voter grouping or in composition of leadership."[44] In such states even the strongest factional leader must, for the most part, content himself with a following that, at best, can poll a bare one-third of the vote. All southern states except Virginia and Tennessee, in the attempt to sidestep some of the consequences of this splintering, have adopted what is known as the second or "run-off" primary. This primary is held from two to five weeks after the first primary, with only the two leading candidates for each office on the ballot. There is some indication that this device tends to perpetuate the multifactionalism whose alleged evils call it into existence. Where there is one key election, which a group must win if it is not to remain out of office for the next year or two, the system encourages splinter groups to merge into two large factions, and heavily penalizes those that stand aloof. Where there is a run-off, this is not the case.[45]

THE NOMINATING PROCESS

Since the primary election, which is in theory a nominating procedure, plays in the southern one-party states the role played by general elections in

[42] For a general discusion of the three major types of factionalism in southern one-party politics, see Key, *Southern Politics in State and Nation,* pp. 298-302. For specific discussions of bifactionalism in North Carolina, Tennessee, and Virginia, see Key, pp. 211-15, 62-75, 20-34, respectively.

[43] Cf. *ibid.,* Chs. 6 and 8. See also Allan P. Sindler, "Bifactional Rivalry as an Alternative to Two-Party Competition in Louisiana," *American Political Science Review,* Vol. XLIX (September, 1955), pp. 641-62.

[44] *Ibid.,* p. 301; see also Chs. 3, 5, 7, 9, 11, and 12 for descriptions of the multifactional states.

[45] *Ibid.,* pp. 419-23.

the two-party states, the southern equivalent of the nominating process in other areas takes place *prior to* the primary. The nature of this pre-primary nominating process varies from state to state, taking one shape where one type of factionalism prevails and another shape where another type prevails. In the bifactional states, each faction determines and announces its candidates by internal negotiation and discussion not dissimilar to that which occurs in party caucuses in the two-party states. In the states marked by personalism, the perennial leaders and the leaders of their opposition call the tricks on nominations pretty much as the spirit moves them. And in the multifactional states, the candidates enter the primaries for the most part on their own initiative, although pre-primary negotiations among the various factions of the moment usually reduce the number of "serious" candidates for a major state-wide office to from three to five.[46]

PARTY FINANCE

Key estimates that the typical successful gubernatorial candidate in the South spends from $100,000 to $200,000 on his campaign, although a respectable (but rarely successful) showing can be made for less.[47] Since there are few definite and formal political organizations to conduct fund-raising campaigns, the money for a particular candidate's war chest comes largely from a handful of wealthy contributors, usually businessmen who either wish to do business with the state or wish to be heard on such matters as tax policy or state regulation of the businesses in which they are interested. Contributors of both varieties, it is believed, usually expect and receive assurances of fairly specific benefits if the candidate they help finance is successful, and as a result the manipulation of politics by the "interests" is more direct and more obvious than outside the South, where campaign funds are raised by permanent and independently powerful party organizations.[48]

In the light of the foregoing considerations, we conclude that the Democratic parties in the southern one-party states resemble the major parties in the two-party states in some respects. But at certain crucial points the former differ sharply from the latter; and Key is quite correct in saying that "the term 'political party,' in its standard connotation, has only limited applicability in a description of the politics of the South."[49]

The Southern Republican Parties

THEIR HISTORY

Frederick Douglass, the great nineteenth-century Negro leader, warned his followers never to forget that "the Republican party is the ship, all else

[46] *Ibid.*, Ch. 19.
[47] *Ibid.*, pp. 464-70.
[48] *Ibid.*, Ch. 22.
[49] *Ibid.*, p. 385.

the sea." From 1865 until the advent of the New Deal in 1933, such Negroes as had the vote in the Solid South and (in the North as well) seem to have stuck to that principle, and the principle seems to have paid off. The Republican leaders fought loyally for the Negroes' rights, especially their right to vote; in general, the Democratic leaders did not. And the Negroes voted loyally, when and where they voted at all, for the party of the Great Emancipator.

In the South from 1870 to about 1900, the Republican parties included politicians and voters of both races. Or, to be more accurate, each included a black faction, made up of Negro politicians and voters, and a white faction, which frequently fought each other for control of the Republican organizations far more energetically than they fought the Democrats for public office. In Georgia, for example, the Republican party, even as late as the 1870's, rolled up a respectable vote in each election and held a substantial number of seats in each legislature. By 1886, however, black and white factionalism had so split the party that it did not even put up candidates for state offices.

By the time of the first World War, these fights had been decided, in every state except Mississippi, in favor of the "lily-white" [50] factions. Most of the white voters by this time had moved over to the Democrats, and most Negroes had been excluded from politics altogether. So matters stood, generally speaking, until the period of the New Deal, when the pro-Negro policies of the national Democratic party caused most Negro voters outside the South to break with the Douglass principle and shift their allegiance to the "sea." And, though it did not show up in the electoral totals, a parallel though less drastic shift of sentiment occurred among Negroes in the South, so that when in 1944 the Supreme Court broke down the barriers against Negro participation in politics, the Negroes did *not* flock to the southern Republican parties in very considerable numbers.[51] As far as actually contesting elections is concerned, therefore, the Republican party played no role worth mentioning in southern local politics from the end of the nineteenth century to the present.[52]

TWO KINDS OF SOUTHERN REPUBLICANS

According to Key, there are two types of Republicans in the South, the distinction between which must be kept carefully in mind. First, there are *Presidential Republicans*—persons who regularly participate in the Democratic primaries and vote in general elections for the Democratic candidates for state and local offices, but when it comes to presidential elections, split their ballot

[50] This term was first coined in 1888 in Texas by a Negro Republican leader, Norris Wright Cuney, to describe the white faction that was trying to get control of the party organization away from his faction.

[51] Heard, *op. cit.*, Ch. 17, presents a short history of the southern Republican parties.

[52] The story is told that once, while counting final-election ballots in a rural Mississippi precinct, the judges turned up a vote for the Republican candidate—the first in the history of the precinct. They checked all the election laws to see if this was legal, discovered there was no law against voting Republican, and decided the only thing to do was to count it. Some thousands of votes later in the count, *another* Republican vote turned up! This was too much for the presiding judge, who exploded. "That *proves* it," he cried. "That so-and-so voted *twice!*"

and vote Republican. It is these "Presidential Republicans" who account for the fact that Republican presidential candidates almost always get a considerably higher vote in most of the southern states—Florida and Texas especially —than that cast for Republican state and local candidates (if any).[53] Their identity is in the nature of the case a closely guarded secret, and so most of what we know about them must be inferred from the election returns. But it is interesting to note, in passing, that southern Democratic leaders to some extent encourage—and sometimes lead [54]—such partial desertion to the opposition, presumably on the theory that it increases their bargaining power in Democratic national conventions. Thus in all the southern states except Alabama, the "loyalty pledges" for voters and candidates have been revised so as to apply exclusively to nominees of the *state* Democratic parties, and there is no legal inhibition against voting for Republican presidential candidates. An ever-increasing number of southerners, moreover, do so.[55]

Secondly, there are the so-called *"Mountain Republicans."* In certain areas, for example western North Carolina, eastern Tennessee, and southwestern Virginia, the Republicans are sufficiently numerous to control local governments, elect a few state legislators and an occasional Congressman, and even— though this happens infrequently—challenge Democratic control of the entire state. All these areas happen to be highland areas, whence the name "Mountain Republicans," and they have other common characteristics as well. They are populated, for the most part, by small farmers, with only a small incidence of Negroes. And they have a different political tradition from the rest of the South. In pre-Civil War days, their inhabitants tended to hold moderate views on the slavery issue, and strongly opposed secession. They were reluctant and sometimes rebellious participants in the affairs of the Confederacy, flocked into the Republican party right after the Civil War, and have stayed there ever since. By contrast with the "Presidential Republicans," they are the backbone of such genuine Republican parties as are to be found in the South. North Carolina and Tennessee are *modified* one-party states rather than one-party states because of their Mountain Republicans; and Virginia may well become a modified one-party state in the near future because of its Mountain Republicans.[56]

IN STATE AND LOCAL POLITICS

In the southern one-party states, we repeat, the Republican parties are hardly "parties" at all, and their leaders are party politicians only in a very special sense of the term. As Key says, the "southern Republican leaders—save those who get themselves elected to local offices—are not politicians. . . . They

---

[53] See the table in Key, *Southern Politics in State and Nation*, p. 279.

[54] In the 1952 election, for example, Governor Byrnes of South Carolina and Governor Shivers of Texas publicly advised the Democrats in their respective states to vote for General Eisenhower, the Republican candidate for president.

[55] Key, *Southern Politics in State and Nation*, pp. 434-35; and Heard, *op. cit.*, pp. 137-40.

[56] Key, *Southern Politics in State and Nation*, pp. 280-85.

might be called palace or bureaucratic politicians, since their chief preoccupation is not with voters but with maneuvers to gain and keep control of the
state party machinery, an endeavor that requires convention manipulation at
home and intrigue with national party leaders up North." [57] Often they do not
run any candidates at all—not even for governor. They do almost no electioneering, even on behalf of their party's presidential candidate. Indeed, about the
only reminders the nation has had of their existence have arisen out of their
relations with the national Republican party.

IN THE NATIONAL REPUBLICAN PARTY

The southern Republican organizations have traditionally dealt with the
national party on two matters of—for them—central importance: (1) how
their votes are to be cast in national party conventions, and (2) how federal
patronage is to be dispensed at home when the Republicans control the national government.

Southern representation in the Republican national conventions has now
been reduced to about one-sixth of the total. The southern votes are nevertheless capable of profoundly influencing the course of events, and are therefore
highly prized, as witness the bitter struggle in the 1952 convention between
the Eisenhower and Taft forces over the contested delegations from Texas
and Louisiana.[58] The spirited competition among Republican hopefuls for
southern convention votes is, now almost as much as in the past, a characteristic feature of Republican party politics; and it is alleged that, now almost
as much as in the past, those votes go—quite literally—to the highest bidder.
This, plus the fact that when the Republicans control the national government,
the southern Republican organizations are in the happy position of having
federal jobs to hand out in their respective states, explains why their activities
have little or nothing to do with their nominal task of opposing the Democrats. Their leaders are preoccupied almost exclusively with gaining and maintaining control of their state organizations, and, up to the present anyhow,
apparently have seen no point in pouring their energies and funds into un-
winnable electoral contests with the dominant party. Moreover, this "closed
club" kind of organization has had the support of many national Republican leaders, for it greatly simplifies the latter's twofold task of negotiating
for convention votes and allocating patronage.[59]

There is some evidence, however, that the nature of southern Republican
leadership is beginning to change. Key, pointing out that the twenty-year
patronage drought from 1933 to 1953 has tended to eliminate the old-time
"patronage referee" (i.e., one who allocates patronage jobs), quotes the follow-

[57] *Ibid.*, p. 292.

[58] For an illuminating account of the Taft-Eisenhower contest in Texas, see O. Douglas
Weeks, *Texas Presidential Politics in 1952* (Austin, Tex.: Institute of Public Affairs, University of
Texas, 1953), pp. 50-81.

[59] Heard, *op. cit.*, pp. 96-97, 119-22.

ing plaintive comment from an Arkansas Republican leader: "It's a wonder we have a skeleton force left after being pushed away from the trough for [twenty] years." [60] More and more, Key says, the southern Republican leadership is being infiltrated by businessmen who are more concerned with combating New Deal–Fair Deal regulations than with maintaining white supremacy at all costs. [61] Until, however, this kind of leadership comes to dominate the southern Republican parties, they are likely to remain primarily traffickers in convention votes and federal patronage, and most of the southern states are likely to remain unambiguously in the one-party state column.

Popular Consultation in the Solid South

Key and Heard both argue, in effect, that as devices for popular consultation the southern one-party systems are markedly inferior to the two-party systems of most of the nonsouthern states. Key lists a number of shortcomings of the southern system which, assuming he is correct on the facts, would certainly justify such a conclusion.

First, it develops no real political leadership. As Key says, "The South must depend for political leadership, not on political parties, but on lone-wolf operators, on fortuitous groupings of individuals usually of a transient nature, on spectacular demagogues odd enough to command the attention of considerable numbers of voters, on men who have become persons of political consequence in their own little bailiwicks, and on other types of leaders whose methods to attract electoral attention serve as substitutes for leadership of a party organization." [62]

Second, by failing to develop definite and continuing group leadership, the system produces confusion and bewilderment among the voters. Instead of simplifying the alternatives before the electorate, one-party factionalism, Key asserts, multiplies them, thereby making enormously more difficult the exercise of intelligent choice at the polls. And this, he adds, as much as the meaninglessness of the general elections, explains the widespread apathy and low voter turnout that are characteristic of southern politics.

Third, the system offers the voter only transient factions to choose among, and, this being the case, makes it almost impossible for him to fix any kind of effective responsibility for the conduct of his state and local governments.

Fourth, the "issueless" politics characteristic of the southern systems does not by any means make for moderation, compromise, and consensus. Indeed, politics in the southern states is if anything more intransigent and violent than that in most nonsouthern states.

On Key's showing, in short, the two-party systems are better instruments of popular consultation—that is, they are more nearly in accord with the model

[60] Key, *Southern Politics in State and Nation*, p. 292 n.
[61] *Ibid.*, pp. 292-95.
[62] *Ibid.*, p. 16.

of democracy presented in Chapters 2 and 3—than are the one-party systems of the Solid South.[63]

The Future of the Solid South

During the 1952 presidential election, the Republican candidate campaigned in the South for the first time in a long while. The Republicans, moreover, carried four of the southern states (Florida, Tennessee, Texas, and Virginia), and came close to carrying three others (Louisiana, North Carolina, and South Carolina). At the present writing there are a total of seven Republican members of the House of Representatives from the eleven southern states. Many observers have asked whether this portends the permanent cracking of the Solid South and the early restoration of two-party politics in the southern states.

The most extensive and careful analysis of this question is that attempted by Alexander Heard before the 1952 election. Heard predicts that the Solid South will come eventually to two-party politics, but will do so as a result of the southern conservatives' permanently abandoning the Democratic party and turning to the Republican party as the best agency for resisting "creeping socialism" in state and nation. This could happen, of course, only when these conservatives become willing to subordinate the race question to other questions; but Heard believes that events are moving them in that direction, and will do so increasingly as time passes. He points to such things as the increasing dispersion of the Negroes, the consequent attenuation of black-belt pressures, the industrialization of the South, the legal eclipse of the white primary, and the ever-increasing urgency of economic issues. All these factors, he says, are reasons for believing that the race question cannot permanently blanket and suppress internal southern white dissension over other issues. He is not willing to make a specific prediction as to *when* the South will finally abandon its one-party systems, but he appears to believe that the moment is not far off.[64]

The journalist Samuel Grafton, who toured the southern states for *Collier's* magazine during the 1952 campaign and tried to assess the prospects of the Republicans, became convinced that there is a trend away from the Democrats among both voters and politicians. It is strongest and most noticeable, he concluded, in Texas—where economic issues (such as the question of federal or state ownership of the offshore oil deposits) are most prominent and where the race question is least on people's minds.[65]

Key, on the other hand, argues that while the 1952 presidential election means that future *presidential* elections will involve more serious contests in

---

[63] Cf. *ibid.,* pp. 302-11.

[64] Heard, *op. cit.,* pp. 146-56, 247.

[65] Samuel Grafton, "The Republican South," *Collier's,* Vol. CXXX (September 27, 1952), pp. 17-19.

all the southern states than they ever have involved before, this does not mean that state and local elections will move in the direction of genuine two-party conflict. Only when the southern Republicans build organizations at *all* levels, and begin to nominate able and attractive candidates and work hard for their election, he concludes, will genuine two-party systems appear in the South.[66]

Vermont's One-Party System

The only one-party system outside the South is that of Vermont. Unfortunately, however, we have at our disposal no study of Vermont's politics and parties comparable to Key's panoramic study of southern politics.[67] The evidence we have, however, seems to bear out the following statement by a prominent southern Democrat made after touring Vermont: "I am a Rotarian, a Democrat, and a Methodist in North Carolina. It is a condition not vastly different from that of a Rotarian, a Republican, and a Congregationalist in Vermont."[68]

No Democrat has held elective state office or won a seat in Congress in Vermont since the first Republican state convention was held in 1854.[69] Not even the most solid southern state can top this as a record for voter loyalty to one party. Unlike that of the Solid South, however, Vermont's one-party system does not seem to owe its existence to any single situational factor, but rather to several such factors. Among these, Robert Mitchell lists: (1) the absence of any large cities (the largest city, Burlington, has a population of 33,155); (2) the homogeneity of the population, made up as it is almost entirely of small farmers, merchants, and professional persons; (3) a deep and widely accepted historical tradition that glorifies, among other things, abolitionism and the Republican party; (4) a political tradition shaped in large part by the ascendancy, during the first fifty years after the Civil War, of the Grand Army of the Republic (a powerful organization of pro-Republican veterans of the Union army, whose slogan was, "Vote as you shot!"); and (5) a long-standing custom of leaving all genuinely hot and divisive political issues to be settled by popular referenda, and in such fashion that neither the Republican party nor the state officials need to take a stand on them. Thus

[66] V. O. Key, Jr., "Solid South: Cracked or Broken?" *New Republic*, Vol. CXXVII (December 1, 1952), pp. 9-11. Weeks comes to approximately the same conclusion regarding Texas, where, he says, there may be a permanent increase in Presidential Republicans, but where genuine two-party politics on the state and local levels is still a long way off: *op. cit.*, pp. 108-11. For a discussion of the future of southern parties written after the Supreme Court's decision on segregation in the schools, see Isabel Paterson, "Southern Breakthrough," *National Review*, Vol. I, No. 5 (December 21, 1955).

[67] The best description of Vermont politics and parties the present writers have come across is that by Robert W. Mitchell, "Unique Vermont," *American Mercury*, Vol. LX (March, 1945), pp. 336-40.

[68] Jonathan Daniels, *A Southerner Discovers New England* (New York: The Macmillan Company, 1940), pp. 239-40.

[69] Mitchell, *op. cit.*, p. 336.

issues that might breed dissatisfaction with and real opposition to the dominant party are siphoned off into the referendum process, and the Republican party in state and local affairs hardly rubs shoulders with them.[70]

The Republican party in Vermont, according to one observer, is "under such loose control from the top that . . . you can run for office in Vermont on the Republican ticket without permission from any individual or organization. The party has no boss, unofficial or otherwise." [71] Since every candidate starts more or less from scratch as far as organization is concerned, the man who is serious about winning must spend quite a lot of money on his campaign. The victors, consequently, are usually men of wealth, or at least men whom the wealthy wish to see win. No small farmer, for example, has ever been elected governor of Vermont, although the small farmers are the largest single occupational group in the state.[72] All this sounds very much like the "multifactionalism" characteristic of many of the southern one-party states. During the Progressive era a half-century ago, we may note in this connection, Vermont politics became bifactional for a time; but the Progressive faction and the old-guard faction eventually merged, and multifactionalism (or the "absence of machine politics," as Vermonters prefer to say) has been characteristic of the state's politics ever since.[73]

The Vermont Democratic party also is not unlike its Republican counterparts in the southern one-party states. It is a tightly organized, rather cliquish affair, closely managed by five or six men at the top. As one commentator has noted, "the same candidates run repeatedly in election after election, and newcomers have difficulty breaking into this exclusive coterie of losers. As a result, some disgruntled young Democrats feel that the leadership of their party is more interested in maintaining its control of the organization than it is in conducting a winning election campaign against the Republicans." [74]

On the whole, then, one-party politics in Vermont appears to operate in its essentials like one-party politics in the South. There is not in Vermont, as there is in the South, a single overriding issue that tends to discourage and confuse dissension on other issues; and this, together with the frequent use of the referendum, perhaps brings popular consultation in Vermont a mite closer to the democratic model than popular consultation in the South. The many similarities between Vermont and southern one-party politics—despite the many social and economic differences between the two areas—suggest that one-party systems are substantially alike no matter where in the United States we find them.

[70] *Ibid.*, pp. 336-37.
[71] *Ibid.*, p. 338.
[72] Earle Newton, *The Vermont Story* (Montpelier, Vt.; Vermont Historical Society, 1949), p. 253.
[73] W. A. Flint, *The Progressive Movement in Vermont* (Washington, D. C.: American Council on Public Affairs, 1941).
[74] Mitchell, *op. cit.*, pp. 338-39.

The Modified One-Party Systems

The evidence presented in Chapter 7 and in the foregoing pages of the present chapter seems to add up to this conclusion: From the standpoint of appropriateness to our model of democracy, there *are* significant differences between two-party systems in general and one-party systems in general. The American party system, however, includes several instances of the *modified* one-party type; and before we can complete our survey of the types of party systems in American politics, we must raise this final question: What difference does it make if there is present an opposition party that almost always tries to win and, even though it wins infrequently, usually polls a substantial vote? In other words, How do the American modified one-party systems compare with those of the other two types?

Because political scientists have done much more research and writing upon the national party system than upon the state party systems, this is no easy question to answer.[75] Key's study of southern politics, however, includes useful descriptions of parties and politics in two modified one-party Democratic states (North Carolina and Tennessee), and suggests a number of contrasts between politics in those states and politics in the unmodified one-party states. By taking his discussion as a point of departure, and adding what evidence is available about the other modified one-party states, we can at least venture some tentative generalizations about systems of this type.

THE GENERAL NATURE OF THEIR POLITICS

In both North Carolina and Tennessee, the statewide modified one-party system is a matter not of substantial opposition by a second party in all sections of the state, but rather of actual domination by the second party in some sections of the state. In North Carolina, the Republicans have great strength in the western counties, and control certain enclaves in other parts of the state.[76] In Tennessee, Republicans dominate politics over the entire eastern third of the state.[77] In the areas mentioned the Republicans normally hold most of the county and municipal offices. In North Carolina, the congressional districts are gerrymandered in such fashion that the Republicans cannot use their strength to elect a U.S. representative.[78] In Tennessee, however, the districting is such that the Republicans can usually fill at least one and often two congressional seats. The best-known of the Tennessee Republican representatives, B. Carroll Reece, has been elected fourteen times, and was Republican National Chairman from 1946 to 1948. In both states, the Republican-dominated areas provide the bulk of the hard-core Republican vote in elections for state

---

[75] Cf. Key, *Politics, Parties, and Pressure Groups*, p. 325 n.

[76] Key, *Southern Politics in State and Nation*, pp. 219-22.

[77] *Ibid.*, pp. 75-78. See also William Goodman, *Inherited Domain: Political Parties in Tennessee* (Knoxville: Bureau of Public Administration, University of Tennessee, 1954).

[78] *Ibid.*, pp. 224-25, esp. Figure 43.

offices. The total Republican vote for state offices depends upon the number of Democrats who choose to vote against their own party's candidates; it almost never results in a Republican majority, as witness the fact that Tennessee has elected a Republican governor only once (in the Republican landslide of 1920), and North Carolina has never done so. In presidential elections, of course, the Republicans pick up a certain number of "Presidential Republican" votes.[79]

A similar pattern of second-party strength is to be found in Kentucky, where twenty-two counties go Republican even in the years when the Democrats pile up their biggest majorities over the state as a whole,[80] and in New Hampshire, where the cities of Manchester and Nashua rarely fail the Democratic party though the rest of the state almost always goes Republican.[81]

A good many at least of the modified one-party states have a second characteristic in common: They are states whose pre–Civil War history was one of real two-party competition, but in which the now-dominant party, having established its overlordship right after the war, has maintained it without interruption ever since. This has been the pattern in the southern and Democratic modified one-party states of North Carolina and Tennessee, and in their northern and Republican counterparts: Maine,[82] New Hampshire,[83] and Pennsylvania.[84]

THE NATURE OF THE DOMINANT PARTIES

The Democratic organizations in both Tennessee and North Carolina— far more at least than the Democratic organizations in the one-party southern states—look and act like the party organizations in the two-party states. They are tightly knit, do a great deal of electioneering against the Republicans, and see to it that their internal divisions remain within the bounds of bifactionalism.[85] In the one-party areas of these states, however, personalism and multifactionalism tend to prevail.

In the northern modified one-party states, similarly, the dominant party's internal strife tends to be distinctly bifactional. An excellent example here is North Dakota, where the Republican primaries are now contested by two fairly distinct factions: the old Non-Partisan League faction, led by Senator William Langer, and the Republican Organizing Committee, formed in 1943 to combat N.P.L. "radicalism," and led by Fred Aandahl.[86] This kind of

[79] Republican presidential candidates carried North Carolina in 1928 and 1952, and Tennessee in 1920, 1928, and 1952.

[80] Jasper B. Shannon, "Political Behavior in Kentucky, 1930-1940," in *A Decade of Change in Kentucky Government and Politics* (Louisville, Ky.: Bureau of Governmental Research, 1943), pp. 3-15.

[81] Penn Kimball, "New Hampshire," *New York Times Sunday Magazine*, March 9, 1952, p. 7.

[82] Claude E. Robinson, "Maine—Political Barometer," *Political Science Quarterly*, Vol. XLVII (June, 1932), pp. 161-84.

[83] Kimball, *op. cit.*

[84] "F. G. L." in the *Nation*, Vol. CLIX (September 9, 1944), pp. 289-91.

[85] Cf. Key, *Southern Politics in State and Nation*, pp. 62-75, 223-24.

[86] Carey McWilliams in the *Nation*, Vol. CLXXIV (March 29, 1952), pp. 295-96.

intraparty politics, of course, contrasts sharply with the kind of multifactional-ism we noted above in Vermont Republican politics.

In Key's opinion, there is a direct causal relation between the bifactionalism of the Democrats' politics in North Carolina and Tennessee and the fact that they face Republican opposition strong enough to constitute a genuine, if not immediate, threat to their control of their respective states. As he puts it:

> The cohesiveness of the majority faction [in the North Carolina and Tennessee Democratic parties] points to the extraordinary influence of even a small opposition party. In both North Carolina and Tennessee, the majority Democratic factions de-rive unity from the opposition of Republicans; in both states the Democrats of the counties with substantial Republican votes accept state leadership and discipline in the battle against a common foe. . . . Republican opposition contributes to the creation of one tightly organized Democratic faction. By the same token existence of one relatively cohesive faction generates within the Democratic party an opposi-tion group, producing something of a bi-factionalism within the dominant party.[87]

In other words, the presence of an opposition party affects the character of the dominant party in the modified one-party states, and thus accentuates the differences between the politics of the latter and the politics of the one-party states.

THE NATURE OF THE OPPOSITION PARTIES

The opposition parties in the modified one-party states almost always run candidates for the statewide offices, and electioneer for those candidates even though they know their chances of winning are slight if not negligible. In the one-party states, by contrast, the opposition parties often do not put up candi-dates at all, and almost never do any all-out electioneering, which, with good reason, they regard as a waste of time, energy, and money.

The opposition parties in the modified one-party states make their nomi-nations by the same *formal* procedures (primaries and conventions) as the dominant parties. The actual task, however, is more nearly that of persuading someone to fight the good but hopeless fight than that of choosing among rival contenders for the highly desirable and much-sought-after honor of the party's nomination.[88] In his study of the 1944 Iowa primary election, for example, Professor Kirk Porter was able to show that genuine contests were far more frequent in the Republican primary than in the Democratic.[89]

The opposition parties in these states, then, do perform functions that, from the standpoint of our model of democracy, are highly significant. They offer the voters an alternative that, on Key's showing, simply does not exist

---

[87] Key, *Southern Politics in State and Nation*, p. 300; see also pp. 223, 228.

[88] See Malcolm B. Ronald's portrayal of the informality of the Democratic party's nominating procedures in the Dakotas: "The Dakota Twins," *Atlantic Monthly*, Vol. CLVIII (September, 1936), pp. 359-65; and T. D. Lyons, " 'Politix' in Dakota," *Commonweal*, Vol. XXXIV (August 22, 1941), pp. 417-20.

[89] Kirk Porter, "The Deserted Primary in Iowa," *American Political Science Review*, Vol. XXXIX (August, 1945), pp. 732-40.

in the one-party states; and that in itself would be enough to put the party systems in which they function considerably closer to our model than the party systems in which no opposition is present. Moreover, the opposition parties, as we have seen, evoke in the organizations and primaries of the dominant parties a degree of cohesion and responsibility that is almost completely lacking in the dominant parties of the one-party systems, and thus clarify the choices that the voter must make. In short, these opposition parties more than pay their way as far as democracy is concerned.

However, the lot of workers and leaders in opposition parties in modified one-party areas is not made any happier by the fact that these parties perform significant functions. In some respects it is considerably more frustrating to adhere to and work for an opposition party that has little chance than one that has no chance at all. As Heard well points out:

The frustration may be greatest where the party is strongest. A conscientious North Carolina [Republican] party officer noted that in a state like Alabama party leaders can relax and catch what votes happen to come their way: They know at the outset they don't have a chance. In North Carolina, however, the size of the party imposes an obligation. The dutiful officer labors to do the best he can. His reward is failure; he never quite gets into the winning bracket.[90]

Senator Richard L. Neuberger, a Democratic politician in predominantly Republican Oregon, tells a story that underscores this point very well:

When my wife was on the board of the local League of Women Voters, someone nervously brought up the fact that she was a Democratic precinct committeewoman. This was contrary to the impartial principles of the league, which is one of the community's most useful organizations.

My wife smiled sweetly across the table at the objector. "Aren't you a Republican precinct committeewoman, Frances?" she asked.

"Well, yes," admitted Frances, "but I don't think that's exactly the same thing." [91]

Our point is that workers in the opposition parties of modified one-party areas are entitled, for what it is worth, to console themselves with the thought that they are making possible the continuance of a more democratic party system than their part of the world would have but for their efforts, and with the further thought that, if everything were to break just right some day, they would even win. And who can say that everything won't break just right—some day!

[90] Heard, *op. cit.*, p. 98.

[91] "Two-Party Blues in a One-Party State," *New York Times Sunday Magazine*, February 1, 1953, p. 16.

Chapter 9

PARTY MEMBERSHIP

What Kind of Group Is a "Political Party"?

American political parties are a special case under the general heading "political parties"; and political parties are a special case under the general heading "human groups." Before we can profitably discuss the nature of party membership in the United States, therefore, we must first raise and answer these questions: What is a human group? And *what kind* of human group is a political party?

Contemporary social science draws a distinction between mere *aggregates* of human beings, such as the persons waiting at a gate in Grand Central Station at 11:50 A.M. to catch the twelve o'clock express to New Haven, and *groups* of human beings, assigning to the latter certain characteristics that the former do not possess, namely: the members of a *group* may be observed *to interact* with one another in *certain recurring patterns of behavior;* to be *associated together for certain purposes;* and to stand over against one another in *certain relationships.*[1] Groups possess these characteristics, to be sure, in greater or lesser degree; and the question of where *exactly* to draw the line between groups and aggregates is therefore less simple than our foregoing statement of the distinction between them might seem to suggest. But the kind of group we are concerned with in this book possesses them in marked degree.

The crucial points at which to observe a group are, then, the *interactions, associations,* and *relationships* among its members; and if we ask, "What kind of human group is a political party?" what we had best mean by the question is, "In what way do the interactions, associations, and relationships character-

---

[1] For our previous discussion of the nature of politics and political groups, see pp. 84-87. For a more extended discussion of the various types of human aggregates, see George C. Homans, *The Human Group* (New York: Harcourt, Brace and Company, 1950), pp. 10-17, 84-86; David B. Truman, *The Governmental Process* (New York: Alfred A. Knopf, 1951), pp. 23-26; John W. Bennett and Melvin M. Tumin, *Social Life, Structure and Function* (New York: Alfred A. Knopf, 1949), Ch. 10; and Richard Centers, *The Psychology of Social Classes* (Princeton: Princeton University Press, 1949), pp. 27-28.

istic of political parties differ from those characteristic of human groups in general?"

We cannot attempt a full and complete answer to this question—the theory of political parties is not sufficiently developed for that. But we can make three statements about the observable interactions, associations, and relationships characteristic of political parties which are generally accepted by students of the subject.[2]

(1) The members of a political party are *organized,* i.e., they are associated together as a result of *conscious and deliberate choice,* which is reflected in an *agreement,* written or unwritten or both, as to how they shall go about pursuing their collective ends; and the relationships between them are established, in large part, by this agreement.

(2) The *purpose* for which members of a party associate together is to gain control, *for the party*—not, as in the case of the so-called Communist party, for some other organization (see Chapter 19)—of the personnel and policies of government.

(3) The *interactions* between party members revolve around—and take their shape from—the major activities in which the members engage in order to achieve the party's purposes: *making nominations, contesting elections,* and *"organizing" public officials.*

To repeat the definition first given in Chapter 5, *a political party is an autonomous organized group that makes nominations and contests elections in the hope of eventually gaining and exercising control of the personnel and policies of government.*[3]

Party Membership in the United States

WHO PARTICIPATES IN PARTY ACTIVITIES?

Let us ignore, for the moment, certain difficulties that arise when we ask, "What constitutes *membership* in a party?" and speak merely of persons who *participate,* in one way or another, in the various activities that are the business of a political party—in short, let us for the moment speak of *participants.* Now the first thing to notice about party participants is that they differ greatly in the amount of time, energy, and resources they put into party activities, so that we may divide them into categories according to the time, energy, and resources they contribute. And we may exhibit these categories as a series of concentric circles, one for each level of participation, as in the diagram on page 200.[4]

[2] Cf. pp. 85-87 and the authorities cited in footnotes 2 and 3 of Chapter 5.

[3] P. 85.

[4] These levels of participation are, admittedly, rather arbitrary—in the sense that each category could be broken down into subcategories, and any two adjacent categories could be combined into a single category. But they correspond in general to current usage in the literature of political parties, which in turn corresponds to groupings that any observer of the participants would readily discern for himself.

At the core of the party are the *leaders,* whose recommendations as to the party's nominees, policies, campaign strategy and tactics, and allocation of funds are in general accepted and followed by the other party members; whose time, energy, and resources are most completely at the party's disposal; whose names the general public and the party members most clearly identify with the party. Here we find the candidates, the chairmen and members of party committees and conventions, and the "bosses."

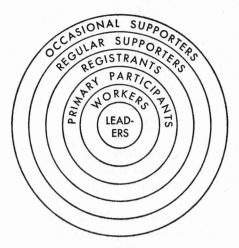

In the next circle are the *workers,* who canvass voters, prepare and distribute campaign literature, make speeches, solicit funds, and carry on the thousand and one other activities through which the party tries to win elections. Here are the precinct captains, the "ward heelers," the "cogs in the machine," the "organization men." For some of them party work is a profession, their way of making a living, a full-time job. For others it is an absorbing after-hours avocation. From all it requires a commitment to devote a considerable portion of their time and energy to the party at frequent intervals and, if need be, at short notice.

In the next circle are the *primary participants,* who attend party caucuses, vote in party primary elections, and in general participate in the party's nominating process—at least to the extent of ratifying or rejecting the candidates selected by the leaders and actively supported by the workers.

Next we come to the *registrants,* who have formally indicated to some public agency their adherence to the party. By no means all of these regularly participate in the party's caucuses or vote in its direct primary elections; normally, indeed, only about 10 to 30 per cent of the total registered voters bother to vote in such elections.[5]

[5] Cf. Dayton D. McKean, *Party and Pressure Politics* (Boston: Houghton Mifflin Company, 1949), pp. 114-15; V. O. Key, Jr., *Politics, Parties, and Pressure Groups,* 3rd ed. (New York: Thomas Y. Crowell Company, 1952), pp. 415-17; and Howard R. Penniman, *Sait's American Parties and Elections,* 4th ed. (New York: Appleton-Century-Crofts, Inc., 1948), pp. 449-50.

The next circle belongs to the *regular supporters*—persons who regard themselves (often with some pride) as "Democrats" or "Republicans," who regularly vote the straight party ticket, and for whom an occasional vote for a candidate of the opposition party is a step to be taken only in emergencies and after considerable soul-searching. Many of them do not vote in the primaries, but most of them vote for their party's candidates in most general elections, or even if they don't vote, still have their impact on the outcome by being outspokenly "for" the party.

At the outermost limits of party participation stand the *occasional supporters,* who describe themselves as "Democrats" or "Republicans" but sometimes split their party's ticket, or desert to the opposition entirely, in general elections. Only in the broadest sense, let us concede, can such persons be said to participate in any of the party's characteristic activities.

WHO SHOULD BE CONSIDERED A "PARTY MEMBER"?

Having thus identified the levels of participation in the activities of a political party, we must next ask: How many of the participants may properly be called "party *members"?* Take the national Democratic party, for instance: Are all the 27,312,217 persons who voted for Adlai Stevenson in 1952 members? Or shall we reserve the term "members" for registered Democrats—even if they voted for Eisenhower? Or for those who voted in the party's primaries? Or for those who actually got out and worked for the election of the Democratic candidates?

Well, the reader may ask, what difference does it make? The answer is that it makes at least this difference: Questions keep arising as to the possibility, or desirability, or both, of increasing democracy *inside* our party organizations; the good health of our democracy is alleged by many informed observers to depend on how we answer them; and yet, clearly, we can hardly begin to answer them until we have a clear picture of the relevant constituencies. The question "Is the Republican (or Democratic) party organization sufficiently democratic?" for instance, might be answered Yes if we think only of those in our first two circles as members, and No if we include those in the third circle.

Some writers have argued, to be sure, that effective decision-making power in political parties is in fact *always* located in a few leaders or "bosses," not in the rank-and-file party "members"; if this is correct, it matters little whom we include as party members. Perhaps the best-known formulation of this theory is that of the Swiss-Italian sociologist, Robert Michels, who, after an extensive investigation of European socialist parties before World War I, concluded that without exception they were organizations whose formal constitutions, however democratic, were meaningless as compared to their real internal power structure. These parties, he observed, invariably followed one and the same pattern: tight oligarchical control by party leaders, supine and unwitting subservience on the part of the party "masses." Michels proceeded to derive from his findings what he called the "iron law of oligarchy," according to which there is an inevitable and irresistible tendency in *every* human organization for power to concentrate itself in the hands of a few leaders, so that democracy is an unattainable will-o'-the-wisp.[6]

A great many American writers have seen something like Michels' "iron law" at work in American parties, have called vigorous attention to their alleged domination by bosses, and have offered a wide variety of proposals as to what could and should be done about it. Some, echoing Michels' very words, have concluded that parties are inherently oligarchical, and must therefore be abolished altogether if we are ever to achieve true democracy in the United States.[7] Others have argued that parties, though they have indeed been oligarchical up to now, can be made democratic via legal regulation—concretely, by wresting control from the bosses and lodging it in the rank-and-file party members, which calls for perfecting the direct primary and using it for *all* nominations.[8] And still others have contended that boss control, while probably unavoidable, should not cause us undue worry: the parties, even though boss-controlled, will continue to be useful agencies of democratic government so long as the voters at large are in a position to displace today's oligarchy with some competing group of leaders. Democracy, for these writers, is a matter of the people's being free to choose between rival party oligarchies; it consists in a certain relationship, that of competition, *between* the parties, and is not to be achieved by operating on the relation between leaders and rank and file *within* the parties.[9]

Whatever the differences in emphasis among the writers here in question, all of them are recognizably committed to what may be called the *ticket-voter* conception of party membership, according to which any citizen of the Republic who more or less regularly *votes* for the candidates of a given party must be deemed a full-fledged member of that party, with the same claim to an equal share in its decision-making processes as those who assume greater obligations toward the party and tender it greater services. This same ticket-

---

[6] Robert Michels, *Political Parties: A Sociological Study of the Oligarchical Tendencies of Modern Democracy,* translated by Eden and Cedar Paul (London: Jarrold and Sons, 1915). A similar position is taken by Gaetano Mosca, *The Ruling Class,* translated by Hannah D. Kahn, edited and revised by Arthur Livingston (New York: McGraw-Hill Book Company, 1939), especially p. 53.

[7] Cf. Albert M. Kales, *Unpopular Government in the United States* (Chicago: University of Chicago Press, 1914), pp. 67-68; James Schouler, *Ideals of the Republic* (Boston: Little, Brown and Company, 1908), pp. 209-10; and Daniel G. Thompson, *Politics in a Democracy* (New York: Longmans, Green and Company, 1893), pp. 45-50.

[8] Cf. the various proposals of the Committee on Political Parties of the American Political Science Association for "intraparty democracy" in "Toward a More Responsible Two-Party System," *American Political Science Review,* Vol. XLIV (September, 1950), Supplement, pp. 17-18, 20-24, 65-69, 70-83. See also Frank J. Goodnow, *Politics and Administration* (New York: The Macmillan Company, 1900), pp. 166-67, 232-33, 248-49.

[9] Cf. Henry Jones Ford, "The Direct Primary," *North American Review,* Vol. CXC (July, 1909), pp. 1-14; and E. E. Schattschneider, *The Struggle for Party Government* (College Park, Md.: Program in American Civilization, University of Maryland, 1948), pp. 38-40.

voter conception of party membership, moreover, dominates current thinking about parties and their problems so completely that it is possible to point, in the contemporary literature of the subject, to only one prominent political scientist who repudiates it: E. E. Schattschneider. To insist on this concept, he argues, is to drive a wedge between membership and obligation in political parties that would be unthinkable, intolerable even, in any other private association, be it church, luncheon club, or fraternal society. Moreover, he adds, it is merely our habit of thinking of party membership in this loose way that lends plausibility to the charges of boss control and oligarchy in American parties, which from his point of view are very wide of the truth. As he puts it:

A more realistic theory, closer to the facts, can relieve us of the nightmarish necessity of doing the impossible. Let us suppose that the concept of the party membership of the partisans is abandoned altogether. If the party is described as a political enterprise conducted by a group of working politicians *supported* by partisan voters who approve of the party but are merely partisans (not members of a fictitious association), the parties would seem less wicked.[10]

PARTY "IDENTIFICATION" AND PARTICIPATION

The study of popular political attitudes in the 1952 presidential election by the Survey Research Center of the University of Michigan indicates that most Americans, like most American commentators on politics, hold the "ticket-voter" conception of party membership explicated above. Most Americans, according to the S.R.C.'s findings, "identify" themselves with a particular party (that is, regard themselves as "members" of the Republican or Democratic parties), but do not feel that they are obligated thereby to work actively (or, say some, even vote) for that party's nominees.[11]

The Michigan investigators asked their national cross section of 1,614 respondents the question, "Generally speaking, do you usually think of yourself as a Republican, a Democrat, an independent, or what?" Forty-seven per cent replied "Democrat," 27 per cent "Republican," 22 per cent "independent," and 4 per cent mentioned a minor party or had no opinion.[12] The interviewers further refined these party identifications by asking those who had identified themselves with a party, "Would you call yourself a strong (R) (D) or a not very strong (R) (D)?" And those who had identified themselves as independents were asked, "Do you think of yourself as closer to the Republican or Democratic party?" Only those who replied that they were closer to neither

---

[10] *Party Government* (New York: Rinehart & Company, Inc., 1942), p. 59. Italics in the original. For a general summary and criticism of these opposing conceptions of party membership, see Austin Ranney, *The Doctrine of Responsible Party Government* (Urbana: University of Illinois Press, 1954), pp. 17-19, 155-57.

[11] Angus Campbell, Gerald Gurin, and Warren E. Miller, *The Voter Decides* (Evanston, Ill.: Row, Peterson and Company, 1954), Ch. VII.

[12] The National Opinion Research Center asked the same question in October, 1944, and got the following answers: 39 per cent "Democrat," 29 per cent "Republican," 29 per cent "independent," and 3 per cent minor party or no opinion: reprinted in Hadley Cantril, ed., *Public Opinion, 1935-1946* (Princeton: Princeton University Press, 1951), No. 47 on p. 580.

party were actually classified as "independents."[13] The respondents distributed themselves among the various categories as shown in Table 9.

TABLE 9   *Distribution of Party Identification Within Regions* [14]

Party Identification	North-East	Mid-West	South	Far West	Total Sample
Strong Democrat	18%	17%	31%	22%	22%
Weak Democrat	18	25	32	24	25
Independent Democrat	13	9	8	10	10
Independent	8	7	2	7	5
Independent Republican	9	8	5	6	7
Weak Republican	18	15	8	13	14
Strong Republican	14	18	6	16	13
None, minor party, or not ascertained	2	1	8	2	4

Seventy-four per cent of the respondents, in other words, identified themselves more or less strongly with one or the other of the major parties; 17 per
cent regarded themselves as "closer" to one than to the other; and only 5 per
cent regarded themselves as "independents," with no party preferences of any
kind. The Michigan investigators further learned that the respondents' party
identifications were highly correlated with various other kinds of political attitudes and behavior: a relatively high proportion of the "strong" party identifiers, for example, expressed the belief that a man should vote a straight ticket
out of "party loyalty" even if he does not like some of his party's candidates.
Relatively few of the respondents in the "strong Democrat" and "strong Republican" categories, moreover, had switched from one party to the other in
previous elections; and a relatively high proportion of them voted for their
party's candidates in 1952.[15]

The Michigan researchers also found, however, that a relatively small proportion of the "strong" party identifiers actually *worked* for the nominees of
their party in 1952. The relation of party identification to political participation[16] is shown in Table 10.

13 For a discussion of the voting behavior of persons who classify themselves as "independents," see Samuel J. Eldersveld, "The Independent Vote: Measurement, Characteristics, and Implications for Party Strategy," *American Political Science Review*, Vol. XLVI (September, 1952),
pp. 732-53; and Philip K. Hastings, "The Independent Voter in 1952: A Study of Pittsfield,
Massachusetts," *American Political Science Review*, Vol. XLVII (September, 1953), pp. 805-10.

14 Table 7.1 in Angus Campbell, Gerald Gurin, and Warren E. Miller, *The Voter Decides*
(Evanston, Ill.: Row, Peterson and Company, 1954), p. 93. This and other material from this
book is reprinted by permission.

15 Campbell, Gurin, and Miller, *op. cit.*, pp. 94-107.

16 The study set up three categories of political participation: a "Low" category for respondents who did not even vote; a "Medium" category for those who voted but did nothing
else; and a "high" category for those who voted and also gave money, attended rallies, and/or
rang doorbells and the like.

TABLE 10 *Relation of Party Identification to Political Participation* [17]

Political Participation	Strong Dem.	Weak Dem.	Ind. Dem.	Ind.	Ind. Rep.	Weak Rep.	Strong Rep.
High	30%	19%	26%	22%	32%	29%	42%
Medium	46	50	48	52	46	49	50
Low	24	31	26	26	22	22	8

"Strong" party identifiers, in other words, were more likely than respondents in the other categories to report a "high" level of participation in the 1952 election. But well over half of them did nothing more than vote, and almost one-quarter of the "strong Democrats" did not "participate" even to that extent.

In sum, the findings suggest that most Americans regard themselves as "members" of one major party or the other. Their attachment to a particular party, along with their attitudes toward particular candidates and particular issues in particular campaigns, helps determine not only how they vote but also *whether* they vote. For the most part, however, they apparently do not feel that their identification with and "membership" in a party—however strongly they may feel about it—obligates them to do more than vote for its candidates in most elections. In other words, they understand the term "party member" to cover not merely "party workers" and "party leaders," but a great many other persons as well.

LEGAL DEFINITIONS OF PARTY MEMBERSHIP IN THE UNITED STATES

The ticket-voter conception of party membership, which, as we have seen, is held by most Americans as well as by most American political commentators, has clearly had a decisive influence upon current legal definitions of party membership in the United States. Each of the states now stipulates in its election laws what persons may participate in the nomination-making stage of the political party process, so that we may fairly speak of a general pattern of legal party membership for the country as a whole.[18]

First, most of the state statutes draw no distinction between party membership and voting affiliation, so that the most anyone is asked to do in order to qualify legally as a member of a party is to go through some registration procedure or cast some sort of vote. In other words, no state demands work on behalf of a party's candidates or contributions to its campaign funds as prerequisites for becoming a legal party member.

[17] Table 7.11 in Campbell, Gurin, and Miller, *op. cit.*, p. 108.
[18] The most exhaustive study of legal definitions of party membership in the United States is Clarence A. Berdahl, "Party Membership in the United States," *American Political Science Review*, Vol. XXXVI (February, April, 1942), pp. 16-50, 241-62. The discussion in the text is largely drawn from this study.

Second, most of the states set up some sort of legal test that one must meet, and so establish one's *bona fides,* in order to be considered a member of a party and vote in its primary elections. In general, that is to say, the statutes are based on two assumptions: that only Republicans should vote in Republican primaries, and only Democrats in Democratic primaries; and that no person should vote for more than one nominee for each public office in any particular primary election.

Here, however, we must distinguish between "closed-primary" states and "open-primary" states. In the former, all who wish to vote in a party's primary must stand ready to meet a party-affiliation test of some kind. Three such tests are now in use: (1) *The past allegiance test.* In Ohio, for example, the voter whose claim to be a member of a party is challenged must take an oath that he supported the party's candidates *in the last general election.* (2) *The present affiliation test.* In South Dakota, the challenged voter must swear that he is "in good faith" a member of the party in question and "a believer in its principles as declared in the last preceding national and state platforms." (3) *The future intention test.* In Missouri, the challenged voter must take an oath to support the party's nominees in the next general election. Some states, be it noted, employ a combination of past allegiance, present affiliation, and future intention tests. At present, thirty-five states use some type of closed primary.[19]

In the open-primary states, on the other hand, the voter meets his "test" by merely requesting the ballot of the party of which he chooses to be a "member." In Wisconsin, for example, the election officials hand each voter the primary ballots of *all* parties, each of which is printed on a separate sheet. The voter detaches the ballot of the party of his choice, marks it, then drops it into the ballot box and his rejects into the box for waste ballots. In these states, as in the closed-primary states, the voter is permitted to participate in the primary of only one party at any given election, so that the primary is as much a *party* primary as that in a closed-primary state. But the sole test of his party affiliation is his decision, as of this moment, to mark this party's ballot rather than that one's. At present, eleven states use the open primary.[20]

Washington alone among the states permits the voter to participate in more than one party's primary at a given election. Ever since 1935 it has used the so-called "blanket" primary, in which the voter may, if he wishes, cast a vote for his choice among the Republican candidates for governor, then cast one for his choice among the Democratic candidates for senator, etc., switching from party primary to party primary as he moves down the ballot from office to office. The only restriction upon him is that he may not vote in two or more party primaries for one and the same office. The Washington primary

[19] Clyde F. Snider, *American State and Local Government* (New York: Appleton-Century-Crofts, Inc., 1950), p. 133.
[20] *Ibid.*

system thus differs from a nonpartisan primary [21] only in one respect: it does not withhold from the voter the party affiliation of the candidates.

Third, the statutes—except in the open-primary states—designate some authority or agency that is to prescribe the test of party affiliation and determine how it shall be applied. In some states this agency is the party itself, and its state convention or state central committee lays down the qualifications a voter must have in order to vote in the party's primary. In other states the legislature retains this power in its own hands. Methods for *applying* the tests vary markedly from state to state, despite the fact that there are, basically, only two systems to choose from: (1) *the challenge system,* where the voter simply declares his party affiliation, but is open to challenge by anyone present on the grounds that he is not a bona fide member of the party whose ballot he is requesting, and can meet the challenge only by swearing an oath that he satisfies the legal requirements for affiliation with that party; and (2) *the party registration system,* where the voter must register, in advance of the primary election in which he wishes to participate, as a party member. This he does either on a special party-registration day, or at the time he registers for the general election. The registering authorities, under this system, furnish the election officials a roster of registered party members for each party, and that roster answers all questions as to who can vote in which party's primary (a voter is not entitled to *any* primary ballot unless his name appears on one of the rosters; if it does appear, he receives the ballot of the party for which he has registered). Those who register as "independents" can vote in the general elections, but are automatically barred from the primaries.

Fourth, no one has yet devised an effective legal method for *enforcing* tests of party membership. We have seen that some states require would-be participants in a party's primary to swear that they "believe in the party's principles," or that they have supported the party's candidates in the past general election, or that they will support them in the next election. In the last analysis, however, there is nothing the election officials can do except take the voter's word (on oath, to be sure) on these matters: "believe in" is difficult to define for purposes of enforcement, and discovering the "party principles" of an American major party would call for a major research project, no two of whose members would necessarily come out with the same results. Nor, given the secrecy of the ballot in general elections in all forty-eight states, is the test of having voted in a certain way in the past or intending to do so in the

[21] A nonpartisan primary is one in which (a) the ballots bear no party names or designations, (b) any qualified voter can vote, and (c) the *two* candidates for each office who poll the largest vote in the primary become the candidates in the final election. (In some cases, if a candidate receives an absolute majority in the primary, he is declared elected without the subsequent "run-off" election.) Several states use the system for making nominations for a considerable number of local officials (mayors, aldermen, police magistrates, school board members, etc.). Minnesota and Nebraska use it for making nominations for the state legislature. Cf. *ibid.,* pp. 133-34.

future any easier to enforce, for all its apparent simplicity. Only the voter knows how he has voted in the past, or how he intends to vote in the future; and after the next election only he will know whether his intention to vote in a certain way was sincere, and, if so, whether it remained firm up to and including the last minute. Nor is there any way around this difficulty that is not inconsistent with the secret ballot.

As the foregoing considerations would lead us to expect, the only "bolters" whose legal right to remain in the party has ever even been challenged have been persons who have publicly supported candidates of the opposition party. For the most part, such persons have belonged to the party "worker" or "leader" categories of participants, not to the "registrant" or "supporter" categories. And only a few attempts have been made—for the most part in the South—to impose legal sanctions even on bolters of this type (i.e., bolters who have shouted from the housetops that they were deserting the party's nominees and violating its loyalty pledges); and these attempts appear to warrant the general conclusion that the legal sanctions cannot be counted on even when they are invoked. In 1924, for example, a number of Texas Democrats who had unsuccessfully opposed "Ma" Ferguson for Democratic nominee for governor openly supported the Republican nominee in the general election; and two years later the Democratic party attempted to bar them from the Democratic primary on the ground that they had violated their loyalty pledge—only to be told by the Texas Supreme Court that such a pledge is a matter of "moral restraint" only, and cannot be used to prevent a person from voting in a primary.[22] In 1928, for a contrasting example, a number of prominent southern Democrats openly supported Hoover for president, and one of them, Senator J. Thomas ("Tom-Tom") Heflin of Alabama, was excluded from running for senator in the 1930 Democratic primary by the state Democratic executive committee, whose ruling was duly upheld by the Alabama Supreme Court.[23] But the Heflin case appears to be without parallel, and must, in any case, be considered side by side with the Love case, which was *sub judice* about the same time. Thomas B. Love, who, like Heflin, was a "Hoovercrat," was successfully excluded from running for lieutenant governor in the Texas Democratic primary in 1928 by a county executive committee;[24] but when, in 1930, the state executive committee tried to exclude him from running for governor in the Democratic primary, the Texas Supreme Court, in line with the earlier decision we have noted, went to his rescue. Since the statute had imposed no penalty for violation of the candidates' pledge of future loyalty, it held, that pledge was "a purely moral obligation binding no longer than it could be conscientiously performed."[25]

We must note, however, that *both* Heflin and Love were soundly beaten

[22] *Briscoe v. Boyle,* 286 S.W. 275 (1926).
[23] *Wilkinson v. Henry,* 128 So. 362 (1930).
[24] *Love v. Taylor,* 8 S.W. (2d) 795 (1928).
[25] *Love v. Wilcox,* 28 S.W. (2d) 515 (1930).

in the 1930 primaries, so that what the evidence adds up to is not that vociferous bolters can always bolt with impunity, but that effective sanctions are more likely to be imposed by party members than by the courts or the law. But even the party members, it seems, seldom get around to punishing bolters.[26]

In summary, the definitions contained in the laws of the forty-eight states have the effect of admitting to party membership *everyone* who belongs to *any* of the six categories of participants in party activities that we included in our diagram a few pages back. A party member is anyone who has a legal right to participate in the party's formal nominating process; and the only legal qualification a voter must meet in order to acquire that right is that of having declared to some public authority that he is a member, plus, at most, that of having taken an oath of party loyalty which, given the secrecy of the ballot, is *ipso facto* unenforceable.

"RAIDING"

One objection to such a loose legal definition of party membership that we have not yet noticed is that it invites "raiding"—i.e., the invasion of one party's primaries by voters belonging to another party. In the open-primary states there are no barriers against such an invasion; and in many of the closed-primary states, especially those with no party-registration requirements, there are no effective barriers. Even in the closed-primary states requiring party registration any voter who possesses a strong will and a certain elasticity of conscience can circumvent the barriers.

A party may have either of two motives for raiding another party's primary, and raiding may occur either by spontaneous action on the part of the rank-and-file voters of the raiding party, or by "command" (possibly via public announcement, possibly via discreet whispering) of the raiding party's leaders. The objective may be to bring about the nomination of the weakest of the opposition's candidates, and so to better the raiding party's chances of victory in the final election. In the 1938 primaries in Minnesota, for example, many Democrats and Republicans entered the Farmer-Labor primary to vote for Hjalmar Petersen and against Elmer Benson for the gubernatorial nomination, on the ground that Petersen's violent attacks on the Benson administration had made him highly unpopular with the Farmer-Labor rank and file, and he would be easier to beat than Benson in the general election.[27] In the 1928 election in New Jersey, Democratic Boss Frank Hague decided that the best way to elect a Democratic governor was to bring about the nomination of one Morgan F. Larson as the Republican candidate; so he passed the word about among his Democratic followers, and sent an estimated 22,000 Demo-

[26] Cf. V. O. Key, Jr., *Southern Politics in State and Nation* (New York: Alfred A. Knopf, 1949), pp. 432-38; and Berdahl, *op. cit.*, pp. 34-35.

[27] Berdahl, *op. cit.*, p. 42. Unless otherwise noted, all the examples of "raiding" given in the text are drawn from pp. 39-50 of the Berdahl study.

crats (including a number of Democratic election officials and Hudson County Democratic County Committee members) into the Republican primary. The maneuver, though successful at the first stage, backfired on Hague: Larson won the general election, and avenged himself by getting some laws passed regulating "Hagueism." [28]

Secondly, the voters of one party may raid another party's primary because they believe their party's candidate is unlikely to win the general election, and they would like to have a say as to which of several opposition candidates is to fill the office in question; i.e., they enter the opposition party's primary and help determine its results, though they have no other intention than to vote for their own party's candidate in the general election. Members of the minority party in modified one-party areas often feel that they have much to gain, from the standpoint of electoral influence, by undertaking maneuvers of this type. In Wisconsin, for example, Democrats used to enter the Republican primaries in large numbers and throw their support to the La Follette "progressive" faction against the "old-guard" faction; and in the same state, more recently (1952), a large number of Democrats entered the Republican primary in an attempt—unsuccessful, as it turned out—to prevent the renomination of Senator Joseph R. McCarthy. Nor does this kind of thing happen only in the open-primary states. South Dakota Democrats have for many years and in considerable numbers voted in the "closed" Republican primary for the "progressives" and against the "regulars." And in Illinois, also a closed-primary state, downstate Democrats often vote in Republican primaries [29] and Cook County Republicans often vote in Democratic primaries. (In the late 1930's, indeed, Cook County party leaders, both Republican and Democratic, issued pleas to their respective rank-and-file voters *not* to "raid" on their own initiative—i.e., to stay home and vote in their own primaries unless the leaders asked them to do otherwise.)

Sometimes "raiding" becomes so taken for granted that the leaders of various factions of one party openly bid for the support in their primary of members of the opposition party. Thus in New Jersey in the 1930's, so many Democrats regularly voted in Republican primaries ("one-day Republicans," they were called) that the various Republican faction leaders frequently made open bids for their support, and a number of bipartisan "deals" were made in the process.

The practice of "raiding" has received rough treatment at the hands of a good many political scientists, on the ground that it reduces the whole idea of party membership to nonsense and so constitutes a serious barrier to the development of "responsible" parties in the United States. In general, they

[28] Dayton D. McKean, *The Boss: The Hague Machine in Action* (Boston: Houghton Mifflin Company, 1940), pp. 69-71.

[29] In 1952, for instance, a number of Champaign County Democrats voted in the Republican primary in order to support candidates pledged to Eisenhower for seats in the national Republican convention.

point to the looseness and unenforceability [30] of the present legal tests for party membership as the heart of the problem, and recommend that the tests be stiffened enough to place genuine barriers in the way of would-be raiders.[31]

Other political scientists see a partial solution to this and other problems posed by the ticket-voter conception of party membership in pre-primary conventions, now actually provided for by law in several states, and held for the purpose of letting the party leaders nominate a slate of organization candidates, to be designated on the primary ballot as such. This system, the argument runs, makes it easy for the genuine party members to distinguish, in casting their votes, between genuine party candidates and false ones.[32]

The American Political Science Association's Committee on Political Parties, on the other hand, looks for a solution mainly to "positive measures to create a strong and general agreement on policies" among the members of each party, rather than such negative measures as punishing rebels and dissidents among those who claim to be members of the party. They propose, among other things: (1) regular and frequent local party meetings, in which the rank and file can discuss party policy and communicate their views to the upper echelons of the organization; (2) improving the process of drafting national party platforms and programs, and thus promoting increased identification of local party members with the national party and its program; and (3) the general adoption of the closed primary, condemnation of the "blanket" primary, and encouragement of pre-primary nominations.[33] These reforms, they trust, will not only make American parties more responsible; they will also aid in achieving "intraparty democracy"—a topic to which we shall return in the next chapter.

Conclusion

The current thinking, both of most political scientists and of most laymen, as to who may properly be considered members of our political parties, with a legal right to participate in their decision-making processes, is carried

---

[30] An election official who knows his man, however, can sometimes enforce even the present tests. William Howard Taft tells how he and a Republican judge prevented the infiltration of Irish-Catholic Democrats into a Republican primary in Cincinnati. When the first of the raiders, Michael Flannigan, presented himself at the polls, Taft challenged him, and Flannigan prepared to swear, as he had on many past occasions, that he was a bona fide Republican. The judge, however, "produced a Bible and demanded, in deep tones, of the would-be voter that . . . he should place his hand upon the Book, and repeat after him: 'I solemnly swear, in the presence of Almighty God, as I shall answer at the last day of Judgment, that I am a Republican'—[The judge] had not gotten further when Flannigan jerked his hand away, retreated from the poll, muttering 'To h—l with the vote.'" *Popular Government* (New Haven: Yale University Press, 1913), pp. 107-09.

[31] Cf. Berdahl, *op. cit.,* pp. 49-50, 261-62; McKean, *Party and Pressure Politics,* pp. 220-21; and Penniman, *op. cit.,* pp. 441-42.

[32] Cf. Key, *Politics, Parties, and Pressure Groups,* pp. 413-15; *A Model Direct Primary System,* the report of the National Municipal League's Committee on the Direct Primary, Joseph P. Harris, chairman; and "Toward a More Responsible Two-Party System," pp. 72-73.

[33] "Toward a More Responsible Two-Party System," pp. 20-21, 27-28, 65-73.

on for the most part in ticket-voter terms, and may be summarized as follows: Any person who is willing to declare publicly his adherence to a party should be considered a full-fledged member of that party and legally entitled to vote in its primary elections.

The ticket-voter conception of party membership has been embodied in the laws of all forty-eight states. For, despite the differences in detail among them, all the states require from a would-be voter in a primary only that he be a qualified voter and that he publicly state his party preference to some public authority, either by registering with a particular party or by asking for its ballot on election day. He may, to be sure, be asked to take an oath that he has supported or will support the party's principles and/or nominees; but he alone, given the secrecy of the general-election ballot, can say whether he is swearing to a truth or a falsehood. It is therefore not too much to say that a man (or woman) becomes a Republican (or Democrat) in the United States merely by *saying* to the designated public authority that he *is* a Republican (or Democrat)—and it does not make any difference, as regards his right to vote in the Republican (or Democratic) primary, whether he has always voted the straight Democratic (or Republican) ticket in general elections and keeps on voting it (provided he keeps this fact to himself).

"Joining" one of our major parties, then, calls for practically no expenditure of effort, and requires no commitments [34]—from the man or woman who is content with "belonging" in the minimum, legalistic sense of the term. If, on the other hand, a man or woman wishes to "get into party politics," i.e., to be a party member in the activist sense of the term, he must in some fashion hook up with one of the party "organizations." What these agencies are, how they relate to each other and to the legal party "members," and the role they perform in the American party system, are the topics dealt with in our next chapter.

[34] Joining at least some minor parties is less easy by far, and the demands on the member, once he is in, are enormously greater. We examine this point in greater detail in Chapter 19.

Chapter 10

FORMAL PARTY
ORGANIZATION

The Concept of "Party Organization"

"ORGANIZATION" IN GENERAL

Perhaps no other concept figures so prominently in the literature of social and political groups as that of *organization,* from which we derive such basic distinctions as that between "organized" and "unorganized" groups, and that between the "good organization man," or the "good organizer," and the "poor organization man," or "poor organizer."

Political parties are by common consent "organized" groups, and in the present chapter we propose to fix attention on their *formal* organization to the virtual exclusion of other aspects of their life and activity. It would be advisable, therefore, to be clear as to just what we understand the term "organization" to mean when applied to a social or political group.

One of the most helpful brief discussions of this point is Professor Rudolf Heberle's. He writes:

> We say a group is organized if certain of its members are authorized *to give orders to members of the group and to represent the group* in relations with outsiders and other organized groups. Organization consists in attributing to certain members definite *powers* and *duties* relevant to the functioning of the group; these certain members are thereby authorized to *demand and prohibit particular actions* from other members, and *expect obedience* to their requests. The empowered persons act, within the sphere of their authority, not as private individuals, but as agents of the group; they do so also in relation to outsiders. Their actions are regarded as actions of the entire group. Since, in the ideal case, all of the functions delegated in this way are essential and interdependent, the *officers of an organized group can be compared to the organs of a living body,* hence the term *organization.*[1]

---

[1] Rudolf Heberle, *Social Movements* (New York: Appleton-Century-Crofts, Inc., 1951), pp. 269-70. Italics added.

In other words, when fifteen college students turn up on the same evening at a picnic ground, and end up having a meal together, they are indeed a group (e.g., they interact with one another), but an *unorganized* group. Why? On Professor Heberle's showing, because none of them is authorized to give orders to the other members, or to represent the group vis-à-vis the outside world. If, however, they have communicated with each other beforehand, agreed to meet at the ground at a certain time, and worked out arrangements whereby A is to buy the food, B is to see to the drinks, C is to provide the transportation, and D is to bring along a ball and a bat, then they are at least a rudimentary form of *organized* group.[2] And if they communicate with one another regularly for this or some similar purpose (e.g., they are a softball team out to win in the intramural league), then they are a less rudimentary form of organized group.[3]

"Organization," in our view, refers to certain more or less *recurring* patterns of activity, more or less *shared* by *individual members* of a *group,* in a way that more or less approximates a "rational" allocation of the functions performed among the persons performing them. It thus includes the procedures by which the members of the group make decisions about the "division of work, allocation of duties, authority relationships, lines of communication, and so forth" that enable the group as a whole to perform its characteristic activities. In studying a group's organization, that is to say, we must fix attention on its characteristic activities. And this, in the case of political parties, points us toward the making of nominations and the contesting of elections.[4]

"FORMAL" AND "INFORMAL" ORGANIZATION

Students of social and political groups often draw a distinction—a refinement of the concept we have just been considering—between "formal" and "informal" organization. "Formal organization," as defined by Simon, Smithburg, and Thompson, is "the pattern of behavior and relationship that is *deliberately* and *legitimately planned* for the members of the organization."[5] The key phrases here, evidently, are "deliberately planned" and "legitimately planned." The first, as we read it, suggests the idea of taking thought: it tells us that the formal organization of a group is not a happenstance, not a pattern that the members of the group fell into by chance, but a *construct,* built by conscious effort on the part of some of the group's members (conceivably,

---

[2] Cf. *ibid.,* p. 270. George Homans defines "organization" as the relationship between the scheme of activities of a group (in the example in the text, buying and preparing the food, riding to the picnic ground, eating the food, throwing and batting the ball, etc.) and the scheme of interaction among the members of the group (A's effect on the actions of B, B's on A's, A's on C's, etc.): *The Human Group* (New York: Harcourt, Brace and Company, 1950), pp. 106, 239.

[3] The notion of regularity and the notion that organization is a matter of more or less are both clearly presupposed in Professor Heberle's definitions.

[4] Cf. Herbert A. Simon, Donald W. Smithburg, and Victor A. Thompson, *Public Administration* (New York: Alfred A. Knopf, 1950), p. 85.

[5] *Ibid.,* p. 86. Italics added.

of course, on the part of all of them). And because it is the result of conscious thought, such a pattern usually lends itself readily to formulation in symbols, whether verbal (as in a constitution or set of by-laws) or nonverbal (as in a chart). It need not, on the other hand, have been so formulated in order to qualify as "formal," and certainly all of it need not—as witness certain aspects of the British Constitution, e.g., the general understanding that the monarch always accepts the advice of his ministers, which is certainly part of the formal organization of the British government but has no basis in positive law. The formal organization of most groups, however, is embodied in a written constitution regarded as not subject to change without further conscious thought, which gives us a second sense in which formal organization is "deliberately planned." [6] In short, the rules governing most groups' formal organization are relatively definite, easy to find, and easy for the newcomer to learn because he can usually be told where to go in order to consult them.

The phrase "legitimately planned," as the writers we cite use it, is equivalent to "planned by consent of the group's members," or if not that, "planned in accordance with rules and procedures to which the members have consented." The procedures and relationships that make up a group's formal organization, in other words, are always open to challenge (in a way that those making up its informal organization are not) on the grounds that the proprieties, whatever these happen to be in the group in question, have not been observed, that they are a departure from the constitution or by-laws, that they are not backed up by the members' consent, etc. The term refers, in other words, to certain ideas in the minds of the members of the group, and also to the relation between these ideas and certain procedures and relationships. [7]

We come now to the notion of "informal organization," which we need, say Simon, Smithburg, and Thompson, because

almost always the actual pattern of behaviors and relationships of the members of an organization will depart slightly or widely from the formal plan of organization. The actual pattern may differ from the formal plan in two ways; (1) the formal plan may be incomplete—it may not include the whole pattern of behavior as it actually develops; and (2) some portions of the actual pattern of behavior may be in contradiction to the plan. By *informal organization* is meant the whole pattern of actual behaviors—the way members of the organization really do behave—insofar as the actual behaviors do not coincide with the formal plan. [8]

The difference between "formal" and "informal" organization, then, is often one of *degree* only, not of kind, as far as both "deliberateness" and "legitimacy" are concerned. The dividing line between them, therefore, is at some points blurred and elusive, and in using the two terms it is well always to remember that the phenomena they denote are not always easy to classify.

[6] Cf. Heberle, *op. cit.*, p. 270.
[7] Cf. Simon, Smithburg, and Thompson, *op. cit.*, pp. 85-87.
[8] *Ibid.*, p. 87.

For example: A private at an army post wishes to get a week-end pass. The table of organization and printed regulations of the post, if he reads them, tell him that his pass must be granted by the captain of his company. His buddies, however, assure him that that is not how it really works: "Cap'n, he don't bother his head with such things. He signs all the pass applications Sarge sticks under his nose." The "formal" organization chart, in other words, puts the decision as to whether our private will get his pass in the hands of the captain; the "informal" organization puts it in the hands of the sergeant, and if our private wants results he will certainly be better advised to treat the informal organization as the real one. On the other hand, the fact that the sergeant and not the captain makes this type of decision is one that everybody knows and acts upon, so that a rookie seeking a pass is told as a matter of course to see the sergeant. And this raises the question, How "informal" is the organization that locates the pass-giving power in the sergeant? The difference between "formal" and "informal" in such a situation either disappears, or boils down to a difference between the written and unwritten (i.e., the set of rules according to which the captain has the power is written down, and that according to which the sergeant has it is not written).

This is not, however, to say that the whole distinction between "formal" and "informal" is pointless. There is growing agreement among present-day political scientists that to fail to look behind the formal organization of a group at the operative realities of its day-to-day activity is to repeat what, on the record, is one of the most dangerous blunders the political observer or analyst can make. Early American political science, because of its almost exclusive concentration upon the legal structure of government,[9] was especially prone to this type of blunder; and many modern observers feel that we have yet to fight ourselves entirely free of the misunderstandings about the actual operation of American government that we have inherited from it.[10] But blunders are also possible in the other direction. In the case cited, all that is needed in order for the current informal organization to go by the board is for the

[9] See David Easton, The Political System (New York: Alfred A. Knopf, 1953), pp. 152-59, for a general discussion of the nature and consequences of the legalistic-formalistic bias of early American political science. For a discussion of the effect of this bias in delaying the study of political parties, see Austin Ranney, "The Reception of Political Parties into American Political Science," Southwestern Social Science Quarterly, Vol. XXXII (December, 1951), pp. 183-91.

[10] Another example of the importance of studying "informal" organization in politics and government is this: Under the Eisenhower administration, the Secretary of State (John Foster Dulles) and the Director of Central Intelligence (Allen Dulles)—the heads of two agencies whose jurisdictional conflicts have been for many years a major Washington headache—happen to be brothers, so that, to some degree at least, clashes between the two agencies, whose formal organizational relations are unchanged, can be talked out within one and the same family. Clearly, the political observer who tries to analyze the relation between the two agencies without taking into account this new factor in the situation would be sleeping at the switch. Or, to choose an example somewhat closer to the subject matter of this book, the relations between national headquarters of the party in power and the White House belong entirely to the informal organization of our political system, and yet, by common consent, are of crucial importance in its actual operation.

present captain or present sergeant to be replaced. Thus the observer who fixed attention on the informal to the exclusion of the formal might find, one morning, that he had been overlooking an important constant in the situation.

We might conclude, therefore, that the fullest understanding of how a given social or political group actually operates requires the study of both its formal and its informal organization.[11]

In the present chapter we are primarily concerned with the *formal* organization of the American major parties (we shall take up their informal organization in Chapter 11). This, in the light of the foregoing discussion, we can define as the deliberately and legitimately planned pattern of behavior and relationships maintained by members of our major parties in the making of nominations, the contesting of elections, and the other activities in which the parties engage.[12]

The agencies, rules, and allocations of authority that make up the "formal" organization of the American major parties are to a considerable extent provided for or regulated *by law*—provisions in certain state constitutions, acts of Congress, and, most conspicuously, acts of state legislatures. The parties' legal status, therefore, is the appropriate starting point for the present phase of our inquiry, and to it we now turn our attention.

The Legal Status of American Parties

IN GENERAL [13]

Until the latter part of the nineteenth century, political parties were largely "unknown to the law" in the United States. There were almost no statutes, national or state, directly regulating or even recognizing party organization and activities, and the courts took the general position that questions touching upon the regulation of parties are "political," and therefore outside the province of the judiciary. Only after the Civil War, when there was a sharp increase in popular concern over party "corruption" and "boss rule," [14] did our legislatures begin to regard the direct regulation of party organization and

[11] In some instances organizations entirely outside the "formal" (i.e., legal) organizations of the parties have become as elaborate as and more important than the latter. In Wisconsin, for example, both the Republican and Democratic parties have developed "voluntary committees" outside the formal-legal party machinery in order to evade the straitjacket restrictions laid on the formal organizations by the state laws regulating party machinery. Each "voluntary committee" now controls its particular party, and each is recognized and dealt with as *the* party organization in the state by the respective national committees of the two parties. Cf. Frank J. Sorauf, "Extra-legal Parties in Wisconsin," *American Political Science Review,* Vol. XLVIII (September, 1954), pp. 692-704.

[12] In Chapter 9 we defined "party members" simply as all persons who engage in these characteristic party activities.

[13] By far the most thorough study of the legal status of American parties is that by Joseph R. Starr, "The Legal Status of American Political Parties," *American Political Science Review,* Vol. XXXIV (June, August, 1940), pp. 439-55, 685-99.

[14] For a review of the amount and nature of post–Civil War concern with political parties, see Ranney, *op. cit.*

activity as one of their responsibilities, and to operate on the surmise that it could best be discharged by the rapid multiplication of statutory enactments.

The present legal status of American parties is a matter of countless rules emanating, according to little or no pattern or logic, from four distinct sources: (1) *State constitutions*. Some 17 states have written provisions directly applying to parties into their fundamental laws. The constitutions of the other 31 states do not so much as mention them; nor does the national constitution. (2) *Acts of Congress*. There are a handful of federal statutes, the best-known of which are the Hatch Acts, which directly regulate party activities. Their impact, however, is out of proportion to their number. (3) *Acts of state legislatures*. These account for the great bulk of the enactments directly applying to political parties. The 48 states without exception now have statutes subjecting parties to some forms at least of regulation. (4) *Court decisions*. The courts, state courts for the most part, have laid down a number of rules applying to party affairs which, in the absence of legislation on the points involved, have the force of law. The courts are often called upon to rule on the constitutionality of statutes governing the parties; and while they generally rule favorably on such statutes, they are always present as a *potential* source of decisions that would change the status quo as regards the legal status of political parties.

THE LEGAL CHARACTER OF POLITICAL PARTIES

Where there are no statutes specifying otherwise, the courts have generally held that political parties—and their various executive committees—have the status of *unincorporated nonprofit associations*. They have, on this showing, no corporate existence apart from the individuals who compose them; they cannot, for example, sue or be sued except by joining the names of the members and/or officers together as plaintiffs or defendants. A party as such, therefore, cannot enter into contracts, though an individual representing a party may do so—the resultant liability, however, being exclusively his, and his only in his capacity as an individual. This state of affairs is, of course, subject to change by statute, and in two states, New York and Louisiana, certain party officers are, for certain purposes, legally responsible in their party capacity. Elsewhere, however, the parties remain unincorporated nonprofit associations.

The courts have generally held that political parties have a legal right to exist, and that this right cannot be destroyed by ordinary legislative acts. Some courts have treated this right as derivative from the right of individual citizens to vote (the logic here being: deny to parties the right to exist, and you deny to individuals the right to organize and belong to parties, and thus restrict their right to vote). Other courts have held the right to be inherent in the idea of a "free government." The general rule, in any case, is that legislatures may regulate and restrain the organization and activities of political parties, but have no constitutional power to destroy a political party outright. The major parties, certainly, have a clear and unqualified right to exist, and other parties too except that they may have to meet certain legal specifications as to what constitutes a party, and, in some states, must have programs that do not run afoul of the law. For a number of states have statutes that put small parties and new parties at great disadvantage vis-à-vis the established major parties, and may destroy them or keep them from being born; and some states prohibit subversive parties altogether.

In six states, any small party or new party is under no disabilities at all; that is, it enjoys as a matter of course the same status and privileges as the established major parties. It can get the names of its nominees printed on the official final-election ballot, for example, or use the state's facilities and financial resources for its direct-primary elections, by merely making application to the proper authorities. Everywhere else in the United States, however, the small or new party enjoys privileges of this character only if it can fulfill certain requirements that are explicitly laid down in a statutory definition of a "political party." The ostensible purpose of such requirements is to reserve the privileges of parties to organizations whose popular following has reached a certain size, usually expressed in terms of a share of the vote for governor or some other officer voted for generally throughout the state, and the requirements range from 1 to 25 per cent of the total vote. Or, as in New York and Texas, no organization is a party that did not poll a specified minimum number of votes (50,000 and 100,000, respectively) at the last election.[15]

If all the definitions were like the two just noted, and the matter were left at that, no new party could ever get on the ballot, and no small party, once put off, could ever get back on. In most of the 42 states here in question, however, a party can get on (or back on) the ballot by petition. In Illinois, for example, a new party must collect at least 25,000 valid signatures on its petition for recognition, so distributed as to include at least 200 registered voters in each of at least 50 counties—the idea being, apparently, to discourage not so much small organizations (25,000 is a quite small percentage of the Illinois vote) as organizations with a purely local following. In some states, the number of signatures required is so small as to make the petition a mere formality, in others so large as to make it improbable that any new organization will ever meet it. And in a few states, no procedure whatever is provided whereby new or small parties can actually get their candidates' names on the ballot under their own party label: they must either run their men as independents, or not run them at all.

The statutes containing such requirements have been challenged a number of times in the courts as a denial of equal protection of the laws and as a violation of the general right of a party to exist. The courts have consistently held, however, that the relevant statutes are constitutional, and that there is no constitutional obligation on the legislature's part to extend to new or small parties the same privileges it extends to the established major parties.[16]

[15] Starr, *op. cit.,* p. 452.
[16] *Ibid.,* pp. 454-55.

THE STATUS OF SUBVERSIVE PARTIES

A number of states have taken measures to keep political parties regarded as subversive from getting nominees on the final-election ballot. As of January 1, 1951, eight states (Arkansas, California, Illinois, Kansas, Maryland, Oklahoma, Wisconsin, and Wyoming) exclude any groups with an official party name that includes the word "communist," and any group directly or indirectly connected with the Communist party of the United States. Fourteen states (the above states plus Alabama, Delaware, Indiana, Ohio, Pennsylvania, and Tennessee) exclude all organizations advocating forcible or unlawful overthrow of the government. Twelve states (the list just given less Alabama and Pennsylvania) exclude groups that advocate or carry out programs of force, violence, sabotage, sedition, or treason, and a number of states specifically bar persons who advocate and/or are members of organizations that advocate violent and unlawful overthrow of the government, or are affiliated, directly or indirectly, with the Communist party of the United States, both from becoming candidates for and from holding elective office (the latter phrasing being a safeguard against subversives who might get themselves elected under the banner of one of the established parties).[17] In Illinois, for example, the petition or certificate of nomination for any candidate for any offices must include the following sworn statement:

I, ..., do swear that I am a citizen of the United States and the State of Illinois, that I am not affiliated directly or indirectly with any communist organization or any communist front organization, or any foreign political agency, party, organization or government which advocates the overthrow of constitutional government by force or other means not permitted under the Constitution of the United States or the constitution of this State; that I do not directly or indirectly teach or advocate the overthrow of the government of the United States or of this State or any unlawful change in the form of governments thereof by force or any unlawful means.[18]

Since few statutes of the type just mentioned have, at the present writing, been challenged in the courts, there remains some doubt about their constitutionality, although there is a marked nationwide trend toward legislation placing disabilities upon subversives, and in general the courts have gone along with the trend. For the moment, in any case, these statutes are part of the laws of several states, and as such have implications regarding the general right of parties to exist that are highly significant, whether or not they are a marked departure, as they are often alleged to be, from our traditional practices. For their tacit premise, to which many voters and legislators are now without doubt deeply committed, is that no party has a right to exist unless it looks to the perpetuation of democratic government in the American com-

---

[17] These statutes are summarized in Walter Gellhorn, ed., *The States and Subversion* (Ithaca, N. Y.: Cornell University Press, 1952), Appendix A, pp. 404-07.

[18] *Illinois Election Laws, 1953*, Article 7, Section 10.1.

munity—or, to put it a little differently, that persons and organizations that repudiate the community's consensus should as a matter of course be excluded from the political rights and privileges it extends to other persons and organizations.

REGULATION OF PARTY ORGANIZATION
AND ACTIVITIES BY STATUTE

Most of the laws applying to political parties regulate their organization and activities, and address themselves, again in accordance with no nationwide pattern, to one or another of the following five matters:

Membership. Each of the 48 states, as we noted in Chapter 9, specifies by law what persons may participate in direct primaries and party caucuses, and in doing so in effect determines which persons are, from the legal point of view, party members.

Organization. Each of the 48 states has statutes prescribing the nature, the manner of selection, the functions, and thus, to a greater or lesser degree, the powers of the party committees and conventions. In some states, especially in the South, these statutes are broad and loose, and leave the parties a good deal of room to move around in. But the major trend over the years has been in the direction of specific and detailed prescriptions.

Nominating Procedures. Most candidates for most offices in most states are now nominated by direct primaries; and even where they are nominated by caucuses and conventions, the procedures are for the most part governed by fairly strict legal provisions.

Party Finance. Most states now prescribe who may and who may not contribute to a political party, how much a single individual may contribute, etc. There are also some federal statutes on this point.

Corrupt Practices. All the states now have some kind of legislation aimed at "cleaning up" the expenditure of party funds; and this legislation also has been supplemented and rounded out by federal statute. Some of the statutes require publication of the parties' campaign receipts and expenditures; others also list in greater or lesser detail the activities on which party funds can lawfully be spent, limit the amount that can be spent, and so on.

REGULATION OF PARTIES BY THE COURTS

The state courts, when asked to regulate this or that aspect of internal party affairs in the absence of applicable statutes, have frequently held that the internal affairs of parties are "political," not "judicial," matters; i.e., they have refused to intervene. The general rule, as matters now stand, appears to be that the courts follow a "hands-off" policy in this area unless jurisdiction has been specifically conferred upon them by statute, or the matter in dispute is regulated by statute, or, in their view, some basic civil right is at stake.[19]

[19] Starr, *op. cit.,* pp. 695-96.

Most of the courts have, in particular, disclaimed any power on their part to settle intraparty factional disputes. These are brought to them from time to time in the form of suits over disputed nominations in party primaries and conventions, and their refusal to take jurisdiction is usually explained on the grounds that they would be performing a "political" function if they did not refuse. Where they have assumed jurisdiction and settled such a dispute, accordingly, they have been careful to argue the matter in such fashion as not to claim any inherent (that is, nonstatutory) power to do so. In some states, on the other hand, the power to settle such contests has been specifically vested in the courts, though a more common arrangement is for the legislature to set up a special tribunal to act as a canvassing and reviewing board for disputed nominations. A few state legislatures have lodged the nomination-reviewing power in the parties' own committees, and the relevant statutes have consistently been upheld by the courts.[20]

The general position, then, is that the courts avoid regulating parties except as the statutes require them—or at least empower them—to do so.

LEGAL PROTECTION OF THE PARTY LABEL

In addition to regulating party organization and activities, some states provide specific statutory protection for party "labels." The purpose here is to prevent the independent candidate from calling himself an "Independent Republican" or "Regular Democrat" or "Jeffersonian Democrat," and thus picking up some votes that would not come his way without the appeal of the party name or a close approximation thereto. Various formulas have been elaborated for extending statutory protection to each party's exclusive right to the use of its name by forbidding other parties, or independent candidates, from exploiting it in any way.[21]

The Formal Organization of American Parties

IN GENERAL

The formal organization of an American political party is an intricate network of committees, conventions, and officers, for the most part provided for by statute. In general, there is a distinct committee and/or convention for every geographical area or election district of a certain kind (e.g., the area over which the resident voters elect such and such a public official). Party organization is therefore closely tied, for the most part, to certain levels of election organization—as we should expect, since parties are primarily nomination-making and election-contesting bodies, and the most obvious and convenient bases for the various parts of their organization are, evidently, election districts.

[20] *Ibid.*, pp. 696-99.
[21] Clarence A. Berdahl, "Party Membership in the United States," *American Political Science Review*, Vol. XXXVI (April, 1942), pp. 243-45. See also Starr, *op. cit.*, pp. 690-92.

The various committees, conventions, and officers do not—in theory, law, or fact—generally form a neat, pyramidal, hierachical pattern, with lines of responsibility and authority clearly established, either over the country as a whole or in any particular state; and insofar as the term "organization" implies any such pattern, its use here is misleading. Take, for example, the situation in Illinois, where the members of the state central committee are elected directly by the primary voters in congressional districts, one from each district. But each congressional district has its own so-called congressional committee, made up of the chairmen of all the county central committees within its boundaries. Each county central committee, in turn, consists of all the ward, township, and precinct committeemen in the county (they, as a group, elect the county chairman). In other words, the pattern appears fairly neat and hierarchical until we come to the top of the pyramid, the state central committee, which in no sense emerges from the committees further down, and, indeed, results from an entirely different process of selection. And, as if all that were not already complicated enough, delegates to national conventions are picked partly by primary voters in congressional districts, and partly by the state convention! And none of the committees or conventions mentioned have any legal power, or, for that matter, any considerable influence, over any other.[22]

Describing formal party organization, therefore—given the danger that by speaking of "levels" of party organization we may give the false impression that it is all symmetrical and sensible like the chart of a field army with its precisely defined "echelons" reaching down through corps all the way to company —is a difficult undertaking at best. The most satisfactory way to go about the task, it seems to us, is to take it a "level" at a time and pause at every opportunity to remind the reader that the lines of authority and responsibility back and forth between the levels mostly have no legal basis, vary tremendously from state to state, and in any particular state are a matter for careful, moment-to-moment observation and study.

THE MAJOR LEVELS OF ORGANIZATION AND THEIR ACTIVITIES

Precinct Committeemen and "Captains." Every state is divided by law into "precincts"—small voting districts, each with a specific polling place and a set of election officials, judges, and clerks, where qualified resident voters cast their ballots in all county, state, and national elections, referenda, etc.[23] Precincts vary in size from around 200 voters in California up to around 2,000 in Massachusetts, and all the states have some precincts with as few as half a dozen voters, these being in mountain or desert areas where, if the precincts were enlarged to include any more voters, some of those voters would have to spend all day traveling in order to cast their votes.[24] The precincts them-

[22] *Illinois Election Laws, 1953,* Article 7, Sections 7-8.

[23] In most states these basic voting districts are legally designated "precincts"; but in a few (e.g., New York) they are called "election districts."

[24] Joseph P. Harris, *Election Administration in the United States* (Washington, D. C.: The Brookings Institution, 1934), pp. 206-08.

selves are not, be it noted, constituencies in the strict sense of that term; i.e., they do not return any *public* official whose job it is to represent the precinct as such. The smallest constituency in most states is the "ward," which is a district within a municipality having the mayor-council or council-manager form of government for the election of members of the city council.

Over most of the country, however, the voters of each party do pick—by direct primary in most of the states, by precinct caucus in the remainder—a *precinct committeeman,* who does "sit" for the precinct as such and is, where he exists, the basic elected party official. The chief exceptions here are the large cities in certain states, where the party voters in each ward elect a *ward committeeman* as the basic elected party official.[25] The ward committeeman then *appoints* precinct leaders, who take charge of party work in the lesser districts within their respective wards. The latter officials are usually known as precinct *captains* in order to distinguish them from precinct *committeemen,* who, as we have seen, are elected. There is also a bewildering variety of elected party officials from the basic party units in non-urban areas, e.g., township committeemen, village committeemen, parish committeemen, etc.

Since, however, the typical party official elected from the base is the precinct committeeman, we may conveniently confine our description to his tasks, and how he goes about performing them—not in any particular precinct, but in an imaginary typical precinct in a typical urban community in a typical state. Some of our data for this purpose have been drawn, as noted, from other writers who have described party organization,[26] the remainder from personal observation in cities as remote and different from one another as Oklahoma City, Evanston, New Haven, Urbana, Richmond, and Geneva (New York).

There appears to be general agreement among students of American parties that Frank R. Kent's classic statement of the precinct committeeman's functions, though written many years ago, can stand virtually unchanged today. The precinct committeeman, according to Kent, is the crucial point at which to observe party organization:

While he is the smallest, he is also, by long odds, the most vital [unit in the party machine]. . . . He is the bone and sinew of the machine. He is its founda-

[25] In Illinois, for example, the law provides that in cities with a population exceeding 200,000, the ward committeeman shall be the basic elected party official: *Illinois Election Laws, 1953,* Article 7, Section 8, Paragraph (b).

[26] The standard textbooks on American parties all contain useful, though brief, accounts of the role and activities of precinct committeemen. The most thorough treatments, however, are to be found in the following: Frank R. Kent, *The Great Game of Politics,* rev. ed. (Garden City, N. Y.: Doubleday & Company, Inc., 1923, 1930), pp. 1-5; Sonya Forthal, *Cogwheels of Democracy, A Study of the Precinct Captain* (New York: William-Frederick Press, 1946); Harold F. Gosnell, *Machine Politics: Chicago Model* (Chicago: University of Chicago Press, 1937); David H. Kurtzman, *Methods of Controlling Votes in Philadelphia* (Philadelphia: Dissertation in Political Science, University of Pennsylvania, 1935); William E. Mosher, "Party and Government Control at the Grass Roots," *National Municipal Review,* Vol. XXIV (January, 1935), pp. 15-18, 38; and Leon Weaver, "Some Soundings in the Party System: Rural Precinct Committeemen," *American Political Science Review,* Vol. XXXIV (February, 1940), pp. 76-84.

tion and the real source of its strength. If he does not function, the machine decays. If he quits, the machine dies. He is the actual connecting link between the people and the organization, and he is the only connecting link—the only man in the machine who has any point of direct contact with the voters, who knows anything about them, who has any real influence with them. All that the boss has in the way of power comes from the precinct executives. All that the machine has in the way of substance and solidity, he gives it. Without him there is no machine. He is the indispensable cog in the wheel.[27]

The principal commodity in which the parties deal, as Kent clearly recognizes, is *votes*: just as an army succeeds or fails as its combat troops on the front line advance or retreat, no matter how well stocked are its PX's or how entertaining its U.S.O. shows, so a major party succeeds or fails as it musters at the polls more or fewer votes than its rival and so wins or loses elections. And it is the precinct committeemen whose performance adds up to success or failure, since it is they who maintain the steady, intimate, and face-to-face relationship between the party organization and the voters which actually delivers or fails to deliver votes. The precinct committeeman, to continue our analogy, is the front-line soldier, and if there is any advancing to be done it is his feet that will do it. Unless he does his job well, therefore, the master strategic and tactical plans of the party generals and colonels are not likely to come off. And, just as an army is unlikely to leave any front-line positions in an area of actual combat unmanned, but may leave some unmanned in areas where no real combat has taken place for some time, so party practice with respect to the deployment of precinct committeemen varies from area to area in proportion to the intensity of combat. Where genuine two-party conflict prevails, these posts are likely to be generally manned. In the modified one-party areas, the dominant party, according to the evidence we have been able to find, sees to it that most of its precinct-committeemen posts are manned, but the second party often has many that are not (it is not really engaged in combat, and doesn't take the trouble). In the one-party areas, the second party is likely to have most, sometimes nearly all of them, unfilled.[28]

In carrying out his tasks, the precinct committeeman has three main objectives: (1) to identify and get acquainted with those voters in his precinct who are sympathetic to his party or to him personally and can be counted upon to vote as he wants them to in both final elections and primaries—and to keep them "regular"; (2) to make sure that the voters just mentioned get properly registered and get to the polls on election day; (3) to try to persuade waverers and independents and even, at the margin, adherents of the opposition party to support the party's ticket in particular elections. The third is,

[27] From: *The Great Game of Politics* (rev. ed.), by Frank R. Kent, pp. 1-2. Copyright 1923, 1930, by Doubleday & Company, Inc. See also Gosnell, *op. cit.*, pp. 51-52.

[28] See, for example, our discussion in Chapter 8 of the relative activity in the primaries of the dominant and second parties in the modified one-party states.

it should be emphasized, by all odds the low-priority objective of the three, and many precinct committeemen almost entirely neglect it.

The precinct committeeman, in his attempt to accomplish the above objectives, divides his efforts among the following three major activities:

CANVASSING. He and his aides go from door to door in the precinct, "ringing doorbells," finding out which voters view his party with favor, learning whether or not those who do are properly registered, and (soon after) seeing to it that those who are not registered get on the books. He may tarry with a doubtful voter long enough to put the case for his party, but he is hardly likely to let this interfere with any call which may help firm up the allegiance of someone already on his side. For this latter, it cannot be overemphasized, is his central function.[29]

SOCIAL SERVICE. By way of creating and maintaining good will for himself and his party, the precinct committeeman often carries on a number of social-service activities in his precinct. Any social gatherings, clubs, picnics, athletic teams, and the like, that he can promote for the voters in his precinct and get credit for in their eyes, are likely to tighten his hold on the votes he controls, and may get him control of some new ones.[30] His axiom is that votes are most dependable when they are expressions of gratitude, and that the most dependable way to earn gratitude is to do favors. In a study of party organization in Chicago in the late 1920's and early 1930's, Professor Gosnell listed the following types of services that precinct captains made it their business to perform for individual voters: They made, to their poorer constituents, outright gifts of food, coal, rent, and money. They helped get people jobs in the city government, used "pull" to have streets and alleys fixed up, taxes and assessments adjusted, permits granted, and building and zoning ordinances eased, and put precinct residents in contact with relief agencies. They furnished legal aid, and went to their constituents' assistance when they got into scrapes with the law. They helped immigrant constituents to obtain naturalization papers, and ex-service constituents to qualify for the state veterans' bonus. They attended funerals and weddings, and tried (when called upon) to smooth over domestic difficulties between husbands and wives, parents and children.[31] Social service on this scale is, to be sure, far more the business of precinct committeemen in large cities like Chicago than of those in rural areas and small towns.[32] But even in the latter, the precinct committeeman must not be above running errands, or fail to keep his constituents reminded that he is an ever-available friend.

ELECTION-DAY ACTIVITIES. The payoff for the precinct committeeman, as we have already noted, comes in the form of valid votes cast for his ticket in

[29] Cf. Forthal, *op. cit.*, pp. 50-54.
[30] *Ibid.*, pp. 46-50.
[31] Gosnell, *op. cit.*, p. 71.
[32] Cf. *ibid.*, pp. 81-84; and Kurtzman, *op. cit.*, p. 11.

primary and general elections. Consequently, he has a number of things to do on election day by way of making sure that the voters he has been cultivating all these months actually go to the polls and vote. If he has done his pre-election job well, he should know pretty well which persons will cast the kind of ballot he wants cast, and his task on election day itself is simply to make sure that these persons don't fail to get to the polls and don't mutilate their ballots once they are there—which means that they must be briefed on how to mark a ballot properly. Getting reliable voters to the polls, similarly, is a matter of reaching all of them by telephone early in the day, maintaining an automobile service ready to transport them to the polls and home again, providing baby sitters for those who have young children, and stationing a representative at the polling place who, by keeping a running check as to which voters on the list have voted, is able to say at any moment which of them have not yet turned up and may need some further prodding.

Such, then, are the objectives and methods of the precinct committeeman. In most states, the statutes provide for city committees as well, made up either of the precinct committeemen from all the city precincts or the ward committeemen from all its wards, according as the former or the latter are the basic elected party officials, and headed by a city chairman of their own choice. Some states provide for township committees or borough committees parallel to the city committees and made up, like them, of committeemen from the basic lower level. Such committees, as a rule, are active in and important for local and municipal elections only; the party has other machinery for overseeing campaigns in national and state elections.

County Committees and County Chairmen. The next generally important level of party organization above the precinct committeeman is that of the county committee. In some of the states county committee members are now picked by the county convention, itself an assembly of the precinct, ward, and township committeemen from all over the county; and in other states they are named by the party candidates for county office. In most of the states, however, the county committee is made up of all the basic elected party officials, that is, precinct, ward, and township committeemen, in each county; and there appears to be a marked trend, in any case, away from all arrangements that use, as county committeemen, party officials not directly elected by the voters.[33]

The county committeemen's job is to select the county chairman, who is the most powerful local (i.e., less than statewide) party official, so that winning the office is a much-sought-after token of success as a local party leader—the more because the powers and functions of the office are not all located within the county's territorial limits. Within the county, the chairman supervises and advises the precinct committeemen and city and township committees, oversees county and local nominations, and presides over the distribution

[33] Cf. Hugh A. Bone, *American Politics and the Party System* (New York: McGraw-Hill Book Company, Inc., 1949), pp. 430-31.

of patronage.[34] Outside it, in most states, he is ex officio a member of the party's congressional committee for the district in which he lives, and, in many states, even an ex officio member of the state central committee, though this is true in by no means all of the states.

Entirely apart from their formal status and powers, the county chairmen are widely regarded as key figures in the informal or "actual" power structure of the state parties. Candidates for a party's nomination for statewide office, for example, can hardly hope for success unless they can count upon the active support of a substantial number of county chairmen. Certainly, the Gallup poll and the newspapers share this view of the county chairmen's "importance." For when it is the opinions of the "grass-roots" party organization that they are after, they turn to the county chairmen as a matter of course.

In most states there are, besides the committees already mentioned, district committees of various sorts—congressional committees, (state) senatorial committees, judicial committees, etc. These committees are made up, for the most part, either of all the county chairmen in the district, or of all of its precinct, ward, and township committeemen; only in a few states are they elected by the party voters. Their ostensible function is to recommend candidates for the offices to be filled from their particular districts, and then to help conduct the campaign on their behalf. Actually, however, these arrangements are usually worked out beforehand by precinct committemen and/or county chairmen, so that the district committees have little to do except ratify decisions that have already been made.

The State Central Committees and State Chairmen. The next significant level of party organization above that of the county committee and county chairman is that of the state central committee. There is considerable variation from state to state in the composition, manner of selection, and even official title of the state committee ("state central committee" appears to be the most usual designation). But they are at least enough alike in source and function to justify the statement that, both individually and collectively, they play a crucial role in American party organization.

Let us note, first, the wide variety of procedures by which the members of the state central committee are selected in different states. In some states they are selected by direct primary, the most frequent unit being the congressional district, and after that the county and the senatorial district.[35] In other states members are selected in other ways: in some, for example, the committee is simply the county chairmen sitting as a body; in others, it is an assembly of all the county comitteemen; in still others, the state committeemen are picked by the state convention. And all this makes for conspicuous differences as to the source from which the members receive their mandate to sit on the com-

---

[34] I.e., of those public jobs whose incumbents are determined by the political party in power. In a later chapter we shall discuss in some detail the nature and role of patronage.

[35] Howard R. Penniman, *Sait's American Parties and Elections,* 4th ed. (New York: Appleton-Century-Crofts, Inc., 1948), p. 350.

mittee: here it is the state convention, there the county convention, and yonder the county or congressional-district committee. The most common source, however, is the direct primary, with the rank-and-file voter choosing one member from each congressional district, county, or senatorial district.

The powers of the state central committee, which are in all states prescribed by law, are (as implied above) notably greater in some states than in others. In some the committee's discretionary powers are very slender and its activities are largely confined to the more or less automatic performance of certain functions—not, however, inconsiderable ones—imposed upon it by the statutes. In most states, however, the committee has powers, to return to an army analogy, not unlike those of a general staff—especially in the one-party states of the Solid South, where the statutory regulation of party organization is less detailed than in any other section of the country, and where the state central committees of the parties have, therefore, more room in which to improvise and write their own ticket.[36]

According to Frank R. Kent, "the key to the political machine, the hallmark of the boss, the sign that he is in the saddle—is control of the state central committee." [37] Just why control of that committee is so important to the "boss" is accounted for, at least in part, by the range of its activities, which Professor Key succinctly summarizes as follows:

Included in the powers of state committees (but not necessarily within the powers of any single committee) are such matters as the following, when not otherwise regulated by law or by party rule: issuance of the call for the state convention, selection of temporary officers for the convention, preparation of an official list of delegates, fixing the time of the primary, prescribing standards for party membership for participation in the primary, making nominations to fill vacancies by death or disqualification in the party slate of nominees, canvassing and certifying results of primaries, deciding primary contexts, generally supervising the party's primaries.[38]

In most states the state chairman of the party is selected by the central committee from among its own members; in a few he is chosen from outside the committee by one process or another. He may or may not "control" the committee, but he is invariably one of the leading figures in the state party organization and is likely to be the leading figure—and thus a powerful figure in the national party and also in the national convention (as we shall see in greater detail in Chapter 13). This we may confirm by noting some of the

[36] As we noted in Chapter 8, the southern states have moved away from statutory regulation of party organization in an effort to preserve the white primary—concretely, by giving the Democratic party the status of an entirely private association. This effort, as we have seen, has been aborted by the Supreme Court's decision in *Smith v. Allwright* (1944), but the southern states have not responded to that decision by turning back to elaborate regulation of party organization.

[37] *Op. cit.*, pp. 144-45.

[38] V. O. Key, Jr., *Politics, Parties, and Pressure Groups*, 3rd ed. (New York: Thomas Y. Crowell Company, 1952), pp. 347-48.

prominent party leaders who have been state chairmen: James A. Farley, Jacob Arvey, Earl Warren, J. Henry Roraback, and Boies Penrose. In a word, the state central committees and the state chairmanships are crucial loci of power in both of our major parties.

The National Committees and National Chairmen. The national committees of both major parties are made up of one man and one woman [39] from each of the 48 states plus the District of Columbia, Alaska, Hawaii, and Puerto Rico—and, in the case of the Democrats, plus the Virgin Islands and the Canal Zone.[40] Since 1952, the Republicans have added a "bonus seat" on their national committee for each state which, at the preceding election, elected Republican presidential electors, or elected a Republican governor, or elected a majority of Republicans in the total delegation to Congress. The occupants of these "bonus seats" are the state chairmen of the respective states entitled to such seats. All the other members are formally selected for four-year terms by the national conventions of their respective parties. In actual practice, however, the committeeman and committeewoman for each state and territory are picked by some kind of machinery within its state or territorial party organization, and the national convention merely elects as a matter of course whatever names have been passed along to it by the state parties. Concretely, one of four methods is used in selecting members of the national committee: either the state or territorial convention (as in 22 states and territories) selects them, or the state or territorial delegation to the national convention (as in 16) selects them, or the state or territorial central committee (as in 9) selects them, or the voters (as in 7) elect them in a direct primary.[41] Some members of the national committee are powerful and active leaders in the party organizations of their respective states; but as a general rule they are prominent business and professional men and women who, while active to some extent in state party affairs, give much less time and attention to them than do the real leaders in the state party organization.[42]

The national committee is not, for either party, the formally supreme rule-making and policy-forming body, since that role is reserved for the na-

[39] Women were first given official positions in national party politics in 1892, when three women were seated as alternates at the Republican national convention. After the passage of the nineteenth amendment, both parties saw the writing on the wall, and proceeded (the Democrats in 1920 and the Republicans in 1924) to give women equal representation on their national committees: Marguerite J. Fisher and Betty Whitehead, "Women and National Party Organization," *American Political Science Review*, Vol. XXXVIII (October, 1944), pp. 895-903.

[40] Although the national parties had maintained informal nationwide correspondence committees previously, the first formal national party committee was set up by the 1848 Democratic national convention. The Republicans set up such a committee at their first convention in 1856.

[41] Dayton D. McKean, *Party and Pressure Politics* (Boston: Houghton Mifflin Company, 1949), pp. 208-09.

[42] Cf. Wallace S. Sayre, "Personnel of Republican and Democratic National Committees," *American Political Science Review*, Vol. XXVI (April, 1932), pp. 360-62; and Peter H. Odegard and E. Allen Helms, *American Politics*, 2nd ed. (New York: Harper and Brothers, 1947), pp. 287-90.

tional convention, to which the committee is formally subordinate.[43] On the other hand, it is, as the convention is not, a continuous going concern, so that there are numerous functions, related to the nomination and election of the party's candidates for president and vice-president, with respect to which it exercises power not unlike that of the convention when it is in session. Thus the committee (usually in January of the presidential-election year) sets the time and place for the national convention, and issues the official call to the delegates. It prepares, for recommendation to the convention, a slate of temporary officers, and draws up a temporary roll of delegates. Disputes often arise in the committee over these matters, and, since they are usually fought out among the leading factions of the national party, easily become important early skirmishes in the developing struggle for the presidential nomination itself.[44] In 1952, for example, the Republican National Committee, when it drew up its temporary roll of delegates, had to decide between rival Taft and Eisenhower delegations from Texas, and the fight over this issue in the committee was readily recognized by both the Taft faction and the Eisenhower faction as one that, both for the sake of strength on the convention floor and for reasons of prestige, had to be won. And the committee's decision in favor of the Taft delegation, though later reversed by the convention, was deemed a significant victory for Taft.[45]

In recent decades, moreover, the national committees have taken on a number of activities that go forward continuously between the national conventions. For example, both now sponsor publications of various sorts,[46] carry on research, and, as occasion seems to demand or invite, make policy pronouncements. These are, clearly, activities that call for permanent functionaries (e.g., a secretary and a treasurer), and for division of labor between special-purpose staffs (each has, for example, a Women's Division and a Publicity Division).[47] They maintain permanent headquarters in Washington, with office space for their staffs and convenient meeting places for the national committees and other party bodies.[48]

[43] Cf. Penniman, op. cit., p. 319. The most complete discussion of the origins, composition, and activities of the national committees available is that in Penniman, pp. 315-24. Kent, op. cit., pp. 150-55, has a useful discussion of the subject, as also do Key, Bone, and McKean.

[44] Cf. Key, op. cit., p. 340, n. 3.

[45] O. Douglas Weeks, Texas Presidential Politics in 1952 (Austin, Tex.: Institute of Public Affairs, University of Texas, 1953), pp. 71-73.

[46] The Democratic National Committee in 1953 converted the Democratic Digest into a magazine of cartoons and condensed articles, modeled on the Reader's Digest, with a view to developing, over and above a subscription list, a considerable newsstand distribution. The Republican National Committee in January, 1954, offered free to all who asked for it a new newsletter type of publication, called Straight from the Shoulder; A Journal of Political Fact.

[47] For detailed descriptions of the publicity division of one of the major parties, see Theodore M. Black, Democratic Party Publicity in the 1940 Campaign (New York: Plymouth, 1941); and Thomas S. Barclay, "The Publicity Division of the Democratic Party, 1929-30," American Political Science Review, Vol. XXV (February, 1931), pp. 68-71.

[48] The Democratic National Headquarters is now at 1001 Connecticut Avenue, N.W., Washington 6, D. C., the Republican National Headquarters at 1625 I Street, N.W., Washington 6, D. C.

The national party chairman is a further instance of the divergence between formal and informal organization in American parties. According to the rules, he is selected by the national committee. Actually, he is as often selected by persons outside the committee, and he may not even be a committee member at the time of his election. In presidential-election years, selecting the national chairman is the undoubted and never-challenged prerogative of the presidential candidate, who normally replaces the incumbent chairman with his own man,[49] and if he wins, is likely to make him Postmaster General in the new cabinet,[50] replacing him as chairman with another man of his own choice. The national chairman of the defeated party, on the other hand, is apt to remain in his post for some time after the election—as did John D. M. Hamilton, John J. Raskob, Hugh Scott, and Stephen A. Mitchell. But this is not a foregone conclusion; for defeat in an election may precipitate a post-election struggle among committee factions, in which the chairman may be involved. A recent instance of such a struggle was that in which the Taft faction in the Republican committee replaced Hugh Scott, who had been selected as chairman by presidential candidate Dewey in 1948, with their own man, Guy Gabrielson, in 1949. Dewey's inability to force the retention of Scott is an illustration of the general rule that the defeated presidential candidate does not exercise the successful candidate's prerogative of putting or keeping his own man in the national chairmanship as a matter of course. He may put or keep his man there, but not because of any authority dumped into his lap by tradition.

Neither the Democratic nor the Republican national chairman, be it noted, is in any sense the "national boss" of his party. He holds his post either at the pleasure of a presidential candidate or a president, or at that of the committee's dominant faction, and not because of any power he holds in his own right. (Even such powerful and popular chairmen as Mark Hanna and James A. Farley, to name only two, were removed when the presidents who had put them there withdrew their support.) His tasks are to organize winning campaigns, to keep relations cordial among the various state and local elements of the national party, and to carry on the publicity and research work of the national office. His chances for holding on to his job are in any case no greater than his proficiency (or his ability to convince party leaders that he is proficient) at these tasks—the first especially. He is not thought of—and usually does not think of himself—as a maker of legislative policy or a party spokes-

---

[49] For example, when the Republican national convention met in 1952, Guy G. Gabrielson was the party's national chairman; but Mr. Eisenhower, shortly after his nomination, selected Arthur Summerfield, then national committeeman from Michigan, as national chairman. When the Democratic convention met, the national chairman was Frank McKinney. After his nomination for the presidency, Governor Stevenson picked Stephen A. Mitchell of Chicago, who had never been a member of the committee, as national chairman.

[50] As President Eisenhower did with Mr. Summerfield in 1953. Other prominent national chairmen who have become Postmaster General are James A. Farley, Frank Walker, and Will Hays.

man on public affairs; and when he steps forward in the latter capacity, few people treat what he says as an official statement of his party's views.[51]

The national chairmen do, however, symbolize the *organizations* of their respective parties as no one else does. This helps explain why the leaders of each party feel that the reputation of their national chairman must be above reproach, and that, if his probity is called into question, he must either prove himself—to use the phrase President Eisenhower coined in another but not dissimilar matter—"clean as a hound's tooth" or step down. That this is so is confirmed by three recent episodes involving the national chairman of one or another of the major parties. In 1951, William M. Boyle, Jr., Democratic National Chairman, was criticized for having allegedly accepted legal fees from a firm that had borrowed money from the Reconstruction Finance Corporation, and not long after resigned—because of "ill health." (President Truman emphasized that he had not asked for Boyle's resignation. But the point raised against Boyle had by no means been cleared up to everybody's satisfaction, and the general feeling among Washington reporters, in any case, was that great pressure had been put on him to step down by party leaders other than Mr. Truman.) The lightning struck next—or, to anticipate, the next *two* times—at the Republican National Chairman; first at Guy Gabrielson, whose law firm had allegedly been retained by a concern that had received loans from the R.F.C. prior to the time he had become national chairman; then, in 1953, at Wesley Roberts. Gabrielson, though promptly called upon to resign by a number of Republican congressmen, insisted that he had done nothing improper, rode out the storm, and kept his job until replaced by Summerfield in 1952. Wesley Roberts of Kansas, who became Republican Chairman upon Summerfield's elevation to Postmaster General following the successful Republican campaign of 1952, resigned after only a few months at his post, after a committee of the overwhelmingly Republican-controlled Kansas legislature had concluded that he had "intentionally violated the spirit of the Kansas lobby law." A national weekly, though ready to assure its readers that Roberts had done nothing contrary to either the law or public morality, put the point we are making here very well in its concluding comment: "As some others before Roberts have learned, a national political chairman of this era must have a record which avoids the appearance of evil." [52]

Congressional and Senatorial Committees. The national committees of both major parties are, for the most part, oriented toward the executive branch of the national government. They do, to be sure, put a high priority on carrying a maximum number of congressional seats, but their primary concern is always with electing a president and seeing him "succeed" in a way that will maximize the chances of re-electing him or, should he not wish to run, of electing the next party nominee. Many members of Congress, indeed, feel that the national committees of their respective parties are too much involved with the

[51] Cf. Key, *op. cit.,* p. 342; Penniman, *op. cit.,* p. 325.
[52] *Time,* March 30, 1953, p. 18.

presidency, at least too much so to function satisfactorily as a general staff in campaigns for congressional seats. Therefore the members of both parties in both houses of Congress have for some time maintained, for the performance of the latter function, their own distinct national campaign committees.

The first such committee was formed by the Republicans in the House of Representatives in 1866. The war between the Republican Congressmen and President Johnson over reconstruction policy was already raging, and the former had good reason to feel that the regular national committee, which Johnson dominated, would be running his errands, not theirs. They proceeded, therefore, to set up a campaign committee of their own, made up of members selected by a joint caucus of Republicans in both houses, to ride herd on the elections for the House. The Democrats followed their example, though not until 1882. After the passage in 1913 of the Seventeenth Amendment, providing for the direct popular election of senators, the Republicans created in 1916 still another committee, which now does for senatorial elections what the old committee had done hitherto in elections for the House. The Democrats created their committee for senatorial elections two years later.

The senatorial committee of each party is picked by the chairman of the party's Senate caucus. The number of members varies from five to ten, all senators who are not up for election, and they serve for two years. The Republican congressional committee includes one representative from each state with Republican representation, that representative being selected by the entire Republican delegation from that state. The Democratic congressional committee is similarly constituted, except that its chairman has the privilege, rarely exercised up to now, of naming for each state a woman committee member, who need not be a representative.

The task of all four committees is to supply speakers, literature, and sometimes funds for the campaigns of party candidates in doubtful districts. Although formally quite independent of the national committees, the congressional and senatorial committees often work closely with them, especially in presidential years, when the issues of the presidential election are—more, of course, in some districts than in others—closely tied up with the issues at stake in the congressional elections. They are somewhat less overshadowed by the national committees in the "off-year" elections, but on the whole they appear to constitute the least important and powerful level of party organization.[53]

Local, State, and National Conventions. We have, up to this point, fixed attention exclusively on the formal party committees, because it is they that control and conduct the bulk of party activity. But state and local party conventions, although, as we shall see in a later chapter, they have sharply declined in importance since the late nineteenth century, must not be permitted to slip entirely from our purview.

There is no hard-and-fast distinction between a "committee" and a "convention." Both are representative party assemblies whose members have been

---

[53] Cf. Penniman, *op. cit.*, pp. 312-15; and Key, *op. cit.*, pp. 345-46.

selected by certain constituencies of legal party members; both meet periodically to transact party business; both are, in most states, provided for and regulated by law. The party convention, however, tends to be a much larger assembly than the committee on its level of formal party organization; and it tends to meet a good deal less frequently (e.g., once or twice a year) than that committee. Thus, while the distinction may not be etymologically sound, it is an accepted part of the vocabulary of American politics, is deeply embodied in the statutes concerning parties, and is a distinction without a difference only in an occasional borderline case (such as that noted in footnote 54).

In a few states, nominations to local and county offices are still made by local and county conventions rather than in direct primaries or by party committees; but this is quite rare, and the general rule is that local and county conventions play a small and rapidly disappearing role in formal party organization.[54] The state conventions, on the other hand, are quite otherwise. In over half the states, for example, they pick some or all of the state's delegates to the national conventions, and thus have a considerable impact upon the process by which candidates for president are nominated. Many of them adopt platforms, which sometimes differ materially from the national platforms,[55] and frequently avail themselves of their legal authority, which is fairly clear, to act as governing body for the party in matters not covered by the statutes. They therefore symbolize the non-national or federal aspect of our party system, much as the national party conventions, though made up of state delegations, symbolize its national aspect. In the latter, the centripetal forces are at their strongest; in the former, the centrifugal forces have their occasional day.

The national party conventions, unlike the state and local conventions, are at least as powerful today as they were a century ago. They nominate the candidates for president and vice-president; and in them reside the supreme rule-making and policy-formulating powers of the national parties—insofar as the latter, given their essentially federal base, may be said to have such powers. Each national convention, in other words, is the apex of its party's formal organization—to the extent that a loose collection of legally independent and semi-independent agencies, which is what each major party is, can be said to have an apex.

Conclusions

Such, then, are the levels of formal organization in the American major parties, and such the agencies which, under the laws of the several states, preside over the parties' nomination-making and election-contesting activities. The various committees, chairmen, and conventions do not, we repeat, add up—

[54] In Illinois, for example, the county "convention" is simply the legal title for a meeting of the county central committee: *Illinois Election Laws, 1953*, Article 7, Section 9, Paragraph (a).

[55] For example, the Texas Democratic Platform of 1952 was largely given over to blasting the nominees, record, and platform of the national Democratic party: Weeks, *op. cit.*, p. 88.

either from the point of view of the lawyer or from that of the political observer concerned merely with how things work—to a neat, pyramidal, hierarchical pattern. Indeed, the relevant statutes in most states tend to make party agencies at different levels quite independent of one another, so that one of the safest statements we can make about American parties is that their *formal* organization, at least, has as its characteristic feature the fragmentation and scattering of power among numerous local, state, and national authorities.

In the light, however, of our discussion early in this chapter of "informal" or "actual" organization as opposed to "formal" organization, the reader may well be asking himself at this point: Is this the *actual* organization of American parties? Are the parties really like that? Do all these committeemen and chairmen really have a say in the parties' decisions? Is the actual power fragmented and scattered in the way the formal structure seems to suggest, or does it, rather, prove to be highly centralized the moment one looks behind the formal structure at the hidden realities of day-to-day party politics?

One way of getting at answers to such questions is to inquire into the nature of leadership and followership in American parties. That inquiry we undertake in the next chapter.

Chapter 11

INFORMAL PARTY
ORGANIZATION:
PARTY WORKERS
AND LEADERS

In the preceding chapter we described the *formal* organization of American political parties and found that it is highly decentralized. In the present chapter we turn our attention to the *informal* organization of the parties, with a view to determining whether it shows a higher degree of centralization. Concretely, we shall discuss the first two of the six categories of party "members" that we noted in Chapter 9: (1) *party workers*—those persons who regularly and actively participate in the parties' nomination-making, election-contesting, and other activities; and (2) *party leaders*—those persons who regularly initiate and direct party activities and, normally at least, make the proposals that the parties' other members respond to. And we shall be concerned primarily with the relationships among these persons that fall under the general headings "leadership" and "followership."

Party Workers

WHAT MANNER OF MEN?

In 1944, the National Opinion Research Center asked 2,560 persons in various parts of the country this question: "If you had a son just getting out of school, would you like to see him go into politics as a life work?" They answered as follows: "Yes," 18 per cent; "No," 69 per cent; "It depends" and "undecided," 13 per cent. About half of those who answered "No" gave as the main reason for their answer their belief that politics is fundamentally dishonest, and that graft and corruption go hand in hand with it as a matter of course. Forty-eight per cent of all the respondents agreed with the statement that "it is almost impossible for a man to stay honest if he goes into politics." [1]

[1] National Opinion Research Center, *The Public Looks at Politics and Politicians*, Report No. 20, March, 1944.

The results of this survey are hardly surprising. The word "politician" undoubtedly suggests to many Americans a contemptible and untrustworthy fellow—a "trimmer" and "compromiser," a man without principle or integrity. And, to judge by such familiar epithets as "party hack" and "ward heeler," party workers are widely regarded as belonging to the lower reaches of the genus "politician": for both expressions suggest to many people the stereotype of a man in a derby hat who chews endlessly on a dead cigar, knows all the angles, especially all the angles that have to do with raids on the public treasury, is forever swearing undying allegiance to the Boss (with bad grammar, of course), switches unhesitatingly to a new boss when the patronage and graft cease to roll in, and stands always ready to profess *any* belief or opinion likely to prove popular with the voters.[2] This picture of politicians is, moreover, more common among the well educated and the well to do than in other segments of the population. And so also are the attitudes toward party leaders and party workers that we might expect to go hand in hand with it.[3]

The apparent high incidence of these attitudes among the upper income and educational levels, implying as it does a proportionate lack of confidence in the process by which political power is won and held under our system, has created great anxiety in certain quarters, so that it is now possible to point to a nationwide organization, the Citizenship Clearing House, whose express purpose is to try to persuade college students over the country to adopt other attitudes. This organization, which was founded by Arthur T. Vanderbilt, Chief Justice of the Supreme Court of New Jersey and a leader of that state's Republican organization, encourages college men and women to go into politics and become active in political parties. This it does by such activities as urging political science instructors to keep their charges reminded that they can go into party politics and remain respectable and uncontaminated. To date, however, there is no indication that the clearing house regards its mission as accomplished.

The prevailing animus against party workers may or may not be justified by the facts. But it is a genuine factor in American politics and helps to ex-

---

[2] J. T. Salter tells the following story: "Taxpayers of Westchester County, New York, held a mass meeting last week in White Plains to protest the cost of their State Government. One speaker suggested that the Republican Legislature adopt a greatly reduced budget, let Democratic Governor Lehman veto it if he dare. State Senator Pliny W. Williamson (Republican) expostulated: 'You wouldn't want the Courts and State institutions and offices closed for lack of funds, would you?'

" 'Yes!' roared the taxpayers.

" 'Well,' stammered the Senator, 'if that's your attitude, I'm all for it.' ": "The Politician and the People," *Journal of Politics,* published by the Southern Political Science Association in cooperation with the University of Florida, Vol. I (August, 1939), p. 258.

[3] In the survey reported above, the various educational-level groups responded as follows: 57 per cent of those who had gone no further than grammar school, 76 per cent of those who had gone as far as high school, and 81 per cent of those who had gone to college answered "No" to the initial question; 34 per cent of the lower-income group, 73 per cent of the middle group, and 78 per cent of the upper group answered "No": *Ibid.*

plain some of the latter's distinctive characteristics. We shall have more to say about it in Chapter 20.

Most of us have probably met and talked with a party worker at some time or other, so that our picture of party workers is based, in part, on personal experience. Perhaps some of us have made it our business to seek out party workers at every opportunity, so as not to have to depend entirely on evidence from casual reading and hearsay. Happily, however, these are not the only alternatives open to us, since we also have at our disposal the results of several more or less systematic studies of party workers by various political scientists, of which the most recent examples are William E. Mosher's study of precinct committeemen in eighteen upstate New York cities in 1932,[4] Harold F. Gosnell's [5] and Sonya Forthal's [6] studies of precinct captains in Chicago in the 1930's, David H. Kurtzman's study of precinct committeemen in Philadelphia in the 1930's,[7] and Leon Weaver's study of precinct committeemen in ten downstate rural Illinois counties in 1938.[8]

By combining the results of some of the studies just mentioned, the present writers have constructed Tables 11 and 12, which show the incidence of

TABLE 11   Distribution of Formal-Education Levels Among Precinct Committeemen [9]

Educational Level	18 NEW YORK CITIES (1932)		CHICAGO (1936)		DOWNSTATE ILLINOIS (1938)		
					Dem. Prec. Com.	Rep. Prec. Com.	
	Prec. Com.	Gen. Pop.	Prec. Com.	Gen. Pop.			Gen. Pop.
Grammar school or less	55.3 *	60.6	40.1	59.9	54	58	60.4
High school	33.0	27.9	39.6	29.9	33	20	28.9
College and professional	11.7	9.6	20.3	9.7	13	22	9.8
Not ascertained	—	1.9	—	.5	—	—	.9

* All figures are percentages of members of the group at the particular educational level and in the particular occupational category.

[4] William E. Mosher, "Party and Government Control at the Grass Roots," *National Municipal Review,* Vol. XXIV (January, 1935), pp. 15-18, 38.

[5] Harold F. Gosnell, *Machine Politics: Chicago Model* (copyright 1937 by the University of Chicago Press).

[6] Sonya Forthal, *Cogwheels of Democracy: A Study of the Precinct Captain* (New York: William-Frederick Press, 1946).

[7] David H. Kurtzman, *Methods of Controlling Votes in Philadelphia* (Philadelphia: Dissertation in Political Science, University of Pennsylvania, 1935).

[8] Leon Weaver, "Some Soundings in the Party System: Rural Precinct Committeemen," *American Political Science Review,* Vol. XXXIV (February, 1940), pp. 76-84.

[9] In both Table 11 and Table 12, the figures for the precinct committeemen in the New York cities are drawn from Mosher, *op. cit.;* the figures for the Chicago precinct captains are taken from Gosnell, *op. cit.,* p. 57; the figures for the precinct committeemen in the ten downstate Illinois counties are drawn from Weaver, *op. cit.* The comparative figures for the general population in each area are taken from the Bureau of the Census, *Sixteenth Census of the United*

(1) persons of various formal-education levels, and (2) persons belonging to various occupational groups, among precinct committeemen on the one hand and among the general population on the other.

TABLE 12   Distribution of Occupations Among Precinct Committeemen

Occupation	18 NEW YORK CITIES (1932)		CHICAGO (1936)	
	Prec. Com.	Gen. Pop.	Prec. Com.	Gen. Pop.
Government employees	19.3 *	5.5	48.3	4.3
Professions	9.2	9.4	11.0	7.7
Merchants and executives	12.0	10.1	28.1	10.2
Clerks, salesmen, laborers	59.5	58.5	12.6	63.4
Others and not ascertained	—	16.5	—	14.4

* All figures are percentages of members of the group at the particular educational level and in the particular occupational category.

We have, as yet, no quantitative studies of other characteristics of party workers. On the basis of personal interviews with 600 Chicago precinct captains, however, Forthal reports the following impressions as to the kind of men they are:

> Friendliness and a desire to cooperate were the predominating personal characteristics observed during the interviews, along with a certain cautiousness and suspicion, even extending to fear and evasiveness. Sincerity, forcefulness, loquacity, and humor declined in frequency. Qualities even more rarely found were cunning, ostentation, and self-satisfaction. . . . The captains in foreign areas invariably spoke the language of the locality as well as English. In the good residential areas, the precinct captains possessed poise, fluency, and a degree of pompousness. In all the areas, docility to the superior in the party hierarchy was an outstanding characteristic.[10]

Gosnell, also writing on precinct captains in Chicago, states that they reflect the race or nationality of the dominant ethnic group in their "areas":

> In the areas where there is a concentration of Negro population, both the Republican and Democratic parties had Negro committeemen. In the areas where persons of Polish descent are found, the parties kept a Zintak, a Konkowski, a Rosenkowski, a Kucharski, a Golusinski, and a Peska as committeemen; and in areas where many persons of Italian extraction are located, the committeemen bore such names as Serritella, Pacelli, Vignola, and Porcaro. . . . The same principle that

States: 1940; Characteristics of the Population (Washington, D. C.: Government Printing Office, 1943).

[10] Forthal, op. cit., p. 42.

the dominant group should be represented was followed in the sections populated largely by Jews.[11]

And Forthal adds that the precinct captains resemble their constituencies in social and economic status.[12]

The foregoing data, as far as they go, suggest the following generalizations: The formal-education level of party workers tends to be a little higher than that of the general population in their localities. They tend to mirror their constituents in point of racial and national origins and social and economic status. In certain other respects, however, they tend to differ from the general population. When their party is in power, for instance, the incidence of government employees among them rises (for obvious reasons) well above that among the general population.[13] And, according to Forthal, "since they form a professional or occupational class, they are stamped by certain common traits. . . . The quality of friendliness appears with greatest frequency among the 600 precinct captains, and it may therefore be called a characteristic of the group." [14] All of which, be it noted, is at sharp variance with the widespread notion that party workers as a class are less bright and less well educated than Americans in general.

The fact that so many party workers hold government jobs when their party is in power might seem to indicate that the desire for personal economic gain is *the* motive that drives men and women into party work. But before we leap to that conclusion let us look at the available data concerning the motivations of party workers.

WHY DO THEY GO INTO POLITICS?

The evidence we have on this question indicates that the expectation of economic reward is indeed one—but *only* one—of the reasons why party workers go into politics. Forthal lists two others: friendship with or obligation to some party member; and the prestige, excitement, and fascination of "the great game of politics." A few persons here and there, she says, perhaps become precinct workers because of their desire for "clean government" and "civic betterment" or because of their wish to see the opposing party defeated. But these appear to be neither very compelling nor very common reasons for going into politics.[15]

[11] *Op. cit.*, pp. 44-45.

[12] *Op. cit.*, p. 45.

[13] In addition to the data presented in Table 12, Kurtzman reported that 58 per cent of the precinct committeemen in Philadelphia were on the city and county payrolls: *Op. cit.*, pp. 47-54. Gosnell reported that in 1928, when the Republicans were in power in Illinois, three-quarters of the Republican ward committeemen in Chicago held elective or appointive government jobs; but in 1934, when the Republicans were out of power, only one-sixth held such jobs: *Op. cit.*, pp. 39-41.

[14] *Op. cit.*, p. 45.

[15] *Ibid.*, pp. 36-41.

Forthal's conclusions on this point are borne out by the testimony of two prominent Democratic leaders, both of whom worked their way up in party politics from the precinct level to the national chairmanship. James A. Farley writes:

Those people who are inclined to imagine that patronage, and patronage alone, is the only thing that keeps a political party knit together are off on a tangent that is about as far wrong as anything humanly could be. . . . To put it plainly, people who think that individuals become active in politics merely for the sake of being "in on the spoils" underestimate the idealism of their fellow citizens. Politics is the national sport of the American people—not baseball, or football, or any other athletic game. . . . People are just as selfish, and just as unselfish, in politics as they are in any other human endeavor.[16]

And Edward J. Flynn writes:

Most of our Captains earn more in private industry than any but a few top political jobs pay. Captains are Captains for a variety of reasons. Some like the excitement of working with a political party. Some have their egos satisfied by the distinction it gives them among their neighbors. Some hope for promotion within the party. Some (but all too few) work because they have made a study of party policies and principles and believe in them.[17]

Finally—and for what it is worth—party workers are of course aware of their reputation as greedy, low-life despoilers of pure government, but tend, it seems, to think well of themselves and of each other and to place a high valuation on the work they do. Gosnell reports, in this connection, a highly instructive interview with a Chicago precinct captain, who laid it on the line as follows with the university investigator sent to see him:

"When anyone gets into trouble with the law—petty thieving, trouble with a relief investigator—or when he loses his job or is about to be evicted, or when a kid gets in with a bad gang and starts staying out all night, in cases like this it is not the relief agency or social welfare agency that the harassed voter first goes to, but rather to the precinct captain who stands in with the law, who will not talk down to him but will treat him as a friend in need, and who is waiting for him in the local tavern or in the ward headquarters, where there is a full time secretary who knows just who can handle him."

When the interviewer, Gosnell continues, ventured to slip in a word for a nearby settlement house, the precinct captain interrupted bitterly:

"Oh, forget that bunk. You innocent, well-meaning middle-class people who have never seen a hungry and moneyless family in your life, who have only a vague idea of how the political and legal and business racket is run, who don't know the right people to talk to in evictions, or tort cases, you think you can come in here and help the poor. You can't even talk to them on their own level, because

<hr />

[16] James A. Farley, *Behind the Ballots* (New York: Harcourt, Brace and Company, 1938), p. 237.

[17] Edward J. Flynn, *You're the Boss* (New York: The Viking Press, 1947), p. 22.

you're better, you're from the University. I never graduated from high school, and I'm one of them." [18]

HOW TO "GET INTO" POLITICS

Any teacher of political science now and then finds himself called upon to answer the question, "How do I go about getting into politics?" The questioner, moreover, not infrequently adopts the same tone he would use if he were asking how to gain admission to some exclusive secret society, the mysteries of which are closed to ordinary mortals and can be revealed only by the elect who are already initiated—or, failing that, by some expert who has thoroughly researched the matter.

One safe answer to the question would be: "It depends on what you mean by 'getting into politics'—for the phrase evidently means different things to different questioners. Do you mean: How does one get a party's nomination for public office? Then the answer appears to be that you must either persuade a party organization to support you, or go out and round up a lot of votes for yourself in a party primary, or make yourself such salable political material that the party will come begging you to run. Do you mean: How does one become an influential adviser of a powerful political figure, a Colonel House or a Louis McHenry Howe? Then you should make yourself so useful to a prominent political leader that he can hardly do without you, as House made himself useful to Woodrow Wilson and Howe to Franklin Roosevelt. Or do you mean: How does one become a party worker? For then the answer is quite simple and the necessary steps are easy to take. You simply present yourself to a local party official, e.g., your precinct committeeman or city chairman, and make known your availability. He will start you out canvassing voters, or addressing envelopes, or driving voters to the polls, or performing some other chore he wants done—but probably not, at first anyhow, one that is other than menial. From then on, you are 'in politics.' In short, there is nothing to it, any more than to becoming a party registrant or a party voter. But—be warned—the w-o-r-k in the term 'party worker' is intended literally: you are supposed to *do* things; these things require time and effort; and the recognition and the rewards tend to be proportional to the time and effort expended.

"Or, finally, do you mean: How does one become a party *leader*—that is, achieve the power to initiate, direct, and sometimes control a party's decisions as to nominees, policies, distribution of patronage, etc.? If so, then the answer is considerably more complex than the other answers given above—if for no other reason than that the question calls for a prior inquiry into the nature and conditions of party leadership."

American political parties, let us remind ourselves, are *a particular kind of social group*. They have, that is to say, some traits in common with all social groups and some traits peculiar to themselves. If, then, we wish to under-

[18] Gosnell, *op. cit.,* p. 70.

stand the nature of the leadership-followership relations that obtain within them, we must take into account both what is known about the phenomenon of leadership *in general* (i.e., in all social groups) and what is known about the "special case" of American party leadership.

Leadership in General

THE MEANING OF "LEADERSHIP"

The word "leader" appears to have at least three fairly distinct meanings. It denotes either (1) a man whose *attainments,* in terms of a particular standard or set of standards and values, rank "high" when compared to the attainments of his contemporaries, as when we call the late Albert Einstein a "leader" among contemporary physicists or of T. S. Eliot a "leader" among contemporary poets; or (2) a man to whom the persons engaged in a particular activity "defer" because of the "status" he enjoys (whether officially or unofficially), as when we speak of the Joint Chiefs of Staff as the nation's "military leaders," or of a famous Parisian couturier as a "fashion leader"; or (3) a man who *emits stimuli* that are "responded to integratively by the members of [a] group" in such fashion as to forward the performance of whatever activities are characteristic of that particular group—as, for example, when a football coach "leads" the team by designing its plays and determining its practice routines, or when the quarterback calls the team's signals in a game.[19] These three meanings of "leader" are not, of course, mutually exclusive, since, for example, a T. S. Eliot might well be regarded as a "leading" poet in all three senses. But they are, for our purposes, worth keeping apart, because it is clearly the third of the three that we are dealing with when we speak of party leadership.[20] Professor Alvin W. Gouldner clearly has our third meaning in mind when he speaks of a leader as an "individual in a group who, in *some* situations, has the *right* to issue *certain* kinds of stimuli which tend to be accepted by others in the group as obligations." And the third meaning is also presupposed in his shrewd distinction between "leadership" and "domination," which turns on what he calls *legitimacy,* that is, the feeling of obligation on the part of the followers not imposed by force or threat of force. (Note, however, his at-first-blush rather surprising point that there is no hard-and-fast

[19] These three meanings of "leadership" follow closely the formulation by Mapheus Smith in Alvin W. Gouldner, ed., *Studies in Leadership* (New York: Harper and Brothers, 1950), p. 15. See also the definition of leadership in David B. Truman, *The Governmental Process* (New York: Alfred A. Knopf, 1951), pp. 188-89. For general summaries and critiques of the current literature on political leadership in particular, see Lester G. Seligman, "The Study of Political Leadership," *American Political Science Review,* Vol. XLIV (December, 1950), pp. 904-15; and Malcolm Moos and Bertram Koslin, "Political Leadership Reexamined: An Experimental Approach," *Public Opinion Quarterly,* Vol. XV (Fall, 1951), pp. 563-74.

[20] The "titular" leader of a party is, to be sure, a leader in the second sense; and there may be a hint of the first meaning in the term "great party leader" when, as in some discussions of the two Roosevelts, Wilson, Lincoln, and Jackson, what is being attributed to the leader is not merely leadership but virtuosity and statesmanship as well.

dichotomy between "leaders" and "followers," since the latter also emit stimuli that affect the former.)[21]

THE FUNCTIONS OF LEADERSHIP

What follows is a description of the activities of a *model* leader—in the sense of the word "model" that we attempted to explain in Chapter 2—and not of any actual leader. Every actual leader in every actual human group is likely on occasion and with greater or lesser effectiveness to perform at least some of the functions mentioned; but no actual leader performs all of them effectively all the time. In short, what we are after here is a measuring stick with which to determine the quality and dimensions of any actual leader.

The analysis of leadership functions we present follows, in broad outline, that of the sociologist Paul Pigors, according to whose terminology a leader in any social group, and any *organized* group especially, performs one "general" function, that of *representation* (technical and psychological), and three "specific" functions: initiation, administration, and interpretation.[22]

Representation. The representative function of the leader, says Pigors, has two main aspects. The first has to do with the outside world, that is, speaking for the group on the one hand and listening or hearing for it on the other. A small group, such as a committee, may find it feasible to transmit and receive its communications collectively; but a group of any size is certain (as we learn from observing the behavior of groups) to need an authorized spokesman; and the latter becomes, on Pigors' showing, the group's "technical" representative. As we put it in Chapter 4, he "presents again" the members of the group, by "standing in their place and presenting on their behalf what they would present if they were there."[23]

The second aspect of the leader's representative function has to do with the group's need for a person or persons who symbolize and typify its purposes, interests, values, etc., that is, represent it not by speaking and hearing for it (though the same person or persons may do that also), but, so to speak, by merely *being* what they are. The leader, in this aspect, "embodies the traits, the outlook, even the sins of the larger group,"[24] and becomes, if you like, its "realized ideal."[25] The characteristics that enable him to do this—to be, in Pigors' phrase, its "psychological representative"—vary, to be sure, from group to group; and in no group, perhaps, could an exhaustive list of them be set down in black and white. It might be his accent, or the clothes he wears, or the kind of life he has led, or the jokes he tells and the jokes he laughs at—

---

[21] Gouldner, *op. cit.*, pp. 15-21. See also Paul Pigors, *Leadership or Domination* (Boston: Houghton Mifflin Company, 1935), *passim*, for a discussion of legitimacy as one of the traits that distinguish "leadership" from "domination."

[22] *Op. cit.*, Chs. 10-13.

[23] Cf. p. 61.

[24] Alfred de Grazia, *Public and Republic* (New York: Alfred A. Knopf, 1951), p. 5.

[25] Cf. Bernard Kutner, "Elements and Problems of Democratic Leadership," in Gouldner, ed., *op. cit.*, pp. 459-67.

anything and everything that the group members, consciously or unconsciously, react to as truly representative of *their* group as distinguished from other groups.

To be a group's "psychological representative" is not, be it noted, to possess personal qualities that add up to a composite picture of the qualities of the group members. Franklin D. Roosevelt, for example, won numerous followers among persons in the lower income and educational-level brackets and was widely regarded as a highly successful leader, though he himself came from a patrician background, had considerable wealth, spoke with a Harvard accent, and in various ways invited the epithet, "country squire in the White House." [26] Similarly, we sometimes hear that John L. Lewis, the head of the United Mine Workers, cannot "really represent" the coal miners, because, unlike them, he lives in luxury and is chauffeured about in a Cadillac. On Pigors' showing, however, the question to ask is not whether he *is* representative in some absolute sense, but rather whether his constituents *regard* him as representative. Bernard Barber says:

When he is the executive of a democratic association representing lower-class people, it is also necessary for the leader to have the established symbols of status and power, since in our society access to these symbols is granted to all men. When their executives have these symbols, the lower-class membership can feel that "our power" is adequate, for they know that these are the necessary instruments of achieving their interests. To this extent, therefore, it is useless for opposing interests to try to undermine the authority of leaders by exposing their possession of upper-class status and power. The members may even take vicarious pleasure in the middle-class status, remuneration, and style of life of their leaders.[27]

Initiation. A perennial question in every social group is, "What shall we do now?" Any group, accordingly, needs some person or persons to whom its members can habitually look for suggestions. The suggestions may or may not be accepted (the more "democratic" the group, for example, the less certain they are to be accepted automatically); and in one and the same group at a given moment different suggestions may be forthcoming from different quarters, the rank and file being asked, in effect, to choose among them. But initiation is one of the functions a group counts on from its leadership; or, to put it the other way around, the members are sure to regard those who perform the function of initiation—and so help the group's desires, resentments,

[26] Fillmore H. Sanford, for example, in 1949 asked 963 Philadelphians, many of them from the lower income and educational-level brackets, what they thought of Roosevelt as a leader. Ninety-six per cent replied that he was a good leader, and the reason most frequently given for the answer was some such statement as that Roosevelt was "a good man," or a "man who liked people": "The Follower's Role in Leadership Phenomena," in Guy E. Swanson, Theodore M. Newcomb, and Eugene L. Hartley, eds., *Readings in Social Psychology*, rev. ed. (New York: Henry Holt and Company, 1952), pp. 328-40.

[27] Bernard Barber, "Participation and Mass Apathy in Associations," in Gouldner, ed., *op. cit.*, pp. 494-95.

and enthusiasms to channel themselves into purposeful action—as belonging to its leadership.

Administration. As we noted in Chapter 10, a further characteristic of every organized group is that when it has determined upon a course of action, someone must identify the activities called for and allocate the group's members and material resources among them. This is the leadership function known as administration, of which we can say, as we did of initiation, that the revelant decisions are not necessarily absolute (since the last word in many groups lies with the membership as a whole), and that there may well be alternative decisions for the group to choose among. But the task of thinking through the allocation problem and coming up with proposals cannot in most groups be performed by the rank and file, and must therefore be entrusted to the leaders.

Interpretation. Finally, in any group problems arise from time to time that cannot be handled by simple appeal to existing rules, policies, and understandings. The latter can hardly be devised so as to cover all possible situations, and some situations are sure to present themselves in which the group must act without taking time for the process by which it normally arrives at new rules, policies, and understandings. At such moments someone must "adapt" the existing ones to the new circumstances, and must do so without compromising group unity. This is the leadership function of interpretation, and the person or persons to whom the group looks for its performance will, as a matter of course, be among its leaders.

Conceptually, it makes no difference whether we think of our four functions as being performed in a given group at a given moment by a single leader, or by a number of leaders, each "specialized" to one or more of them. Our point is merely that every organized group has among its members some person or persons who perform them, whether continuously or sporadically, and whether well or ill. And our next question becomes: On what kinds of persons do leadership functions tend to devolve, and why on these persons rather than on other members of the group? What, in other words, makes a man a leader?

WHAT MAKES A LEADER?

The Personality-Trait Explanation. The vast and growing literature on leadership offers two major types of answer to the question, What makes a leader?: one that runs in terms of "personality traits," and a second that runs in terms of "situations." Until fairly recently, most writers on the subject gave the first type of answer, which holds that certain men are leaders because they happen to have "leader-type personalities," which is to say because they happen to possess certain personal characteristics that dispose other men (who, in turn, have "follower-type personalities") to follow their lead. Here, for example, is sociologist Emory S. Bogardus' statement of this view of the matter:

Leadership is personality in action under group conditions. It includes dominant personality traits of one person and receptive personality traits of many persons. It is interaction between specific traits of one person and other traits of the many, in such a way that the course of action of the many is changed by the one.[28]

The personality-trait explanation of leadership continues to dominate the professional literature on political parties. Professor McKean, for example, in his discussion of what makes certain men successful party leaders, points to such personality traits as glandular balance, health and strength, intelligence, practical education, ambition, courage, sensitivity to group or party opinion, willingness to compromise, political imagination and inventiveness, humaneness, sympathy, ability to read and assimilate rapidly, and the gambler's willingness to take chances.[29] And Professor Bone, again for example, stresses the leadership qualities of skill in oratory, showmanship, and a "sense of social direction." [30]

The Situational Explanation. A growing number of sociologists and social psychologists, basing themselves upon recent empirical studies of leadership in various types of group, now reject the personality-type approach, and hold that the type of personality that provides successful leadership in one kind of group and situation does not necessarily provide it in all groups and situations. They hold that the personality traits of a successful leader in a political party, for example, differ greatly from the personality traits of a successful conductor of a symphony orchestra, and these, in turn, from those of a pennant-winning baseball manager. There are, that is to say, no leadership traits that are *equally* effective in *all* groups and situations, and any explanation of leadership that runs in terms of such traits is bound to be false.[31] Leadership, in short, is *specific* to particular situations and groups. As Fillmore H. Sanford puts it:

Leadership is a *relation* between leader and follower, as marriage is a relation between husband and wife and friendship a relation between two people. If we want to learn about marriage we do not study only husbands or only wives. We have to study the relation that exists between them. The same thing holds for friendship or enmity or partnership or leadership.[32]

[28] Emory S. Bogardus, *Leaders and Leadership* (New York: D. Appleton-Century Co., 1934), p. 3. For a summary of the literature urging this approach to the analysis of leadership, see Ralph M. Stodgill, "Personal Factors Associated with Leadership: A Survey of the Literature," *Journal of Social Psychology*, Vol. XXV (1948), pp. 35-71; and for another such summary see Gouldner, ed., *op. cit.*, pp. 21-25.

[29] Dayton D. McKean, *Party and Pressure Politics* (Boston: Houghton Mifflin Company, 1949), Ch. 11. See also the list in Charles E. Merriam and Harold F. Gosnell, *The American Party System*, 4th ed. (New York: The Macmillan Company, 1949), pp. 155-63. Merriam and Gosnell go on to suggest, however, that too little is yet known about the nature of party leadership to justify any sweeping or dogmatic generalizations: *Ibid.*, p. 163.

[30] Hugh A. Bone, *American Politics and the Party System* (New York: McGraw-Hill Book Company, Inc., 1949), Ch. 18.

[31] Cf. Gouldner, ed., *op. cit.*, pp. 25-41; Joseph W. Eaton, "Is Scientific Leadership Selection Possible?" in *ibid.*, pp. 616-17; and Truman, *op. cit.*, pp. 189-93.

[32] Fillmore H. Sanford in Swanson, Newcomb, and Hartley, *op. cit.*, p. 329.

Sanford goes ahead to urge some hypotheses that seem to him to merit further consideration:

> In a concrete leadership situation the follower's deeplying attitudes and needs are present as background determinants of his reaction to the leader, but there are also *situationally determined needs* that arise. The need to achieve a group goal or the need to adjust to here-and-now demands is imposed on the more persistent patterns of needs, making new demands on the leader. In a life-or-death situation the follower's need for warm approval is likely to be less important than his need to survive. He will thus be less likely to accept the "nice guy" as a leader, more likely to follow the man who appears able to help solve the immediate and pressing problem. It is possible to state this sort of observation as a definite hypothesis: the more psychologically significant the group goal, the greater the follower's emphasis on the leader's competence to assist in achieving that goal. A corollary to the hypothesis is as follows: the more *clearly perceived* the goal, and the more visible is progress toward it, the more follower emphasis there will be on the functional competence of the leader.[33]

No one would suggest that contemporary social science is able to provide a full and documented account of why some men become leaders and other men do not. There is, however, a growing tendency among social scientists to seek the answer to such questions in the special character of the particular group in question, in the demands made upon it by the total situation in which it is caught up, and in the psychological and technical needs, in the context of that situation, of the leaders and followers who compose it.

Political parties, as noted above, are a special kind of group, whose major purpose is to gain and exercise control of government by making nominations binding on all the members and (at least in the two-party and modified one-party areas) by contesting elections. What, now, can we say about the nature and distribution of leadership in American political parties?

The Nature of Party Leadership

"BOSSES" AND "LEADERS"

What Are They? Much of the literature on American parties makes a great deal of a supposed distinction between "party bosses," who head something known as "machines," and "party leaders," who head something known as "organizations." For some writers, indeed, this distinction is as clear and definite as that between chalk and cheese, and can be applied, for purposes of political analysis, by anyone who grasps the relevant criteria.[34] Bosses, we are told, differ from leaders in the following respects:

---

[33] *Ibid.*, pp. 338-39. Italics in the original.

[34] For descriptions by present-day writers of the differences between "bosses" and "leaders," see E. E. Schattschneider, *Party Government* (New York: Rinehart and Company, Inc., 1942), Ch. VII; McKean, *op. cit.*, pp. 270-92; and D. W. Brogan, *Politics in America* (New York: Harper and Brothers, 1954), pp. 123-24. For examples of earlier writers who made use of this

MOTIVES. The "boss" seeks private economic gain, and power for the sake of power. The "leader," by contrast, seeks the success of his party in order to get its program and principles adopted—and, some would add, to forward the public (as opposed to his own selfish) interest.

METHODS. The "boss" relies on patronage, graft, and various forms of intimidation and even violence. The "leader," by contrast, relies on his ability to persuade party workers and voters of the righteousness of his principles.

RESPONSIBILITY. The sources of the "boss's" power are secret and obscure; he relies on "manipulation," rather than on his ability to carry voters with him in free and open elections. The "leader's" power, by contrast, is the free gift of the electorate, to which he appeals with principles, logic, and facts; it is, in consequence, "responsible" power, which that of the boss, by definition, never is.

Some writers, to be sure, handle the distinction between "bosses" and "leaders" somewhat more cautiously, and in effect treat it as a "matter of degree" (so that a given party bigwig could be a leader in some respects and a boss in other respects)—but still capable of serving as a useful tool of analysis.[35] Only a handful of writers are prepared to go all the way with "boss" Edward J. Flynn and recognize that the two sets of terms denote the same phnomena, and merely express a distinction between two ways of reacting to those phenomena.[36] (It is, writes Flynn, "only the 'leader' you don't like who is a 'boss,' and the 'organization' that you don't like that is a 'machine.' " [37]

How Useful Is the Boss-Leader Typology? In the opinion of the present writers, the classification of party leaders into "bosses" and "leaders" confuses rather than clarifies the issues at stake in any discussion of American parties and politics. One objection to it is that by fixing attention on the purity or impurity of the participants' motives, it draws us into a kind of "good-men-versus-bad-men" analysis of politics. And in the present writers' opinion, the task of the political scientist is to understand *what* party leaders do and *why* they do what they do, not to speculate about whether their motives are good or bad.[38]

distinction, see Woodrow Wilson, "Leaderless Government," in R. S. Baker and W. E. Dodd, eds., *The Public Papers of Woodrow Wilson: College and State* (New York: Harper and Brothers, 1925), Vol. I, pp. 336-59; A. Lawrence Lowell, *Public Opinion and Popular Government* (New York: Longmans, Green and Company, 1913), pp. 139-40; Frank J. Goodnow, *Politics and Administration* (New York: The Macmillan Company, 1900), pp. 139, 169-70, 174; and William B. Munro, *Personality in Politics* (New York: The Macmillan Company, 1924), pp. 79 ff.

[35] Cf. Howard R. Penniman, *Sait's American Parties and Elections*, 4th ed. (New York: Appleton-Century-Crofts, Inc., 1948), pp. 357-65.

[36] It might be noted in this connection that V. O. Key, Jr., *Politics, Parties, and Pressure Groups*, 3rd ed. (New York: Thomas Y. Crowell Company, 1952), one of the most recent and most popular textbooks on the American party system, says nothing about "bosses" as distinguished from "leaders."

[37] *Op. cit.*, pp. 231-32.

[38] Ostrogorski repeatedly pointed out that there are *no* "good" party leaders. The respectable party "leaders" in both British and American politics, he said, are every bit as "bad" as the disreputable "bosses"—an excellent reason, he thought, for condemning the whole institution of

The second objection to the "boss-leader" typology is this: The dichotomy between the "responsibility" of the "leader" and the "irresponsibility" of the "boss" has no counterpart in reality. The party leaders usually classified as "bosses"—the William Tweeds, Richard Crokers, Charles F. Murphys, Tom Pendergasts, and Frank Hagues—for the most part did *not*, in point of fact, exercise absolute power, or have so firm a hold on what power they had as to be able to keep it indefinitely. Even at the height of their power, most of them were up against strong opposition both within their own parties and from the other major party, and many of them were eventually overturned.[39] They were not, to be sure, "responsible" in the sense that they ran for and were elected to a public office called "the boss-ship"; but they *were* responsible in the sense that their position within their parties ultimately depended upon their ability to provide their followers with patronage, favors, and power; and this ability, in turn, depended upon the voters' approval of the kind of government their "machines" were providing. "Boss" Ed Flynn's testimony on this point is instructive:

> It is one of our political legends that bosses never pay attention to the public. Of course the legend will not stand up against any logical analysis, for it must be rather obvious that a political boss can survive only so long as he wins elections, and equally obvious that the only way to win elections year after year is to know what the voters want and give it to them. . . . For always the primary purpose is to win an election.[40]

The third objection is that the assumed distinction between the methods of the "boss" and the methods of the "leader" does not, in fact, help us much when it comes to separating the sheep from the goats. Thomas E. Dewey, whom most writers who use this typology would probably describe as a "leader" instead of a "boss," notoriously used the distribution of patronage and favors to maintain his New York organization, and relied upon contributions from business corporations to support it—although these "methods" belong, properly speaking, over in the bosses' column.[41] To put the point bluntly: *any*

permanent political parties: *Democracy and the Organization of Political Parties,* translated by Frederick Clarke (New York: The Macmillan Company, 1902), Vol. I, pp. 352, 529; Vol. II, pp. 195, 216, 224, 285, 406.

[39] Harold Zink, after a study of twenty municipal "bosses," concluded: "Not one of the score of city bosses under study has enjoyed an unbroken rule of absolutism throughout his career as overlord, however powerful he may ordinarily have been. Only a few have approached complete domination even for a majority of the years that they have ruled. Some bosses, in spite of all their efforts, find it impossible to control completely": *City Bosses in the United States* (Durham, N. C.: Duke University Press, 1930), p. 47.

[40] Flynn, *op. cit.,* p. 221; see also p. 110 for an account of how a coalition of New York Democratic "bosses" were defeated (1932) when they tried to block the nomination of Herbert Lehman for governor against the wishes of the party workers.

[41] Cf. Robert G. Spivack, "New York," in R. S. Allen, ed., *Our Sovereign State* (New York: The Vanguard Press, Inc., 1949), pp. 76-78; Charles W. Van Devander, *The Big Bosses* (New York: Howell, Soskin, 1944), pp. 311-12; and Warren L. Moscow, *Politics in the Empire State* (New York: Alfred A. Knopf, 1948), *passim.*

successful party leader avails himself—and *must* avail himself—of most of the methods of maintaining leadership that the typology associates exclusively with "bosses." [42]

In short, there is little to be gained, and much clarity and insight to be lost, by distinguishing party "leaders" from a different species called party "bosses." In what follows, therefore, we shall speak only of party "leaders," and attempt to keep to ourselves any sentiments of approval or disapproval we may feel toward this specific leader or that one.

SOME GENERALIZATIONS ABOUT PARTY LEADERSHIP

Although the literature on political parties contains very little systematic analysis of party leadership, it does now provide us with a considerable number of "case studies" of party leaders.[43] And the evidence presented in them, supplemented by the writers' own observations, seems to us to warrant the following generalizations about the nature of leadership in American parties:

Party Leadership Is "Specific" to Particular Situations. We noted above that there is growing agreement among present-day social scientists that there are *no* personality traits common to all leaders of all groups, and that leadership is best thought of as highly differentiated, i.e., specific to particular groups and situations. There are a number of reasons for believing that this is the most fruitful approach to leadership in American political parties. For one thing, the studies of local "bosses" we have available make it very clear that a wide variety of human types have become bosses, so that the classic stereotype of the "derby-hatted, sport-suited, flashy-jewelried, plug-ugly boss, with coarse, brutal features, protruding paunch, and well-chewed stogy," is often quite wide of the mark.[44] Boies Penrose, "boss" of Pennsylvania Republicans

---

[42] In his novel, *All the King's Men*, Robert Penn Warren has his leading character, Willie Stark (who bears a certain resemblance to Huey Long), say: "Dirt's a funny thing. Come to think of it, there ain't a thing but dirt on this green God's globe except what's under water, and that's dirt too. It's dirt makes the grass grow. A diamond ain't a thing in the world but a piece of dirt that got awful hot. And God-a-Mighty picked up a handful of dirt and blew on it and made you and me and George Washington and mankind blessed in faculty and apprehension. It all depends on what you do with the dirt. That right? . . . You can't inherit [goodness] from anybody. You got to make it . . . and you got to make it out of badness. . . . And you know why? Because there isn't anything else to make it out of.": *All the King's Men* (New York: Harcourt, Brace and Company, 1946), pp. 50, 272.

[43] Some of the leading case studies of recent party leaders are: Charles E. Merriam, *Four Party Leaders* (New York: The Macmillan Company, 1926); Wayne C. Williams, *William Jennings Bryan* (New York: G. P. Putnam's Sons, 1936); Henry F. Pringle, *Theodore Roosevelt* (New York: Harcourt, Brace and Company, 1931); H. C. F. Bell, *Woodrow Wilson and the People* (Garden City, N. Y.: Doubleday & Company, 1945); Mary E. Dillon, *Wendell Willkie* (Philadelphia: J. B. Lippincott Company, 1952); Harold F. Gosnell, *Champion Campaigner: Franklin D. Roosevelt* (New York: The Macmillan Company, 1952); John Gunther, *Roosevelt in Retrospect* (New York: Harper and Brothers, 1950); Dayton D. McKean, *The Boss: The Hague Machine in Action* (Boston: Houghton Mifflin Company, 1940); William M. Reddig, *Tom's Town* (Philadelphia: J. B. Lippincott Company, 1947); J. T. Salter, ed., *The American Politician* (Chapel Hill, N. C.: University of North Carolina Press, 1938); R. S. Allen, ed., *Our Fair City* (New York: The Vanguard Press, Inc., 1947); Zink, *op. cit.;* and Van Devander, *op. cit.*

[44] Zink, *op. cit.*, pp. 63-65.

for many years, majored in political economy at Harvard, and lived to write a learned book entitled *A History of Ground Rents in Philadelphia;* [45] Frank Hague neither smokes nor drinks, and has no paunch; [46] and Tom Pendergast, far from being a back-slapper, was "strictly business" about politics, and his associates thought him cold and austere. [47]

Secondly, the particular methods used by successful party leaders do, when subjected to study and analysis, clearly vary with the situations in which they operate. One famous southern "boss," Huey Long, operated in a one-party state where the "better" people had for many years provided respectable and dignified government that did nothing for the underprivileged. Long set out to rally the "red-necks" against the entrenched aristocrats; and where demagogic oratory, bribery, patronage, intimidation, and violence seemed to him likely to forward his purposes, he made uninhibited use of them, and ended up with a near-dictatorship on his hands. But he consistently delivered the goods on his promises to the depressed groups, who certainly regarded him as their great benefactor. [48] Another southern "boss," Senator Harry F. Byrd of Virginia, has used methods so different from Long's as to seem to belong to another world. His organization, unlike Long's, has to reckon with a certain amount of opposition from the other major party, and in any case must do business with an electorate that is somewhat more prosperous and better educated than Long's. The Byrd organization, in consequence, while it exercises tight and pervasive control over the Democratic party and the government of Virginia, operates always with dignity and decorum, relying mainly upon the unobtrusive distribution of patronage to key party workers on the one hand, and the maintenance—again unobtrusive—of conditions favorable to the dominant business interests on the other. [49]

Another contrast that points up this lesson is that between Vito Marcantonio of New York City's East Harlem district and Frank Hague of Jersey City and Hudson County, New Jersey, both widely regarded as "bosses." Marcantonio "did business" with the Communists, openly espousing their policies and interests, and relying on the Communist party for the corps of expert canvassers and organizers he had to have in order to bring off the well-nigh incredible feat now associated with his name: that of winning for himself, in a multi-party district within a multi-party city, and election after election,

---

[45] Walter Davenport, *Power and Glory: The Life of Boies Penrose* (New York: G. P. Putnam's Sons, 1931), pp. 97-98.

[46] McKean, *The Boss,* Ch. 1.

[47] Reddig, *op. cit.,* pp. 133-35.

[48] Harnett T. Kane, *Louisiana Hayride* (New York: William Morrow and Company, 1941), describes in detail the character and methods of the Long machine, but explains the whole phenomenon in terms of the voters' supineness and of Long's Svengali-like political genius. V. O. Key, Jr., on the other hand, explains Long's success in terms of the failure of the "better people" in Louisiana to improve the lot of the underprivileged. Key confirms the widespread impression that Louisiana voters in Long's day had only the two alternatives of "a venal administration with a dynamic program, or an honest, do-nothing administration belonging to the corporations": *Southern Politics in State and Nation* (New York: Alfred A. Knopf, 1949), pp. 164, 168.

[49] Key, *Southern Politics in State and Nation,* pp. 21-27.

the nominations of *all* parties for U.S. representative.[50] Frank Hague's methods were at the other end of the spectrum, although his electorate, like Marcantonio's, included large numbers of men and women to whom he might have appealed in the Marcantonio manner. Instead he "moved in" on the Communists, and on the trade unions as well, and made his running battle with both an important source of the strength that, year after year, kept him in power.[51]

Another contrast that is in point: Sheriff Birch Briggs of Polk County, Tennessee, gained control of the dominant party in a one-party area by using intimidation and violence, by stuffing ballot-boxes, and by "running errands" for the one dominant business in his area.[52] But an equally famous and successful rural "boss," Joseph Sickler of Salem County, New Jersey, with nothing to work with but the *second* party in a modified one-party area, merely made the most of his skill as a public speaker and his ability to bring people to like and respect him—that is, he acted, for most purposes, like a "leader." [53]

The evidence, we repeat, does not bear out the notion that there is a single type of personality and a particular set of methods associated with party leadership in all situations. At most it appears to warrant two additional *general* statements as to how leader-follower relations "work" in the typical local situation in a political party.

The Leader's First Business Is to Control His Own Party. Whether a would-be party leader is operating in a two-party, one-party, or modified one-party area, his task is to get control first of his own party's activities and policies—that is, to think of beating the opposing party as, so to speak, a second phase of the task, posterior to the first both in logic and in time. Winning primary elections, in other words, is the *central* function of the party leader, from precinct committeeman on up:

His standing in politics, his place in the organization, and, in most cases, his job at the City Hall or Courthouse, depend upon his ability to carry his precinct in the primaries for the machine candidates. He can afford to lose the precinct in the general election. That will not hurt him much. It may not be his fault. He may be a Democrat in a Republican stronghold and the most he is expected to do is to make a good showing. But there is no excuse for him to lose in the primaries. He must deliver the goods there. If he cannot carry his precinct in the primaries he loses his position as precinct executive, he loses his political pull, and, in all probability, his political place. All hope of promotion in the machine is gone from him.[54]

[50] Richard Rovere, "Vito Marcantonio: Machine Politician, New Style," *Harper's*, Vol. CLXXXVIII (April, 1944), pp. 391-98.

[51] McKean, *The Boss, passim.*

[52] Van Devander, *op. cit.,* pp. 186-91.

[53] Robert C. Brooks, "Sickler of Salem County: A Study of Rural Politics," in J. T. Salter, ed., *op. cit.,* pp. 328-47.

[54] From: *The Great Game of Politics* (rev. ed.), by Frank R. Kent, pp. 2-3. Copyright 1923, 1930, by Doubleday & Company, Inc. See also Kent, pp. 10-11; and Van Devander, *op. cit.,* pp. 9-10.

The Leader's Position Ultimately Depends on the Voters. Despite what some writers have had to say, as noted above, about the "irresponsibility" of "bosses," the evidence indicates that the power of *any* party or factional leader depends in the last analysis on what the voters do in the primary and general elections. Immediately, to be sure, it depends upon what his followers within the party or faction think of him; but this, in turn, depends in large part on their judgment as to how well he has steered the group toward its objectives. Even if he is the "nicest guy" in the world, they will hardly retain him as party or factional leader when they decide, once and for all, that he is steering it badly, and that with him at the helm there will be no dividends of patronage, power, or prestige in return for the efforts they are expending. And one important point to grasp here is that a judgment as to his success or failure can hardly be made without an eye to the past, current, and probable future behavior of the voters.

"Failure" and "success" mean, to be sure, different things in different party groups and in different situations. In two-party areas, both parties think of success as winning general elections and parceling out the rewards that accrue to the victor; and the objective of each major faction in each party is to dominate the parceling-out process. This, however, means winning *both* primary and general elections, and the party or faction leader will be judged with that in mind. In one-party areas, by contrast, success is a matter of winning primaries and dominating caucuses—alike for factions in the dominant party and for factions in the second party, where the big thing is merely to control the party organization and so control whatever national patronage may turn up. In the modified one-party areas, success has much the same meaning it has in the two-party areas: the second party must roll up a substantial percentage of the vote and, now and then at least, win an election; the dominant party must see to it that the second party's victories don't occur too often.

But all this is to say, as intimated above, that the success of every party and faction in the nation is determined by how it performs at the polls—in some kind of election. And since the party or factional leader's power depends on his ability to lead his followers to success rather than failure, his own position ultimately depends upon what the voters do to his party or faction at election time. It is therefore highly significant that the studies of such famous "bosses" as Ed Crump of Memphis, Jim Curley of Boston, Tom Pendergast of Kansas City, and Frank Hague of Jersey City, all make the point that their power, when the chips were down, depended basically not on vote stealing or violence but on one simple fact: that the ordinary voters in their areas were generally satisfied with the kind of government they provided. And most of them, on occasion at least, discovered the hard way that when the voters grow dissatisfied, the "boss" loses part or all of his power.[55] The party

[55] On the sources of Crump's power, see Gerald M. Capers, "Memphis, Satrapy of a Benevolent Despot," in R. S. Allen, ed., *Our Fair City,* pp. 211-34; and Key, *Southern Politics in State and Nation,* pp. 58-69. On Curley, see Louis M. Lyons, "Boston: Study in Inertia," in R. S. Allen,

leader, in short, however much he might like to concentrate solely upon the immediate members of and workers in his particular organization, cannot afford to ignore the voters: he may perhaps ignore some of them over long periods and most of them over short periods; but never many of them for very long.

THE "DO'S" AND "DON'TS" OF PARTY ACTIVITY

Another interesting sidelight upon the leader-follower relationship in American parties is provided by the available data concerning party leaders' and workers' views on how to succeed in politics.

Both leaders and workers in American parties seem to agree that the man who wishes to get ahead in a party must be loyal to those above and below him in the hierarchy, and must have a reputation for telling the truth. Lying to his associates, in other words, or welshing on some commitment he has made to them, is *the* unforgivable sin and is punished relentlessly; as Jim Farley puts it, men who go back on their word "never get anywhere, because no one trusts them. They dig their own political graves by deception and treachery. If there is one type of man who can't succeed in politics, it's the man who habitually lies." [56] When Tom Pendergast, shortly before he died, gave his valedictory on his political career, he rested the case for his being accounted a worthy citizen on the single claim: "I've never broken my word. Put this down: I've never broken my word to any living human being I gave it to. That is the key to success in politics or anything else." [57]

Another point on which party leaders and workers appear to be virtually unanimous has to do with the claims of the man who knows precinct-level politics at first hand to be listened to against those of the man who knows about politics only what he has read in books and newspapers. "He's never polled a precinct" is the politician's equivalent of the businessman's slur, "He's never met a payroll." As Frank Hague told George Creel:

Politics is a business. That's what the reformers don't get. They think it's a sort of revival meeting, with nothing to do but nominate some bird who's never seen a polling place, make a lot of speeches about clean government, and then sit back and wait for voters to hit the sawdust trail. It's a laugh. You got to have *organization,* and not for just a few weeks before election, but all the year 'round. . . . According to reformers, the average American can hardly wait for election day so he can exercise the sovereign right that the forefathers bought with their blood. That's another laugh. A full fifty per cent of voters have got to be coaxed or dragged to the polls. Honest, I hate to think what would happen to democratic

ed., *Our Fair City,* pp. 16-36. On Pendergast, see Reddig, *op. cit.* On Hague, see McKean, *The Boss,* and George Creel, "The Complete Boss," *Collier's,* Vol. XCVIII (October 10, 1936), pp. 13, 58-60.

[56] Farley, *Behind the Ballots,* p. 23.

[57] Quoted in Reddig, *op. cit.,* p. 385. See also Zink, *op. cit.,* p. 63; McKean, *The Boss,* p. 99; and Brooks, *op. cit.*

government if it wasn't for the boys in the wards and precincts who spend their nights ringing doorbells and licking stamps.[58]

Boies Penrose, though Harvard-trained and the author of learned works on government, pressed the same point when someone asked him why congressmen and state legislators had to take orders from him:

Look here, you and I don't talk the same language. You speak from the book. I speak from experience. I don't think you'd understand me if I did answer. I'll tell you what you do. You go out into your own home ward or district and get busy. Work with the boys. Help them get out the vote. And after a year of that come in again. We'll talk facts, not morals.[59]

Many successful party leaders believe that friendliness toward and sincere affection for one's associates are musts for the man who wishes to rise in a party hierarchy.[60] While he was national chairman of the Democratic party, for example, Jim Farley used to keep on file at national headquarters the names of all the people—over 150,000 in all—who were working for the party in precincts all over the nation. At least once during every campaign each of these workers received a personal letter from Farley on party-headquarters stationery, thanking him for his work. As he explained:

Here's the reason why I write a letter. The receiver knows that it was intended for him personally and no one else in the world and, far more important, he can keep that letter telling about the fine help he rendered in electing the President of the United States, or the Governor, or the Senator, until his dying day. I know because I've seen them time and again—frayed, soiled, and tattered from being exhibited on a thousand different occasions but still holding together somehow or other. In fact, in the early days, I kept one or two such communications myself and was proud of them. . . . An army is seldom stronger than its infantry forces, and a political army is never stronger than its corps of workers. Having come up through the ranks from the lowest rung on the political ladder, I know and appreciate fully what their efforts mean to the success of the Democratic ticket.[61]

Party "Cohesion" and "Discipline"

WHAT THESE WORDS MEAN IN PARTY POLITICS

When social scientists speak of group "cohesion," they refer to the extent to which, in a given situation, group members can be observed to work to-

[58] Creel, *op. cit.*, p. 13.

[59] Quoted in Davenport, *op. cit.*, p. 187.

[60] Cf. Jim Pendergast's views in Reddig, *op. cit.*, p. 28; and Joseph Sickler's views in Brooks, *op. cit.*

[61] Farley, *op. cit.*, p. 193. Not all successful party leaders, be it noted, fit into the implied Farley formula. Frank Hague, Tom Pendergast, Thomas E. Dewey, Charles F. Murphy, and Richard Croker have all been described by their associates as "reserved," "cold," and even "unfriendly." Friendliness and warmth are perhaps less highly valued in party leaders than loyalty, faithfulness to obligations, and technical know-how.

gether for the group's goals in one and the same way. A party caucus in a legislative assembly, for example, is "cohesive" on matters of foreign policy insofar as its members vote alike on foreign-policy measures; and a party is "cohesive" at election time to the extent that its members actively support the party's official nominees.

"Cohesion" must not be confused—the more since there is some conceptual overlap—with "discipline." By the latter term social scientists mean two things: (1) cohesion of such character that followers regularly accept and act upon the commands of the leader or leaders, i.e., the cohesion of a crack army regiment as opposed to the cohesion of a Quaker meeting; and (2) availability to the leader of ways and means of inducing recalcitrant members to accept and act upon his commands.

Some writers deplore the alleged absence of discipline in American parties. The latter, they say, score low on both the counts just noted: their members do not obey their leaders' commands, and the leaders are not in position to get them to do so by imposing sanctions; furthermore, to come back to "cohesion," the members of American parties cannot be counted on to act alike in given situations.[62] Whether or not this is merely, or even largely, because of the lack of "discipline" is in the opinion of the present writers a difficult question, and not one to be answered in terms of uncriticized tacit assumptions. Let us, by way of getting into the problem, look first at the sanctions available to American party leaders.

METHODS OF DISCIPLINE IN AMERICAN PARTIES [63]

Such discipline as we find in American parties is usually enforced via one or more of the following methods:

Patronage. When party leaders have public jobs to give to party workers, they tend to appoint to them those party workers who have cooperated and followed orders in the past and are likely to do so in the future.[64] Since, as we have already noted, the desire for economic gain is one (though by no means the only one) of the more urgent reasons why people go into politics, the capacity to dole out jobs in this way is, as far as it goes, an effective disciplinary weapon at all levels of party organization. As Joe Guffey, senator from Pennsylvania and "boss" of its Democratic organization during the New Deal era, put it: "Patronage always helps. I believe in rewarding the fellows who've

---

[62] Cf. Schattschneider, *Party Government*, pp. 196-98. In Chapter 17, we shall review the evidence as to how much "cohesion" American parties actually display inside the national, state, and local governments.

[63] For an extended discussion of discipline in American parties, see Key, *Politics, Parties, and Pressure Groups*, pp. 349-65. See also Bone, *op. cit.*, pp. 369-72.

[64] The term "patronage" originally meant favors—usually sinecures of one kind or another—that an aristocratic "patron" gave his "retainers" as rewards for faithful service; e.g., the "pocket-borough" seats in the pre-1832 House of Commons, which were distributed, on a straight patron-retainer basis, by the noblemen who controlled them.

done the work. When a job comes vacant, I just try to think who deserves it." [65] And Ed Flynn wrote with equal frankness:

> How do I maintain the majority support of the [Bronx County, New York, Democratic] Executive Committee? To begin with, I always see to it that the key party workers have some sort of exempt [i.e., from merit-system civil-service examinations] positions if they want them. . . . The families also—sons, daughters, husbands, wives—of the District Leaders are taken care of in some way or other. Sometimes they are given exempt positions, and sometimes they get help from us in the line of civil service promotion. . . . I have the final word about who should be appointed to positions that control exempt jobs.[66]

If there were enough jobs, and *if* party leaders had a sufficiently free hand in doling them out, they could presumably do something about the lack of discipline of which the writers just mentioned complain. But there is one further *if*—namely, *if* they wanted party discipline badly enough to change the entire character of the American party system in order to get it.

Purges. Party leaders sometimes attempt to unseat recalcitrant party workers and lesser leaders (whom they have been unable to bring to heel otherwise) by beating them in primaries and caucuses. The only recent attempts at "purges" on a national scale are associated with the names of Franklin Roosevelt (1938) and Harry Truman (1946).[67] But the purge, particularly that directed at a faction, is a common disciplinary measure on the state and local political levels.

The Leader's Prestige. The leader's most dependable and effective disciplinary "weapon," however, is the belief among his followers (based on their appraisal of his past record and the extent to which he keeps them convinced of the rightness of his present position) that the policies, nominees, and tactics he recommends are those most likely to achieve the party's goals. But records vary all the way from unrelieved failure to invariable success (some party leaders live and die without losing an election); so the prestige weapon is available to different party leaders—and to a given party leader in different situations—in varying degrees. Few are so successful or convincing that they can neglect other weapons in their attempt to maintain the degree of discipline that they are shooting for.

WHEN ARE AMERICAN PARTIES MOST COHESIVE?

The available evidence indicates that the members of American parties are far more cohesive on questions having to do with the selection of public officeholders than on questions having to do with the formulation of public policy. In the Congress and in our state legislatures, for example, we seldom find *all*

---

[65] Quoted in Joseph Alsop and Robert Kintner, "The Guffey," *Saturday Evening Post*, Vol. CCXC (March 26, 1938), pp. 98-101.

[66] Flynn, *op. cit.*, p. 224. See also Key, *Politics, Parties, and Pressure Groups*, pp. 352-55. In Chapter 16, we shall have more to say about the role of patronage in the life of the parties.

[67] For an account of these "purges" and their results, see pp. 286-89.

the legislators of one party voting together on a legislative issue; [68] but on matters having to do with the "organization of the house"—selecting the speaker, allocating memberships on the various committees, etc.—votes almost always follow strict party lines.[69]

We are in the presence of this same phenomenon whenever we see two leaders of the same party, known to disagree profoundly on this or that issue of public policy, supporting each other at election time. In 1952, for example, candidate Eisenhower supported and received support from Senators McCarthy (Wisconsin) and Jenner (Indiana), though both gave every indication that they did not see eye to eye with him on certain—to them, anyway—urgent public questions. At the same time, Senators Russell (Georgia) and Long (Louisiana) and Speaker Rayburn (Texas) were supporting and receiving support from candidate Stevenson, though his stand on state ownership of off-shore oil deposits and a national civil-rights program differed sharply from their own.

The cohesion of the parties where nominations and elections are concerned cannot be explained in terms of "discipline" (i.e., the leader's forcing his reluctant followers into line). The reason appears to be simply this: The members of each of the major parties, however much they may differ on other matters, put a high valuation on their party's winning elections and controlling government personnel; otherwise they would not be members. They know, moreover, that unless they close ranks and avoid working at cross purposes, victory will go as a matter of course to the other party. So they close ranks and avoid working at cross purposes—not because they have been "ordered" to and will have sanctions imposed on them if they do not, but because it would be foolish not to.

The two *parties* appear to be much alike from the standpoint of leadership and discipline. But it is quite otherwise with the several *levels of organization* within each party.

The Incidence of Leadership and Discipline in American Parties

IN THE NATIONAL PARTIES

The Presidential Candidates. Most students of American politics agree that the major parties get a brief taste of something approximating effective leadership during presidential campaigns, when each party has staked its fortunes on its nominee and, in the nature of the case, must either concede him a commanding position, or deny it to him and so invite disaster in November. In each party, accordingly, the presidential nominee names the national chairman, provides the interpretation of the party platform that is generally con-

---

[68] We shall examine the evidence on this point in detail in Chapter 17.
[69] Cf. Schattschneider, *op. cit.,* pp. 196-97; and Bone, *op. cit.,* p. 370.

sidered to be *the* official one, calls the tricks on general campaign strategy, and speaks officially for the party on policy matters. He exercises, in other words, a kind of authority that simply does not exist within an American national party at any other time, and, other things being equal, can count on keeping it until the "honeymoon" is over. Here again, however, it is not a question of discipline: He has no effective method for bringing into line local party organizations or leaders who decide to "bolt" the ticket or drag their feet. His authority rests on the simple fact that he everywhere heads the party's ticket, and that the ticket is unlikely to fare much better in any locality than he does.[70]

The President. In 1908, Woodrow Wilson, then an academic political scientist who had yet to hold his first elective public office, wrote:

> [The president] cannot escape being the leader of his party except by incapacity and lack of personal force, because he is at once the choice of the party and of the nation. He is the party nominee, and the only party nominee for whom the whole nation votes. . . . He may be both the leader of his party and the leader of the nation, or he may be one or the other. If he lead the nation, his party can hardly resist him. His office is anything he has the sagacity and force to make it.[71]

But political scientists of subsequent decades have, in general, agreed only in part with Wilson. To the extent that the party in power *has* any national leadership between elections—so runs the more recent formulation—it comes for the most part from the president; but a man can be president and still find himself unable to provide much leadership, and incapacity and lack of personal force may not be the only reasons for his failure to provide more. He is indeed, in the eyes of the public, the legitimate enunciator of party policy; but his party in Congress is as likely to ignore that policy as to put it into law. He can use patronage and purges in the attempt to get rid of the worst rebels, but such disciplinary measures, even if they achieve their immediate objective (which they do not always do) may backfire and prove costly in the extreme. Professor McKean seems amply justified, therefore, in saying that the president's party leadership is "at best a working but shifting and uncertain coalition of the President and his supporters in Congress."[72]

Wilson, be it noted, had somehow convinced himself that if the president proves himself a strong leader of public opinion and a strong executive inside the formal government, this will as a matter of course give him a strong hand inside his *party*. Few informed observers would put it so today, and Wilson himself might well have put it differently after his stint in the White House. For Herbert Croly, after watching Wilson's own effort to translate presidential

---

[70] Cf. Howard R. Penniman, *Sait's American Parties and Elections*, pp. 326-27; and Key, *Politics, Parties, and Pressure Groups*, pp. 351-53. But see our discussion of the limited effectiveness of the "coattail effect" in Chapter 17.

[71] Woodrow Wilson, *Constitutional Government in the United States* (New York: Columbia University Press, 1908), pp. 67, 69.

[72] McKean, *Party and Pressure Politics*, p. 637. See also Key, *Politics, Parties, and Pressure Groups*, p. 710; and Merriam and Gosnell, *The American Party System*, pp. 185-86. We shall return to the subject of presidential party leadership in Chapter 17.

leadership into leadership of the Democratic party, found himself driven to the conclusion that Wilson had lessened his effectiveness as a *party* leader by making the presidency the kind of thing he had dreamed of at Princeton. As Croly said, a man determined to be a strong president and a strong party leader

> . . . can, of course, hide behind the fiction of partisan responsibility, whenever he wants to avoid speaking to his party about a legislative proposal upon which he is likely to encounter serious resistance; but no suavity of manner and no amount of wise self-restraint in the employment of his power can obscure the real facts of the situation. At the final test the responsibility is his rather than that of his party. The party which submits to such a dictatorship, however benevolent, cannot play its own proper part in a system of partisan government. It will either cease to have any independent life or its independence will assume the form of a revolt.[73]

Our point here is confirmed by current usage of the term "presidential leadership," by which contemporary political scientists clearly mean leadership by the chief executive *of the rest of the government,* not leadership of the majority party by its official head; the latter, if mentioned at all, is brought in merely as an element in, or aspect of, "presidential leadership." And it is further confirmed by the fact that the major disciplinary weapons at the president's disposal—the veto, the threat of veto, and the appeal to public opinion over the heads of congressmen—lend themselves to use by the *executive* against the *legislature,* not to use of a *party leader* against *party members.*[74]

The Defeated Presidential Candidate. The newspapers often speak of a defeated presidential candidate as "titular head" of his party. A more accurate designation would perhaps be "the closest approximation to a titular head his party can point to"—and, even in calling him that, we should be well advised to remind ourselves that he is titular head only to the extent that people generally choose to think of him, and accept him, as such. For the defeated candidate has even less reason than the president to think of himself as *the* leader of his party, and notably less opportunity to become leader. He holds no official party position, and has therefore no formal capacity to speak for the party; nor is there any party post to which he can aspire that would give him that capacity.[75] In short, his claims to speak for his party are—and are generally understood to be—about as strong as his chances of being renominated at the

---

[73] Herbert Croly, *Progressive Democracy* (New York: The Macmillan Company, 1914), pp. 345-46. Reprinted by permission of The Macmillan Company.

[74] Cf. Pendleton Herring, *Presidential Leadership* (New York: Farrar and Rinehart, Inc., 1940); Merriam and Gosnell, *op. cit.,* pp. 186-89; and Key, *Politics, Parties, and Pressure Groups,* pp. 710-12.

[75] This is in sharp contrast to the situation in Great Britain, Canada, Australia, New Zealand, and South Africa. In each of these nations the statutes provide for a salaried official known as the "Leader of Her Majesty's Loyal Opposition," which office is invariably held by the leader of the party that holds the second largest number of seats in the lower house of the national legislature. See Dean E. McHenry, "Formal Recognition of the Leader of the Opposition in Parliaments of the British Commonwealth," *Political Science Quarterly,* Vol. LXIX (September, 1954), pp. 438-52.

next convention. And since in most instances his chances are—and are generally understood to be—very slim indeed,[76] neither the general public nor the leaders and workers in his party are likely to regard any pronouncement on public policy from him as a statement *by his party*.[77]

Congressmen. Insofar as the second party in national politics has anyone at all who is regarded as its spokesman and symbol, it is more likely to be a leading congressman than the party's most recent presidential candidate.[78] During the Republicans' long period in opposition (from 1933 to 1953, broken only by their control of Congress from 1947 to 1949), it was Senator Robert A. Taft of Ohio who received the sobriquet of "Mr. Republican," and not Herbert Hoover, Alfred Landon, Wendell Willkie, or Thomas E. Dewey. And, at the present writing, Senators Johnson, Symington, and Russell and Speaker Rayburn are at least as strong candidates for the title of "Mr. Democrat" as Adlai Stevenson. Neither Senator Taft nor any of the congressional Democrats mentioned, on the other hand, exercised leadership in his party that was significantly more effective—as far as rallying party members behind his views on public policy was concerned—than that of the defeated presidential candidate. Some members of both the majority and minority parties in Congress usually become prominent and respected political leaders; but their power to mobilize the entire membership of their respective parties behind them is, as a rule, highly limited.

The status of leadership and discipline in the national parties appears, in summary, to be this: The most effective leadership in both national parties is that exercised during presidential campaigns by the presidential candidates, when the parties' main objective is to win the election. *Between* elections, neither party has any very effective national leadership, or maintains any significant degree of discipline. Such leadership as the majority party has is indeed exercised by the president; but "presidential leadership" is for the most part attempted outside party channels, and the president is rarely an effective party leader. Nor are the prominent congressional leaders of the majority party in any better position to provide party leadership. Congressional leaders of the minority party have often been regarded as the party's spokesmen, but they have never succeeded in bringing about cohesion among the party's followers. Thus, as we suggested above, American national parties are most cohesive on matters connected with winning elections and least cohesive on matters connected with the formation of public policy between elections; and each party has yet to develop the forms of leadership and/or the methods of discipline that would make it cohesive even on major policy issues.

[76] Of the twenty-eight major-party presidential nominations made in the twentieth century, only three have gone to persons who had previously won such nominations but lost the elections (Bryan in 1900 and 1908, and Dewey in 1948).

[77] Cf. Penniman, *op. cit.,* pp. 327-29; and Bone, *op. cit.,* p. 380.

[78] Cf. Merriam and Gosnell, *op. cit.,* pp. 190-91.

IN THE STATE AND LOCAL PARTIES

The studies of leadership in American parties noted above point to cases in which the party organization of an entire state has, over a period of years, accepted strong leadership, and even acquiesced in a high degree of discipline. Among the more notable recent instances are the Long organization in Louisiana, the Dewey organization in New York, and the Byrd organization in Virginia; and some earlier examples are the Quay-Penrose organization in Pennsylvania, the La Follette-Progressive organization in Wisconsin, and the Roraback organization in Connecticut.

The consensus among students of American parties, however, seems to be this: Party organizations with effective leadership and discipline are most commonly found not at the state level but at the county and city levels.[79] Thus most of the famous "bosses," though concerned with and influential in state and national politics, have been primarily county and city leaders. For example, Tom Pendergast's power was largely confined to Kansas City and Jackson County, the Cermak-Kelly-Nash "machine's" to Chicago and Cook County, Frank Hague's to Jersey City and Hudson County, and Ed Crump's to Memphis and Shelby County. In other words, state leadership and discipline, where they appear, are likely to rest on the leader's commanding position in some county or city within the state.

The Decentralization of American National Parties

The foregoing discussion of the incidence of leadership and discipline among the various levels of American parties warrants at least one firm conclusion: *American national parties are decentralized*—not only in their "formal" organization, as we noted in Chapter 10, but also in their "informal" organization; for the leader-follower relations of discipline and leadership tend to be stronger at the base of the national parties' pyramids than at their top, and achieve maximum strength only at the bottom.[80]

Many writers deplore the decentralization of American national parties, and attribute to it most of the latter's "deficiencies." Only a few writers have raised their voices to say that it is unavoidable or even desirable in a nation like the United States. We shall return to this question in our final chapter. For our present purposes it is enough to conclude, as most students of American parties have concluded, that neither major party's "informal" organization at the present time possesses a single locus of *national* leadership, authority, and discipline, and that in both parties leadership is scattered among a great many state and local organizations.

[79] Cf. *ibid.*, pp. 192-93; and Schattschneider, *op. cit.*, pp. 142-51.

[80] See, for example, Schattschneider's statement that American parties are so decentralized that the national parties are really "ghost" parties, and that the state and local bosses have no real superiors: *Op. cit.*, p. 164.

PART FOUR

Major Activities of American Parties

Chapter 12

MAKING NOMINATIONS: PROCESS, MACHINERY, AND CONTROL

With the present chapter we begin the phase of our inquiry that we have entitled "Major Activities of American Parties." The general plan for this phase is as follows: Chapters 12-17 will deal with the major activities of the two "major" parties, thus leaving to Chapters 18 and 19 what we have to say regarding the nature, activities, and role of the minor parties.

Our immediate concern, that is to say, is with those major party activities that throw the most light on the parties' role in our total governing system, and with the typical theater for those activities, the two-party areas (one of which is the nation as a whole), not the one-party areas. (In Chapter 8, we noted some of the special traits of the parties' nomination-making and election-contesting activities in the one-party and modified one-party areas.) The first of the major parties' activities with which we shall deal is that of making nominations.

The Nominating Process

ITS NATURE

An Election-winning Process. Suppose some good fairy were to appear at a meeting of any human organization—a college fraternity, a Rotary club, a Y.M.C.A.—and say to its members: "I propose to give to the most deserving member of this group the following prizes: a guaranteed tax-free annual income of $1,000,000, irresistible charm for the opposite sex, perfect digestion, and complete peace of mind. But I want *you* to elect the one among you who should have these good things, and so I shall now pass out slips of paper on which you will write the name of the group member who should receive my gifts. The member with the most votes wins." There is little reason to doubt that we can predict the outcome of this election: a tie for first among many candidates—each with one vote.

Suppose, however, that two members of the group, A and B, somehow or other get advance notice of the good fairy's intentions. Suppose further that A says to B, "Look, you and I can win this election if we cooperate. You vote for yourself, and I'll vote for you too. That will give you two votes, and since each of the others will vote for himself, you'll win, and then we can split up the take!" In this case, the only way the other members of the group can hope to beat the A-B organization is by forming a counter-organization, i.e., by agreeing to pool their votes also, and to cast them for someone other than B.

The agreement of A and B to vote for B is tantamount to a *nomination;* and the process that results in their voting for B instead of A or someone else is essentially the same as the process that in the 1952 Republican National Convention, for instance, resulted in the passing up of Taft and Warren in favor of Eisenhower. Any group of persons who wish to elect one of their number to office in a larger group to which they belong must, among other things, concentrate their strength behind a single group member—must, that is to say, select a "candidate" behind whom to unite in the election. Making a nomination, then, is an indispensable first step in the larger process of winning an election.[1]

A Boiling-down Process. Theoretically, the American voter has a free choice among all the persons constitutionally eligible for, say, the presidency. In practice, however, the alternatives open to him are to vote for the Republican or the Democratic candidate, or to "throw away" his vote by casting it for the candidate of some third party.[2] Once the major parties confront him with their nominees, the voter who wishes to influence the course of events by casting his vote finds himself choosing not among all persons constitutionally eligible, but between two persons only, one of them certain to be elected.

Consider, on the other hand, what choosing a president would be like *in the absence of* nominations. There are about 60,000,000 persons who fulfill the constitutional requirements, and all of them, theoretically, could put themselves forward as candidates. But since the records, personalities, and policies of 60,000,000 potential presidents are clearly somewhat more than the average

[1] Cf. E. E. Schattschneider's discussion of the relationship between the degree of dispersion of votes and the necessity of organization in democratic elections: *Party Government* (New York: Rinehart & Company, Inc., 1942), pp. 38-48.

[2] Very few voters choose the latter alternative. In 1952, for example, a total of 428,638 persons voted for all third-party candidates for president, as against the 61,960,898 who voted for the two major-party candidates.

voter could be expected to take into account, *some* kind of process for "boiling down" the 60,000,000 alternatives to a number that the voter *can* be expected to consider and choose among is indispensable. Here also there are a good many theoretical possibilities: voters might, for example, consider only members of their immediate families, or they might consider only persons recommended by their newspapers. But *any* process used would reduce itself, in effect, to the making of nominations and would confront the voter with a "limited choice" among "nominees."

A Party Process. In the United States, as in all modern democracies, nominations are in fact made for most (although not all) public offices by *political parties,* rather than by the newspapers, the League of Women Voters, the political commentators, or any other *deus ex machina* that we might call on instead.[3]

ITS SIGNIFICANCE

For the Community. Most people, when they think of the process by which a democracy fills its public offices, tend to regard it as mainly a matter of elections, not nominations, and for good reason. The "Get-out-the-vote" drives conducted by our civic organizations, for example, are aimed exclusively at the final step in the process, when the nominees already stand over against one another as opponents. And, again for example, many a high-school civics class has been told in so many words that while it is our duty as good citizens to vote in general elections, it is not our duty to vote in primary elections— the latter being, after all, *party* affairs. And large numbers of students must have taken their civics lessons to heart; all states outside the South (where, as we have already seen, the primary elections *are,* in effect, the final elections) almost invariably show a vastly smaller vote in the primaries than in the general elections.[4]

A strong case can be made out, however, for the proposition that what people would be well advised to put foremost in their minds when they think of office filling in a democracy is nominations and not elections. When the major parties nominate their presidential candidates, they reduce the number of potential presidents from 60,000,000 to 2; while voters in the general election reduce the number only from 2 to 1. And even if we agree that the first 59,999,500 who are eliminated at the nomination stage are persons whom no one would ever have seriously considered, the next 498 can hardly be thrown out without making choices that, little accustomed though we are to think of it that way, are of crucial significance for the nation's future. Most voters, in short, begin to play their role in the process only at a late moment, when only Number 499 and Number 500 are left (and when who knows how many philosopher-kings, each capable of leading the nation forward to the good life,

[3] Cf. Schattschneider, *op. cit.,* pp. 50–53.
[4] See the figure in Charles E. Merriam and Harold F. Gosnell, *The American Party System,* 4th ed. (New York: The Macmillan Company, 1949), p. 311.

have been passed up as "unavailable"). As Schattschneider puts it, "The parties frame the question and define the issue [as to who shall be elected]. In doing this they go a long way toward determining what the answer will be." [5]

For the Parties. There are many reasons for regarding the making of nominations as the most crucial of the parties' activities. For one thing, this activity, more than any other, distinguishes parties from other types of political organizations. Pressure groups like the NAM and CIO, for example, frequently appeal to the voters for support of particular candidates and policies, and try to persuade public officials to act in certain ways; but only political parties nominate candidates and present them to the voters as official representatives of the sponsoring organizations.[6] And the surest test for determining whether a particular political organization is properly called a "party" or a "pressure group" is to put it this question: Do you nominate candidates and run them in your own name as your own official representatives? [7]

In the second place, a party's chances of winning a given election depend first (although not exclusively) upon its ability to make a *binding* nomination, i.e., one that the party leaders and workers will unite behind and work for. If its forces are divided among several candidates, it can hardly hope to win the election from an opposition party that *is* united.[8]

Finally, most students of political parties agree that those who control a party's nominating process control the party itself. For it is they who can extend and withdraw the party label, they who determine what face the party will turn toward the electorate, and they who, if their party's candidate wins the election, will have a say-so regarding the distribution of whatever perquisites of office the successful candidate, who is necessarily beholden to the person or persons who got him the nomination, may command.[9] Consequently, those party leaders and workers who hope to control their party regard *intra*-party contests as even more important than contests with the opposition party, however much they may also want to win the latter. Frank Kent drives this point home with great lucidity:

[5] *Op. cit.,* p. 51.

[6] In 1952 the NAM worked for the election of Eisenhower, and the CIO worked for Stevenson. But both pressure groups supported men nominated by *parties;* and there has never been an officially labeled NAM or CIO candidate for president.

[7] Frederick W. Dallinger called attention to the fact that the growth of American party organization was closely connected with the growth of party nominating methods: *Nominations for Elective Office in the United States* (New York: Longmans, Green and Company, 1897), p. 44. See also Chapter 5 of the present book.

[8] Note, for example, what happened to the Whig party in 1836, when it failed to agree upon a single national candidate for president, and confronted the electorate with no less than *three* official Whig candidates: Hugh White in the South, William Henry Harrison in the West, and Daniel Webster in the East. The Democrats, by contrast, united behind Martin Van Buren in all sections, and won the election hands down: Wilfred E. Binkley, *American Political Parties: Their Natural History* (New York: Alfred A. Knopf, 1944), p. 160.

[9] Cf. Schattschneider's statement that "a party must make nominations if it is to be regarded as a party at all. By observing the party process at this point one may hope to discover the locus of power within the party, for he who has the power to make the nomination owns the party": *Op. cit.,* p. 100.

It ought to be plain why the primaries are so vital to the machine, and why it is a matter of political life and death to the precinct executive to carry his precinct in the primaries. The machine can lose its candidate time after time in the general election without greatly diminishing its strength or loosing the grip of its leaders. Of course, it is disheartening to the rank and file and it greatly lessens the number and quality of the political pies for distribution to the faithful. It could not be kept up too long without causing a revolt in the organization, but, I repeat, the machine cannot be smashed by defeating its candidates at the election. But if it loses in the primaries, it is out of business. Any organization that cannot carry the primary election is a defunct organization. It either politically disappears or it makes peace and amalgamates with the faction that defeated it.[10]

Nominations as Elections in the One-Party Areas [11]

In Chapter 8, we noted the methods used by the southern whites in their attempt to make the Democratic primaries, in effect, the final elections; and we observed some of the ways in which they have thereby affected the nominating process in those states. The South, however, is by no means the only area in the United States in which the nominees of a particular party are invariably successful in general elections. Professor Cortez A. M. Ewing, for example, studied the results of all elections (some 10,572 in all) held from 1896 to 1946 for seats in the national House of Representatives, and tabulated the size of the pluralities rolled up by the winners. His results are set forth in Table 13.

TABLE 13   Sectional Distribution of Congressional Pluralities by Percentages in Sectional Categories [12]

Plurality	East	South	Border	Middle West	West	U.S.	U.S. Less South
Over 50%	10.3	71.8	4.8	7.8	13.3	25.5	9.2
40-50%	8.0	4.8	1.9	5.2	5.5	5.6	5.9
30-40%	12.3	5.8	9.5	9.3	9.4	8.8	9.9
20-30%	18.0	5.5	11.5	16.3	17.3	13.6	16.5
10-20%	23.6	6.3	26.5	25.1	25.5	20.0	24.8
0-10%	27.8	5.9	50.8	36.2	29.0	26.5	33.7

Ewing's figures indicate that there are many one-party and modified one-party congressional districts *outside* the South, though more of them in the

[10] From: *The Great Game of Politics* (rev. ed.), by Frank R. Kent, pp. 11-12. Copyright 1923, 1930, by Doubleday & Company, Inc.

[11] For a general discussion of this topic, see V. O. Key, Jr., *Politics, Parties, and Pressure Groups,* 3rd ed. (New York: Thomas Y. Crowell Company, 1952), pp. 425-30.

[12] Cortez A. M. Ewing, "Primaries as Real Elections," *Southwestern Social Science Quarterly,* Vol. XXIX (March, 1949), p. 296.

South than in any other section. And we learn from the same source that the number of one-party districts has increased markedly since 1896. Of the representatives elected between 1896 and 1920, 21.6 per cent received 75 per cent or more of the vote in their districts; of those elected between 1922 and 1946, however, 29 per cent received 75 per cent or more of the vote. Similarly, 37.7 per cent of the representatives elected in 1898 got over 60 per cent of the vote in their districts, while through the period 1916-1946, 50 per cent or more did so in every election except in 1932 and 1934.[13] The decline in the number of two-party congressional districts since 1896 merits careful attention, and we shall have a word to say about it below.

We are sometimes told that the voter in a one-party area has about as much choice as one in a two-party area, the only difference being that the former makes his choice in the primary election of the dominant party and not in the general election. The available evidence does not, however, bear this out. V. O. Key's recent study of nominations for state legislative posts in selected areas does, to be sure, show that far more contests take place in the primaries of parties with a good chance to win the general election than in the primaries of parties with little or no chance to win (while the voter who votes in the primary of the second party in a modified one-party or one-party area often has no choice whatever).[14] But Julius Turner's study of primary contests in the "safe" congressional districts (i.e., those in which the winner regularly receives 60 per cent or more of the popular vote) between 1944 and 1950 points strongly in the other direction: voters in the primaries of the dominant parties in such areas often have no choice at all. His data are summarized in Table 14.

TABLE 14 *Proportion of Safe Districts in Which Two or More Candidates Ran in Primaries of Dominant Party* [15]

Section	Number of Elections in Safe Districts	Number of Primary Elections Contested	Percentage
South	395	227	57.5
Northeast	222	66	29.7
Border	62	43	69.4
Central	207	95	45.9
West	79	52	65.8
Total	965	483	50.1

[13] *Ibid.*

[14] V. O. Key, Jr., "The Direct Primary and Party Structure: A Study of State Legislative Nominations," *American Political Science Review*, Vol. LXVIII (March, 1954), pp. 4-6.

[15] Julius Turner, "Primary Elections as the Alternative to Party Competition in 'Safe' Districts," *Journal of Politics*, published by the Southern Political Science Association in cooperation with the University of Florida, Vol. XV (May, 1953), p. 201.

TABLE 15   *Percentages of Unopposed Nominations in Southern Primaries, 1900-1948* [16]

	DEMOCRATS			REPUBLICANS *		
			Per Cent			Per Cent
	Total	Unop-	Unop-	Total	Unop-	Unop-
Type of Office	Races	posed	posed	Races	posed	posed
Statewide	944	248	26.3	160	63	39.8
Intermediate	1,235	465	37.6	199	72	36.2
Local	1,293	704	54.4	12	11	91.7
Total	3,472	1,417	40.8	371	145	39.1

* Most of these data are from Oklahoma, a Democratic modified one-party state.

Finally, Professor Ewing's study of primary elections for all offices, local, state, and national, in the southern states between 1900 and 1948 produced the data presented in Table 15.

The evidence presented by these three studies, then, indicates that contests—and no contest, no choice for the voters—do tend to occur more frequently in the primary elections of parties whose candidates are expected to have a good chance to win in the general elections. It also indicates, however, that even in the primaries of the dominant parties in the one-party and modified one-party areas many elections go uncontested—with the result that numerous officals are virtually appointed by the leaders of factions within the dominant parties, with the ordinary voter having little or no influence upon the outcome.

The Size of the Nominating Job

ELECTIVE OFFICES IN THE UNITED STATES

Their Number. The United States has not only a vast number but also a rich variety of governmental units—the nation as a whole, the states, and, within the states, counties, municipalities, townships, school districts, park districts, drainage districts, sanitary districts, etc.; and most of these units are governed by *elective* officers. Richard S. Childs, when he attempted to calculate the total number of our elective offices, concluded that there are well over five hundred thousand, distributed among the various types of units somewhat as shown in Table 16.

Our major parties, to be sure, divide their energies by no means equally among these categories of elective offices. They usually fight hard (in the two-party areas at least) to capture federal and state offices; they hardly ever contest school-board and special-district elections; they put up a struggle for most

[16] Cortez A. M. Ewing, *Primary Elections in the South* (Norman: University of Oklahoma Press, 1953), p. 52.

TABLE 16 *Elective Offices in the United States* [17]

Governmental Unit	Number of Units	Estimated Number of Elective Offices per Unit	Total Estimated Elective Offices per Type of Unit
U.S.A.	1	533	533
States	48	—	10,000
Counties	3,049	12	36,588
Municipalities	16,677	8	133,416
Towns and townships	17,338	8	138,704
School districts	63,407	3	190,221
Special districts	5,950	6	35,700
Total	112,420	—	545,162

county, municipal, town, and township offices, though the energies they channel into such struggles vary greatly from situation to situation, office to office, and election to election. Even with the school districts and special districts out of the picture, be it noted, nominating candidates for so many offices and seeing them through the general election is a staggering task.

The Character and Size of the Constituencies. The constituencies [18] from which all these public officials are elected differ greatly in character and size, both from category to category—states, congressional districts, counties, municipalities, wards, townships, school districts—and within each category. The president and vice-president are elected by a national constituency with a total population of over 165,000,000; U.S. senators and certain state officials are elected by statewide constituencies, in states with populations ranging from 160,083 (Nevada) to 14,830,192 (New York). The average congressional district has a population of around 350,000, but some have populations of around 900,000. The average parliamentary constituency in Britain, by contrast, has a population of 81,000; in France, 66,000; in the Netherlands, 100,000; and in Switzerland, 24,000. [19]

As we noted in Chapter 4, most of our constituencies are "single-member districts," i.e., they elect only one person for a particular office in a particular election. But a substantial number of them, such as legislative districts in some states, school districts, and municipalities with either the commission form of government or some form of proportional representation, fall into the category of "multiple-member districts."

The "Long Ballot." For the reason just noted, the average American voter is a member of several different constituencies that elect different kinds of

[17] Richard S. Childs, *Civic Victories* (New York: Harper and Brothers, 1952), p. xv.

[18] As used here, the term "constituency" denotes any geographic area in which voters elect one or more public officials.

[19] See the table of comparisons in Childs, *op. cit.*, p. 55.

public officials to run different kinds of governmental units. In order to save expense and trouble, most states try to hold as many of the elections as possible at the same time; a few states, indeed, hold *all* their elections for all public offices together. Most American voters, accordingly, do their voting on what political scientists call a "long ballot"—i.e., one on which the voter chooses among several candidates for each of several offices for each of several governing units, one therefore that presents him with a formidable list of names and, by necessity, uses up a good "long" piece of paper.[20]

Many writers regard the long ballot as the least defensible peculiarity of the American electoral system. They argue as follows: Forcing the voter to make so many choices at so many elections and for so many offices precludes his casting an independent, reasoned, and intelligent ballot. He can hardly know even the names of all the candidates, let alone their respective qualifications for the offices they seek. Thus he is likely, out of desperation if not laziness, either to vote "straight," that is, for all the nominees of a particular party, or to abstain from voting altogether, or to vote in only a few of the better-publicized contests. The "long ballot," these writers contend, takes the power to select public officials away from the individual voter and places it in the eager and grasping hands of the ticket makers, the party "bosses." [21]

The National Short Ballot Association, established in 1908, reflected this point of view about American elections, and conducted a vigorous campaign of education and propaganda in favor of a sharp reduction in the number of elective offices. It worked hand in glove with certain other reform movements, such as that urging the adoption of the commission and council-manager forms of municipal government, and in 1919 became part of the National Municipal League. Its teachings have not gone entirely unheeded: certain state and local governments now have fewer elective offices than they used to have. But the short-ballot movement still has a long way to go before it can safely shut up shop; over the country as a whole, the ballot is still "long" by the movement's standards, and the trend toward shortening it appears to have tapered off in recent years.[22]

WHAT NUMEROUS ELECTIONS DO TO THE PARTIES

Leaving aside for the moment the question of whether the long ballot is or is not to be deplored, the American political system does require, by comparison with the political system of any other democratic nation, a great many elections for a great many public offices for a great many governing units. And

[20] The ballots in Great Britain and other parliamentary democracies, where voters are called upon to make a choice for only one office at a given election, are by contrast "short."

[21] For a recent statement of this position, see Childs, *op. cit.*, Ch. V. See also Key, *Politics, Parties, and Pressure Groups*, pp. 654-57; and Howard R. Penniman, *Sait's American Parties and Elections*, 4th ed. (New York: Appleton-Century-Crofts, 1948), Ch. XXV, "The Overburdened Voter."

[22] Richard S. Childs is the founder and long-time leader of the short-ballot movement. For his summary of its progress to date, see *op. cit.*, Chs. IX-XXII.

this has certain consequences for our political parties, two of which are worth noting at this point.

First, it means that American parties have a great many more nominations to make and a great many more elections to contest than parties in other democratic nations; and that the sheer *volume* of the parties' work must be taken into account in any assessment of their character and the role they play. For, as we shall note in detail in this and subsequent chapters, the volume of work is reflected in such matters as the role of patronage, the relationship between leaders and workers, and the relationship between party leaders and party workers on the one hand and party supporters on the other.

Second, it helps to maintain the independence of the state and local parties; or, to put this a little differently, it strengthens the hand of each level of party organization vis-à-vis its "superior" in the "hierarchy." Political parties are primarily nomination-making and election-contesting groups, and, this being the case, their organization must, we repeat, correspond to that of the electoral system. Our numerous state and local constituencies, offices, and elections render absolutely necessary, in other words, state and local party organizations, to make local nominations and contest local elections as the national party organizations make national nominations and contest national elections.

The Evolution of Nominating Machinery in America

The evolution of nominating machinery in America is closely related to the general institutional development of political parties (see Chapter 5). In tracing it, we may usefully break it down into the following five major phases: [23]

(1) From early colonial times until about the time of the Revolution. Most nominations for elective offices in the colonial governments were made by one or the other or both of two methods: those who wished to hold office simply made public announcement of their candidacies, or announcement was made on their behalf by primitive versions of the "caucus"—i.e., by small, informal, irregular, and secret gatherings of some of the community's leading citizens, brought together on a basis of straight co-optation.[24] Gradually, however, as lines were drawn in colonial politics between the Whig-Patriot and Tory-Loyalist "parties" and the struggle between them grew more and more

[23] The account in the text is drawn largely from the following sources: Dallinger, *op. cit.*, pp. 5-44; M. I. Ostrogorski, *Democracy and the Organization of Political Parties*, translated by Frederick Clarke (New York: The Macmillan Company, 1902), Vol. II, pp. 1-204; and Ernst C. Meyer, *Nominating Systems* (Madison, Wis.: published by the author, 1902), pp. 2 ff.

[24] Despite the informality of such nominating procedures, some attempts were made to insure minimum standards for the nominees they produced. Just how minimum those standards were is shown by a 1683 New Jersey regulation, which required the official nominators to swear that they would not name anyone "known to them to be guilty for the time, or to have been guilty for a year before, of Adultery, Whoredom, Drunkenness, or any such Immorality, or who is insolvent or a Fool": Quoted in Charles E. Merriam and Louise Overacker, *Primary Elections*, rev. ed. (Chicago: University of Chicago Press, 1928), p. 8, n. 1.

intense, both developed continuing organizations of a less irregular and more formal character: correspondence committees, patriotic societies, and, most important of all, so-called "parlor caucuses"—that is, self-constituted, usually secret gatherings of "party" leaders, some of which, by the time of the Revolution, had a continuing membership and highly regularized procedures. The most famous of them was the "Boston Caucus Club," John Adams' description of which we quoted in Chapter 5.

(2) From the Revolution to the launching of the new national government in 1789. During this period, nominations for elective offices in the new state governments and for members of the national Congress were made by various methods: correspondence among "party" leaders, mass meetings of local "party" members, recommendations by prominent citizens, and, most commonly, by caucuses, which assumed during this period the form in which we know them today. Before the end of the period, however, there had emerged, in a few states, a new method of making nominations for statewide and county offices, namely, conventions of delegates elected *ad hoc* by local "party" groups. These conventions, to be sure, did not have the settled status and the rules governing procedure and membership that we now associate with the delegate convention; and they met irregularly and infrequently. But it is worth noting that these were the years during which the convention became available as an alternative.

(3) From about 1789 to about 1830. In the 1790's, as we noted in Chapter 5, the conflict between the Federalists and the Jeffersonian Republicans crystallized all over the nation, and each group developed into something closely resembling a modern political party. Each party soon included among its prime objectives the election of its adherents to offices selected by statewide and national constituencies; and since the caucuses and conventions mentioned above were mostly local affairs, designed for nominating candidates for local offices, the parties found themselves obliged to develop new machinery, designed with an eye to the larger constituencies. The Jeffersonians, who were the first to recognize this necessity, solved the problem temporarily, in many of the states, by setting up the so-called "legislative caucus," which brought together the Jeffersonian members of the state legislature for the purpose of picking a gubernatorial candidate. The Federalists soon imitated the Jeffersonian legislative caucus, and for the next thirty-odd years both parties used it continuously for making nominations for statewide offices. On the national level, the Federalist party took the lead: beginning in 1800, its representatives and senators met in secret caucus and agreed upon candidates for president and vice-president. The Republican party promptly provided themselves with the equivalent of the Federalist "Congressional Caucus," and used it for nominating presidential candidates until 1824. From an early date, however, the Republicans held open sessions.

Almost from the moment of their establishment, the legislative and congressional caucuses drew a heavy barrage of unfavorable criticism, mainly from the Jacksonian Democrats within the Republican party, who denounced the caucuses as aristocratic, immoral, and oversusceptible to manipulation by the "wire pullers." Through the final years of the period here in question some of the legislative caucuses were abolished under Jacksonian pressure, and some were "diluted" (by the addition of delegates elected by party groups outside the legislatures) in an attempt to meet the Jacksonians' criticisms. On the national level, the Congressional Caucus kept on going, though under increasing fire, until 1820, but by 1824 it had fallen so low in public estimation that less than a third of the eligible Republican participants bothered to attend (by this time the Federalist party had passed out of existence, and the Republicans had the national field to themselves); and those who did attend brought further ridicule and condemnation upon the whole institution by passing up Jackson and nominating the near-nonentity, William H. Crawford.

(4) From about 1830 to about 1900. As we have already noted, some nominations were being made by conventions as early as the 1780's, and the incidence—as well as the respectability—of such nominations gradually increased over the ensuing years until, by 1830, conventions had entirely displaced the legislative caucuses in most of the states. The first national nominating conventions met to name candidates for president and vice-president in 1831 (the newly formed Anti-Masonic party) and 1832 (the Jacksonian Democratic party). From then until the end of the century the delegate convention was the most common method of making nominations, though we must note that the local caucus continued to be used for naming candidates for *local* offices in many areas. The period 1830-1900, accordingly, witnessed the emergence of the state and local party committees that have been, ever since, a characteristic feature of our party system. (They came into existence, as we observed in Chapter 5, because the conventions, which named them, had to make provision for carrying on party work in the intervals between conventions.) Like the legislative-caucus system it replaced, however, the convention system came under increasingly heavy attack as the years passed—and the criticisms sounded very much like those which had previously been directed at the caucus. Conventions, their opponents argued, are undemocratic, not truly representative of the party rank and file, subject to manipulation, bribery, and corruption, and caught in the iron grip of the "bosses." And by the turn of the century or thereabouts, the critics had mustered strength enough to overthrow the convention system in most areas and replace it with our present system of making nominations.

(5) From about 1900 to the present. On September 9, 1842, the Democrats of Crawford County, Pennsylvania, nominated a candidate for public office by direct primary, and thus became the originators of a new fashion in nominating machinery that—tailored as it is to avoid the kind of charges then directed against the caucus and the convention—has since shown itself to have a well-nigh irresistible appeal for those who determine the nature of our elec-

toral system.[25] Through most of the nineteenth century, as it spread first to other localities in and around Pennsylvania and then to more distant places, it continued to be called the "Crawford County System." It did not, to be sure, gain its first legal foothold until the end of the century, when several states in the South and West adopted laws making its use optional for local and state nominations; and not until 1903 did the first state (Wisconsin) enact a law requiring its use for most nominations. But over the next decade and a half events moved swiftly in its favor, so that by 1917 all but four states had adopted the compulsory direct primary for some or all statewide offices, and by 1956 all the states had done so.[26]

American Nominating Machinery Today

THE LEGAL REGULATION OF NOMINATIONS

Until 1866, the parties' caucus and convention nominating procedures were entirely unregulated by and "outside of" the law. The first steps toward legal regulation of nominations were taken by California (March, 1866) and New York (April, 1866). The California law, directed at various forms of corruption and bribery, was "optional" in character, i.e., its sanctions applied only to those political parties or other organizations that voluntarily invoked them. The New York law, though mandatory for all political organizations, went no further than to prohibit improper attempts to influence the vote of primary electors. From 1866 to 1900, a number of other states adopted laws, some optional and some mandatory, prohibiting various types of fraud in caucuses, conventions, and direct primaries. And since 1900, all the states have enacted laws regulating primary elections, with the result that the legal provisions governing primary elections are now at least as elaborate as those governing general elections.[27]

The great bulk of the laws regulating nominating procedures, like those

[25] James H. Booser, "Origin of the Direct Primary," *National Municipal Review*, Vol. XXIV (April, 1935), pp. 222-23.

[26] For the history of the adoption of direct-primary laws, see Merriam and Overacker, *op. cit.*, Ch. V. For many years Connecticut was the only state which did not use the direct primary. In 1955, however, Connecticut adopted a system which is a peculiar combination of a pre-primary convention, a referendum, and a closed primary. The new system works as follows. Party delegate conventions meet and select a nominee for each office, and these nominees are certified to the public authorities as "party-endorsed" candidates. During a period of fourteen days after the convention, any candidate who received at least 20 per cent of the votes in the convention for the nomination to any office may, by petition, file or have filed on his behalf a "candidacy" for that nomination. If one or more such candidacies are filed, a regular closed primary is held to choose the nominee from among the "party-endorsed" and the petitioning candidates; and whichever receives the largest number of votes is declared the party's official nominee for the office. If no candidate petitions for a primary within the designated period, the "party-endorsed" candidate is automatically declared the official nominee.

[27] For the history of the growth of legislation regulating nominating procedures, see Merriam and Overacker, *op. cit.*, pp. 4-39.

regulating party organization and membership, are *state* laws. In general, they deal with such matters as eligibility for a party's nomination, eligibility for voting in a party's primaries, the conditions under which party primaries are to be held and the votes to be counted, and the methods of nomination to be required or authorized for this office or that one. As matters now stand, thirty-three states require that all nominations for all offices be made by direct primary. And fifteen states require nominations for some offices to be made by direct primary, and those for other offices to be made by caucuses, by conventions, or by a combination of the two.[28]

THE NATURE OF THE VARIOUS NOMINATING METHODS

Caucuses. Strictly speaking, a "caucus" is any face-to-face assembly of the members of a party or faction that is held for the purpose of determining its candidates and policies. Thus a meeting at which Democratic members of the U.S. Senate select a floor leader or decide upon parliamentary strategy is a "caucus"; and a strategy conference held in a "smoke-filled room" by the supporters of one of the aspirants to a particular party's presidential nomination is also a "caucus." [29] But when we speak of the caucus as a nominating device, we normally assign to the term a somewhat narrower meaning, namely, that of face-to-face assembly of *party members* as contrasted with *delegates of party members*. A few states still permit caucuses to be used for the nomination of candidates for local offices and for the selection of delegates to nominating conventions for larger constituencies. In the (relatively few) situations where the caucus is still used, however, it only faintly resembles the caucuses of the eighteenth and early nineteenth centuries. In the latter the party leaders exercised strict, though informal (i.e., non-legal) control over admission, and voting was conducted according to *party* rules and procedures; while in the present-day caucus, state laws, not party rules, determine who can attend and what procedures must be followed. State laws, however, do not always use the term in the narrow sense we have just explained. In some states, for example, it is applied to a procedure whereby the polls are kept open at a certain place for a specified number of hours on a prescribed day, and legally qualified party members can come in at any time and vote by secret, state-supervised ballot, a procedure hardly distinguishable from what is generally called a "direct primary." And some states provide for "nonpartisan caucuses," in which party names and membership requirements are not permitted to intrude! [30] But the main point to grasp is that caucuses have been reduced to a minor—and highly inconspicuous—role in our total machinery for making nominations.

[28] *Book of the States, 1954-1955* (Chicago: Council of State Governments, 1954), Vol. X, table on p. 83.

[29] For various theories concerning the derivation of the term "caucus," see Ostrogorski, *op. cit.,* Vol. I, p. 120.

[30] Cf. Clyde F. Snider, *American State and Local Government* (New York: Appleton-Century-Crofts, 1950), pp. 128-29.

Conventions. A nominating convention is an assembly of *delegates,* selected in whatever manner by the members of a party, whose purpose is to determine its official candidates and policies. As we have already observed, this was the prevailing nominating procedure in the United States through most of the nineteenth century, though it lost ground rapidly after 1900. Today only a few states, including, however, New York and Indiana, use it for some or all statewide offices. (A somewhat larger number of states, as noted above, still use it for making nominations for certain local offices.) [31] Like the caucus, the convention used to be governed entirely by party rules. Today, however, state and local conventions are more or less closely regulated by state law; and only the national nominating conventions continue to be governed largely (but not entirely) by party rules.

By far the best-known nominating conventions are, of course, those held by the national parties every presidential year for the purpose of naming candidates for the presidency and vice-presidency. We shall devote Chapter 13 to an examination of the nature and role of these conventions.

Petitions. In some states, would-be candidates for some offices can get their names on the general-election ballot by filing a petition signed by a specified number of voters. Nomination by petition is the sole formal method of nomination in most of the world's democracies. In Great Britain, for example, becoming an official candidate for a seat in the House of Commons is simply a matter of filing with the "returning officer" a statement of one's name, address, and business, together with the names of ten registered voters who support one's candidacy—a "proposer," a "seconder," and eight "assenters." [32] In the United States, nomination by petition is used for all candidates in many nonpartisan municipal and judicial elections; and in some states, filing a petition is the only way that third-party and "independent" candidates can get their names on the general-election ballot.

Most nominations for most elective offices in the United States today, however, are made by direct primary.

THE DIRECT PRIMARY

In General. Under the direct primary, nominations are made *directly* by the party "members" themselves, not *indirectly* by the latter's "representatives" (as in conventions), and by secret ballot, not open voting (as in most caucuses). There are several varieties of direct primaries, each of which we shall presently describe; but they are all based upon the notion that *primary* elections (i.e., elections in which members of a particular party determine who shall be its nominees) should be conducted as nearly as possible in the same

---

[31] A few states also use the so-called "pre-primary convention" system, a kind of hybrid between the convention system and the direct primary, which we shall note in greater detail below.

[32] Cf. R. B. McCallum and Alison Readman, *The British General Election of 1945* (London: Oxford University Press, 1947), p. 28.

manner as *general* elections (i.e., those in which the voters decide which nominees shall be elected to public office). Thus all variants of the direct primary have at least these three features in common with the typical general election in the United States: (1) they are regulated for the most part by law, not party rules; (2) they are conducted by public officials, not party officials; and (3) any citizen who satisfies certain legal requirements can participate without the party leaders' having any say in the matter, one way or the other.

In general, direct primaries involve the following procedures: The aspirant to a party's nomination for office gets his name on the primary ballot—either (a) by filing a petition signed by a specified number of party members in his constituency,[33] or (b) by announcing his candidacy and paying a fee into the state treasury. In about half the states, anyone, including a member of another party, is legally free to run in any party's primary; in California, indeed, the law expressly permits such "cross-filing," and it is common practice. In most of these states, the candidate who wins the nominations of both parties can accept only one of the two; but in California the law permits him to accept both, provided only that he has carried the primary of his own party.[34]

After the filing period has elapsed, the state prints the ballots and determines what persons are eligible to vote in each party's primary.[35] It then conducts the election almost exactly as it conducts general elections, counts the votes, declares the results, presides over the review of contested elections, and prints the names of the winners on the general-election ballot.

The direct-primary system differs from state to state on only one major point: the mode of determining *who can vote* in the primary of each party. In this connection there are three main types of primaries: "closed," "open," and "blanket."

Closed Primaries. A "closed primary" is one in which a voter who wishes to vote in a party's primary must first pass a "test" of affiliation, the purpose being to make sure that only the "members" of that party shall have a voice in determining its nominees. (In Chapter 9 we noted that the two main tests now in use are the "challenge" and party registration.) The main advantage

[33] In some states the requirement is expressed as a percentage (varying considerably from state to state) of the party's vote for a specified office (e.g., the governorship) at the last general election; in others it is a set figure. Such petitions should not be confused with the kind of petition a candidate files to get his name on the *general*-election ballot. Usually the latter type of petition requires more signatures than the former.

[34] On "cross-filing" and its effects, see Robert W. Binkley, Jr., *Double Filing in Primary Elections* (Berkeley: University of California, Bureau of Public Administration, 1945); and Evelyn Hazen, *Cross Filing in Primary Elections* (Berkeley: University of California, Bureau of Public Administration, 1951). The relevant California statutes were recently amended, however, and now provide that every candidate in a primary must have his party affiliation printed alongside his name, thereby telling the voter whether the candidate is "native" or "foreign" to the party whose nomination he is seeking. Most observers believe this new provision will lessen the likelihood of a Republican's winning a Democratic nomination and vice versa.

[35] See pp. 205-09 for the kinds of qualifications prescribed by the various states for eligibility to vote in primaries.

the closed primary's proponents claim for it is that it tends to discourage "raiding" and "colonizing" by members of the opposition, and thus to promote the integrity, unity, and responsibility of the parties.[36] At present, thirty-eight states employ the closed primary in one form or another.[37]

Open primaries. An "open primary" is one in which a voter who wishes to vote in a party's primary may do so without having to pass any test of affiliation whatever. In some states, the voter gets the ballots of all parties, marks one, and deposits the others in a special box for unused ballots. In other states, he receives a ballot with the names of the candidates for nomination in all parties printed on it in separate columns for each party. He is instructed to make choices in the column of one party only, and warned that if he votes in the columns of more than one party his ballot will be thrown out. The main advantage claimed for the open primary is that it tends to preserve the secrecy of the voter's party affiliation and thus to protect him from any sort of punishment or retaliation for his choice among the parties. Nine states now use this system.[38]

The Washington "Blanket Primary." Since 1936, the voter in the state of Washington has marked a primary ballot on which the names and party affiliations of all candidates of all parties for a given office are printed under a distinct heading for that office. He votes for one candidate under each heading, and is not restricted to the candidates of any one party for all offices. Washington's is the only primary system in which the voter can "split" his vote among the parties, and several political scientists have condemned it on the ground that it "corrupts the meaning of party" and is "a barrier to the development of a program-conscious attitude among party members."[39] Ogden's study of the actual operation of the system, however, indicates that there is only a little more ballot splitting in the primaries than in the general elections, and that the blanket primary has not significantly harmed party organization or "regularity."[40]

THE IMPACT OF THE DIRECT PRIMARY UPON THE PARTIES

Has It "Democratized" Them? The early-day advocates of the direct primary believed that it would "democratize" the parties' internal structure because it would take the nominating power away from the "bosses" and give it

---

[36] Note, for example, the plug for the closed primary in the report of the Committee on Political Parties of the American Political Science Association, "Toward a More Responsible Two-Party System," *American Political Science Review,* Vol. XLIV, Supplement (September, 1950), p. 71.

[37] *The Book of the States, 1954-1955,* table on p. 83.

[38] *Ibid.*

[39] "Toward a More Responsible Two-Party System," p. 72.

[40] Daniel M. Ogden, Jr., "The Blanket Primary and Party Regularity in Washington," *Pacific Northwest Quarterly,* Vol. XXXIX (January, 1948), pp. 33-38. See also Claudius O. Johnson, "The Washington Blanket Primary," *Pacific Northwest Quarterly,* Vol. XXXIII (January, 1942), pp. 27-39.

to the "members." [41] Its opponents believed that the direct primary, by destroying the power of party leaders over nominations, would cause the parties to "disintegrate" by reducing them to congeries of confused and confusing factional disputes. [42]

Most present-day commentators agree that the direct primary has fulfilled neither set of expectations—not even the forecast, common to both, that it would destroy the party leaders' power over the nominating process. Most primary elections, they contend, are won by "organization" candidates, as likely as not the same candidates who would have won had the direct primary never been invented, so that the "machines" are about as much in control of nominations as they ever were; and there is no evidence that the cohesiveness and "responsibility" of the parties have been affected one way or the other by the displacement of the caucus and the convention. Most of these commentators, however, would oppose abolition of the direct primary, on the grounds not that it has broken the power of many "bosses," but that it does oblige the party leaders to put up candidates who can survive the give-and-take of a primary-election struggle, and also provides the party members with a last-resort "shotgun-behind-the-door," which they can use whenever the leaders try to put over something outrageous. [43]

Has It Hastened the Trend to One-Partyism? Earlier in the present chapter we presented data pointing to an increase in the incidence of one-party areas, and to the coincidence of the increase with the heyday of the direct primary. We must now pause to inquire—since the fact that two events happen simultaneously does not prove that one of them "causes" the other—whether there is any reason to suppose that the coincidence is other than accidental. This question could be answered empirically only if we were in a position to set up a controlled experiment (for instance, by taking two similar modified one-party counties side by side, one with and the other without the direct primary, and observing what happens)—which we are not. And no amount of data confirming the coincidence would bring us any closer to proof

[41] See, for example, the argument of Frank J. Goodnow that the direct primary "will put into the hands of the people the same control over nominations as they now have over elections": *Politics and Administration* (New York: The Macmillan Company, 1900), pp. 248-49. See also Goodnow, pp. 166-67, 232-33.

[42] See, for example, the argument of Henry Jones Ford that the direct primary is "a wholesale scheme of party disintegration," *Annals of the American Academy of Political and Social Science,* Vol. XVI (September, 1900), pp. 177-88. See also Ford's article, "The Direct Primary," *North American Review,* Vol. CXC (July, 1909), pp. 1-14.

[43] For general evaluations of the direct primary, see Penniman, *op. cit.,* pp. 440-50; Dayton D. McKean, *Party and Pressure Politics* (Boston: Houghton Mifflin Company, 1949), pp. 224-26; Hugh A. Bone, *American Politics and the Party System* (New York: McGraw-Hill Book Company, Inc., 1949), pp. 517-18; Merriam and Gosnell, *op. cit.,* pp. 306-15. For descriptions of its operation in particular states, see James K. Pollock, *The Direct Primary in Michigan, 1909-1935* (Ann Arbor: University of Michigan Press, 1943); Boyd A. Martin, *The Direct Primary in Idaho* (Stanford: Stanford University Press, 1947); L. M. Holland, *The Direct Primary in Georgia* (Urbana: University of Illinois Press, 1949); and a series of articles in the *Annals of the American Academy of Political and Social Science,* Vol. CVI (March, 1923).

of a causal connection. Our inquiry, therefore, must be raised to the level of theory. Let us *assume* two similar modified one-party counties side by side, one with and the other without the direct primary, and let us ask whether the former, in the nature of the case and by contrast with the latter, would be likely to develop toward one-partyism. The present writers think it would, and for two reasons. First, just to the extent that one party is dominant over the other, voters can "make their votes count" by voting in the dominant party's primaries, which they can do only if there are such primaries, and which they will learn to do increasingly as time passes. And second, just to the extent that one party is dominant over the other, promising young men with political ambitions will offer themselves as candidates in the dominant party's primary, which again they can do only if there are such primaries. And the effect in both cases is to weaken progressively the second party by draining off interest in what it is doing by comparison with what the dominant party is doing, and by starving its leadership of bright young men who mean business about politics. Or, to put it the other way around, the second party's chances of holding the interest of the rank and file, and of attracting capable potential leaders among the young, are enormously greater in the county which has no direct primary.[44]

Has It Affected the Control of Nominations? The direct primary has undoubtedly increased the volume and added to the complexity of the tasks that party leaders and workers have to perform: it has nearly doubled the number of elections for which they must organize, work, and gather funds. It seems probable that it has also altered, to some extent, the character of the contests within each party for control of the nominating process. Before its adoption, these contests were fought out among party leaders and party workers, i.e., among persons belonging to the party's innermost circles. Under the direct-primary system, by contrast, persons outside these circles—those who vote in the party's primary but are not party leaders or party workers—take part in the contests, and in a sense have the last word as to their outcome. This, of course, is all to the good as far as the partisans of the direct primary are concerned: what they want is genuine "intraparty democracy," and precisely what they mean by this is control of the nominating process by the rank-and-file "members," not the "bosses." [45] Any assessment of the effects of the direct primary or of the thinking underlying it must, therefore, turn finally upon answers to the question, Where *does* control of the nominating process now reside in American parties?

[44] These models were suggested by the data presented in Joseph P. Harris, "A New Primary System," *State Government,* Vol. XXI (July, 1948), p. 141; and in Key, "The Direct Primary and Party Structure," pp. 14-20. Neither Harris nor Key, be it noted, argues that the direct primary has *caused* the increase in one-partyism, but both concede that it may have.

[45] Cf. the report of the Committee on Political Parties of the American Political Science Association, where it is argued that "party responsibility includes also the responsibility of party leaders to the party membership" and that "the internal processes of the parties must be democratic": "Toward a More Responsible Two-Party System," p. 23.

Control of Nominations in American Parties

Those who have studied the control of nominations in American parties seem to agree on two propositions: (1) Most nominations are *leader-controlled,* i.e., *not* controlled by the rank-and-file party members (who rarely rise up, take the "shotgun" out from "behind the door," and pass over organization candidates in favor of candidates opposed by the party leaders). And (2) the nominating process is *decentralized,* in the sense that nominations for national public offices are more often controlled by state and local party leaders than by national leaders. Let us examine the evidence on each of these two points.

LEADER CONTROL

The Evidence. Few attempts have been made to measure precisely what effects the direct primary has actually had on the control of nominations. What evidence we have on this point consists of statements made by students of the subject on the basis of personal observation of the general workings of the system over a number of years. But certainly the consensus among these students is that the party organizations or "machines" usually put forward slates of carefully selected candidates, back them in the primaries, and elect them, often with little or no opposition.[46] Ewing's and Turner's studies of the effects of incumbency on primary elections tend to bear this out, since they show that incumbents who seek renomination win about 90 per cent of the time and are unopposed about half the time.[47]

Key's recent study of nominations for state legislative posts suggests, however, that the organization's power over nominations varies according to the type of party system. In the primaries of the dominant parties in the one-party and modified one-party areas, his figures indicate, competition is keener than in the primaries of either party in the two-party areas, and the keener competition tends to weaken organization control.[48] This, to be sure, is what we should expect in the light of our discussion in Chapter 8, where we saw that the organizations of the dominant parties in the one-party areas play little or no role in the making of nominations. In the "multifactional" one-party areas especially, the direct primary has undoubtedly lessened the power of the few leaders at the top of the party hierarchy to make nominations; so that the Democratic primaries in such states as Arkansas, Florida, and Mississippi probably resemble more closely the utopia of the partisans of the direct primary than those in the two-party states or the bifactional one-party states.

One other point in connection with leader control of direct-primary elections merits notice: In most areas notably fewer persons vote in the primaries

[46] Cf. Penniman, *op. cit.,* pp. 442-43; McKean, *op. cit.,* pp. 224-26; Bone, *op. cit.,* pp. 532-33; and Merriam and Gosnell, *op. cit.,* pp. 306-08.

[47] Ewing, *Primary Elections in the South,* pp. 59-63, 71; Turner, "Primary Elections as the Alternative to Party Competition in 'Safe' Districts," pp. 208-09.

[48] Key, "The Direct Primary and Party Structure," pp. 14-16.

than in the general elections. The absence of centrally gathered statistics for primary elections in all the states makes it difficult to document this point for the whole nation over any specific period of time. But the Bureau of the Census did gather such statistics for the 1942 primary and general elections, and its results are shown in Table 17.

TABLE 17   Relative Participation in the Primary and General Elections of 1942 [49]

(The figures indicate the vote in the primaries as a percentage of the vote in the general elections.)

Percentages	Number of States	Identity of the States
Under 35	4	Colorado, Maine, Massachusetts, Utah
35-44.9	8	Indiana, Iowa, Michigan, New Hampshire, New Jersey, Ohio, Wisconsin, Idaho
45-54.9	4	Kansas, Maryland, Nebraska, Nevada
55-64.9	6	Illinois, Kentucky, Missouri, Pennsylvania, Vermont, Washington
65-74.9	6	Minnesota, Montana, New Mexico, South Dakota, West Virginia, Wyoming
75-84.9	3	California, North Dakota, Oregon
85-99.9	1	North Carolina
Over 100	11	Alabama, Arizona, Arkansas, Florida, Georgia, Louisiana, Mississippi, Oklahoma, South Carolina, Tennessee, Texas

(Data not available on the other states)

As we have already pointed out, winning primaries is high-priority business for party leaders and workers. They see to it, therefore, that *their* voters get to the polls, in good or bad weather and however dull the contests may appear to the casual observer. Consequently, "organization" votes are likely to be the hard core of the total vote in any direct primary election; and the smaller the total vote, the more likely it is that the nominations will be controlled by the leaders rather than the rank and file. If this line of reasoning is correct, however, the low level of participation in the primaries reflected in Table 17 suggests that in most areas most nominations are indeed controlled by party leaders.[50]

[49] This table is a revised presentation of the data given in Charles E. Merriam and Harold F. Gosnell, *The American Party System*, 4th ed. (New York: The Macmillan Company, 1949), Figure 10 on p. 311. Reprinted by permission of The Macmillan Company. See Frederic H. Guild, "The Operation of the Direct Primary in Indiana," *Annals of the American Academy of Political and Social Science*, Vol. CVI (March, 1923), pp. 172-80, for an account of how low voter participation in the Indiana primaries tightened "boss" control of the party organizations.

[50] Note that of the eleven states with a larger vote in the primaries than in the general election, ten are either one-party or modified one-party states. This is what we should expect from our analysis of the role of the primary in such states in Chapter 8.

The Pre-Primary Convention. The party organization, say some political scientists, is charged with the responsibility for conducting campaigns for the party's nominees; and its choices as to who those nominees shall be should, therefore, have some kind of inside run in the primary, just as the rank and file should be in a position to reject organization candidates when they wish. Nor, they add, is there any reason why one of these "should's" must be sacrificed to the other: let the law require a "pre-primary convention" of party leaders for the purpose of naming *their* slate of candidates for the primary; let the organization candidates be designated as such on the primary ballot; and then let anti-organization candidates get themselves on the ballot by petition. Formalizing the organization's position in this way, they contend, will bring about the proper balance between the power that should accompany the organization's responsibility, and the rank and file's indisputable claim to the last word.[51] New Mexico, Utah, Colorado, Rhode Island, Nebraska, and Massachusetts now employ one or another version of the pre-primary convention.[52]

DECENTRALIZATION

In Chapter 11 we noted that the nearest an American party ever gets to having a national leader is when its president-elect tries to induce members of Congress bearing the same party label as himself to support a legislative program put forward in his name. We also noted that not all of his fellow partisans are likely to string along with him, and that if some of them openly rebel against his "leadership" this means only that American politics are functioning in their normal manner. A word is now in order about the weapon some presidents have turned against some or all of the recalcitrants, namely, the "purge," the purpose of which is to get rid of the rebels by keeping them from being renominated. For we shall have a clearer grasp of the relative strength of national and local party leaders over the nominating process once we have seen how the purges attempted in the past have worked out.

A Brief History of Recent Presidential "Purges." In 1910, President William Howard Taft and his conservative Republican advisers tried to block the renomination of such progressive Republican senators as Dolliver, Cummins, Beveridge, and La Follette. The Taft group withheld patronage from the rebels and contributed money and speakers to their opponents in the primaries. Every one of the rebels, however, retained the support of the organization in his state, and was renominated.[53]

In 1918, President Wilson moved vigorously to accomplish the defeat of anti-administration Democrats in the primaries of five southern states. Among other things, he wrote a public letter to the Democratic national committee-

---

[51] Cf. Joseph P. Harris, *A Model Direct Primary System* (New York: The National Municipal League, 1951), pp. 20-31.

[52] See R. N. Ballard, *The Primary Convention System in Utah* (Salt Lake City: Institute of Government, University of Utah, 1947); and C. B. Judah and O. E. Payne, *New Mexico's Proposed Pre-Primary Designating Convention* (Albuquerque: University of New Mexico, 1950).

[53] Key, *Politics, Parties, and Pressure Groups,* pp. 355-56.

man from Georgia, opposing the renomination of Senator Hardwick and endorsing his opponent, William J. Harris. Said Wilson:

> Senator Hardwick has been a constant and active opponent of my administration. Mr. William Harris has consistently and actively supported it. In my opinion, the obvious thing for all those who are jealous of the reputation of the party and the success of the government in the present crisis is to combine in support of Mr. Harris.[54]

Unlike Taft's, Wilson's purge was effective; his candidates—with, however, the help of the local organizations involved—won four of the five contests in which he intervened.

In 1930, President Hoover openly endorsed the nomination of Carroll Reece for Congressman from Tennessee. Reece's unsuccessful opponent charged that Hoover, by taking such a step, was clearly guilty of "an attempt at political dictatorship in a free country." [55]

In 1946, President Truman sought to block the renomination of Roger C. Slaughter for Congressman from Missouri, on the grounds that he had tried, as a member of the powerful House Rules Committee, to obstruct Truman's legislative program. Truman enlisted the help of the powerful local Pendergast organization and the local CIO-PAC, left the campaign against Slaughter up to them, and got his man.[56]

In 1950, Truman announced that he was supporting Emery Allison for the Democratic senatorial nomination from Missouri (he would not, he said, "dabble" in the politics of other states than his own). The Missouri organization, however, threw its support to Thomas C. Hennings, Jr., and defeated Allison.[57]

We have left until last, and for discussion under a separate heading, the most spectacular—and unsuccessful—of attempted presidential "purges," namely, Franklin D. Roosevelt's intervention in the primaries in 1938.

The "Purge" of 1938.[58] Despite his "landslide" triumph in the 1936 presidential election and despite the huge Democratic majorities in both houses of Congress, President Roosevelt failed four times in 1937-1938 to get the support he expected and felt entitled to from Democratic representatives and senators. His candidate for the Senate majority-leadership, Alben W. Barkley, squeaked through by a bare 38-37 margin. Opponents of his Court Reorganization bill carried with them enough Democratic votes to defeat it. Some Democrats helped to defeat his Administrative Reorganization bill (or, as its opponents called it, "the dictator bill"). And the Democratic chairman of the House

---

[54] Quoted in Raymond Clapper, "Roosevelt Tries the Primaries," *Current History*, Vol. XLIX (October, 1938), pp. 16-17.

[55] *Ibid*.

[56] New York *Times*, July 19, 1946, pp. 1, 36; and August 7, 1946, pp. 1, 2.

[57] New York *Times*, January 6, 1950, pp. 1, 8; and August 3, 1950, p. 46.

[58] The most complete account of the 1938 "purge" that has come to the present writers' attention is William C. Hise, *President Roosevelt and the Democratic "Purge" of 1938* (unpublished M.A. thesis, University of Illinois, 1949).

Rules Committee, Representative John J. O'Connor of New York, for a long while kept his Wages and Hours bill from reaching the floor.

Angered by the opposition of the anti–New Deal Democrats, Roosevelt and a group of his New Deal advisers (the press called the latter the "elimination committee") set to work to prevent the rebels' renomination in the 1938 primaries.[59] In a "fireside chat" delivered over the national radio networks on June 24, 1938, Roosevelt announced his intention to intervene in some Democratic primaries. He explained his purposes as follows:

As President of the United States, I am not asking the voters of the country to vote for Democrats next November as opposed to Republicans or members of any other party. Nor am I, as President, taking part in Democratic primaries. As the head of the Democratic party, however, charged with the responsibility of carrying out the definitely liberal declaration of principles set forth in the 1936 Democratic platform, I feel that I have every right to speak in those few instances where there may be a clear issue involving these principles or involving a clear misuse of my own name.

Do not misunderstand me. I certainly would not indicate a preference in a State primary merely because a candidate, otherwise liberal in outlook, had conscientiously differed with me on any single issue. I should be far more concerned about the general attitude of a candidate toward present-day problems and his own inward desire to get practical needs attended to in a practical way. We all know that progress may be blocked by outspoken reactionaries and also by those who say "Yes" to a progressive objective, but who always find some reason to oppose any proposal to gain that objective. I call that type of candidate a "Yes, but" fellow.[60]

For the most part, Roosevelt confined himself, for purposes of the purge, to public statements for or against certain candidates. He endorsed the renomination of Senators Barkley of Kentucky, Bulkley of Ohio, and McAdoo of California, all pro–New Deal Democrats, and opposed the renomination of Senators Smith of South Carolina, George of Georgia, and Tydings of Maryland, all anti–New Deal Democrats. His appeal in each case was to "members" of the Democratic party, not to the state and local party organizations; nor is there any evidence that he made any serious attempt to enlist the latter on his side.[61] Senators Barkley and Bulkley won their primaries, but few observers regarded them as owing their victories, to any considerable extent, to Roosevelt's endorsement. Senator McAdoo was defeated. And all three of the proscribed anti–New Deal senators were renominated, and with votes to spare. With only one to go—the contest involving Representative O'Connor of New

---

[59] According to *Time,* the "purge was originated at a meeting in the Georgetown home of Harry Hopkins by a group consisting of Hopkins, Harold Ickes, Joseph Keenan, Robert H. Jackson, David K. Niles, James Roosevelt, Thomas G. Corcoran, and Benjamin Cohen": *Time,* Vol. XXII (September 12, 1938), p. 22.

[60] New York *Times,* June 25, 1938, p. 3.

[61] See Hise, *op. cit.,* Ch. V, for an account of the techniques of the "purge."

York—most observers were ready to write off the "purge" as a complete failure.[62]

But Roosevelt, according to "Boss" Edward J. Flynn of the Bronx, now changed his tactics: he telephoned Flynn and asked him to take charge of the primary campaign against O'Connor. Flynn, though in general opposed to "purges," acceded to Roosevelt's request—in large part, apparently, out of personal dislike for O'Connor. And, working through and with the party organization in the district concerned, without any help or interference from Washington, Flynn saw to it that his candidate defeated O'Connor, though by a narrow margin. "It is interesting to me to note," Flynn drily remarks in his autobiography, "that this is the only victory the President obtained in his 'purge.' "[63]

In a word, in the only instance in which he enlisted the help of the local party organization, Roosevelt successfully "purged" a rebel Democrat; where he relied on direct public appeals to the rank and file, the rebels were renominated. And the unavoidable inference here as with the other presidential "purges" is that in any contest between local party leaders and a national party leader over a local nomination, the former are likely to win.

Decentralized control of the nominating process undoubtedly gets in the way of strong presidential party leadership, that is, of the kind of party discipline that would enable a national party leader, once in the White House, to force his legislative program through the Congress. But it also undoubtedly reflects the wishes of the typical party leader on the state and local level, who is deeply committed to the view that the party organization *in each constituency* should determine who the party's candidates for offices elected from that constituency will be, and that for party leaders outside the constituency to "dictate" to the local organization violates all the rules of the game. James A. Farley was echoing the sentiments of most organization men when he pronounced the following judgment upon the 1938 "purge":

I knew from the beginning that the purge could lead to nothing but misfortune, because in pursuing his course of vengeance Roosevelt violated a cardinal political creed which demanded that he keep out of local matters. Sound doctrine is sound politics. When Roosevelt began neglecting the rules of the game, I lost faith in him. I trace all the woes of the Democratic party, directly or indirectly, to this interference in purely local affairs. In any political entity voters naturally and rightfully resent the unwarranted invasion of outsiders.[64]

---

[62] Most political analysts at the time deemed the "purge" hastily conceived, badly planned, and ineptly executed. Cf. Clapper, *op. cit.;* Walter Millis, "The President's Political Strategy," *Yale Review,* Vol. XXVIII (September, 1938), pp. 1-18; Turner Catledge, New York *Times,* July 10, 1938, section IV, p. 3; and Arthur Krock, New York *Times,* September 18, 1938, p. 18.

[63] Edward J. Flynn, *You're the Boss* (New York: The Viking Press, 1947), pp. 149-51.

[64] James A. Farley, *Jim Farley's Story; the Roosevelt Years* (New York: McGraw-Hill Book Company, Inc., 1948), pp. 146-47.

Chapter 13

MAKING NOMINATIONS: THE NATIONAL CONVENTIONS

We have seen in the preceding chapter that the national organs of the American major parties take little part in and have scant influence on the process by which candidates are nominated for seats in the two houses of Congress and for state and local offices—that, in a word, the business of making nominations for public office in the United States is a near-monopoly of the state and local party organs. But the reader will have noted that we have said nothing thus far about nominations for the offices of president and vice-president. Here we encounter an altogether different situation; for ever since 1831, presidential and vice-presidential candidates have been nominated in both major parties and in most minor parties by national delegate conventions of party members.[1]

The general rule, then, is nominations by state and local party organs, and nominations for the presidency and vice-presidency are the one exception to the rule. A word is perhaps in order, therefore, as to why the exception seems to us so significant as to warrant our devoting an entire chapter to it. The reason is, quite simply, that the presidency, with its enormous prestige, power, and patronage, is the greatest single elective prize available to American parties, which accordingly work far harder and spend far more money trying to capture it than any other public office. Nominating and campaigning for its presidential candidates is, in consequence, the central *raison d'être* of a national party, and its central preoccupation. If, then, we are to understand what the American national parties are like, and how they both resemble and differ from the state and local parties, one of the things we must do is form a clear idea of the process by which presidential candidates are nominated.

[1] For an account of the origins and development of the national conventions, see pp. 102-03, 276.

The Formal Structure of the National Conventions

THE RULES

The first national conventions of both major parties adopted rules governing their own proceedings and provided for the calling of subsequent conventions. Since then, each convention of each party has been conducted under rules of its own adoption.

It is often said that a party's national convention is its "supreme governing body." Upon closer examination, however, it appears that the convention of neither party exercises anything properly describable as "supreme power." The two parties, moreover, differ notably in their views as to how much power the convention ought to exercise. The Republicans tend to regard the national convention as the governing body of the national party, with full power to make rules—not only for the conduct of the convention itself, but also for the procedures in the states by which the delegates to the convention are selected. Thus when two delegations from the same state ask to be seated at the convention, the Republican convention usually determines which of the two has the more just claim under the *national* rules, then seats that entire delegation.[2] Moreover, each Republican convention adopts a full set of rules for the governing of all national party organs, which remain in effect until the next convention. Often, to be sure, the convention merely re-enacts the existing rules; but sometimes—as in 1952—fairly drastic changes are put through, and not without resentment on the part of the losers in the preceding struggle.[3] Let us bear in mind, however, that the rules in question apply almost exclusively to the internal functioning of the *national* convention and *national* committee; they do not, that is to say, involve any effective control of the state and local Republican parties by the national party organs.

The Democrats entrust to their national convention even less power than the Republicans do. Democratic conventions adopt rules for their own proceedings—usually the rules of the preceding convention. Unlike the Republi-

[2] See Paul T. David, Malcolm Moos, and Ralph M. Goldman, *Presidential Nominating Politics in 1952* (Baltimore: The Johns Hopkins Press, 1954), Vol. I, pp. 85-86, 158-59. This five-volume report of the Cooperative Research Project on Convention Delegations in 1952, sponsored by the American Political Science Association, is the most comprehensive and detailed study yet made of the national conventions, and the data for the present chapter are in large part drawn from it. With respect to the Republican attitude toward the national convention as rule maker, the report states: "There was a point, early in the history of the presidential primary movement, when the Republican party was prepared to assert that national party rules took priority over the local laws of any state on some aspects of delegate selection. The rules were soon amended to recognize state law, where it clearly exists and is pertinent; but the prerogatives of the Republican national convention were again asserted vigorously in dealing with the delegate contests of 1952."

[3] See *Official Report of the Proceedings of the Twenty-Fifth Republican National Convention, 1952* (Washington, D. C.: published by the Republican National Committee, 1952), pp. 289-300, for the rules adopted in 1952. See also *ibid.*, pp. 278-89, for an account of the floor fight and roll-call vote on the proposal to enlarge the membership of the national committee and thus reduce the proportion of women members.

cans' rules, however, which are codified into a set of formal party statutes, the Democrats' rules are a kind of "common-law" collection of resolutions adopted by previous conventions, decisions by previous convention chairmen, and "the customs and usage of the Convention."[4] (Every four years, nevertheless, the national committee has someone—in recent years, Clarence Cannon—collect the rules and print them in pamphlet form.) And, again unlike the Republicans, the Democrats have for the most part operated on the principle that the selection of delegates is strictly the business of the states. Where two rival delegations from the same state ask to be seated, and the party organization of that state has been unable to resolve the conflict, the Democrats have often, though not always, refused to decide between them and seated *both* delegations, splitting the vote between them.[5]

THE APPORTIONMENT OF VOTES

Evolution of the Existing Rules. The processes by which the convention delegates are selected are now largely controlled by the election laws of the various states. The national conventions control, and impose uniformity upon, *only* (a) their own procedures, and (b) the rules determining the number of votes and delegates to which each delegation is entitled. Their powers over (a) and (b), we may note in passing, date back to the first conventions of each of our major parties. In the first Democratic national convention in 1832, the *number of delegates seated* from a given state corresponded to no observable principle of allocation, and varied considerably from state to state. But for purposes of transacting the convention's business, each delegation was allotted a number of *votes* in the convention equal to its votes in the electoral college—an easy and convenient rule to apply, and one that had the further assumed advantage of giving each delegation a voice in the selection of the party's nominee commensurate with its potential impact—or, more correctly, that of the state it represented—upon the final election. Later each state's delegation was allotted *two* votes for each of its state's votes in the electoral college.

The first Republican national convention in 1856 adopted—and its successors over several decades retained—this same rule, despite the continual and increasing protest from the northern Republicans, who contended that it gave the southern Republicans a voice in the selection of the nominee out of proportion to their likely contribution to his victory in the election. The discontent on this score came to a head after the 1912 convention, at which William Howard Taft, largely because of his hard core of southern supporters, won the nomination over Theodore Roosevelt, who promptly formed a third party and thereby gave the Democrats an easy victory in the election. This being precisely the sort of disaster the northern Republicans had been predicting for decades, the 1916 Republican convention was unable to say them nay: it

---

[4] *Democratic Manual* (prepared by Clarence Cannon for the Democratic National Committee, and published by it, 1952), p. 2.

[5] David, Moos, and Goldman, *op. cit.,* Vol. I, pp. 85-86, 158-59.

adopted a plan, elaborated between elections by the national committee, giving extra or "bonus" votes to delegations from states carried by the Republican presidential candidate in the preceding election. The Democrats did not begin to award "bonus" votes until 1944.[6]

Apportionment Rules for the 1952 Conventions. In summarizing the apportionment rules for the 1952 conventions, we must first distinguish between *votes* and *delegates*. A delegation's total number of *votes,* is, so to speak, its share of the convention's formal decision-making power; its total number of *delegates,* on the other hand, is the number of *persons* in its ranks who are entitled to cast votes. It should be noted that a Republican rule (Rule 3) specifically prohibits any state or territory from sending to the convention more delegates than it has votes; and each and every delegate to Republican conventions, accordingly, casts one full vote. Under Democratic rules, however, the total number of convention delegates can (and in practice usually does) exceed the total number of votes. This is so because each state is permitted to send *two* delegates for each *one* of its "at-large" (see below) votes, each delegate being entitled to cast only a *half*-vote. And in 1952, some states were also permitted, on the national committee's recommendation, to have some "district" (see below) delegates, each entitled to cast only a half-vote.[7] In the 1952 Democratic convention, accordingly, the *votes* totaled 1,230 and the *delegates* totaled 1,642.

The following rules governed the apportionment of *votes* among the various delegations to the 1952 national conventions:

REPUBLICAN RULES [8]

A. DELEGATES-AT-LARGE [9]

1. Four delegates-at-large from each state.

2. Two additional delegates-at-large for each representative-at-large in Congress from each state.

3. Four delegates-at-large for Alaska, six each for the District of Columbia and Territory of Hawaii, three from Puerto Rico, and one from the Virgin Islands. Four additional delegates-at-large from each territory which elected a Republican as its delegate to Congress at the last preceding election.[10]

---

[6] *Ibid.,* Vol. I, pp. 159-61.

[7] *Ibid.,* Vol. I, p. 161.

[8] From *Official Report of the Proceedings of the Twenty-fifth Republican National Convention, 1952,* pp. 16-17. The apportionment rules governing the 1956 Republican convention are printed on pp. 289-90. See also David, Moos, and Goldman, *op. cit.,* Vol. I, pp. 159-61, for a summary of the 1952 apportionment rules for both conventions.

[9] A "delegate-at-large" represents an entire state, rather than a particular congressional district within a state.

[10] Edward J. Flynn explains the practice of awarding votes to the territories—which, of course, have no voice in the election of a president—thus: "While no territories vote in Presidential elections, they have been given the right to elect delegates to national conventions because of their interest in appointments made by the President, such as governor, federal judges, marshals, etc.": *You're the Boss* (New York: The Viking Press, 1947), p. 88, n. 1.

4. Six additional delegates-at-large for each state carried by the Republican nominee in the last preceding presidential election; or, if the state was not carried by the Republican presidential candidate but was carried by the Republican nominee in the most recent election for U.S. senator, or governor, it receives six additional delegates-at-large.

B. DISTRICT DELEGATES [11]

1. One district delegate from each congressional district which cast 2,000 or more votes for any Republican presidential elector in the last preceding presidential election or for the Republican candidate for U.S. representative in the last preceding congressional election.

2. One additional district delegate for each congressional district casting 10,000 or more votes for any Republican elector in the last preceding presidential election, or for the Republican candidate for U.S. representative in the last preceding congressional election.

C. ALTERNATES

One alternate is chosen for each delegate, and is authorized to cast the delegate's vote when the delegate is not present.

DEMOCRATIC RULES [12]

1. Two votes for each senator and representative in Congress from each state.

2. Four additional votes for each state which cast its electoral votes for the Democratic candidate in the last preceding presidential election.

3. Six votes each for Alaska, the District of Columbia, Hawaii, and Puerto Rico; two votes each for the Virgin Islands and the Canal Zone.

Distribution of Votes by Types in 1952.[13] Of the 1,206 total votes in the 1952 Republican convention, 789 (65.4 per cent) were congressional-district votes; 229 (19.0 per cent) were at-large votes other than bonus votes; and 188 (15.6 per cent) were bonus votes. Of the 1,230 total votes in the 1952 Democratic convention, 858 (69.8 per cent) were congressional-district votes; 260 (21.1 per cent) were at-large votes other than bonus votes; and 112 (9.1 per cent) were bonus votes.

Distribution of Votes by Regions in 1956.[14] The following two tables show

---

[11] A district delegate is one who represents the party in a particular congressional district within a state.

[12] From the *Democratic Manual,* pp. 12-14.

[13] These data are drawn from the table in David, Moos, and Goldman, *op. cit.,* Vol. I, p. 161.

[14] The data for Table 18 are drawn from the Chicago *Tribune,* December 2, 1955, p. 3. The data for Table 19 are drawn from the New York *Times,* November 18, 1955, p. 16. It should be noted that in preparing for its 1956 convention, the Democratic National Committee sought to increase the number of votes and delegates by declaring the following apportionment rules: each state was given at least as many votes as it had had in the 1952 convention; in addition, a four-vote bonus was given to each state that had either voted for Stevenson in the 1952 election or elected a Democratic governor or U.S. senator from 1952 through 1955. The

the distribution of votes by regions in the two 1956 conventions. A glance at Table 18 reveals that the bulk of the voting power in the Republican convention was located in the Northeast and the Middle West, but the South (as a result of Republican successes in that region from 1952 to 1955) was not far behind.

TABLE 18   Distribution of Votes by Region in the 1956 Republican Convention

Region	Cong. Dist. Votes	Votes at Large	Total Votes	Per Cent of Total Votes
Northeast	252	120	372	28.1
South	235	90	325	24.6
Middle West	254	124	378	28.6
West	104	120	224	16.9
Territories	0	24	24	1.8

And Table 19 indicates that the bulk of the voting power in the Democratic convention was about equally shared by the Northeast, Middle West, and South, with the latter region having the largest single block of votes.

TABLE 19   Distribution of Votes by Region in the 1956 Democratic Convention

Region	Cong. Dist. Votes	Votes at Large	Total Votes	Per Cent of Total Votes
Northeast	256	108	364	26.5
South	240	152	392	28.6
Middle West	258	98	356	25.9
West	104	126	230	16.8
Territories	0	30	30	2.2

HOW THE DELEGATES ARE SELECTED

Types of Delegate-Selection Systems.[15] The election laws of each of the forty-eight states now regulate, in varying detail, the selection of delegates to the national conventions. Most states require both parties to use the same system; a few states, however (Alabama, Florida, and Georgia, for example), leave open to the state central committee a choice between alternative systems.

Committee also agreed to a larger number of delegates with half-votes, so that if all the states availed themselves of their maximum quotas, the 1956 Democratic convention would have a grand total of 1,372 votes, 2,744 delegates, and 1,896 alternates.

[15] See *ibid.,* Vol. I, pp. 162-85; and V. O. Key, Jr., *Politics, Parties, and Pressure Groups,* 3rd ed. (New York: Thomas Y. Crowell Company, 1952), pp. 447-51.

Delegate-selection systems, in consequence, differ from state to state. The interested reader should examine the relevant statutes of his own state.

The systems in use differ primarily as regards the degree of formal-legal influence exercised by rank-and-file party voters through direct primaries. From this standpoint, we can identify three main types of delegate-selection systems.

SELECTION BY PARTY COMMITTEES AND CONVENTIONS. In some states the entire delegation to the national convention is picked either by the state central committee, or by the state convention, or by a combination of the state convention (which names the at-large delegates) and district conventions (which name the district delegates). In most states the law empowers the state and district conventions to instruct the delegates to vote for a particular presidential candidate at the national convention. Since, however, few local conventions bind their delegates in this manner, most convention-selected delegates go to the national conventions uninstructed.[16]

SELECTION BY DIRECT PRIMARIES. In some states the party voters, acting through a direct primary, select the entire delegation to the national convention. But the relevant direct-primary arrangements vary sharply from state to state, particularly as to whether, and in what way, the elected delegates are legally pledged to vote for a particular presidential candidate at the convention. In some direct-primary states, each individual candidate for convention delegate indicates on the ballot his preference among the presidential hopefuls and, if elected, is legally pledged to vote for that candidate at the convention until released by him. In other states, consolidated slates of delegate candidates pledged to specific presidential hopefuls are printed on the ballot, and the members of the winning slate are legally obligated to vote for their man at the convention until he releases them. And, finally, there are states in which the ballot offers no indication of the delegate candidates' preferences among the presidential candidates. In some of these states, to be sure, the voters, in selecting delegates, indicate their preference among various national presidential candidates; but for the most part these "preferential polls" are regarded as a sort of "popularity contest," since the results are purely "advisory" (i.e., are not binding upon the elected delegates). The remaining states provide their elected delegates with no formal indication whatever of the party voters' wishes. We shall have more to say below about the role and importance of the presidential primary.

SELECTION BY A COMBINATION OF CONVENTIONS AND DIRECT PRIMARIES. Some states have their district delegates selected by direct primaries and their at-large delegates selected either by the state convention or by the state central committee of the party. In such states the district delegates are never legally bound to vote for any particular presidential candidate, even if—as, for example, in Illinois—the law provides for a preferential poll.

Incidence of the Several Delegate-Selection Systems. In 1952, the national conventions of the major parties differed sharply in this regard.

---

[16] Cf. David, Moos, and Goldman, *op. cit.,* Vol. I, p. 45.

REPUBLICANS.[17] Of the 53 state and territorial delegations to the 1952 Republican national convention, 20 included only delegates selected by state and territorial conventions; 15 were mixtures of delegates selected by state conventions and delegates selected by district conventions; 4 included only delegates selected by state and territorial committees; 10 included only delegates selected by direct primary; 2 were mixtures of delegates selected by direct primary and delegates selected by state conventions; 1 was a mixture of delegates selected by direct primary, delegates selected by state convention, and delegates selected by district conventions; and 1 was a mixture of delegates selected by direct primary and delegates selected by the state central committee. Of the total of 1,206 delegates, 463 (38.4 per cent) were picked by state and territorial conventions, 174 (14.4 per cent) by district conventions, 36 (3.0 per cent) by state and territorial committees, and 533 (44.2 per cent) by direct primary.

DEMOCRATS.[18] The parallel breakdown of the 54 state and territorial delegations to the 1952 Democratic national convention was as follows: 30 included only delegates selected by state and territorial conventions; 7 included only delegates selected by state and territorial committees; 13 were made up of delegates selected entirely by direct primary; 2 were made up partly of delegates selected by direct primary and partly of delegates selected by state committees; and 2 were made up partly of delegates selected by direct primary and partly of delegates selected by state conventions. Of the 1,230 total *votes*, 593½ (48.2 per cent) were cast by delegates picked by state and territorial conventions; 86 (7.0 per cent) by delegates picked by state and territorial committees; and 550½ (44.8 per cent) by delegates picked by direct primaries. Of the 1,642 total *delegates*, 877 (53.4 per cent) were selected by state and territorial conventions; 123 (7.7 per cent) by state and territorial committees; and 639 (38.9 per cent) by direct primary.

THE ROLE OF THE PRESIDENTIAL PRIMARY

The reader may have been wondering why there has been so little discussion of the presidential primaries, which receive so much attention from the newspapers and from radio and television commentators. The answer is that the publicity the presidential primaries receive—they are the *only* part of the pre-convention contests among candidates that goes forward under public scrutiny—represents their major impact upon events. They *do* drum up interest in the election, and in some at least of the personalities involved, and to some extent, no doubt, affect opinion as to who is likely to win; so that, for example, defeat in a particular primary—especially one in which no "favorite son" (see below) is running—may be very damaging indeed to a candidate's chances of winning the nomination.[19]

[17] Data drawn from *ibid.*, Vol. I, Table 1 on pp. 42-44.
[18] Data drawn from *ibid.*, Vol. I, Table 2 on pp. 56-59.
[19] The following are often cited as instances in which a defeat in a single primary was

The fact remains, however, that at present a candidate, theoretically at least, could sweep *all* the primaries and still lose the nomination; for, as the figures cited in our preceding section indicate, in the 1952 conventions of both parties less than half of the votes (44.2 per cent in the Republican convention and 44.8 per cent in the Democratic) were cast by delegates selected by direct primaries, and many of these votes were not legally committed to any particular candidate. Party voters, it would seem, have less formal *direct* influence upon the choice of presidential candidates than upon that of candidates for most other offices in the United States.[20]

Some political scientists and politicians deplore this situation, and argue that the presidential primary should be *the* method for making presidential nominations. We shall have more to say about this proposal in the concluding section of the present chapter.

WHAT KINDS OF PERSONS ARE THE DELEGATES?

The most comprehensive study of this question to date was made in 1952 by the Cooperative Research Project on Convention Delegations. It requested the delegates to that year's conventions to fill out questionnaires concerning their personal backgrounds and characteristics; and while the returns were by no means complete, and while the data, at least as reported, suggest no conclusions of a precise character, the project's report does appear to support the following broad generalizations.[21]

(1) Some of the delegates and alternates were incumbent senators, congressmen, governors, state legislators, and local officials; but most delegates and alternates did not hold and had never held public office.

(2) A high proportion of the delegates held or had held *party* office of one kind or another. Most of the delegations, for example, included at least the most prominent state party officers—the state chairman, the national committeeman and committeewoman, and some county chairmen.

(3) About half the delegates had been delegates or alternates at earlier national conventions, although some state party organizations, apparently determined to have as many party workers as possible attend at least one national convention, made it their practice to send nobody a second time.

(4) Almost all of the delegates paid their own expenses—i.e., received no financial assistance either from the state party organizations or from organizations supporting particular candidates.

(5) An overwhelming majority of the delegates were white males.

fatal to a candidate's chances for the nomination: Willkie's defeat in the 1944 Wisconsin primary, Stassen's defeat in the 1948 Oregon primary, and Truman's defeat in the 1952 New Hampshire primary (after which, although not necessarily because of which, he announced that he would not be a candidate for re-election).

[20] See pp. 278-81 for the predominance of the direct primary as the method for making nominations for most local, state, and national offices.

[21] These generalizations are based upon the present writers' collation of the data on the individual delegations presented in the last four volumes of David, Moos, and Goldman, *op. cit.*

Thus, most of the delegates to the 1952 conventions were "party leaders" and "party workers," and only a handful were "party voters" or "party registrants." We shall point out some of the implications of this fact in a later section of the present chapter.

FORMAL CONVENTION PROCEDURES

Pre-Convention Activities. Over a year before its convention is due to assemble, the party's national committee reaches a tentative decision as to (a) the day on which the convention will assemble, (b) the city that will play host to it, and (c) the number of votes to which, under the party rules, each delegation will be entitled. Making the last of these decisions usually involves only a simple exercise in arithmetic, but making the other two often poses more difficult problems. In deciding (a), for example, the national committee must first decide how long it wants the pre-convention and post-convention campaigns to be; [22] and in deciding (b), it must choose among the cities preferred by this party faction or that, and thus favor one faction over another. [23] Not until a half-year later, at a further meeting held for the purpose of confirming its preliminary decisions on these points, does it issue the official Call for the Convention, and thus set the convention machinery—particularly the delegate-selection machinery described above—actually in motion. [24]

Over the ensuing months, the national committee performs—besides the routine task of completing physical arrangements for the convention—two functions, either of which may affect considerably the probable fortunes of leading candidates, or of any candidate organization seeking to wrest control of the party from the "ins." It compiles a "temporary roll" of delegates as returns are certified to it from the states and territories, and in doing so makes preliminary decisions (the last word here lies with the convention itself) as

[22] In preparing for the 1956 conventions, the national committee of each party explored the possibilities of holding its convention a month later than usual (middle or late August instead of, as in years past, middle or late July). Presumably this change was intended to shorten the expensive and wearisome post-convention campaign; but it would also have the effect of *lengthening* the *pre*-convention campaigns, and there was no public discussion of the consequences of such a step. The main snag the committees came up against was the fact that the laws of several states set deadlines for the certification of presidential candidates ranging from seventy to ninety days before the November election. On assurances from these states that the relevant laws would be changed, however, the Republicans chose August 20 and the Democrats August 13. We shall deal with this matter again in Chapter 17.

[23] The practice has long been for both parties to choose the same city, since using the same facilities as the other party permits both parties to get them at a much cheaper rate than each would pay if it were the sole user. In preparing for its 1956 convention, however, the Republican national committee selected San Francisco despite the Democrats' prior choice of Chicago. Many observers believed the committee made this choice because they expected President Eisenhower to be renominated and did not wish his renomination to take place in the stronghold of the anti-Eisenhower wing of the party.

[24] In preparing for its 1952 convention, the Republican National Committee made its preliminary decisions on May 11, 1951, and issued the official Call on January 18, 1952. For the text of this Call, see the Republican *Proceedings*, pp. 16-23. The Democratic National Committee made its preliminary decisions on May 25, 1951, and issued its official Call on February 5, 1952. For the text of the Democrats' Call, see their *Proceedings*, pp. 5-7.

to the disposition of all disputed seats (it may, for example, have two lists of delegates certified to it from a given state and thus have to recommend which delegates shall be seated). And it draws up a "slate" of "temporary officers" to preside during the initial "temporary organization" phase of the convention.

Temporary Organization. The convention conducts the first phase of its business—by no means necessarily so brief as its title would seem to imply— under a "temporary organization." The chairman of the national committee presides over the opening session, at which the Call is read, nominations for temporary officers are made and voted upon, and the temporary rules—usually those that governed the last preceding convention—are proposed and adopted—with any amendment the convention, which pauses at this point to hear, discuss, and vote on motions for changes in the rules, may see fit to embody in them.[25]

The temporary organization of the convention involves, besides the officers just mentioned, four temporary committees. These committees are chosen at the opening session, and promptly retire. Their deliberations account for the often considerable prolongation of the temporary-organization phase of the convention. They include: (1) the Committee on Rules, which will draw up and propose the adoption of the set of rules that will govern the convention in its "permanent organization" phase; (2) the Committee on Resolutions, which will write and propose the adoption of the "platform"; (3) the Committee on Credentials, which will take up all contests for convention seats, canvass (via formal hearings) the conflicting claims of the contestants, and bring in recommendations as to who shall be seated; and (4) the Committee on Permanent Organization, which will nominate a slate of permanent officers for the convention, and consider and report on any proposed changes in the party's national rules.

Each delegation names two members of the Resolutions Committee and one member of each of the other three. The committee "appointments," in consequence, though nominally made by the chairman, merely ratify decisions taken by the individual delegations.

Once the temporary committees have been put to work, the chairman of the national committee hands the gavel over to the temporary chairman, who proceeds (in most conventions at least) [26] to deliver the "keynote speech." This speech is called the "keynote" because it is supposed to set the tone for the

---

[25] The 1952 Republican convention's dramatic and crucial fight over the "fair-play" amendment took place at this juncture. We shall discuss the nature and significance of this fight later in the present chapter.

[26] Normally the temporary chairman will have been chosen in large part because of his reputation as a spellbinder; but he must have a public record that entitles him to speak for the party on the issues of the day. In the 1952 Republican convention, however, the keynote speech was given by General Douglas MacArthur, while the temporary chairman was a regular Republican politician, Walter S. Hallanan of West Virginia. The 1952 Democratic convention followed the usual procedure of having the temporary chairman, Governor Paul Dever of Massachusetts, deliver the keynote address.

party's whole drive for the presidency and whip up enthusiasm for the cause among the party's adherents, both at the convention and out over the country.

The convention, at this stage, has nothing to do but await the reports of the temporary committees; yet it does not wish, with the eyes of the nation upon it, to appear idle—as it might if the delegates did their waiting in their hotel rooms, or in restaurants and taverns. It therefore needs fillers, not too irrelevant to its mission, with which to pass the time; and tradition requires it to use for this purpose speeches by various eminent party leaders—senators, congressmen, governors, ambassadors, national committeemen and committee-women, candidates for offices in key states, and elder party statesmen.[27] The longer the wait, the more fillers it needs.[28]

Permanent Organization. The convention enters a new phase as, one by one, the temporary committees bring in their reports. The Committee on Permanent Organization proposes a slate of permanent officers, who are elected forthwith. The permanent chairman then takes the chair, and history marks time as he bows to tradition and makes *his* speech. The Rules Committee proposes a set of rules for the convention, and they are adopted. The Credentials Committee proposes a permanent roll of delegates for the convention—though here approval by the convention may be had for the asking, or it may not. The last word with respect to contests over seats lies with the convention, which, moreover, may take cognizance of any contest that—perhaps because of its merits, perhaps because of its implications for the struggle over the presidential nomination—it chooses to take cognizance of. Finally, the Committee on Resolutions reports the platform it has written, and the convention makes it its own.

Writing the Platform. The Resolutions Committee starts to work a week or so before the convention begins (that is, a week or so before its members are formally elected!). With or without its full membership present, it proceeds to hear testimony from representatives of interested groups on the real or imagined issues of the day. But it never finishes its work before the convention assembles, and seldom finishes it before the convention has heard reports from the other temporary committees. Little by little, it draws up a platform, which, as a general rule, is adopted by voice vote. Sometimes, however, the committee's report precipitates an all-out fight on the floor, and a roll-call vote must be taken on this or that "plank" (a notable recent example of such a fight being the bitter contest over the civil-rights plank in the 1948 Democratic convention). We shall comment on the national platforms and the part they play in the American party system later in the present chapter.

[27] In the 1952 Republican convention, for example, Herbert Hoover, the party's most recent successful presidential candidate, spoke, while Mrs. Franklin D. Roosevelt was among those who addressed the 1952 Democratic convention.

[28] The 1952 Republican convention opened on July 7, and the last temporary committee reported on the afternoon of July 10. The 1952 Democratic convention opened on July 21, and the last temporary committee reported on the afternoon of July 23. A little business was transacted in the intervals, to be sure, but most of the time was taken up by speech making.

When it has heard and voted on all the temporary committees' reports, the convention, having completed its permanent organization, is at last ready to get down to its main business.

Selecting the Nominees. The secretary of the convention calls the roll of the delegations in alphabetical order, and each as its name is called does one of three things: (1) presents a candidate for president, (2) yields its "place in line" to another delegation so that the latter may present its candidate, or (3) passes. Presenting a candidate means putting a member of the delegation up to make a nominating speech, which is immediately followed by a "demonstration" by the candidate's supporters—a mixture of elements drawn from such familiar American folkways as the parade, the pep rally, and the New Year's Eve celebration. This is followed by several brief seconding speeches on behalf of this same candidate, some of them at least by members of other delegations than the one presenting the candidate. The reading of the roll of the delegations is then resumed, and a second delegation presents a candidate. And this process is repeated until all the delegations have been called and all the candidates nominated.[29]

With the last candidate nominated, the convention turns to the grim and tedious business of balloting. The secretary or a "reading clerk" calls the roll of the delegations, and the chairman of each delegation instructs him as to how its vote is to be recorded: for example, "Eisenhower 20, Taft 10." Any member of a delegation can, when the chairman has announced its vote, demand that the delegation be "polled." The clerk must then call out the name of each individual member of the delegation, and record his vote in accordance with his own oral instructions. Many persons who watched national convention proceedings for the first time in 1952 expressed annoyance at this practice. "Why," they asked, "should a delegate wish his delegation to be polled when all it does is consume time?" One of four motives apparently underlies such a request: (1) a determination to correct a suspected inaccuracy in the chairman's report; (2) a desire for a little publicity, or, more concretely, a desire to have the folks back home hear first one's name, then one's voice, and perhaps even see one's face over a national hook-up; (3) a desire to expose a fellow delegate who is voting for a candidate other than the one he is committed to (i.e., to make him—literally—stand up and be counted); or (4) to accomplish precisely that to which our anonymous critic is objecting: i.e., to delay the proceedings in order to keep some delegation further down the list from having to vote until, perhaps, some current interdelegation negotiations have been completed. We have no evidence as to the incidence of these four motives, but the third, which brings the poll within the orbit of state and local politics, is undoubtedly often present, as is the fourth.

In times past, both parties operated under the so-called "unit rule," which requires each delegation's *entire* vote to be cast in accordance with the wishes

[29] A candidate does not have to be formally nominated in order to have votes cast for him; but in most instances all "serious" candidates are formally nominated and seconded.

of a *majority* of its members. The Republicans abandoned the unit rule completely in their 1876 convention, and have never re-adopted it. In present-day
Democratic conventions, however, the rule applies to some delegations but not
to others: The 1912 Democratic convention repealed its long-standing rule
that *all* delegations must use the unit rule, and specifically prohibited its application to any delegate elected by direct primary (on the ground that delegates
so elected are responsible to the voters only). The rules now in force in Democratic conventions, however, provide that where a delegation is picked by a
state party convention or party committee rather than by direct primary and
the "state convention has instructed its delegation to observe the unit rule,
the [national] convention will enforce it." [30]

After all the delegations have voted, the votes are totaled and the results
announced. In the conventions of both parties a simple majority of the votes [31]
is required to nominate. If no candidate receives a majority, the list must be
gone through again—and again and again until a majority does swing behind
one of the candidates, and makes him the nominee.[32] Custom—backed up by
the patent interest of the party in "unity" behind its candidate—calls for a motion by a member of some losing faction to "make the nomination unanimous,"
and his motion usually carries by voice vote.[33]

With its presidential candidate nominated, the convention must now repeat the procedure just described for its vice-presidential nominee. For several
reasons, however, things now move much more rapidly, and the atmosphere
becomes one of relative relaxation: (1) the struggle for control of the convention has, so to speak, already been decided, and is unlikely to be resumed; (2)
a new factor enters the picture—the wishes of the presidential nominee himself; (3) the convention needs a "balanced" ticket, and a great many possibles
are eliminated out of hand because they can bring the ticket no strength it
does not already have; in other words, the convention now has a narrower
range of choices than in the earlier balloting; [34] (4) everyone is tired and ready

[30] *Democratic Manual,* pp. 43-44. For the origins and abandonment of the unit rule, see
Henry L. Stoddard, *Presidential Sweepstakes* (New York: G. P. Putnam's Sons, 1948), p. 42.

[31] *Votes,* not delegates (see above). Until 1936, the Democratic party required a two-thirds
majority to nominate. See pp. 182-83 for an account of how and why the party dropped this
rule.

[32] The world's record for endurance balloting was set by the Democrats in 1924, when their
convention was still on its feet in the 103rd round! In 1952, no such demands were made on
the delegates' staying powers: General Eisenhower was nominated on the first ballot, Governor
Stevenson on the third.

[33] Not always: the losers, on good grounds or bad, may feel so strongly about what has
happened as to deny this courtesy to the winner. To date, however, only the Democrats have had
trouble on this score: their convention failed to make unanimous the nominations of Stephen
Douglas in 1860, Grover Cleveland in 1884, William Jennings Bryan in 1896, Franklin D. Roosevelt in 1932, and Harry S. Truman in 1948: Stoddard, *op. cit.,* p. 23.

[34] In 1955 President Eisenhower gave to a press conference one of the most frank and authoritative accounts we have of how the process of selecting a vice-presidential nominee actually
works. The story of the selection of Richard M. Nixon for the Republican nomination in 1952,

to go home. A further highly intangible factor here is what we might call America's characteristic mood of optimism about the vice-presidency, candidates for which appear to be nominated on the tacit assumption that the presidential nominee, if elected, could not possibly be gathered to his fathers before his term of office has expired. Vice-presidential candidates, in short, are easier to nominate than presidential candidates because the delegates—and the American people generally, it would seem—don't much care who gets to be vice-president.

The Nominees Accept. Over a long period in the past, the nominees were duly sought out at their homes and notified of their good fortune by committees which the conventions named for this purpose; and custom required each nominee to reply to the committee with an "acceptance speech." In 1932, however, Franklin Roosevelt, after being nominated by the Democrats, flew from New York to Chicago and delivered his acceptance speech at the convention itself. Apparently this has now become settled custom: in 1952, both nominees delivered their acceptance speeches before their respective conventions.

All its business having been completed, the convention now adjourns *sine die.*

The Struggle for the Nomination

THE NATURE OF THE STRUGGLE

Millions of Americans have now watched all or some of a national party convention over television, or at least listened in on one by radio. The formal convention procedures we have just described, though not raised to the level of familiarity of, say, the World Series, must have been more or less well known to the reader before he began to read the present chapter, and may have struck him as not worth going into at such length. If so, he should be more than ready to join us in thinking through the two questions we are about to raise, namely: What do the conventions teach us about the nature of our national parties? And what do they teach us about the role of the national parties in the American system?

Let us notice, to begin with, that the national parties can be looked at from several distinct points of view. As one group of political scientists has put it:

Viewed nationally, American parties can be examined either as loose coalitions of national factions . . . , or as federations of state parties, which in turn have

as told by Mr. Eisenhower and reported by *Time,* was as follows: Immediately after his nomination for the presidency, Eisenhower was "asked to name his running mate," but declined on the ground that his long absence abroad had left him somewhat out of touch with domestic politics. After some reflection, he jotted down a list of seven names, including Nixon's. He and his advisers agreed that the final choice must be "young, liberal, forceful, and from either the East or West Coast—with West preferred." They decided that only Nixon fulfilled all these qualifications, and passed the word around. "That evening Dick Nixon was formally nominated by acclamation": *Time,* June 13, 1955, pp. 25-26.

their own factional character. Or the whole structure may be viewed in three dimensions, in which the national party is treated as both a coalition of national factions and a federation of state parties. The national factions are then treated in part as groupings of state factions, cutting across the federal nature of the national parties.[35]

It should be clear from our description that the overriding purpose of a national nominating convention is to put the *party*—the *national* party—in the best possible position to win the presidential election in November, and that, when things go reasonably well, the convention contributes to the accomplishment of this purpose in at least three ways: (1) It awards the presidential nomination to that one of its leaders who seems, upon mature deliberation, most likely to win. (2) It unites all factions of the party behind the nominee, and helps elicit from party workers throughout the nation the zest for and devotion to hard work that the campaign will demand. (3) It drums up general popular interest in and enthusiasm for the party's candidate and cause.

Some critics of the American party system contend that this is—or *should* be (these, though different things, sometimes get confused in the minds of some critics)—only *one* of the convention's purposes. It acts, they say, or should act, as a deliberative body, with clear responsibility to debate and clarify the great issues of the day and formulate a forthright program of basic principles and specific measures; and it should also serve as *the* governing body over the several elements of which the national party is composed. And they have proceeded, basing their proposal on this contention, to recommend the holding of national conventions in "off years" as well as in presidential years.[36] Nor have these critics gone entirely unheeded. The national committees of both parties took the recommendation under advisement in 1954. However, they ended up rejecting it, which suggests that the leaders of both parties take a different view of the matter, and attribute to the national convention a much narrower function than these critics wish it to have.

From the standpoint of a particular faction—national, regional, state, or local—within the national party, to be sure, the convention takes on a somewhat different meaning. As it participates in the convention, such a faction seeks not only to help nominate a winner, but also to make sure that its wishes, interests, preferences, prejudices, etc., are duly reflected both in the selection of candidates and in the writing of the platform. "He will be the best vote getter" is perhaps an unanswerable argument for nominating Candidate A *from the national party's point of view;* but if A is pledged to a policy that a particular faction deems abhorrent, the argument is not unanswerable *from the standpoint of that faction.*

[35] David, Moos, and Goldman, *op. cit.,* Vol. I, p. 11. Cf. E. E. Schattschneider, *Party Government* (New York: Rinehart & Company, Inc., 1942), pp. 156-58.
[36] See the proposals by the Committee on Political Parties of the American Political Science Association in "Toward a More Responsible Two-Party System," *American Political Science Review,* Vol. XLIV (September, 1950), Supplement, pp. 38, 55-56.

In short, the first and most important thing to keep in mind when trying to understand the national conventions is that what the delegates do (each of them, remember, belongs to a faction) is determined partly by their wish to nominate a winner and partly by their wish to win and keep a strategic position in the party for their faction. Each faction wishes to be listened to— not merely heard but *listened to*—when party decisions are taken; it knows it will be listened to only if it is valued; and it watches jealously for every word and deed that presupposes or implies a particular valuation placed upon it. In the words of Pendleton Herring:

> What has our experience with national party conventions demonstrated their basic purpose to be? It is to find a man whom a majority of the voters will agree to support. . . . The convention is designed to unite diverse sections and rival leaders behind a man, and to whip up the enthusiasm of party workers to fight for his election. This involves not questions of public policy but problems of party strategy.[37]

TYPES OF CANDIDATES

In the 1952 Democratic convention, no less than fourteen men received votes for the presidential nomination, and in the Republican convention five. By no means all of the nineteen, however, thought of themselves (or were regarded by those who voted for them) as serious contenders for the nomination. Names are sometimes presented and votes cast for them for other reasons.

Perhaps the best way into this phase of our problem is to list three categories, to one of which any man whose name is placed in nomination is pretty certain to belong.[38]

Presidents Still in Office. Any incumbent president who is both eligible for another term and regarded as willing to accept the nomination (which he is until and unless he has flatly, vigorously, and unambiguously eliminated himself) is a well-nigh certain winner of the nomination.[39] In part this is because of his patronage (which means that many of the delegates are beholden to him) and his prestige and power (which mean that a delegate will think twice before risking his displeasure). But there is another and, in the opinion of the present writers, more urgent reason: Failure to nominate him for re-election is tantamount to a public confession by the party that the administration it put in office is indefensible—and reason and instinct alike keep the delegates reminded that such a confession is a poor start toward winning the next election. If, therefore, an incumbent president is still in the field, the other types of candidates we are about to notice are unlikely to appear at all.

---

[37] E. Pendleton Herring, *The Politics of Democracy* (New York: Rinehart & Company, Inc., 1940), pp. 228-29. For other statements of this same general position, see James Bryce, *The American Commonwealth* (London: Macmillan and Company, 1889), Vol. II, pp. 187-89; and Herbert Agar, *The Price of Union* (Boston: Houghton Mifflin Company, 1950), pp. 345-47.

[38] This typology is a somewhat revised version of that suggested in David, Moos, and Goldman, *op. cit.*, Vol. I, pp. 186-88.

[39] The last incumbent president who actively sought renomination and failed to get it was Chester A. Arthur in 1884.

National Leaders with Maximum "Availability." These are men who have truly national reputations and followings, who are not dependent upon their home-state organizations for their main support, and who seem to possess in high degree the mysterious political characteristic we Americans call "availability." It is difficult to say in so many words just what "availability" consists of (it is commonly talked about as though it were the presidential-politics equivalent of "glamour" in a female movie star), though some writers have attempted to do just that;[40] suffice it to say that it is the elusive something which a Franklin Roosevelt, a Tom Dewey, a Dwight Eisenhower, and an Adlai Stevenson all had in common (but Roosevelt more of than Dewey and Eisenhower more of than Stevenson), and that a man who wishes to be president has to convince first the other party leaders, then the delegates to the convention, and then the nation that he has plenty of it.[41]

"Favorite Sons." It is common practice for a delegation that is not yet committed to any candidate of the foregoing types to present the name of, and cast its votes on the early ballots for, the most prominent party figure in its home state. If that leader is also a man who has won repute outside his state—like Stassen and Warren in 1952—his followers may indulge the hope of a deadlock among the leading candidates that will force the convention to turn to him. Even if he is little known outside his own state (as, in 1952, were Fulbright of Arkansas, Dever of Massachusetts, and Williams of Michigan), the delegation may have much to gain by voting for him: specifically, solidifying the state organization and complimenting its leader, and keeping the delegation in a "flexible" position, i.e., in the position of being sought after by the leading national candidates and thus increasingly able, as the number of votes not committed to leading candidates declines, to exact important concessions in return for its vote. In any case, keeping this man's name before the con-

---

[40] *Time*, for example, once made an attempt to identify the elements of "availability." An "available" candidate, it said, must pass these ten tests: (1) He must have a solid American background, as humble as possible; (2) he must look good—but not too good—in newsreels and portraits; (3) he must be healthy and vigorous; (4) he must have an attractive wife and children; (5) he must be successful—but not too successful; (6) he must identify himself with a popular national issue; (7) he must let someone, preferably the electorate, decide to make him a candidate; (8) he must be acceptable to old-line party leaders; (9) he must have some well-heeled backers, concealed as carefully as possible; and (10) he must let the voters see him, as often and auspiciously as possible: *Time*, Vol. XLI (April 26, 1943), pp. 18-20. Most political scientists would add: He must come from the right state, i.e., a two-party state that has a substantial number of electoral votes.

[41] We have accepted current usage here, and spoken of "availability" as if it were a *quality* possessed by some persons and not by others and universal to all political situations. It seems probable, however, that people mean by a man's "availability" merely his chances of winning, and nothing more. A man's chances of winning depend on many considerations, all of which have to do with his relationship to the total political situation in a given presidential year. These chances can be listed and analyzed with a view to seeing how he stacks up against his rivals, so that in a given year we can conclude that his chances are excellent. But there seems no good reason, in such a case, for referring his excellent chances back to a quality that he possesses and putting a name to that quality. In other words, "availability," like "leadership" (see Chapter 11 above), is specific to concrete political situations, not a *quailty* possessed only by certain persons and universal to all situations.

vention through ballot after ballot builds him up, possibly to the point where he may become a contender in his own right at some future convention.

THE PURSUIT OF VOTES

What the candidates and their organizations are looking for at the convention is *not* enthusiastic and lengthy demonstrations on the floor, or loud cheers from the gallery, or laudatory editorials in the newspapers, or at least not these things as such, but *votes*—getting them in the first instance, and then holding them through ballot after ballot against the blandishments of other candidates. Others may forget this, but the practical politician cannot afford to. "I shall never forget," writes James A. Farley, "standing in the balcony in 1932 in Chicago when Governor Ritchie was placed in nomination. They put on a great show—a great parade. I walked out on the balcony. He and I stood there alone, and I put my arm on his shoulder. I said: 'Bert, that's a great reception for you,' and just as he saw me he said: 'Unfortunately there's not a single delegate in the whole demonstration.' "[42] As far as the realities of the convention were concerned, in other words, the demonstration might just as well never have occurred.

This means that the candidates and their advisers must give careful thought to the question, Why do delegates vote for a particular candidate, or, variously, why do they switch their votes from one candidate to another at some point in the balloting? James A. Farley and Edward J. Flynn, two old hands at trying to win votes and influence delegates, have testified that the primary motivation of most delegates is their desire to see the convention nominate a man who will win in November—not the man whom they like best or who they think would make the best president, but the man who can *win*.[43] Many of them come to the convention with their minds already made up as to which of the candidates best fills the bill; but when they get to the convention, they may discover that their man hasn't a chance of getting the nomination, and, if this happens, they switch their votes to the man they think is going to get it—in the familiar phrase, they "get on the bandwagon." No doubt some votes are switched as a result of "deals" among the delegations' leaders, but the usual reason appears to be a conviction on the delegate's part that the man he is switching to is going to win the nomination and the election.[44]

[42] James A. Farley, "How Conventions Are Run," *U.S. News & World Report,* Vol. XXXII (June 27, 1952), pp. 40-46. Copyright by *U.S. News & World Report,* an independent weekly news magazine published at Washington.

[43] Many observers of the 1952 Republican convention concluded that a clear majority of the delegates admired Senator Taft more and believed that he would make a better president than General Eisenhower. But a majority also believed that Eisenhower could win in November, and Taft could not. So—in some instances, no doubt, not without some heartache—they cast their votes for Eisenhower. See above, however, our point that somewhere along the line loyalty to a party faction enters the picture, and sets limits within which even the desire to win in November must operate.

[44] Farley, *loc. cit.;* and Flynn, *op. cit.,* pp. 96-97.

The political scientists who studied the 1952 conventions came to the conclusion that the convention itself, as it progressed, considerably affected the attitudes of the delegates toward the nomination and toward the party:

Most delegates arrived with their frame-of-mind attuned to the parochial concerns of county, congressional district, state, and region. But physical removal from their previous surroundings was quickly followed by the intense emotional pressures of the convention environment. Delegates found themselves engaging in discussions with other delegates from the opposite ends of the country, with a corresponding enlargement of points of view and a reinforcement of the emotional attachments to party that—for regular party people—are second only to religious and patriotic feeling in their intensity. In the end, most of the delegates were thinking less about the constituents in their home districts and more about the problems of their party as a national organization with a national constituency—one, moreover, that could not win unless it could appeal effectively to a majority of the entire American electorate.[45]

PRE-CONVENTION CAMPAIGNS

The organizations of those candidates for the nominations who seriously believe they have a chance to win start their campaigns for delegate votes anywhere from six months to two years before the convention actually assembles. They usually adopt one or another or a combination of the three following plans of campaign: (1) public appeal to the electorate with an eye mainly to the presidential primaries; (2) private talks with the members of the various state and congressional district conventions that will name delegates to the national convention; and (3) private talks with delegates who have already been selected. There are various techniques at their disposal for persuading the delegates to vote for their man: The organization provides itself with reliable intelligence about the delegates, so as to find out which ones are irrevocably committed to another candidate, and which are worth working on. It makes it its business to besiege the latter with personal letters, telegrams, and telephone calls. It arranges for its candidate to meet with the uncommitted delegates and try to sell himself to them in person. It sets up an elaborate and inviting headquarters in the convention city, where it must be ready to hand out lapel buttons, provide entertainment, and offer refreshments. It makes broad appeals to public opinion through the regular media of mass communication. When the convention assembles, the organization knows, if it has done its pre-convention job well, how its man is running and what it must do to put him over. If it has done it badly, its man is probably too far behind the leaders ever to catch up.[46]

[45] David, Moos, and Goldman, *op. cit.*, Vol. I, p. 193.

[46] For an account of the 1952 pre-convention campaigns, see David, Moos, and Goldman, *op. cit.*, Vol. I, pp. 24-56. For an account of Roosevelt's classic pre-convention campaign in 1930-1932, see James A. Farley, *Behind the Ballots* (New York: Harcourt, Brace and Company, 1938), Ch. II; and Flynn, *op. cit.*, Chs. 8 and 9. For the 1948 pre-convention campaigns, see Roy V. Peel, "The 1948 Preconvention Campaigns," *Annals of the American Academy of Political and Social Science*, Vol. CCLIX (September, 1948), pp. 75-89.

THE ROLE OF THE PLATFORMS

The critics of the national convention system often single out the platforms as one of its most nonsensical and useless features.[47] Their bill of particulars includes the following items: The platforms are written far too hastily and under conditions of pressure that render impossible calm and thoughtful deliberation upon national problems and party principles;[48] the "planks" are now vague, now equivocal, and now silent altogether about controversial questions, clear and unambiguous only on questions that have already been settled—"full of sound and fury, signifying everything";[49] and, since few voters read the platforms or take them into account in chosing between the parties, and since they are not and are not intended to be binding upon the party's candidates in any case, the energies that go into them are largely wasted.[50]

Convention delegates nevertheless seem to take the platforms quite seriously. In the 1948 Democratic convention, for example, not only was there a bitter floor fight over the civil-rights plank, but several southern delegates, once their side lost the fight, went home and began to organize support for a third-party candidate. It can, admittedly, be argued that this is an "extreme case"; but it is also part of the historical record, and in and of itself is enough to write a question mark beside the proposition that the platform, no matter what it says, is of little importance in explaining American party behavior.

In short, the critics who approach party platforms and platform-writing procedures in the manner just noted miss the crucial point. The function of a national convention, as we have seen, is *not* that of enunciating principles and laying down rules to bind the many variegated elements of which the national party is composed. It has, rather, at least three main functions: (1) nominating a man who can win; (2) uniting behind him all the party's resources and support that will be needed for an all-out, nationwide effort on his behalf; and (3) appealing with maximum effectiveness to a maximum number of interest groups in the electorate as part of the party's effort to mobilize enough popular support to win in November. Insofar as it contributes to the performance of those functions, the platform pays its way. Accordingly, the proper question to ask and answer about it is: Does it so contribute? To ridicule it, and chide the "pols" for taking it more seriously than they should, on the grounds that it does not contribute to some function that the convention does *not* have, is wide of the mark—even if the critic is prepared to show that the convention *should* have that other function.

[47] For the most comprehensive criticism of the present-day platforms, and for a series of proposals for improving them, see "Toward a More Responsible Two-Party System," pp. 30, 50-56.

[48] Cf. Charles E. Merriam and Harold F. Gosnell, *The American Party System,* 4th ed. (New York: The Macmillan Company, 1949), pp. 72-75.

[49] Peter H. Odegard and E. Allen Helms, *American Politics,* 2nd ed. (New York: Harper and Brothers, 1947), p. 535.

[50] Cf. Dayton D. McKean, *Party and Pressure Politics* (Boston: Houghton Mifflin Company, 1949), pp. 236-38.

The platform, once we look at it in the manner just indicated, will be seen at once to play a highly strategic role in the struggle for the nomination, the quest for party unity, and the pursuit of votes. It is, to be sure, written and adopted *before* the presidential candidate is nominated. But there is good reason for this: It must reflect the ideas and aspirations of each of the major contenders for the nomination in a way that will enable the eventual winner to stand on it, and still leave each of the eventual losers feeling that he and the interests, groups, and ideas he represents have not been repudiated by the party. And any platform that does that well contributes a great deal to the party's chances for unity and victory in November—which, let us repeat once more, is the only justification it needs in the eyes of the party leaders and workers.[51]

FIGHTS OVER THE RULES AND CONTESTED DELEGATIONS

Other aspects of the convention's proceedings likewise become more understandable when we remember that the struggle for the nomination and the search for unity are among the major drives that power its formal activities. Each of the 1952 conventions, for example, witnessed rancorous floor fights over the rules and over the seating of contested delegations. The ammunition, in all these fights and on both sides, was an impressive array of high-sounding arguments, appealing now to the law of the land, now to its traditional political doctrines, and now to lofty principles of justice and equity. The competing candidates' respective stakes in the outcome of the fights were hardly mentioned. But if we forget about the ammunition, and look at the disposition of forces on the field of battle, we shall not long be deceived as to what the real issues were. For instance, at the opening session of the Republican convention, the so-called "fair play" amendment to the temporary rules, offered by Governor Langlie of Washington, an Eisenhower supporter, precipitated an acrimonious debate which was duly followed by a roll-call vote. The amendment provided that no delegate whose seat was in dispute (except for delegates placed on the temporary roll by a two-thirds vote of the national committee) should be permitted to cast a vote on any issue. In the debate, the *talk* was of fair play; but the reality behind the talk, as even the most casual spectator clearly saw, was the simple fact that the Taft faction was counting on a total of sixty-eight seats from the three contested delegations of Texas, Louisiana, and Georgia, and the Eisenhower faction was determined to deny it these seats. The passage of the amendment was, accordingly, a grave defeat for the Taft cause, and the subsequent seating of all three pro-Eisenhower

[51] For an application of this type of analysis to the 1952 platforms and conventions, see Austin Ranney, "The Platforms, the Parties, and the Voter," *Yale Review*, Vol. XLII (September, 1952), pp. 10-20. The classical exposition of this interpretation of the role and value of the platforms is that by Herring, *op. cit.*, pp. 230-37. See also Agar, *op. cit.*, pp. 346-47; Key, *op. cit.*, pp. 462-64; Howard R. Penniman, *Sait's American Parties and Elections*, 4th ed. (New York: Appleton-Century-Crofts, Inc., 1948), pp. 481-86; and Hugh A. Bone, *American Politics and the Party System* (New York: McGraw-Hill Book Company, Inc., 1949), pp. 550-54.

delegations the *coup de grâce* that made that cause hopeless—all this, remember, before a nominating speech had been made or a single ballot cast.[52]

Similarly, the controversy over the "loyalty pledge" rule in the Democratic convention had the look—initially, at least—of an ideological contest between northern liberals and southern conservatives, with no candidate interests as such involved; but it can be seen in retrospect to have turned finally on the struggle for the nomination. Senator Moody of Michigan had proposed a resolution prohibiting the seating of any delegate until he had given the Credentials Committee assurances that he would "exert every honorable means available to him in any official capacity he [might] have, to provide that the nominees of [the] convention . . . appear on the election ballot under the heading, 'Name or Designation of the Democratic Party.'"[53] This proposal was intended to prevent a repetition of the "Dixiecrat" bolt of 1948, in the course of which the bolters managed to get the "States' Rights" nominees on the ballots of four southern states as the official Democratic nominees. The resolution was debated on the level of high principle, with the liberals arguing that the national convention's nominations should be binding on all state and local organizations, and the southerners defending the principle of states' rights and the autonomy of the state and local parties. The convention passed the resolution by voice vote, but the real battle, as we know now, was merely postponed, and did not occur until the wild and confused night session on the convention's fourth day, when the fur began to fly over an announcement by Governor Battle of Virginia to the effect that neither his delegation nor the delegations from Louisiana and South Carolina could give the assurances demanded by the Moody resolution. Permanent chairman Rayburn promptly ruled that the three delegations in question could cast no votes, then found himself entertaining a motion by delegate Sasscer of Maryland that the Virginia delegation be seated anyway. Rayburn construed the motion as an appeal from his ruling, and ordered a roll-call vote. That vote—despite the fact that many delegates were by no means clear as to what was being voted on—was duly held, and for a moment seemed likely to produce the following inconclusive result: 351½ for seating Virginia, 462½ against, and 416 still deciding. Before the vote was announced, however, Jacob Arvey of Illinois, a leader of the Stevenson faction, reappeared on the floor, and the convention suddenly learned that Illinois was changing its vote from 45-15 against seating the Virginia delegation to 52-8 *for* seating it. This precipitated a flood of vote-switching into the "for seating" column, and the vote finally announced was 650½ for seating to 518 against. And before long the Louisiana and South Carolina delegations were also seated.

Now: On the level of high principle, what had happened was that the southerners had won the battle, the liberals having either let themselves be

---

[52] For a running account of this whole fight, see David, Moos, and Goldman, *op. cit.*, Vol. I, pp. 68-76, 87.

[53] *Official Report of the Proceedings of the Democratic National Convention, 1952*, p. 55.

outsmarted or abdicated on their avowed ideals. Many liberal delegates and observers, indeed, bitterly condemned Arvey and Stevenson, and were on the point of concluding that Stevenson, despite his reputation, was no liberal at all. But we know now, from subsequent disclosures by Arvey, that he was striking a deftly concealed blow if not for liberal principle, at least for the prospects of the leading liberal candidate. Arvey realized, he said, that the Kefauver forces were trying to drive the southerners—who would never vote for Kefauver anyway—out of the convention, so as to reduce the total votes and therefore the size of the majority needed for a Kefauver nomination. And that move the Stevenson forces had to block at all costs.[54] In short, the fight over the rules in the Democratic convention, like that in the Republican convention, was in the last analysis decided with an eye to the struggle for the nomination.[55]

The relation between contested-delegation fights and the struggle for the nomination is even easier to see, since the contesting delegates' preferences among the leading candidates are usually known to everyone in the convention. Floor fights over who shall be seated are, therefore, almost invariably tests of strength between candidate organizations, and are so clearly understood to be just that that the contending factions go to little trouble to try to make them look like something else. The 1952 Republican convention, where the Eisenhower forces combined victory in the "fair play" rules fight with victory in seating the pro-Eisenhower delegations and so dominated the proceedings almost from the beginning, is the classical example—not so much because the stakes were more thinly disguised than usual (which they were), but because the contest fights occurred under the magnifying glass of the national television networks.[56]

The Conventions Evaluated

THEIR CRITICS

From their origins in 1831 to the present time, the national nominating conventions have been subjected to a continuous barrage of criticism which, if anything, has grown milder as the decades have passed. According to

[54] Jacob Arvey, as told to J. M. Madigan, *Reporter*, Vol. IX (November 24, 1953), pp. 19-26, esp. p. 24. For a useful summary of this whole fight, see David, Moos, and Goldman, *op. cit.*, Vol. I, pp. 101-06, 112-17, 124-31, 136-51.

[55] There is at least one precedent for the Democratic "loyalty pledge" fight: In the 1880 Republican convention, Roscoe Conkling, the leader of the faction wishing to renominate U. S. Grant, feared a large-scale bolt if his man won. He therefore introduced a resolution providing that no delegate should be seated unless he would first swear to support the convention's nominee, whoever he might be. This aroused a storm of indignant opposition, and Conkling, fearing the resolution was harming Grant's chances of getting the nomination, finally withdrew it: Stoddard, *op. cit.*, p. 80.

[56] For a useful summary of the fight over the contested delegations in the 1952 Republican convention, see David, Moos, and Goldman, *op. cit.*, Vol. I, pp. 76-85.

Thomas Hart Benton, a Democratic leader of Jackson's day, the conventions are undemocratic, produce weak presidents, and usurp the people's right to pick their own president:

> Until this system is abolished, and the people resume their rights, the elective principle of our government is suppressed; and the people have no more control over the selection of the man who is to be their President, than the subjects of kings have over the birth of the child who is to be their ruler.[57]

John C. Calhoun objected to them so strongly that he refused in 1844 to let his name be presented to the Democratic convention, and said flatly that no such convention could represent the popular will. "I hold it impossible," he declared, "to form a scheme more perfectly calculated to annihilate the control of the people over the presidential election, and vest it in those who make politics a trade, and who live or expect to live on the government." Calhoun, indeed, openly favored a return to the congressional caucus, which he regarded as having produced better results all the way around.[58]

Perhaps the most widely quoted condemnation of the conventions is that of M. I. Ostrogorski, writing in 1902. He described the delegates as "a greedy crowd of office-holders, or of office-seekers, disguised as delegates of the people," and the platform as "a collection of hollow, vague phrases, strung together by a few experts in the art of using meaningless language, and adopted still more precipitately without examination and without conviction." Worse still, he wrote further, the convention does its work under intolerable pressure from the "mob" in the galleries:

> Cut off from their conscience by selfish calculations and from their judgment by the tumultuous crowd of spectators, which alone made all attempt at deliberation an impossibility, [the delegates] submitted without resistance to the pressure of the galleries masquerading as popular opinion, and made up of a *claque* and of a raving mob which, under ordinary circumstances, could only be formed by the inmates of all the lunatic asylums of the country who had made their escape at the same time.

In a word, Ostrogorski could account for the fact that this "colossal travesty of popular institutions" manages to place good if not great men in the presidency only by "repeating the American saying: 'God takes care of drunkards, of little children, and of the United States!'"[59]

These themes are echoed—together with a few new ones—in the criticism directed against the conventions in our own day, though the style of language has changed and the prose reverberates less colorfully. This criticism, whether

---

[57] Thomas Hart Benton, *Thirty Years' View* (New York: D. Appleton and Company, 1856), Vol. II, pp. 595-96.

[58] Quoted in Benton, *op. cit.,* Vol. II, pp. 596-99.

[59] All these quotations are from M. I. Ostrogorski, *Democracy and the Organization of Political Parties,* translated by Frederick Clarke (New York: The Macmillan Company, 1902), Vol. II, pp. 278-79. Used with the permission of The Macmillan Company.

from publicists [60] or from political scientists,[61] boils down to the following indictments: (1) The conventions are not sufficiently representative—i.e., the apportionment of the delegates does not properly reflect the numbers of party voters in the various states; (2) they respond to the wishes of party leaders and workers rather than of party voters; (3) the conventions are too large and unwieldy, and, in consequence, (4) they are too subject to wire pulling and (5) they go forward in an atmosphere of confusion, childish horseplay, and irrationality not conducive to calm deliberation on party principles, programs, and men; (6) they are too exclusively tied to making presidential nominations and therefore cannot act as the parties' national governing organs and deliberative assemblies; and (7) the vice-presidential nominations are always made hastily, for strictly political reasons, and without serious regard to the grave possibility that any vice-president may become president.

PROPOSALS FOR REFORM

The authors and popularizers of these indictments have proposed a number of reforms, each calculated to remove or modify one or another of the conventions' alleged shortcomings. These vary greatly in detail, but by and large they are based on three major contentions: (1) The size of the conventions should be sharply reduced. (2) The conventions should meet biennially . instead of in presidential years only. And (3) the influence of party voters should be greatly increased, mainly by stepping up the proportion of delegates selected by direct primaries or, better still, having *all* the delegates so selected.[62]

THE CRITICS CRITICIZED

In the present writers' opinion, the first point that must be made in any appraisal of the conventions and of their critics is this: The conventions *as they are today* are an integral part of our present party system, and highly appropriate to that system. One of the latter's principal features, as we have noted repeatedly, is that its national major parties are *decentralized:* They are composed of a number of more or less autonomous state and local parties, over which *no* national party organ has any effective control. Consequently any convocation of these local units for the purpose of naming and uniting behind a single candidate and platform is bound to be more like a diplomatic con-

[60] Cf. Thomas L. Stokes, "Getting Nominated Is an Intricate Business," *New York Times Sunday Magazine,* April 20, 1952, pp. 9, 67-68; and James Reston, "The Convention System: A 5-Count Indictment," *New York Times Sunday Magazine,* July 11, 1948, pp. 7, 36-38.

[61] Cf. Penniman, *op. cit.,* pp. 504-06; and Bone, *op. cit.,* pp. 559-62. The most comprehensive attack made by political scientists upon the present nominating conventions is that by the Committee on Political Parties of the American Political Science Association in "Toward a More Responsible Two-Party System," pp. 28-29, 38, 74.

[62] See Louise Overacker, *The Presidential Primary* (New York: The Macmillan Company, 1926), for an account of the arguments for and the early history of the presidential primary movement. See David, Moos, and Goldman, *op. cit.,* Vol. I, Ch. 6, for a summary of recent proposals for the presidential primary. For the advocacy of this and other reforms, see "Toward a More Responsible Two-Party System," p. 38; and Estes Kefauver, "Indictment of the Political Convention," *New York Times Sunday Magazine,* March 16, 1952, pp. 9, 59-63.

ference of independent sovereign states than a session of the legislative body of a single sovereign state.[63]

Secondly, the horseplay and high jinks to which so many critics of the conventions take exception are probably indispensable to the performance of the conventions' function. The delegates are ordinary Americans, called upon, we repeat, to nominate a winner and rally a national party behind him. Their behavior, like their opinions and ideas, reflects the norms of American society. The delegates, obliged as they are to keep open their communications with the broad reaches of the population, possess about that degree of refinement and austerity that one finds, and expects to find, in any type of convention made up of ordinary Americans—a national convention of furniture dealers, say, or an American Legion convention—that is, that degree of refinement and austerity that is consistent with getting down off your high horse, making some noise and, in general, whooping it up.[64]

Thirdly, we hear sometimes that the conventions are primarily "shows," put on by the politicians for the amusement of the masses, who in the old days read about them in the newspapers, later listened to them on the radio, and, most recently, watched them on television. Those who urge this point were indeed ready in 1952, when the conventions were first telecast, with the suggestion that this new development would force the politicians to improve the show—shorten speeches, shorten or eliminate demonstrations, refrain from acrimonious public intraparty bickering, etc. But the 1952 conventions, on these counts at least, were pretty much like the conventions in the dark ages before the 21-inch screen. Most of what goes on at the conventions, in point of fact, is intended for the *participants,* not the spectators.

Fourthly, the conventions do accomplish the participants' purposes. They normally nominate men who are good vote getters, and they normally unite the many elements of the national parties behind the nominees. Moreover, there is no reason to suppose that the men placed in the presidency by this system have been notably inferior to the men who rise to positions of eminence in the other representative democracies, where quite different party processes prevail.[65]

[63] Cf. Schattschneider, *op. cit.,* p. 102; and Agar, *op. cit.,* p. 347.

[64] A distinguished French observer of the 1936 conventions, M. Raoul de Roussy de Sales takes a notably less dim view of the free-and-easy atmosphere of American nominating conventions than one is likely to find in American writings about them. "Quite often during these conventions," he tells, "some of my American friends apologized to me for what was going on before our eyes. They thought that I should form an unfavorable opinion of the irresponsible levity and the uncontrolled exuberance of these thousands of people supposedly assembled for a serious purpose. But I think that if those who attend conventions are so lighthearted and so obviously cheerful it is because they know by instinct that whatever is done or said does not matter very much. They do not consider politics a tragic business because they do not have to—not yet": "Notes on the Conventions," *Atlantic Monthly,* Vol. CLVIII (September, 1936), pp. 308-09.

[65] Cf. Harold J. Laski, "The Conventions and the Presidency," *Harper's,* Vol. CLXXXI (July, 1940), pp. 166-71; James M. Burns, "The Case for the Smoke-filled Room," *New York Times Magazine,* June 15, 1952, pp. 9, 24-26; and Key, *op. cit.,* pp. 474-76.

Finally, if we examine closely the standard criticisms of the conventions, we can see that they are really directed at our party system as a whole. The criticisms are based upon the assumption that the national conventions *should* be the real governing bodies of the national parties, with real power to bind the state and local parties on program and men alike, and the further assumption that the conventions *should* represent the party voters instead of the party workers and leaders. The kind of conventions which the critics hope to bring about by their proposed reforms might well be appropriate to a system of highly centralized parties acting as rubber stamps for their party voters. But it would be highly *in*appropriate to our present system of decentralized parties, run largely by party workers and leaders.[66]

Thus the question of whether or not we should reform our national conventions along the lines mentioned above really turns upon the more basic question of whether we wish to retain our party system or fix ourselves up with a different one. *That* question we reserve for consideration in the concluding section of this book.

[66] Cf. D. W. Brogan's judgment that "the Convention, imperfect organ of representative government as it is, is an essential part of the American system. . . . For the Conventions do something that no other organ of the American system of democracy does: they provide a meeting place for a representative sample of all types of politicians, amateur and professional; they supply, however imperfectly, one great need of the American system, the nationalising of party politics, and they are a substitute for a missing class in American political life, a group of universally recognized political leaders": *Politics in America* (New York: Harper and Brothers, 1954), p. 234.

Chapter 14

CONTESTING ELECTIONS: ELECTORAL MACHINERY

Having made its nominations by one of the processes described in the preceding two chapters, any political party that means business about winning elections must next concentrate its energies on getting its candidates *elected* over the opposition's nominees. Thus it becomes vitally concerned with that group of party activities which we have referred to now and then as the contesting of elections. These include canvassing, campaigning, driving voters to the polls, furnishing the officials who count the ballots, etc. But a party conducts its election-contesting business, like its nomination-making activities, within the context of certain electoral machinery which the community prescribes.

The purpose of the present chapter is to give the reader a general picture of the electoral machinery of the United States, the kinds of problems it poses for the parties, the procedures the parties follow in attempting to cope with those problems, and the impact of the machinery upon the nature and activities of the parties themselves.

The Legal Regulation of American Elections

Article I, Section IV, of the national Constitution provides that "the times, places, and manner of holding elections for Senators and Representatives shall be prescribed in each State by the legislature thereof; but the Congress may at any time by law make or alter such regulations. . . ." Up to the present time, Congress has exercised this power only to the extent of requiring that senators and representatives be chosen on the first Tuesday after the first Monday in November of every even-numbered year, that they be elected by secret ballot, and that, except in the case of congressmen at large, they be elected from *districts*. Congress has also prescribed that presidential electors be elected on the first Tuesday after the first Monday in November of every fourth year, and, further, that the electors in all the states cast their votes on the same day (usually early in December). It has also enacted laws regulating campaign contributions, expenditures, and "corrupt practices" in elections in which national officers are selected, and has provided for the settlement of disputed elections.

Aside from these rather minor congressional regulations, however, American elections—for local, state, *and* national offices—are conducted under *state* and not under national laws.[1] Here, then—as we did with party membership and with the nominating process—we must begin our survey of American electoral machinery by noticing how the legal details of that machinery vary from state to state.

The Principal Elements of American Electoral Machinery

REGISTRATION [2]

The History and Purpose of Registration Machinery. Over most of the United States until well into the nineteenth century the would-be voter had only to present himself at the polling place and, in the absence of an official challenge of his eligibility, cast his ballot—with no questions asked.[3] If challenged, he had only to sign an affidavit affirming his qualifications, or perhaps produce unchallenged voters from the district who were prepared to testify in his behalf, in order for the challenge to be set aside. Any such simple arrangement, however, clearly presupposes a situation in which the voters and election officials are likely to know each other personally—that is, the kind of situation that obtains in a rural neighborhood. It could produce satisfactory results over the country as a whole only so long as the latter was predominantly rural—which, as we know, it gradually ceased to be through the nineteenth century. In the cities, the arrangement was an open invitation to such fraudulent practices as "repeating" and "voting the graveyard," and—in view of the hard fact that the city precinct election official could not say out of personal knowledge who was eligible and who was not—could hardly be defended. Beginning shortly after the Civil War, therefore, a number of states adopted registration laws; and by the turn of the century, all the states had established one or another of the available registration systems.

[1] The Fourteenth, Fifteenth, and Nineteenth Amendments to the National Constitution, of course, limit the states' freedom to regulate the suffrage.

[2] Joseph P. Harris, *Registration of Voters in the United States* (Washington, D. C.: Institute for Government Research, 1929), is still the most detailed discussion of this subject, although it is now out of date in many respects. Of the recent textbooks on American parties, Howard R. Penniman, *Sait's American Parties and Elections,* 4th ed. (New York: Appleton-Century-Crofts, 1948), Ch. XXVI, contains most information on registration.

[3] There were a few exceptions to this general rule: Massachusetts had set up a kind of registration for some elections in some localities as early as 1800; and most of the other New England states had followed suit by the time of the Civil War.

The purpose of any system of registration, as the foregoing paragraph suggests, is to see to it that all votes cast in elections are cast by eligible voters. And the fool- and scoundrel-proof means of accomplishing this purpose is to furnish the election officials in each election district a list, prepared *before* election day, of all persons in the district who have satisfied the legal requirements for voting (age, citizenship, length of residence, etc.). Such a list, or "register," is of course no better than its built-in-guarantees against falsification and exploitation by the unscrupulous. What it does, for the most part, is to make sure that decisions as to who is eligible shall not be postponed until election day, and to create at least the possibility that they shall be made on a full canvass of the evidence (i.e., with due procedure).[4]

Types of Registration Systems. Although the details of registration systems vary considerably from state to state, the two main questions that need to be asked in order to understand any particular system are: Is it "periodic" or "permanent"? And is it "direct" or "indirect"? A *periodic registration* system is one in which, at specified intervals ranging from one to ten years, the existing register of voters is abandoned, and an entirely new one drawn up. In 1953, two states used this system for all elections at all levels, and twelve states used it for some elections at some levels.[5] A *permanent registration* system is one in which one and the same basic list is continued indefinitely, and is brought up to date from time to time via specified procedures for removing and adding names. The advantages of permanent over periodic registration, which most present-day political scientists stoutly affirm (and which were first urged by Professor Joseph P. Harris in 1929 [6]), are said to be twofold: It costs less money, and it provides somewhat surer guarantees against fraudulent voting.[7] Either of these two apparently well-documented claims would appear to be reason enough for adopting it, and, in general, the political scientists' counsel on this matter has prevailed. By 1953, no less than thirty-four states used permanent registration for all elections at all levels, and twelve states used it for some elections at some levels.[8] A system of *direct* or *personal registration* is one in which the would-be voter must himself take the steps by which his name gets on the register, i.e., he must either present himself in person to a registration official, or send in an application by mail. Over half the states at present use this system. A system of *indirect or nonpersonal registration* is one in which the registration officials are themselves responsible for getting the voter's name on the list. A few states use the latter system for all elections; many states use it for some elections at some levels.

[4] The most recent compilation of the various state statutes on registration is Council of State Governments, *Registration for Voting in the United States,* rev. ed. (Chicago, 1946).

[5] *Book of the States, 1954-1955* (Chicago: Council of State Governments, 1954), Vol. X, table on pp. 80-81.

[6] *Op. cit.,* p. 19.

[7] Cf. Penniman, *op. cit.,* pp. 608-11.

[8] *Book of the States, 1954-1955, loc. cit.*

ELECTION ORGANIZATION: THE MAIN "LEVELS" [9]

Statewide Supervision and Control. Each state government exercises some direct control over the several types of election held within its borders. For this purpose, it has at hand two instruments, which it may use either singly or in combination. The first of these is the *election laws*. The typical body of state statutes regulating elections is extremely complex and reflects a determination on the part of the legislators to impose upon the activities of election officials at intermediate and election-district levels a rigid and uniform pattern that will leave no detail to chance or discretion. Most observers agree, however, that the legislators might very well have saved themselves their pains. Local election officials are far too numerous to be supervised effectively; moreover, since they themselves interpret and apply the statutes, the very complexity of the laws may operate to give them a greater power of decision.

The second agency of control is found in the *supervisory powers granted to statewide officials*. In some states the governor, and in a few states a state board of elections, exercises supervisory powers over local election officials, though in no case powers great enough to add up to effective control of elections. In most states the secretary of state is the "chief election officer"—but this title means only that he performs certain clerical services in connection with elections all over the state:

He publishes the election laws, receives the official returns and usually tabulates the results for the official canvassing board, certifies to the county officers in charge of printing the ballots the names of candidates for state offices, certifies the form of the ballot and the working of referendum propositions, and attends to various other clerical details in connection with state elections.[10]

Intermediate Supervision and Control. The statutes of most states provide for some kind of election-supervising authority intermediate between statewide officials and voting-district officials. In some states this authority resides in special boards or commissions of elections, one of which is provided for each county or city in the state, or short of that in other states, for the more populous counties or cities. Usually these boards are, by law, bipartisan, and their members are appointed: county election boards by the governor, and city election boards by the mayor. Over most of the nation, however, the law requires a local official or set of officials, such as the county clerk, the mayor and council, or the county board of supervisors, to take on the task of supervising the activities of the voting-district officials.[11]

---

[9] Joseph P. Harris, *Election Administration in the United States* (Copyright by the Brookings Institution, 1934), remains the most detailed survey of election administration in the United States, although, like his work on registration, it is out of date in a number of respects. Among the recent textbooks on parties, Penniman, *op. cit.,* Ch. XXVII, has the most detailed discussion of the subject.

[10] Harris, *Election Administration in the United States,* p. 101. For a summary of the various methods of statewide supervision and control of elections, see Harris, pp. 96-108.

[11] *Ibid.,* pp. 108-20.

Voting-District Supervision and Control. This brings us to the "bottom" level of election organization, that is, to the officials responsible for the actual conduct of elections in the actual voting districts themselves.[12] These officials, says Harris, "determine the character of elections."[13] Concretely, they see to such matters as "the arrangement of furniture and voting equipment within the polling place; opening of the polls, examination of voting machines and ballot boxes, opening of ballot packages, administering oaths to inferior election aides; general supervision and conduct of the voting process, including distribution and receipt of ballots, keeping of voters' lists and district register, giving of instructions to electors, etc.; and finally, tallying of votes and certification and delivery of returns to a central agency."[14] They are usually designated as "election judges" or, in a few cases, "election inspectors"; their assistants are usually designated as "election clerks." In some states there are as few as three judges per voting district, and in other states as many as ten; and in most states they are appointed, for terms ranging from one to four years, by the intermediate supervisory officials previously mentioned. Over most of the nation the law requires that voting-district boards be bipartisan— with, however, the majority party in each district getting a majority of the seats; and one result of this has been that their members are in practice named on recommendation by the local party organizations. (The precinct committeeman usually names such election judges and clerks as his party is entitled to in his precinct.)

The voting district—the precinct and the ward—is, as noted above, the theater in which the voters' ballots are actually cast and counted; and the intermediate and statewide officials, whatever their nominal authority as defined by law, are nowhere in a position to exercise effective supervision over what goes on within the voting district. The actual electoral machinery over the nation is thus far more decentralized than the relevant statutes indicate. Effective supervision and control of the machinery rests ultimately in the hands of the precinct and ward election judges, and could be transferred elsewhere only by creating further machinery on a vast and costly scale.[15]

BALLOTS

The History of the Ballot in the United States.[16] In colonial times, votes were cast in some elections by written ballots, in others by "corn" and "bean"

---

[12] These are usually "precincts" for county, state, and national elections, "wards" and "townships" for municipal elections, and various *ad hoc* "districts" for elections for such agencies as school boards, sanitary districts, park districts, etc.

[13] *Ibid.,* p. 126.

[14] Murray H. Shusterman, "Choosing Election Officials," *National Municipal Review,* Vol. XXIX (March, 1940), p. 186.

[15] Harris, *Election Administration in the United States,* pp. 126-48.

[16] The standard work on the early history of American elections is Cortlandt F. Bishop *History of Elections in the American Colonies* (New York: Columbia College, 1893). For the history of the ballot in the nineteenth and early twentieth centuries, see Eldon C. Evans, *A History of the Australian Ballot System in the United States* (Chicago: University of Chicago Press, 1917).

ballots, and in yet others *viva voce,* the election officer calling for the "Yea's" and "Nay's" or a show of hands on whatever issue was being decided. The last method, still in wide use in private organizations and for some purposes in legislatures and town meetings, appears to have been used more commonly than the other two.

From revolutionary days until the early nineteenth century, on the other hand, the usual voting procedure was for the voter to write on a slip of paper the names of the candidates he favored and hand it over to the election judge, who in turn dropped it in the ballot box. This went by the board when party leaders, knowing that many of their supporters could not write and that for many who could, writing out a ballot was too heavy a chore to do willingly, began to have the names of their particular party's nominees run off on slips of paper by professional printers, so that all the voter had to do was accept a copy of the slip prepared by the party of his choice, carry it with him into the polling place, and hand it to the election judge for deposit in the ballot box. The offices to be filled were, as we know, numerous, so that the leader who wished to include the names of all his candidates often found himself passing out long narrow strips of paper that looked like railway tickets. So it was that a party's list of candidates for a particular election came to be— and still is—known as its "ticket." [17]

This system of voting soon came under sharp criticism, on the grounds that it helped the buyers of votes to see to it that the voters they corrupted delivered the goods, that it made for intimidation of other voters, and that, in general, it facilitated abuses of the democratic voting process. In due time, this criticism translated itself into a demand for the adoption of a system of voting generally known (because it was first used in Australia, in 1856) as the "Australian ballot." Harris defines the latter as "an official ballot, printed at public expense, by public officers, containing the names of all candidates duly nominated, and distributed at the polls by the election officers." [18] The notion of the "Australian ballot" also usually involves the element of *secrecy:* the ballot must be cast and counted in such a manner that no one can determine how a particular voter voted. [19] The first American state to adopt the Australian ballot was Kentucky, which did so in 1888. Kentucky's example was soon imitated by several other states, and this type of ballot is now used for all elections in each of the forty-eight states. (The last state to fall in line was South Carolina, which adopted it for all elections as recently as 1950.) [20]

For useful short summaries of this history, see Spencer D. Albright, *The American Ballot* (Washington, D. C.: American Council on Public Affairs, 1942), pp. 14-30; and Harris, *Election Administration in the United States,* pp. 150-54.

[17] Albright, *op. cit.,* p. 20.

[18] Harris, *Election Administration in the United States,* p. 154.

[19] In the British Commonwealth, the term further denotes a ballot that offers no indication of the candidates' party affiliations; in the United States, by contrast, an "Australian ballot" may or may not indicate party affiliation.

[20] Clyde F. Snider, *American State and Local Government* (New York: Appleton-Century-Crofts, 1950), p. 142.

Ballot Forms.[21] Ballots [22] differ considerably in form from state to state, despite the fact that all of them fall under the general heading "Australian." The major differences, however, have to do with the following four choices which ballot designers must make. The ballot must be of either:

(1) The party-column type or the office-group type. The *party-column ballot* lists all the candidates of a particular party in a single vertical column, the lists being printed side by side in such fashion that the names of all candidates for a particular office are in a horizontal line across the ballot. In 1953, thirty states were using this type of ballot.[23] The *office-group ballot,* by contrast, lists the candidates of all parties for a particular office in a vertical column under the heading for that office, and so discourages, or rather is said to discourage, "straight-ticket" voting by forcing the voter to consider the individual merits of each candidate for each office. Eighteen states now use it.

(2) The party-circle type or the no-party-circle type. On a *party-circle ballot,* each party participating in the election has its circle, printed at the top of the ballot, and the voter has only to make his "X" in the circle of the party of his choice in order to vote for all of its candidates. The purpose of this arrangement is, of course, to facilitate straight-ticket voting. Twenty-six states now use this type of ballot. In the other twenty-two, the voter can vote a straight ticket only by marking an "X" for each individual candidate of the party of his choice.

(3) The party-emblem type or the no-party-emblem type. Fourteen states now print on their ballots some kind of identifying emblem—an American flag, an eagle, a rooster, a plow, or whatever—at the head of each party's column or alongside each party's candidates, presumably to help the not-too-literate voter distinguish between the various party lists. The remaining thirty-four states permit no such emblems.

(4) Of the type permitting "write-ins" and "paste-ons" or of the "no-Johnnie-come-lately's" type. Most states offer the voter some means of voting for candidates whose names, usually because they became candidates after the deadline for getting on the ballot, do not appear on the ballot. Of these, the majority simply leave a blank line at the bottom of the list of candidates for each office, and here the voter "writes in" the name of the person he wishes to vote for. A few states permit him to "paste on" the ballot a gummed sticker bearing the name of a person whose name is not printed on the ballot. The states that forbid election officials to take cognizance of write-ins or paste-ons we may speak of as having the "no-Johnnie-come-lately's" type of ballot.

The ballots of some states have peculiarities not referable to any of these

[21] The most detailed discussion of this subject is to be found in Albright, *op. cit.* Harris, *Election Administration in the United States,* Ch. V, also has a useful summary of the various American ballot forms.

[22] We are here concerned only with the traditional *paper* ballot. Voting machines will be described in a later portion of the present chapter.

[23] This and all subsequent data about the incidence of types of ballot forms among the states are drawn from the *Book of the States, 1954-1955,* Vol. X, table on p. 82.

four choices. But the ballots of most states take their shape from the decisions legislators have made in each of the four areas of choice we have just noted.

Election Activities before Election Day

For purposes of examining how American electoral machinery usually works, let us fix attention on what happens in the "typical" precinct (a) before, (b) in the course of, and (c) after election day.

Before election day, the machinery goes into motion with the *call for the election*, which emanates from either the intermediate or the statewide supervisory officials. This proclamation designates the date on which the election is to be held and lists the offices to be filled. If the election is one in which national officers—senators, representatives, and presidential electors—are to be chosen, it must, by act of Congress, be held on the first Tuesday after the first Monday in November of the even-numbered years.[24] Forty-seven of the states invariably satisfy this requirement. The forty-eighth, Maine, enjoys a special dispensation permitting it to hold its congressional elections (but *not* its elections for presidential electors) along with its state elections in September of even-numbered years. Maine has no doubt been encouraged to keep on doing this because of the nationwide publicity lavished on it in virtue of its somewhat spurious reputation as a national political barometer ("as Maine goes, so goes the nation").[25] Many states elect state and local officials along with congressmen and senators in their November elections in order to avoid the expense of holding separate elections. The remainder make their elections for state and local officials a separate affair altogether, partly, it seems, out of the belief that if the two types of election are held simultaneously, the electoral verdict in the second is unduly influenced by the voting trend in the first. In no state are *all* elections held in November of even-numbered years.[26]

After the call for the election has been issued, the precinct boundaries are fixed, the polling places for the precincts chosen, and the election judges and clerks selected and announced. These matters are usually the responsibility of some local authority, such as the county board of commissioners or the city council.[27] The hours during which the polls will be open are fixed (over most of the country by the state legislature) and announced. In most states the polls stay open from eleven to twelve hours, opening as early as 6:00 A.M. and closing no later than 7:00 P.M.

[24] Representatives are chosen in *every* even-numbered year, and presidential electors in *every other* even-numbered year. In normal circumstances, a senator is chosen in a particular state in two out of every three even-numbered years. In common parlance, a year in which presidential electors are chosen is known as a "presidential year," and a year in which only representatives or representatives and senators are chosen is known as an "off year."

[25] Cf. Claude E. Robinson, "Maine—Political Barometer," *Political Science Quarterly*, Vol. XLVII (June, 1932), pp. 161-84.

[26] Cf. Albright, *op. cit.*, p. 32.

[27] Harris, *Election Administration in the United States*, p. 207.

Election-Day Activities

CASTING THE BALLOTS

The Steps in Casting a Ballot. Upon entering the polling place on election day, the voter must first be *identified*. This involves giving his name and address to the election board, who duly check it against the register of voters that has been certified to them by the appropriate authority, thus establishing his *eligibility*. The latter may, however, at once be called into question by a *challenger,* that is, someone appointed by one of the parties or candidates to remain on guard through election day against this or that type of electoral fraud. If challenged, the voter must take an oath that he is the person he claims to be and is duly qualified to vote. If not challenged, or if, having been challenged, he has taken the required oath, the voter receives his ballot from one of the judges, proceeds with it into a booth, and marks it. In most states this is a matter of making "X's" within the squares alongside the names of the candidates he wishes to vote for, or, if he wishes to vote a straight ticket, in the party circle of the party of his choice. In a few states, however, he votes by scratching out all the names except those of the candidates he favors; and in a few other states he can use either method of marking his ballot.[28] Having marked it, he hands his ballot to one of the judges, who promptly deposits it in the ballot box.

So it goes at the polling place for most voters in most elections in most states. A word now about absentee voting and about voting machines, which make for a slightly different procedure where they are used.

Absentee Voting.[29] Most states now make it possible for persons who cannot be present in their precinct on election day to cast a vote and have it counted with everybody else's. The relevant procedures vary somewhat from state to state, but the general pattern is as follows: (1) Within a specified period before election day, the voter must apply to an intermediate supervisory election officer (in many states, the county clerk) for an "absentee ballot." The application, which may be made either in person or by mail, involves the voter's taking an oath to the effect that he is duly qualified and will be absent from his precinct on election day. (2) The voter receives from the election officer the same ballots he would have found waiting for him at the polling place, marks them, places them in an official envelope, and executes an oath (printed on the back of the envelope) to the effect that he is a qualified voter and has marked the ballots in secret. (3) He hands or mails the envelope to the election officer, who, in turn, delivers it to the

---

[28] Albright, *op. cit.,* pp. 65-69.

[29] The most detailed recent studies of absentee voting are: James K. Pollock, *Absentee Voting and Registration* (Washington, D. C.: American Council on Public Affairs, 1940); and Paul B. Steinbicker, "Absentee Voting in the United States," *American Political Science Review,* Vol. XXXII (October, 1938), pp. 898-907.

election board of the voter's precinct. (4) On election day the precinct officials remove the ballots from the envelope and deposit them in the ballot box.

In view of the fact that only a small percentage of the total votes in any
American election are cast in this fashion, this question might be asked: Since,
other things being equal, absentees from an election might fairly be expected
to cancel each other out, do we need, in "normal" times, to go to all this
trouble to protect the voter against the temporary disfranchisement he allegedly
suffers by being away from home on election day? The answer, of course, is
that the times are *not* normal: the nation maintains, and seems likely to maintain through the foreseeable future, a large military establishment, which means
that on any election day hundreds of thousands of citizens are as a matter of
course unable to vote in their home precincts. Accordingly, failure to maintain
absentee voting arrangements with a minimum of red tape and inconvenience
would result in disfranchisement on a scale that the originators of the idea
of local-residence voting requirements certainly never had in mind. Thus in
1944 Congress enacted a "soldier-vote" law enabling military personnel to
vote absentee more easily in the presidential election of that year,[30] and a number of states have lately smoothed the way for absentee voting by servicemen
by appropriate changes in their relevant laws.

Voting Machines. The normal polling procedure based on written ballots
has for a long time been under heavy fire from political scientists and publicists interested in the good health of the democratic process. It is, they
charge, unduly expensive; it maximizes the possibilities of fraud and error;
and it has, in any case, been rendered obsolete by the now highly perfected
voting machine. The use of voting machines, these writers argue, would be
preferable to the old system even if it were equally expensive, and lent itself
equally to fraud and error; but in fact it works out much cheaper in the long
run, both in money and frayed nerves, and reduces the chance of fraud and
error almost to the vanishing point.

The voting machine was first invented in Europe, around the middle of
the nineteenth century, and its major imperfections were eliminated well before the end of the century. In America, its use in a regular election was first
authorized (by the State of New York) in 1892, since which time most states
have adopted it for some or all of their voting subdivisions. Some states, for
example, require the use of the voting machine in counties and cities with
a population above a certain figure. There seems no doubt that its vogue is
constantly increasing.[31]

In their present form, voting machines lend themselves equally well to
party-column or office-group balloting; and if the constituency wishes to provide for party-circle voting, the machines can take care of that too. There is

---

[30] Boyd A. Martin, "The Service Vote in the Elections of 1944," *American Political Science
Review,* Vol. XXXIX (August, 1945), pp. 720-32.

[31] Cf. Albright, *op. cit.,* Ch. IV; and Penniman, *op. cit.,* pp. 635-40.

even a machine that can be used for the simpler forms of proportional representation.

In general, voting machines affect the procedure described above as follows: The voter, having been identified, steps into a booth and draws a curtain, which automatically unlocks the machine for his use. He proceeds to vote either a split ticket (by pulling the levers opposite the names of individual candidates) or a straight ticket (by pulling one of the party levers). If he changes his mind before leaving the booth, he can rearrange the levers in any manner he chooses, since the machine stays unlocked until he leaves. When he has pulled the last lever, he opens the curtain, which action automatically locks the machine and registers his vote upon the "counter" dials for all the candidates for whom he has voted.

When the polls are closed, the compartment containing the counter dials is unlocked by the election officials and the totals are read off and reported. This, of course, is much simpler and easier than the endless shuffling of papers involved in tallying paper ballots. For those who are fascinated by "the great game of politics" it also provides a moment of more concentrated and focused drama in a long and usually dull day than the process of counting paper ballots can provide. The precinct party leaders will usually be on the spot to see the machine opened; and they and the election officials (most of whom, be it noted, are active party workers) can tell at a glance how their efforts have been rewarded. For the district party leader in particular this is the crucial moment; the figures on the dials will tell him whether he can point with pride to his district's showing, regardless of the over-all outcome of the election, or whether he will have some explaining to do when the results are analyzed by his party superiors. The equivalent satisfaction or disappointment comes much more slowly for the district party leader in a precinct where paper ballots are used; for in such a precinct the results emerge only gradually and bit by bit from the tedious process described below.

COUNTING THE BALLOTS

The polls close, and the election board turns at once to counting ballots. Here, as with other aspects of election machinery, there is much variation from state to state as to the procedures followed (over most of the country the law prescribes them in minute detail). In general, however, the following steps are involved: First, the number of ballots in the ballot box must be checked against the poll list. Second, the ballots must be sorted into two piles, one of "straight" ballots and one of "split" ballots. Third, each party's "straights" must be counted, and one vote tallied for each of each party's candidates for each one of that party's "straight" ballots. Fourth, the "split" ballots must be scanned one at a time, and a vote tallied for each candidate each time his name is marked on a ballot. Each judge, theoretically, must look on as each ballot is sorted and tallied; but it is notorious that in actual practice the judges tend to divide the work up, and so hasten the longed-for moment when everybody can at last go home. When all the tallies are completed, they are added together to make a precinct total for each candidate; then the "returns" (i.e., the totals for each candidate) are entered on the official form provided for this purpose, signed by all the judges, and delivered, along with the ballots, to the intermediate supervisory officials.

All these chores are, at best, exacting and wearisome, the more since they are usually performed late at night by election judges who have already, before sitting down to them, spent twelve long hours identifying voters and checking poll lists, and since they are often performed amid confusion and disorder, with too many people around, and not only around but talking. In most states, every party and every candidate is privileged to have a *watcher* present (often he is the same person who has served during voting hours as challenger). The watcher's task is to observe the counting, call irregularities and errors to the judges' attention, and serve as a witness of the results reported by the judges should they later be challenged. Harris believes that the chances both of fraud and of honest error are at their highest during the counting process, partly because of the latter's unavoidable cumbersomeness and partly because the officials who conduct it are tired and ought to be home in bed.[32]

Activities after the Election

THE CANVASS AND RECOUNTS

Within a specified period after the election, the intermediate supervisory officials conduct the *official canvass*. They go over the totals from each of the precincts, add them up, and announce and certify the official results. This, however, is a purely clerical function, since the officials in question have no power to go behind the precinct officials' tallies in order to rectify errors, round out incomplete returns, or ferret out suspected frauds. The power to make official recounts is vested in other officials, who alone can question the validity of the returns from the precinct election boards.

In most states, any candidate, or any group of citizens interested in a particular referendum measure, can secure a recount of the votes, in some cases merely on demand, in others by offering some evidence at least of error or misconduct in the original count. In some states recounts are supervised by the courts; over most of the nation, however, they are supervised by a legislative body, either the state legislature or the city council within whose jurisdiction the error or misconduct is alleged to have occurred. In general, the procedure for a recount is as follows: Having brought together representatives of all interested parties, candidates, and organizations, the officials authorized to conduct the recount re-examine the ballots, determine the validity of each individual ballot, recount and retally the votes for each candidate, and

[32] Harris, *Election Administration in the United States,* pp. 220-46.

announce the revised official results. In some states the courts are authorized to review the decisions of the recounting authorities; in most states the latter's decisions are final.[33]

The Special Case of Presidential Electors

A BRIEF HISTORY OF THE ELECTORAL COLLEGE

The electoral-college system for selecting the president and vice-president has posed a number of special problems for the conduct of elections in the forty-eight states. That system was devised by the Founding Fathers as a middle course between popular election and "mob rule" on the one hand and congressional selection on the other (congressional selection was believed to be incompatible with the principle of separation of powers). The framers of the Constitution expected that the electors, each of whom presumably would cast his vote on the basis of his own individual judgment rather than on the basis of his commitment to some organized political group, would rarely give a majority to a single candidate. Accordingly, they provided (in Article II, Section I, later altered by the Twelfth Amendment) that in each election in which no candidate receives a majority of the electoral votes, the House of Representatives shall choose among the three candidates having the largest pluralities, with each state's delegation having one vote. It is clear that the framers expected that in most presidential elections the electoral college would nominate and the House of Representatives would elect.[34]

In specifying how the electors shall be chosen, the Constitution (Article II, Section I) provides merely that "each State shall appoint, in such Manner as the Legislature thereof may direct, a Number of Electors, equal to the whole Number of Senators and Representatives to which the State may be entitled in the Congress." During the early years of the Republic, electors from most of the states were chosen by the state legislatures, so that in only a few states have electors always been chosen by popular election. By 1832, however, the electors were popularly elected in every state except South Carolina (which did not provide for popular election until after the Civil War); and ever since that year the leading political parties in each state have presented "tickets" of candidates for elector, each pledged to vote for his respective party's national nominees for president and vice-president. Until the end of the nineteenth century, to be sure, the would-be electors appeared on the ballots of the states

---

[33] *Ibid.*, pp. 305-14.

[34] The Founding Fathers' expectations in this regard were, of course, seldom realized. The nominating function was assumed by the Federalist and Republican parties in the late 1790's, and from that time to the present the electors have cast their votes for the nominees of their particular parties. Only two elections have been thrown into the House of Representatives: that of 1800, in which *both* Republican candidates, Jefferson and Burr, received majorities, thereby leading to the adoption of the Twelfth Amendment (which provided, among other things, that each elector shall cast separate ballots for president and vice-president); and that of 1824, at which time the nation had something very like a national multiple-party system.

as individual candidates, though their party affiliations and the particular presidential candidates to whom they were pledged were generally known by the voters. And these implicit pledges have been consistently redeemed, not in general because of any laws obligating electors to vote for the national nominees of their respective parties, but because of the strength of party ties and, more and more as time has passed, because the custom is so deeply rooted that no elector would think of violating it. Only twice since the 1816 election has an elector voted for a candidate other than the nominee of his party.[35] In short, the political parties have been mainly responsible for turning the electoral college, originally intended as a guarantee against a popularly elected and popularly controlled presidency, into a sort of score board for an electoral process which, according to most observers, has virtually made the presidency a genuinely plebiscitary office.

Around the turn of the century, some of the states formally recognized the "party rubber stamp" character of the electors. First Massachusetts (1892), then Minnesota (1901), began to group all the candidates for elector for each party together under the party's label; and soon Kansas (1897) and Wisconsin (1901) were printing the names of each party's nominees for president and vice-president at the head of its list of candidates for elector. The next logical step came in 1917, when Nebraska adopted the *presidential short ballot,* which omits the names of individual candidates for elector and bears only the names of the nominees for president and vice-president of the several parties. An "X" marked in the box beside a party's nominees (there is only one box for each party, so that the voter cannot split his ticket for the two offices) constitutes a vote for each of that party's candidates for elector.[36]

THE PRESENT STATUS OF PRESIDENTIAL ELECTORS [37]

Arrangements regarding the nomination, election, and instruction of electors are by no means the same over the country as a whole, though we may note that each of them is handled in the same way by at least a majority of the states.

Nomination. As of 1948, there were 27 states in which the nomination of presidential electors was left to the state conventions of the several parties, 10 in which it was left to some party organization other than the state convention, 7 in which nomination was by direct primary, and 3 in which nomi-

---

[35] In 1820, William Plumer of New Hampshire, though pledged to vote for the Republican party's nominee, James Monroe, voted in the electoral college for John Quincy Adams on the ground that "only Washington deserved a unanimous election." In 1948, Preston Parks of Tennessee, who was elected on the official Democratic ticket, voted in the electoral college for Thurmond, though Harry Truman was the official nominee of the national Democratic party and of the Tennessee Democratic party. We shall consider this episode in greater detail below.

[36] See Albright, *op. cit.,* pp. 99-107, for a brief history of the election of presidential electors.

[37] The most recent survey of this subject is Ruth C. Silva, "State Law on the Nomination, Election, and Instruction of Presidential Electors," *American Political Science Review,* Vol. XLII (June, 1948), pp. 527-29.

nation might be by either the primary or the convention method. The remaining state, Pennsylvania, has adopted the unique practice of entrusting the nomination of electors for each party to its presidential nominee.

Election. As of 1953, there were 27 states using the presidential short ballot (see above), and 21 that stuck to some more traditional practice.[38] Of the latter states, 5 printed the names of the candidates for elector only, omitting the names of the nominee for president and vice-president, while the remainder either used a ballot bearing the names both of the candidates for elector and of the presidential and vice-presidential candidates, or required that the names of candidates for elector appear on the ballot, but permitted the names of the presidential and vice-presidential candidates to appear also if the latter's party organization so determined.

Instruction. The ballot laws of most states are clearly based on the assumption that a party's candidates for elector will, if elected, vote in the electoral college "as instructed"—i.e., for the candidates for president and vice-president designated as that party's official candidates by the state party agency that is authorized by law to perform this function. Only two states, however, have statutes actually *requiring* electors to vote their "instructions." We may note in passing that a number of problems relating to the legal status of presidential electors' instructions arose during the 1948 election, when the "Dixiecrats" sought to capture the Democratic party organizations in the southern states. The "Dixiecrats" argued that a state Democratic party is completely independent of the national party and can, if it chooses, instruct its electors to vote for presidential and vice-presidential candidates other than those named by the party's national convention. In the four states they carried (Alabama, Louisiana, Mississippi, and South Carolina), the "Dixiecrats" did capture the official Democratic party machinery, and did name candidates for elector pledged to Thurmond and Wright.[39]

PRESTON PARKS AND THE TENNESSEE "REVOLT" OF 1948

For the most striking recent departure from the normal behavior pattern for presidential electors we must look to the 1948 election in Tennessee. The Democratic state convention, meeting in April, chose its prescribed twelve candidates for elector. When, however, the Democratic national convention nominated Truman and Barkley and adopted a vigorous federal civil-rights platform, and some southerners responded by launching a "States' Rights" party and nominating Governors Thurmond and Wright for president and vice-president, three of the Tennessee Democratic candidates for elector— Malcolm Hill of Sparta, Walter P. Armstrong of Memphis, and Preston Parks of Somerville—declared that, if elected, they would vote for Thurmond and Wright and not Truman and Barkley. Armstrong later withdrew his candidacy, and the state executive committee replaced him with a pro-Truman

---

[38] *Book of the States, 1954-1955,* Vol. X, table on p. 82.
[39] See pp. 427-31 for an account of the "Dixiecrat" movement.

candidate. Hill and Parks, however, were duly nominated as candidates for elector by the States' Rights party of Tennessee, so that when the November election came around their names appeared twice on the ballot. The popular votes, when tallied, produced the following curious results: 270,402 votes for the Democratic candidates for elector, among them Hill and Parks, and 73,815 votes for the States' Rights candidates, among them Hill and Parks. Hill promptly announced that he would bow to the electorate's "overwhelming preference" for Truman, and cast his vote in the electoral college for Truman, not Thurmond. Parks, by contrast, ignored the popular vote and, when the electoral college met at Washington on December 13, 1948, cast his vote for Thurmond.[40] Whether Parks (or Hill, by voting for Truman) violated his "instructions" is a question that can be decided, evidently, only on the basis of a prior answer to the question, Was the Democratic nomination, because first in point of time, more binding than the States' Rights nomination? Certainly Parks did not so regard it.[41] Parks' "revolt" did not, of course, affect the actual outcome of the electoral college's decision; had it done so, it would presumably have raised issues of an extremely dramatic character. But the next Parks revolt *might* affect the outcome, and it is well for students of the American political system to keep themselves reminded that the electoral college, however innocuous in the typical election, involves areas of indeterminacy that are potential dynamite.

Another recent incident is worth noting in this connection. In 1952, the executive committee of the Alabama Democratic party required its candidates for elector to sign a pledge committing them, if elected, to "aid and support the nominees of the National Convention of the Democratic party for President and Vice-President of the United States." One candidate, Edmund Blair, refused to take the pledge, and sought a writ of mandamus to compel Ben F. Ray, chairman of the executive committee, to certify his nomination in spite of his refusal. The national Constitution, he argued, clearly intends electors to be free to vote as they see fit, and requiring them to pledge their votes to particular candidates is clearly unconstitutional. The Alabama Supreme Court upheld Blair's contention; but the United States Supreme Court, by a five to two vote, reversed the state court's decision, holding that custom and usage have sanctioned "instruction" of presidential electors by party agencies. Noth-

[40] See the New York *Times,* November 4, 1948, p. 2, and December 14, 1948, p. 35, for the details of this story.

[41] Arthur Krock pointed out that Hill's home county has less than 500 Negroes in a total population of 16,000, whereas Parks' home county has more Negroes than whites. Moreover, Krock quoted Hill as saying that if by voting for Thurmond he could have thrown the election into the House of Representatives, he would have done it: New York *Times,* December 16, 1948, p. 28. We learn from the same source that Senator Ellender of Louisiana told President Truman, shortly after the election, that he was trying to persuade the electors of his state—who had been elected on the Democratic ticket with Thurmond and Wright as the official Democratic candidates—to violate their instructions and vote for Truman instead. Truman replied that, all things considered, he "didn't want them": New York *Times,* November 25, 1948, p. 39.

ing in the Constitution, the Supreme Court concluded, prohibits reinforcement of this custom and usage by a legally imposed pledge.[42]

Election Frauds

Post-election charges of electoral fraud—some subsequently substantiated and some subsequently disproved—have been a characteristic feature of American politics ever since the beginnings of the Republic. In 1790, for example, General Anthony Wayne was elected to a seat in the House of Representatives from Georgia, and was duly seated. His defeated opponent, James Jackson, "contested" his election, charging that there had been fraud at the polls; and the House, having investigated the charges, voted to oust Wayne and declare his seat vacant.[43] In 1954 a majority of the Senate Subcommittee on Privileges and Elections, reporting on the New Mexico senatorial election of 1952, alleged that 55,000 voters had been denied the right of secret ballot, that 17,000 ballots had been altered fraudulently, and that 13,000 ballots had been counted and then burned, thus estopping any possible inquiry into whether they had been properly cast and tallied.[44] The full Senate later voted down a motion to declare the seat in question vacant; but few stepped forward to insist that the election had been entirely free of fraud.[45] Similar incidents could be cited for every election year between 1790 and 1954, and for each level of American government. No discussion of American electoral machinery would be complete, therefore, if it did not take note of the various types of fraud, whether successful or not, which have accompanied its operation, and seek to estimate the incidence of fraud in the current conduct of elections.

TYPES OF FRAUD [46]

Registration Frauds. These generally take the form of "padding the register," that is, putting or keeping on the register of eligible voters the names of persons no longer living, persons who have moved away, or—where daring matches ingenuity—persons invented by the perpetrators of the fraud—all, of course, with a view to having their votes cast by trusted repeaters on election day.[47]

Ballot-Casting Frauds. Here we include such practices as *repeating,* that is, sending the same person from precinct to precinct to vote under some of the fraudulent names on the "padded" register, or *ballot-box stuffing,* which is a

[42] *Ray v. Blair,* 343 U.S. 214 (1952).

[43] Harris, *Election Administration in the United States,* pp. 315-16.

[44] Cf. the Hearings before the Subcommittee on Privileges and Elections, United States Senate, 83rd Congress, 1st Session, on the Contest of Patrick J. Hurley v. Dennis Chavez.

[45] New York *Times,* March 24, 1954, pp. 1, 15.

[46] Cf. the discussion in Harris, *Election Administration in the United States,* pp. 37-75; and in Albright, *op. cit.,* pp. 43-46.

[47] The story is told that all the signers of the Declaration of Independence were still voting regularly in all local, state, and national elections in Philadelphia on the eve of World War I!

matter of running up the tally on your side by getting into the ballot-box appropriately marked illegal ballots (usually a difficult feat to bring off without the connivance of the precinct election officials). The latter type of fraud usually occurs shortly before the polls close, when the names of qualified voters who have not put in their appearance can be spotted and ballots cast for them. Another practice worth mentioning is *chain voting,* sometimes called the "Tasmanian dodge." An official ballot is procured somehow in advance of the election, marked for the right candidates, and handed to a "dependable" voter, who tucks it under his coat, goes to the polls, gets his blank ballot from the judges, enters the booth, switches the two ballots, then hands the marked ballot to the judge and the blank ballot, which he carries away under his coat, to his contact outside the polls—so that it also can be marked for the right candidates and then be traded, in the manner just described, for a new blank ballot. The purpose of the chain, of course, is to see to it that votes, once bought and paid for, are actually cast in the manner desired. Finally, there is outright *intimidation and violence,* especially coercive steps calculated to scare known opposition voters and challengers away from the polls. (In Harris' opinion, this sort of thing is much less common today than a century ago.[48])

Ballot-counting Frauds. One practice in this category is that of *altering and spoiling ballots,* e.g., piling up your candidate's vote by writing X's in on uncompleted ballots, or reducing your opponent's vote by making illegal marks on opposition ballots so that they will be thrown out. (For the latter purpose, the spoiler merely conceals an almost imperceptible sliver of graphite under a fingernail, and gets busy when nobody is looking.) Another practice is that of *substituting* ballots—that is, replacing opposition ballots with favorable ones. Still another is *making false counts and false returns,* or *altering returns,* as when the officials conducting the official count and canvass deliberately return totals padded in favor of the party or the candidate they prefer.

In the very nature of the case, as noted above, these frauds for the most part require at least the connivance of the precinct election officials. Most students of the subject, indeed, agree that the most effective way of preventing election frauds lies not in passing elaborate election laws and prosecuting those who violate them, but in fixing attention on the caliber of precinct judges and clerks.[49]

HOW OFTEN ARE FRAUDS PERPETRATED?

On the basis of the evidence now available, we can estimate only in the most general and impressionistic way the incidence of fraud in American elections. Most present-day students lean to the view that our elections are still far from pure, but are much improved in comparison with American elections of the 1850's; and we are often told that electoral frauds are now more com-

[48] Harris, *Election Administration in the United States,* p. 316.
[49] Cf. *ibid.,* pp. 377-82.

mon in urban than in rural areas.[50] Professor Harris, who has probably studied this subject more thoroughly than any other recent analyst, concluded in
1934 than "honest elections have become the established rule in most sections
of the country, and boisterous conduct at the polls is confined to a few large
cities. Election frauds have not disappeared, but they are going." [51]

The Parties' Election-contesting Jobs

We noted in Chapter 12 that the sheer number of elective offices and the
resultant frequency of elections at all levels of American government except
the national impose a heavy burden of nomination-making chores on any
American party seriously contending for power against serious opposition,
although both parties escape it to some extent in the modified one-party areas,
and almost entirely in the one-party areas. We can now venture a similar
statement about the parties' election-contesting activities: If they are seriously
contending for power against serious opposition, they have a great many jobs
to do between the time the nominations have been made and the time the final-
election results are announced. The outsider may be inclined to think that all
the parties have to do is campaign, and that if they campaign well they will
win elections automatically. But any party worker or leader knows better;
given the character of American electoral machinery, a party that means business has on its hands a long list of chores that have little or nothing to do with
campaigning in the ordinary sense of that term.[52] Of these we must notice at
least the following:

(1) *Getting voters registered.* What a party needs from those who approve
its candidates and program is not so much support, though this helps, but
votes. Other things being equal, it would rather have Citizen A's mild support
backed up by a vote than Citizen B's enthusiastic support eventuating in just
talk. And since no one can vote unless properly registered, the party's first
task is to make sure that its supporters get their names on the register. More

---

[50] Cf. V. O. Key, Jr., *Politics, Parties, and Pressure Groups,* 3rd ed. (New York: Thomas Y.
Crowell Company, 1952), pp. 644-48; Hugh A. Bone, *American Politics and the Party System*
(New York: McGraw-Hill Book Company, Inc., 1949), pp. 667-69; Dayton D. McKean, *Party
and Pressure Politics* (Boston: Houghton Mifflin Company, 1949), pp. 365-67. Such studies of
recent "bosses" as Dayton D. McKean, *The Boss: The Hague Machine in Action* (Boston:
Houghton Mifflin Company, 1940), and William M. Reddig, *Tom's Town* (Philadelphia: J. B.
Lippincott Company, 1947), deal at length with the amount and type of frauds practiced by their
protagonists, and conclude that fraud was a very small and unimportant factor in their power.
The two volumes on present-day state and local governments edited by Raymond S. Allen,
Our Fair City (New York: The Vanguard Press, Inc., 1947) and *Our Sovereign State* (New
York: The Vanguard Press, Inc., 1949), convey—without much supporting evidence—the impression that election frauds are normal practice in the United States. Between 1940 and 1953, we
may note in passing, thirty of the elections for seats in both houses of Congress have been contested, but all the contests were dismissed by the congressional investigating committees, and no
seat was declared vacant. For the record before 1940, see Vincent M. Barnett, Jr., "Contested
Congressional Elections in Recent Years," *Political Science Quarterly,* Vol. LIV (1939), pp. 187-215.

[51] *Election Administration in the United States,* pp. 319-20.

[52] Campaigning *per se* will be discussed in Chapter 15.

concretely, it must (a) identify its supporters, (b) find out which ones are not registered, and (c) keep after them until they have taken all the necessary steps for getting registered.

(2) *Getting the voters to vote.* With its supporters properly registered, the party's next job is to make sure that they vote. This often means, for one thing, providing them with transportation to the polls, and answering the telephone or baby-sitting for them while they are on their way to and fro. It also means stationing someone at the polling place to keep a running check on which of the party's supporters have turned up and which have not, so that, a few hours before the polls close, he can relay the no-shows' names to headquarters and let it go to work on them. The party must also ascertain which of its supporters are to be out of town on election day, and see to it that they cast absentee ballots.

(3) *Getting the voters to mark their ballots properly.* An improperly marked ballot is no better, from the party's point of view, than a ballot not marked at all. The party must, therefore, do what it can to make sure that its supporters mark their ballots correctly. To this end, it distributes properly marked sample ballots to its supporters and urges them to study the sample so carefully that they cannot fail to reproduce it. And if the party's fortunes should depend, because of last-minute developments, on "write-ins" or "paste-ons," it must redouble its efforts in this department.

(4) *Making sure the ballots are counted and the results reported correctly.* Since properly marked ballots by properly registered voters do no good unless they are counted and reported accurately, the party must make sure that its election officials and its watchers know the law and see that it is enforced. Or, if that is a counsel of perfection, it must at least make sure that the counting and reporting process does not illegally discriminate *against* its candidates.

(5) *Making sure that the opposition obeys the law.* The party must do all it can to detect and prevent such illegal practices by its opponents and their supporters as voting ineligible and unregistered voters, casting illegally marked ballots, improperly counting, tallying, reporting, and canvassing the results, and engaging in any of the several types of frauds described above.

(6) *Contesting recounts.* If the party leaders feel they can prove fraud against the opposition in an election which the former have lost, they must demand—and follow through on—recount proceedings. And vice versa: if the opposition demands a recount, they must defend their candidates' totals.

Not every party in every area, of course, performs all these chores in all elections, or performs any of them exhaustively. But any party that means business about winning elections and faces serious opposition must *try* to perform them as well as it can. And no major party in a two-party area which consistently performs them badly or not at all can reasonably hope to win many elections.

The foregoing discussion has focused upon what we may call the "safe" votes—those which can be depended upon to produce valid tallies in favor of the party's candidates, so long as the mechanics of the voting process have been adequately performed and the safeguards adhered to. But no major party in a two-party area can ever afford to take its voters for granted. It must strive constantly to retain the votes it has, and to secure as many new votes as possible. How American parties go about achieving these goals is the subject of our next chapter.

Chapter 15

CONTESTING
ELECTIONS:
WINNING THE VOTES

In the two-party areas, as we know, the major parties' prime objective is winning elections. The payoff for them, therefore, is *votes,* as the payoff for, say, a manufacturer is sales. The manufacturer either sells his line or he fails, and he cannot laugh off his failure by proving to himself or somebody else that his product beats the world in quality; and the political party either gets enough votes to win elections or it fails, and it cannot laugh off *its* failure by proving how superior its candidates are or how cogent and courageous its policies. For party and manufacturer alike, offering a good sound product and backing it up with a good sound organization are valued goals, but *intermediate* goals, valued because—or insofar as—they put the product over with the consumers.

There is, therefore, a sense in which *all* the activities of American parties—making nominations, writing platforms, campaigning, organizing government, and the rest—are "electioneering." Those who conduct them, that is to say, must always be asking themselves these questions: What will the voters think of what we are doing? Will it help us win the next election?

American parties, however, expend far more energy and far more money on "campaigning" [1] than parties in other self-governing countries. In a parliamentary democracy, for example, an election may come at any moment, and therefore the parties' representatives in the government campaign continuously —lest they be caught off guard. By American standards, to be sure, their "campaigns," save for the month immediately preceding a general election, are extremely leisurely and low-pressure affairs. [2] With us, by contrast, the intervals between elections are in general specified by law, and everybody knows, therefore, that the party in power can be displaced only after the specified interval

---

[1] Here used in the strict sense of the term, to mean the direct appeals to the voters made in the period immediately preceding a particular election and calculated to win votes in that election.

[2] Cf. Herman Finer, *Theory and Practice of Modern Democracy,* rev. ed. (New York: Henry Holt and Company, 1949), p. 589.

has run its course. Our election campaigns, accordingly, last longer (usually three months at least), and our parties spend far more energy and money on them than those in the parliamentary democracies.[3] To return to our analogy: if the manufacturers of automobiles could make sales only on one legally specified day every two years, their sales campaigns would be scheduled for the period immediately preceding that specified day, and would assume a level of intensity during that period that is unnecessary when, as at the present time, sales may be made at any time.

The purpose of the present chapter is to describe the campaigning activities of American parties—their goals, their organization, their techniques, and their effect upon the voters.

How to Win Votes: The Politicians' Theory

The leaders—the men who direct our parties' campaigns—face problems in "strategy" and "tactics" no less urgent and difficult than those our military leaders are called upon to solve in directing our military campaigns when the nation is at war. In deciding what steps to take and what order to take them in, party leaders, like generals, try to rely as little as possible on intuition (hunches) and coin flipping, and as much as possible on cool calculation based on the results of reflective analysis of past experience—i.e., *theory*. And the first step toward understanding the kind of campaigns they conduct is to come to grips with the theory on which they proceed.

The politicians' theory involves, on the one hand, a set of notions about what makes voters vote as they do, and, on the other hand, a set of notions about how parties, on the basis of those voter motivations, can maximize the votes for their candidates. No one, however, has ever attempted to set down a systematic and authoritative statement of even its major propositions, so that the student who wishes to take a look at it has to piece it together for himself—partly from published statements by political leaders who have written about campaigning, and partly from observation of what the parties actually do during campaigns.

WHAT MAKES VOTERS VOTE FOR ONE
CANDIDATE INSTEAD OF ANOTHER?

There appears to be general agreement among politicians upon the following propositions as to what makes voters vote as they do:

(1) The "against" vote is stronger than the "for" vote—that is, voters vote both "for" and "against" persons, parties, and states of affairs, but they

---

[3] Cf. Peter H. Odegard and E. Allen Helms, *American Politics*, 2nd ed. (New York: Harper and Brothers, 1947). D. W. Brogan argues that the greater frequency of elections and the intermingling of national and state politics in the United States means that many American officeholders, especially members of the House and the president, who must get along with them, "must be thinking of elections virtually all the time": *Politics in America* (New York: Harper and Brothers, 1954), pp. 235-36.

tend to be more conscious of—and easier to mobilize about—what they are against than what they are for. Thus voters who dislike or deplore a particular party or candidate are more likely to vote, without prodding and pushing from other people, than voters who merely like or approve of a party or candidate.[4] In the current jargon of the social sciences, the man with negative reactions to one of the parties or candidates is more likely to go to the polls than the man with positive reactions.

(2) Voters tend to vote for whatever they identify with "more pork chops" and against what they identify with "fewer pork chops"—that is, they try to cast their votes in such a manner as to protect and advance their own economic interests.

(3) Voters tend to vote for the party and candidate likely to view with favor—and forward the interests of—their ethnic group, and against the party and candidate who seem to them to "look down" on it or work against its interests.[5]

(4) Voters gravitate toward and are activated by candidates with attractive personalities, shun and turn a deaf ear to candidates with unattractive personalities.[6]

(5) Most voters like to be on the popular and winning side, so that wayerers, in deciding how to vote, weigh their expectations as to which party or candidate is likely to win along with their expectations as to which is likely to do the better job.[7]

(6) Most voters are not much interested in politics, and, if left to themselves, tend to be "politically inert." The campaigner therefore has to persuade voters that it is "important" for them to vote, that is, that they have a genuine stake in the outcome of the election. Few voters will go to the polls under their own steam: the organization has to *get* them there.

(7) Nobody, not even the pollsters, can foretell with certainty what the voters will do in a given election. Overconfidence, therefore, is a luxury no party or candidate can possibly afford; and the best course, no matter how much evidence there may be that an election is in the bag, is to take no chances, and campaign as hard as time and resources permit.

[4] Cf. Oliver Carlson and Aldrich Blake, *How to Get into Politics: The Art of Winning Elections* (New York: Duell, Sloan, and Pearce, 1946), p. 119; and Turner Catledge, "The ABC's of Political Campaigning," *New York Times Magazine,* September 22, 1940, p. 9.

[5] See, for example, Samuel Lubell's discussion of the parties' catering to Italo-Americans, Irish Catholics, Polish-Americans, and German-Americans: *The Future of American Politics* (New York: Harper and Brothers, 1951), pp. 66-75, 222-25, 52, 133-34, 159-60.

[6] Cf. Raymond E. Baldwin (former governor of and U.S. senator from Connecticut), *Let's Go into Politics* (New York: The Macmillan Company, 1952), p. 92. James A. Farley wrote that one of the main reasons for Franklin D. Roosevelt's success with the voters was that so many of them regarded him as a warm, affectionate, solid, and reliable human being: *Behind the Ballots* (New York: Harcourt, Brace and Company, 1938), pp. 318-20.

[7] Cf. Roy V. Peel and Thomas C. Donnelly, *The 1932 Campaign* (New York: Farrar and Rinehart, Inc., 1935), p. 143.

HOW CAN A PARTY MAXIMIZE ITS VOTES?

On the basis of the foregoing notions about voter motivations and behavior, the politicians have developed a set of notions about how a party or candidate should go about winning the largest possible number of votes:

(1) The basis for any successful campaign is a well-planned and effective *organization,* extending from the top-level strategists all the way down to the precinct workers. One central purpose of the campaign is to induce as many voters as possible to prefer *your* candidates to the opposition's, and this necessitates (a) identifying those voters who do prefer your candidates, and (b) getting them to go to the polls and cast valid votes on election day. Both (a) and (b) clearly call for a substantial number of loyal, tireless, enthusiastic workers at the county and precinct level. As for effective top-level organization, it will prevent the lost motion and working-at-cross-purposes that characterize badly organized campaigns, and minimize the dangers of unpredictable adverse developments in the campaign.[8]

(2) The wisest campaign strategy is to be always on the offensive, i.e., never to be maneuvered into a defensive or apologetic position. Many voters, as we have seen, regard politics as a dirty business anyway, and this means that they are more ready to believe charges than alibis. Since, moreover, voters tend to be against things rather than for them, they are more disposed to "identify" with the attackers in any political scrap than with those who are attempting to repel the attack. Similarly, the appropriate response to an attack is to mount an immediate counterattack, preferably more vigorous and hard-hitting than the attack it is intended to counter; and the appropriate response to a "charge" or "exposé" is a still more damaging countercharge or counterexposé. (In a pinch, however, accusing your opponents of "smearing" and "mudslinging" may turn the trick.)[9]

(3) In making your "pitch" to the voters, take care not to scatter your fire. Stick to a few simple, easily grasped appeals, dramatize them, hammer away at them. Talk about the issues *your* side thinks it can win on, not those raised by your opponents.

(4) Be careful not to offend or antagonize any economic, ethnic, or religious group that might give your candidates substantial support. Attack only those groups which you know beforehand won't support your side whatever you do or say; and avoid irritating even these groups unnecessarily.[10]

---

[8] This point is strongly emphasized by most of the politicians who have written about the art of campaigning: Cf. Baldwin, *op. cit.,* p. 100; Edward J. Flynn, *You're the Boss* (New York: The Viking Press, 1947), Ch. 13; and Allen Morris (campaign manager for former Governor Fuller Warren of Florida) in Fuller Warren, *How to Win in Politics* (Tallahassee, Fla.: Peninsular Publishing Company, 1949), pp. 112-13. It should also be remembered, however, that few campaign organizations actually achieve such perfect coordination: Cf. Roy V. Peel and Thomas C. Donnelly, *The 1928 Campaign* (New York: Richard R. Smith, Inc., 1931), pp. 36, 87, 106.

[9] Carlson and Blake, *op. cit.;* Catledge, *op. cit.;* V. O. Key, Jr., *Politics, Parties, and Pressure Groups,* 3rd ed. (New York: Thomas Y. Crowell Company, 1952), pp. 488-98.

[10] Richard L. Neuberger, successful Democratic candidate for U.S. senator from Oregon in

(5) Try to put over a picture of the opposition's candidate—if these are the worst things that can plausibly be said about him—as a "politician," job-hungry, ineffectual, and unimportant. Let the hatchet-work on the opposition candidate be done, however, by persons other than your leading candidate, who must not appear to be "indulging in personalities" or "mudslinging." [11] Meantime, try to get across to the voters a picture of your candidate as a "statesman," but a man whose achievements have not "gone to his head" or caused him to lose the "common touch."

(6) If the election appears to be close or if your side appears to have the edge, act and talk as if you—and everybody else—knew that victory is sure to be yours. If you can do this convincingly enough, a greater or lesser number of waverers will "jump on the bandwagon." But you must be careful, at the same time, not to encourage overconfidence or apathy within your own organization and among your own supporters.[12]

(7) Given the sheer number of voters to be reached in the typical American constituency, a party must rely in large part on the mass-communications media. But this does not alter the fact that the best way for a candidate to "sell" himself and win support for his program is to appear *personally* before as many voters as possible and speak to them. Voters like to vote for a man who has stood in their presence, whose voice they have heard unmediated by electronics, and with whom, therefore, they feel they have had some sort of personal contact—the more personal, and the more of it, the better. This is why hand-shaking is something the candidate dare not leave off his agenda,[13] and why even television appearances, though in a sense they bring the candi-

---

1954, puts this point strongly in his article about the campaigns in which he has participated: "I Run for Office," *Harper's,* Vol. CXCIV (February, 1947), pp. 153-59. See also Richard L. Neuberger, *Adventures in Politics* (New York: Oxford University Press, 1954); Charles W. Smith, *Public Opinion in a Democracy* (New York: Prentice-Hall, Inc., 1939), pp. 168-89; and Charles Michelson, *The Ghost Talks* (New York: G. P. Putnam's Sons, 1944), p. 45.

[11] Thus in the 1936, 1940, and 1944 presidential campaigns, Franklin Roosevelt did not mention his opponents by name; the "belittling" campaigns against them were conducted by other Democratic politicians. See Theodore M. Black, *Democratic Party Publicity in the 1940 Campaign* (New York: Plymouth Publishing Company, 1941), pp. 107 ff.; and Charles Michelson's account of the strategy used in 1936, New York *Times,* November 15, 1936, s. 4, p. 10.

[12] Most observers stress the illusion-of-victory technique: Cf. Key, *op. cit.,* pp. 488-98; Catledge, *op. cit.;* and Black, *op. cit.,* pp. 109-10. There is some reason to believe, moreover, that a "bandwagon effect" does exist in voting behavior, although no one can say exactly how far-reaching it is or what its psychological determinants are: Cf. Donald T. Campbell, "On the Possibility of Experimenting with the 'Bandwagon' Effect," *International Journal of Opinion and Attitude Research,* Vol. V (Summer, 1951), pp. 251-60. In the 1954 congressional elections, be it noted, the Republican leaders were convinced that they were behind as they went into the last weeks of the campaign, but generally took the line that the election could still be pulled out of the fire by extra-hard work by the party organization and by all-out campaigning by President Eisenhower.

[13] Most of the practicing politicians emphasize this point over and over again: Cf. Baldwin, *op. cit.,* p. 92; Farley, *op. cit.,* pp. 162-65; Warren, *op. cit.,* Chs. 2 and 5; and Harold R. Bruce, "Presidential Campaigns," in Edward B. Logan, ed., *The American Political Scene* (New York: Harper and Brothers, 1936), pp. 127-69.

date "closer" to the voter than he can possibly get to them in a large public meeting, are a poor second-best to personal appearances. This makes campaigning very strenuous for the candidate, even where there is little travel involved, and makes it an ordeal of marathon proportions where travel is involved. But it wins votes, and politicians, votes entirely aside, derive some satisfactions from it. Adlai E. Stevenson, the Democratic presidential candidate in 1952, testifies to both of these points:

You must emerge, bright and bubbling with wisdom and well-being, every morning at 8 o'clock, just in time for a charming and profound breakfast talk, shake hands with hundreds, often literally thousands, of people, make several inspiring, "newsworthy" speeches during the day, confer with political leaders along the way and with your staff all the time, write at every chance, think if possible, read mail and newspapers, talk on the telephone, talk to everybody, dictate, receive delegations, eat, with decorum—and discretion!—and ride through city after city on the back of an open car, smiling until your mouth is dehydrated by the wind, waving until the blood runs out of your arms, and then bounce gaily, confidently, masterfully into great howling halls, shaved and all made up for television with the right color shirt and tie—I always forgot—and a manuscript so defaced with chicken tracks and last-minute jottings that you couldn't follow it, even if the spotlight weren't blinding and even if the still photographers didn't shoot you in the eye every time you looked at them. (I've often wondered what happened to all those pictures.) Then all you have to do is to make a great, imperishable speech, get out through the pressing crowds with a few score autographs, your clothes intact, your hands bruised, and back to the hotel—in time to see a few important people.

But the real work has just commenced—two or three, sometimes four hours of frenzied writing and editing of the next day's immortal mouthings so you can get something to the stenographers, so they can get something to the mimeograph machines, so they can get something to the reporters, so they can get something to their papers by deadline time. (And I quickly concluded that all deadlines were yesterday!) Finally sleep, sweet sleep, steals you away, unless you worry—which I do.

The next day is the same.

But I gained weight on it. Somehow the people sustain you, the people and a constant, sobering reminder that you are asking them to entrust to you the most awesome responsibility on earth. It was a glorious, heart-filling, head-filling odyssey for which I shall be forever grateful to my party, to my staff and to my fellow Americans. Their faces are a friendly, smiling sea of memory stretching from coast to coast.[14]

---

[14] Adlai E. Stevenson, *Major Campaign Speeches* (New York: Random House, 1953), pp. xi-xiii. See also the account of the rigors and rewards of campaigning by another Illinois Democrat, Paul H. Douglas, "Running for Office Means What It Says," *New York Times Magazine,* September 5, 1948, pp. 5, 41.

Campaign Organization [15]

REGULAR PARTY MACHINERY

A party or candidate about to launch a campaign must first "get organized," that is, decide what jobs need to be done and divide them up among the available workers. In most campaigns this is, to begin with, a matter of assigning or reassigning functions within existing party machinery—the national committee, the state committees, and the various county, city, district, and other local committees, down to the precinct committeemen. These cannot be counted on, to be sure, to go all out for each party candidate as a temporary organization especially created on his behalf would go all out for him. But they are "there" at the beginning of *every* campaign, and usually take at least some responsibility for pushing the *entire* ticket. In the typical state and local campaign, indeed, they are not only the organizational nucleus, but the entire organization.

In preparing campaigns for such "major" offices as the presidency, U.S. senatorships, and governorships, the regular organizations must, first of all, "grow" enough to take on the tasks that have to be performed. The national committee must increase its staff in such of its permanent divisions as research and publicity, and create new divisions, such as speakers' bureaus, labor divisions, Negro divisions, and opinion-survey divisions, to handle special campaign activities.[16] Similarly with the state committees and, to some extent, with the county, congressional-district, and city committees, which are likely to find themselves called upon to recruit and supervise a number of additional canvassers, speakers, publicity men, and envelope addressers. Indeed, one component of the regular party machinery—the congressional and senatorial campaign committees, which supply speakers, literature, and funds for the parties' candidates in doubtful states and congressional districts—is active *only* during campaigns.[17]

[15] Convenient discussions of campaign organization are to be found in Key, *op. cit.,* pp. 480-83; Odegard and Helms, *op. cit.,* pp. 598-602; and Hugh A. Bone, *American Politics and the Party System* (New York: McGraw-Hill Book Company, Inc., 1949), pp. 575-79.

[16] With regard to the national committees' expanded regular divisions during campaigns, see Black, *op. cit.;* Thomas S. Barclay, "The Publicity Division of the Democratic Party, 1929-30," *American Political Science Review,* Vol. XXV (February, 1931), pp. 68-72, and "The Bureau of Publicity of the Democratic National Committee, 1930-32," *American Political Science Review,* Vol. XXVII (February, 1933), pp. 63-66; Ralph D. Casey, "Party Campaign Propaganda," *Annals of the American Academy of Political and Social Science,* Vol. CLXXIX (May, 1935), pp. 96-105, and "Republican Propaganda in the 1936 Campaign," *Public Opinion Quarterly,* Vol. I (April, 1937), pp. 27-44; and C. A. H. Thomson, "Research and the Republican Party," *Public Opinion Quarterly,* Vol. III (April, 1939) pp. 306-13. On the special activities of a speakers' bureau, see William J. Walsh, "How to Use a Speakers' Bureau in a Political Campaign," *Public Opinion Quarterly,* Vol. III (January, 1939), pp. 92-106. And for an interesting account of the use of opinion-polling research by the Democratic National Committee in the 1952 campaign, see the article by Lewis Anthony Dexter, who directed the experiment: "The Use of Public Opinion Polls by Political Party Organizations," *Public Opinion Quarterly,* Vol. XVIII (Spring, 1954), pp. 53-61.

[17] See pp. 233-34.

Electioneering, in short, is one of the regular party organization's major activities, and the regulars usually constitute at least the core and perhaps the whole of the party's campaign organization.

AUXILIARY AND "FRONT" ORGANIZATIONS

In many state and national campaigns and in some campaigns for local offices, the regular party organizations share their electioneering activities with auxiliary and "front" organizations of one sort or another. The theory on which these organizations are formed and proceed is that large numbers of voters view the regular parties as such either with indifference or with positive disapproval, and can be reached only by organizations that "put principle above party"—that is, work for particular causes or candidates "regardless of party labels." These organizations run to one or another of the following three types:

The Permanent Independent Organization. Organizations of this type seek to bring together "independents" with common economic interests or a common socio-economic point of view, and make it their business to bring about the nomination and election of candidates likely to favor those interests or reflect that point of view. Between elections, they issue pronouncements on public policy, now for general propaganda or educational purposes, now with a view to affecting party platforms. During campaigns they "endorse" particular candidates and set up machinery for canvassing, getting voters registered, issuing campaign literature, and getting voters to the polls—the same sort of machinery, that is to say, that the regular party organization keeps in motion during the weeks preceding an election. Sometimes they work hand in hand with the party organizations whose candidates they favor, but not always. For the party regulars, in the very nature of the case, wish to appeal to the broadest possible constituency and, other things being equal, do not wish their man to be identified with a particular set of interests or a particular point of view; they frequently tend, therefore, to view the independents with a distrust that readily translates itself into tension and mutual antagonism.[18]

Perhaps the best-known (and most successful) of these organizations is the Political Action Committee of the Congress of Industrial Organizations, which was formed in 1943 to work for pro-labor, pro-CIO, and "liberal"-"internationalist" policies and candidates. The PAC marshaled considerable strength behind Roosevelt in 1944 and Truman in 1948, and continues to be a valuable (and valued) ally of the Democratic party in most elections. (Some observers, indeed, hold that the PAC, in some areas in which it is active, has done a more effective and more professional job of electioneering on behalf of Democratic candidates than the latter's regular party organizations.[19])

[18] For a general discussion of the role and activities of these organizations, see Florence B. Widutis, "Action Dynamics of Citizen-Organizations in National Elections," *International Journal of Opinion and Attitude Research*, Vol. III (Summer, 1949), pp. 193-204.

[19] Cf. Key, *op. cit.*, pp. 78-79. For a detailed account of the PAC's activities in the 1944 campaign, see Joseph Gaer, *First Round, The Story of the CIO Political Action Committee* (New York:

Other examples are Labor's League for Political Education, which was created in 1947 by the American Federation of Labor and has been active in presidential and congressional elections since 1948; and Americans for Democratic Action, founded in 1947. The newest is For America, launched in 1954 to "combat super-internationalism and interventionism in both political parties" and to work for a new party alignment.[20]

The Candidate Organization. In many national and state elections, "general-citizen" organizations spring to life and go to work, not for entire party tickets, but for particular candidates. Notable recent examples are the Citizens for Eisenhower and Volunteers for Stevenson organizations, which raised large sums of money and conducted vigorous campaigns for their respective candidates in the 1952 presidential election. Volunteers for Stevenson dissolved (as a national organization at least) after the election, but Citizens for Eisenhower has remained active; it endorsed and campaigned for certain Republican candidates in both the primary and general congressional elections of 1954.[21]

The "Front" Organization. This type of organization, by contrast with the candidate organization, does not "spring" to life; it is created, and once created controlled, by the regular party organization to take on certain election chores that the latter cannot perform for itself. It rarely bears a party label, or at least not that of the party it fronts for (thus we have Democrats for Eisenhower, Businessmen for Stevenson, Servicemen's Wives to Re-elect Roosevelt, Jeffersonian Democrats for Dewey, etc.); and what, typically, it amounts to is merely a collection of names (bona fide, to be sure) on a letterhead or in a newspaper advertisement. It serves two main purposes. It helps the party it fronts for to put over the impression that its candidate commands support outside its own ranks, and thus strengthens his appeal for the "independents" and the disaffected partisans of the opposition. And it enables the party to solicit, collect, and spend campaign funds without identifying itself as the recipient, and so circumvent the legal limitations upon the amount of money

Duell, Sloan and Pearce, 1944). For accounts of its formation and objectives, see Richard Rovere, "Labor's Political Machine," *Harper's,* Vol. CXC (June, 1945), pp. 592-601; and Matthew Josephson, *Sidney Hillman, Statesman of American Labor* (Garden City, N. Y.: Doubleday and Company, 1952). For a general account of the role of the CIO in politics, see Fay Calkins, *The CIO and the Democratic Party* (Chicago: University of Chicago Press, 1952).

[20] This organization was created by, among others, Colonel Robert R. McCormick, General Robert E. Wood, John T. Flynn, Clarence E. Manion, and Hamilton Fish. According to the last, the organization intended to recruit 5,000,000 voters, and would start out with a war chest of $500,000: New York *Times,* May 8, 1954, p. 6. Mr. Fish has since withdrawn from For America, on the grounds that his colleagues were unwilling to channel the group's energies and funds into nomination-making and election-winning activities—i.e., unwilling to combat the PAC and LLPE on the latter's own ground.

[21] Citizens for Eisenhower is not unique in this regard. The Independent Citizens' Committee of the Arts, Sciences, and Professions for Roosevelt, formed for the 1944 campaign, reorganized in 1945 as a continuing body and dropped "for Roosevelt" from its title. It was absorbed in 1947 by the Progressive Citizens of America; this, in 1948, became the nucleus of the Progressive Party, which nominated Henry Wallace for the presidency (see pp. 449-50).

it and its candidates can spend.[22] We shall examine this subterfuge in greater detail in Chapter 18.[23]

Campaign Techniques

CHANNELS OF APPEAL

Political parties and candidates direct their appeals to the voters through two main kinds of channels:

Personal Contacts. As we have seen above, many politicians believe that voters are likely, other things being equal, to vote for the candidate who has stood in their presence and spoken to them, so that they think of him as a *person* rather than as a face on a billboard or a voice on the radio. The good campaign manager will see to it, therefore, that his candidate makes every personal appearance he can possibly squeeze into the period between his nomination and election day. Audiences range in size all the way from tens of thousands in a civic auditorium, a football stadium, or a baseball park to the small handful of party faithfuls gathered about the rear platform of the campaign train at a "whistle stop" or at some partisan's home for a "coffee" or "tea." [24] Similarly the canvassing activities of precinct workers are for the most part a matter of personal contacts, though the purpose here is more often to get information about the voters' party preferences and registration status than to influence their opinions.[25]

Mass Communications. Because of the sheer number of voters involved in national, statewide, and congressional elections,[26] candidates make personal appearances before only a small fraction of their potential supporters. Thus the main channels for their appeals to the voters necessarily have to be those that reach large numbers of them simultaneously—and, for that very reason, *impersonally:* newspaper advertisements, radio spot-announcements and

[22] Cf. Carlson and Blake, *op. cit.,* p. 48. A Senate committee investigating campaign finance in the 1944 presidential election concluded that it was impossible to determine accurately the total number of nonparty organizations, but compiled a list of 177, including such names as Girls Who Save Their Nickels to Elect a Republican President Club, Independent White Democrats, National Independent Committee of German-Americans for the Reelection of Roosevelt, and the People's Committee to Defend Life Insurance and Savings: U.S. Senate, Special Committee to Investigate Presidential, Vice-Presidential, and Senatorial Campaign Expenditures in 1944, 79th Congress, 1st Session, Report (1945), Appendix VII, pp. 134-37.

[23] "Front" organizations sometimes become so numerous as to cause confusion. In the 1944 campaign in New Haven, Conn., for example, there was an Independent Citizens' Committee for Roosevelt, an Independent Citizens' Committee for McMahon (the Democratic candidate for U.S. senator) and an Independent Citizen's Committee for Geelan (the Democratic candidate for U.S. representative). Having noted the duplication of effort and wasted motion among these three committees, one waggish observer suggested the creation of an over-all coordinating committee for their activities, and that it be called The Independent Citizens' Committee to Support Every Candidate on the Democratic Ticket!

[24] For a detailed description of "whistle-stop" campaigning by both presidential candidates in 1948, see the *New Yorker,* October 9 and October 16, 1948.

[25] See pp. 225-27 for a description of precinct workers' activities.

[26] See p. 272 for a discussion of the sizes of the various American constituencies.

speeches, television spot-announcements and speeches, postcards and letters, handbills and posters, lapel buttons, pamphlets and comic books, windshield and envelope stickers, and so on.[27] Even in contests for local offices in relatively small constituencies, parties and candidates often employ some of these media.

"MUDSLINGING"

Are American campaigns really as "dirty" as we sometimes hear? The parties often accuse one another, certainly, of "smears" and "mudslinging," and we noted in a previous chapter that many Americans would unhesitatingly answer the question we have just posed in the affirmative.[28] But there are wide differences of opinion as to which campaign appeals are "mudslinging" and which are legitimate criticisms of the other fellow's record and policies. Republicans, for example, denounced Democratic talk about the "Hoover depression" in 1932 and the "Giveaway program" in 1954 as "smear tactics," and Democrats answered that these phrases accurately described Republican performance when in office. Democrats, similarly, pointed to Republican charges in 1952 and 1954 that the Democrats had been "soft on communism" and "unwilling to win or end the Korean war" as "smears," and Republicans replied that the facts spoke for themselves.

According to one widely accepted definition, "mudslinging" is a matter of using an opponent's race or religion as an argument against him, or trying to win votes by casting aspersions upon his loyalty, personal morality, and honesty, instead of confining discussion to his stand on issues or his performance in office: and on this showing, there is indeed a good deal of "mudslinging" in American campaigns. As recently as the 1928 presidential election, for example, a nationwide "whispering campaign" (i.e., a campaign not openly and officially conducted by any organization) rang the changes on the charge that, since the Democratic candidate, Alfred E. Smith, was a Roman Catholic, he would, if elected, run the government on orders from the Pope. In the 1940 presidential campaign, there were unofficial pamphlets intended to identify the Republican candidate, Wendell Willkie, with fascism, and the Democratic candidate, Franklin D. Roosevelt, with communism.[29] In the 1950 Maryland senatorial campaign, a newspaper-type throwaway featured a "composite" photograph depicting the Democratic candidate, Millard Tydings, in friendly conversation with Earl Browder, a former leader of the American Communists.[30]

[27] Cf. Key, *op. cit.*, pp. 479, 498-99.

[28] See pp. 237-38.

[29] These pamphlets are summarized and excerpted in Hugh A. Bone, *"Smear" Politics: An Analysis of 1940 Campaign Literature* (Washington, D. C.: American Council on Public Affairs, 1941).

[30] See the Report of the Committee on Rules and Administration, United States Senate, on the Maryland Senatorial Election of 1950, Senate Report No. 647, 82d Congress, 1st Session (1951).

It can be argued, however, that American campaigns, at least at the national level, are less "dirty" than they used to be. George Washington's opponents called him an "impostor," a "crocodile," and a "hyena," and accused him of personally looting the U.S. Treasury. Jefferson's referred to him as "the anti-Christ in the White House," and accused him of having had a bastard son by a part-Negro woman. Jackson was described as the son of a common prostitute and a mulatto man, Lincoln as a "clown," a "drunkard," a "despot," a "gorilla," etc., and Andrew Johnson as "an insolent, drunken brute in comparison with whom Caligula's horse was respectable." [31] Against such a background, present-day American presidential campaigns are clearly on the genteel (and colorless) side, although the incidence of "mudslinging" in local campaigns may be somewhat higher.

Checking on the Results

Naturally the directors of campaigns want to know during the campaign how things are going, how their appeals are being received by the voters, what further appeals might help, and where the latter are likely to help most. In recent years some campaign headquarters have begun to use the public opinion polls as a means of finding out how their appeals are going over with the voters, and to include in their staffs men and women skilled in polling techniques.[32] Most national and state campaign directors, however, remain convinced that the most accurate and reliable sources of information about how the campaign is going and how the election is going to come out are the local party leaders. The precinct committeeman, most of them believe, has a better "feel" of what is going on in his precinct, the county chairman of what is going on in his county, and the state chairman of what is going on in his state, than anyone else. Sample-survey polls may confirm what the organization already knows; but a smart organization politician, basing his opinions on the candid reports of the local leaders, has more confidence in these reports than in those emanating from Dr. Gallup and the other pollsters.[33]

Does Campaigning Influence Votes?

Campaigning absorbs much of the energy and almost all of the money spent by American parties, and, in national and state elections at least, the amounts of both involved are by any standards impressive. The question there-

[31] Samuel Hopkins Adams, "Presidential Campaign Slanders," *Life,* Vol. XVII (October 2, 1944), pp. 53-60.

[32] See Dexter, *op. cit.;* and Jacob K. Javits, "How I Used a Poll in Campaigning for Congress," *Public Opinion Quarterly,* Vol. XI (Summer, 1947), pp. 222-26.

[33] Charles Michelson testifies that James A. Farley's forecast of the 1936 presidential election, in which Farley predicted exactly the states to be carried by each party, was based entirely on reports from state and county Democratic leaders: New York *Times,* November 15, 1936, s. 4, p. 10.

fore arises: Do those who engage in campaigning take it too seriously, and pour into it energies and funds that would accomplish more if utilized in some other way? The following paragraphs summarize the available evidence on this point.

POLITICAL SCIENTISTS' VIEWS

The political scientists who have attempted answers to the foregoing questions are in general agreement that campaigning *does* influence voting behavior to some degree. But they are by no means agreed upon the nature of its impact, or upon its importance relative to other factors that affect voting behavior.[34]

The American system of elections-by-the-calendar, according to one group of writers, disposes us to exaggerate the impact of campaigning and in extreme cases to think of all votes as being determined in the campaign period. In point of fact, as Professor Truman puts it, "our elections are not likely to be understood until they are studied as a continuous process in which the campaigns and the balloting are at most climaxes." [35] And within this process, it is argued, votes are determined to a very considerable extent by the total national situation—*by events*—and by the voters' understanding (correct or incorrect) of how the parties and candidates they are choosing among have affected that situation.[36] In 1932, for example, many voters were sick of living in a depressed economy and had become convinced that the Hoover administration was not going to do anything about it. And it seems probable that no amount of clever campaigning by the Republicans could have prevented such voters from voting for the Democrats in that year's election.[37] The Democrats, in

[34] Of the various writers who have commented on this question, Harold F. Gosnell is the most deeply convinced that campaigning plays a crucial role in determining the outcome of elections, and argues that it is often decisive: "Does Campaigning Make a Difference?" *Public Opinion Quarterly*, Vol. XIV (Fall, 1950), pp. 413-18. He explains much of Franklin D. Roosevelt's success as a vote getter in terms of his skills as a campaigner: *Champion Campaigner: Franklin D. Roosevelt* (New York: The Macmillan Company, 1952). Peel and Donnelly contend that nobody really knows how much difference campaigns make or whether this appeal is more effective than that one, and believe that much campaign money "is spent unwisely and for questionable ends": *The 1928 Campaign*, pp. 42-43. Key points to the paucity of trustworthy data, and to the fact that they are limited to presidential campaigns: *Op. cit.*, pp. 505-09. See also David B. Truman in *The Pre-Election Polls of 1948* (New York: Social Science Research Council, Bulletin No. 60, 1949), pp. 244-49. Other writers conclude that campaigning probably makes some difference, though no one can say precisely how much or what kind of difference: Cf. Hugh A. Bone, *American Politics and the Party System*, pp. 590-92; Odegard and Helms, *op. cit.*, pp. 635-37; and Turner Catledge, "Is Campaigning Worthwhile?" *New York Times Magazine*, October 15, 1944, p. 10.

[35] David B. Truman, "Some Political Variables for Election Surveys," *International Journal of Opinion and Attitude Research*, Vol. V (Summer, 1951), pp. 249-50.

[36] Bernard Berelson, "Events as an Influence upon Public Opinion," *Journalism Quarterly*, Vol. XXVI (June, 1949), pp. 145-48.

[37] But see the argument by Thomas Wilkinson and Hornell Hart that there is no statistical evidence to support the widely held notion that depressions result in defeats for the party in power and prosperity results in victories for it: "Prosperity and Political Victory," *Public Opinion Quarterly*, Vol. XIV (Summer, 1950), pp. 331-35.

other words, went into the campaign with an indeterminate but possibly very large number of votes already won, and these should not be attributed to the campaign they conducted. In 1952, similarly, some voters at least had broken with the Democrats because of their belief that the latter were mishandling the domestic security program, the problem of corruption, and the Korean war, and would have voted for the Republicans no matter what kind of campaign they conducted.

THE RESULTS OF SAMPLE-SURVEY STUDIES

There have been at least three large-scale attempts by social scientists to study voting behavior via repeated interviewing of panels of voters selected by sampling procedures.[38] Taken together, they are the source of the most reliable and useful information we possess about the nature and extent of the influence of campaigning on voting behavior, and on the relative effectiveness of various campaigning devices.

The following generalizations are suggested by the findings in these studies:

(1) Many voters make up their minds before the campaign even begins, and so are not likely to be converted by electioneering. The greatest proportion of these early deciders are persons who strongly identify themselves with a particular party [39] and are likely to support any candidates on its ticket and to turn a deaf ear to the opposition party's propaganda.[40] The Lazarsfeld study of the 1940 presidential election found that 49 per cent of all the voters had decided in May how they were going to vote, and duly carried out their decision in November. Of the remainder, 28 per cent were "crystallizers"—those who had no vote intention in May but later acquired one; 15 per cent were "waverers"—those who had a vote intention in May, then fell away from it to indecision or to the other party during the campaign, but finally returned

---

[38] These are (1) the pioneer study of the 1940 presidential election by the sociologist Paul F. Lazarsfeld and his associates, who interviewed a panel of 600 voters in Erie County, Ohio, selected by standard sampling methods, once a month from May to November and reported their results in Paul F. Lazarsfeld, Bernard Berelson, and Hazel Gaudet, *The People's Choice: How the Voter Makes Up His Mind in a Presidential Campaign* (New York: Duell, Sloan and Pearce, 1944); (2) the study of the 1948 presidential election by a group of social scientists, who interviewed panels of voters (varying in size from 1,029 in one interview to 814 in another) in Elmira, New York, four times between June and November and reported their results in Bernard R. Berelson, Paul F. Lazarsfeld, and William N. McPhee, *Voting* (Chicago: University of Chicago Press, 1954); and (3) the study of the 1952 presidential election by the Survey Research Center of the University of Michigan, whose researchers interviewed a national panel of 1,614 respondents both before and after the election, and reported their results in Angus Campbell, Gerald Gurin, and Warren E. Miller, *The Voter Decides* (Evanston, Ill.: Row, Peterson and Company, 1954).

[39] Cf. the discussion of "party identification" on pp. 203-05.

[40] Such a voter was the college janitor who proudly told a professor that he had never voted for a Republican. The professor, who prided himself on his independence, somewhat scornfully remarked, "I don't suppose you'd even vote for Almighty God if He ran on the Republican ticket." The janitor replied indignantly, "Almighty God wouldn't run on the *Republican* ticket!"

to their original choice in November; and only 8 per cent were "changers"—those who had a vote intention in May but voted for the other party in November.[41]

Other studies suggest that the time at which voters make up their minds and the amount of vote shifting varies considerably from campaign to campaign. The Survey Research Center, for example, asked respondents both in 1948 and in 1952 to fix the time at which they had reached a decision. The results are shown in Table 20.

TABLE 20   *Time of Voter Decision in 1948 and 1952*[42]

Time of Voter Decision	Dewey Voters	Truman Voters	All Voters	Eisenhower Voters	Stevenson Voters	All Voters
Before the conventions	42%	36%	37%	27%	35%	31%
At the time of the conventions	34	22	28	40	27	34
During the campaign	13	14	14	18	24	20
Within 2 weeks of election	3	14	9	10	7	9
On election day	2	3	3	1	4	2
Do not remember	2	1	1	1	—	1
Not ascertained	4	10	8	3	3	3

The data, in short, point to at least these conclusions: In every campaign a great many voters have such firmly fixed voting intentions that campaign propaganda is not likely to change their votes. The proportion of such voters, however, varies considerably from one campaign to another; and in every campaign there are many voters whose intentions are *not* solidly fixed. These are the voters whose votes could conceivably be changed by electioneering.

(2) Most voters expose themselves to at least *some* campaign propaganda; so the parties need not fear that they are firing their broadsides at targets that are not there.[43] The Lazarsfeld study, however, concluded that the voters who "consume" the most propaganda are also the persons who have the firmest voting intentions and are thus least likely to be affected by it. Moreover, voters tend to read and listen only to the propaganda of the party they intend to vote for anyway; and most voters who show a high degree of interest in

[41] Paul F. Lazarsfeld, Bernard Berelson, and Hazel Gaudet, *The People's Choice*, 2nd ed. (New York: Columbia University Press, 1948), Ch. III.

[42] These data are presented in Table 2.4 on p. 18 of Campbell, Gurin, and Miller, *op. cit.*, and include data derived from the earlier Survey Research Center study of the 1948 presidential election, reported in Angus Campbell and R. L. Kahn, *The People Elect a President* (Ann Arbor, Mich.: Institute for Social Research, 1952). For further evidence of the considerable amount of last-minute vote shifting in 1948, see Raymond A. Bauer, Henry W. Riecken, and Jerome S. Bruner, "An Analysis of Voting Intentions: Massachusetts, 1948," *International Journal of Opinion and Attitude Research*, Vol. III (Summer, 1949), pp. 169-78.

[43] Cf. Lazarsfeld, Berelson, and Gaudet, *op. cit.*, Ch. XIV; and Campbell, Gurin, and Miller, *op. cit.*, pp. 32-33.

the campaign and expose themselves to a great deal of propaganda listen mostly to the side they *agree* with.[44]

It should be noted, however, that the Lazarsfeld study indicates that most of the persons who either switch their voting intentions or make up their minds late in the campaign are more influenced by personal contacts than by mass-communications propaganda; and while some of these are contacts with party precinct workers, more of them are with friends and business associates who, in casual conversation, propagandize for their favorite candidates. The latter sort of propaganda is more effective than the mass-communications variety, the Lazarsfeld group suggests, for several reasons. It happens to the voter in the ordinary course of events rather than by conscious *choice* on his part (as when he turns on a political speech on television or reads party litera- ture or advertisements). It enables the persuader to shape his arguments to the particular kind of resistance shown by each "persuadee." It can take ad- vantage of every man's desire to be well thought of by his associates, and of the fact that a man is more likely to trust someone he knows personally than some impersonal and remote organ of party propaganda.[45]

Which of the mass-communications media is most effective in exercising such influence as they do exert? The sample-survey studies do not answer this question. The Lazarsfeld study suggests, rather tentatively, that radio in 1940 was a more effective propaganda channel than newspapers, magazines, or party literature.[46] Many politicians now believe that television is the most effective mass-communications medium.

In short, such evidence as the sample-survey studies have produced—it is, be it noted, far from definitive—suggests that most of a party's expensive mass- communications propaganda is seen and listened to by voters who are already convinced; and that the voters who do change their minds during a campaign are more likely to be induced to do so by the conversation of friends and asso- ciates than by television speeches or radio spot-announcements aimed at them by the parties. But this does not mean that the parties' campaigning activities are largely useless; it only means that they are not very effective in inducing opposition voters to switch sides.

(3) The Lazarsfeld group found that the parties' campaigning activities have, in varying degrees, three main effects: (1) *Conversion,* i.e., winning over voters who originally preferred the opposition. Only a small proportion of the voters, it seems, are influenced to this extent, but it is interesting to note that some are.[47] (2) *Reinforcement,* i.e., influencing voters to hold firm to their original preferences [48] by supplying them with reasons for doing so, by re-

---

[44] Lazarsfeld, Berelson, and Gaudet, *op. cit.,* pp. 89-91.

[45] *Ibid.,* Ch. XVI.

[46] *Ibid.,* pp. 125-34.

[47] *Ibid.,* Ch. X.

[48] That campaigns have this sort of impact on a good many voters was by no means un- known to party leaders before the Lazarsfeld study was published. Turner Catledge once asked

minding them that many other voters feel as they do, and by counteracting the possible corrosive effects of opposition propaganda.[49] (3) *Activation,* i.e., inducing voters to translate their preferences and intentions into actual votes cast on election day. This, according to the Lazarsfeld group, is the major effect of campaigns, and the process involved appears to be more or less as follows: To begin with, party propaganda arouses interest in the election on the part of persons who have hitherto felt no concern about it one way or the other. As their interest grows, they consume more propaganda, and finally begin to select the propaganda that fits in with their original party preferences. And by the time election day rolls around, they are sufficiently seized of the justice of that party's position, and of the "importance" of the election, to take the trouble to vote. Thus the main effect of a party's campaign is to convert preferences into votes by actually getting to the polls persons who will support its ticket *if* they vote at all.[50]

The sample-survey studies generally conclude, along with most political scientists, that campaigning does win a party some votes that it would not otherwise get.

THE POLITICIANS' VIEW

What about the men who actually do the campaigning? Since they continue to campaign, they obviously think it wins enough votes to justify the effort and expense. But on what sort of grounds?

We have a candid and revealing statement on these questions from Charles Michelson, who was Director of Publicity for the Democratic National Committee during the 1930's. Following the Democrats' landslide victory in the 1936 presidential election, he was asked how, in his opinion, the Democrats' campaigning activities had affected the election results, and confessed that it seemed to him in retrospect "that we were frequently fighting shadows." *"Probably,"* he continued, "the result of the election would have been just the same had neither the Democratic nor the Republican national committee functioned at all." Why, then, did the Democratic leaders conduct such an elaborate and expensive campaign? Because, Michelson replied, *"It was up to us to take nothing for granted."* [51] In other words, a major party must win votes in order to accomplish its prime objective of winning elections. If there is even an off-chance that campaigning may play a substantial role in winning the votes—and the social scientists agree with the politicians that there is reason to believe that it *can* play such a role—then no party that means business

a prominent party leader whether campaigning really changes anyone's mind, and received this reply: "Ah, my boy, you miss the point if you think a campaign is meant to change votes. Ninety per cent of the purpose of every revival is to convince the converted": *New York Times Magazine,* October 15, 1944, p. 10.

[49] Lazarsfeld, Berelson, and Gaudet, *op. cit.,* Ch. IX.

[50] *Ibid.,* Ch. VIII.

[51] New York *Times,* November 15, 1936, s. 4, p. 10. Emphasis added.

about winning elections can afford, within the limits of its available resources, to campaign any less energetically than the opposition.[52]

The Basic Character of American Campaigns: "Propagandistic" or "Educational"?

Much of the existing literature on American political parties assumes that their campaigning activities are essentially "propagandistic" rather than "educational,"[53] and describes in greater or lesser detail the "propaganda techniques" used by the parties in campaigns. In the opinion of the present writers, however, American campaigns are at least as "educational" as they are "propagandistic." They are, be it remembered, a characteristic activity of American political parties, which, we contend, faithfully reflect the character of American society.[54] They are planned and executed according to the set of rules summarized early in the present chapter by the sort of men who have achieved leadership in the American party systems. These leaders are neither propagandists nor educators, but—because they make nominations and contest elections—a little of both, but not much of either. Considered in general terms, the campaigns they run show the following characteristics:

(1) American campaigns do not provide a sober canvass of the major political, economic, and social issues of the day, calculated to give the voters anything comparable to what a university professor would regard as knowledge about and understanding of these issues. This is so partly because the system requires that the major issues—the ones on which the most crucial decisions will be made between this campaign and the next one—either be avoided or be touched upon only marginally by the campaign strategists on both sides. And it is partly because their mood and manner—like that of American advertising campaigns, American religious campaigns, and even American "educational" campaigns—is not that of the classroom. In short, one of the rules, implicit in those we have already noted, is this: Don't overtax the intellectual capacity of the masses of voters. Or, variously, don't as-

---

[52] For accounts of the contrasting campaigning practices in the one-party and modified one-party areas, see V. O. Key, Jr., *Southern Politics in State and Nation* (New York: Alfred A. Knopf, 1949), pp. 317-29, 400-05; Alexander Heard, *A Two-Party South?* (Chapel Hill: University of North Carolina Press, 1952), pp. 115-17; and O. Douglas Weeks, *Texas Presidential Politics in 1952* (Austin: Institute of Public Affairs, University of Texas, 1953), pp. 89-96.

[53] Among present-day political scientists there are no generally agreed and precise definitions of these terms; but most writers agree that "propaganda" connotes manipulation of other people's attitudes by the propagandist for his own ends, while "education" connotes instructing people in "the truth" for the good of the whole community. For various definitions of both concepts, see the following: Harold D. Lasswell, "The Theory of Political Propaganda," *American Political Science Review*, Vol. XXI (August, 1927), pp. 627-31; Frederick C. Bartlett, *Political Propaganda* (Cambridge: Cambridge University Press, 1940); and Leonard W. Doob, *Public Opinion and Propaganda* (New York: Henry Holt and Company, 1948). The most complete bibliography is Bruce L. Smith, Harold D. Lasswell, and Ralph D. Casey, eds., *Propaganda, Communication, and Public Opinion: A Comprehensive Reference Guide* (Princeton: Princeton University Press, 1946).

[54] See Chapter 21.

sume that the voters, insofar as they pay attention to you at all, do so out of a desire to be instructed (some may, but not enough to affect the election results). But not overtaxing the intellectual capacity of the audience is as sound a rule in education as in propaganda.

(2) American campaigns do oversimplify even the issues they deal with, and in doing so indeed hew close to the classic rules of propaganda as laid down by such experts as Adolf Hitler and Joseph Goebbels. But we must not conclude from this that they oversimplify out of any intent on the part of the strategists to patronize or manipulate the voters. For one thing, the over-simplification is clearly a matter not of strategy in the Hitler-Goebbels sense, but of tacit and spontaneous agreement by *two* sets of strategists, who as the campaign proceeds tacitly negotiate with one another as to which not-very-relevant and not-very-urgent issues to treat as "the" issues. The problem, as the strategists on both sides necessarily see it, is not the Hitler-Goebbels problem of how to impose an ideology and a program despite the best efforts of the opposition to impose theirs, but how to square off to opponents whose ideology and program are almost identical with their own—how to keep on saying for weeks and weeks what the opposition is saying, and yet give it a sufficiently different twist and sound to keep the campaign interesting. The parties, in short, are actors in one and the same show; each needs the other to perform well, lest the audience get bored and stay home on election day. And for another thing, there is every reason to believe that the oversimplification reflects, as much as anything else, an honest effort on the part of both sets of strategists to explain what the election is about to *themselves*. They, hardly less than the voters, are overwhelmed by the scale and complexity of the problems to be dealt with by the government they seek to control. And to suppose that they say to each other in their midnight councils: "The real issues are these, but the voters wouldn't understand them, so let's keep quiet about them," is to overlook both the rapport between American party leaders and American voters and the deep respect with which the former regard the latter. The rule, if conscious rule there be, is: Choose issues appropriate to the American political system, and discuss them in such a way as to capture and retain the interest of the American people and to bring some of them, who might not otherwise have done so, to vote for our side.

(3) Even the previously mentioned rule about "pork chops" must be grasped in the context of the system. It means neither that the strategists regard the voters as motivated exclusively or even primarily by economic considerations, nor that American party leaders so conduct campaigns as to subordinate other issues to economic issues, nor, finally, that they are prepared to contemplate any drastic redistribution of pork chops. Here, as in other respects, the parties are as careful as, say, Ford and General Motors to approach their "customers" each with approximately the same commodity; and neither deceives itself, any more than do Ford and General Motors, as to whether total sales are going to be greatly affected by what is said via the

mass-communications media. The rule is: Don't go after new supporters with appeals that might lose you many old ones.

(4) The same considerations as in the foregoing paragraph apply to the strategists' handling of America's many delicate conflicts of interest and aspiration between ethnic groups. One party may, over a number of years, gradually win from the other party a considerable proportion of the voters belonging to a particular ethnic group, as the Democrats appear, in recent years, to have taken away from the Republicans a sizable part of the Negro vote. But the process by which this is accomplished does not reflect itself recognizably and as such in the party's campaign appeals, where the rule is: Avoid issues between ethnic groups.

(5) To picture American campaigns as the unfolding of the plans of the master strategists at the top flies in the face of what we know about the internal organization of American parties. A propaganda machine is *ipso facto* centralized; it cannot, given the character of its mission, tolerate improvisation in its lower echelons; the "line," *because* it constitutes a carefully devised assault upon the less rational susceptibilities of the recipients, must originate at the top and descend to the bottom with the obligatory force of a command. An American national party, on the other hand, is *ipso facto* decentralized; given the character of its organization, it cannot prevent improvisation in its lower echelons; and any "line" adopted at the top will be effective at the bottom just to the extent that those at the bottom recognize it as meeting *their* standards of appropriateness, honesty, and fair play; commands, as we have observed repeatedly in the preceding chapters, play no role in the process.

(6) One who views an American campaign as a chess game between two teams of high-powered general-staff officers armed with the latest know-how about manipulating the masses not only misses the point; he also misses the fun. An American party campaign is, in the nature of the case, a comedy of errors, which stands in the same relation to a genuine propaganda operation as, say, the annual congressional baseball game to the first game of a World Series. The catcher has no way of signaling for a low one inside, and the chances are that the pitcher—assuming there's only one in the box, and that the bat boy is willing to let him have the ball for a moment—doesn't know how to throw one. No one knows, when he hits the ball over the fence, whose score the run will be added to, so in general the players economize their energies, and seem to prefer foul tips to home runs. Since the real score is going to be chalked up—on another day, and in another ball park—in a popularity contest, the players worry very little about their batting and fielding averages—which, in consequence, run pretty low. And the fun of watching the spectacle consists precisely in understanding that this is the kind of game it is.

(7) The general impact of each campaign *is* educational, in the sense that it does focus public attention for a few brief weeks each quadrennium (and, to some extent, each biennium) on public affairs, and does involve the com-

munication of a certain amount of more or less apposite information and argument about those affairs. If its mood is not that of the university classroom, it is also not that of Nuremberg and Red Square—and, since there are two sets of loudspeakers, each of which is prepared to call the other a liar if it strays too far from the truth, it *cannot* be that of Nuremberg and Red Square. "Slogans" and "symbols"—irrational symbols if you like—figure prominently in it, but so do facts about the national debt, and reasonably sober reflection about American foreign policy. And—what is most important from the standpoint of our inquiry in this book—it educates the American people with respect to the special character of their political system, gives them a "feel" for the special character of their politics, and instructs them in the special character of their own role in those politics.

Chapter 16

PAYING THE BILLS

Items in the Bills

CAMPAIGN EXPENDITURES

All party activities, as we have pointed out repeatedly, are undertaken with a view to winning elections; and in one sense, therefore, all the money the parties spend in connection with those activities belong under the heading of campaign expenditures. For the moment, however, let us distinguish between "campaign expenditures" in the strict sense (those made during particular campaigns and intended to help win particular elections), and "between-elections expenditures" (those made at other times and intended to advance the party's cause in all elections).

A party's bills for campaign expenditures, as just defined, usually include the following major items: [1]

General Overhead. Most campaign organizations maintain campaign headquarters, and this involves expenditures for such items as office space, office equipment and supplies, telephone service, postage, and staff salaries (unless these are carried on some other party budget); and the larger the constituency in which the election is being fought, the larger the staff and the more expensive the headquarters facilities required. The national party committees, for example, hire not only numerous clerical workers, but also—among others —research workers, speech writers, publicity experts, and pollsters. (Nor do the various party headquarters account for all the expenditures; besides the

---

[1] This classification of campaign expenditures generally follows that in Louise Overacker's *Money in Elections* (New York: The Macmillan Company, 1932), Ch. II, especially pp. 20-46. This work remains the most comprehensive and most authoritative study we have of this subject, and Professor Overacker has supplemented it with articles in the *American Political Science Review* on the presidential elections of 1932, 1936, 1940, and 1944. See also James K. Pollock, *Party Campaign Funds* (New York: Alfred A. Knopf, 1926). These and most other studies of money in American politics concentrate for the most part upon presidential elections, so that there is relatively little literature on the role of money in state and local elections.

headquarters serving the entire ticket, there are often separate headquarters for several of a party's leading candidates.)

Professor Louise Overacker, writing in the early 1930's, estimated that 20 to 40 per cent of all campaign expenditures belong in the "overhead" category.[2] Given the enormous and increasing outlays for radio and television at the present time, however, the proportion of overhead expenses to total expenses has probably shrunk since she made her estimate.

Field Activities. This item includes all expenses incurred in the attempt to establish *personal* contacts between the organization and the voters: For example, costs of meetings and rallies, salaries and travel expenses for speakers, organizers and "advance men," and salaries for canvassers.

Publicity. This heading covers the cost of all general appeals directed impersonally—through the mass-communications media for the most part—at voters in the mass: payments for newspaper advertisements, campaign literature, mats and "boilerplate" editorials for newspapers, billboards, posters, lapel buttons, automobile stickers, etc.

The largest single item here is now the payments for radio and television programs and spot-announcements, which have grown to such proportions in recent years as to require the parties to allocate to publicity a much larger share of their total campaign budgets than in the past (in the 1930's, according to Professor Overacker, about half the budget went for publicity).[3] In the 1952 election, for example, a 15-minute program on a single TV station in Ohio cost $750,[4] and the average national "simulcast" (i.e., a program broadcast simultaneously on radio and television), cost the Democratic National Committee $52,670 ($33,305 for CBS-TV, $11,365 for CBS radio, and $8,000 for advance newspaper advertisements). These figures, moreover, relate to a simulcast that the party arranged well ahead of time; costs were approximately 50 per cent higher when arrangements were made at the last minute and time had to be pre-empted (that is, when the networks had to cancel regular commercial broadcasts in order to make room for the political broadcast).[5] The National Volunteers for Stevenson's broadcast from Madison Square Garden shortly before the election cost $120,000 (plus $12,000 for advance newspaper advertisements),[6] and the Citizens for Eisenhower-Nixon's hour-long election-eve broadcast $267,000.[7] On the basis of admittedly fragmentary reports, the New York *Times* concluded in 1952 that the national

[2] Overacker, *Money in Elections,* p. 22.

[3] *Ibid.,* pp. 23-24.

[4] Testimony of Representative Clarence J. Brown, in U.S. House of Representatives, Special Committee to Investigate Campaign Expenditures, 1952, 82nd Congress, 2nd Session, Hearings (1952), p. 15. These hearings will henceforth be cited as House Committee Hearings, 1952.

[5] Testimony of Stephen A. Mitchell, Chairman of the Democratic National Committee, in House Committee Hearings, 1952, pp. 150-54.

[6] Testimony of Hermon D. Smith, Chairman of Volunteers for Stevenson, in House Committee Hearings, 1952, pp. 29-31.

[7] Testimony of Walter Williams, Chairman of Citizens for Eisenhower-Nixon, in House Committee Hearings, 1952, p. 115.

organizations for Eisenhower had spent a total of $2,083,400 for radio and television alone, and the national organizations for Stevenson $1,428,400.[8]

Grants to Other Party Organizations. The national committees of both parties often give lump sums to the congressional and senatorial campaign committees and to needy state and local party committees, thus enabling them to make expenditures they could not otherwise afford; and, conversely, state and local committees which can afford it sometimes give money to the national committees. In 1944, for example, the last year for which such figures are available, the Democratic National Committee gave nineteen state central committees a total of $148,815, and received from twenty-two state central committees a total of $276,549. The Republican National Committee in the same year sent $14,400 to one state central committee and received $1,249,286 from thirty-two state central committees.[9] Such transfers, as these figures clearly show, account for a considerable share of some party organizations' campaign expenditures.

Special Election-Day Activities. This heading covers a number of "legitimate" outlays such as those for telephone squads, drivers and automobiles, baby sitters, challengers, and watchers, and may include illegal or "twilight" (i.e., legal but shady) outlays for the outright purchase of votes or for the indirect bribery of voters (as by hiring large numbers of "election-day workers," who merely cast their votes and then take the rest of the day off).[10]

BETWEEN-ELECTION EXPENDITURES

Most expenses, as we have pointed out above, are incurred during campaigns. As we saw in Chapter 10, however, many American party organizations remain active and continue to spend money in the intervals between campaigns—above all the national committees, which accordingly have large permanent clerical staffs and publicity divisions, and a year-in-year-out publication program that includes party newspapers and magazines and various other types of literature. (The Democratic National Committee's publicity division was created not only between elections, but in the leanest between-election period the party has ever lived through, that from 1929 to 1931.) [11] Many state and local party organizations also keep up a steady round of meetings and rallies between elections, and in addition maintain fairly ambitious canvassing programs.

[8] New York *Times,* December 1, 1952, pp. 1, 16-17.

[9] U.S. Senate, Special Committee to Investigate Presidential, Vice-Presidential, and Senatorial Campaign Expenditures in 1944, 79th Congress, 1st Session, Report (1945), appendices XI-XIV, pp. 242-43. This report will henceforth be cited as Senate Committee Report, 1945.

[10] Cf. Overacker, *Money in Elections,* p. 23. See also Edward J. Flynn, *You're the Boss* (New York: The Viking Press, 1947), pp. 112-13, for an account of how election-day money was spent in the Bronx during his regime.

[11] See Louise Overacker, "Campaign Funds in a Depression Year," *American Political Science Review,* Vol. XXVII (October, 1933), pp. 769-83, for an account of how the Democratic National Committee went ahead with its publicity activities despite the large debt left over from the 1928 campaign.

CAMPAIGN BUDGETS

To conclude our discussion of what parties spend money for, let us take a look at two campaign budgets, the first actual and the second hypothetical, and see how the various items compare with one another.

In the 1944 presidential election, the Democratic National Committee allocated its expenditures as follows:[12]

Chairman's activities
Chairman's office .... $ 44,454.00
Contributions to other organizations 230,315.75
V-P candidate's expenses 11,988.69
Absentee voters, labor, etc. 19,631.77
Treasurer's activities 147,117.07
Secretary's office 411.79
Publicity division
Radio 757,344.09
Other 264,438.05
Women's division 59,364.39
Speaker's bureau 13,982.88
Negro division 74,599.24
Overhead expenses 241,218.46
Grand total $1,864,866.18

On the basis of their campaigning experience, Oliver Carlson and Aldrich Blake suggest the following minimum budget for a candidate for a seat in a state legislature from a metropolitan constituency containing four distinct communities:[13]

1. Miscellaneous and reserve fund	$300	
2. Literature and campaign cards	150	
3. Precinct workers	500	
4. Precinct workers manager	150	
		$1,100
5. Advertisements in 4 community papers	640	
6. Advertisements in labor and ethnic organs	160	
		800
7. Billboards	500	
		500
8. Letterheads, envelopes, and postage	200	
9. 2 stenographers at $100 each	200	
10. 1 radio program on a major station	200	
		600
11. Distribution of literature	100	
12. Rent of 4 headquarters at $25 each	100	
13. 4 headquarters managers at $50 each	200	
14. Bumper signs for cars	50	
15. Quarter cards	50	
		500
Total budget		$3,500

[12] These figures are given in Louise Overacker, "Presidential Campaign Funds, 1944," *American Political Science Review*, Vol. XXXIX (October, 1945), pp. 899-925.
[13] Oliver Carlson and Aldrich Blake, *How to Get into Politics: The Art of Winning Elections*

The Size of the Bills

The *total* campaigning bill for most American elections is anybody's guess, and the best guess is pretty certain to be several million dollars off. The one thing that is certain is that the *actual* expenditures are much larger than the *reported* expenditures. Many of the committees that spend money during campaigns make no public report of their expenditures. (Most county committees, for example, file no reports with either federal or state authorities.) [14] Many of the reports that *are* filed with public authorities are inaccurate and incomplete, sometimes intentionally so, and in any case are scattered and hard to collate. The party committees that do report expenditures have good reason to play down the amount of money that passes through their hands.[15] And there are numerous expenditures by individuals which, in the nature of the case, are known only to a few persons.

We can, however, form a rough idea of the sums involved in a presidential election by examining some reported-expenditure statistics together with two expert calculations of total expenditures. Some observers estimate that over a million dollars was spent on behalf of each of at least three 1952 presidential aspirants (Eisenhower, Taft, and Kefauver) merely in trying to capture the *nomination* of one of the parties.[16] Vastly larger sums were spent in the general-election campaign. According to the New York *Times,* the *reported* expenditures in 1952 totaled $32,155,251,[17] and Congressman Clarence J. Brown, adding to this figure his estimate of the unreported expenditures, told a congressional committee that he would not like to pay out of his own pocket the sums spent in excess of $80,000,000.[18] *U.S. News & World Report* esti-

(New York: Duell, Sloan and Pearce, 1946). For a comparison with actual (though incomplete) figures, see the data on the average expenditures of candidates for the national House of Representatives given in U.S. House of Representatives, Special Committee to Investigate Campaign Expenditures for the House of Representatives, 1950, 81st Congress, 2nd Session, Report (1951), p. 20. This report will henceforth be cited as House Committee Report, 1951.

[14] Statement of Committee General Counsel Gillis W. Long in House Committee Hearings, 1952, p. 147. The county committees that do report spend a great deal of money. In the 1944 election in Pennsylvania alone, for example, the Democratic county committees spent $407,363, and the Republican county committees spent $957,250—a total of $1,264,613: Senate Committee Report, 1945, Appendix X, pp. 241-42. The Chairman of the Allegheny County (Pa.) Republican Committee testified in 1952 that his committee alone spent about $330,000 and the Democratic committee in his county spent about $150,000—a total of almost $500,000 in a single Pennsylvania county in the 1952 election alone: Testimony of Thomas E. Whitten, House Committee Hearings, 1952, p. 146.

[15] Cf. Overacker, *Money in Elections,* pp. 378-79.

[16] Cf. *U.S. News & World Report,* December 19, 1952, pp. 38-44. These estimates are not out of line with the recorded costs of previous pre-convention campaigns: General Leonard Wood's supporters spent $1,773,000 and Governor Lowden's $415,000 in trying to win the Republican nomination in 1920. The Hoover pre-convention campaign in 1928 cost $395,000, and the Roosevelt pre-convention campaign in 1932 cost $185,000: "The Presidential $ $ $," *Fortune,* Vol. XXII (July, 1940), pp. 47-49, 105-12.

[17] New York *Times,* December 1, 1952, pp. 1, 16-17.

[18] House Committee Hearings, 1952, p. 12.

mated the total cost of the election at between $80,000,000 and $100,000,000! [19]

These figures may, at first glance, seem disproportionately high; but if we bear in mind the fact that great corporations like General Motors, Ford, and Chrysler each spend from $11,000,000 to $37,000,000 *annually* to advertise their wares, and consider that the parties must appeal, in large part via the same mass-communications media, to a potential electorate of 90,000,000 once every four years, they fall pretty much into line with what we should fairly expect.[20]

A word now about the cost of campaigns for other offices. Senator Paul H. Douglas concluded from his own experience that a serious candidate for U.S. senator in a populous state must have a campaign fund of between $150,000 and $200,000.[21] Henry V. Poor, an unsuccessful candidate for the House of Representatives in a New York City district in 1952, spent over $15,000 in his campaign, and speaks of this figure as a *minimum* budget for a campaign for such an office.[22] And in the light of what we know about the economics of certain senatorial campaigns in the past, the estimates of Douglas and Poor seem, if anything, low. In the 1926 Pennsylvania Republican senatorial primary, for example, candidate Vare spent $785,000 and candidate Pepper $1,800,000! In the Illinois Republican senatorial primary of the same year, the two leading candidates spent, between them, over a million dollars.[23]

In short, the man who wishes to run for a major public office in the United States must have either (a) a not too small personal fortune that he is willing to invest in the enterprise, or (b) friends or an organization, or both, behind him willing to put up the money.[24] And in view of the increasing reliance upon radio and television as campaign media, the sums needed are likely to increase rather than diminish.[25]

[19] *U.S. News & World Report,* December 19, 1952, pp. 38-44.

[20] In 1954, American businessmen spent a total of $594,000,000 on advertising. Among the corporations spending the most were: General Motors ($37,300,000); Ford Motor Co. ($17,999,-000); Chrysler Corp. ($11,787,000); and Colgate-Palmolive Co. ($10,990,000): *Time,* June 13, 1955, p. 97. For a comparison of the size of the parties' campaigning bills and the size of the corporations' advertising bills, see John W. Lederle, "Political Committee Expenditures and the Hatch Act," *Michigan Law Review,* Vol. XLIV (1945), pp. 290-99; and V. O. Key, Jr., *Politics, Parties, and Pressure Groups,* 3rd ed. (New York: Thomas Y. Crowell Co., 1952), pp. 531-32.

[21] Paul H. Douglas, "What It Costs to Run," *Atlantic Monthly,* Vol. CXC (August, 1952), pp. 43-46.

[22] Henry V. Poor, "What It Costs to Run for Office," *Harper's,* Vol. CCVIII (May, 1954), pp. 46-52.

[23] Overacker, *Money in Elections,* pp. 278-83.

[24] The student must not be misled by the occasional "pauper" campaign he reads about in the newspapers, such as "Alfalfa Bill" Murray's campaign for governor of Oklahoma, in which the candidate took up collections at the public meetings he addressed "in order to get to the next town." All this means is that the real money is being spent by the candidate's friends, supporters, and potential beneficiaries.

[25] See Louise Overacker, *Presidential Campaign Funds* (Boston: Boston University Press, 1946), p. 34, for the reported-cost figures of presidential campaigns in the 1928, 1940, and 1944 elections. For figures for the 1932 election, see her article, "Campaign Funds in a Depression Year," *American Political Science Review,* and for figures for the 1936 election, see her article, "Campaign Funds in the Presidential Election of 1936," *American Political Science Review,* Vol. XXXI

Raising the Money

WHERE THE MONEY COMES FROM [26]

Contributions. Since parties and candidates in the United States get no direct grants from the public treasury, they finance themselves largely out of contributions from private sources, of which there appear to be three main categories:

CONTRIBUTIONS FROM CANDIDATES. Since the candidate normally has a big stake in the outcome of the election, he must expect to be one of the first sources to which the campaign treasurer turns in his quest for funds. How much he is expected to contribute depends on, among other things, his reputed financial worth, the prestige and salary attaching to the office he seeks, and the manner in which he was nominated (if he was "drafted," he can put up some resistance to party duns, but not so if he sought the office). If he cannot contribute the amount expected from him out of his personal resources, he must get busy and tap the resources of his friends and supporters. For if the word gets around in the organization that he is a cheapskate, or that he is trying to wangle a free ride, no future nominations are likely to come his way.

CONTRIBUTIONS FROM PATRONAGE JOBHOLDERS AND PARTY WORKERS. Party leaders expect "gratitude" from incumbents of remunerative public posts who owe their appointments to the party's influence, and it is clearly understood among party workers (they learn it long before they become appointees) that this gratitude will express itself in continued loyalty to the party, which in turn requires regular contributions to the party's campaign funds. The standard practice is for the officeholder to contribute a percentage (usually between 1 and 3 per cent) of his official salary.[27] The civil-service laws of the national government and of some of the states, as we shall note in detail later, put certain obstacles in the way of this traditional practice; but they can easily be circumvented—for example, by having the jobholder purchase a ticket or two to the annual Jefferson-Jackson Day or Lincoln Day dinner at $100 a plate.

CONTRIBUTIONS FROM "THE GENERAL PUBLIC." No matter how generous the candidates and jobholders are, however, they are too few in number to provide more than a small fraction of what the party needs for its campaign. The bulk of the money, accordingly, must come from nonparty sources—that is, from supporters and sympathizers among the general public, or from organized groups and corporations that have an interest in the outcome of the election.

(June, 1937), pp. 473-98. The *Congressional Quarterly* pointed out that the *reported* total expenditures ($13,700,000) for all candidates in the 1954 congressional elections were the highest in history: *Congressional Quarterly*, Vol. XIII (April 15, 1955), p. 369.

[26] For the most complete general discussion of this question, see Overacker, *Money in Elections*, Ch. VI.

[27] See Flynn, *op. cit.*, p. 15, for an account of how jobholders were assessed in the Bronx; and see Dayton D. McKean, *The Boss: The Hague Machine in Action* (Boston: Houghton Mifflin Company, 1940), Ch. 8, for the parallel practice in Hudson County, New Jersey.

A number of studies have been made of such contributions to party funds, and they all conclude that the bulk of the funds from public sources come from the wealthy. There are, to be sure, numerous small donations from private citizens with modest incomes, but as Table 21 clearly shows, any party that placed exclusive reliance upon them would be courting financial disaster.

TABLE 21 *Percentages of Total Contributions by Size of Contributions* [28]

| | 1928 | | 1932 | | 1936 | | 1940 | | 1944 | |
Size of Contribution	Dem.	Rep.	Dem.	Rep.	Dem.	Rep.	Dem.	Rep.	Dem.	Rep.
$1,000 and over	69.7	68.4	58.1	64.9	45.4	50.0	32.7	42.1	51.2	57.1
$100 to $999	16.3	21.9	14.5	23.4	18.0	23.9	17.3	30.7	25.2	33.9
Less than $100	12.5	8.2	16.0	9.1	18.5	13.5	23.3	13.4	23.6	9.0
Not allocated	1.5	1.5	11.4	2.6	18.1	11.6	26.7	13.8	—	—

Contributions to the Democrats' war chest for the 1952 election followed the previously established pattern: Stephen A. Mitchell, Chairman of the Democratic National Committee during the campaign, stated that while his committee received 126,000 contributions, 95 per cent of which were for less than $500, no less than 65 per cent of the total sum received was accounted for by contributions *in excess* of $500.[29] Persons who have had a hand in raising campaign funds seem to agree, moreover, that soliciting small contributions from numerous individuals burns up a good deal of what is contributed before it is contributed, and calls for hard work that might better be expended on other party activities; for most Americans apparently feel no obligation to contribute to the campaign funds of the party they prefer.[30] In short, the parties not only *must* rely heavily upon large contributions from a few wealthy donors (because they cannot finance themselves without such contributions), but considerations of convenience and efficiency also point them toward the large contributors.

Loans. Party expenditures during a campaign often exceed current contributions, and not always because the party managers have miscalculated the latter. Party managers apparently feel about campaigning the way most Americans feel about fighting a war: Get the job done, win the fight, and worry about the expense *after* the victory has been won! So, like the government during the war, they finance current operations by anticipating future contribu-

---

[28] The figures for 1928, 1932, 1936, and 1940 are given in Overacker, *Presidential Campaign Funds*, p. 14. The figures for 1944 are given in Overacker, "Presidential Campaign Funds, 1944," *American Political Science Review.*

[29] House Committee Hearings, 1952, p. 151.

[30] In June, 1948, the Gallup poll asked its respondents, "If you were asked, would you contribute five dollars to the campaign fund of the party you prefer?" Twenty-nine per cent replied "yes," and 71 per cent "no": Reprinted in the *Public Opinion Quarterly*, Vol. XII (Fall, 1948), p. 564.

tions—i.e., by borrowing. Sometimes, indeed, they have it both ways, by borrowing and *not* anticipating future income, since some of the "loans" they arrange are really disguised gifts—from persons who do not wish to be identified as large contributors to the party or who wish to report what they contribute as a "bad debt" and get back, later, some tax benefits.[31] Usually, however, deficit financing is accomplished via bona fide loans, which must be repaid by contributions after the election is over.[32]

WHAT MAKES PEOPLE GIVE?

According to Carlson and Blake, campaign funds are made up of:

Coppers—from the general public; plus

Nickels—from the candidates' personal friends; plus

Silver—from persons who hate the opposition and want some kind of revenge; plus

Gold—from persons who want something from the winner.[33]

The individuals in each of these categories *may* have any one or more of a wide variety of reasons, conscious and unconscious, for contributing. They may hope to get or keep a public post, which may be anything from a postmastership to an ambassadorship; to advance and protect the interests of the economic grouping or class with which they identify themselves,[34] or of another economic grouping or class about whose lot they have "feelings of guilt"; to obtain tariff advantages, government contracts, concessions, etc.; to

[31] According to *U.S. News & World Report,* under present tax laws and rulings by the Bureau of Internal Revenue, an individual may "lend" any amount of money to a party, make some kind of "effort" to collect after the campaign, and if he cannot collect, call it a "non-business bad debt" and write it off as a short-term capital loss. The effect is to avoid state and national ceilings on the size of donations, evade gift taxes, and limit income-tax liability. The magazine makes no guess, however, as to how often, or on what scale, party donors have actually taken advantage of the law in this fashion: *U.S. News & World Report,* Vol. XXXII (May 9, 1952), pp. 28-31.

[32] The party that loses will, for obvious reasons, have a harder time paying off its deficit than the party that wins. After the 1928 election, for example, the Democratic party was $1,-600,000 in the red, and in 1932 it had managed to cut its debt by only two-thirds: Cf. Louise Overacker, "Campaign Funds in a Depression Year," *American Political Science Review,* Vol. XXVII (October, 1933), pp. 769-83. The Democratic party also came out of the 1952 election with a considerable deficit, which was finally paid off largely by $100-a-plate dinners, with speeches by the defeated candidate, Adlai E. Stevenson, as the main attraction.

[33] *Op. cit.,* pp. 50-57. See also the comments by campaign manager Allen Morris in Fuller Warren, *How to Win in Politics* (Tallahassee, Fla.: Peninsular Publishing Company, 1949), Ch. 10.

[34] Few persons who contribute to party funds to protect their own—and their friends'—economic interests ever say so as plainly as did Henry Clay Frick, the steel tycoon, on a certain occasion. Frick and a number of other heads of large corporations contributed heavily to Theodore Roosevelt's war chest in the 1904 campaign on the understanding, according to Frick, that there would be no "trust-busting" of *their* corporations. After the election, however, Roosevelt nevertheless initiated a series of antitrust prosecutions against several of the firms in question, and Frick, mentioning a specific secret conference at the White House, told a reporter: "Why, Roosevelt fairly went down on his knees to us in his fear of defeat, and said that he would be good and leave the railroads and the corporations alone if we would only give him this financial help. We did, but he didn't stay put in his second term. We got nothing for our money": Quoted in David Loth, *Public Plunder: A History of Graft in America* (New York: Carrick and Evans, Inc., 1938), pp. 268-69.

help a particular candidate win a particular office, out of personal liking or admiration for him, or a conviction that he will forward the public interest; to help achieve victory for a party because it espouses a particular "ideology" or program; [35] or to get rid of a party solicitor to whom, for whatever reason, it is difficult to say no; or—but let the reader make his own list, for as yet we have no empirical studies concerning contributors' motives (and if and when we do have, since the respondents may fib to the investigators, we may not be much the wiser).

The one thing it seems safe to say is that most people normally let loose of money only in the expectation, or at least hope, of getting something in return for it, and, presumably, contribute to parties with an eye to the things a victorious party is able, once in office, to deliver. We have some knowledge of what these things are, and, starting from them, can with some confidence "construct" the appropriate motives. We must, however, be careful to avoid the pitfall of attributing to the givers of coppers more lofty and altruistic motives than to the givers of gold. The millionaire who contributes to the Republicans in the expectation that his profits will go up and his surtaxes down deserves no medal for altruism. But the $115-a-week automobile worker who votes for the Democrats in the expectation that the White House will support the next UAW strike deserves no medal either (and political scientists are not, or should not be, in the business of awarding medals anyhow). Each, presumably, believes his equivalent of Secretary Wilson's famous dictum, "What is good for General Motors is good for the Nation." But the American party system leaves all of us free to give to a party, and by giving put pressure on it to behave as we want it to, for any reason—selfish, unselfish, or both— that seems good to us.

The Legal Regulation of Party Finance

WHY REGULATE?

Some commentators on American politics have seen great dangers to the republic, actual or potential or both, in the fact that our parties get their funds in the everybody-free-to-contribute-for-his-own-reasons manner we have just described, and in certain other aspects of party finance.[36] Some have pointed with alarm to alleged corrupt expenditures, the purchase of votes in particular, and attributed them in part to the parties' having too much money at their disposal. Others have dwelt on the possibility that, as Will Rogers once put it, American elections might be "decided by bullion and not by ballot," yet

[35] For a canvass of this question, see Overacker, *Money in Elections,* Ch. VII; and *Fortune,* July, 1940, pp. 47-49, 105-12.

[36] Professor Overacker points out that "the meagre accounts which we have of ancient election methods show that 'campaigning' has gone on in every age where there were elections, that money played an important part in this campaigning and that the control of the use of money agitated ancient as well as modern lawmakers": *Money in Elections,* p. 5. See *ibid.,* pp. 5-19, for a brief historical account of the use of money in elections and of attempts to regulate it by law.

others on the possibility that rich men will control the government by exacting favors for their contributions, and still others on the possibility that patronage and graft will demoralize the civil service and so undermine our democracy—in each case with the recurrent themes that the dangers would be less if the parties were put on shorter money rations and if they obtained their funds in a different way.

The dangers in question are, of course, matters of grave import for the student of democracy and political parties, and we shall return to them in the final section of this chapter. For our immediate purposes it is enough to point out that American lawmakers have to a considerable extent shared these apprehensions, and have sought to guard against their realization by passing laws regulating party finance. To these laws we now turn our attention.

STATE REGULATION

Early American ventures in the regulation of party finance were modeled upon the British Corrupt Practices Act of 1883, which bans two categories of campaigning practices: "corrupt practices" (e.g., bribery and "treating" of voters), which carry relatively severe penalties; and "illegal practices" (e.g., transporting voters to or from the polls), which carry somewhat lighter penalties. (On the enforcement side it requires each candidate to appoint an election agent to answer for his obedience to the laws and report his receipts and expenditures.) The 1883 law received much favorable publicity in the United States, and before long (1890) New York became the first American state to place on its books a statute regulating party finance. In the course of the next thirty-five years, 44 states imitated New York's example.[37]

All 48 states now regulate party finance in one way or another, with, however, marked variation from state to state in details.[38] Nearly all (45 states) require parties, candidates, or both to file official statements of expenditures.[39] Nearly all (40 states) require them to file official statements of receipts. A great many (32 states) stipulate who may or may not contribute, usually by prohibiting contributions from corporations and labor unions, and a similar number (29 states) limit the *type* of expenditures, mainly by prohibiting such "corrupt practices" as bribery or intimidation of voters. More than half (31

---

[37] For the content and influence of the British Corrupt Practices Act of 1883, see Earl R. Sikes, *State and Federal Corrupt-Practices Legislation* (Durham, N. C.: Duke University Press, 1938), pp. 123-25; and Overacker, *Money in Elections*, pp. 212-17. For a useful summary of the regulation of party finance in other nations, see James K. Pollock, *Money and Politics Abroad* (New York: Alfred A. Knopf, 1932). For the most complete general history of the adoption of such legislation in the United States, see Pollock, *Party Campaign Funds*, Ch. II.

[38] The most recent general summary of the state laws regulating party finance is S. Sydney Minault, *Corrupt Practices Legislation in the 48 States* (Chicago: Council of State Governments, 1942).

[39] The figures on the incidence of each type of regulation among the states are taken from the *Book of the States, 1954-1955* (Chicago: Council of State Governments, 1954), Vol. X, table on pp. 78-79.

states) put a ceiling on the *amount* of expenditures *by* candidates; and some (18 states) put a ceiling on total expenditures *on behalf of* candidates.

Provisions for enforcement also vary markedly from state to state, but in general the initiative for starting prosecutions and invoking penalties is left to private individuals, either the defeated candidate or some party official, rather than to the public authorities.

FEDERAL REGULATION [40]

Congress has passed three major statutes regulating campaign finance: the Pendleton Act of 1883, the Federal Corrupt Practices Act of 1925, and the Hatch Political Activities Acts of 1939 and 1940. These apply only to general and special elections in which federal offices (including seats in the two houses of Congress and in the electoral college) are at stake, and do not apply to *primary* elections or conventions in which candidates for the offices named are selected.

The main provisions of the federal regulatory laws are as follows:

(1) Ceilings are imposed on the total amount of expenditures *by* (but not *on behalf of*) individual candidates. A candidate for the House of Representatives may spend up to $2,500, or, alternatively, a figure arrived at by multiplying the total number of votes cast in the election in question for the office contested by 3¢, but in no case more than $5,000. A candidate for the Senate may spend up to $10,000, or, alternatively, a figure arrived at by multiplying the total number of votes cast in the contest by 3¢, but in no case more than $25,000. If, moreover, the state the candidate seeks to represent in Congress imposes a lower ceiling than that imposed by federal law, the state ceiling governs.

(2) Ceilings are imposed on the total expenditures of national political committees. No national political committee (that is, any group that spends money to influence the outcome of elections in two or more states) may in any calendar year receive or spend more than $3,000,000.

(3) Ceilings are imposed on contributions by individuals. No individual may in any calendar year contribute more than $5,000 to any candidate or any political committee. (Note, however, that an individual may give up to $5,000 each to as many candidates and committees as he likes.)

(4) Contributions from certain sources are prohibited. No corporation and no labor organization may contribute funds in connection with any election in which a national office is at stake.

(5) Solicitation of funds from and by federal employees is sharply restricted. Officers and employees of the United States (including members of

---

[40] For convenient summaries of federal legislation regulating party finance, see the Report of the Special Committee of the House of Representatives to Investigate Campaign Expenditures, 82nd Congress, 1st Session (1953), pp. 71-76. This report will henceforth be cited as House Committee Report, 1953. See also John W. Lederle, "Political Committee Expenditures and the Hatch Act," *Michigan Law Review.*

Congress) are prohibited from soliciting or receiving political funds from or donating them to other such officers and employees. (Persons *not* employed by the federal government can solicit and receive contributions from federal officers and employees, provided the transaction takes place off federal premises.) [41]

(6) Electioneering activities by public employees paid out of federal funds are prohibited. The Hatch Acts forbid any public officer or employee below the "policy-making" level in the executive branch to take "any active part in political management or in political campaigns," and similarly restrict any state or local employee whose principal activity is in connection with a function financed in whole or in part by federal funds. What the persons covered by the acts cannot do without "taking part, etc." is a highly complicated question, a detailed answer to which would carry us too far afield. They can, according to rulings the courts have laid down in interpreting the acts, express political opinions in private conversations, but not in public speeches; they can attend party rallies and conventions as spectators, but not as organizers or delegates; they can wear—but not distribute—party lapel buttons. They cannot, in short, engage in any *overt* electioneering activity that goes beyond letting others know where they stand politically.[42]

(7) Reports of contributions and expenditures are made mandatory. Each candidate for the House of Representatives and for the Senate must file (with the Clerk of the House and the Secretary of the Senate respectively) two statements of his receipts and expenditures, one before and one after the election. And each national political committee must file with the Clerk of the House several times each year a statement of its current receipts and expenditures.

THE RESULTS OF LEGAL REGULATION

Students of American party finance seem generally agreed that legal regulation has proved far from effective. Four conclusions seem justified:

(1) *The ceilings on contributions by individuals are easily circumvented.* The purpose of such ceilings is, as we have noted, to prevent the wealthy from "buying" elections by pouring vast amounts of money into the campaign of a particular party or candidate; and to this end federal law, as we have also noted, prohibits any person from contributing more than $5,000 to a single candidate or party committee. On the face of it, however, such a rule invites contributors, while observing its letter,[43] to violate its spirit as much as they like. A man cannot give more than $5,000 to, say, the Republican National Committee; but he can, in strict literal conformity with the rule, give $3,000 to the committee, another $3,000 to Citizens for Eisenhower-Nixon, and an-

[41] L. V. Howard, "Federal Restrictions on the Political Activity of Government Employees," *American Political Science Review*, Vol. XXXV (June, 1941), pp. 470-89.

[42] Cf. *ibid.;* and Ferrel Heady, "The Hatch Act Decisions," *American Political Science Review*, Vol. XLI (August, 1947), pp. 687-99.

[43] Most contributors go the law one better by limiting each contribution to $3,000, since a federal gift tax must be paid on any contribution in excess of $3,000.

other $3,000 each to the New York Republican Central Committee, the Nassau County Citizens for Eisenhower, and the Elect a Republican Congress Committee; and, having done all that, he can also have his wife, his 30-year-old son, his 27-year-old daughter, *and* his four 3-year-old grandchildren all give similar amounts to these same committees. There is, moreover, reason to believe that this is what wealthy donors in fact do. In the 1944 election, for example, the Du Pont family contributed $109,832 (31 individuals in the Du Pont family contributed to a total of 58 organizations); the Pew family $96,995 (9 individuals, 60 organizations); the Mellon family $59,500 (6 individuals, 30 organizations); the Rockefeller family $53,400 (9 individuals, 27 organizations); and the Vanderbilt family $38,000 (7 individuals, 19 organizations).[44]

(2) *The ceilings on expenditures by national committees are completely disregarded.* The purpose of the ceilings, as we have seen, is to limit the amounts spent on campaigns (concretely, the federal law prohibits any "national political committee" from receiving or spending more than $3,000,000 in any calendar year). Here also the letter of the law is scrupulously observed, so that since 1940 neither party's national committee has exceeded the limit.[45] But each presidential campaign from 1940 to the present has brought its rash of national "independent" committees of one kind or another, each formally separate and distinct from the others and from any national party committee, and each, therefore, legally free to spend up to the $3,000,000 limit.[46] In the 1952 election, for instance, the national Citizens for Eisenhower-Nixon organization collected and spent $1,450,000; and the 16,000 state and local Eisenhower-Nixon clubs spent another $1,500,000.[47] The National Volunteers for Stevenson spent $740,000, and the state and local Volunteers organizations spent at least as much.[48] Meanwhile, of course, both national party committees were busy raising and disbursing funds, with the result that total *reported* expenditures rose to $32,000,000—but without anyone's violating the legal limitation of $3,000,000!

(3) *The prohibitions against contributions by labor organizations and corporations are consistently evaded.* The Smith-Connally Act of 1943 prohibits contributions by "any labor organization . . . in connection with any election at which [any national offices] are to be voted for." But by 1944, as if in

[44] Senate Committee Report, 1945, Appendix VIII, pp. 140-51. Wealthy families use the same procedure to evade ceilings on contributions to individual congressional candidates: see the report on individual contributions in the 1954 congressional elections in the *Congressional Quarterly*, Vol. XIII (April 15, 1955), pp. 396-404.

[45] In 1944, the Republican National Committee officially reported receipts totaling $2,999,999.48!

[46] Pollock points out that such committees operated in presidential campaigns before the passage of the Hatch Acts. *Party Campaign Funds*, pp. 55-61. But since 1940 there have been many more of them, most of them have spent far more money than their predecessors, and where the party committees used to frown on and try to discourage the formation of such "independent" committees, they now encourage them in every way possible: Cf. Senate Committee Report, 1945, p. 7.

[47] Testimony of Walter Williams, House Committee Hearings, 1952, pp. 109-15.

[48] Testimony of Hermon D. Smith, House Committee Hearings, 1952, pp. 27-35.

response to the act, the CIO had created the Political Action Committee, and by 1947 there was a Labor's League for Political Education that made no secret of having been sponsored by the AFL. Both have been able to claim immunity from the Smith-Connally prohibitions: they are, they insist, independent of their respective unions and are thus not "labor organizations" within the meaning of the act; and the money they spend, they insist further, goes into propaganda and educational activities that have no connection with any political party, and therefore cannot be regarded as "contributions" to parties and candidates. Both contentions have been upheld by the courts, with the result that unions continue to participate in political campaigns on a large scale, and these particular provisions of the Smith-Connally Act, as far as the purposes of its authors are concerned, are inoperative.[49] LLPE, for example, spent $242,661 in the 1952 election.[50]

Corporations likewise have found it easy to circumvent restrictions on their political activity—for example, by means of the "educational" programs of such organizations as the National Association of Manufacturers and the Chamber of Commerce. These organizations are no less busy during campaigns than their labor counterparts at trying to affect voter preferences and are financed by the nation's corporate wealth; and many corporations, moreover, make even more direct contributions via the purchase of blocks of tickets to $100-a-plate party dinners.

(4) *Presidential campaigns are more decentralized than formerly.* Thus they have become more expensive and more difficult to regulate. The independent committees we have mentioned, not only the PAC type of organization but the Citizens for Eisenhower-Nixon type as well, *are* independent of the national party committees, and sometimes plan and conduct their campaign activities without even consulting the party committees; and both national party chairmen in the 1952 campaign have since testified that the resulting absence of central campaign direction has, from the parties' point of view, numerous disadvantages. As Democratic Chairman Mitchell put it:

As we all know, separate committees are required [sic] by the law. But you are not able to have a coordinated campaign and the lack of coordination, it is inefficient, and more money is spent by numerous committees, in my judgment, than would be spent if the direction of the campaign were by one. . . . The law does prohibit unified management of a campaign. In the case of the Stevenson-Sparkman campaign, the operation of the various committees, the volunteers, entirely outside of the question of funds, was such that we found ourselves colliding in attempting to get a radio or television program, or radio or television time.[51]

[49] Cf. Overacker, "Presidential Campaign Funds, 1944," *American Political Science Review.*
[50] Testimony of James L. McDevitt, Director of LLPE, in House Committee Hearings, 1952, p. 101. See also Joseph Tanenhaus, "Organized Labor's Political Spending: The Law and Its Consequences," *Journal of Politics,* Vol. XVI (August, 1954), pp. 441-71.
[51] House Committee Hearings, 1952, pp. 148-49. For Republican National Chairman Summerfield's testimony to the same point, see House Committee Hearings, 1952, p. 56.

Most observers would agree with Professor Overacker's judgment that while legal regulation of party finance in America has probably greatly reduced the incidence of some of the most-disapproved corrupt campaign practices (such as the outright bribery of voters), it has done little or nothing to limit the amount of money spent on politics or to even things up as between rich candidates and poor candidates.[52] And most observers would endorse her conclusion that

The Hatch Act limitations were included in an act which purported to "Prohibit Pernicious Political Practices." One might almost parody it to read: "An Act to *Promote* Pernicious Political Activities." It defeats its own purpose by encouraging decentralization, evasion, and concealment. Worst of all, it makes difficult if not impossible that publicity which is essential to full understanding of who pays our political bills—and why.[53]

Many would also agree with Charles Michelson's statement that

The result of the legislation was to make constructive criminals of all the officials of the two great parties. . . . Not since the Volstead Act has there been so general a side-stepping of the law by people who are normally classed as decent citizens.[54]

THE FLORIDA LAW OF 1951

In 1951, the State of Florida drastically revised that part of its election code which regulates campaign expenditures—with the result, in the opinion of one admiring observer, that we now have "the first comprehensive attempt to adjust state regulation of campaign finance to the facts of contemporary political life." [55] Each candidate in a primary or general election must, under the new law, appoint a campaign treasurer, to whom all contributions to the candidate's campaign must be sent. The treasurer must deposit them in a designated depository within twenty-four hours after their receipt. All expenditures must be financed by vouchers against the deposits so created. When the campaign is over, the depository bank must report the candidate's deposits and withdrawals to the Secretary of State. And at varying intervals *during* the campaign—every week for candidates for governor and U.S. senator, and every month for other candidates—each treasurer must report to the Secretary of State his receipts to date, the names of the donors, and the amount and character of each expenditure. The treasurers' reports must, as they come in, be made available for the newspapers.[56] No single individual may contribute more

---

[52] Cf. Overacker, *Money in Elections,* pp. 378-79.

[53] *Presidential Campaign Funds,* p. 45.

[54] Charles Michelson, *The Ghost Talks* (New York: G. P. Putnam's Sons, 1944), p. 207. See also Carlson and Blake, *op. cit.,* p. 48.

[55] Elston E. Roady, "Florida's New Campaign Expense Law and the 1952 Democratic Gubernatorial Primaries," *American Political Science Review,* Vol. XLVIII (June, 1954), pp. 465-76.

[56] In the 1952 gubernatorial primary campaign, these reports were given prominent space in a number of papers over the state.

than $1,000, and no person financially interested in horse racing, dog racing, liquor licenses, or profit-making public utilities that require public franchises may contribute to any campaign fund.

Interested Floridians appear to regard the workings of the new law with great satisfaction, and some commentators have pointed to it as an excellent model for other states, and the federal government as well, to follow.[57] The whole question of the proper legal regulation of campaign finance is, however, only one aspect of the larger problem of money in American politics—a problem to which we shall return in the final section of the present chapter.

Patronage and Graft in American Politics

The term "patronage," as it is normally used, refers to the practice of making appointments to public office as rewards for services to a political party or political leader. It is usually contrasted with the "merit system," which is the practice of awarding appointments to public office solely on the basis of technical competence, as determined either by competitive examination or by credentials. It is impossible to say, on the basis of information now available, exactly what percentage of all the public jobs in the United States are filled by patronage and what percentage by the merit system. This much can be said, however: Although merit-system jobs are far more numerous at all levels of government today than they were fifty years ago, there are still a great many patronage appointments, particularly at the state and local levels.[58]

"Graft" is a more inclusive concept; it is defined by Professor Key as "the abuse of control over the power and resources of the government for the purpose of personal or party profit."[59] The term includes, among other things, favoritism in awarding government contracts or in spending public funds, writing laws so as to give special privileges to certain groups, administering laws so as to favor one competing group over another, and so on. In the present chapter, however, we are not concerned with the kind of graft whose object is the purely *personal* profit of the grafter, but rather with that whose object is the sort of gratitude on the part of the beneficiary that will dispose him to give money to a *party*.

Opinions differ sharply as to the present incidence of graft in the United States. Scandals, say some observers, are notably less frequent, the sums involved more modest, and the resultant public anxieties less urgent than in the past (e.g., the days of "Boss" Tweed, the Whiskey Ring, and the *Crédit*

---

[57] Cf. Roady, *op. cit.;* and the testimony of Robert A. Gray, Secretary of State of Florida, in House Committee Hearings, 1952, pp. 172-90.

[58] As of 1952, only nineteen states had comprehensive merit-system laws. Most of the other states, like the federal government, had merit-system requirements for filling some but not all jobs: Cf. Richard S. Childs, *Civic Victories* (New York: Harper and Brothers, 1952), p. 275.

[59] V. O. Key, Jr., *The Techniques of Political Graft in the United States* (Chicago: private edition, distributed by the University of Chicago Libraries, 1936), p. 5.

Mobilier).[60] But they have not disappeared: such phrases as "mink coats," "deep freezes," and "five-percenters" have taken on a political coloration in recent years, and "corruption"—along with "communism" and "Korea"—is believed by many to have been a major cause of the Democrats' defeat in the 1952 presidential election.

Current political morality, though it officially puts both patronage and graft on the disapproved list, tends to wink at the former, and comes down hard only on the latter. Graft, accordingly, insofar as it still plays a role in American politics, does so in whispers behind closed doors; in other words, graft is not today an accepted means to party ends, but patronage still is.[61] Now and then, moreover (as we shall note in a moment), a more-candid-than-most party leader or party worker speaks up frankly in defense of patronage, and many of the negotiations relating to its distribution are conducted more or less out in the open.[62]

THE FUNCTIONS OF PATRONAGE

The primary function of patronage is to serve as the mortar that binds together the blocks, and so maintains the strength, of party organization. As we have noted many times before, the core of any successful party operation is the small band of workers who will faithfully carry on its activities when the prospects for victory are dim as well as when they are bright, and when the party's candidates are dull and uninspiring as well as when they are glamorous. The occasional volunteer workers whose enthusiasms are fired by particular candidates or issues in particular elections are always welcome; but at best they are temporary allies, whom no sensible party leader would count on as bone and marrow for his organization. And most party leaders firmly believe that the only kind of precinct workers they dare put their definitive bets on are those who hope to get some personal economic gain (usually in the form of a patronage job) for their services to the party; so that handing out patronage jobs—or at least holding forth the hope of such jobs—is generally regarded by party men not only as legitimate, but as the most practical and sensible way of keeping precinct workers faithfully and steadily at their tasks.

Patronage also provides a source of campaign funds (via assessments of jobholders, as explained above). The huge and increasing costs of campaigns and the relative scarcity and poverty of patronage jobholders, however, have made this aspect of patronage far less crucial than it was a half-century ago.[63]

[60] Cf. Flynn, *op. cit.,* p. 61.

[61] For some useful and suggestive studies of the problem of graft in American politics and in American life in general, see John T. Flynn, *Graft in Business* (New York: The Vanguard Press, 1931); Loth, *op. cit.;* and the literature on "bosses" cited in Chapter 11.

[62] Few present-day party leaders, by contrast, would publicly defend the famous distinction between "honest graft" and "dishonest graft" made by the old Tammany boss, George Washington Plunkitt, in the early 1900's. See William L. Riordan, *Plunkitt of Tammany Hall* (New York: Alfred A. Knopf, 1948), pp. 3-8.

[63] Cf. Key, *The Techniques of Political Graft in the United States,* pp. 68-75.

Finally, patronage is a major weapon, which factions can employ in intraparty contests for control of the organization. In any showdown contest for the loyalty and support of party workers, the faction that dispenses the party's patronage over any considerable period of time has, naturally enough, the inside run.[64]

FARLEY'S RULES FOR HANDING OUT PATRONAGE

For a frank and authoritative explanation of how patronage is handed out by party leaders there is no better place to turn than to a public statement from James A. Farley about the situation the Democrats faced when they came to power in 1933. They had, he says, some 150,000 federal patronage jobs to fill (out of a total of 750,000 federal posts)—and some ten applicants for each job. Farley, whom President Roosevelt had put in charge of allocating the jobs, promptly found himself inundated by a flood of letters from all over the country. "They demanded jobs which I had never even heard of," he writes—among others, some that sounded like leg pulls:

When I received the first letter asking for appointment to the position of Custodian of the Craters of the Moon I thought the man was joking. It wasn't until I had received several other letters asking for the same position that I realized the Craters of the Moon is one of our finer national monuments in the West and that the position of custodian is much coveted.[65]

Farley had to invent machinery for breaking the log jam. He had a dossier prepared for each applicant. And the dossiers were evaluated, one by one, in accordance with the following tests: [66]

(1) Who recommended the applicant? If he is not recommended by a party leader (a Congressman, a national party committeeman, a state or local chairman), he is eliminated from further consideration.

(2) Is he qualified? If there is reason to believe that the applicant cannot handle the job he is applying for, he is either dropped or shifted to another job, no matter how eminent the persons recommending him.

(3) Is he loyal to the party and its program? If the applicant has done little or nothing to help win recent elections, he is dropped in favor of one who has been active. And, where at all possible, a person who believes in the president's program is preferred to one who does not.

(4) Was he F.R.B.C.—For Roosevelt Before Chicago? If two or more applicants for the same job pass the other tests, the job is given to the one who actively supported the Roosevelt cause in the pre-convention campaign. "Bandwagon jumpers" come second.

---

[64] Cf. *ibid.*, pp. 75-81.

[65] James A. Farley, "Passing Out the Patronage," *American Magazine*, Vol. CXVI (August, 1933), pp. 20-22, 77.

[66] The most complete statement of these rules is in *ibid.* See also Farley, *Behind the Ballots* (New York: Harcourt, Brace and Company, 1938), pp. 271-72; and Oliver McKee, Jr., "The Job-Master General," *North American Review*, Vol. CCXXXVII (February, 1934), pp. 119-26.

Though there are changes in emphasis from time to time and from place to place, most patronage is still distributed according to rules that closely follow the Farley pattern.

THE ROLE OF PATRONAGE

Patronage and the "spoils system" have had—and have today—numerous critics. And, to judge by the steady (if not rapid) advance of the merit system at all levels of American government, the critics' arguments have deeply affected public policy. Their main charges against the patronage system, today as in the past, are that it debauches the government service by sluicing into it technically incompetent personnel, that it lowers the morale of government employees by generating an atmosphere of job insecurity, and that it corrupts the political morality of the nation by treating venality and jobbery as natural and normal. A few critics add the further charge that patronage injures the parties themselves, by turning them into job-dispensing agencies and thus deflecting their attention from their proper task—the formulation of public policy [67]—and by giving the "ins" a powerful and unfair advantage over the "outs." [68]

Patronage also has its modern defenders, who, like Andrew Jackson, argue that the spoils system does far more good than harm. Their case for patronage consists of two main arguments: (1) Governmental policies should be administered by men who believe in them, and the best way to ensure this is to have the policies of the majority party carried out by active adherents of that party.[69] (2) Democratic government cannot operate without political parties; political parties, however, cannot operate without a solid core of hardworking precinct workers and leaders; and few people will devote the necessary time and energy to party activities without the kind of hope of personal economic reward that patronage provides.[70]

The practical politicians' philosophy of patronage has been well stated by Mr. Farley:

The patronage is a reward to those who have worked for a party victory. It is also an assistance in building party machinery for the next election. It is also—and this the public usually forgets—the test by which a party shows its fitness to govern. Every bad appointment comes home to roost eventually. . . . As . . . a politician I would reward those who have worked for the Democratic party. I would try to build strong Democratic organizations in the states. I would try, by the test

[67] Cf. James K. Pollock, "The Cost of the Patronage System," *Annals of the American Academy of Political and Social Science,* Vol. CLXXXIX (January, 1937), pp. 29-34. This entire issue of the *Annals* is devoted to the subject of patronage and the civil service.

[68] Thomas J. Haggerty, "Spoils and the 'Racket,'" *Annals of the American Academy of Political and Social Science,* Vol. CLXXXIX (January, 1937), pp. 17-21.

[69] Cf. Raymond Baldwin, *Let's Go into Politics* (New York: The Macmillan Company, 1952), pp. 132-33.

[70] Cf. Edward J. Flynn, *op. cit.,* pp. 20-25; Frank Hague, as quoted in George Creel, "The Complete Boss," *Collier's,* Vol. XCVIII (October 10, 1936), pp. 13, 58-60; and William Turn, "In Defense of Patronage," in the January, 1937, issue of the *Annals,* pp. 22-28.

of loyalty, to be sure that every man in the Roosevelt administration was whole-heartedly working for Roosevelt. Realizing that party success is largely dependent on party unity, I would fight to see that patronage was equitably distributed. I would try to diminish envy and rancor by giving rewards to ability. I would re-frain from making a single *personal* appointment. . . .[71]

The Problem of Money in American Politics

PROPOSED REFORMS IN REGULATORY LEGISLATION

Many commentators on American politics and elections, including both academic political scientists and members of recent congressional committees that have investigated the subject, are agreed that our laws regulating campaign finance need reworking. Current proposals for reform, and current arguments in support of those proposals, are of interest not only because they may become public policy but also for the light they throw on current American thinking about the problem of money in politics.

Most commentators on the problem would agree with the following three sets of statements about it: [72]

(1) The most effective regulatory device is *publicity*. Its great advantage, we are told, is that it provides the political system with an excellent self-cor-recting mechanism. If, that is to say, one candidate is known to be spending many times as much as his opponent, or if he is known to be receiving huge contributions from the "fat cats," the voters are likely to feel that he and his friends are trying to "buy" the election, and will vote against him. Similarly, and for the same reason, a rich man is not likely to lavish outsize contributions on particular candidates if he knows beforehand that the fact of his doing so will become public knowledge. Full publicity, then, is the best way to keep elections from being controlled by the rich; and present state and federal legis-lation should be revised so as to provide for the centralized accounting of and responsibility for campaign funds, and for *pre*-election publication of each candidate's and party's receipts, donors, and expenditures.

[71] Farley, "Passing Out the Patronage," *American Magazine*, p. 77.

[72] The case for these proposed reforms is most fully stated in Professor Overacker's *Money in Elections*, Ch. XIV. It can also be found in Professor Pollock's *Party Campaign Funds* and in his article, "Campaign Funds and Their Regulation in 1936," *American Political Science Review*, Vol. XXX (June, 1936), pp. 507-12; and in Hugh A. Bone, *American Politics and the Party System* (New York: McGraw-Hill Book Company, Inc., 1949), pp. 641-48. Active politicians who make the same arguments include Paul H. Douglas, *Ethics in Government* (Cambridge, Mass.: Harvard University Press, 1952), pp. 65-85; William Benton, "To Stem the Tide of Political Dol-lars," *New York Times Magazine*, December 9, 1951, p. 19; and Richard L. Neuberger, "It Costs Too Much to Run for Office," *New York Times Magazine*, April 11, 1948, p. 20. See also Robert Bendiner, "How Much Does Your Vote Cost?" *Collier's*, Vol. CXXX (September 20, 1952), pp. 24-27. Each of the three most recent congressional committees that have in-vestigated this problem have recommended changes in the federal laws along the lines sum-marized in the text: see Senate Committee Report, 1945, pp. 80-84; House Committee Report, 1951, pp. 21-26; and House Committee Report, 1953, pp. 57-58.

(2) While legal ceilings on expenditures and on contributions by individuals have the laudable purpose of trying to give the poor candidate an even chance with the rich candidate, there is no satisfactory way of defining a "fair" ceiling, and in any case such ceilings are too easily evaded to be worth bothering with.

(3) The sensible way of giving poor candidates a more even break with rich ones is to provide various kinds of official aid for *all* candidates: free mailing privileges, free radio and TV time, perhaps even outright grants from the public treasury to all campaign funds.

THE NATURE OF THE MONEY PROBLEM

The above statements all rest, clearly, upon the premise—now explicit, now tacit—that in politics as in every other aspect of American life, *money talks*. In other words, when we speak of "the problem" of money in American politics, what we are saying is that money can and often does determine the outcome of elections, and that we think it should not do so. Big money, according to these commentators, buys big campaigns; and big campaigns usually prevail over little campaigns; and this violates the basic democratic principle of political equality. If, that is to say, the rich can control the government by buying the votes of the poor, whether directly through bribery or indirectly through elaborate campaigns and expensive mass propaganda, then the principle that each member of the community should have the same chance as his fellows to participate effectively in the community decision-making process goes by the board.

Now, if money does indeed swing elections in the way this argument presupposes, then its inadequately regulated use in our elections *is* a major barrier to the fuller realization of democracy in the American system. But let us, before accepting that conclusion, examine the proposition that money swings elections.

THE ROLE OF MONEY IN AMERICAN POLITICS

As we noted above, most of the money spent in American politics goes to pay for campaigns. And in Chapter 15 we drew several conclusions about the role of campaigns that bear repeating here: Campaigning does affect a party's chances of winning elections, but is only one factor among many other factors ("events," traditional voter loyalties, the personalities of the candidates, etc.). It remains to be shown, in other words, that even the cleverest and most costly campaign can transfer *major* blocs of voters from one candidate or party to another. And if it cannot induce large numbers of voters to vote for a candidate or party they would not otherwise have voted for, then it can decide, at most, only close elections.

Do more expensive campaigns in fact usually carry the day against less expensive campaigns? Or, to put the same question a little differently, is the amount of money spent on a campaign a reliable index of its prospects for victory? We have very little empirical evidence to go on here, but what we have does not, in the present writers' opinion, warrant affirmative answers to these questions. The sociologist George Lundberg, to be sure, when he studied the 1928 elections in a number of New York counties on the one hand, and certain states on the other, concluded that in 145 out of 156 elections, the side that spent the greater sums won. "These figures indicate," he writes, "that *in fourteen cases out of fifteen, campaign expenditures, as reported, constitute an absolutely reliable index of the outcome of the election.*" [73] But all that Lundberg's figures in fact show is that in the 1928 elections he studied, the Republicans—who normally won the elections in those days—spent more money than the Democrats; they do *not* show that the Republicans won the elections *because* they spent more money. [74]

Nothing could be more certain, moreover, than that the country has seen many an election won by the party or candidate that spent the lesser sums in the campaign. The Democrats have spent less than the Republicans in every presidential campaign in the twentieth century, for example, and yet have won seven times out of fourteen. And, finally, even if we had data comparable to Lundberg's on all recent elections at all levels, and even if they showed that the party with the larger campaign fund has won a high percentage of them, we could not safely conclude that campaign funds have been *the* determining factor, because we would have no grounds for rejecting the obvious alternative hypothesis—which is that the winning party was going to win the elections it won in any case, and found it easy, for that reason, to raise money.

In summary, all one can say about the role of money in American politics is this: Most of the money is spent on campaigning, and campaigning is only one of the factors that determine the outcome of elections. If, in a given election, the other factors balance out about evenly for both parties, a heavy preponderance of money on one side might, conceivably, decide the election in its favor. But this is a far cry from saying, as the commentators we have in mind either say or imply, that money regularly *does* decide American elections. [75] Nor is there any reason to believe that money plays a more important role in American politics than it does in other aspects of American life: The poorer party, or candidate, that is to say, is no worse off than, say, the poorer litigant in a lawsuit, or the poorer college in its contest with richer colleges for professors, students, and winning football teams. In other words, the prob-

[73] George Lundberg, "Campaign Expenditures and Election Results," *Social Forces,* Vol. VI (March, 1928), pp. 452-57. Italics in the original.

[74] Lundberg, let us note in all fairness, never comes right out and says this. The reader can decide for himself whether it is implied in the sentence quoted.

[75] The position taken in the text is, in general, also taken by Overacker, *Money in Elections,* pp. 86-93; Key, *Politics, Parties, and Pressure Groups,* pp. 562-64; and McKean, *Party and Pressure Politics,* pp. 359-61.

lem of money in American politics is a "special case" of the general problem of money in American society.[76]

To the character of American society, and the extent to which our political parties reflect it, we turn our attention in the final three chapters of this book.

[76] For two recent discussions of the problem from this point of view, see Douglas, *Ethics in Government;* and George A. Graham, *Morality in American Politics* (New York: Random House, 1952).

Chapter 17

PARTY GOVERNMENT
IN STATE
AND NATION

The Model of Responsible Party Government

The activities of American political parties that we have described in the preceding five chapters are merely means to one central and overriding end, that of winning public office for their nominees. We turn now to a different kind of party activity, for which we must look *inside* the formal governmental machinery after the election is over, when the successful nominees are actually filling the offices to which they have been elected. And the question we shall wish to keep in mind as we describe this kind of party activity—a key question, incidentally, for our whole inquiry in this book—is this: Do the party labels under which most American public officials go into office determine, or at least influence, their behavior while in office? To what extent, in other words, is a legislator's, an executive's, an administrator's, or a judge's affiliation with one of our major parties rather than the other *predictive* of his behavior in his official capacity?

Many American scholars believe that these questions are the most crucial that can be asked about a party system; for they believe that a party system merits approval or disapproval according to the answers it furnishes to them. These questions, in other words, touch upon the key points involved in the doctrine of responsible party government, which, as we noted in Chapter 6, has many adherents among present-day American theorists of party.[1]

When it is behaving in accordance with the model of democratic party behavior envisoned by these theorists, a party regards winning elections not as an end in itself, but rather as the appropriate means for accomplishing its *proper* end—which is the translation of its platform, program, and principles into actual public policy. Once in command of a majority of the votes and public offices, therefore, the majority party's leaders introduce in the legislature bills embodying the party program; all the party's members in the legis-

[1] See pp. 151-52; see also pp. 525-27.

lature loyally support and vote for these bills; and the party leaders make sure that the resulting laws are faithfully carried out by the administrative agencies. When the parties act in this manner, the argument runs, the majority party is clearly and unequivocally *responsible* for what the government does or does not do; and at the next election the voters hand down a *meaningful* verdict of approval or disapproval of that party by giving it another term in office or turning it out of power.[2]

In the concluding chapters of this book we shall have more to say about this responsible-party-government model as compared with our own model of democracy on the one hand, and with the going concern that is the American political system on the other. In the present chapter we shall attempt merely to describe the role our parties observably play inside our formal governmental machinery at both the national and state levels.

The Role of Party in the National Government

IN CONGRESS

The most visible and formalized manifestation of party activity inside the machinery of the national government is the "organization" (organization, that is, in a special technical sense of the term which differs from that used in earlier chapters) of Congress by the parties at the beginning of each session. In this sense, organization includes the election of officers and the assignment of members of Congress to the various congressional committees and other agencies, some "formal," i.e., created by the official rules of the two houses, and some "informal," i.e., created by purely party understandings and not to be found in the rules of the houses.[3]

Party Agencies in Congress.[4] Independently—or for the most part independently—of the committees and officers (the formal organization) of the two houses, each of the parties in each house has a formal organization of its own, consisting of the following.

---

[2] For a more complete description of this model and its sources and present-day advocates, see Austin Ranney, *The Doctrine of Responsible Party Government* (Urbana: University of Illinois Press, 1954).

[3] This meaning of "organization" is not remote from ordinary speech, which refers to the "organization" meeting of a new club. Note that, as used in Congress, the term says nothing one way or the other about the mobilization of party members behind particular bills or programs; when we say, therefore, that the Democrats "organized" the 84th Congress, we do not suggest that, as a party, they controlled all its activities, or worked hand in hand in the committees or on the floor in support of particular bills.

[4] Useful descriptions of the party agencies in Congress are to be found in George B. Galloway, *The Legislative Process in Congress* (New York: Thomas Y. Crowell Company, 1953), pp. 331-50; Floyd M. Riddick, *The United States Congress, Organization and Procedures* (Washington, D. C.: National Capitol Publishers, Inc., 1949), pp. 42-52, 86-102; Harvey Walker, *The Legislative Process* (New York: The Ronald Press Company, 1948), pp. 176-79; and Estes Kefauver and Jack Levin, *A Twentieth-Century Congress* (New York: Duell, Sloan and Pearce, 1947), Ch. 8. For a description of the setting up of party organization in the first week of an actual Congress (the 81st, meeting in January, 1949), see Stephen K. Bailey and Howard D. Samuel, *Congress at Work* (New York: Henry Holt and Company, 1952), pp. 66-95.

THE CONFERENCE. The most inclusive of the party agencies in Congress is the conference, which consists of all the members "in good standing"[5] of one of the parties in one of the houses.[6] It is, in theory at least, the basic governing body for each party in each house: it selects the members of the other party agencies described below and has the authority to determine the party's position on proposed legislation and other matters. But even in theory the conference has only very limited governing powers. The rules which govern the conference's proceedings either, as with the Republicans, specifically state that no conference decision on legislative matters is binding upon any member,[7] or, as with the Democrats, provide all the "escape clauses" a member needs in order not to be bound by a conference decision that he dislikes.[8]

THE COMMITTEE ON COMMITTEES. Each conference turns over to a "committee on committees" the task of making nominations for the standing committees of its house and the various other offices it must fill. The House Democrats use, as a committee on committees, the holdover members plus, when they have been named, the new members of the House Committee on Ways and Means; the Senate Democrats and the Republicans in both houses ask each state delegation to name one member of the committee on committees. The conference has, but rarely uses, the power to turn down any recommendation made by its committee on committees.

THE POLICY COMMITTEE. Each conference selects a "policy" committee or a "steering" committee, which becomes its general staff for such purposes as planning floor strategy, recommending conference "stands" on proposed legis-

[5] For a detailed historical account of what has determined membership in congressional caucuses and conferences, see Clarence A. Berdahl, "Some Notes on Party Membership in Congress," *American Political Science Review,* Vol. XLIII (April, June, and August, 1949), pp. 309-21, 492-509, and 721-35. Berdahl's account suggests that the worst sin a congressman can commit—which is, from the parties' standpoint, to bolt his party's ticket in a presidential election —has by no means always resulted in his being barred from his party's conference.

[6] Both parties in both houses used to call it the "caucus," but in recent years the Senate Democrats and the Republicans in both houses have passed up "caucus" in favor of "conference," presumably on the grounds that "conference" breathes dignity and "caucus," which suggests a furtive meeting of politicians rather than a consultation among statesmen, does not. Only the House Democrats continue to call their most inclusive agency a "caucus."

[7] Rule VI of the Senate Republican Conference Rules states: "No action by the Conference upon any matter pending or to be proposed in the Senate shall be binding in any way on members casting their votes thereon." These rules are reprinted in George B. Galloway, *The Legislative Process in Congress* (New York: Thomas Y. Crowell Company, 1953), pp. 332-34.

[8] Rule 7 of the House Democratic Caucus Rules provides: "In deciding upon action in the House involving party policy or principle, a two-thirds vote of those present and voting at a Caucus meeting shall bind all members of the Caucus: *Provided,* The said two-thirds vote is a majority of the full Democratic membership of the House; *And provided further,* That no member shall be bound upon questions involving a construction of the Constitution of the United States or upon which he made contrary pledges to his constituents prior to his election or received contrary instructions by resolutions or platform from his nominating authority." And according to Rule 8, he may be released from any caucus decision by notifying the caucus or the floor leader of his desire to be released. These rules are reprinted in John M. Mathews and Clarence A. Berdahl, *Documents and Readings in American Government,* rev. ed. (New York: The Macmillan Company, 1940), pp. 433-34.

lation, and, in general, keeping things—and, insofar as this is possible, conference members—moving, and moving in a desired direction. Before 1946, these committees were purely unofficial party organs in both houses. The Legislative Reorganization Act of that year, however, authorized each house to create a majority policy committee and a minority policy committee, and to furnish each of them a staff paid out of official congressional funds. The House of Representatives has not availed itself of this authorization: its Democratic "steering committee" and its Republican "policy committee," now as in the past, are purely unofficial (i.e., party, not congressional) entities, made up of the speaker, the majority (or minority) leader, and the whips as ex officio members, and enough elected members, one from each of a number of regional zones, to bring the total strength to approximately twenty.

The Senate, on the other hand, did act on the authorization, and so has its official majority policy committee and official minority policy committee. The Senate Democrats also maintain a separate steering committee whose membership only partially overlaps that of the official policy committee; [9] the Republicans have only the latter.

THE PATRONAGE COMMITTEE. Each house of Congress has a number of employees (doorkeepers, pages, capitol police, congressional post-office workers, etc.) whose positions are available for patronage appointments.[10] Such patronage is controlled by the patronage committee of the majority party, but the minority party is also permitted its share, being allowed to name assistants to a number of majority positions. The majority party's patronage is dispensed by the chairman of its patronage committee, and each state is given its share in proportion to the number of members it contributes to the total party representation in the house. The jobs are parceled out among individual members in each delegation in order of seniority, so that members relatively far down on the seniority list usually get no patronage.

THE FLOOR LEADER. Each party conference in each house picks a floor leader, referred to as "majority leader" or "minority leader," who is more active and conspicuous than any other party dignitary in his house—so that being named floor leader is one of the highest honors a congressman can receive. He is, so to speak, the "quarterback" of his party's "team" in his house. He does not decide who shall play on the team, or what plays the team shall use, although he has considerable say in both areas; but within the limits of the plays and members he has at his disposal, he calls the plays on the floor itself. He and his counterpart in the other party generally determine, between them, how the house shall allocate its time, in what order various items of business shall come up, and what matters are sufficiently noncontroversial to be disposed of by unanimous-consent procedure. If, for example, the other side attempts an un-

[9] In the 83rd Congress (1953-1955), the Republicans had a majority policy committee of twelve members with a staff of twelve. The Democrats had a minority policy committeee of nine members with a staff of four, plus a steering committee of fifteen members: Galloway, *op. cit.*, pp. 331, 335.

[10] See Galloway, *op. cit.*, pp. 338-39, for a list of these posts.

expected parliamentary maneuver, which can be countered, and its potentially unpleasant consequences avoided, only by a quick decision as to what to do, the floor leader is authorized to make the decision. The majority leader is, among other things, the official channel of communications between the party in his house and the president, but not in the sense that he becomes—or is regarded as—"the president's man," that is, an overseer working for the president.[11] The floor leader's position is never awarded purely on the basis of seniority: no one, on the other hand, is likely to be named to the post until he has spent many years in his house.

THE WHIPS. Each conference selects a chief whip, and the House conferences select a "deputy" or "chief assistant" whip and a number of assistant whips. Their major function is to serve as a channel of two-way communications between the party leaders and the rank-and-file members, and to make sure that a maximum number of the latter are present when a vote is to be taken on any matter in which party interests are at stake. The chief whip is usually heir presumptive, if not heir apparent, to the position of floor leader; and even the assistant-whip posts carry with them a good deal of prestige.

THE SPEAKER OF THE HOUSE AND THE PRESIDENT PRO TEMPORE OF THE SENATE. The speaker, as a general rule, holds no party office except a position on the steering committee; but the fact that his party conference has chosen him to preside over the House stamps him as its leader, and this, with the majority leader as his chief assistant, he continues to be even after his elevation.[12] Like the floor leaders, therefore, he is not picked on a straight seniority basis, yet is sure to be a man with many years' service in the House behind him. The majority party conference picks him from among its own members; he is then formally elected by the House in a straight-party-lines vote—over the candidate of the minority party, who, after his defeat, usually becomes minority leader.

The office of president pro tempore of the Senate, since his sole function is to preside over the Senate in the absence of the vice-president, is a post of honor that, unlike the speakership, carries with it no leadership responsibilities. The majority conference usually hands it, more or less perfunctorily, to its most senior member (like the speaker, he is subsequently elected on the floor in a straight-party-lines vote, with the most senior senator of the minority party as his "opponent").[13]

[11] See Riddick, op. cit., pp. 88-100, for a more detailed description of the floor leaders' duties and powers.

[12] In sharp contrast with the Speaker of the British House of Commons, who upon his elevation to his post cuts off all party ties.

[13] The Republicans in both houses generally make a practice of dividing up the prominent party leadership positions among several members, while the Senate Democrats usually have the floor leader serve as chairman of the conference, policy, and steering committees. Thus the 84th Congress (1955-1957) opened as follows:

All four party conferences met on January 4, 1955, the day before Congress opened officially. The Senate Democratic conference elected Lyndon B. Johnson (Tex.) as majority leader, chairman of the policy committee, and chairman of the conference; Earle C. Clements (Ky.) as whip; Thomas C. Hennings, Jr. (Mo.), as secretary of the conference; and Walter F. George (Ga.), the

The Selection of Members of Congressional Committees. Since 1910, both the Senate and the House have elected members of their standing committees, who therefore owe their posts, *de jure,* to the house to which they belong. Actually, however, as we should expect from what we have seen in the foregoing sections, both houses merely ratify, at the election stage, the results of a process that goes forward inside—and between—the party conferences. The committee on committees of the majority party first decides, in consultation with the minority party, how many members each party is to have on each committee.[14] Each committee on committees then draws up a slate of members for its party's quota on each committee. These slates are then ratified—usually without objection—by the respective party conferences, and are then ratified—always without objection—by the parent body.

Thus the parties' committees on committees actually select the members of standing committees. But this does not mean that the committees on committees have a free hand in the matter. For one thing, custom requires that each section of the nation be represented, if possible,[15] in each party's membership on each committee; and the custom is religiously observed. And, for another thing, the seniority principle—according to which a member who served on a particular committee in the previous Congress must be reassigned to it if he wishes to be—is so firmly established that a committee on committees will violate it only when it has the most urgent reasons for doing so.[16]

Geographical considerations and seniority do constitute major limitations on the committees' freedom of action; but this is not true of such considera-

most senior Democrat, as president pro tempore. The Senate Republican conference elected William F. Knowland (Calif.) as minority leader, Eugene D. Millikan (Colo.) as chairman of the conference, Leverett Saltonstall (Mass.) as whip, and Milton R. Young (N. D.) as secretary of the conference. They also picked Styles Bridges (N. H.) as the new chairman of the policy committee to replace Homer Ferguson (Mich.), who had been defeated for re-election to the Senate.

The House Democratic caucus picked Sam Rayburn (Tex.) as speaker, John W. McCormack (Mass.) as majority leader, and Carl Albert (Okla.) as chief whip. The House Republican conference elected Joseph W. Martin, Jr. (Mass.), as minority leader and Leslie C. Arends (Ill.) as chief whip. Charles A. Halleck (Ind.), who had been majority leader in the 83rd Congress, was given no official post, but has subsequently been described as "assistant floor leader": New York *Times,* January 5, 1955, p. 1.

[14] The Senate custom is to have party strength in each committee reflect as closely as possible party strength in the whole Senate. Thus if the Democrats have 51 per cent of the Senate seats, and there are to be a total of 23 members of, say, the appropriations committee, the Democrats will claim 12 committee posts and assign 11 to the Republicans. The House custom is for the majority party to claim half again as many ways and means committee posts, and twice as many rules committee posts, as it gives to the minority party, and to have the other committees reflect comparative party strength in the House: Galloway, *op. cit.,* pp. 279-81.

[15] That is, if the committee is large enough—as, for example, the House rules committee is not—and if the section has representation in the house in question—as, after a landslide, some sections do not.

[16] For a discussion of geographical and seniority factors in the selection of members of standing committees, see Paul D. Hasbrouck, *Party Government in the House of Representatives* (New York: The Macmillan Company, 1927), pp. 41-43; Roland Young, *This Is Congress* (New York: Alfred A. Knopf, 1943), pp. 105-08; and Bertram M. Gross, *The Legislative Struggle* (New York: McGraw-Hill Book Company, Inc., 1953), pp. 274-77.

tions as commitment to the party's platform or loyalty to the party's ticket in elections. The committees do not, for example, normally regard it as part of their business to punish bolters by depriving them of committee assignments, even important committee assignments, though these are the richest gifts a party organization in Congress can offer to one of its members, and bolting the party's ticket in an election is, from the party's point of view, a grave offense.[17] Bolters have been punished on occasion by a committee on committees, but such punishment is certainly the exception and not the rule. In the 1948 election, for example, a number of Democratic congressmen (notably Senator Eastland of Mississippi) actively supported the "Dixiecrat" candidate for president, and Democratic Senator Glen Taylor of Idaho actually ran for vice-president on the Progressive ticket; but when the 81st Congress met in January, 1949, both Senator Taylor and the "Dixiecrat" congressmen kept the committee posts they had held in the preceding Congress. (Another consideration may, to be sure, have entered into the decision not to punish the '48 Democratic bolters, namely, that the Democrats needed all the votes they could get in order to organize the 81st Congress, and were not likely to risk the bolters' voting with the Republicans.) [18]

In short, party committees select the members of congressional committees; but considerations of party regularity and loyalty do not, in general, influence these decisions.

The Control of Congressional Time. Each house of Congress has more to do during its plenary sessions, at which all bills must be formally acted upon, than it can hope to accomplish. Time, therefore, is at a great premium, and the allocation of precious minutes among the matters urgently demanding consideration is one of the most difficult and delicate problems each house— and the party leaders and conferences within it—must face and, somehow, solve, as witness the figures presented in Table 22.

The control of plenary-session time is lodged primarily in the majority leaders of the two houses (but, in the House of Representatives, in the speaker also). The majority leader makes up and revises the schedule according to which matters are to be taken up, arranges for expediting noncontroversial measures by use of unanimous-consent procedure, and in general tries to do for his house what a dispatcher does for a railroad.

The majority leader's control is, however, far from absolute. He must work in close cooperation with the minority leader as he establishes the schedule, lest the minority set up a hue and cry about "gag rules" and "steam rollers" that might prove embarrassing at election time. He must see to it that no sizable bloc of his own party feels that its proposals are not getting a fair chance to be heard and acted upon. And in the House of Representatives, any schedule he establishes will prove effective only if the rules committee—which, in view of the seniority of its members, he rarely if ever controls—goes along

---

[17] Cf. Berdahl, *op. cit.*
[18] Cf. Gross, *op. cit.*, p. 279.

TABLE 22 The Pressure of Business in the Eighty-third Congress [19]

Item	SENATE		HOUSE	
	1st Session	*2nd Session*	*1st Session*	*2nd Session*
Time in plenary session	763h, 35m	1,198h, 17m	506h, 47m	525h, 56m
Measures reported and placed on calendars	969	1,852	1,019	1,423
Time per measure in plenary session	47 minutes	39 minutes	29 minutes	22 minutes
Public bills enacted into law	109	162	179	331
Private bills enacted into law	75	313	152	462
Per cent of private bills of all bills enacted into law	40.7	65.9	45.9	58.2

with it, while in the Senate, he never knows when his schedule will be set aside by a filibuster.

The majority leader is, in other words, a railroad dispatcher with a lot of people to please and a lot of conflicting interests to reconcile—e.g., the wishes of his party conference, those of the president and the administration, those of the minority party, and, in the House, those of the rules committee—a railroad dispatcher, in short, who must rewrite the railroad's timetable from day to day and from moment to moment, instead of receiving it from on high and never deviating from it. The demands of his party's platform are, at most, *among* the many things he must keep in mind, and they are not necessarily at the top of the priorities list.[20]

The Firmness of Party Lines in Congress. According to the responsible-party-government model outlined at the beginning of this chapter, *all* the members of the majority party in the legislature vote alike on the legislative questions that arise. Any legislature which does not maintain rigid party lines, therefore, does not conform to the model: the majority party within it is not acting *as a party,* and so cannot *as a party* be held responsible, in any meaningful sense, for how the government is being run; and the minority party, since it is not acting *as a party* either, cannot meaningfully put itself forward as a responsible alternative, committed to running the government in some other way. *Responsible* party government, as the model portrays it, is a matter of firm lines, high cohesion, and effective discipline in both parties.

Now, party lines in the Congress of the United States, as commentators on American parties have been pointing out for many decades, are not nearly

[19] The data for this table are given in the *Congressional Record,* Vol. 100, December 14, 1954, p. 1099.

[20] Cf. Riddick, *op. cit.,* pp. 99-101; Galloway, *op. cit.,* pp. 549-50; Hasbrouck, *op. cit.,* pp. 101-05; and Joseph P. Chamberlain, *Legislative Processes, National and State* (New York: D. Appleton-Century Company, 1936), pp. 314-15.

as rigid as those of the model. Most votes, in Senate and House alike, range Democrats and Republicans against Democrats and Republicans, not Democrats against Republicans, and on such a scale that it is often impossible to identify a Republican or Democratic "stand" on the issue at stake at all. One of the earliest statements we have about the nonrigidity of party lines in Congress dates back to 1834—a complaint by a Jacksonian Democratic member of the House of Representatives from New York to the editor of a newspaper in his district:

I wish, my dear sir, that organization, according to the New York school, was a little more the order of the day here. Then something like concert of action could be secured upon party questions, and we should not meet with those defeats to which the want of organization constantly exposes us. At the commencement of the session of 1829, the administration had a majority in the lower house of about sixty, and yet, the friends of the president could hardly ever carry a question. You would be disgusted at the arrogance and magnificent air with which southern politicians claim an exemption from the shackles of party. They swell like frogs at the fountain when a party question is broached, and generally demonstrate their independence by voting with the opposition. How short would be the career of a New York politician who would thus misrepresent his constituents! [21]

And apparently Congress has not changed much, in this regard, over the ensuing century, as witness the following statement from a leading student of American parties in 1942:

The roll calls in the House and the Senate show that party votes are relatively rare. On difficult questions, usually the most important questions, party lines are apt to break badly, and a straight party vote, aligning one party against the other, is the exception rather than the rule. The vote is sometimes unanimous or nearly unanimous; that is, the parties are occasionally in substantial agreement. Often both parties split into approximately equal halves. . . . [This is] *the most important single fact concerning the American parties.* He who knows this fact and knows nothing else, knows more about American parties than he who knows everything except this fact.[22]

There is some evidence, mostly from recent empirical studies of party voting in Congress, that the statements just quoted somewhat exaggerate the congressman's independence vis-à-vis his party affiliation, and, indeed, that no simple statement of the situation (since, as we shall see, congressmen are less

21 Quoted in Berdahl, *op. cit.,* p. 721.

22 E. E. Schattschneider, *Party Government* (New York: Rinehart and Company, Inc., 1942), pp. 130-32; italics in the original. See also Ernest S. Griffith, *Congress: Its Contemporary Role* (New York: New York University Press, 1951), pp. 151-52; and the testimony of George H. E. Smith, then research assistant to the minority leader of the Senate, before the La Follette–Monroney Committee: Joint Committee on the Organization of Congress, 79th Congress, 1st Session, *Hearings* (1946), pp. 361-64. James M. Burns argues that party behavior in Congress is such that behind the façade of our "two-party" system, we really have in Congress a *multiple-*party system, lacking only formal labels for the various blocs. He also argues that party affiliation is a factor of negligible importance in determining how congressmen vote: *Congress on Trial* (New York: Harper and Brothers, 1949), p. 35, and Ch. III, "The Impotence of Party."

independent on some matters than on others) could possibly be accurate. The oldest study we have in this area, A. Lawrence Lowell's inquiry into party voting in Congress, in some state legislatures, and in the British House of Commons in the nineteenth century, dates, to be sure, from 1901.[23] But Elston E. Roady's study of party voting in Woodrow Wilson's first administration,[24] that of John B. Johnson, Jr., of party voting in the United States Senate from 1880 to 1940,[25] and the most comprehensive of all, Julius Turner's study of all roll-call votes in the House of Representatives in the sessions of 1921, 1930-1931, 1937, and 1944,[26] have given us large amounts of new data to take into account in our generalizations about party regularity.

All of these studies have attempted quantitative measurement of the firmness of party lines in Congress, using for this purpose one or more of the following three indices. (1) *The party vote.* Lowell, the first to use this index, defined a "party vote" as a roll call in which 90 per cent or more of the members of one party vote "Yea" and 90 per cent or more of the members of the other party vote "Nay." (2) *The index of party cohesion.* This index, originally devised by Stuart Rice,[27] measures the "unity of a party on a roll call, regardless of the position of other parties . . . by dividing the number of votes cast by the party members who were in the majority in the party on the roll call, by the total number of party members who voted." The result obtained "will range from 50 to 100, and is converted, for convenience of presentation, to the scale of 0 to 100, and is called the index of cohesion . . . [so that the] lowest possible party cohesion [where half the party members vote "Yea" and the other half vote "Nay"] is 0; the highest, or perfect cohesion [where all the party members vote one way] is 100." [28] (3) *The index of likeness.* This index, also initially developed by Rice,[29] measures "the difference between two groups in the degree of support given to a motion . . . by subtracting the percentage of 'yea' votes cast by one group from the percentage of 'yea' votes cast by the other, and subtracting the result from 100. . . . The index of likeness ranges from 0 to 100, with 0 representing complete dissimilarity of voting behavior [where, for example, the Republicans vote 100-0 "Yea" and the Democrats vote 100-0 "Nay"], and 100 perfect similarity [where, for example, the Republicans and the Democrats both split 50-50]." [30]

[23] "The Influence of Party upon Legislation in England and America," *Annual Report of the American Historical Association for the Year 1901* (Washington, D. C.: Government Printing Office, 1902), Vol. I, pp. 321-542.

[24] Elston E. Roady, *Party Regularity in the Sixty-third Congress,* unpublished doctoral dissertation in political science, University of Illinois, 1951.

[25] John B. Johnson, Jr., *The Extent and Consistency of Party Voting in the United States Senate,* unpublished doctoral dissertation in political science, University of Chicago, 1943.

[26] Julius Turner, *Party and Constituency: Pressures on Congress* (Baltimore: The Johns Hopkins Press, 1951).

[27] Stuart Rice, *Quantitative Methods in Politics* (New York: Alfred A. Knopf, 1928), pp. 208-09.

[28] Turner, *op. cit.,* p. 26.

[29] *Op. cit.,* pp. 209-11.

[30] Turner, *op. cit.,* pp. 36-37.

The results of these studies are summarized in the following tables.

Table 23 shows the *average cohesion* of American parties in recent sessions of the House of Representatives and, for purposes of comparison, the cohesion of French parties in the 1930 session of the Chamber of Deputies.

TABLE 23   *Average Cohesion of French and American Parties* [31]

FRENCH CHAMBER OF DEPUTIES (1930)		U.S. HOUSE OF REPRESENTATIVES		
Party	*Average Cohesion*	*Year*	*Party*	*Average Cohesion*
Communist	100	1921	Rep.	74.4
Socialist Français	99		Dem.	69.4
Socialist	98	1928	Rep.	57.8
Union Rep.-Dem.	95		Dem.	61.3
Dem. et Social	94	1930-31	Rep.	62.3
Rep. de Gauche	92		Dem.	69.6
Dem. Populaire	91	1933	Rep.	71.7
Radical Socialist	91		Dem.	63.1
Independent	77	1937	Rep.	70.2
Gauche Social Rad.	75		Dem.	53.9
Gauche Radical	53	1944	Rep.	70.8
Rep. Socialist	37		Dem.	56.0
Ind. de Gauche	27			

Table 24 shows the *proportion of party votes* in selected sessions of the House of Representatives with, for purposes of comparison, the proportion of party votes in selected sessions of the British House of Commons:

TABLE 24   *Proportion of Party Votes to All Roll-Call Votes* [32]

BRITISH HOUSE OF COMMONS		U.S. HOUSE OF REPRESENTATIVES	
Year	*Per Cent Party Votes*	*Year*	*Per Cent Party Votes*
1924-25	94.4	1921	28.6
		1928	7.1
1926	94.8	1930-31	31.0
		1933	22.5
1927	96.4	1937	11.8
		1944	10.7
1928	93.6	1945	17.5
		1946	10.5
		1947	15.1
		1948	16.4
Average	94.9	Average	17.1

Table 25 shows the historical trends in party votes in the American House of Representatives, and, we may note in passing, appears to indicate that party

[31] *Ibid.*, Table 2, p. 27.
[32] *Ibid.*, Table 1, p. 24.

votes, the nearest approximation we have in our terminology to the kind of votes envisaged by the responsible-party-government model, are becoming less, not more, frequent as the decades pass.[33]

TABLE 25   Percentage of Party Votes Cast in Selected House Sessions, 1845-1948 [34]

Year	President	Percentage of Party Votes
1845-47	Polk (D)	10.7
1863-65	Lincoln (R)	30.2
1887-89	Cleveland (D)	13.6
1897-99	McKinley (R)	50.9
1899-1901	McKinley (R)	49.3
1921	Harding (R)	28.6
1928	Coolidge (R)	7.1
1930-31	Hoover (R)	31.0
1933	Roosevelt (D)	22.5
1937	Roosevelt (D)	11.8
1944	Roosevelt (D)	10.7
1945	Roosevelt (D)—Truman (D)	17.5
1946	Truman (D)	10.5
1947	Truman (D)	15.1
1948	Truman (D)	16.4

Nor, to judge from the results of an attempt by the present writers to measure party cohesion in the 83rd Congress (1953-1955) by a sampling of the roll-call votes in both houses, have party lines moved significantly closer to the responsible-party-government model in the years since the Turner study.[35] In terms of the Rice Index of Cohesion, the House Republicans scored, on the average, 65.7, and the House Democrats 47.2; the Senate Republicans scored, on the average, 67.7, and the Senate Democrats 53.1. In the 83rd Congress, in short, Republican cohesion in the House appears to have been approximately the same as during the years studied by Turner (see Table 23 above), and Democratic cohesion in the House was actually lower than Turner found it to be during several of the years he studied. (We may note, for what it is worth, that both parties scored slightly higher in the Senate than in the House, and that the Republicans scored higher than the Democrats in both houses.)

Party Affiliation as a Factor Influencing Congressmen's Votes. In the study referred to above, Turner attempted to compare the strength of major-

[33] The frequency peak for party votes came in the Republican administrations of 1897-1901; and they were notably less frequent in the Roosevelt and Truman administrations than in those of thirty or forty years earlier.

[34] *Ibid.*, Table 3, p. 28.

[35] In preparing this survey, the present writers used the roll-call figures reported in the *Congressional Quarterly* for both sessions of the 83rd Congress, and tabulated only those roll calls which seemed to them to be on major issues. This amounted to a total of 32 roll calls for both sessions in the House, and a total of 41 for the Senate.

party affiliation as a factor influencing congressmen's votes with the strength of each of three other factors—urban or rural character of constituencies, foreign-born or native-born character of constituents, and geographical-sectional location of constituencies. His method was to construct a series of synthetic "parties" (by including in one "party" all the representatives from predominantly rural constituencies, by including in another all the representatives with predominantly native-born constituents, by including in still another all the representatives from the Northeast, and so on), to measure the average cohesion of each synthetic "party" in congressional voting, and to compare it with that of the actual Democratic and Republican congressional parties. We need not, for our purposes, report his results in detail; suffice it to say that he found a higher degree of average cohesion in the actual parties than in the "rural" or "native-born" or "northeastern" or other synthetic congressional "parties." On the basis of this data, Turner concluded that "party pressure seems to be more effective than any other pressure on Congressional voting, and is discernible on nearly nine-tenths of the roll calls examined." [36] In other words, Turner's study shows that in determining their votes congressmen tend to respond to whatever pressure or pressures seem most likely to unseat them if ignored or resisted. These pressures include *both* party affiliation and the special natures of the various constituencies. In the cases where the two kinds of pressure are in conflict, however, the former appears to be more influential more often than the latter.

In their respective studies, Turner and Johnson found other noteworthy tendencies in congressional voting behavior: Republicans tend to be more cohesive than Democrats,[37] and both parties tend to be more cohesive when they are in the minority than when they are in the majority.[38] Johnson, however, contends that statements of this kind are misleading, in that they distract attention from the major variable involved in the problem of party cohesion, namely, *the character of the issue being voted on*. Some issues, he thinks, divide the Congress sharply along party lines, so that the parties show a high degree of cohesion; some divide it along party lines, but not sharply, so that the parties show a lesser degree of cohesion; and some do not divide it along party lines at all, so that the parties show a low degree of cohesion. In the next section we shall attempt to summarize the available data bearing upon this issue-to-issue approach to congressional voting.

How Party Cohesion Varies from Issue to Issue. The evidence presented by Turner [39] and Johnson [40] appears to warrant the following generalizations: (1) The Democrats in Congress generally vote for lowering tariffs; the Republicans generally vote for maintaining or increasing them. (2) The Demo-

---

[36] *Op. cit.,* p. 23; see also p. 33.

[37] *Ibid.,* p. 25, n. 11.

[38] *Ibid.;* Johnson, *op. cit.,* pp. 254-56. See William B. Munro, *The Invisible Government* (New York: The Macmillan Company, 1928), p. 81, for an explanation of why this is so.

[39] *Op. cit.,* Ch. III.

[40] *Op. cit.,* pp. 258-73.

crats generally favor a tax structure with a narrow base and high surtaxes on large incomes; the Republicans generally favor a tax structure with a broad base and low surtaxes on large incomes. (3) The Democrats generally favor federal regulation of wages and hours; the Republicans generally oppose it. (4) The Democrats generally favor public ownership or regulation of public utilities (particularly electric power); the Republicans generally oppose it. On most other issues—public works, states' rights, armaments, veterans' claims, women's rights, the merit system, etc.—both parties show a low degree of cohesion and adopt inconsistent stands from session to session; the differences between them over any save the very briefest periods of time, that is to say, are negligible.

The question, How firm are party lines in Congress? does not, then, lend itself to a simple answer. All one can say is that it depends on the issue; for party lines are firm on some issues, less firm on others, and not firm at all on still others.

The Role of Party in Congress: A Summary. In terms of the evidence canvassed in the foregoing pages, what over-all statements appear to be in order about the general role of party in Congress?

First, it seems clear that the party leaders have little or no "disciplinary" or "command" power over the rank-and-file members of their respective parties in Congress. Both party conferences in both houses meet infrequently, and they seldom attempt to "bind" their members to vote a particular way.[41] The floor leaders and whips do, on occasion, seek to persuade party members to vote a certain way on a certain bill; but they never "order" or "command" them to do so, and for good reason: their power to enforce commands being extremely limited, nothing is to be gained by issuing them, and something—namely, the capacity to persuade in some future situation—is likely to be lost.[42]

Second, there is no locus of concentrated power in either house of Congress that might enable a party to translate its program into legislation via steam-roller or push-button tactics. The power of a congressional majority is highly fragmented, so that bits and pieces of it are lodged in floor leaders, standing committees, committee chairmen, presiding officers, and rules committees, among whom there may be countless differences of opinion and emphasis;[43] there are, besides, administration spokesmen and pressure-group spokesmen, not represented on the floor at all;[44] and there is, finally, the

[41] Kefauver and Levin, for example, point out that the Caucus Rooms, which are the largest and handsomest halls in their respective congressional office buildings, have for some time been used almost exclusively for committee hearings that draw large audiences. The party caucuses meet so seldom that these rooms are rarely needed as meeting places for them: *Op. cit.,* pp. 99-100. For the story of the decline of the caucuses, see Young, *op. cit.,* pp. 94-96; Galloway, *op. cit.,* p. 330; and Hasbrouck, *op. cit.,* pp. 28-29.

[42] Young, *op. cit.,* p. 248.

[43] If not about the policy to be embodied in legislation, then about the pace at which the house in question is to move in the desired direction.

[44] Cf. Griffith, *op. cit.,* pp. 19-20; Galloway, *op. cit.,* pp. 327-28; Gross, *op. cit.,* p. 68; and Young, *op. cit.,* pp. 83-84, 88-89, 91, 93-94.

minority, which for a number of reasons (the rules of the game as the congressmen understand them; the public sympathy the minority will command if they can show the rules are being violated; and the fact that tomorrow the minority may be the majority, and may retaliate) must not be pushed too hard.

Third, there is no evidence of a trend, of the kind desired by the proponents of the responsible-party-government model, toward a type of formal organization in the two houses that would concentrate power in the majority party's hands and allow it to run things according to its own lights. The Legislative Reorganization Act of 1946 was intended to accomplish some such purpose;[45] but it has failed to achieve it.[46] Nor, in the view of such writers as Pendleton Herring and Bertram Gross, was there ever any good reason to expect any other result; for, they hold, the basic reason for the "weakness" of party government in Congress lies not in any "deficiencies" in formal organization, but in the basic character of the parties themselves (which that organization reflects), and specifically in the fact that party nominations for members of Congress are *locally,* not nationally, controlled. As Herring puts it:

If a party is to be held responsible for the enactment of a legislative program, there must be a sufficient concentration of power in the party leaders to enable them to hold their following in line. One effective means is to permit party leaders to determine who should be nominated as representatives of the party. This is a key power sometimes disregarded in discussions of cabinet responsibility under parliamentary government. If we were ready to abolish direct primaries and grant to the national party organization the initial selection of Congressional candidates the disagreements between executive and legislative branches would become insignificant and few. Our problems would be translated to a different area. Control of the national party machine would be the great prize.[47]

Finally, the parties—for all that their role in Congress little resembles that in which the responsible-party-government model casts them—do affect the course of events, and do affect it in large part through the influence of party affiliation on the behavior of the individual congressman; on some issues, indeed, party affiliation apparently *determines* his vote, just as the advocates of responsible-party-government wish it to on all issues. Party agencies determine the composition and personnel of the committees and allocate the available floor time in both houses. In a word, any description of congressional operations that concentrated exclusively on the activities of the parties would cer-

[45] Cf. the hearings cited above, and the Joint Committee on the Organization of Congress, 79th Congress, 2nd Session, *Report* (1946) (Senate Report No. 1011).

[46] For further suggestions for reforming congressional organization so as to provide for better party government, see the report of the Committee on Political Parties of the American Political Science Association, "Toward a More Responsible Two-Party System," *American Political Science Review,* Vol. XLIV (September, 1950), Supplement, pp. 56-65.

[47] E. Pendleton Herring, *Presidential Leadership* (New York: Farrar and Rinehart, Inc., 1940), pp. 23-24. See also Gross, *op. cit.,* pp. 65-67.

tainly be wide of the facts; but so would a description that failed to take those activities into account.[48]

IN CONGRESSIONAL-PRESIDENTIAL RELATIONS: "PRESIDENTIAL LEADERSHIP"

The Theory of Presidential Leadership. Some theorists of American parties who believe that only concentrated and effective leadership could enable our national parties to play a "responsible" role in legislation and government have lost faith in reorganization and reform *inside* Congress as the means of getting it. They now pin their hopes, rather, on the development of "presidential leadership," which is a shorthand expression for a future state of affairs in which the president would be fully accepted as *the* leader of his party, and members of his party in Congress, following his orders, would loyally support the party's (i.e., the president's) legislative program.

The best-known and most forceful exposition of this point of view is still that advanced by Woodrow Wilson in his *Constitutional Government in the United States* (1908), which he wrote while he was still an academic political scientist and had not yet begun his active political career. His argument, briefly summarized, is as follows: The president can, if he chooses to do so, become the unchallenged leader of his party, because (a) as the only important national officer elected by *all* the people, he is in a position to mobilize public opinion behind his program to an extent that no congressman or group of congressmen could hope to equal, and (b) he can, making the most of the fact that the presidency is the prize that an American national party values above all else, demand adherence to his program on the twofold ground that the party owes him a debt of gratitude for his having won it, and that making a good record during his administration will strengthen the party's hand in future elections. As Wilson pointed out, the president cannot escape being the leader of his party "except by incapacity and lack of personal force, because he is at once the choice of his party and of the nation."

He is the party nominee and the only party nominee for whom the whole nation votes. . . . He can dominate his party by being spokesman for the real sentiment and purpose of the country, by giving direction to opinion, by giving the country at once the information and the statements of policy which will enable it to form its judgments alike of parties and of men. . . . He may be both the leader of his party and the leader of the nation, or he may be one or the other. If he lead the nation, his party can hardly resist him.[49]

The Development of Presidential Leadership. The presidency, contrary to the expectations of the framers of the Constitution, has indeed become the primary source of leadership and dynamism in the American political system;

[48] Cf. Griffith, *op. cit.,* pp. 148-51; and Gross, *op. cit.,* p. 68.

[49] *Constitutional Government in the United States* (New York: Columbia University Press, 1908), pp. 67-69. See also Norman J. Small, *Some Presidential Interpretations of the Presidency* (Baltimore: The Johns Hopkins Press, 1932), Ch. V; and Ranney, *op. cit.,* Ch. 3.

this no contemporary political scientist, however unsympathetic he might be with Wilson's tendency (as revealed in the passage just quoted), would deny.[50] The president is today—to use an often-repeated metaphor—"the keystone of our governmental arch," in the sense that he and his establishment hold the whole governmental structure together and keep it moving. But it does not necessarily follow from all this that the president is in a position to provide the kind of party leadership that Wilson had in mind. In point of fact, the "strong" presidents who have built the modern presidency have relied far more upon *extra*-party weapons of leadership (their ordinance powers as Chief Executive, their dominance over foreign policy, their veto power, their power as Commander in Chief, and, above all, their role as "leader of public opinion,") than upon the weapons they hold in virtue of their "headship" of a political party. The president's relations with the Congress, moreover, are today acknowledged to be the Achilles' heel of his general position,[51] and only two presidents, Thomas Jefferson and Woodrow Wilson, have made serious and sustained efforts to use the majority party in Congress as their major channel for exercising legislative leadership.[52] In a word, *general* presidential leadership has become a conspicuous feature of our national government; but presidential *party* leadership has contributed little or nothing to this development. In the next section we shall see why.

Factors That Facilitate Presidential Leadership. The literature of presidential leadership puts great emphasis on certain potential strengths allegedly inherent in the presidential office and certain weapons that the president can, if he chooses, use on others when he needs to bring them into line. These are:

PATRONAGE. One weapon the president is often said to be able to count on when he seeks to persuade members of his party in Congress to mobilize behind his program is patronage—that is, appointments to federal jobs, his to bestow or withhold, that they would like to have for their followers back home. The consensus among present-day students of the presidency, however, is that presidential patronage is in point of fact a leadership weapon of extremely limited usefulness. Most of the jobs the president has at his disposal, for one thing, are handed out in the early months of any new administration; and through the remaining three-plus years the larder is empty, and therefore

---

[50] Cf. Herring, *op. cit.*; Wilfred E. Binkley, *The President and Congress* (New York: Alfred A. Knopf, 1947); Edward S. Corwin, *The President: Office and Powers* (New York: New York University Press, 1941); Harold J. Laski, *The American Presidency* (New York: Harper and Brothers, 1940); Louis Brownlow, *The President and the Presidency* (Chicago: Public Administration Service, 1949); and George Fort Milton, *The Use of Presidential Power, 1789-1943* (Boston: Little, Brown and Company, 1944).

[51] Lawrence H. Chamberlain studied the legislative history of ninety major acts of Congress passed from the 1890's to the 1940's, and found that presidential influence was preponderant in nineteen, congressional influence preponderant in thirty-five, presidential and congressional influence about equal in twenty-nine, and pressure-group influence preponderant in seven: *The President, Congress, and Legislation* (New York: Columbia University Press, 1946).

[52] Cf. Corwin, *op. cit.*, pp. 19-20, 266, 271-75; Milton, *op. cit.*, Chs. III, V, and VIII; and Burns, *op. cit.*, pp. 174-77.

not tempting.[53] The Senate, for another thing, confirms a presidential appointment to a federal position located within a single state only if the appointee is acceptable to the senior senator or the state and local party leaders in that state,[54] so that, for many jobs, the patronage power is less in the president's hands than in those of the state and local leaders of the president's party.[55]

THE "COATTAIL EFFECT." A winning presidential candidate usually gets around 7 per cent more votes than the total cast for candidates on his ticket for the House of Representatives,[56] and some observers have concluded from this that a sizable number of the representatives and senators elected in a presidential year "ride in on the president's coattails," that is, owe their election to the extra votes they received from having run on the same ticket with the presidential candidate. These congressmen, it is argued, know that their electoral destiny depends upon the president's popularity, and are therefore more than ready to follow his lead on legislative matters—that is, to help him make the kind of record that will get *all* of them re-elected; and a determined and resourceful president can convert this "coattail effect" into a potent weapon of legislative leadership by threatening to withhold his endorsement from recalcitrant congressmen and holding it out as a reward to congressmen who go down the line for his program.

Professor Malcolm Moos has recently studied the alleged "coattail effect," however, and has found that (a) when the data are subjected to rigorous analysis the effect turns out to be far less common than some observers have supposed it to be, (b) "coattailing often involves a reversal of mount and rider," the presidential candidate, that is to say, often riding on the coattails of the congressman, and (c) in any case, relatively few congressmen have any reason to think that their chances for re-election depend to a significant degree on the personal popularity of their party's presidential candidate.[57] The presidential candidate's vote, to be sure, is likely to be larger than the congressman's, but the reason for this, Moos contends, is that many voters make a choice for president but do *not* make one for representative.[58] Of the 435 congressional districts,

[53] Cf. E. Allen Helms, "The Presidency and Party Politics," in Robert S. Rankin, ed., *The Presidency in Transition* (Gainesville, Fla.: The Journal of Politics, 1949), pp. 48-49.

[54] The practice of withholding confirmation until the senior senator is satisfied is known as "senatorial courtesy," presumably because confirming without his being satisfied would be discourtesy on the part of his fellow senators.

[55] Cf. Helms, *op. cit.,* pp. 56-57; and Griffith, *op. cit.,* pp. 142, 151.

[56] In 1952, for example, Eisenhower received a total of 33,936,000 votes (or 55 per cent of the total), while Republican candidates for the House of Representatives got a national total of 28,399,000 votes (or 50 per cent of the total), and Republican candidates for the Senate (with, of course, contests in only about a third of the states) got a national total of 23,242,000 (or 53.7 per cent of the national two-party total).

[57] Malcolm Moos, *Politics, Presidents and Coattails* (Baltimore: The Johns Hopkins Press, 1952).

[58] In 1896, about 99 per cent of the persons who made a choice for president also made a choice for representative; but in the period from 1920 to 1948, an average of only about 90 per cent voted for both offices: *Ibid.,* p. 17.

moreover, some 120 (mostly in the South) are strictly one-party areas, where a congressional candidate's chances of winning depend little, if at all, on how well or badly his party's presidential candidate fares in the election; and some 210 are predominantly, if not completely, one-party areas, where, again, the congressional candidate can safely forget all about the "coattail effect." Only 105 of the districts are what Moos calls "marginal" (i.e., areas in which the winner's share of the popular vote has not gone above 55 per cent since 1940), and of these only 42 are "critical-marginal" (i.e., areas in which the winner's share of the popular vote has not gone above 51.5 per cent since 1940).[59] Only in these "marginal" and "critical-marginal" districts—about one-fourth of the total—can the "coattail effect," according to Moos, possibly be worth a congressional candidate's losing sleep over; and some of these are areas in which the candidate for representative sometimes runs *ahead* of the presidential candidate on his ticket (so that the president "rides in on the coattails of the representative").[60] Moos's study indicates, in short, that while the "coattail effect" may operate in some districts in some elections, there are many districts in which it is negligible and many others in which, if it is present at all, no president would dare count on it as a means of curbing a rebellious congressman.[61]

Factors That Inhibit Presidential Party Leadership. The factors that allegedly facilitate presidential party leadership, as we have just seen, do not for the most part stand up under critical examination. But even if that were not the case, the factors working *against* presidential party leadership of the type envisaged by Wilson are both numerous and formidable.

THE RECURRENT PHENOMENON OF DIVIDED PARTY CONTROL. During the years 1955-1956, the United States had a Republican president and a Senate and House of Representatives controlled by the Democrats, so that President Eisenhower, had he cast himself in the role envisaged by the proponents of "presidential leadership," would have been courting defeat for his legislative program: he had either to pick up some support from Demcoratic legislators (which, according to the presidential-leadership doctrine, he had no business doing) or, failing that, to rely exclusively upon, and so "lead," the Republicans in Congress, and write off his legislative program as hopeless. Nor was this an unprecedented situation in the history of American government: Of the 44 Congresses, beginning with that elected in 1868 and ending with that elected in 1954, 13 (or 29 per cent) have confronted the president with at least one house controlled by the other major party.[62] The danger of such divided control is, therefore, something that any president must keep in mind as he thinks forward to the next election—especially when he receives expert advice to ignore

---

[59] *Ibid.*, pp. 24-25.

[60] *Ibid.*, pp. 93-108.

[61] *Ibid.*, pp. 115, 123-24.

[62] The data for party control of Congress before 1948 are taken from the charts in Louis H. Bean, *How to Predict Elections* (New York: Alfred A. Knopf, 1948), pp. 15, 19.

the desires and feelings of the opposition party and stake everything on the loyalty and solidarity of his own party. To antagonize and irritate the minority party in Congress today is to tempt fate; for tomorrow they may be the majority party.

THE LACK OF CENTRALIZED POWER IN CONGRESS. We have noted above that power in Congress is not concentrated in the hands of any individual or group; it is, rather, shared by many individuals and many groups—the speaker, the floor leaders, the standing committees, the standing-committee chairmen, etc. And what this means, for purposes of the present discussion, is that even if the president did win the complete support and loyalty of a particular set of congressional leaders (e.g., the floor leaders of his party),[63] he would not thereby win that of his party in Congress; for no single set of party leaders in Congress can deliver the support of that party's rank-and-file congressmen.

THE PRESIDENT'S LIMITED LEASE OF POWER. As a president moves from the beginning to the end of his legal tenure, the strength he derives from his patronage power and the "coattail effect" (if any) fades away; and, other things being equal, his capacity to lead his party and to some extent his capacity to lead the government itself fade with it. A first-term president, in the absence of some obvious reason why he cannot be re-elected, can keep these capacities more or less intact, and, up until the passage of the Twenty-Second Amendment, a second-term president could do so too, by refusing to divulge his plans, and so keeping himself in the running as a candidate for re-election to a third term. Since the amendment went into effect, however, a president's tenure is limited to two elective terms or a total of ten years in office, and no second-term president can talk himself around the fact that he will soon be a retired elder statesman, flirting with the possibility of running for the Senate but, meantime, able to affect events only via an occasional appearance on a national television network.

THE POPULAR BELIEF IN "INDEPENDENCE." When members of the president's party in Congress "refuse to be dictated to" and proclaim to the world that they are voting, and will continue to vote, "as their conscience dictates" and "in accordance with the will of the people," even if this involves opposing White House policy, one thing they can count on is a round of applause from the general public—much of it, indeed, from persons who do not agree with their stand on the specific issue in question. The applause will not, to be sure, be unanimous, since some voices will be raised in protest against their "obstructionism" and "uncooperativeness" and their "inability to see that the executive and the legislature must work together"; but nothing can be more certain than that large numbers of Americans dislike the idea of a "rubber-stamp Congress," and breathe more easily when they know that Congress, including the president's own partisans in Congress, is showing its "independence" and "in-

---

[63] By no means a sure thing, as witness the fact that in the course of 1954, Senator William Knowland, the Republican floor leader, openly opposed President Eisenhower on at least two major issues—the McCarthy censure and Far Eastern policy.

tegrity." [64] There are, moreover, at least three good reasons why this is precisely what we should expect by way of popular reaction when such a clash occurs: (1) the congressman being "little" and the president being "big," the former, like the Orioles when they meet the Yankees, can levy upon the nation's huge reserves of latent sympathy for the underdog; (2) the objection to a "rubber-stamp Congress," however inconvenient it may be from the vantage point of the responsible-party-government advocates, has behind it a good deal of traditional American constitutional theory—it is, in other words, a logical application of the idea of separation of powers; and (3) there is, as we shall note in Chapters 21 and 22, no evidence that the teachings of the responsible-party-government school, which might indeed some day replace our traditional constitutional doctrine on this point, have yet converted large numbers of the nation's electorate. In any case, no president is likely to be ignorant of or to fail to take into account the fact that conspicuous use of the big stick against "independent" congressmen may well cost him more support, both congressional *and* popular, than it gains him.

THE DECENTRALIZED NATURE OF THE PARTIES. Besides being likely (as we have just seen) to prove costly to any president who uses it freely, the big stick has this further disadvantage in American politics: it is pretty certain, when used inside a party, to fail of its purpose. The real centers of command and control over the big decisions a party must make—whether to take a stand on this issue or that one, what program to put forward, what strategy to adopt, whom to nominate for what office, whether to withhold the official party label here and bestow it there—are, we repeat, located at the *state and local* levels of our major parties rather than at their national levels. And this means that no president, even if backed up by, say, the national chairman and the appropriate floor leader, can when the chips are down coerce a party member in Congress into voting a particular way. For the only threat that could be counted on to turn the trick, that is, the threat to read him out of the party if he refuses, cannot, in the very nature of the case, be brought into play.

The five "factors" which we have just noted do not warrant the conclusion that the president is in *no* sense the leader of his party in Congress. But they cast grave doubts on the possibility of his becoming the kind of party leader some contemporary theorists are calling upon him to be. The president, like his party's leaders in Congress, will have at any moment just that position of leadership with respect to his fellow partisans in the legislature that he can win and hold by cajolery, by persuasion, and by happening to want the same things they want; and he will weaken, not strengthen, that position by attempting to issue commands to them from on high. In a word, the permanent,

---

[64] Thus many of the congressmen who have won reputations as "real statesmen"—men like George W. Norris, Robert M. La Follette, William E. Borah, and Paul H. Douglas, for example— have won a considerable part of their prestige by *opposing* presidents of their own parties, not by faithfully supporting them.

institutionalized presidential party leadership Woodrow Wilson envisaged might or might not be a good thing from the standpoint of democracy; but, our parties and our formal governmental structure having been and being what they are, it has not existed in the past, is not discernible today, and is an improbable development within the foreseeable future.[65]

IN THE ADMINISTRATIVE AGENCIES

Patronage appointments to administrative posts are today, as they have been in the past, the channel through which the political parties have had their most conspicuous impact on the national government service. The party out of power may make some campaign promises that it intends to welsh on, but the promise of "a real shakeup in the bureaucracy down in Washington" is not one of them.[66] A new administration can be counted on to regard the permanent civil service, with its tenure appointments, as in large part a barrier to the achievement of its goals, and to exercise considerable ingenuity in finding ways to circumvent its rules and get more and more of its sympathizers on the payroll. On the other hand, no one can say beforehand how much of this sort of thing it will be in a position to do, in part because the situation of any incoming administration with regard to the number of jobs available is unique [67] and in part because the high prestige the merit-system civil service laws enjoy among the general public oblige any new administration to avoid at least the appearance of a frontal attack on the "merit system." But there are many ways to avoid the appearance of a frontal attack on the "merit system" and still get the party's friends on the payroll: making provisional appointments, getting specific positions exempted from civil service procedures, creating new agencies in the place of old ones, etc. According to one uncompromising enemy of the spoils system, even today "civil service commissioners desiring to enforce the merit spirit will find themselves thwarted by the contamination of a patronage environment." [68] And we have the word of one authority on public administration that "political favoritism is still the principal handicap to good administration despite the gains of the last six decades." [69] While, therefore, an incoming political party does not turn the government service inside out, as it was expected to in the days of Andrew

[65] For similar statements of this view of the general nature of presidential party leadership, see Herring, op. cit., pp. 25-26; Laski, op. cit., pp. 11-16, 138-54, 159-60, 245-46; Helms, op. cit.; L. H. Chamberlain, op. cit., pp. 267-71; and Griffith, op. cit., pp. 42-43.

[66] This promise is a "natural" for the party out of power: it creates enthusiasm among the job-hungry workers in its ranks, and it appeals to voters who feel that a "new broom" will indeed sweep clean" in Washington.

[67] The Eisenhower administration was harshly criticized by many Republicans during its early months for "keeping too many New Dealers and Trumanites on the payroll"—and by many Democrats for "ruining the civil service by packing it with spoilsmen."

[68] John M. Pfiffner, Public Administration, rev. ed. (New York: The Ronald Press, 1946), pp. 234-37.

[69] Leonard D. White, Introduction to the Study of Public Administration, rev. ed. (New York: The Macmillan Company, 1939), p. 287.

Jackson and George Clinton, there is still enough patronage to merit careful attention on the part of its leadership.

IN THE COURTS [70]

The Supreme Court. Most—though not all—appointees to the Supreme Court are more or less active members of the president's own party, with a reputation (which, as the two Roosevelts learned, cannot always be depended upon) for sharing his views about the Constitution and public policy. President Washington established the precedent by appointing five good Federalists to the first Court,[71] and subsequent presidents, with few exceptions, have followed it.[72]

Even in the early years of the Republic, senators fought many a hot fight over the confirmation of Supreme Court appointees, in many of which the contestants were divided along straight partisan lines. Between 1789 and 1894, for example, no less than twenty presidential appointments to the Supreme Court failed to be confirmed by the Senate. Since 1894, on the other hand, the Senate has turned down only one appointee (Parker), and has put up serious protest and opposition to only four (Brandeis, Stone, Hughes, and Black). In each of the latter five cases, moreover, it was not the nominee's party affiliation but his philosophy and views on social and economic matters that were called into question.[73] Thus few commentators in recent years have accused the Court of making its decisions on *partisan* grounds; and the only role that the parties appear to play in the politics of the Supreme Court is in the initial selection of appointees.

The Other Federal Courts. Partisan influence plays a somewhat different role in the selection of the judges of the other federal courts. From 1885 to 1941, 517 of the 545 appointments to the district courts (or 94.8 per cent) went, like Supreme Court appointments, to men of the president's own party (most of the remaining 5.2 per cent were southern Democrats appointed by Republican presidents).[74] But appointments to the district courts are normally regarded as subject to "senatorial courtesy," so that the judges are in actual fact picked by state and local party leaders. Judgeships are, indeed, among the most attractive patronage jobs these leaders have at their disposal, and any attempt by the president to bypass "senatorial courtesy" in their selection is

[70] The most complete recent general discussion of this question is that in Peter H. Odegard and E. Allen Helms, *American Politics,* 2nd ed. (New York: Harper and Brothers, 1947), pp. 168-77.

[71] Washington, as we noted in Chapter 6, held strong notions about parties, and would have said—to himself as well as to others—that he was appointing, not men of party, but men of sound views upon and unshakeable loyalty to the new Constitution.

[72] Cf. Helms, *op. cit.,* p. 53.

[73] Joseph P. Harris, *The Advice and Consent of the Senate* (Berkeley: The University of California Press, 1953), p. 303.

[74] *Ibid.,* pp. 314-24.

sure to be resented, resisted, and, other things being equal, defeated.[75] It has often been proposed, accordingly, that the judgeships be "taken out of partisan politics," but no such proposal has yet won enough support to be regarded as "practical politics." [76]

The president has a much freer hand in selecting judges for the courts of appeal, the tax court, the customs court, and the like, because the districts involved group several states together. But the appointments go as a matter of course to members of the president's party.

In short, party affiliation plays a highly important role in the *selection* of federal judges, particularly for courts below the Supreme Court. But there is no reason to suppose that American judicial decisions are influenced by the party ties of the judge or judges concerned.

THE ROLE OF PARTY IN THE NATIONAL
GOVERNMENT: A SUMMARY

The evidence presented in the foregoing pages shows that the parties have their main impact on governmental affairs between elections by deciding who shall fill the key positions in the formal policy-making agencies. In nominating candidates for the presidency, the vice-presidency, and the 531 members of Congress, the parties determine which few persons among the many millions of Americans constitutionally eligible for these strategic positions shall bring *their* values, *their* loyalties, *their* ideas, and *their* interests into the making of public policy. In selecting the speaker, the floor leaders, and the chairmen and members of the standing committees, the parties determine who shall occupy the posts that command access to the nation's statute book. In making patronage appointments, they put *their* men into key positions in the nation's administrative agencies and, below the Supreme Court level at least, its courts; and even the members of the Supreme Court itself owe their elevation to it, at least in part, to their affiliation with the president's party. In a word, after winning an election the majority party's central function inside the national government is to *organize* it (in the special sense of this term noted at the beginning of the present chapter).

The parties *as such,* on the other hand, appear to have much less to do with determining what laws are passed and what administrative and judicial policies their appointees follow after they are installed in their respective posts. For example, party cohesion is usually weaker, and party affiliation a less powerful vote-influencing factor, in the Congress of the United States than in the

[75] President Hoover attempted in 1929 to ignore senatorial courtesy in connection with certain district-court judgeships, but the Senate consistently turned down his own nominations, and he finally had to give in and suggest names acceptable to the senators. President Truman tried in 1951 to appoint some district judges in Illinois without consulting Senator Douglas, and, like Hoover before him, ran into a blank wall of opposition.

[76] Cf. Odegard and Helms, *op. cit.,* pp. 174-76; and Harris, *op. cit.,* pp. 314-24.

legislatures of most of the world's other democracies; and certainly the parties' impact on congressional voting behavior and presidential-congressional relations is far more modest than most advocates of responsible party government and presidential leadership think it should be. And party influence is even less evident in the determination of national administrative and judicial decisions.

It would be quite incorrect, however, to say that the parties play no role whatever in the formulation of national governmental policy. Party affiliation, our evidence shows, is one of the most reliable bases we have for predicting how congressmen will vote, at least on certain issues. And, in certain circumstances anyhow, control of both the presidency and Congress by the same party does provide a measure of coherence and "teamwork" in our complex and fragmented mosaic of formal governmental structures. Thus, while the policy-making activities of American parties fail conspicuously to meet the standards set for them by the advocates of responsible party government, any account of the national policy-making process that left the parties completely out of the picture would be highly inaccurate and misleading.

We have seen that the *national* parties' chief weakness, from the standpoint of the responsible-party-government doctrine, lies in their lack of a *centralized* system of *command* leadership. No party leader or set of leaders—neither the president nor the floor leaders nor the policy committees—is in a position to *command* a congressman to vote this way or that or to punish him if he ignores their wishes. Such party leadership as we find on the national level is a leadership of persuasion, cajolery, and pleading, not a leadership of commands backed up by sanctions that can effectively be imposed upon the disobedient.

This is what we should have expected to find. Everything we have learned in the preceding chapters about the national parties' activities outside the formal government has indicated that the parties have no centralized command leadership in their *extra*governmental activities either. We have seen, with respect to one extragovernmental activity after another—nominating, platform writing, election fighting, and money raising alike—that the parties are *decentralized,* and thus, in the nature of the case, not set up for the giving and enforcement of commands from the center. All we have added to the picture in the foregoing pages, then, is a line showing that the parties behave in their *intra*governmental activities much as they do in their *extra*governmental activities.

We have also noted, however, that the extragovernmental activities of some state parties, by contrast with those of the national parties, are subject to a considerable degree of centralized direction and control; and it remains to ask whether this is true of their intragovernmental activities as well.

The Role of Party in the State Governments

IN THE LEGISLATURES [77]

Party Organization. In Chapter 7 we noted that the party systems of the forty-eight states all belong to one or another of three types: the two-party system, the modified one-party system, and the one-party system; and in subsequent chapters we have called attention to the sharp differences from state to state as regards election and primary laws, party organization, and nominating procedures. It will therefore come as no surprise to our readers to be told that there is no single formula which will summarize the role played by political parties inside the states' formal governmental structures.

Two states, Nebraska and Minnesota, elect members to their legislatures on ballots without party designations, and are therefore said to have "nonpartisan" legislatures.[78] In the forty-six states that have partisan legislatures, according to the recent report of the Committee on State Legislatures of the American Political Science Association (henceforth referred to as the "Zeller report"), the incidence of the various types of party agencies in our state legislatures is as shown in Table 26.

The Zeller report states that majority-party agencies exercise strong control over the formal organization and procedures of the houses in 28 senates and 29 houses, moderately effective control in 6 senates and 5 houses, and weak or no control whatever in 11 senates and 10 houses. Minority parties are reported to have "strong" legislative organizations in 18 states, "moderately strong"

[77] The most comprehensive recent study of this subject is that conducted by the Committee on State Legislatures of the American Political Science Association. The committee sent questionnaires on the 1949-1951 biennium to two or more competent persons in each state, and got back at least one from each state and two or three from most states. The results are reported in Belle Zeller, ed., *American State Legislatures* (New York: Thomas Y. Crowell Company, 1954), of which Chapter 12 is devoted to "Party Organization and Control." O. Douglas Weeks published his own summary of the material in the chapter just mentioned in "Politics in the Legislatures," *National Municipal Review*, Vol. XLI (February, 1952), pp. 80-86.

Most of the standard textbooks on state government have little to say about the role of party inside the formal governmental structures. Several useful studies of this question in specific states are: William J. Keefe, "Party Government and Lawmaking in the Illinois General Assembly," *Northwestern University Law Review*, Vol. XLVII (March-April, 1952), pp. 55-71; W. Duane Lockard, "Legislative Politics in Connecticut," *American Political Science Review*, Vol. XLVIII (March, 1954), pp. 166-73; Warren Moscow, *Politics in the Empire State* (New York: Alfred A. Knopf, 1948), pp. 166-76; Samuel K. Gove and Gilbert Y. Steiner, *The Illinois Legislative Process* (Urbana: University of Illinois, Institute of Government and Public Affairs, 1954); Dean R. Cresap, *Party Politics in the Golden State* (Los Angeles: The Haynes Foundation, 1954), Ch. V; and Thomas C. Donnelly, *The Government of New Mexico* (Albuquerque: University of New Mexico Press, 1947), pp. 98-101.

[78] Nebraska adopted its unicameral and nonpartisan legislature in 1934 as the result of a successful campaign against "party politics in the legislature." Minnesota, on the other hand, adopted nonpartisan elections for legislators in 1913 as the result of some complicated legislative maneuvering and without any serious debate on the merits of nonpartisan legislative elections: Cf. Charles R. Adrian, "The Origin of Minnesota's Nonpartisan Legislature," *Minnesota History*, Vol. XXXIII (Winter, 1952), pp. 155-63.

TABLE 26   *Party Agencies in the State Legislatures* [79]

Agency	Status	Senate	House
1. Majority caucus	Existent	25	24
	Existent, but of little or no significance	8	9
	Nonexistent	15	14
2. Majority party leadership of presiding officers	Strong	14	35
	Moderate	5	1
	Weak	27	9
3. Steering or policy committee	Existent	11	11
	Occasional	5	4
	Nonexistent	23	24
4. Rules or sifting committees as majority party agencies	Existent	13	14
	Occasional	7	7
	Nonexistent	20	19
5. Floor leaders	Existent	31	30
	Occasional	6	6
	Nonexistent	7	8
6. Committee on committees	Existent	9	0
	Nonexistent	39	47

ones in 10 states, and "weak" organizations, or no organization at all, in 18 states. In two states, North Dakota and Virginia, the rival factions within the dominant parties maintain continuous organizations of such strength as to create a close approximation to a well-organized two-party system inside their legislatures.[80] In Minnesota, there is a strong "liberal-conservative" split behind the nonpartisan façade, and each faction maintains a caucus and other agencies similar to those maintained by parties elsewhere. No such factional division or organization is to be found, on the other hand, in Nebraska's nonpartisan legislature.[81]

Of the twenty-five majority caucuses reported, only thirteen meet frequently, or attempt to control their party members' votes on legislative matters. The other twelve caucuses normally meet only at the beginning of each session, and confine their activities to picking their parties' nominees for such chamber offices as speaker, sergeant-at-arms, etc.[82]

The Zeller report, in a word, seems to confirm what numerous students of state government have been saying for some time: that party organizations in state legislatures for the most part have far less impact on events than the

[79] This is a slightly revised version of Table 11 on p. 195 of Zeller, *op. cit.* (Information was not obtainable for all party agencies in all states.)

[80] *Ibid.*, pp. 193-94.   [82] *Ibid.*, pp. 194-95.

[81] *Ibid.*, pp. 211-12.

comparable organizations in Congress, and that this statement applies even in the "organizing" phase of a newly elected legislature.[83]

Party Cohesion. The Zeller report also presents the available data as to party cohesion in the legislatures of the various states. In 17 states the parties show a high degree of cohesion, in 11 a moderate degree, and in 20 a low degree.[84] Some recent intensive studies of party voting in particular state legislatures, moreover, confirm the committee's findings in this regard. Lockard, for example, after studying all roll-call votes in the Connecticut legislature (classified by the Zeller report as having strong cohesion) from 1931 to 1951, scored the Senate Republicans 86.2 for average cohesion, the Senate Democrats 82.5, the House Republicans 82.9, and the House Democrats 86.7. In the Senate, he found, majorities of the two parties were on opposite sides of issues 83.5 per cent of the time, and in the House 80.7 per cent of the time. The Connecticut legislature, on this showing, comes considerably nearer to the responsible-party-government model of cohesion than Congress or the legislatures of most of the other states.[85] Warren Moscow reports that in the New York legislature (also classified by the Zeller report as having strong cohesion) voting along party lines is taken so much for granted that most bills are passed by the following "short roll call" procedure: The clerk calls only the names of the floor leaders and of the first and last members of the house listed alphabetically, and unless a member specifically asks to be recorded otherwise, he is counted as having voted like his floor leader (with the curious result that a vote of, say, 135 to 12, is possible with only 90 members actually present on the floor). In the 1945 session, the Senate passed 1,482 bills out of 1,660 in this manner, and the Assembly 1,403 out of 1,603.[86] On the other hand, the Zeller report's classification of the Illinois General Assembly as having moderate party cohesion seems to be less justified. Keefe's study of all roll calls in the 1949 and 1951 sessions showed that more than half of all roll calls were unanimous, that in more than three-quarters of all roll calls 90 per cent or more of the members of both parties voted on the same side, and that less than 5 per cent of the votes were "party votes" (which Keefe defined as a roll call in which 80 per cent or more of the members of one party vote "Yea" and 80 per cent or more of the members of the other party vote "Nay").[87]

[83] Cf. *ibid.*, p. 213. See also Clyde F. Snider, *American State and Local Government* (New York: Appleton-Century-Crofts, Inc., 1950), pp. 187-88; Austin F. Macdonald, *American State Government and Administration,* 4th ed. (New York: Thomas Y. Crowell Company, 1950), pp. 205-06; and Oliver P. Field, Pressly S. Sikes, and John E. Stoner, *Bates' and Fields' State Government,* 3rd ed. (New York: Harper and Brothers, 1949), pp. 199-200.

[84] Zeller, *op. cit.,* Table 9 on pp. 190-91. The "weak party cohesion" group includes the two states (North Dakota and Virginia) in which the committee found high cohesion and elaborate organization in the factions within the dominant parties. For another general survey of party cohesion in state legislatures, see Malcolm E. Jewell, "Party Voting in American State Legislatures," *American Political Science Review,* Vol. XLIX (September, 1955), pp. 773-91.

[85] Lockard, *op. cit.*

[86] Moscow, *op. cit.,* pp. 175-76.

[87] Keefe, *op. cit.*

Applying the Zeller report's classification of state legislatures by degree of party cohesion to the two-party, modified one-party, and one-party classification previously established in the present book produces the results presented in Table 27.

TABLE 27   Party Cohesion in the State Party Systems

COHESION IN THE TWO-PARTY STATES			COHESION IN THE MODI-FIED ONE-PARTY STATES			COHESION IN THE ONE-PARTY STATES		
Strong	*Moderate*	*Weak*	*Strong*	*Moderate*	*Weak*	*Strong*	*Moderate*	*Weak*
Colo.	Ill.	Ariz.	Iowa	N. H.	Ky.	Vt.		Ala.
Conn.	Mont.	Calif.	Kans.	S. D.	Me.			Ark.
Dela.	Nev.	Minn.*	N. C.		N. D.†			Fla.
Ida.	Ohio	Neb.*	Pa.		Okla.			Ga.
Ind.	Utah	N. M.			Ore.			La.
Md.	Wash.				Tenn.			Miss.
Mass.	Wis.							S. C.
Mich.	Wyo.							Tex.
Mo.								Va.†
N. J.								
N. Y.								
R. I.								
W. Va.								

* Nonpartisan legislatures.
† Strong factional cohesion within dominant party.

The pattern revealed in Table 27 is what our analysis of the nature of politics in each type of party system should have led us to expect. The incidence of strong party cohesion is greatest by far among the two-party states and least by far among the one-party states; and the modified one-party states, as in most other respects, occupy a middle position between these two extremes.[88]

In short, party cohesion is stronger in a few state legislatures than that in Congress, about equal to that in Congress in a few others, and considerably weaker than that in Congress in most state legislatures.

IN GUBERNATORIAL-LEGISLATIVE RELATIONS: "GUBERNATORIAL LEADERSHIP"

The Theory of Gubernatorial Leadership. The governor of each state, according to some political scientists, should provide the kind of governmental and party leadership that, as we have seen, a certain school of political scientists expects the president to provide in the nation as a whole. The governor no less than the president, they argue, occupies a highly strategic position, and

[88] The Zeller report comes to the same general conclusion: Cf. Zeller, *op. cit.,* pp. 205-11.

can use his patronage power, his leadership of public opinion, and his "coat-tail" vote-getting leadership to induce members of his party in the legislature —where they are usually in the majority—to adopt his legislative program; he has only to make it clear to them that failure to accept his leadership will seriously endanger their party's chances of retaining the governorship and their own chances of re-election.

Some writers, indeed, feel that the governor has certain advantages over the president in this regard. For one thing, they argue, the presidency is the end of the line for any ambitious party leader; he can hope for no higher office. The governorship, by contrast, is often a steppingstone to larger opportunities: a seat in the United States Senate, a position in the president's cabinet, a seat on the federal bench, perhaps even the presidency itself. The governor, in a word, is more likely than the president to convince himself that whipping his party's members into line behind his program is worth his while.[89] For another thing, these writers argue, our state parties are better disciplined and more tightly knit than our national parties, so that the governor, by comparison with the president, has a relatively well-organized party at his command to begin with.[90] And in any case, they contend, all the reasons that point to the desirability of presidential leadership for the nation and for the national parties apply with equal force to gubernatorial leadership for the states and the state parties.

The Development of Gubernatorial Leadership. In the early years of the nation the state governors, generally speaking, had little power, alike from the standpoint of their formal position as specified in the state constitutions, and as regards actual leadership in the decision-making activities of their states. Beginning in the latter half of the nineteenth century, however, most of the states revised their constitutions, and in doing so greatly increased the governors' powers; so that by the end of the century there were governors like Hiram Johnson in California and the elder La Follette in Wisconsin, whose popular and legislative leadership had a profound impact on events.

Not until the 1920's, however, did the governors begin to make themselves felt as *party* leaders, and so take the final step toward the strong governorship that we find in most of the states today.[91]

The Present Status of Gubernatorial Leadership. The status and strength of gubernatorial leadership, according to the scholars who have looked into the matter, varies considerably from state to state. Professor Lipson, for instance, finds that the governor in some states normally exerts a kind of influence that, within his own sphere, compares favorably with that of any official in any democratic government in the world, while in other states the governor is

[89] Cf. Field, Sikes, and Stoner, *op. cit.*, pp. 266-68.
[90] Cf. Joseph P. Chamberlain, *op. cit.*, pp. 286-88.
[91] For a useful historical account of the development of gubernatorial leadership, see Leslie Lipson, *The American Governor, From Figurehead to Leader* (Chicago: University of Chicago Press, 1939), pp. 47-61.

merely one among several leaders. But even where gubernatorial leadership is normally strong, this is in part due to the personalities of particular governors and the circumstances surrounding particular administrations, and may therefore be enormously weakened overnight. Nowhere is it so "institutionalized" that it can be counted on to remain strong, no matter who the incumbent is and what circumstances surround the administration.[92]

Where the governor *is* normally a strong leader, Lipson further concludes, his *party* leadership contributes notably more to his position than the president's party leadership ever contributes to his position.[93] The Zeller report states that gubernatorial party leadership is a source of strength for general gubernatorial leadership in fifteen of the two-party states and three of the modified one-party states, but (as we should expect) in none of the one-party states.[94] As genuine interparty competition for control of the state governments declines, in other words, the governor's leadership of his party declines, and so contributes less and less to his power and influence in general.

Where we find strong gubernatorial party leadership, it appears to follow much the pattern described in the following statement by the majority leader of the Illinois Senate in 1953:

> Not only is it important that legislation be drafted in keeping with the policy of the administration, but it is also important that the time and efforts of the Legislature be freed from legislation which will encounter an executive veto. Every Monday night the Speaker of the House, the majority leader of the House, the majority whip of the House, the President pro tem of the Senate, the majority whip of the Senate meet with the Governor on the subject of legislation pending or proposed, in connection with which we generally invite the proponents of any particular measure that is then very current, or the chairman of the committee before which some special and important legislation is pending. We go over the legislation, its potentialities, whether it is feasible, whether it is desirable, and we thresh it out as well as we know how.[95]

Factors Inhibiting Gubernatorial Party Leadership. The big items here are the ever-present danger that the governor's party will lose control of one or both houses of the state legislature and the ever-present problems arising out of the fact that the governor cannot control his own party.

THE THREAT OF DIVIDED PARTY CONTROL. When we discussed presidential party leadership in Congress, we saw how the danger that the opposition party may win control of both houses of Congress forces a president to pay some

---

[92] *Ibid.,* pp. 222-26.

[93] *Ibid.,* pp. 206-15.

[94] *Op. cit.,* pp. 206-07, 209-10.

[95] Statement by Illinois State Senator George Drach, quoted in Gove and Steiner, *op. cit.,* pp. 12-13. Gove and Steiner go on to say (p. 13): "Some measures never make the Monday night meetings and floor leaders have been known to ask a bill's sponsor during a committee hearing whether a proposal has been cleared with the Governor." See also Moscow, *op. cit.,* pp. 178-82, for a description of the importance and processes of gubernatorial party and legislative leadership in New York.

heed to its desires and feelings, instead of relying solely upon the loyalty and solidarity of his own party. And we saw further that 29 per cent of the Congresses elected from 1868 through 1954 were controlled by the party opposed to the president.

The same consideration estops the governor of a state from working solely through his own party in the legislature; in many states, indeed, the governor's party is more likely, statistically speaking, to lose control of the legislature than the president's party is to lose control of Congress, and this reflects itself in great circumspection on the governor's part in his relations with the opposition. V. O. Key, Jr., and Corinne Silverman, on the basis of data from all gubernatorial and legislative elections in all the states with partisan legislatures from 1931 to 1952, found that one and the same party controlled both the legislature and the governorship in all sessions in only fifteen states, including the eleven southern states and the following one-party and modified one-party states: Vermont, Oklahoma, New Hampshire, and South Dakota. In fourteen of these fifteen states the same party was in control all the time; only in South Dakota were there simultaneous shifts in control of both branches. In all the remaining thirty-one states, control was divided some of the time (from 9.1 per cent of the sessions up to 72.7 per cent).[96] Key and Silverman further found that approximately one-third of the elections studied gave the control of the governorship to one party and control of one or both houses of the legislature to the other,[97] and that a popular gubernatorial candidate could not be counted on to "pull" a majority of his party's legislative ticket into the legislature on his "coattails." Even where the victorious governor got from 50 to 55 per cent of the popular vote, the opposition party still won control of one or both houses of the legislature as often as not, and even where the governor's percentage rose to 55 to 60 per cent of the vote (as it did in some 50 per cent of the elections) the opposition still gained control of one-third of the legislatures.[98] Except in the one-party states, therefore, divided party control of the state government is a familiar situation.

Key and Silverman found that "the proportion of the period in which a division of party control prevailed increases roughly as states come to be characterized by fairly even party competition." In the two-party states there was divided party control during from 40 to 70 per cent of the legislative sessions studied![99] Thus in the states where one condition of responsible party government—namely, genuine two-party competition—prevailed, another condition of such government—namely, control of all the branches of the state government by a single party—was *least* likely to prevail. In most states outside

---

[96] "Party and Separation of Powers: A Panorama of Practice in the States," in Carl J. Friedrich and J. Kenneth Galbraith, eds., *Public Policy* (Cambridge, Mass.: Graduate School of Public Administration, Harvard University, 1954), pp. 383-85. See especially Table 1 on p. 384.

[97] *Ibid.*, pp. 386-88, especially Table 2 on p. 387.

[98] *Ibid.*, pp. 388-89, especially Table 3 on p. 389.

[99] *Ibid.*, pp. 383-85.

the South, the Democrats were the victims of divided party control far more often than the Republicans. Eighty per cent of the governors who faced legislatures controlled by the opposition were Democrats, and only 20 per cent Republicans.[100] The main cause for the Democrats' handicap in this regard is that in many nonsouthern states the rural areas are, mathematically speaking, heavily overrepresented in at least the upper house of the legislature, and that this gives the Republicans what amounts to continuous and undisputed control. In such two-party states as California, Connecticut, Massachusetts, New Jersey, New York, and Wisconsin, the Democrats have never at any time held control of the governorship and *both* houses of the legislature.[101] In those states, therefore, the kind of "party government" and "gubernatorial party leadership" urged by some political scientists can be provided only by the Republicans.[102]

THE DECENTRALIZATION OF STATE PARTIES. In many states control of the governorship and both houses of the state legislature by no means guarantees firm gubernatorial party leadership; much less does it guarantee responsible party government. We have already noted that in the one-party states neither gubernatorial *party* leadership nor *party* responsibility has any real meaning, and that in most of the modified one-party states they mean very little. We can now go further and say that even in many of the two-party states the governor has no real power to command the members of his party in the legislature, and most, like the president in his dealings with Congress, rely largely on persuasion and cajolery. For in the states as in the nation, party nominations for legislative positions are *locally* controlled, and the central party agencies have no formal and little actual power to withhold the party label from a locally selected candidate or legislator who refuses to abide by the governor's leadership. As Lipson puts it:

> In the days when candidates were chosen at party conventions, stricter party discipline was the rule. Today, candidates with little or no party allegiance can win the nomination in the primary and, once elected to the legislature, behave as independents.[103]

In a word, from the standpoint of party and general governmental leadership, some governors have more power than the president, some have about as much, and most have considerably less.

IN THE ADMINISTRATIVE AGENCIES

The literature on public administration has even less to say about the role of party in the state administrative agencies than it does about the role of party in the national bureaucracy. There are, however, reasons for believing

100 *Ibid.*, p. 392.
101 *Ibid.*, pp. 408-09.
102 Cf. *ibid.*, pp. 403, 406-07.
103 *Op. cit.*, p. 213.

that the states lag far behind the national government in eliminating party considerations from the administrative process. In many states, for one thing, relatively few administrative posts are covered by merit-system laws, so that a relatively high proportion of such posts are filled by patronage appointments. For another thing, allegations of "corruption" in the awarding of state contracts and of "protection" accorded by state officials to vice and gambling rings continue to figure with such prominence in our newspapers as to suggest that the power of party leaders on the state level is still capable of being translated into illicit financial gain. The whole subject, however, is one that awaits more serious scholarly research, and is, in consequence, one about which we know little or nothing that merits inclusion in the present survey.

IN THE COURTS

In the Selection of Judges.[104] In the United States at present, the judges of state courts are selected as follows: [105] In nineteen states, all judges are elected on a partisan ballot (i.e., one on which the party affiliation of each candidate is printed); in five states, judges of the higher courts are elected on a nonpartisan ballot, and judges of the lower courts are elected on a partisan ballot; in five states, judges of the higher courts are appointed, and judges of the lower courts are elected on a partisan ballot; in one state, judges of the higher courts are appointed, and judges of the lower courts are elected on a nonpartisan ballot; in five states, all judges are appointed; and in thirteen states, all judges are elected on a nonpartisan ballot.[106] In short, a majority of our state judges are elected on partisan ballots, and state political parties generally regard electing their candidates to certain kinds of judgeships—particularly those with power to probate wills and preside over business failures, bankruptcies, and receiverships—as worthy of the most strenuous and expensive campaigning— in part, no doubt, because the judges' power to appoint receivers and executors of estates gives them vast amounts of patronage to dispense. In partisan elections for most other kinds of judgeships—even those for judges of the superior and supreme courts—the parties generally confine themselves to nominating candidates, and campaign little or not at all.

Most commentators on our state judicial systems deplore the popular election of judges in any form, and are particularly opposed to partisan elections for judicial posts. Men are nominated, it is contended, because they enjoy the favor of party leaders, and are elected because the leaders enjoy favor with the

---

[104] The most complete description of the various state systems for selecting judges (as of 1943) is given in Evan Haynes, *The Selection and Tenure of Judges* (Berkeley, Calif.: The National Conference of Judicial Councils, 1944), Ch. II.

[105] The figures for the number of states employing each type of judge-selecting system are taken from the *Book of the States, 1954-1955* (Chicago: Council of State Governments, 1954), Vol. X, Table 2 on p. 436.

[106] For an illuminating discussion of party "endorsements" in one system of nonpartisan elections, see Malcolm C. Moos, "Judicial Elections and Partisan Endorsement of Judicial Candidates in Minnesota," *American Political Science Review*, Vol. XXXV (February, 1941), pp. 69-75.

voters, all with a bare minimum of attention to the "learning in the law" and the "judicial temperament" that good judges ought to have. No judge, it is further contended, can maintain the proper attitude on the bench if his mind is on future elections; and the way to free judges from preoccupation with such irrelevancies is to have them appointed.[107]

In the Performance of the Judicial Function. The present writers do not feel competent to comment on the underlying premises and logical consequences of the argument just summarized, and will confine themselves to pointing out that the writers on state judicial systems never go quite so far as to state in so many words that, once on the bench, partisan-elected judges grant special favors to their party organizations and fellow partisans;[108] the literature of the "problem" proceeds, rather, by insinuation, and with scant recognition that the implicit charges against the bulk of the nation's bench are so grave that they might well be avoided until they can be properly documented. No student of the state judicial systems has yet seen fit to investigate systematically the role of party in the performance of the judicial function; in the absence of such studies the only verdict which can justly be rendered on this charge against the parties is neither "Guilty" nor "Not Guilty," but rather the old Scottish verdict of "Not Proven."

THE ROLE OF PARTY IN THE STATE GOVERNMENTS: SUMMARY AND COMPARISON WITH THE NATIONAL GOVERNMENT

In certain respects party plays substantially the same role inside the governments of all the forty-eight states, and in certain other respects the role of party varies considerably from state to state. Let us speak first of the extent to which the parties play the same role in all the states.

Party considerations appear to have more influence in selecting administrative personnel in the states generally than they have in the selection of national administrative personnel, primarily because of the relatively higher proportion of the latter covered by merit-system laws. Parties appear to exert about as much influence in the selection of state judges as they do in the selection of federal judges; and, again, there is no convincing evidence that partisan considerations play an important role in the making of judicial decisions at either level. Finally and most important, in most of the state governments and in the national government alike, the *main* (though not the only) activity of parties is that of selecting from the total number of persons legally eligible for the key positions of government the few who will actually occupy those positions—a function which they accomplish at both levels mainly by their nominating and electioneering activities.

---

[107] Cf. Snider, *op. cit.,* pp. 275-78; W. Brooks Graves, *American State Government,* 3rd ed. (Boston: D. C. Heath and Company, 1946), pp. 673-74; and Laurance M. Hyde, "Judges: Their Selection and Tenure," *Journal of the American Judicature Society,* Vol. XXX (February, 1947), pp. 152-58.

[108] Cf., however, Macdonald's statement that "judges chosen by popular vote may reasonably be expected to be cogs in the dominant political machine": *Op. cit.,* p. 260.

When, however, we raise the question of what role the parties play *as parties* in directing the formation of state legislative policy and assuming responsibility for how the state governments are run, we cannot answer it with any very specific comments about *the* role of party in these matters; for, as the evidence presented in the foregoing pages indicates, there is great variation from state to state in what the parties do in this regard. We have learned, however, that we can classify the states according to the nature and dimensions of the governmental role their parties perform in matters other than the selection of governmental personnel; and such a classification results in these three main groups of states: (1) Those in which party plays at least as important a role as it plays in the national government in such matters as "organizing" the legislature, dividing the legislature into two cohesive party groups opposing each other on most matters of public policy, and providing the agencies and channels for close cooperation between the majority party in the legislature and the chief executive. Party intragovernmental activities in such states as Connecticut and New York, in fact, usually resemble the models of responsible party government and executive party leadership much more closely than do the equivalent party activities in the national government. (2) States in which the parties play some part in these matters, but usually play a less important role than is played by parties in the class of states just mentioned and in the national government. (3) States in which the parties play little or no discernible part in the direct formulation of governmental policy.

We have further learned that most of the states in category (1) above are also in the category of two-party states (according to our classification in Chapter 7), that most of the states in category (2) are modified one-party states, and that most of the states in category (3) are one-party states. On this showing, therefore, it seems reasonable to conclude that as party competition declines, the parties are likely to play a less significant intragovernmental role. In other words, in every respect save one, the two-party states come closer to the responsible-party-government model than do the modified one-party and one-party states. The exception has to do with divided party control between the executive and the legislature, which is more frequent in the two-party states than in the others.

Finally, it is clear that *no* American party system, state or national, measures up to the responsible-party-government standard fully and in every respect. A few state party systems may come close to doing so, but the national party system and most of the state party systems are for the most part remote from the party-government model. Whether this is a good or a bad thing for America from the standpoint of democracy is a question we reserve for the final chapters of this book.

PART FIVE

The Nature and Role of the Minor Parties

Chapter 18

BOLTERS, FARMER-LABOR PARTIES, AND LABOR PARTIES

What Is a "Minor Party"?

Up to this point we have confined our description of the American party system to the membership, organization, and activities of the two so-called "major" parties. Actually, however, there are many other organizations in the United States that fit our definition of a political party as "an autonomous organized group that makes nominations and contests elections in the hope of eventually gaining and exercising control of the personnel and policies of government"; and while, for some purposes, they can be ignored (as we have been ignoring them except for an occasional passing reference), no account of our party system would be complete that did not include them.

In the 1952 presidential election no less than *seventeen* parties other than the Republicans and Democrats officially nominated candidates for the presidency; and of these, eleven managed to get their candidates on the ballots of one or more of the states. The particulars are shown in Table 28.

Each of the seventeen, as the table clearly shows, accounted for a "minor" (not to say insignificant) share of the votes cast, and had a "minor"

TABLE 28   *Minor Parties in the 1952 Presidential Election* [1]

Party Name	Presidential Candidate	Number of States Where Listed on the Ballot	Total Popular Vote
Liberal	Adlai Stevenson	1 (N. Y.)	416,711
Progressive	Vincent Hallinan	25	75,927
American Labor	Vincent Hallinan	1 (N. Y.)	64,211
Prohibition	Stuart Hamblen	20	72,769
Socialist Labor	Eric Hass	21	30,376
Socialist	Darlington Hoopes	16	20,189
Christian Nationalist National America First	Douglas MacArthur	8	17,205
Socialist Workers	Sarrell Dobbs	7	10,306
Poor Man's	Henry Krajewski	1 (N. J.)	4,203
American	Mrs. Mary Kennedy	0	—
American Vegetarian	Daniel J. Murphy	0	—
Church of God Bible	Homer A. Tomlinson	0	—
Greenback	Fred C. Proehl	0	—
United	Oliver Amlie	0	—
Washington Peace	Mrs. Helen Jensen	0	—

(not to say infinitesimal) chance of electing its presidential candidate.[2] But each did nominate a candidate, did try to get him on the ballot, and did campaign for him more or less energetically; and each does, therefore, qualify as a political party.

The purpose of the present chapter is to present a brief historical account of these minor parties and their predecessors, and to fit them, in terms of their character, activities, and impact, into our picture of the American party system.

Before we undertake that task, however, a word is in order about the terminology we shall be using. The term "minor party" usually refers to any party other than the two major parties *in a two-party system*,[3] and is thus used interchangeably with the term "third party," which denotes a party that nominates candidates and electioneers for them, but rarely or never finishes better than third, usually wins no public offices, and accounts for only a small fraction of the popular vote. A "third party," in other words, is *any* party which seldom finishes better than third, not that party which regularly finishes third instead of fourth or sixth or seventeenth. In the 1952 election, for example, the Poor Man's Party was as much a "third party" as the Progressive Party.

[1] The data are taken from *The World Almanac for 1954* (New York: The New York World-Telegram and Sun, 1954), pp. 581, 583.

[2] Out of a total vote for all parties of 61,679,882, the seventeen minor parties accounted for 711,847 votes, or 1.1 per cent. Note, however, that over half of the latter were cast for Stevenson, a major-party nominee also running as a minor party's nominee in one state.

[3] The larger and smaller parties in a *multiple-party system*, for example, are seldom referred to as "major" or "minor."

Which of the parties that have played a role in American politics are, then, to be regarded as "third parties"? The answer is: This depends on which of our party systems, and what point in time, you have in mind. In the American *national* party system, from 1868 to the present day, *all* parties other than the Democrats and Republicans have been third parties.[4] On the other hand, in certain state and local party systems during certain periods the Democrats or the Republicans have been third parties. In state elections in Minnesota in the 1920's and 1930's, for example, the Farmer-Labor party normally polled either the largest or the second-largest vote, and the Democrats were clearly a third party. In state elections in Wisconsin in the 1930's, similarly, the Progressives, not the Democrats, were the Republicans' main opposition. And in city elections in Milwaukee, Wisconsin, Bridgeport, Connecticut, and Reading, Pennsylvania, the Socialists have traditionally beaten one or the other or both of the "major" parties.

In most state and local party systems through most of the period since the Civil War, however, the Republicans and Democrats have been, as they have in the national party system, the major parties, and all other parties have been "minor."

Types of Minor Parties in American Politics

American politics have seen the rise (but seldom much of a rise) and fall of many minor parties through the decades since 1789. All of them, however, have played substantially the same role vis-à-vis the party system, and, great as the differences between them may seem to be from the ideological point of view, they show certain marked similarities as well. In this and the following chapter, we shall attempt to identify certain prominent types of minor parties, to describe the major characteristics of each type, and to summarize the careers of the more notable examples of each type. Our general discussion of the role of minor parties will thus be postponed until the concluding section of Chapter 19.[5]

Factions Bolting from the Major Parties

In Chapter 13 we noted that one grand objective of a major party in a presidential campaign is to keep all its factions united behind and working

[4] In the 1912 presidential election, the Progressive party finished second and the Republicans third. Nevertheless, the Progressive party was generally regarded (and quite properly, on our showing) as a "third party."

[5] The best general descriptions of American minor parties of all types are: William B. Hesseltine, *The Rise and Fall of Third Parties* (Washington, D. C.: Public Affairs Press, 1948), particularly for the bibliographical appendix; Wilfred E. Binkley, *American Political Parties: Their Natural History* (New York: Alfred A. Knopf, 1944); Thomas H. Greer, *American Social Reform Movements* (New York: Prentice-Hall, Inc., 1949; and, for the earlier minor parties, Fred E. Haynes, *Social Politics in the United States* (Boston: Houghton Mifflin Company, 1924).

for the party's nominee, and that this objective has a certain impact on its nomination-making, platform-writing, and campaigning activities. We observed, further, that the typical major party's factions are often so far apart (in their views on public policy or in their notions as to who would make the best nominee) that keeping them together behind the successful candidate, whose nomination spells defeat for some factions, takes some doing. It is therefore remarkable that the major parties have so seldom failed to do it, and that only four times in our recent history has a faction been so disappointed with a party's platform or candidate as to "bolt the ticket," and put up its own candidate: the Liberal Republicans in 1872, the "Gold Democrats" in 1896, the Progressives in 1912, and the "Dixiecrats" in 1948. But such a bolt [6] is a theoretical possibility at any national convention, and the story of what happened on the four occasions mentioned merits careful attention from every student of American parties. That story, occasion by occasion, is as follows.

THE LIBERAL REPUBLICAN BOLT OF 1872 [7]

In the late 1860's and early 1870's, a number of Republican leaders, of whom the most prominent were Carl Schurz, Lyman Trumbull, and Charles Francis Adams, put increasing pressure on the Republican administration to adopt certain national reforms (such as civil-service legislation, lower tariffs, and less punitive treatment of the ex-Confederates); eventually, having failed to get any attention for their demands, they decided to prevent the re-election of the incumbent Republican president, Ulysses S. Grant. As a beginning, they organized a separate "liberal" faction in several states, and in 1870, two years before the national election, they defeated an administration candidate for the governorship of Missouri. They failed, however, to block Grant's renomination in the 1872 Republican national convention. Faced with a choice between knuckling under and bolting, they chose the latter course and proceeded to issue a call for a "Liberal Republican" convention in Cincinnati.

What they had intended, of course, was a Liberal Republican rally, which would as a matter of course nominate Adams. But the Cincinnati convention had hardly assembled when control of its proceedings slipped out of their hands and into those of a group of professional Republican politicians who had no interest in reform, but simply felt they were not getting their fair share of the patronage under the Grant administration. These interlopers proceeded to nominate Horace Greeley, himself a spoilsman and protectionist and thus hardly less objectionable to the Liberals than the administration candidate; and for a while there was talk of a second attempt at a Liberal convention. But the final decision went against it, and the Liberals ended up

---

[6] Generally speaking, the purpose of the bolters is *not* to set up a permanent third party, but to defeat the parent party's candidate in this election and subsequently to drive a hard bargain in the negotiations to restore party unity.

[7] The most complete account is Earle D. Ross, *The Liberal Republican Movement* (New York: Henry Holt and Company, 1919).

rallying behind Greeley on the ground that anyone, even Greeley, was preferable to Grant—as, curiously, did the Democrats also, by refraining from nominating a candidate of their own and endorsing the Liberal Republican nominee. Even so, Grant won, by a vote of 3,597,000 to 2,834,000 (the latter figure being 44 per cent of the total).

After the election, the Liberal leaders abandoned third-party tactics, returned to the Republican fold, and in due time were generally credited with forcing the nomination of "reform" Republican candidates in 1876 (Hayes) and 1880 (Garfield).

THE "GOLD DEMOCRATS" OF 1896 [8]

In the 1896 election a single issue dominated American politics: Should gold remain the basic monetary unit, or should silver be given a position of equality with it? Generally speaking, the industrial East and persons in the upper economic brackets everywhere favored the gold standard, and the agricultural West and South and persons in the lower economic brackets everywhere demanded bimetallism. Far more than is usual in American politics, moreover, each side was deeply convinced of the rightness of its own position and of the immorality and insanity of the opposing one.

The Democratic national convention of 1896, dominated by the silver forces, wrote a strong bimetallist platform, nominated for president William Jennings Bryan, the "boy orator of the Platte," whose name was synonymous with the free-silver cause, and promptly found itself with a bolt on its hands. The bolters, easterners and middle-westerners in the main, held a rump convention at Indianapolis, wrote a strong pro–gold-standard platform, and named John M. Palmer of Illinois as the "National Democratic party's" candidate for president. Judging from the election results, they might have saved themselves the trouble: Palmer received 134,645 (.09 per cent) out of a total of 14,160,000 votes cast. By 1900, silver had ceased to be much of an issue, and most of the "Gold Democrats," despite Bryan's renomination, returned to the Democratic party.

THE PROGRESSIVES OF 1912 [9]

During the years 1890-1917, American politics were deeply influenced by "progressivism," a nationwide politico-literary movement whose standard bearers on the book- and article-writing side were publicists like Lincoln Steffens, Henry D. Lloyd, Ida M. Tarbell, and Herbert Croly, and, on the political side, leaders like William S. U'Ren, George W. Norris, Robert M. La Follette, and Theodore Roosevelt.

[8] The best account of this rather obscure group of bolters is in Edward Stanwood, *A History of the Presidency*, new ed. (Boston: Houghton Mifflin Company, 1928), Vol. I, pp. 557-61.

[9] The best general description of the progressive movement is Benjamin P. DeWitt, *The Progressive Movement* (New York: The Macmillan Company, 1915). The events leading up to the 1912 bolt are well described in Kenneth W. Hechler, *Insurgency, Personalities and Politics of the Taft Era* (New York: Columbia University Press, 1940). The best descriptions of the 1912

The progressives had looked upon American politics and found them bad, but not irremediably bad. The basic trouble, they held, was that the machines with their bosses and the greedy "interests" had snatched control of all our levels of government—local, state, and national alike—from the people. To blame this on democracy and to conclude that the ideals of democracy are impractical ideals, they argued, was to overlook the fact that those ideals had never yet been put into effect, that "the cure for the ills of democracy is more democracy," and that the reforms that would give us "more democracy" were ready at hand: direct election of U.S. senators, direct primaries, the initiative, the referendum, and the recall, the merit system, government control of the "trusts," lower tariffs, government conservation of natural resources, etc.[10]

The first political expression of the progressive movement was a series of state and city factional rebellions inside the two major parties. In the early 1900's Robert La Follette was elected Governor of Wisconsin, Hazen Pingree Governor of Michigan, Samuel "Golden Rule" Jones Mayor of Toledo, and Tom Johnson Mayor of Cleveland. The first conspicuous progressive move in national politics did not come until 1909, when a group of insurgent Republican congressmen, led by La Follette in the Senate and Norris in the House, tried unsuccessfully to defeat the Payne-Aldrich Tariff Act. The next year the insurgent Republicans in the House joined with the Democrats to strip "Old-Guard" Speaker Joseph Cannon of many of his formal powers, and the struggle between the progressives and the Old Guard became open warfare on a nationwide scale. Two years after that, in the 1912 election, the bolt occurred, in the manner described below.

The Progressives, determined to block the renomination of President William Howard Taft, first mobilized behind the candidacy of Senator La Follette; but when ex-President Theodore Roosevelt suddenly announced his own candidacy and wrapped himself in the mantle of a progressive program, they switched their support to him. At the 1912 Republican national convention, however, the Taft forces were in complete control. Taft's renomination, therefore, was a foregone conclusion, and Roosevelt and progressivism promptly disappeared from sight under the administration's steam roller.[11] The Progressives responded by holding a rump convention in Chicago, drawing up a strongly progressive platform, and nominating Roosevelt for president and

Progressive party are to be found in such biographies of its leaders as Claude G. Bowers, *Beveridge and the Progressive Era* (Boston: Houghton Mifflin Company, 1932); Edward N. Doan, *The La Follettes and the Wisconsin Idea* (New York: Rinehart & Company, Inc., 1947); Belle C. La Follette and Fola La Follette, *Robert M. La Follette* (New York: The Macmillan Company, 1953); Henry F. Pringle, *Theodore Roosevelt, A Biography* (New York: Harcourt, Brace and Company, 1931); and George E. Mowry, *Theodore Roosevelt and the Progressive Movement* (Madison: University of Wisconsin Press, 1946).

[10] The fullest and most forceful expositions of the general progressive point of view are to be found in Herbert Croly's books, *The Promise of American Life* (New York: The Macmillan Company, 1909); and *Progressive Democracy* (New York: The Macmillan Company, 1914).

[11] Political scientists frequently cite the 1912 Republican convention as the clinching evidence for the axiom that an incumbent president *cannot* be defeated for renomination, even if the individual members of the convention would like, in their heart of hearts, to be rid of him.

Governor Hiram Johnson of California for vice-president. And Roosevelt, in due course, gave the new party the nickname by which it is now known: "I feel as fit," he told an inquirer after his health, "as a *bull moose!*"

Roosevelt waged a typically strenuous campaign, and, insofar as its purpose was merely to beat Taft, waged it successfully: he polled 4,123,206 popular votes (29.6 per cent of the total) and 88 electoral votes as against Taft's 3,484,529 popular votes and 8 electoral votes. But the real beneficiary of the bolt was the Democratic candidate, Woodrow Wilson, who, with a mere plurality (6,290,-818) of the popular votes, ended up with 435 electoral votes—and the presidency.

Several Progressive leaders, notably Senator Albert J. Beveridge, spoke out after the 1912 election in favor of keeping the party alive and contesting future elections. Roosevelt, however, failed to warm to the idea; the party polled only about half of its 1912 vote in the 1914 congressional elections; and Roosevelt himself delivered it the *coup de grâce* in 1916, when he endorsed the regular Republican nominee, Charles Evans Hughes. Many commentators, however, believe that in the course of its brief career the Progressive party changed the face of American politics, for one thing by forcing the Democrats, under Wilson, to put through a program of progressive legislation, and for another by consolidating control of the Republican party in the hands of the Old Guard, who were to keep it for at least a generation after 1912.[12]

THE "DIXIECRATS" OF 1948 [13]

As we noted in Chapter 8, the southern wing of the Democratic party has for many decades bitterly resisted, both in national Democratic conventions and in the national government, all attempts by nonsoutherners to alter traditional Negro-white relations in the South. We also noted, however, that the southerners' influence on the writing of national Democratic platforms and the selection of Democratic presidential nominees has declined markedly since the early days of the New Deal. The major turning point here was the 1936 convention, when the New Dealers forced the abolition of the two-thirds rule, which the southerners—correctly or incorrectly—regarded as giving them the power to veto unacceptable nominees and platform planks. For since then the nonsouthern Democrats, who control some three-quarters of the votes in the national convention, have courted the Negroes and other minority groups in the large northern industrial states by demanding equal treatment of all races. And during World War II, President Roosevelt drove home the point that the Democratic party was not the captive of its southern wing by issuing his fa-

---

[12] Cf. Greer, *op. cit.,* p. 100.

[13] The most useful published accounts of the Dixiecrat movement are in Alexander Heard, *A Two-Party South?* (Chapel Hill: University of North Carolina Press, 1952), Ch. 2; and in V. O. Key, Jr., *Southern Politics in State and Nation* (New York: Alfred A. Knopf, 1949), pp. 329-44. The present writers have also found most helpful Robert S. Friedman, *The Dixiecrats in the 1948 Election* (unpublished M.A. thesis in political science, University of Illinois, 1950) and Emile B. Ader, *The Dixiecrat Movement* (Washington, D. C.: Public Affairs Press, 1955).

mous Fair Employment Practices Order,[14] and by having himself and his wife photographed with the leaders of such pro-Negro organizations as the National Association for the Advancement of Colored People.

The first hints of an intention on the part of the southern Democrats to strike back came in 1944. In that year the Mississippi Democratic convention released its electoral-college nominees from any obligation to vote along party lines, and some of the latter duly announced that they would *not* vote for Roosevelt, the national Democratic nominee.[15] And in Texas, when it became clear that the pro-Roosevelt faction had won control of the state Democratic convention, the extreme anti-Roosevelt group, calling themselves the "Texas Regulars," withdrew to name their own slate of electors. They accounted, to be sure, for only 135,439 votes, as against 821,605 for the pro-Roosevelt electors; but theirs was "the first effort in recent history by any southern group to leave the national Democratic party without joining the Republican party,"[16] and as such was a harbinger of what was to happen in 1948.

The 1948 revolt was precipitated by Roosevelt's successor, President Harry S. Truman, whose Commission on Civil Rights published in 1947 a report recommending that the federal government take action to guarantee certain rights—voting and employment rights, among others—to southern Negroes, and thus alerted the white southerners to the imminence of new attacks on southern race relations from the North. Nor did they have long to wait: in February, 1948, Truman sent a message to Congress calling for the enactment of an anti-lynching law, measures protecting the Negroes' right to vote, and a national fair-employment-practices law. Over the following weeks, Truman turned a deaf ear to the chorus of protest—with all southern voices included except those of the out-and-out southern liberals—that came up from the South, where the indignation was yet the greater because of the widespread conviction that Truman himself (coming as he did from the border state of Missouri) could hardly believe sincerely in his civil-rights proposals. To the southerners, they could only be explained as a crass bid for the Negro and liberal vote in the North. Before the ink of the president's signature on this message was dry, at any rate, several southern leaders, among them Governor Fielding Wright of Mississippi, Governor J. Strom Thurmond of South Carolina, Governor Ben Laney of Arkansas, and Governor Jim Folsom of Alabama, were speaking ominously of a southern bolt and, more concretely, of the need for a conference of "states' rights Democrats." And they meant business; the threatened conference actually convened (in Jackson, Mississippi) in early May, vigorously denounced the Truman program, and resolved to reassemble after the Democratic na-

---

[14] This order prohibited any plant holding a government defense contract from discriminating in its hiring and firing against any person because of his race or national origin.

[15] Governor Thomas L. Bailey, who was pro-Roosevelt, scotched the rebellion by taking advantage of a nearly forgotten statute and persuading the *legislature* to name pro-Roosevelt nominees for elector.

[16] Friedman, *op. cit.*, p. 5.

tional convention if the latter renominated Truman and failed to repudiate his program.

The convention, meeting in early July, took up the southerners' gauntlet. The majority of its platform committee, to be sure, attempted to keep the peace by proposing what most northern liberals regarded as a "mild" civil-rights plank, but the southerners themselves forced the issue by moving to substitute for it a vigorously worded states' rights plank. The convention not only voted them down, but approved a motion by Hubert Humphrey, later senator from Minnesota, to substitute a national civil-rights plank with "teeth" in it. As soon as the vote on Humphrey's motion was announced, the entire Mississippi delegation and half the Alabama delegation walked out of the convention. The remaining southerners gave their votes for the nomination to Senator Russell of Georgia; and when Truman was renominated, northern-southern feeling was so bitter that no one even proposed the customary courtesy motion to make the nomination unanimous.

The projected second states' rights conference met in Birmingham on July 17, adopted a strong states' rights and anti-Truman platform, and "suggested" (they did not officially use the term "nominate") Governor Thurmond for president and Governor Wright for vice-president. Presumably no one present expected Thurmond and Wright to be elected; the strategy was, rather, to win enough electoral votes in the southern states to prevent a Truman or a Dewey majority in the electoral college, and so throw the election into the House of Representatives, where it would be decided on a one-vote-per-state basis that might enable the southerners to exact a no-interference pledge from one of the parties. And, in any case, the northern Democrats would learn once and for all that the Democratic party cannot afford to ride roughshod over southern ideas and feelings. As Governor Wright put it at the Birmingham convention:

This is the South's great opportunity, it is a chance to prove to the nation that we are the Democratic Party. We have saved the Democratic Party in the past and we will save it in the future. But we will not save it for those who have crashed into the party, seized control and led it astray. Those people thought we were bluffing. They thought they could bluff us, well, we called their bluff.[17]

The bolters' basic plan for winning the electoral votes of the southern states called for capturing the official machinery of the Democratic party in each state, and getting Thurmond and Wright on the ballot not as third-party candidates but as the official nominees of the Democratic party. This, however, they were able to bring off in only four states: Alabama (where Truman did not appear on the ballot at all), South Carolina, Mississippi, and Louisiana; everywhere else they had to run as "States' Rights Democrats." Thurmond-Wright spokesmen made token sorties into a few states outside the South and appeared on the ballot in four nonsouthern states (Kentucky, North

[17] Quoted in Friedman, op. cit., p. 68.

Dakota, Maryland, and California), in which they polled a total of 14,489 votes; but the bolt, despite its claim to be a national movement, remained a family affair—as its popular nickname, "Dixiecrats," implied—among southerners.

In the November election Thurmond carried the four states in which he was the official Democratic nominee, and won one electoral vote in Tennessee, for a total electoral vote of thirty-nine.[18] In the remaining southern states except Georgia, where he ran second, Thurmond ran well behind Dewey. In the South as a whole he polled 1,154,096 votes (or 22.5 per cent of the total vote) to Truman's 2,559,764 votes (50.1 per cent of the total)—far short, be it noted, of the vote needed to throw the election into the House. If the Dixiecrats *had* managed to capture all the electoral votes in the South, the electoral totals would have been 215—instead of 303—for Truman, 189 for Dewey, and 127 for Thurmond, and the election *would* have been thrown into the House. The Dixiecrats' basic plan, in other words, was strategically sound; but they failed to persuade enough southern Democratic leaders to join their rebellion and help get Thurmond and Wright on the ballot as the official Democratic nominees.

The Dixiecrat revolt of 1948 must not, however, be written off as having produced no practical results. There is reason to believe, for one thing, that it served to sharpen factional lines in most southern Democratic parties, and thus to make southern one-party politics a little less amorphous than they had been in the past.[19] And in the 1952 Democratic national convention, the non-southern Democrats were visibly more careful about stepping on southern toes than they had been in previous conventions—though not so careful as to encourage southerners in the belief that they have regained the veto power they once claimed.

In the 1952 election, with no Dixiecrat candidate in the field, the Republicans—possibly but not necessarily as a result of the 1948 bolt—fared better in the South than they had since 1928. Eisenhower, the Republican nominee, carried four southern states (Florida, Tennessee, Texas, and Virginia), lost by close margins in four (Louisiana, Mississippi, North Carolina, and South Carolina), and made a creditable showing in the three others. Some commentators, notably Senator Karl Mundt (Republican of South Dakota), have suggested, in the light of such developments, that the southern Democrats officially merge with the Republicans in a nationwide conservative and states' rights party.[20] At the present writing, however, there is no evidence that Senator Mundt has found any significant number of supporters south of the Mason-Dixon Line. The Dixiecrats will, in the opinion of skilled observers of southern

---

[18] See pp. 332-33 for the peculiar circumstances in which Thurmond received this electoral vote.

[19] Cf. Heard, *op. cit.*, pp. 27-28.

[20] Cf. Karl Mundt, "The GOP Should Merge with the Dixiecrats," *Collier's*, Vol. CXXVIII (July 28, 1951), pp. 20, 45-46.

politics, continue as an identifiable faction inside the national Democratic party, and will not seek the status of a third party or set up in business as the southern wing of the Republican party.[21]

National Farmer-Labor Parties [22]

We come now to a group of minor parties, all of them postdating the Civil War, that have this in common: they have arisen out of a conviction on the part of certain organized farmer and labor groups that the agricultural and "working-class" elements of the population receive less than a fair share of the nation's bounty, that attempts to press their claim to a fair share on the major parties by pressure or "balance-of-power" tactics are in the nature of the case futile, and that their only hope for justice lies in bringing together all the nation's dispossessed groups in a third party, large and powerful enough to call the tricks on national economic policy. Do not farmers and workers—so runs the argument, generation after generation—make up a majority of the population? If they do, why should a party clearly devoted to their interests not sweep the nation like wildfire? And—by way of reply to the point that third parties never win in the United States—how about the Republican party, which finished second in its first national election (1856) and won the presidency in its second attempt (1860)? Does its history not prove that a new party *can* succeed in American politics? [23] Here, in a word, is a group of minor parties launched with the firm intention not only of remaining indefinitely in business, but with the confident expectation of capturing, at a fairly early date, the entire machinery of the government of the United States.

We shall confine our attention to three major examples of this kind of party: the "Greenbackers," the "Populists," and the Progressives of 1924.

THE "GREENBACKERS" [24]

After the Civil War, American farmers, particularly farmers who depended on wheat and corn for their cash income, were caught in a squeeze between the low prices they received for their crops and the high prices of the things they had to buy. Many of them became convinced that the best way out—for them and for the nation—was a quick rise in prices, which could be

---

[21] Cf. Key, *op. cit.;* and Heard, *op. cit.*

[22] The most complete general accounts of these parties are: Nathan Fine, *Labor and Farmer Parties in the United States, 1828-1928* (New York: Rand School of Social Science, 1928); Murray S. Stedman, Jr., and Susan W. Stedman, *Discontent at the Polls, A Study of Farmer and Labor Parties, 1827-1948* (New York: Columbia University Press, 1950); and Joseph R. Starr, "Labor and Farmer Groups and the Three-Party System," *Southwestern Social Science Quarterly,* Vol. XVII (June, 1936), pp. 7-19.

[23] Fine points out that many of the nineteenth-century third-party movements were buoyed up and inspired by the rapid rise of the Republicans, and figured that it would take but one or two campaigns before they too would elect a president: *Op. cit.*, pp. 178-79.

[24] The best descriptions are in Fine, *op. cit.,* pp. 67-72; Haynes, *op. cit.,* pp. 160-63; and Greer, *op. cit.,* pp. 69-73.

brought about by inflating the currency. So they demanded further issues of the "greenbacks," or paper money, that had helped finance the war. And when the major parties flatly rejected inflation in favor of a "sound currency," as both had clearly done by the mid-1870's, a number of farmer organizations proceeded (1875) to form the Independent Party, popularly known as the "Greenbackers," to press for more paper money by third-party tactics. In the 1876 election, the new party's nominee for president was Peter Cooper, the 85-year-old New York philanthropist who had founded Cooper Union. He received a mere 81,737 votes out of a national total of 8,412,000.

In 1878 the Greenbackers, having united forces with several labor organizations, broadened their program to include certain demands for labor legislation, changed their name to the National Party, and concentrated their attention on the congressional elections. Things began to look up: "Greenback-Labor" (for so the party was now called in popular discussion) candidates polled a national total of more than a million votes, and several were elected. The party's leaders, impressed no doubt by calculations as to what would happen if its 1876-1878 rate of growth could be maintained, accordingly went into the 1880 presidential election with a great show of confident optimism. Having nominated James B. Weaver, a Greenbacker congressman from Iowa who had been a general in the Union army, they staged the first "whirlwind campaign tour" in American political history, putting their candidate through an endless round of personal appearances and speechmaking in state after state. But the 1876-1878 tide, instead of continuing to rise, had turned. Weaver polled only 308,578 votes out of a national total of 9,218,000; and the party's rank-and-file supporters in the farms and in the factories appear to have written it off as a hopeless venture. For its nominees—General Benjamin F. Butler in 1884 and Alson J. Streeter in 1888—each received only a small fraction of the disappointingly small vote cast for Weaver; and after the 1888 election the party, in part because large numbers of its leaders and supporters went over to the Populists, simply disintegrated.

THE "POPULISTS" [25]

The collapse of the Greenback-Labor party left the farmers and workers temporarily disillusioned about third-party activity, but not about political activity in general. Beginning in the early 1880's, farmers all over the South and Middle West began to form local organizations, which exerted local pressure (e.g., on state legislators and congressmen) on behalf of their demands for economic justice. And after a few years these organizations coalesced into two huge regional farmers' federations, the "Southern Alliance" (officially known as the National Farmers' Alliance and Industrial Union) and the "Northern Alliance" (officially known as the National Farmers' Alliance). The Alliances adopted broad programs, including such demands as monetary

[25] The authoritative account is John D. Hicks, *The Populist Revolt* (Minneapolis: University of Minnesota Press, 1931).

inflation through the issuance of more paper money and the free coinage of silver, lower tariffs, a progressive income tax, and government ownership of railroads and telegraphs; and in the late 1880's their strength began to grow by leaps and bounds, not least of all because of the war cry they acquired when an Alliance leader, Mrs. Mary E. Lease, told a farm audience in Kansas, "What you farmers need to do is to raise less corn and more *Hell!*" [26]

By the early 1890's the Alliance leaders had decided that the time was ripe for a national farmer-labor party that would do the job that the Green-back-Labor party had muffed. In 1892, accordingly, representatives of the Farmers' Alliances met with those of several national labor organizations (such as the Knights of Labor) and founded the People's Party. The new party, promptly nicknamed "the Populists," got off to a good start. Its first presidential nominee, the same General Weaver who had been the Green-backer candidate in 1880, polled 1,040,886 popular votes out of a national total of 12,052,000, and, more impressive still, got 22 votes (those of Colorado, Idaho, Kansas, and Nevada) in the electoral college. No minor party had ever done so well in a presidential election; and the wiseacres who were predicting early failure for the movement received a further surprise in the 1894 congressional elections, when Populist candidates polled 1,471,590 votes and several won seats. Unavoidably, the Populist leaders began to indulge dreams—if not of winning the 1896 presidential election, at least of being able to decide the issue between the two major parties and thus name terms to the victor.

In 1896, as we have already noted, free silver was the overriding issue. The Populist convention did not meet until the Democrats had already nomi-nated Bryan and adopted a platform advocating not only free silver, but several other Populist measures as well. The convention, accordingly, faced this di-lemma: Should the Populists content themselves with half a loaf (the Populist measures in the Democratic platform) and go all out for Bryan? Or should they hold out for the whole loaf, and go it alone? The "fusionists," that is, the advocates of half a loaf, won the day, and the Populists nominated Bryan. (They passed up the Democrats' vice-presidential nominee, the conservative Maine banker Arthur Sewall, in favor of Tom Watson of Georgia.) After one of the most strenuous campaigns in American political history, McKinley, the Republican candidate, defeated Bryan by 7,035,000 popular votes and 271 elec-toral votes to 6,467,000 popular votes and 176 electoral votes; the Bryan-Watson ticket received only 222,583 votes as against 6,245,363 votes for the Bryan-Sewall ticket. The Populists, in short, had traded their independence for half a loaf that ended up being no loaf at all.

The party never recovered from its 1896 defeat, which was the more bitter because of the widespread suspicion that it would have fared better in the long run had it chosen the other horn of its dilemma. Most of its leaders and supporters stayed in the Democratic party after the 1896 elections; and the

[26] Quoted in Hicks, *op. cit.,* pp. 159-60.

Populist hard core that fought the 1900, 1904, and 1908 elections, with Watson as its presidential candidate, attracted a mere 115,000 votes even in its best year. The party formally disbanded in 1912.

THE PROGRESSIVES OF 1924 [27]

By the early 1920's many Americans had come to regard the leadership of both major parties as ultra-conservative, and labor and farm groups expressed increasing dissatisfaction at their prospects of persuading either of the parties to take agriculture and labor into account in formulating national economic policy. Before long, talk was in the air about the need for a new third party, and in 1922, with the railway brotherhoods taking the lead, a call was issued for a "Conference for Progressive Political Action" to look into the possibilities. Delegates were invited from such groups as the state federations of labor, the larger farmers' organizations, church social-action groups, the Socialist party, the Non-Partisan League, and the independent (i.e., not affiliated with the AFL) labor unions; and this conference led to a second conference and then a third, at which the decision was finally taken: the CPPA would form a new party, to be called the Progressive party; it would contest the 1924 presidential election; and it would hold its convention on July 4.[28]

The convention met as planned, nominated Senator Robert M. La Follette for president and Senator Burton K. Wheeler for vice-president, wrote a platform calling for, among other things, public ownership of the railroads and water-power resources, direct nomination and election of the president, popular election of federal judges, and encouragement of labor unions and collective bargaining; and set out on one of the more curious campaigns in American political history. For one thing, the new party, called into being as it was almost exclusively with an eye to the struggle for the presidency, contested few congressional, state, and local offices, so that the campaign, by normal American standards, tended to be top-heavy. And so did its organization: unlike the 1912 Progressives, who were able to count on support from numerous Republican state and local organizations, those of 1924 had no grass-roots bases except a handful that it took over temporarily from the Socialists. Finally, while the party got on the ballot in all the states except Louisiana, it suffered greatly from the vagaries of the various state election laws: its candidates were listed as Progressives in some states, as Independents in other states, and as Farmer-Laborites or Socialists in yet others. La Follette, in any

----

[27] The most complete account is Kenneth C. MacKay, *The Progressive Movement of 1924* (New York: Columbia University Press, 1947). The present writers have classified the 1924 Progressives as a farmer-labor party rather than as a bolt from a major party because, while its nominees were both major-party senators, the rest of the party's organization and much of its support came from farmer and labor groups rather than from disaffected adherents of the major parties.

[28] Many national minor parties have held their conventions on Independence Day, Washington's Birthday, or Lincoln's Birthday—as a reminder to the nation, no doubt, that there is nothing inconsistent in radicalism *and* patriotism.

event, carried only his home state of Wisconsin and its thirteen electoral votes, although he polled a national total of 4,822,856 popular votes out of a total for all parties of 28,934,000, and ran second in eleven states.

In 1925 the CPPA reassembled, nominally to decide whether to continue the Progressive party, but actually, since the result was a foregone conclusion, to sentence it to death. The Socialists wished it to go on (and on), but most of the unions and farmer organizations announced that they were pulling out and would henceforth seek to forward their objectives without resorting to third-party methods—as they have subsequently done. The CPPA breathed its last.

Local Farmer-Labor or Labor Parties

Besides the national parties discussed in the preceding section, farmer and worker groups have from time to time organized political parties with primarily state or local objectives. Six examples of such parties may be noted.

THE WORKINGMEN's PARTIES OF THE 1820's [29]

In the late 1820's, labor groups in various eastern cities (especially New York, Boston, and Philadelphia) formed local third parties, generally called "Workingmen's parties," with no apparent purpose but to contest elections for state and local offices. They agitated mainly for free, tax-supported schools open to all children, the abolition of imprisonment for debt, and the public control of monopolies. They never attracted many votes, and following the panic of 1837 they quickly disappeared. Their chief claim to distinction is that they were, if not the first full-fledged minor parties to appear in American politics, at least among the very earliest.[30]

THE "GRANGER" PARTIES OF THE 1870's [31]

The roots of the Granger parties lie not in politics, at least in the usual sense of the term, but in the felt needs of the nation's farmers, in the Middle

[29] The best account of the Workingmen's parties is in Fine, *op. cit.,* pp. 13-18.

[30] Some scholars hold that the first minor party in American politics was the "Quid" party of John Randolph: Cf. John D. Hicks, "The Third Party Tradition in American Politics," *Mississippi Valley Historical Review,* Vol. XX (June, 1933), pp. 4-6. John Randolph of Roanoke, Virginia, was the outstanding Republican leader in Congress during Jefferson's first administration. He broke with the administration in 1806 over the handling of the Yazoo land-fraud case, lost his committee posts, and proceeded to rally around him a small band of congressmen whom he called the *tertium quid.,* i.e., the "third alternative" (the Republicans and the Federalists being the other two). The Quids confined themselves, for the most part, to oppositionist activities inside Congress, never did much electioneering, and thus never became a full-fledged political party. The Workingmen's parties, in the view of the present writers, were the first authentic minor parties in American politics. For further details on Randolph's Quids, see William C. Bruce, *John Randolph of Roanoke,* 2 volumes (New York: G. P. Putnam's Sons, 1929).

[31] The most authoritative accounts of the Granger parties are two works by Solon J. Buck: *The Agrarian Crusade* (New Haven: Yale University Press, 1920); and *The Granger Movement* (Cambridge: Harvard University Press, 1933).

West particularly, for local clubs in which they could get together socially and exchange ideas about their common problems. During the years immediately following the Civil War, quite spontaneously it seems, the idea of such clubs ("granger organizations" they were called, "granger" being a synonym for "farmer") spread over the agricultural sections of the country like a rash. By 1867 they were getting together in a national federation called the National Patrons of Husbandry or, for short, the "Grange."

The local grange meetings did encourage discussion, and what the grangers discussed, at least where wheat and corn were grown, was the high tariffs and the sharp practices of the railroads and grain elevators; and in eleven states the discussion finally led to a decision to organize independent statewide farmers' parties and thus to make the railroads and grain elevators behave. Officially these new parties bore such labels as Independent, Reform, Anti-Monopoly, and Farmers'; unofficially they were all called "the Granger parties." During the years 1873-1875 they attracted numerous supporters—enough, in many of the states in which they appeared, to force the legislatures to pass laws regulating railroads and grain elevators. Success, indeed, is what killed them off: once the desired laws were on the books, the parties lost their *raison d'être,* and promptly began to disappear. After 1876, they were little heard of. (A number of the Granger-party leaders and supporters later became active in the Greenbacker and Populist parties.)

THE NON-PARTISAN LEAGUE [32]

The beginnings of the NPL date back to 1915, when a group of North Dakota farmers requested certain reform legislation but ran up against a flat refusal from the leaders of the Republican party, which then as now completely dominated the state's politics. Under the generalship of Arthur C. Townley, a former Socialist, these farmers organized the NPL and set out to see what could be accomplished via formal organization. Their program, as it finally took shape, called among other things for state ownership of terminal elevators and flour mills, rural nonprofit credit banks, and state-supported hail insurance. As a matter of policy, the League used third-party tactics only where it had failed to get results with its preferred approach, which was to enter League candidates in the primaries of the dominant party in the area under attack, and get them first nominated and then elected as members of that party—whence the adjective "non-partisan" in the League's name, which put the parties on notice that it would as willingly infiltrate one as the other. Where its candidates were defeated in the infiltrated primary, however, the League did on occasion run them in the general election as "independ-

[32] The best descriptions of the Non-Partisan League are: Andrew A. Bruce, *The Non-Partisan League* (New York: The Macmillan Company, 1921); Usher L. Burdick, *History of the Farmers' Political Action in North Dakota* (Baltimore: Wirth Brothers, 1944); and Herbert E. Gaston, *The Nonpartisan League* (New York: Harcourt, Brace and Howe, 1920).

ents" or even with third-party labels—although with little success.[33] At its peak, the League could point to well over 200,000 members, and to sister organizations in several states other than North Dakota. It held the whip hand in North Dakota politics from 1916 to 1920, and became a factor to be reckoned with in Minnesota and South Dakota as well. After 1920, however, its power rapidly declined; and where it did not disappear entirely it became a mere faction of the Republican party.[34]

THE MINNESOTA FARMER-LABOR PARTY [35]

The story of Minnesota's Farmer-Labor party begins not in Minnesota but in far-off New York, and not with a party bidding for agricultural support but with a national Labor party, frankly modeled on that in Britain, and, like the latter, committed to socialism. Founded in 1919, this Labor party added the word "Farmer" to its name in 1920—presumably in the hope of casting its net more widely in that year's presidential election. Parley P. Christensen of Utah, its candidate, polled 250,000 votes, only a few of which, be it noted, were cast in industrial areas. Two years later, control of the national party passed into the hands of the Communists, and its farm supporters deserted it en masse.[36]

The party's strongest state branch, in part because it succeeded in attracting large numbers of former members of the state's Non-Partisan League, was the Minnesota Farmer-Labor party. The latter went right on nominating candidates and contesting elections after the parent national party disappeared, and by the mid-1920's it had sent two of its members to the U.S. Senate. Through the 1930's, it was the Republican party's chief rival for supremacy in state elections, the Democrats having been reduced to third-party status, and it won each gubernatorial election from 1930 to 1936. Its decline dates from 1938, when Harold Stassen, a Republican, unseated Governor Elmer Benson. This defeat and the growing influence of the Communists on the party's leadership combined so to discredit the party as to render a comeback unlikely. In the 1940's, the party was willing enough to join forces with the Democrats in a new Democratic-Farmer-Labor party. After the anti-Communist elements decisively defeated the pro-Communist forces for control of the new party, it became strong enough to elect a U.S. senator (1948 and 1954) and a governor (1954).

[33] For a useful description of the League's various political tactics, see Samuel P. Huntington, "The Election Tactics of the Nonpartisan League," *Mississippi Valley Historical Review*, Vol. XXXVI (March, 1950), pp. 613-32.

[34] See p. 195 for an account of the present status of the Non-Partisan League faction in the North Dakota Republican party.

[35] See Hesseltine, *op. cit.*, pp. 52-54.

[36] For accounts of the 1920 national Farmer-Labor party, see Fine, *op. cit.*, pp. 377-95; and Greer, *op. cit.*, pp. 126-27.

THE WISCONSIN PROGRESSIVE PARTY [37]

From the early 1890's to the early 1930's, the Wisconsin "progressives" were not (if we leave out of account the presidential elections of 1912 and 1924) a third party, but rather a faction within the Wisconsin Republican party. After 1920, however, this group never once supported the presidential candidate of the party to which it nominally belonged; and in 1934 it at last broke away completely from the Republicans and set up in business as a third party: the Wisconsin Progressive party. From then to the end of the decade the Progressives, not the Democrats, were the party the Wisconsin Republicans had to beat (the Democrats, here as in Minnesota, became for the time a third party). In 1934 they elected both a senator (Robert M. La Follette, Jr.) and a governor (Philip La Follette); in 1936 they re-elected the governor; and in 1940 they re-elected the senator (although they had in 1938 lost the governorship). By 1946 the movement had pretty clearly run its course, and the party's leaders decided to take it back into the Republican fold (so that its complete history might well be called "from faction to third party to major party to third party to faction"). Since then the Progressives have either gone over to the Democrats or have operated as a small faction in the Wisconsin Republican party.

THE AMERICAN LABOR AND LIBERAL PARTIES OF NEW YORK [38]

In early 1936, President Franklin D. Roosevelt recommended to certain New Deal labor leaders in New York (among others, David Dubinsky of the International Ladies Garment Workers' Union and Sidney Hillman of the Amalgamated Clothing Workers) the launching of a New York labor party— not for its own sake, but as a device for enabling union members, liberals, socialists, etc., to vote for Roosevelt and his program without stamping themselves with the Tammany-tainted Democratic label. James A. Farley, Edward J. Flynn, and other New York Democratic leaders voiced strong objections, but Dubinsky and Hillman liked the idea and proceeded to found the American Labor party. It duly endorsed Roosevelt in 1936, and polled 275,000 of Roosevelt's 3,293,000 votes in New York. In 1940 it endorsed him again, and polled 417,000 of his 3,252,000 votes in New York.

The ALP did not long, however, remain a mere dodge for getting Roosevelt some votes that he might otherwise have lost. As early as 1937, over vigorous protests from the Democrats, the party supported Fiorello H. La Guardia for Mayor of New York City, and gave him 483,000 votes. Nor did it long succeed in holding together all its original supporters. The Communists, having lost their legal status as a political party because of getting too few votes

[37] See Hesseltine, op. cit., pp. 54-57; and Doan, op. cit.
[38] The best accounts are: Warren Moscow, Politics in the Empire State (New York: Alfred A. Knopf, 1948), Ch. VII; Hugh A. Bone, "Political Parties in New York City," American Political Science Review, Vol. XL (April, 1946), pp. 272-82; and Daniel Bell, "New York's 'Third Parties,'" Common Sense, Vol. XIV (June, 1945), pp. 14-15.

in the 1936 gubernatorial election, in 1938 went over to the ALP en masse, labored mightily (as Communists do when they enter another party) in the ALP's primaries, and captured control of the party's machinery in certain New York City localities. Dubinsky and Hillman promptly disagreed over how to deal with this development: Dubinsky would have excluded the Communists from the party altogether; Hillman would have let them work in the party on the understanding that no Communist would be nominated for any public office. Hillman carried the day, with the result that Dubinsky and his union soon pulled out of the ALP and formed the Liberal party, whose constitution specifically prohibits the admission of any person who believes in any form of totalitarianism. Both new parties, however, endorsed Roosevelt in the 1944 election. The ALP gave him 496,000 and the Liberals 329,000 votes (the Democrats' statewide total was 2,479,000).

After 1944, the Communists were in virtually complete—and notorious—control of the ALP. In 1947, accordingly, the Democratic State Central Committee announced that it would not accept ALP endosement of the Democratic presidential nominee; and in the presidential election of the following year the ALP endorsed Henry Wallace, the national Progressive nominee. The Liberal party, which supported Truman, polled only 223,000 votes (as compared with 2,558,000 Democratic votes), while the ALP drew 510,000 votes for Wallace, which the Democratic Central Committeee may or may not have thrown away by the 1947 announcement. These latter votes decided the statewide election, since there were just enough of them to throw the state to Dewey, the Republican nominee. Thereafter, however, the ALP declined rapidly in strength, the Liberals and Democrats taking over most of its former non-Communist support. In 1952, the ALP endorsed Vincent Hallinan, the national Progressive nominee, but polled only 64,000 votes for him as compared with the 417,000 Liberal votes and 2,688,000 Democratic votes cast for Stevenson, the Democratic nominee.

Chapter 19

THE PARTIES
OF IDEOLOGICAL
PROTEST

Their General Nature

In the preceding chapter we described the careers of the more notable examples of three types of American minor parties: factions bolting from the major parties, farmer-labor parties, and labor parties. Despite the many differences among these parties, they all had this in common: they disagreed with the major parties about how generally accepted American political and social doctrines were to be applied to specific problems, but *not* about those doctrines themselves. All of them, in other words, belonged in the ideological mainstream of American politics. Far from forcing a major issue with the rest of the country on the level of high principle, they avoided even the appearance of doing so.

In the present chapter, by contrast, we shall deal with the minor parties in American history that have staked everything on an idea, or body of ideas, on the grounds not that that idea or body of ideas was sound American doctrine but that it was *correct,* and that the nation's salvation lay precisely in recognizing its correctness. Most of their leaders, indeed, rather prided themselves upon their remoteness from the mainstream and upon the *novelty* of their principles. We may, for that reason, call them the "parties of ideological protest." Concretely, we shall describe the socialist parties, the single-issue parties, the Union party of 1936, and the Communist Party and its satellite, the Progressive party of 1948-1952.

The Socialist Parties

In most of the nations of Europe, workers and trade unions have pressed their demands mainly through the creation and support of Marxist-socialist parties of one variety or another;[1] and the history of the European labor

---

[1] The French Socialists and the Social Democrats of other European nations regard themselves as *the* true Marxists, and the Communists as Leninist-Stalinist corrupters of Marxism. The

movement is, in consequence, intimately tied up with that of the European socialist movement.

In the United States, by contrast, the labor movement has in general given the socialist movement a wide berth.[2] American workers have pressed their demands by such purely "industrial" tactics as forming trade unions and carrying on strikes and boycotts, and by such "balance-of-power" political tactics as supporting major-party candidates who advocate measures favorable to labor in general and unions in particular. Their slogan, urged on them many years ago by Samuel Gompers, the first president of the American Federation of Labor, has been, "Reward your friends and punish your enemies!"; and a corollary of that slogan, as they have applied it, has been, "Organize no third parties; and if someone else organizes a third party, keep out of it." Even when separate organizations for labor political action have appeared in the field, such as the rich and powerful Political Action Committee of the CIO or the equally rich and powerful Labor's League for Political Education of the AFL, they have confined their activities to supporting pro-labor major-party candidates in primaries and general elections.

All this is not to say that the American socialist movement has not had its roots in labor, but rather that only one small segment of the American labor movement has tried to achieve its goals by means of political parties with socialist programs. The parties it has created have been among the most persistent—although hardly the most powerful—minor parties in American political history. At the present time three such parties are sufficiently active in American politics to deserve mention.[3]

THE SOCIALIST LABOR PARTY [4]

Marxist socialism first came to the United States in the 1850's in the intellectual baggage of immigrants from Germany, and our first Marxist or-

British Labor Party differs sharply in this regard from its counterparts on the continent: it has a mere sprinkling of non-communist Marxists and advocates such a brand of non-Marxist socialism as that suggested by its slogans, "the inevitability of gradualness" and "fabianism."

[2] Picking one's way through the highly complicated maze that is the history of the American socialist movement is a task of great difficulty for anyone who cannot work at it full time. The reader who is prepared to undertake this chore beyond the simplified version presented in the text may begin by consulting such works as these: Nathan Fine, *Labor and Farmer Parties in the United States, 1828-1928* (New York: Rand School of Social Science, 1928); Thomas H. Greer, *American Social Reform Movements* (New York: Prentice-Hall, Inc., 1949); and Harry W. Laidler, *A History of Socialist Thought* (New York: Thomas Y. Crowell Company, 1927) and *Social-Economic Movements* (New York: Thomas Y. Crowell Company, 1945). An excellent description of the organization and campaigning activities of the Socialist party is Howard R. Penniman, *The Socialist Party in Action: The 1940 National Campaign* (unpublished Ph.D. thesis in political science, University of Minnesota, 1941).

[3] The fourth present-day Marxist-socialist organization, the Communist Party, is not, according to our definition, a political party at all, any more than John Smith's secretary is his wife because he registers her as such at Atlantic City. We discuss the so-called Communist Party in a later section of the present chapter.

[4] The best account of the Socialist Labor party is in Fine, *op. cit.* The "official" account is Henry Kuhn and Olive M. Johnson, *The Socialist Labor Party during Four Decades, 1890-1930* (New York: New York Labor News Company, 1931).

ganizations, organized on the state and local rather than the national level, appeared in the early 1860's. Some of them called themselves "parties," and in due course affiliated with the First International, which Marx had helped establish in London in 1864. In 1876 the American Marxist groups held a unity convention in Philadelphia and formed a party which, the next year, officially named itself "The Socialist Labor Party of North America."

The SLP from its beginnings was split between two factions: one that accepted electioneering as one among several tactics for overthrowing capitalism, and a second, the anarchist-syndicalist faction, which rejected all forms of political action on the grounds that socialism can come only through strikes, sabotage, and violence. The SLP took on its present character in the 1890's under the leadership of Daniel De Leon, its patron saint, who seized control of it in 1892. De Leon insisted that the party nominate presidential candidates and use campaigns as vehicles for propaganda but reject such "bourgeois" delusions as piecemeal reforms, "bread-and-butter" trade unionism, and alliances with non-Marxist groups.

The party duly nominated a presidential candidate in 1892, and has done so in all subsequent elections. No SLP candidate, however, has ever received over 45,000 votes in a national election.

The SLP now devotes most of its energies to denouncing other socialist parties and labor groups. Its attitude toward itself and toward its rival socialist parties was well expressed by its 1952 presidential candidate, Eric Hass: "We have a Marxist program, the *only* Marxist program being offered to Americans today. We will win because our program is correct. We'll dance a fandango on the grave of the Socialist party!" [5]

THE SOCIALIST PARTY

The Socialist party was founded in 1898 [6] by a group of erstwhile followers of Daniel De Leon, who had come to dislike his all-or-nothing attitude toward politics and the labor movement. For a half-century now it has been for many Americans (few of whom, however, have ever voted for one of its candidates) *the* minor party. Its two great spokesmen, both perennial presidential candidates, have been Eugene V. Debs (who ran five times from 1900 to 1920) and Norman Thomas (who ran six times from 1928 to 1948), each of whom, in the course of his long political career, became a much-sought-after speaker to non-socialist audiences all over the land and, in the opinion of many non-socialists, a respected prophet of moral righteousness, possibly even correct but a little ahead of his times. The party has often polled more votes than any other minor party.[7]

[5] Quoted in "Where Are the Radicals?" *Fortune*, Vol. XLVI (October, 1952), pp. 115, 250-53.
[6] As the Social Democratic party. It adopted its present name in 1901.
[7] From 1904 to 1920, Debs polled votes ranging from 403,000 in 1904 to 911,000 in 1920. A cartoon of the period shows his face with a clock dial superimposed, hands set at 12:00, and the legend: "Runs every four years if wound up properly." From 1928 to 1948, Thomas polled votes ranging from 79,000 in 1944 to 873,000 in 1932.

Like the SLP before De Leon's take-over, the SP has always been a two-faction party: there is, on the one hand, a "moderate" faction that favors gradualist reform, platforms unlikely to offend non-socialists, and alliances with other progressive (not necessarily socialist) groups; and, on the other hand, an "impossibilist" faction, willing to settle for nothing short of all-out socialism immediately, and opposed to alliances with groups not similarly committed to socialist objectives. The moderates have normally controlled the party, so that most Socialist platforms have emphasized a number of not very drastic social and economic reforms, many of which, as the party's members are always ready to point out, were taken over and put into law by the New Deal. During most of its history the Socialist program and leaders have stuck close to the native American tradition of populism and progressivism, which has little in common with the doctrinaire Marxist socialism of Europe (and of the SLP).[8] Most of the party's votes, in consequence, have come from intellectuals, union leaders, and progressives of one sort or another who have wished, in this election or that, to voice a protest against what they regarded as the overconservatism ("stodginess") of the two "old" parties. The SP has long tried to win organized labor to its cause, but, as noted above, might as well have saved itself the trouble. Many of its voters and, indeed, some of its leaders went over to the Democrats during the New Deal days and never found their way back home, so that the SP's strength declined rapidly after 1932.

At the 1950 Socialist convention, Norman Thomas proposed that the party abandon its costly and futile presidential campaigns, run candidates only in localities where they have a real chance of winning, and otherwise act as a sort of Fabian society, whose major function would be to criticize the course of the major parties from an independent socialist point of view. The convention voted him down, however, and in 1952 the party nominated for president Darlington Hoopes of Reading, Pennsylvania, who polled a national total of 20,189 votes.

THE SOCIALIST WORKERS' PARTY [9]

In 1928, the American Communist Party expelled from its ranks a group of "Trotskyites," i.e., followers of Leon Trotsky in his unsuccessful struggle with Josef Stalin for control of the world Communist movement. For a few years thereafter the expellees devoted themselves to stating and restating their claim to be regarded as the "true Communists," spreading the latest word from the

[8] The Socialists' good standing according to American canons of respectability is regarded with great contempt by the adherents of the parties that follow a pure Marxist line. The Trotskyite leader, James P. Cannon, says of the Socialist party that it has always been "regarded as a group of people who are for Socialism but don't mean any harm. That kind of party is always tolerated, but never gains any real serious influence. Throughout the labor movement the leaders and members of the SP were known as people who are for Socialism but who never make any trouble for labor fakers, racketeers, or traitors": *The History of American Trotskyism* (New York: Pioneer Publishers, 1944), pp. 246-47.

[9] The best accounts of this party are in "Where Are the Radicals?" *Fortune,* and James P. Cannon, *The History of American Trotskyism* (New York: Pioneer Publishers, 1944).

"Old Man" (Leon Trotsky), and exposing the Stalinist "Thermidorian" reaction, both in the U.S.S.R. and abroad. In 1936 they briefly entered what their leader called "the heterogeneous Socialist party . . . this centrist mishmash, this headless, helpless party," [10] but withdrew from it almost at once and, in 1938, founded the Socialist Workers' Party. The latter takes an anti-Stalinist line, stressing among other things the fact that its program is even more revolutionary than that of the Communists. Though the tiniest of the Marxist parties, the Socialist Workers have been singled out by fate for singularly rough treatment. During World War II a number of party members were jailed for violating the Smith Act. In 1951, Trotsky's widow suddenly denounced the party for "capitulating to the Stalinists." And in the middle of the 1952 presidential campaign, its presidential candidate, Grace Carlson, suddenly announced that she had had "a change in philosophy" and was leaving the party—to return to the Catholic Church. The party hastily substituted the name of Farrell Dobbs, who polled a national total of 10,306 votes.

Single-Issue Parties

Each of the ideologically based minor parties we have described in the preceding pages has had a program covering a wide range of public issues and involving a wide range of proposals about public policy; each of them, that is to say, has acted in this regard much like the major parties. We have had some minor parties in our history, however, that have been launched—as Ostrogorski felt *all* political parties should be launched [11]—primarily to press an ideological point of view on a *single* public issue. Some of them, to be sure, have been willing to adopt positions on other issues, provided the latter could be kept subordinated to the central issue.

There have been four main instances of this kind of party in American politics: the Anti-Masonic parties of the 1820's and 1830's, the Liberty and Free Soil parties of the 1840's, the "Know-Nothing" party of the 1850's, and the Prohibition party.

THE ANTI-MASONIC PARTIES OF THE 1820's AND 1830's [12]

The anti-Masonic movement was launched, mainly in and around New York, in the late 1820's purely and simply as an expression of its charter mem-

[10] Cannon, *op. cit.*, p. 236.

[11] Ostrogorski argued that the only legitimate excuse for forming a political party is to advance one side of a particular public issue. Once that issue is settled, he declared, the party no longer has any reason to exist and should disband. The worst thing to be said about the American and British major parties, from his point of view, is precisely that they take sides on many different issues, and persist after those issues are settled: *Democracy and the Organization of Political Parties,* translated by Frederick Clarke (New York: The Macmillan Company, 1902), Vol. I, pp. 329-34, 345-46, and Vol. II, pp. 656-68, 671-74.

[12] The best account is Charles McCarthy, "The Anti-Masonic Party," in the *Annual Report of the American Historical Association for the Year 1902* (Washington, D. C.: Government Printing Office, 1903), Vol. I, pp. 365-574.

bers' concern over the allegedly growing power and influence of secret societies in general and the Masonic lodges in particular. At first it did not take the form of a single political party, but rather, as it spread over the country, that of a congeries of local political parties. When, however, the Jacksonian Democrats in the state legislatures stepped forward to defend the Masons against the parties' attacks (Andrew Jackson himself was a high-degree Mason), the movement became, in its immediate impact and significance, a force working against the rise of Jackson. Accordingly, it picked up support from a number of anti-Jackson politicians (including William H. Seward, Thaddeus Stevens, and Thurlow Weed, who were later to become prominent figures in the Whig and Republican parties). It did not organize itself as the national Anti-Masonic party until 1831, when it assured itself a place in history by holding a national nominating convention, the first the nation had ever seen. By this time, however, the name "Anti-Masonic" was, properly speaking, no longer applicable, the "single issue" having ceased to be the influence of secret societies and become that of Jackson's claim to the presidency—as may be seen from the fact that it nominated a strong Mason, William Wirt of Maryland, as its presidential candidate. Wirt won only Vermont's electoral vote in the 1832 election, and the party soon disappeared; its leaders, for the most part, joined the movement to found the Whig party.[13]

THE LIBERTY AND FREE SOIL PARTIES OF THE 1840's

In the 1830's and 1840's, the abolitionist movement was spreading rapidly over the states north of the Mason-Dixon Line. But it, like the socialist movement a half-century later, was a two-faction movement: one faction, led by William Lloyd Garrison, favored staying out of partisan politics, while the second was committed to the view that slavery could be ended only by political means, though not by appealing either to the Whigs or to the Democrats. In 1840 the latter faction decided the time had come to organize a third party and set out on the quest for power. Their Liberty party accordingly came into existence that year, with James G. Birney, a Kentuckian who had freed his own slaves, as its presidential nominee. He polled 7,069 popular votes out of a national total of 2,411,000 in the 1840 election,[14] and was renominated in 1844, when he received 62,300 votes out of a national total of 2,698,000, but got enough votes in New York state to be regarded as responsible for throwing the state, and therefore the whole election, from Whig candidate Henry Clay to Democratic candidate James K. Polk, who was strongly pro-slavery![15]

In the presidential election of 1848 the Liberty party joined forces with the "Barnburner" (i.e., rural) faction of the New York Democrats and the "Con-

[13] Edward Stanwood, *A History of the Presidency*, new ed. (Boston: Houghton Mifflin Company, 1938), Vol. I, pp. 155-64.

[14] *Ibid.*, Vol. I, p. 203.

[15] *Ibid.*, Vol. I, p. 223.

science [i.e., anti-slavery] Whigs" to form the Free Soil party. The new party, with its "four freedoms" slogan, "Free Soil, Free Speech, Free Labor, and Free Men," nominated ex-President Martin Van Buren, who polled only 291,263 votes out of a national total of 2,872,000. In 1848 as in 1844, however, the abolitionists could, with appropriate arithmetic,[16] be shown to have decided the election, this time by drawing enough votes in crucial states away from Democratic candidate Lewis Cass to elect Whig candidate Zachary Taylor.[17] In 1852, they nominated John P. Hale of New Hampshire, who polled 156,667 votes out of a national total of 3,145,000. In 1856, most of the Free Soilers went into the new Republican party.

THE "KNOW-NOTHING" PARTY OF THE 1850'S [18]

Nativism and anti-Catholicism have been potent forces in American life from its very beginnings; but—in large part because of the flood of immigrants that descended on the United States in the 1840's—they cut their widest swath politically in the forties and fifties. Most of the immigrants of that period were Roman Catholics from Ireland and Central Europe; they settled, for the most part, in the big cities of the East, where the Democratic city machines extended them a welcoming and helping hand, so that they ended up voting Democratic *en bloc*. For some Americans, in due course, they came to represent cheap labor and unemployment; for others they were the symbol of perpetual rule by Democratic metropolitan machines; for still others they were a thinly disguised army of the Pope, whose evident mission was to win America, by fair means or foul, for Catholicism.

The story of the "Know-Nothing" party traces back to the founding, in 1849, of a secret society known to its members, the first of whom were New Yorkers who disliked immigrants for one or another of the foregoing reasons, as the Order of the Star-Spangled Banner. This Order, helped along, no doubt, by its having a secret ritual, grip, password, and sign of recognition, quickly spread to other cities over the land, and in due course began, secretly of course, to deliver its members' support to major-party candidates who spoke out against unlimited immigration and "Popery." By 1854, some seventy-five congressmen appear to have been members of the Order; rumors about its size and influence filled the air, and people began to speak of it as the "Know-Nothing *party*" ("Know-Nothing" because its members, bound by their oaths, answered questions about it by outsiders with professions of ignorance) though it was still merely a conspiratorial pressure group.

In 1856, the leaders of the nativist movement, noting the growing popular concern with slavery and fearful lest immigration and Popery go by the

---

[16] There are grave methodological objections to this kind of post-mortem judgment about an election. Such judgments necessarily rely on unprovable assumptions as to how people would have voted *if* other parties and candidates had been in the field.

[17] Stanwood, *op. cit.*, Vol. I, p. 243.

[18] The best account is in Ray A. Billington, *The Protestant Crusade, 1800-1860* (New York: Rinehart & Company, Inc., 1938).

board as issues, decided to come out into the open and form a new political party, to be called officially the "American party." It nominated ex-President Millard Fillmore, a "doughface" (that is, a northerner opposed to federal interference with the extension of slavery), who proceeded to alienate the nativists by conducting a campaign in which their pet anxieties were hardly mentioned (though the pro-slavery plank in the party's platform would probably have driven most of its northern supporters into the newly formed Republican party anyway). Fillmore, in consequence, polled only 874,534 votes out of a national total of 4,054,000, and received the electoral vote of a single state (Maryland). Shortly after the election, the party disbanded in good Ostrogorskian fashion and for the best of good Ostrogorskian reasons: the issue it had been formed to fight had been eclipsed by the slavery issue, which in due course was to help produce the Civil War.

THE PROHIBITION PARTY [19]

The Prohibition party is the third-oldest existing political party in the United States: it named its first presidential candidate in 1872, and has named one in every presidential election since. It has never polled many votes, even by third-party standards,[20] but its determination to contest the next election apparently never flags—despite the pressure it is under from prohibitionists who prefer the tactics used by the Anti-Saloon League and the Woman's Christian Temperance Union to third-party tactics.[21]

During most of its history the Prohibition party has been divided between two quite distinct factions: the "narrow-gaugers," who want the party to take a stand on and argue about the issue of Drink and leave all other issues strictly alone; and the "broad-gaugers," who feel that the party should take stands on other issues than Drink whenever a majority of the members can agree on a position. The "narrow-gaugers" were in control from 1880 to 1900;[22] but from 1904 on, the "broad-gaugers" have been in the saddle and have issued platforms espousing such causes as the direct election of senators, woman suffrage, lower tariffs, and the merit system. A shared belief in the wickedness—

---

[19] The most complete account of the Prohibition party's history and program is D. Leigh Colvin, *Prohibition in the United States* (New York: George H. Doran Company, 1926). For an account of its more recent activities, see Roger W. Babson, *Our Campaign for the Presidency in 1940* (Chicago: National Prohibitionist, 1941).

[20] Its largest total was 258,950 votes out of a national total of 13,523,000 in 1904. In 1952, its candidate, Stuart Hamblen, received 72,769 votes.

[21] Many scholars believe that the temperance organization mainly responsible for the adoption of the Eighteenth Amendment and the passage of the Volstead Act was the Anti-Saloon League, and not the Prohibition party. For an illuminating account of the League's methods and achievements, see Peter H. Odegard, *Pressure Politics: The Story of the Anti-Saloon League* (New York: Columbia University Press, 1928).

[22] In the 1896 election, the "narrow-gaugers" defeated a proposal to include a free-silver plank in the platform, whereupon the "broad-gaugers" seceded and named their own ticket under the label "National Party." No more convincing demonstration of the divisiveness of the free-silver issue in that election has come to light!

and thus the need for the national outlawing—of alcoholic beverages, however, is clearly what has held the party together all these years.

The Union Party of 1936 [23]

The Union party of 1936 fits none of the categories under which we have subsumed the parties discussed above. It was an ephemeral coalition of three ill-assorted ideological protest movements thrown up by the great depression of the 1930's: the Union for Social Justice of Father Charles E. Coughlin, the Townsend Recovery Plan (or Old-Age Pension Plan) of Dr. Francis E. Townsend, and the "Share-the-Wealth" movement, founded by Huey Long and continued, after Long's assassination in 1935, by the Reverend Gerald L. K. Smith. Both the Democrats and the Republicans having turned a deaf ear to the arguments and demands of all three movements, it is hardly surprising that they came together in 1936 in a new Union party, which nominated for president William ("Liberty Bell Bill") Lemke, Republican representative from North Dakota and one-time legal adviser for the Non-Partisan League. The party's platform, a curious mélange of populism, Long-ism, Townsend-ism, and doctrines allegedly drawn from the papal social and economic encyclicals, had certain overtones, later emphasized in Gerald L. K. Smith's speeches, which some observers denounced as fascistic. In the election Lemke polled 892,000 votes out of a national total of 45,604,000, and the party's leaders, presumably having found out what they wanted to know—namely, whether such a party had any future—went their separate ways.

The Communist Party [24]

We have reserved what we have to say about the Communist Party and its satellite, the Progressive party of 1948 and 1952, for this part of the present chapter primarily for this reason: The American Communist Party is not a "political party" in the sense in which we have been using that term in this book. To qualify as the latter, a political organization must be *autonomous,* that is, stand ready to show that it is not a front for some other organization, which for strategic reasons wishes to have in the field what looks like a political party. The disclosures of recent years have made it abundantly clear that

[23] Very little has been written about the Union party. The best account the present writers have been able to find is Herbert Harris, "That Third Party," *Current History,* Vol. XLV (October, 1936), pp. 77-92. See also Walter Davenport, "Mr. Lemke Stops to Think," *Collier's,* Vol. XCVIII (October 17, 1936), pp. 7-8, 25-36.

[24] The literature on the Communist Party is now voluminous. Among the better discussions of the Communist Party in America are: Howard R. Penniman, *Sait's American Parties and Elections,* 5th ed. (New York: Appleton-Century-Crofts, Inc., 1952), Ch. XIII; James Oneal and G. A. Werner, *American Communism,* rev. ed. (New York: E. P. Dutton, 1947); and Benjamin Gitlow, *I Confess* (New York: E. P. Dutton, 1940).

the American Communist "party" is the creature of a conspiratorial under-
ground communist movement, which takes its orders from Moscow and is, in
fact, waging war upon the United States.[25]

The American communist movement has always maintained two levels of
organization: the "open" party, which nominates candidates, holds conventions, and publishes the *Daily Worker;* and the "secret" party, whose members conceal their party membership and carry on the movement's main work
of espionage, sabotage, and the infiltration of government agencies and non-
communist political organizations.[26] The "secret" party's activities are for the
most part illegal, or at least directed toward an illegal purpose; but the "open"
party, until recently, enjoyed all the privileges extended to genuine political
parties in the United States. During its heyday it sometimes nominated candidates for office and ran them under its own label (as, for example, in the
presidential elections from 1924 to 1940). But its chief tactic was to endorse candidates nominated by noncommunist parties (as in the presidential elections
from 1944 to 1952).[27] The highest vote an officially labeled Communist presidential candidate ever got was 101,000 in 1932; but, as we shall note below,
the Communists fared much better when they supported candidates running
under other labels.

Beginning with the Smith Act in 1940, however, and culminating in the
Communist Control Act of 1954, a series of legislative enactments now on
the books has outlawed even the "open" party. Today, when it can hardly be
said to exist, the main channel for participation by the Communist Party in
American elections is, and has been for several years, the American Labor
party and the national Progressive party.

The Progressive Party of 1948 and 1952 [28]

The events that led to the founding of the Progressive party began in
1946, when Secretary of Commerce (and former Vice-President) Henry A.
Wallace publicly attacked President Harry S. Truman, from whom of course
he held his appointment, for his allegedly "red-baiting" and "war-mongering"

[25] Cf. Penniman, *op. cit.,* pp. 240-42.

[26] For descriptions of the operations of the "secret" Communist Party, see Whittaker Chambers, *Witness* (New York: Random House, 1952); and Herbert A. Philbrick, *I Led Three Lives*
(New York: McGraw-Hill Book Company, Inc., 1952).

[27] The recipient of the endorsement might have been committed to a policy that the Communists favored; or he might have had advisers whom the Communists felt they could influence; or his opponent might have been a man whom the Communists had good reason to dislike or fear; etc.

[28] The best accounts are William B. Hesseltine, *The Rise and Fall of Third Parties* (Wash-
ington, D. C.: Public Affairs Press, 1948), Ch. 11; Charles Angoff, "Wallace's Communist-
Front Party," *American Mercury,* Vol. LXVII (October, 1948), pp. 413-21; William H. Hale,
"What Makes Wallace Run?" *Harper's,* Vol. CXCVI (March, 1948), pp. 241-48; and "Where
Are the Radicals?" *Fortune.*

foreign policy. Truman soon gave Wallace the walking papers he had clearly asked for, and through the remainder of 1946 and the following year as well, Wallace acted as editor of the liberal journal, the *New Republic*. He also made a number of speeches before audiences assembled by the Progressive Citizens of America, the extreme left-wing residue of several liberal organizations founded to support Roosevelt in the 1944 election. Then, on December 29, 1947, Wallace announced over a national radio hookup that he would run for president in 1948 on a third-party ticket, and called for a "Gideon's army" of New Dealers and "peace lovers" to rally behind him.

The PCA duly sponsored a national convention, which founded the Progressive party, nominated Wallace for president and Senator Glen Taylor of Idaho for vice-president, and adopted a platform proposing various domestic reforms along extreme New Deal lines and, above all, a policy of rapprochement with the Soviet Union.[29] The only prominent New Dealer besides Wallace who supported the new party, however, was Rexford G. Tugwell; and while, undoubtedly, there were many Progressives who were not Communists, the Communists did, increasingly as the campaign proceeded, dominate the party. Wallace, in any case, polled only 1,157,172 votes out of a national total of 48,402,000, by no means enough to do what the movement had clearly set out to do, which was to defeat Truman.

When the Communist North Koreans invaded South Korea in 1950, Wallace supported American intervention against the Communists and blamed the Soviet Union for the outbreak of the war. After he failed to persuade the Progressive party's leadership to go along with him on both points, he and Tugwell withdrew from the party altogether—and, to judge by the vote in the next election, carried with them most of its 1948 supporters, so that nothing was left of the 1948 organization except a hard core of out-and-out Communists and a sprinkling of sympathizers so close to the Communists that, in the familiar phrase, "If they aren't Communists, they're just cheating the party out of its dues."

The Progressives' 1952 nominee for president was Vincent Hallinan, a wealthy San Francisco lawyer who at the time he was nominated was serving a jail sentence for contempt of court in connection with his defense of the left-wing labor leader, Harry Bridges. He ran on a platform that attributed the Korean war to militarism and greed for profits on the part of the United States, and demanded an immediate cease-fire on any terms, however costly. He polled 140,138 votes out of a national total of 61,680,000.

[29] When three delegates from Vermont moved that the platform clearly disclaim any intention "to give blanket endorsement to the foreign policy of any nation," the convention's leadership choked off discussion of their motion on the grounds that to discuss it would be to make "an insinuation against a friendly ally" and to submit to "anti-Soviet hysteria."

The Role of the Minor Parties

AS VOTE-GETTING ORGANIZATIONS

Success and Failure. In Chapter 15 we noted that the major parties in the American system measure their success and failure almost entirely by the number of votes they poll and the number of public offices they capture. From that point of view, the minor parties in American history have a poor record.[30] In every presidential election since the Civil War, at least one minor-party candidate has entered the lists. No such candidate, however, has ever won an election; only one (Roosevelt in 1912) has finished second; only four (Weaver in 1892, Roosevelt in 1912, La Follette in 1924, and Thurmond in 1948) have received any electoral votes; and only one (Roosevelt in 1912) has managed to swing the election from one major party to the other. Only three (Weaver, Roosevelt, and La Follette) have received as much as 10 per cent of the total national popular vote. And in most elections all the minor parties together have polled well under 10 per cent of the votes.[31]

Nor is the picture with respect to congressional elections notably different. Thirty of the forty-one Congresses elected from 1872 to 1954 have had at least one minor-party senator or representative.[32] No single Congress, however, has had a significant number of minor-party congressmen; the Fifty-fifth Congress, elected in 1896, had twenty-eight, which is the highest number on record, and normally minor-party members account for less than 10 per cent of the total membership. Most minor-party congressmen, moreover, have come from a few localities, for the most part localities west of the Mississippi, where (as we have seen) the farmer-labor parties have had their best innings. And in recent years the number of minor-party congressmen has markedly declined, as have the number of seats contested by minor parties and the minor parties' share of the popular vote.[33]

In certain states and localities at certain times, to be sure, a party other than the Republican or the Democratic has been either the first or the second party; but this is an atypical state of affairs in American politics, and one that does not tend to repeat itself in any particular place. And no third party has ever become the second or first party in national politics. Each of the three new major parties that have entered American politics since 1789—the Jeffer-

---

[30] For a contrary view, see Hicks, "The Third Party Tradition in American Politics," *Mississippi Valley Historical Review*, Vol. XX (June, 1933).

[31] For summaries of the minor parties' record in post–Civil War presidential elections, see Murray S. Stedman, Jr., and Susan W. Stedman, *Discontent at the Polls, A Study of Farmer and Labor Parties, 1827-1948* (New York: Columbia University Press, 1950), Table 1 on p. 34; and Cortez A. M. Ewing, *Presidential Elections* (Norman: University of Oklahoma Press, 1940), Ch. III.

[32] Cf. Stedman and Stedman, *op. cit.,* Chart III on p. 45. These figures do not include congressmen who have classified themselves as "independents."

[33] Cortez A. M. Ewing, *Congressional Elections, 1896-1944* (Norman: University at Oklahoma Press, 1947), pp. 66-74. See also Stedman and Stedman, *op. cit.,* p. 47.

sonian Republicans, the Whigs, and the (1856) Republicans—has *begun* as a major party; that is, it has finished at least second in the first national election it contested. No major party, in other words, has ever resulted (as did the British Labor Party) from a third party's gradual growth in electoral strength.[34] Most national minor parties, moreover, have had relatively short careers (ten years or less); and a mere handful (the Prohibition, Socialist, and Socialist Labor parties) have lasted more than twenty years.

Organization and Attitudes. One reason for the minor parties' general failure to compete successfully with the major parties is that they have, for the most part, lacked certain organizational characteristics that enable the major parties to attract workers and voters. The major parties make the requirements for membership as easy and undemanding as possible; many of the minor parties appear to have gone out of their way to make them difficult and forbidding. The Socialist party, for example, requires a formal application for membership, in which the applicant declares his belief in the party's principles and agrees not to participate in the activities of any other political organization, or otherwise aid in the election of non-Socialist candidates, unless he has been given special permission to do so.[35] And the Socialist Labor party's constitution states: "If any member of the SLP accepts office in a pure and simple trade or labor organization, he shall be considered antagonistically inclined towards the SLP and shall be expelled. If any officer of a pure and simple trade or labor organization applies for membership in the SLP, he shall be rejected." [36] Setting such conditions is hardly likely to maximize any party's membership.

Most national minor parties, again, have had a national headquarters and a national committee, and little else in the way of organization. Unlike the major parties, that is to say, they have not developed strong state and local organizations to serve as bases for their election-contesting activities, and this comparative advantage on the part of the major parties has consistently reflected itself in the election returns. The exceptions here are the minor parties formed by factions bolting from the major parties, which have sometimes carried a number of the parent parties' regular local organizations along with them; but such parties, as we noted earlier in this chapter, are rarely more than brief interludes in the lives of the major parties, and have little in common with other minor parties.[37]

A still further reason for the poor showing of the minor parties lies in

---

[34] Hesseltine, *op. cit.,* p. 9.

[35] Clarence A. Berdahl, "Party Membership in the United States, II," *American Political Science Review,* Vol. XXXVI (April, 1942), p. 259.

[36] Quoted in Fine, *op. cit.,* p. 182.

[37] Cf. Stedman and Stedman, *op. cit.,* pp. 114-17; and Bertram M. Gross, *The Legislative Struggle* (New York: McGraw-Hill Book Company, Inc., 1953), pp. 61-62. The Socialist party has attempted to build up strong state organizations; but over the years the national organization has far overshadowed them: Cf. Greer, *op. cit.,* pp. 49-51.

their characteristic impecuniousness, which prevents their doing many of the things that may be regarded as minima for participating in an American election as a serious competitor. They depend upon dues and other small contributions from devoted members, and these do not add up to anything like the sums available to the major parties from groups and individuals so situated that they can reap immediate rewards (and thus get returns on their investment).[38] Empty or near-empty war chests, let us remember, mean thin campaigns, which must struggle along largely without access to television and radio and without facilities for getting out the vote on election day.

Finally, the minor parties suffer under a disadvantage inherent in their own basic character, or, more precisely, in the motives that drive their leaders to organize them in the first place: from their very beginnings, they stand committed to a fairly specific program, and cannot, like the major parties, direct persuasive appeals to all segments of the community, however inconsistent those appeals. The minor party, in other words, can appeal only to those segments of the community that would like to see its program adopted in all or most of its details—that is, to a limited electorate which the party has already carved out of the total electorate before the campaign ever begins. And having set forth its program, it must count on the voters' coming to it; it cannot go to them.[39] Nor is that all: its leaders, typically, tend to be men for whom, to judge by their observable behavior, "principle" is more important than "power"; and this kind of preoccupation maximizes the likelihood of ideological schisms and fissions which not only weaken the party generally, but also produce organizational splits that are difficult to heal.[40]

Judged by the major parties' standard of winning votes and offices, then, the minor parties in American politics have little to show for their efforts. It remains now to inquire what claims can be made for them in terms of their performance, not as competitors for votes, but in other capacities.

AS PIONEERS OF PUBLIC POLICY

Some students of American politics argue that the minor parties are the "dynamic" element in our party system, that they and only they keep the policy-making process moving ahead toward new, increasingly progressive goals, that this is their proper role, and that, by and large, they have performed it well. If we had only the major parties, the argument runs, new ideas would win acceptance and forward-looking reforms would be adopted only after intolerable delays. The minor parties prevent these delays, and so keep the nation abreast of its destiny and true to its basic values.

[38] For a comparison of expenditures by major parties and minor parties in the 1944 presidential election, see U.S. Senate, Special Committee to Investigate Presidential, Vice-Presidential, and Senatorial Campaign Expenditures in 1944, 79th Congress, 1st Session, Report (1945), pp. 76-77.

[39] Cf. Pendleton Herring, *The Politics of Democracy* (New York: Rinehart & Company, Inc., 1940), pp. 189-90.

[40] Cf. Stedman and Stedman, *op. cit.*, pp. 108-10.

The function of the minor parties, according to these writers, is to feed new ideas—new ideas, moreover, that would otherwise have remained unheard of—into the policy-making process.[41] And the supporting logic runs as follows: The major parties will automatically, given their inherent character, avoid all genuinely controversial and divisive issues that arise in the community, no matter how urgent their resolution may be from the standpoint of the national interest. They must avoid them, because facing them head-on involves taking a stand, and taking a stand loses votes. On the record, moreover, great progressive reforms grow only from controversial and divisive issues; if there are no such issues, there are no reforms. The minor parties, which not only get few votes but know they are going to get few votes, are able to escape such inhibitions and unflinchingly pursue the truth about public policy, whether it poses controversial and divisive issues or not. In short, the task of pushing reforms while they are still new and unpopular has to be done by the minor parties if it is to be done at all. It is, to be sure, a thankless task, since what happens is that once a minor party has done all the hard and unpopular groundwork, and has developed popular interest in and support for some reform, the major parties blithely and without so much as a by-your-leave take over, put the reform on the statute books, and claim all the credit, including that of having thought up the idea in the first place. So it went, the argument concludes, with free public education, abolition of slavery, regulation of railroads and business monopolies, progressive income taxes, woman suffrage, direct election of senators, and social security; and so, presumably, it will continue to go so long as our party system operates in its traditional manner.

Other writers have taken vigorous exception to the above line of argument, on the grounds that it consists, from beginning to end, of a series of unproved—and unconvincing—propositions.[42] The fact that a minor party can be shown to have advocated a particular reform *before* the major parties took it up, for example, is no indication that the latter took it up *because* the former advocated it.[43] The third parties, moreover, have not been alone in

---

[41] The notion that the minor parties serve to feed new ideas into the policy-making process is advanced by, among other writers, Hicks, "The Third Party Tradition in American Politics"; Fred E. Haynes, *Social Politics in the United States* (Boston: Houghton Mifflin Company, 1924), pp. 153-55; Hesseltine, *op. cit.*, pp. 9-10; Hugh A. Bone, *American Politics and the Party System* (New York: McGraw-Hill Book Company, Inc., 1949), pp. 388-90; Peter H. Odegard and E. Allen Helms, *American Politics*, 2nd ed. (New York: Harper and Brothers, 1947), p. 123; and Charles E. Merriam and Harold F. Gosnell, *The American Party System*, 4th ed. (New York: The Macmillan Company, 1949), pp. 59-62.

[42] The doubts summarized in the text are expressed by, among other writers, Herring, *op. cit.*, p. 181; Stedman and Stedman, *op. cit.*, pp. 29-30; Dayton D. McKean, *Party and Pressure Politics* (Boston: Houghton Mifflin Company, 1949), pp. 409-10; and Howard R. Penniman, *Sait's American Parties and Elections*, 4th ed. (New York: Appleton-Century-Crofts, Inc., 1948), p. 262.

[43] Many of the reforms minor parties have advocated have never been adopted. An amusing example is provided by Pendleton Herring, who points out that the Socialist Labor platform of 1892 advocated "the abolition of the presidency, the vice-presidency, and the senate of the

advocating ultimately successful reform proposals: non-party pressure and re-form groups like the Anti-Saloon League, the Civil Service Reform League, the National Municipal League, the American Civil Liberties Union, the National Association for the Advancement of Colored People, and the League of Women Voters, have often supported so-called third-party measures. How do we know that these pressure groups did not provide the leaven that finally made the major parties' bread rise? In short, these writers conclude, the whole question as to how public policy is "pioneered" in American politics is extremely complex, and, for the moment at least, not sufficiently re-searched to admit of broad statements to the effect that the minor parties are *the* "pioneers."

AS SAFETY VALVES FOR DISCONTENT

Any group of Americans which *as a group* wants the government to do something it is not doing, or stop something it is doing, has open to it at least three courses of action: (1) It can operate as a pressure group and "lobby" and employ "balance-of-power" tactics during or· before electoral campaigns; i.e., it can state its case to already-elected public officials, and it can back up its demands by supporting, in primary and general elections, those candidates and parties who seem sympathetic. It can, in other words, try to get its way by "pressuring" the parties from outside; and there is no doubt that American public policy is profoundly influenced, from year to year, by organizations (e.g., the American Medical Association, the Farm Bureau Federation, the American Legion, and the American Federation of Teachers) that confine themselves to this course of action.[44] Let us merely note in passing that "out-side" here means outside: the group must not, if it hopes to use pressure tac-tics successfully, allow itself to be openly and completely identified with one of the parties. (2) It can operate inside a major party, always taking care to maintain its separate identity as a group with policy objectives that it expects to be carried out, and can try to become so necessary to the party's chances of victory that the other factions will go along, to some degree at least, with its policy demands. The classic example of a group that follows this course of action is the southern wing of the Democratic party.[45] (3) It can organize a third party; that is, it can forgo all attempts to persuade, bargain with, and

United States"! Herring comments, "When, if ever, the rest of the country catches up with this proposal, it may be that third parties will no longer be a problem": *Op. cit.,* p. 181.

[44] There is now a vast literature on pressure groups and their activities in American politics. In addition to a number of excellent works on specific pressure groups, there are these general dis-cussions of pressure activity: David B. Truman, *The Governmental Process* (New York: Alfred A. Knopf, 1951); Stuart Chase, *Democracy Under Pressure* (New York: The Twentieth Century Fund, 1945); V. O. Key, Jr., *Politics, Parties, and Pressure Groups,* 3rd ed. (New York: Thomas Y. Crowell Company, 1952), Chs. 2-6; Earl Latham, *The Group Basis of Politics* (Ithaca, N. Y.: Cornell University Press, 1952); Pendleton Herring, *Public Administration and the Public Interest* (New York: McGraw-Hill Book Company, Inc., 1936); and E. E. Schattschneider, *Politics, Pres-sures, and the Tariff* (New York: Prentice-Hall, 1935).

[45] See Chapter 8 for our discussion of the purposes and techniques of the Solid South.

compromise with the leaders of the major parties and the groups that support those parties, and strike out entirely on its own to contest elections and win votes.

Of the above three courses of action, the first and second are far more likely than the third to yield quick—though not necessarily entirely satisfactory—results. For one thing, they permit the group to deal directly with public officials *in office,* and thus give it immediate access to the core of the decision-making process. For another, the relative looseness of major party lines on most matters of public policy leaves most legislators, executives, and administrators relatively free to conclude bargains with widely diverse interest groups. Finally, the fact that most major-party nominations are now made by direct primaries carries the bargaining process one stage further back than it would otherwise go: instead of dealing with nominees the party organizations have picked, an interest group can, by offering support to or threatening to withhold it from the various candidates, affect the nomination itself in a manner favorable to its purposes.[46]

A prospective minor party offers none of these advantages. By organizing such a party, an interest group draws a line between itself and the major parties, cuts itself off from direct access to the decision-making centers, and greatly reduces its bargaining power as compared to the groups that *are* dealing with the major parties. Moreover, the whole structure of our formal government places minor parties and the groups that support them under a number of costly disabilities, as Pendleton Herring well says in the following passage:

Our decentralized government makes it necessary for political parties to establish themselves locally before trying to bridge the gap between state and national jurisdictions. The system of electing our legislature by a plurality vote in single-member districts makes it difficult for minority groups to secure representation. Statutory requirements that parties have a certain minimum number of supporters, moreover, make it impossible for many minor parties to get on the ballot. Our system of government itself condemns the third party to a position of unimportance. . . . In this country . . . a third party leader must usually remain an agitator. No regular way whereby he may enter into the governmental process is provided. A bloc in Congress may be organized without establishing a party; but even if a third party controls a bloc of votes in Congress the most it can hope for is an occasional opportunity to affect the balance of power. Furthermore the control of procedure in Congress by the dominant political party offers little opportunity for minor party representatives to exert any influence. They are placed at a grave disadvantage when it comes to influencing congressional committee action, and they have no way of participating in the election of the party leaders who, in turn, control procedure. The stability of the chief executive is not dependent on a coalition of parties. In fact the character of the chief magistracy is the greatest obstacle to a multi-party system. So great is the prestige of this office that no party can hope

---

[46] This point is well made by Hicks, "The Third Party Tradition in American Politics"; and by Key, *op. cit.,* pp. 302-03.

to attain wide popular support if it has no chance of sending its candidate to the White House.[47]

Despite these disabilities, however, forming a third party has been and still is the indicated course of action for certain kinds of groups. Concretely, any ethnic, class, sectional, or occupational group may come to feel that it has no chance whatever of getting attention for its demands from the major parties and the groups that support them, so that, from its point of view, letting those parties and groups go unchallenged involves complete abdication of its major aspirations and its notions of justice. The members of such a group are likely to feel that the character of the major parties and the *modus operandi* of the party system deprive them of an audible voice in American politics. If so, such a group will be well advised to abandon all attempts at wheedling and compromise, and do independent battle at the polls. On the statistics to date, it can't expect to win. But this is not to say that the attempt is meaningless. In the first place, the statistics of the future *may* not repeat indefinitely the patterns of the past, which is to say that there may—to paraphrase a recent automobile advertisement—be a third party in America's future. In the second place, such a group can at least tell itself that it is pressing forward along the only avenue open to it, which is always a satisfaction of a kind. And finally, the more idealistic and devoted of its members, at least, will draw psychic dividends, as the returns come in from election to election, from standing forth before the nation in lonely righteousness—as witness the following remarks by Eugene V. Debs to a meeting of the Conference for Progressive Political Action in 1925, when the latter group was trying to decide whether to continue the Progressive party:

Do you know that all the progress in the whole world's history has been made by minorities? I have somehow been fortunately all of my life in the minority. I have thought again and again that if I ever find myself in the majority I will know that I have outlived myself. There is something magnificent about having the courage to stand with a few with and for a principle and to fight for it without fear or favor, developing all of your latent powers, expanding to the proportionable end, rising to your true stature, no matter whose respect you may forfeit, as long as you keep your own.[48]

In some political systems the world has seen, any group that gets to feeling that way about itself and the society in which it lives has no course open to it but to organize a revolutionary movement and attempt to tear apart the whole fabric of the society's institutions. In the United States such a group is free to organize a third party, try to win others over to seeing things its way, and so arrive at a meaningful estimate of its actual strength over the country. Regardless of its success, it can have, meantime, the satisfaction of feeling that

[47] Herring, *The Politics of Democracy*, pp. 183-84.

[48] Quoted in Kenneth C. MacKay, *The Progressive Movement of 1924* (New York: Columbia University Press, 1947), p. 234.

it is *doing* something about the sources of its discontent. One mark of the best political system, obviously, is that it breeds no foci of potential revolution. The next best system, it could be argued, is that which provides machinery that makes sure that no group shall set off down the road to revolution—as, surely, many a group has done in other countries than ours—on the basis of a foolish overestimate of the size of its potential following. Our arrangements for third parties do provide such machinery; and the minor parties are, therefore, best regarded as "safety valves" for letting off the steam generated by potentially revolutionary groups, and for letting those groups find out for themselves how much steam they actually are generating.

It becomes clear, from this point of view, that the number and strength of minor parties in American politics at any given time is a measure of how much extreme discontent exists. And that, in turn, is a measure of how well or how badly the major parties and the other policy-making agencies are performing their task of giving each major group in the community enough satisfaction to keep it moving in the mainstream of the nation's politics. As Herring puts it:

The rise of a third party to any position of influence would be a portent of serious rigidities in our political system. It would not indicate a movement to be frowned upon but would suggest rather that our party leaders had failed in their task of harmonizing and adjusting the economic and social forces of their communities.[49]

In short, the "safety-valve" role of the American minor parties must be considered in the context of the whole party system; and that, in turn, must be considered in the context of the whole American social, political, and governmental system. In the concluding three chapters of the present book we shall attempt to describe that system, to identify the role that the American party system plays therein, and to assess that role in the light of the theoretical conditions for democracy discussed in the first four chapters.

[49] Herring, *The Politics of Democracy*, p. 179.

PART SIX

The Role of the American Party System

Chapter 20

THE AMERICAN POLITICAL ENVIRONMENT

Party Systems and Their Environments

In the preceding thirteen chapters we have described various aspects of "the"[1] party system that actually operates in the United States today; and, up to this point in our analysis, we have tried to avoid making judgments as to whether that party system is "good" or "bad," "democratic" or "undemocratic." One can make such judgments, we believe, only in the light of his conception of a *model* party system, which, like any "model,"[2] is a set of ideas about how a party system *should* operate, and not an empirical description of the actual operation of an existing party system.[3]

ACTUAL PARTY SYSTEMS AND THEIR ENVIRONMENTS

In the final chapter of this book, the present writers will attempt to evaluate the American party system according to the model of democracy set forth in Chapters 2 and 3. Before we undertake that task, however, it seems de-

---

[1] The quotation marks here are intended to remind us of the point made in Chapter 7: that the phrase "the American party system" is only a convenient label for the sum of all the American party systems—national, state, and local, and two-party, modified one-party, and one-party.

[2] See pp. 18-22 for discussion of the nature and function of models in political analysis.

[3] See, for example, the widely varying model party systems advocated on the one hand by the adherents of the doctrine of responsible party government (see pp. 384-85) and on the other by M. I. Ostrogorski, in *Democracy and the Organization of Political Parties,* translated by Frederick Clarke (New York: The Macmillan Company, 1902), Vol. II, pp. 658-95.

sirable to round out our description of the actual party system by considering the political environment within which it operates; for the American party system, like any other, can be fully described and understood only by taking account of the fact that it operates *in a particular environment*. It operates, that is to say, in the *American* community—a community with certain physical, demographic, social, economic, ideological, and formal-governmental characteristics that together make it at least somewhat different from any other community in the world. The American environment, we assume, both helps to shape and, in turn, is to some extent shaped by the party system.[4]

We cannot hope, of course, to describe the *whole* American environment within the limited space of the present chapter. We shall therefore concentrate upon the *political* environment—that is, upon those aspects of the total environment that have the most direct impact upon the party system. Accordingly, we shall pay special attention to these matters: (1) the nature of the American community, (2) the dominant ideas Americans hold about matters more or less directly related to political organization, and (3) the nature of our politico-governmental system.[5] Having described the political environment, we shall, in Chapter 21, try to say how that environment has affected the parties and how the parties have affected the environment; and, in Chapter 22, we shall evaluate the role of the party system in the light of our model of democracy.

The Nature of the American Community

WHAT KIND OF PEOPLE ARE WE?

In the first place, the American community has a *large population*. Our present total of over 160,000,000 makes us the fourth most populous nation in the world; only China (463,000,000), India (357,000,000), and the U.S.S.R. (193,000,000) have larger populations than the United States.[6]

In the second place, America is a predominantly *urban* community. The 1950 census reported that 59 per cent of the population live in "urban" areas (i.e., those with populations of 2,500 or more)—this by contrast with the report of the first census in 1790 to the effect that only 5.1 per cent lived in urban areas. Table 29 shows this trend in detail.

In the third place, the United States has perhaps the most *heterogeneous*

---

[4] For example, see Chapter 8 for some preliminary suggestions as to the nature of the interrelationships between the American state one-party systems and their environments.

[5] That is, the regularized, understood, and accepted patterns of behavior Americans normally follow in making their governmental decisions, which patterns are to be found partly in such written documents as constitutions, statutes, court decisions, executive orders, and bureaucratic regulations, and partly in those unwritten agreements that political scientists usually call "customs" and "usages."

[6] These figures are taken from *The World Almanac, 1954* (New York: New York *World-Telegram and Sun*, 1954).

population of all the nations of the world.[7] Some of the major respects in which we differ from each other are as follows.

TABLE 29 Distribution of Americans Among Living Areas of Various Sizes, 1790 and 1950 [8]

Size of Living Area	Per Cent of Population Living in Such Areas		Size of Living Area	Per Cent of Population Living in Such Areas	
	1790	1950		1790	1950
1,000,000 or more	0	11.5	10,000 to 25,000	1.2	8.3
500,000 to 1,000,000	0	6.1	5,000 to 10,000	1.2	5.2
100,000 to 500,000	0	11.9	2,500 to 5,000	1.1	3.7
50,000 to 100,000	0	6.0	Under 2,500	94.9	41.0
25,000 to 50,000	1.6	6.3			

Ethnic Differences. The 1950 census reported that 89.5 per cent of the population were whites, 10.0 per cent were Negroes, and the remaining 0.5 per cent was made up of persons of Chinese, Indian, Japanese, and other descents. Of the white population, 6.7 per cent were born outside the United States, and another 15.7 per cent had as either one or both parents persons who had been born outside the United States. In 1950, therefore, nearly a third of the American population was either non-white or of very recent immigrant status.[9] Moreover, just about every conceivable ethnic strain was represented in the remaining two-thirds of the population: British, Irish, Scandinavian, Central European, Middle and Far Eastern, Latin American, etc.; and at least some of these groups have played an important role in our politics.[10]

Occupational Differences. Americans make their living in a remarkable variety of ways. The 1950 census listed no less than 970 different occupations, and the census takers themselves described the list as far from complete. Considering only the major categories, however, the occupational distribution of Americans is shown in Table 30.

[7] Cf. the statement by two leading sociologists that "as a society the United States is made up of the most heterogeneous assortment of groups and subcultures known for any modern nation. . . . In the United States today we find every conceivable kind of cultural splitting and social differentiation: ethnic cultures based on immigrant groups, religious cultures based on branches of Christianity and a few small folk-like sects; interest groups with particular economic, social, and political values; status and class groupings, with variations in outlook, social values, standards of living, and the like; and regional cultural differences, as between the Deep South and New England, or between rural and urban populations": John W. Bennett and Melvin M. Tumin, *Social Life, Structure and Function* (New York: Alfred A. Knopf, 1949), pp. 607-08.

[8] Adapted from the *Statistical Abstract of the United States, 1954* (Washington, D. C.: U.S. Department of Commerce, Bureau of the Census, 1954), p. 27.

[9] U.S. Bureau of the Census, *U.S. Census of Population: 1950* (Washington, D. C.: U.S. Government Printing Office, 1953), Vol. II, *Characteristics of the Population*, Part 1, U.S. Summary, Table 35 on p. 87. This volume will henceforth be cited as "1950 Census."

[10] Brief histories of each of the major ethnic groups in the United States are given in Francis J. Brown and Joseph S. Roucek, eds., *One America*, 3rd ed. (New York: Prentice-Hall, Inc., 1952), Chs. 3-12. Special attention is given to their political activities in Joseph S. Roucek and Arthur D. Wright, "Political Activities of Minority Groups," in *ibid.*, pp. 426-46.

TABLE 30   Occupational Distribution of Americans, 1950 [11]

Occupation	Per Cent of Population So Employed
Professional, technical, and kindred workers	8.7
Farmers and farm managers	7.7
Managers, officials, and proprietors except farm	8.9
Clerical and kindred workers	12.3
Sales workers	7.0
Craftsmen, foremen, and kindred workers	13.8
Operatives and kindred workers	19.8
Private household workers	2.5
Service workers, except private household	7.6
Farm laborers, unpaid family workers	1.6
Farm laborers, paid, and farm foremen	2.6
Laborers, except farm and mine	6.1
Not reported	1.3

By using still more gross categories than in Table 30, we get these results: 71.2 per cent of the working population were private wage and salary workers, 9.8 per cent worked for the various governments, 17.1 per cent were self-employed, and 2.0 per cent were unpaid family workers.[12]

Religious Differences. Although the compilation of statistics on church membership and religious preferences presents a number of problems (for example, not all denominations report their memberships, and those that do have no uniform reporting method), it has been estimated that there are over 250 religious sects in the United States with a total membership of 90,860,000. In other words, somewhat over half (about 56.7 per cent) of the American people officially belong to a church; somewhat less than half are—officially, at least— "unchurched." Of the church members, 52,890,000 (58.2 per cent) are Protestants; 30,425,000 (33.5 per cent) are Roman Catholics; and 5,000,000 (5.5 per cent) are Jews. The largest Protestant sects are: Baptists (including twenty-four separate varieties), 17,763,000; Methodists (including twenty-two varieties), 11,661,000; Lutherans (including twenty-two varieties), 6,746,000; and Presbyterians (including ten varieties), 3,648,000. We are, therefore, a society with a relatively high proportion of non–church members, and also a predominantly Protestant society with a large Roman Catholic minority and a much smaller Jewish minority.[13]

Educational Differences. Despite our system of free public schools and our laws fixing minimum ages at which children may leave school, there are wide variations in the amount of formal education attained by Americans. The major differences are shown in Table 31.

[11] 1950 Census, Table 53 on p. 101.
[12] *Ibid.*
[13] These data are drawn from *The World Almanac, 1954*, pp. 705-06.

TABLE 31 Years of School Completed by Americans 25 Years Old and Over, 1950 [14]

Years of School Completed	Per Cent of Population
None	2.5
Elementary school	
1-4 years	8.3
5-6 years	9.1
7 years	6.8
8 years	20.2
High school	
1-3 years	17.0
4 years	20.2
College	
1-3 years	7.2
4 years	6.0
Not reported	2.7

The data in Table 31, then, show that 46.9 per cent of the adult population in 1950 had gone no further than elementary school, 37.2 per cent had had at least some high school education, and only 13.2 per cent had had any college education.

Income-Level Differences. The distribution of American families among the various levels of annual income is shown in Table 32. The data in Table 32 show that over half (52.5 per cent) of American families in 1952 received incomes of less than $4,000 per year, and 20.8 per cent received incomes of over $6,000 per year. How much social tension results from these differences

TABLE 32 Annual Income of Families, 1952 [15]

Income Level	Per Cent of Families at That Level
Under $1,000	8.9
$1,000 to 1,999	10.8
$2,000 to 2,999	14.2
$3,000 to 3,999	18.6
$4,000 to 4,999	15.4
$5,000 to 5,999	11.9
$6,000 to 9,999	16.6
$10,000 and over	4.2

[14] 1950 Census, Table 44 on p. 96. These figures suggest a pattern that, like several of the others presented in this chapter, is changing rapidly. The 1960 census will probably show a substantially higher level of formal education in the population.

[15] U.S. Bureau of the Census, *Statistical Abstract of the United States: 1954* (Washington, D. C., 1954), Table 347 on p. 313.

in income levels and from the many other differences among the American people is our next concern.

THE "CIVIL-WAR POTENTIAL" IN AMERICAN SOCIETY

The General Nature of Sociopolitical Conflict. Students of human affairs have long observed that there is competition and conflict among social groups in every human society.[16] The individuals in any society always differ from one another in at least certain respects, such as those discussed above, and a certain amount of "stratification" of the society is unavoidable. Technically speaking, a social "stratum" is simply an aggregate of individuals who happen to share a common characteristic, e.g., blue-eyedness, maleness, a low standard of living, or the Ph.D. degree. The persons in each stratum have goals and values that are at least somewhat different from the goals and values of persons in the other strata; therefore, if people in one stratum are fully satisfied, people in another are bound to be dissatisfied: if thin persons are considered beautiful, fat persons will be unhappy; if Protestants manage to convert a number of Catholics, the remaining Catholics will be unhappy; if inflation makes it easier to pay debts, debtors will rejoice but creditors will complain. Most social scientists, in fact, regard the following proposition as axiomatic: Any given social stratum is, in the nature of things, set over against at least one competing stratum; and *all* the strata in a society can therefore never fully and equally realize their many competing goals and values.

By no means all the persons in all the strata in any society are highly conscious of their position and sharply aware of their competitors; no doubt the members of many strata (e.g., blue-eyed persons) are hardly aware of their common characteristics and certainly do not think of themselves as sharing a common cause with their fellows in social conflict with the opposing strata (e.g., brown-eyed and green-eyed persons). The members of *some* of the strata in any society, however, do become conscious of their common characteristics, are aware of their conflict with the competing strata, and do to some extent direct their behavior accordingly. Social scientists generally refer to the persons in such strata as members of "groups" or "classes";[17] and in every society there is some conflict among the groups over the question of which groups' values and interests will be more satisfied and which less satisfied—over "who gets what, when, and how."[18]

[16] For a highly convenient summary of the agreed-upon propositions about social conflict put forward in the literature of sociology and social psychology, see Robin M. Williams, Jr., "Propositions on Intergroup Hostility and Conflict," in Logan Wilson and William L. Kolb, eds., *Sociological Analysis* (New York: Harcourt, Brace and Company, 1949), pp. 740-76.

[17] For fuller discussions of the concepts "stratum," "group," and "class," see Bennett and Tumin, *op. cit.*, Ch. 10; and Richard Centers, *The Psychology of Social Classes* (Princeton: Princeton University Press, 1949), pp. 27-28.

[18] Cf. Harold D. Lasswell, *Politics, Who Gets What, When, How* (New York: Whittlesey House, 1936). The classical application of this view of social conflict to the special analysis of politics is Arthur F. Bentley, *The Process of Government* (Chicago: University of Chicago Press,

There is, of course, great variation from society to society in the incidence and bitterness of intergroup conflict, and thus in what we may call the society's "civil-war potential"—that is, the total amount of potential intergroup hostility that might, in the absence of effective pacifying and unifying forces, break out into actual shooting civil war. Social scientists generally agree that the variables to fix attention on in estimating the likelihood of peaceful coexistence within a given society are the following: (1) the heterogeneity of the society and the number of strata which result from it; (2) the "visibility" of each group's competitors; (3) the general level of personal and group tension and insecurity; (4) the number and strength of the common interests and other unifying factors in the society; and (5) the channels the society provides for "siphoning off" intergroup conflict.[19] What, according to these tests, are the prospects for *American* society? How great *is* our civil-war potential?

Social Conflict in American Society. In America, as in any other society, certain factors operate to maximize the "civil-war potential," and certain other factors tend to minimize it. The maximizing factors include at least the following:

(1) The *heterogeneity* of the society. We have already noted the complexity of American society, which means that there are a maximum number of bases for setting Americans apart from one another and therefore a maximum number of social strata and a maximum number of at least potentially hostile groups and classes.[20] In order to suggest the range and variety of social conflict, actual and potential, in our society, we present the following list—not intended to be exhaustive—of some of the major types of conflict:[21]

Competition among cities, states, and regions for industry, teachers, labor, population, water, etc.

Competition among business firms for customers.

Competition among buyers for scarce goods.

Competition for jobs among individuals and trade unions.

Competition between labor and management over wages, hours, working conditions, and union status.

Competition among individuals for status, power, and prestige.

Competition among religious groups for membership and status.

Competition among ethnic groups for status, power, and prestige.

Competition among various income-level groups over governmental taxes and expenditures, and for various kinds of special privilege.

1908). Some leading recent examples of the Bentley type of analysis of politics are: David B. Truman, *The Governmental Process* (New York: Alfred A. Knopf, 1951); Bertram M. Gross, *The Legislative Struggle* (New York: McGraw-Hill Book Company, Inc., 1953); and Earl Latham, *The Group Basis of Politics* (Ithaca, N. Y.: Cornell University Press, 1952).

[19] For a summary of the factors affecting the "civil-war potential" in a society, see Williams, "Propositions on Intergroup Hostility and Conflict," in Wilson and Kolb, *op. cit.,* Nos. 1-32.

[20] Cf. *ibid.,* No. 21; and Robin M. Williams, Jr., *American Society* (New York: Alfred A. Knopf, 1951), pp. 469-73.

[21] Cf. the somewhat different list in Jessie Bernard, *American Community Behavior* (New York: The Dryden Press, 1949), Chs. 7-23.

Competition among businessmen, farmers, and workers for favored positions in the economy.

Competition among individuals, pressure groups, and political parties for political power.

Other examples will no doubt suggest themselves to the reader.

(2) The *impersonality* of American society. Most social scientists agree that ours is a highly "impersonal" society—that is, one in which most of us never meet face to face with most of the persons whose activities closely affect our lives. For example, when one of us takes an aspirin, he is committing, however unconsciously, a great act of faith; for, unless he is enough of an analytical chemist to tell by taste and smell that the tablets do indeed contain aspirin rather than arsenic or strychnine (and few of us are), he has to depend upon the honesty and skill of some unknown pill roller and the vigilance of some unknown governmental food-and-drug inspector working in a factory hundreds or thousands of miles away. If either or both of these strangers let him down, he will hardly be able to find them and punch them in the nose.

By the same token, most of us never see most of our "enemies" (i.e., the members of groups competing most vigorously with our own) face to face. To the striker, the boss is a remote figure seen as a sort of devil image bent on keeping the worker ground down, and not, like himself, a human being with both good and bad qualities; and to the boss, the striker is a grubby, lazy, and dangerous radical bent on robbing him of his just profits, and not a worried, harassed, and anxious husband and father trying to increase the size of his paycheck. Two eminent sociologists put it this way:

A more careful examination of the facts might not show that modern man is insensible to the plight of his fellows, *when he knows and understands them,* but that modern society is such that *it is difficult, if not impossible, even for a morally sensitive man or woman to see and appreciate many of the problems and points of view of men and women above and below him or her in the pyramid of social classes and jobs.* It is almost as if the person from each distinct social class lives in another social world; about the "other" worlds, in their real and vital aspects, he knows but little. One may properly wonder whether the industrial manager who drives from the exclusive suburbs to his downtown factory through the neighborhoods of the workingmen's homes knows less about what goes on inside those houses than their inhabitants know about the problems of the Cadillac-driving manager. No one has probably deliberately fostered this separatism, but it has occurred nevertheless, and now constitutes a fundamental and stubborn problem in the solution of economic problems many of which cut across social class lines.[22]

(3) Our *tradition of violence.* The Civil War is by no means the only, but merely the largest-scale, instance in American history in which one group of Americans tried to achieve their goals by doing violent bodily harm to other Americans. In the conflict between labor and management, for example,

---

[22] John F. Cuber and Robert A. Harper, *Problems of American Society: Values in Conflict* (New York: Henry Holt and Company, 1948), p. 19. Italics in the original.

violence has long played a major role: management has employed "goon squads" of strikebreakers and police to crack picket lines with clubs, tear gas, and even rifles; and labor has resisted with methods as extreme as the attempted assassination of intransigent bosses and "scabs." [23] And the continuing violence among the dock workers on the New York waterfront reminds us that this kind of violence is far from being a thing of the past. Our race relations, for another example, have often been characterized by violence. We need not go back as far as the heyday of the Ku Klux Klan after the Civil War for illustrations, but need only point to such recent episodes as the race riots in Cicero, Illinois, in July of 1951, and the various violent attempts in Maryland in 1954 to resist the enforcement of the Supreme Court's order outlawing racial segregation in the public schools. Nor is American politics completely devoid of violence even now. We still read in our newspapers of episodes in certain large cities in which the watchers and challengers of one party are beaten up by the adherents of the other party; as recently as August, 1946, there was a day-long gun fight in Athens, Tennessee, between the Crump-Biggs machine and a group of veterans who were trying to unseat the machine; [24] and in 1954, A. L. Patterson, the Democratic nominee for attorney general, was murdered in Phenix City, Alabama, for political reasons. In short, violence is always simmering just under the surface of several areas of American social conflict, and small-scale civil wars still break out in those areas often enough so that any attempt, such as we are making in the present chapter, to describe the American political environment must take them into account.[25]

FACTORS MAKING FOR CONSENSUS IN AMERICAN SOCIETY

Despite all the forces just described as maximizing our "civil-war potential," intergroup conflict in American society is clearly less bitter and violent than in many other societies—such as, for example, those of France, Italy, South Africa, and certain Latin American nations. This suggests that, along with these divisive factors, American society contains a number of powerful forces making for consensus [26] and social peace, among which must be mentioned at least the following:

The "Unity of Diversity." Although the heterogeneity and complexity of American society noted above does create multifold differences among our people, it also tends to keep any *particular* difference from splitting the com-

---

[23] Cf. Louis Adamic, *Dynamite, the Story of Class Violence in America,* rev. ed. (New York: The Viking Press, 1934).

[24] Cf. Bernard, *op. cit.,* pp. 524-26.

[25] Cf. V. O. Key, Jr., *Politics, Parties, and Pressure Groups,* 3rd ed. (New York: Thomas Y. Crowell Company, 1952), pp. 12-13.

[26] On p. 54 we defined consensus as "the kind of fundamental agreement among the members of the community that exists when they feel for each other that minimum of mutual need that disposes them to conduct their discussion in [a democratic manner], *and* to act with forbearance when divisive issues arise."

munity into warring camps. This means, for one thing, that intergroup conflict is for the most part *noncumulative;* that is, the persons who find themselves in opposite camps on one issue may well find themselves on the same side of another issue, and the interpersonal hostility and resentment generated by the conflict in the first instance is often dissipated by the cooperation in the second. Thus the labor leader and the businessman struggle over wages and hours and union status during the day's bargaining session; but, both being good Catholics, they work together in the evening to secure more public aid for the parochial schools; and the Republican and Democratic opponents in a tough election campaign join forces afterward in a common effort to remove legal ceilings on campaign expenditures. The multiplicity of social groups means, moreover, that no single group is ever likely to be 100 per cent mobilized for any particular fight, since such mobilization could happen only if all the members of the group abandoned all their other interests for the one in question—and that almost never happens.[27] As Williams puts it:

> Without these relatively fluid, crisscrossing allegiances it seems highly probable that conflict would be increased, assuming that class differentiation did not diminish. American society is simply riddled with cleavages. The remarkable phenomenon is the extent to which the various differences "cancel out"—or are noncumulative in their incidence. There is this much realistic sociological meaning in *e pluribus unum.*[28]

Upward Social Mobility. Americans in the lower, underprivileged strata of society have, unlike their counterparts in many other societies, rarely made concerted attempts to overthrow the whole society and put themselves *collectively* on top. Perhaps the basic reason for this has been the widespread belief among such persons that no matter how lowly a man's status may be, he has a real chance to lift himself, by his own individual efforts and merits, up to a sunnier place in the social hierarchy. Nor is this merely a delusion fostered by NAM propaganda, for the fact is that not only has there long been a high degree of "social mobility" in American society, but many more of the mobile individuals have moved up than have moved down the scale. Accordingly, it is a rare American who regards the society as a kind of gigantic conspiracy against his legitimate aspirations and therefore something only to be overthrown as rapidly and as ruthlessly as possible: after all, he personally knows a lot of people who *have* greatly improved their positions, and what others have done he can do.[29]

The Generally High Level of Physical Comfort. Unquestionably some Americans live better than others, and both groups know it. Even the less

[27] Cf. E. E. Schattschneider, *Party Government* (New York: Rinehart & Company, Inc., 1942), pp. 32-34.

[28] Williams, *American Society,* p. 531.

[29] Cf. Elbridge Sibley, "Some Demographic Clues to Stratification," in Wilson and Kolb, *op. cit.,* pp. 642-50. Sibley argues that the educational system has been the main consciously planned agency for producing the high degree of upward social mobility characteristic of American society in the past.

well-off, however, have a high level of physical comfort, not only by contrast with their counterparts in other societies, but also in terms of having enough of most of the necessities and some of the luxuries, so that life is something more than a grim struggle for the minimum conditions of biological existence.

External Pressures. Social analysts for many centuries have pointed out that men tend to set aside their individual differences and societies their internal conflicts in the presence of threats to their individual and collective existence by other societies. Thus wars and rumors of wars and the presence of common enemies have always tended to force groups that would otherwise be divided and quarreling to close ranks. The United States has lived continuously in the presence of what most of its citizens have regarded as real threats to its national existence, first from the Fascists and now from the Communists, since the early 1930's. And the familiar plea, "Let us forget our differences and remember that we are all *Americans,*" unquestionably wins real response and represents for many Americans a genuine longing for and conviction of the necessity of national unity.

Common Interests. In one of the most penetrating passages of one of the great classics of political science, Rousseau wrote:

What made the establishment of societies necessary was, if you like, the fact that the interests of individuals clashed. But what made their establishment possible was the fact that these same interests *also* coincided. *In other words:* It is the overlap among different interests that creates the social bond, so that no society can possibly exist save as there is some point at which all the interests *concerned* are in harmony. Now: society should be governed exclusively in terms of the common interest *of its members.*[30]

In other words, if the *only* important social force in America were the intergroup conflict noted above, then our society could hardly hold together and resist the onslaughts of the Fascists and the Communists; but it *has* held together and *has* resisted those onslaughts. Why? Because, among other reasons, the groups that compose American society do have, along with their differing and "private" interests, certain *common* interests that they can achieve only by holding the society together. This does not mean, of course, that every single American has always preferred to maintain America's political independence above everything else; the activities of the German-American Bund and the Communist Party and its fellow travelers teach us otherwise. It does mean, however, that in the face of the Fascist and Communist threats to our national existence the overwhelming proportion of Americans have as a matter of fact placed the *common* value of preserving the nation above the private values held by the subnational interest groups of which they are members. Thus they have observably *acted* as though they placed the highest value on maintaining, in Williams' words, "the situation in which individuals continue to interact and to avoid conflict on the basis of the gains each anticipates

[30] Jean Jacques Rousseau, *The Social Contract,* translated by Willmoore Kendall (Chicago: Henry Regnery Company, 1954), Bk. II, Ch. I.

from perpetuation of the social framework essential to interaction." [31] In other words, while the Negro wants social equality with the whites, the worker wants a guaranteed annual wage, and the businessman wants relief from his tax burden, most members of all three groups believe—and *act* as though they believed—that they are more likely to achieve these (and other) goals by the kind of intergroup bargaining and compromise characteristic of the American system than by the far different systems characteristic of Communist and Fascist states. "Common interests," then, are not myths that people given to wishful thinking talk about because they shrink from facing the harsh and selfish nature of American life; they are empirically observable factors in the American political environment that the social scientist must take into account in any attempt to describe the latter.

The American Belief System

BELIEF SYSTEMS AND CONSENSUS

Having discussed the general nature of the American community, we now turn to a second aspect of our political environment: the American belief system. The "belief system" of any community is the whole complex of its members' ideas that underlies, informs, and helps to shape its social and political behavior and institutions. It includes not only "values," i.e., the people's notions of what is good and beautiful and just, but also "conceptions of reality," i.e., their ideas about the way things *are* and about the effectiveness of various means for making things as they are more like things as they should be.[32]

A community's belief system, like an individual's, is not a neatly arranged, logically ordered, and internally consistent system of propositions; it is rather a "mesh of struggling inclinations, interests, and ideals, some held conscious and some suppressed for long intervals but all active in bending behavior in their direction." [33] If the only value conflicts in society were conflicts between one group's consistent set of ideas and another group's equally consistent though opposed set, social analysis would be a great deal easier than it is. The fact is, however, that in most communities each individual and each social group holds a number of logically inconsistent and conflicting ideas; and so it is with the belief system of the whole community.

One of the things that distinguish a "community" from a mere aggregation of human beings, however, is the fact that most of the persons living within its boundaries have a certain number of *common* values and beliefs. It is these which underlie the consensus that makes it possible for them to live

---

[31] Williams, *American Society*, p. 520.

[32] For discussions of the general nature and role of belief systems in social and political life, see Gunnar Myrdal, *An American Dilemma*, 9th ed. (New York: Harper and Brothers, 1944), Introduction and Appendix I; and Robert M. MacIver, *The Web of Government* (New York: The Macmillan Company, 1947), pp. 4-6.

[33] Myrdal, *op. cit.*, p. xlviii.

together under a common government. Consensus is not something a society either has or does not have; it is something that a "society," if it has it at all, has in greater or lesser *degree*. The degree of consensus in any given society, moreover, profoundly affects the kind of politico-governmental system it can sustain. If, in other words, most people in a given society hold a large number of commonly understood, commonly acted-upon, and relatively consistent values and beliefs, they are likely to create and maintain one kind of political system; but if, on the other hand, few such common beliefs are held, or if they are not commonly understood and acted upon, or if they include many serious conflicts and inconsistencies, quite a different political system is likely to result. That is why we now raise the question, What kind of belief system do we have in America?

THE "AMERICAN CREED": CONVICTIONS AND CONFLICTS [34]

The American belief system displays at least two striking characteristics. The first of these is *the wide diffusion of a great many common values and ideas throughout the whole society*. A striking number of similar attitudes are held and expressed by most Americans at all levels in all the various strata described above. There seems to be, in other words, an *American* creed—in the sense of a body of ideas held by most Americans regardless of their differing positions in the social hierarchy—to a greater degree than truly *national* creeds can be found in most of the world's other nations. As Myrdal puts it:

The intensities and proportions in which these conflicting valuations are present vary considerably from one American to another, and, within the same individual, from one situation to another. The cultural unity of the nation consists, however, in the fact that *most Americans have most valuations in common* though they are arranged differently in the sphere of valuations of different individuals and groups and bear different intensity coefficients.[35]

The second is *the striking number of inconsistencies and contradictions among these commonly held and widely diffused ideas*. It sometimes seems difficult to escape the conclusion that for every value and belief widely held by Americans there is a contradictory value or belief that is no less widely held. Perhaps the most appropriate way to describe the major items of the American creed, therefore, is to present them as pairs of conflicting ideas.

Idealism and Materialism. Several social analysts have described America as "the most idealistic nation on earth." In support of this contention they point to such data as our tendency to develop our foreign policy in moral terms ("keep the world safe for democracy," "too proud to fight," "the right

[34] Among recent attempts to describe the American belief system are: Myrdal, *op. cit.*, Ch. I; and Williams, *American Society*, pp. 388-440. An older but still useful study is Robert S. Lynd and Helen Merrell Lynd, *Middletown in Transition* (New York: Harcourt, Brace and Company, 1937), Ch. XII. Also very useful is the collection of results of public opinion polls in Hadley Cantril, ed., *Public Opinion, 1935-1946* (Princeton: Princeton University Press, 1951).

[35] Myrdal, *op. cit.*, p. xlviii. Italics in the original.

is more precious than peace") rather than in terms of our "national interest," [36] our humanitarian programs of relief to victims of war and disaster in
other lands, our recurrent waves of "reform" against "corruption" and "vice,"
etc. America is also frequently described by foreigners, however, as "the most
materialistic nation on earth"—a nation whose people know, in Oscar Wilde's
phrase, the price of everything and the value of nothing, who care little for
art or beauty or the gracious life but who care to know about any individual
or nation only how many cars, dollars, telephones, TV sets, bathtubs, tons of
steel, etc., they have. And there is just as good evidence for our "materialism"
as for our "idealism," for we seem to be in fact both materialistic *and* idealistic. A paradox? Very well then, a paradox; but one that we have to face
up to.

Christianity and Secularism. From one point of view we are certainly a
Christian nation. Almost all of us profess a belief in God, the divinity of
Christ, the desirability of attending church, and the beneficial effects of religion. We send our children to Sunday school, open sessions of our legislatures
and our political conventions with prayers, regard atheists as beyond the pale,
and say we believe a person ought to try to live according to Christ's teachings. Yet only a little over half of us belong to a church, and, while many
non–church members undoubtedly attend church, their number is at least
equaled by the church members who show up only on Christmas and Easter,
if then. Along with our Christian slogans of behavior ("love thy neighbor as
thyself," "turn the other cheek," "I am my brother's keeper") most of us also
believe in "an eye for an eye and a tooth for a tooth," "business is business,"
and "God helps those who help themselves." [37]

Capitalism and Collectivism. Most Americans certainly believe that capitalism (or "free enterprise") is the best economic system yet devised and that
"socialism," creeping or galloping, is bad. We believe that men work best
and produce most when they have the incentive of being able to make a profit
and where free competition rewards the efficient and punishes the inefficient;
that tight government regulation of industry should be at most a temporary
emergency measure and not a permanent policy; and that a smart businessman
who makes a good product should be permitted to enjoy the fruits of his skill
without being subjected to a governmentally imposed ceiling on his income. [38]
On the other hand, Americans—including American businessmen—have not
only accepted but *asked for* a considerable amount of collectivism in the
past few decades; and a politician who ran on a platform of repealing social
security, "fair trade" laws, government subsidies to private industry, unem-

---

[36] See, for example, the common conception of the present nature of American foreign
policy in the debate between Hans J. Morgenthau, *In Defense of the National Interest* (New York:
Alfred A. Knopf, 1951), and Thomas I. Cook and Malcolm Moos, *Power Through Purpose: The
Realism of Idealism as a Basis for Foreign Policy* (Baltimore: The Johns Hopkins Press, 1954).

[37] Cf. the polls on American attitudes toward religion in Cantril, *op. cit.,* pp. 699-701, 742-45.

[38] Cf. the polls on American attitudes toward free enterprise and socialism in Cantril, *op. cit.,*
pp. 344-51, 802-03.

ployment compensation, etc., would thereby lose many votes in most areas of the nation.

Success and Security. Most Americans believe that a person should do his utmost to "be a success"—to make as much money, live in as fine a home, and drive as high-powered a car as he can. We have little respect for the man without ambition, and we speak admiringly of "risk capital" and "seizing one's chance to make a killing." On the other hand, our great organized economic interest groups and most individuals seem to be aiming at *security* rather than at being able to make a great killing at the risk of going broke: our business groups press for "fair trade" laws, which establish legally enforced minimum prices and thus prevent "cutthroat" price competition; our farmers clamor for "parity" prices, whether flexible or rigid, instead of taking their chances on boom and bust; and our workers struggle for the guaranteed annual wage and for job and union security. In other words, we believe that interference with "the law of supply and demand" is bad, but we keep right on interfering with it.

Competition and Cooperation. Our commitment to capitalism and its directives for human behavior makes us place a high value on individual competition for individual success. We believe a man should "make his own way," "get only what's coming to him," and "rely on himself instead of sponging on others." Yet our commitment to Christianity and "democracy" makes us value cooperation with our fellows. We believe also in "helping those less fortunate than ourselves," "being a good neighbor," and "working together for the good of the community." [39]

Class Attitudes in a Middle-Class Society. Despite the fact that American society is stratified into the various levels of income, education, status, and prestige that we noted above, very few Americans think of themselves as belonging to an "upper" or "lower" class. The *Fortune* poll in 1940, for example, asked a cross section of Americans the question, "If you had to describe the class to which you belong with one of these three words [upper, lower, middle], which would you pick?" 7.6 per cent replied "upper," 7.9 per cent replied "lower," 79.2 per cent replied "middle," and 5.3 per cent didn't know. [40] When the Princeton Office of Public Opinion Research asked the same question in 1945 and added "working class" as a fourth category, 3 per cent replied "upper," 1 per cent replied "lower," 43 per cent replied "middle," 51 per cent replied "working class," and 2 per cent didn't know. [41] It seems likely, however, that the latter figures indicate only that being "working-class" (in the sense, no doubt, of "I *work* for a living") had become as respectable for many Americans as being "middle-class" used to be.

---

[39] Sebastian de Grazia argues that this particular value conflict lies at the bottom of the low state of consensus and the absence of real community in modern American society: *The Political Community* (Chicago: University of Chicago Press, 1948), Ch. 6. We shall return to his thesis later in the present chapter.

[40] Cantril, *op. cit.,* No. 4 on p. 117.

[41] Reported in Centers, *op. cit.*

The OPOR did find that "radical" social and economic attitudes were more prevalent among those who placed themselves in the "working" and "lower" classes than among those who replied "upper" and "middle." Perhaps their most significant finding for our purposes, however, was the fact that there were many differences in attitudes *within* each of these "classes" and that "class attitudes" in America are at most statistical expressions of *tendency,* not hard-and-fast bodies of consistent ideas uniformly held by all the members of each of the groups of respondents.[42] In short, the Princeton study only confirmed what the Marxist parties in America have, to their despair and disgust, long known, namely, that most Americans simply do not think of themselves as belonging to any "capitalist" or "proletarian" class. Perhaps they should, but the fact is that they do not.

Individualism in a Nation of "Joiners." Most Americans have no objection to a particular *individual's* having more income, prestige, and "success" than the rest of us *if* he has earned his privileges by his own merits and efforts; but most of us strongly resent any *class* distinction and privilege. The aspect of army life most resented by American soldiers in World War II, for example, was the officer–enlisted man social caste system and the special privileges it gave to all officers regardless, allegedly, of their individual merits.[43] The idea that a man should make good *strictly on his own* is one of our most cherished beliefs. Yet we are notoriously a "nation of joiners." Despite all our talk of individualism and self-reliance, most of us belong to a number of organizations, in each of which we pool our resources with those of other individuals to advance various shared interests—economic, social, political, or whatever. In the United States at present there are, in round numbers, 12,000 trade associations, 4,000 chambers of commerce, 70,000 labor unions, 100,000 women's clubs, and 15,000 civic service groups, luncheon clubs, etc.[44] Most of these, of course, are what social scientists call *gesellschaft* rather than *gemeinschaft* organizations; that is, they are formally organized special-interest groups of various kinds rather than traditional groups based on kinship, proximity, and direct and inclusive interpersonal relations among the members.[45] Whether or not, as some writers have argued, our "joinerism" is an effort to alleviate the impersonality and coldness of American life, it certainly is in conflict with our belief in the rugged and self-reliant individual.

Majority Rule and Minority Rights. As we noted in Chapter 1, most Americans believe that "democracy" is the ideal form of government; and most of us also believe that the United States has the most democratic government in the world. Yet many of us also believe that "democracy" means, among

---

[42] Cf. the summary in Centers, *op. cit.,* pp. 208-09, and in Williams, *American Society,* pp. 96-101.

[43] Samuel A. Stouffer *et al., The American Soldier* (Princeton: Princeton University Press, 1949), Vol. I, Ch. 8, esp. p. 379.

[44] Jay Judkins, *National Associations of the United States* (Washington, D. C.: U.S. Department of Commerce, 1949), p. viii.

[45] Cf. Williams, *American Society,* pp. 462-63.

The American Political Environment 475

other things, both that the majority rather than the minority should rule and that a minority should have the power to veto any action of the majority inimical to its welfare. This contradiction, which we analyzed in Chapter 2, has a number of consequences, for our political system in general and our party system in particular, which we shall discuss in detail in the final two chapters.

THE NATURE OF AMERICAN CONSENSUS

In the light of the foregoing considerations, let us now repeat the two general characteristics of the American belief system that we noted at the beginning of our summary of its major items. (1) There are many beliefs and values that are common to most Americans, and our society contains few if any groups that hold unified and internally consistent belief systems that are sharply opposed to equally unified and consistent belief systems held by other groups. (2) There is a good deal of inconsistency and logical contradiction among these various common beliefs, not only in the society as a whole but also within most of the subgroups and social strata into which Americans may be classified. American society is, in these respects, very different from such a society as, for example, that of South Africa, which has almost no beliefs common to all the population but rather is divided into two main groups, each of which has a highly unified and consistent body of beliefs that sharply contradict the beliefs held by the other group.[46]

Sebastian de Grazia argues that American society, as a result of these contradictions in its belief system, has a high degree of "anomie" (that is, "the disintegrated state of a society that possesses no body of common values or morals which effectively govern conduct"). The conflict between the cooperative directives of our religious and political beliefs and the competitive directives of the economic system we believe in, De Grazia continues, deprives us of the "fundament of commonness" that any genuine *community* needs, produces the unease, restlessness, rootlessness, and longing for belongingness characteristic of most Americans, and makes us a mere "society" rather than a genuine community.[47]

In the present writers' opinion, however, it is incorrect to say that because our belief system has so many contradictions, there is *no* consensus in American society. It is more correct, we feel, to say rather that our belief system permits only *a low degree* of consensus as compared with, say, the degree of consensus among the Afrikanders, but a high degree of consensus as compared with the inhabitants of South Africa as a whole. It must also be said that such consensus as we have in America is firm and persistent, and provides

---

[46] For descriptions of the present deep division in South Africa between the Afrikander group and its opponents, see Alexander Brady, *Democracy in the Dominions,* 2nd ed. (Toronto: University of Toronto Press, 1952), pp. 385-99; Arthur Keppel-Jones, "The Dilemma of South Africa," *Behind the Headlines,* Vol. V (November, 1950); and Austin F. Macdonald, "Politics in the Union of South Africa," *Annals of the American Academy of Political and Social Science,* Vol. CCLXXXVIII (July, 1953), pp. 140-52.

[47] *Op. cit., passim.*

the solid and stable foundation on which the American community rests. Our belief system certainly does not permit the kind of consensus and community De Grazia dreams of; but the very fact that it contains many contradictions—which, as we have seen, characterize most of the strata and groups within the society as well as the society as a whole—makes it highly unlikely that tightly knit groups each with its internally consistent belief system will arise within the nation, and, as in South Africa, tear it apart.

In short, the American belief system provides a degree of consensus that is more than adequate for maintaining our present political system, but might be quite inadequate for maintaining a different system (such, for example, as that proposed by the advocates of responsible party government). All this, of course, has important implications for understanding and evaluating the role of the American party system, and we shall recur to it in our final two chapters.

THE AMERICAN ATTITUDE TOWARD POLITICS

Our "Other-directed Society" and the "Inside-Dopesters." In his well-known and influential book *The Lonely Crowd* David Riesman argues that America is fast becoming an "other-directed" society—that is, one in which more and more persons choose their values and beliefs and determine their behavior according to what they think their associates will approve, rather than according to some inner set of convictions about right and wrong implanted in them by their parents (which Riesman calls "inner-direction") or according to the ancient customs and practices of the culture (which he calls "tradition-direction"). Other-directed persons, he continues, have a characteristic attitude toward politics—a kind of apathy and indifference growing from the belief that "people are more important than issues" and that the important thing to know about any political issue is not its rights and wrongs but rather the "inside dope" about which side is going to win. The other-directed person thus approaches politics as an "inside-dopester" rather than as a "moralizer" or as an "indignant"—which latter attitudes, he says, characterize the inner-directed person's approach to politics.[48] Riesman does not argue that every American takes precisely this attitude toward every political issue, but only that more and more Americans, especially those in the "middle class," approach more and more political issues in this manner all the time. Thus politics in America, he believes, is becoming a kind of spectator sport; and our increasing insistence upon "glamour," i.e., attractive *personal* qualities, in our candidates—as distinct from approved stands on public issues—is a sure sign of this growing other-directed apathy toward politics.[49]

American Skepticism About Politics. There is considerable evidence to support Riesman's thesis. A number of social scientists, for example, have

---

[48] David Riesman, *The Lonely Crowd* (New Haven: Yale University Press, 1950). Chapter IX is devoted to the discussion of American attitudes toward politics.

[49] *Ibid.*, pp. 214-21.

tried to find out why we have such low voter-turnouts in most American elections, and they have all concluded that by far the greatest single cause is the feeling of many potential voters that it doesn't really matter very much *who* wins the elections.[50] The public opinion polls report the same attitude. When, for example, the Gallup poll asked a national sample during the congressional elections of 1946, "Do you think it makes a great deal of difference or only a little difference which political party runs the country?" 30 per cent replied "a great deal," 43 per cent replied "little," 21 per cent replied "none," and 6 per cent had no opinion.[51] Further support for Riesman's thesis is provided by Gunnar Myrdal, who, in his study of American social and political attitudes, noted with surprise how many Americans believe that social ills cannot be cured by politics and legislation and how many of the people he and his interviewers talked to apparently considered politics trivial and unimportant.[52] And, as we pointed out in Chapter 11, most Americans do not want their sons to go into politics as a life work; they think politics is a dirty business, and believe it is hard for a man to go into politics and remain honest.[53]

In short, relatively few Americans regard politics as something central to their lives, as the arena in which most of the important decisions affecting their and the nation's future are being made. Most of us have *some* interest in and concern with politics, but assign it a much lower priority than one would gather from reading our newspapers and observing our political campaigns. This too is a crucial aspect of the environment within which our party system operates.

The American Political System

OUR ANTI-MAJORITARIAN CONSTITUTION

The Political Theory of the Constitution. Historians now generally agree that the fifty-five men who wrote the Constitution of the United States in 1787 represented only one of the two major political groups and bodies of political ideas struggling for supremacy at the time. Most of them represented the conservative-mercantilist aristocrats who feared that their opponents, the radical-agrarian democrats, might pull down the whole edifice of orderly government, sound finance, and property rights if events continued as they had under

---

[50] Cf. Charles E. Merriam and Harold F. Gosnell, *Non-Voting* (Chicago: University of Chicago Press, 1924); Paul F. Lazarsfeld, Bernard Berelson, and Hazel Gaudet, *The People's Choice* (New York: Duell, Sloan and Pearce, 1944), pp. 45-49; Angus Campbell, Gerald Gurin, and Warren E. Miller, *The Voter Decides* (Evanston, Ill.: Row, Peterson and Company, 1954), Ch. III; and Bernard Berelson, Paul F. Lazarsfeld, and William N. McPhee, *Voting* (Chicago: University of Chicago Press, 1954), pp. 24-34.

[51] Cantril, *op. cit.,* No. 35 on p. 579. Asking the same question in the 1942 congressional elections, Gallup got these answers: 25 per cent "a great deal," 42 per cent "little," 26 per cent "none," and 7 per cent "no opinion": *Ibid.*

[52] *Op. cit.,* Ch. I.

[53] Pp. 237-38.

the Articles of Confederation and the existing state constitutions, and who had determined therefore to replace the Articles with a new fundamental law that would make it impossible for the radicals to carry out their dangerous and evil designs.[54]

The Founding Fathers came to the Philadelphia convention equipped with a well-thought-out and systematic body of political ideas, and with the firm intention of embodying those ideas in the new constitution.[55] Their political theory was founded upon the conviction that every man is an "atom of self-interest" whose overriding purpose in life is to advance his own (mainly economic) interests regardless of how the interests of others might be affected. In politics, they believed, men seek to gain their private and selfish ends by uniting in "factions" and "parties" with others of like private interests; thus if any such faction or party succeeds in controlling the whole power of government, it will use that power ruthlessly to impose its will upon and pursue its interests at the expense of the rest of the nation.[56] Therefore, not only does the individual citizen need to have his rights and liberties protected against the government, but each group in the community needs to be protected against aggression by other groups. Above all, those who have property need to be protected against the envy and thievery of those who have none.

The danger to property, liberty, and stability is very great indeed, the Founding Fathers were deeply convinced, in a "democratic" government, by which term they meant any government in which popular majorities have the full and unrestrained power to do any fool thing they want to.[57] Any popular majority, they believed, is bound to be composed largely of the ignorant and unpropertied rabble; and the latter's main political goal is to plunder and expropriate the "rich, the educated, and the well-born." The community, they warned, is in very great danger indeed if *any* single faction controls the gov-

[54] The best works on the general political situation in the 1780's are: Merrill Jensen, *The Articles of Confederation* (Madison: University of Wisconsin Press, 1940) and *The New Nation: A History of the United States During the Confederation* (New York: Alfred A. Knopf, 1950); Allan Nevins, *The American States During and After the Revolution, 1775-1789* (New York: The Macmillan Company, 1927); and Charles A. Beard's famous work, *An Economic Interpretation of the Constitution of the United States* (New York: The Macmillan Company, 1913).

[55] Among the more useful secondary accounts of the Founding Fathers' political ideas are those given in Vernon L. Parrington, *Main Currents in American Thought,* one-volume ed. (New York: Harcourt, Brace and Company, 1927, 1930), pp. 267-320; Richard Hofstadter, *The American Political Tradition and the Men Who Made It* (New York: Alfred A. Knopf, 1948), Ch. I; Francis G. Wilson, *The American Political Mind* (New York: McGraw-Hill Book Company, Inc., 1949), Ch. 5; J. Mark Jacobson, *The Development of American Political Thought* (New York: The Century Company, 1932), Ch. III; and J. Allen Smith, *The Spirit of American Government* (New York: The Macmillan Company, 1907). The main primary sources for federalist political theory are, of course, the debates in the constitutional convention, as presented in Max Farrand, ed., *The Records of the Federal Convention of 1787,* 4 volumes (New Haven: Yale University Press, 1913, 1937); and the *Federalist* papers.

[56] Cf. our summary of Madison's theory of politics in the tenth *Federalist* paper, presented on pp. 132-34.

[57] Cf. Gaetano Salvemini, "The Concepts of Democracy and Liberty in the Eighteenth Century," in Conyers Read, ed., *The Constitution Reconsidered* (New York: Columbia University Press, 1938), pp. 105-19.

ernment; but the worst situation of all is that in which a popular majority is in the saddle. And, believing these things, they came to Philadelphia firmly resolved to build insurmountable barriers against democracy. They made no secret, moreover, of their hatred and fear of democracy. Hofstadter summarizes their views as follows:

> Cribbing and confining the popular spirit that had been at large since 1776 were essential to the purposes of the new Constitution. Edmund Randolph saying to the Convention that the evils from which the country suffered originated in the "turbulence and follies of democracy," and that the great danger lay in "the democratic parts of our constitutions"; Elbridge Gerry, speaking of democracy as "the worst of all political evils"; Roger Sherman, hoping that "the people . . . have as little to do as may be about the government"; William Livingston, saying that "the people have ever been and ever will be unfit to retain the exercise of power in their own hands"; George Washington, the presiding officer, urging the delegates not to produce a document of which they themselves could not approve simply in order "to please the people"; Hamilton, charging that the "turbulent and changing" masses "seldom judge or determine right" and advising a permanent governmental body to "check the imprudence of democracy"; the wealthy young planter, Charles Pinckney, proposing that no one be president who was not worth at least one hundred thousand dollars—all these were quite representative of the spirit in which the problems of government were treated.[58]

What the Founding Fathers did want was a "balanced government": power, they thought, "should be divided into parts, usually three parts; each part should derive so far as possible from a separate source; each should be as independent as it can be; and each should be held to its own sphere of action by checks." And their preference for such a government was founded upon the conviction "that government's stability and government's objectives are best accomplished by *a delicate equipoise between equal powers, by mutual jealousies.*"[59] This doctrine of "balanced government," the origins of which go back at least as far as Polybius, was first made popular in America by the writings of Montesquieu (whose authority at the time was such that Madison referred to him in the forty-seventh *Federalist* paper as "the oracle who is always consulted and cited on this subject"),[60] and applied to specifically American problems most notably by John Adams in his book, *A Defence of the Constitutions of the Governments of the United States of America* (1787), which was published shortly before the Philadelphia convention met and was read avidly by most of its members. In accordance with this theory, the Founding Fathers hoped to create a balanced government not only by "separation of powers" and "checks and balances" *within* the new national government, but also by fragmenting the society itself so that determined majority factions

---

[58] Hofstadter, *op. cit.*, p. 4.

[59] Stanley Pargellis, "The Theory of Balanced Government," in Read, *op. cit.*, p. 37. Italics added.

[60] For an account of Montesquieu's influence on the Founding Fathers, see Paul M. Spurlin, *Montesquieu in America, 1760-1801* (Baton Rouge: Louisiana State University Press, 1940).

would be unlikely to emerge. They believed that the people should have *a* voice but not *the* voice in the new government, and they hoped to create a political system in which the government could not take any particular action if any substantial minority were determined that it should not do so. Their whole analysis of the problem is succinctly expressed in the fifty-first *Federalist* paper:

It is of great importance in a republic not only to guard the society against the oppression of its rulers, but to guard one part of the society against the injustice of the other part. Different interests necessarily exist in different classes of citizens. If a majority be united by a common interest, the rights of the minority will be insecure. There are but two methods of providing against this evil: the one by creating a will in the community independent of the majority—that is, of the society itself; the other, by comprehending in the society so many separate descriptions of citizens as will render an unjust combination of a majority of the whole very improbable, if not impracticable. . . . The second method will be exemplified in the federal republic of the United States. Whilst all authority in it will be derived from and dependent on the society, the society itself will be broken into so many parts, interests and classes of citizens, that the rights of individuals, or of the minority, will be in little danger from interested combinations of the majority.[61]

Anti-Majoritarian Devices in the Constitution. In order to achieve the goals outlined above, the Founding Fathers wrote into the Constitution the following devices, all intended to prevent popular majorities (and "factions" or "parties" representing such majorities) from capturing control of the whole power of government.[62]

FEDERALISM. If "power is divided between the national and the state governments, each of which is supreme in its own sphere," then a popular majority bent on destroying property rights must capture control of not one but many governments in order to have its way over the whole nation.

SEPARATION OF POWERS. The power of the national government is distributed among the legislative, executive, and judicial branches, and the legislative power is further divided between two separate and independent houses. These agencies, moreover, are separate in three main respects: (1) *In personnel.* No person can hold office in more than one of the branches of government at any given time. (2) *In the manner of selection.* The members of each agency are selected in a different manner and by a different constituency from the others, the original plan having been for the representatives to be chosen by the voters directly (they were to be the only public officials so selected), senators by the state legislatures, the president by the electoral college (whose members were to be selected as the legislature of each state directed), and judges by presidential appointment with senatorial approval. (3) *In length and stagger-*

---

[61] *The Federalist*, Modern Library Edition (New York: Random House), p. 339.

[62] The standard accounts of the framing of the Constitution are: Charles Warren, *The Making of the Constitution* (Boston: Little, Brown and Company, 1928); Robert L. Schuyler, *The Constitution of the United States, An Historical Survey of Its Formation* (New York: The Macmillan Company, 1923); and, of course, Farrand's *Records*.

ing of fixed terms. Representatives serve for two years, and the entire House comes up for re-election every two years; senators serve for six years, but only one-third of them come up for re-election every two years; the president is elected every four years; and judges serve "during good behavior." In short, the Constitution reflects the framers' determination to make it impossible for the *entire* government to be replaced at any given election.

THE AMENDING PROCESS. By requiring the assent of two-thirds of both houses of Congress and of three-quarters of the states for any formal amendment to the Constitution, the framers provided that any substantial minority represented in either house of Congress or in a portion of the states could effectively block any change in the Constitution desired by a popular majority.

JUDICIAL REVIEW. Although the Constitution does not explicitly grant the courts the power to declare legislative and executive acts unconstitutional and therefore null and void, most historians agree that the Founding Fathers believed that the courts both should and would exercise such a power, so that John Marshall's famous assertion of the power in *Marbury v. Madison* (1803) was no "usurpation" but rather fully in accord with both the wishes and expectations of the framers.

The Development of the Constitution.[63] The Constitution and the politico-governmental system based upon it have, of course, undergone a number of changes since 1789. Among other things, we may note the fact that the national government now has more power vis-à-vis the states than it was thought to have then; the president, the courts, and the bureaucracy now have more power vis-à-vis Congress than they were intended to have; and not only does a far larger proportion of the adult population now have the vote than had it in 1789, but the voters, through such changes as the direct election of senators and the conversion of the electoral college into a rubber stamp for the voters' preferences, now play a more important role in selecting governmental personnel than the Founding Fathers assigned to them.

It cannot be said, however, that all these changes add up to a complete democratization and centralization of the constitutional system. Our present-day system retains a great many old devices and features, and has some new ones, that together make, formally speaking, a close approximation to what the framers intended it to be.

OUR PLURALISTIC POLITICS

How Public Policy Is Made in the United States. Most political scientists agree that when the investigator gets behind the formal-legal façade of the American governments and looks at the actual processes and forces that animate the formal structures, he finds that public policy is made in the United

---

[63] Two standard works on the development of the Constitution are: Alfred H. Kelly and Winfred A. Harbison, *The American Constitution: Its Origins and Development,* rev. ed. (New York: W. W. Norton and Company, Inc., 1955); and Carl B. Swisher, *American Constitutional Development,* 2nd ed. (Boston: Houghton Mifflin Company, 1954).

States for the most part by a process of conflict, bargaining, and ever-shifting and changing alliances among interest groups of all sizes, purposes, and degrees of organization.[64] Only on rare occasions, that is to say, does policy appear to be made in response to the wishes of a homogeneous, self-conscious popular majority made up of individuals acting as such, over the objections of a single opposed minority made up also of individuals acting as such. Consequently, while we can often correctly say that a particular elective official holds his office because a popular majority preferred him to his opponent in the preceding election, we can seldom say with equal accuracy that a particular public policy—flexible farm price-supports, the Marshall plan, reduction of military appropriations, or whatever—has been adopted because a definite popular majority clearly favored it. Majorities and minorities, in fact, almost never meet head on in the manner feared by the Founding Fathers. In recent years, only the debate about immigration policy that led to the McCarran-Walter Act and that about internal security that led to the present federal loyalty program seem to have been close to majority-minority clashes as traditionally conceived.

Our Modern "Concurrent Majority." In a recent penetrating and influential essay,[65] Peter F. Drucker argues that the "concurrent-majority" kind of political system advocated by John C. Calhoun in the 1850's and presumably made an anachronism by the Civil War [66] has in fact become the American way of making political decisions, albeit in a somewhat different form from that envisioned by Calhoun. Drucker, in support of his thesis, argues that each and every substantial interest group in American politics has a veto power over any move by any combination of the other groups which it feels is deeply inimical to its own interests—a "veto power" not in the sense of an ability to block completely any such move, but in the sense of an ability to force at the very least a watering down of the proposal's most obnoxious features and, sometimes at any rate, to prevent its passage in any form. Thus, for example, trade-union leaders were not able, in 1947, to block completely the passage of the Taft-Hartley Act; but they *were* able to get some of what they regarded

---

[64] The most general expositions of this conception of politics in America are Bentley, *op. cit.,* Truman, *op. cit.,* and Latham, *op. cit.* One sign of its general acceptance among present-day political scientists is the fact that it underlies the description of American government and politics in one of the most popular of the recent textbooks on the subject: James M. Burns and Jack W. Peltason, *Government by the People,* 2nd ed. (New York: Prentice-Hall, Inc., 1954). For a useful general description of the nature and activities of the leading organized interest groups, see Key, *op. cit.,* Chs. 2-6. Some informative descriptions of the activities of particular pressure groups are: Latham, *op. cit.;* Stephen K. Bailey, *Congress Makes a Law* (New York: Columbia University Press, 1950); Charles M. Hardin, *The Politics of Agriculture* (Glencoe, Ill.: The Free Press, 1952); Avery Leiserson, *Administrative Regulation, A Study in Representation of Interests* (Chicago: University of Chicago Press, 1942); Wesley McCune, *The Farm Bloc* (Garden City, N. Y.: Doubleday, Doran and Company, Inc., 1943); and Peter H. Odegard, *Pressure Politics: The Story of the Anti-Saloon League* (New York: Columbia University Press, 1928).

[65] Peter F. Drucker, "A Key to American Politics: Calhoun's Pluralism," *Review of Politics,* Vol. X (October, 1948), pp. 412-26.

[66] See pp. 124-26 for an account of Calhoun's ideas.

as its worst features (e.g., the prohibition of industry-wide bargaining and the prohibition of the union shop) struck out. And, for another example, the southern whites were not able, in 1954, to prevent the Supreme Court from outlawing racial segregation in southern public schools; but they were able to prevent the immediate and complete enforcement of the decision for a long time after it was made (at the present writing, eighteen months after the Court's decision, most southern schools remain as segregated as they ever were).

The other side of the picture, says Drucker, is that the public policies which *are* adopted and carried out are necessarily those that have successfully undergone a sort of political milling process. Each group that feels its interests are vitally involved in a particular proposal registers its views about what in the proposal it is willing to accept, what it can be forced to accept, and what it will under no conditions accept; and the final *actual* policy—as opposed, perhaps, to the *formal* policy (see our example of the results of the Supreme Court's anti-segregation decision)—is one that every major group is at least prepared to live with.

Drucker and other writers call this kind of political system "pluralism." [67] They believe that, as it functions in America, it is not any temporary and shameful deviation from the norms of our politico-governmental system but rather the latter's very essence. They believe that we depart from this way of making political decisions only during emergencies, such as wars and depressions, at which times we lapse into a kind of plebiscitary presidential dictatorship.[68] But "pluralism" and the modern "concurrent majority" are the *normal* modes of policy making in the United States, firmly supported by three main factors: (1) the party system, (2) the formal-governmental system, and, most important of all, (3) predominant American attitudes toward government and politics. We shall take up the first of these three factors in Chapter 22; and we shall complete the description of the American political environment in the present chapter by considering briefly the latter two.

PLURALISM IN THE FORMAL-GOVERNMENTAL STRUCTURE [69]

The American formal-governmental structure, as the Founding Fathers intended, does not provide any single locus of power which, once captured, will enable a single interest or party to impose its will upon all the other interests and parties in the nation. On the contrary, governmental power in the United States is notoriously broken into a great many fragments; and the interest or party that possesses any one or two or three of them can keep the others from

---

[67] Cf. Drucker, *op. cit.;* John Fischer, "Unwritten Rules of American Politics," *Harper's,* Vol. CXCVII (November, 1948), pp. 27-36; Riesman, *op. cit.,* pp. 236-44; and Williams, *American Society,* p. 262.

[68] Cf. Clinton L. Rossiter, *Constitutional Dictatorship* (Princeton: Princeton University Press, 1948).

[69] For a brief but suggestive general review of this subject, see Max Lerner, "Minority Rule and the Constitutional Tradition," in Read, *op. cit.,* pp. 191-207.

"ganging up." Moreover, the very fact that there are so many different positions of power to be won is one of the foremost forces preventing the creation in the first place of a single, unified, determined national majority. Such a majority, if it existed, would face a task calling for sustained effort over a number of years—long enough to capture control of *all* the agencies of *all* the governments, national, state, and local, that it would have to control in order to impose its will uniformly throughout the entire nation. Consequently, the lesser groups and interests that would have to join together—and keep themselves mobilized and determined—for such a purpose usually settle for less grandiose but far more attainable goals, namely, capturing control of one agency here and another there. Among the most important devices fragmenting formal-governmental power in the United States today are the following.

Federalism. Despite the increase in the national government's power since 1789, a great many important matters are still dealt with largely or entirely at the state and local levels regardless of the national government's wishes—for example, most of the regulation of nominations, elections, and the franchise, marriage and divorce, education, insurance, contracts, tort liability, licensing of professions and occupations, incorporation of businesses, etc. The national government, moreover, is itself not a dinosaur intent on swallowing up the states; state and local interests, on the contrary, are strongly represented *within* the national government, particularly in Congress, where most representatives and senators pay attention to the interests of their districts and states first and—if there be such a thing in contradistinction to the totality of these local interests—to the interests of the nation as a whole second.[70] Political scientists who believe that "federalism is obsolete"[71] may deplore this state of affairs, but few deny its existence.

Separation of Powers. As we noted above, the Founding Fathers intended separation of powers, fixed terms of office, and the staggered calendar of elections to make it as difficult as possible for any single faction or party to capture control of the whole power of the national government at any one time. While these institutions certainly do not work today just as the men of 1787 intended, they still serve to fragment power in such a way that mutual hostility and resistance among the various branches and agencies is the normal situation in Washington. Swift and cooperative action by all branches and agencies takes place only in times of great national emergency or on those rare occasions when no major interest considers itself sufficiently endangered by a particular proposal to exercise its threat of veto. Many observers have noted that Congress usually acts as though it had a vested interest in resisting presidential leadership and maintaining its own independence;[72] and, while the present

70 Cf. Ernest S. Griffith, *Congress: Its Contemporary Role* (New York: New York University Press, 1951), pp. 139-46.

71 Cf. Harold J. Laski, "The Obsolescence of Federalism," *The New Republic*, May 3, 1939, pp. 367-69.

72 See pp. 402-05 for our discussion of the barriers to effective presidential leadership.

Supreme Court seems, for the moment at least, to regard its power to restrain presidential and congressional action by judicial review as almost in abeyance, it has kicked up its heels on at least one occasion in recent years—when it overruled President Truman's seizure of the steel mills in 1952. Bicameralism, moreover, has combined with separation of powers both in the national government and in many of the states to make for frequent divided party control of the various branches.[73] Separation of powers, in short, still operates to a considerable extent as the framers intended, in that "each department [has] a will of its own," each branch has "the necessary means *and personal motives* to resist encroachments of the others," and the nation is rarely confronted with the possibility of a situation in which "if a majority be united by a common interest, the rights of the minority will be insecure." [74]

The Committee System of Congress. Most students of Congress agree that neither house has a single tightly knit body of leaders possessing the power to ram through whatever legislative program it desires. Power in both houses is largely distributed among the various standing and special committees, each of which has what comes close to complete power over the shape of legislation in its assigned subject-matter area. Drucker suggests that the committees retain their power mainly because "only in the quiet and secrecy of a committee room can sectional compromise be worked out. The discussion on the floor as well as the recorded vote is far too public and therefore largely for the folks back home." [75]

The Filibuster and Threat of Filibuster. In Chapter 8 we noted that the absence of an effective cloture rule in the Senate means that each individual senator, Senate coalition, and Senate committee must always bear in mind the ever-present possibility that an opposing faction may filibuster to death any proposal it is dead set against. This situation constitutes one of the most extreme fragmentations of power and therefore one of the most effective minority veto powers in the entire national governmental system; and it forces each Senate coalition to draw its legislative proposals in such a way that no opposition faction will be so dead set against them as to resort to a filibuster. Despite the relatively unfavorable publicity the filibuster has received, however, it is *not* a strange and inappropriate departure from the basic principles of our formal-governmental system; it is, on the contrary, one more—and an extremely effective—way of fragmenting power, and therefore one of the most powerful weapons a Senate minority and the interests it represents can use to protect themselves against a majority. As we have tried to show in the preceding paragraphs, the American politico-governmental system offers many

[73] Cf. pp. 415-16.

[74] These quotations are taken from the fifty-first *Federalist* paper. Italics added.

[75] *Op. cit.,* p. 415. The classical analysis of the power and role of congressional committees is Woodrow Wilson, *Congressional Government* (Boston: Houghton Mifflin Company, 1885). Wilson's analysis is in many respects supported by such studies as Gross, *op. cit.,* and Griffith, *op. cit.*

such weapons, and fragmentation rather than concentration of power is today, as in 1789, one of the system's basic principles.

American Attitudes Toward Government

How do the American people feel about our pluralistic political system and our complex, decentralized, and fragmented governmental system? Do they hunger for a simpler, more centralized, and more majoritarian system, or are they satisfied with the situation pretty much as it stands? The answers to these questions are clearly fundamental to an understanding of the American political environment and the party system that operates within it, and to any consideration of proposals for changing either the environment or the parties or both.

In the present writers' opinion, by far the most powerful single force sustaining and perpetuating our pluralistic politics is the American belief system. Our main reasons for thinking so are as follows.

First, the American belief system, as we pointed out above, is of such a nature that on most issues popular majorities—each with a common understanding of the particular issue, a common decision to place that issue above all others, and a passionate desire to have its way—simply do not often arise. For each popular majority is itself composed of subgroups, each of which holds many beliefs and values in common with the opposition groups *and* many conflicting beliefs and values among its own members and as between itself and the other groups associated with it on the particular issue. The American belief system, in other words, makes for popular majorities that are *themselves* products of pluralistic bargaining and compromise, and are not, therefore, prepared to force through their own programs regardless of the feelings of the opposition. *Political majorities in America tend to be cross sections, not segments, of the community.*

Second, one of the most important elements of the American belief system is that which places a high value on "liberty" and "minority rights," and never mind whether this is logically inconsistent with that other element of the belief system that values "majority rule." In the words of the late Dean McBain:

As for the United States, despite relatively slight modifications from time to time, and despite our recrudescent vocal explosions against the occasional concrete operation of this or that check, belief in popular sovereignty itself stands little if any higher in our accepted articles of political faith than loyal adherence to this check and balance system. This is by no means an outworn and abandoned tenet in our fundamentalist creed.[76]

[76] Howard L. McBain, *The Living Constitution* (New York: The Macmillan Company, 1941), pp. 200-01. Used with the permission of the Macmillan Company. This edition is a reprint of the first edition, published in 1927 by the Workers Education Bureau Press.

And if one is tempted to exclaim, "But the people *can't* believe in *both* popular sovereignty *and* checks and balances—they're logically contradictory!" the answer, as Dean McBain suggests, is simply: Ah, but they *do!*

Third, most of the evidence we have as to how the American people feel about their governmental system indicates that most of them are quite satisfied with it and highly suspicious of attempts to make major changes in it. When, for example, President Roosevelt attempted to "tamper with the independence of the courts" with his "court-packing scheme" of 1937, he was roundly defeated—although, in typically pluralistic fashion, the Court also soon began to sustain rather than strike down New Deal legislation. Public opinion polls taken at the time all showed substantial majorities against his plan and in favor of maintaining our traditional system of judicial review.[77] In Chapter 12 we noted, for another example, that presidential attempts to influence local nominations have uniformly failed unless they enlisted the aid of the local party organizations; and public opinion polls taken during Roosevelt's attempted "purge" of anti–New Deal congressmen in 1938 all showed majorities of over 60 per cent *against* any such attempt to interfere in local matters.[78] And in Chapter 8, for another example, we observed that the attempt by some senators in 1949 to do away with filibusters by instituting a more effective cloture rule resulted in a *less* effective rule and in establishing the filibuster even more solidly than before.

All of this is not to say that the American people are, completely and all the time, satisfied with their politico-governmental system in all its details and that no change of any sort in it is possible; for the majoritarian elements in our belief system are bound to lead to a certain amount of popular dissatisfaction with the system and its results, especially in times of national emergency. The point is that our pluralistic and to some extent anti-majoritarian governmental system is highly appropriate to and amply sustained by the many anti-majoritarian aspects of the American belief system, by the peculiar kind of low-degree consensus that that belief system permits, and by the whole American political environment within which the American politico-governmental system—*and* the party system—operates; and all of these factors set very real limits upon the nature and dimensions of any change that is likely to be made in either the governmental system or the party system.

[77] Cf. Cantril, *op. cit.*, Nos. 1, 4, 5, 9, and 15 on pp. 148-50.
[78] Cf. *ibid.*, Nos. 2, 14, 17, and 19 on pp. 933-34.

Chapter 21

THE NATURE AND ROLE OF THE AMERICAN PARTY SYSTEM

Our examination of the American party system to this point has of necessity been conducted as a series of related but partial glimpses of various aspects of that system; like the three blind men, we have seized hold of the elephant wherever we could grasp him, and the net impression we have received has been of a series of parts, not of the whole. Our task in the present chapter is to attempt, in the light of what has gone before, a more rounded description of the essential nature of the American party system and its role in American life and politics.

The reader is once again warned, before embarking on this summary, that we are here speaking of "the" American party system as the sum of the national, state, and local party systems, which, as we have often pointed out, may be of either the two-party, one-party, modified one-party, or multiple-party type.

Leading Characteristics of the Major Parties

DECENTRALIZATION

Probably the most striking single characteristic of the Democratic and Republican parties in most areas and at most levels of government is their *decentralization*. Each party is a congeries of autonomous and semi-autonomous local groups of party leaders, workers, and supporters; and while these local groups in each party bear the common label "Democratic" or "Republican," this does not mean there is any common superior who stands over against them all in a posture of *command*. In other words, most Republican and Democratic parties—and especially the national parties—are structurally more like a coalition or alliance among independent sovereign nations than an army with command power flowing downward and obedience obligations flowing upward through a hierarchy.

In Chapters 9-17 we found decentralization to be characteristic of almost every aspect of the parties' organization and activities. The following will serve as illustrations.

Decentralization in the Formal-Legal Organization of the Parties. The numerous committees, caucuses, conventions, and officers that together make up the formal-legal organization of a major party are not—either in theory, in law, or in fact—arranged in a neat, pyramidal-hierarchical structure of super-ordination and subordination. On the contrary, the relevant statutes in most states make each party agency at each "level" of organization more or less independent of the others, and the national conventions, sometimes mistakenly described as the "supreme governing bodies" of the national parties, are authorized only to make rules governing their own proceedings and those of the national committees and other national agencies. They have little or no power, formal or actual, over state and local party agencies.

Decentralization in Their Informal Organization. Neither American national major party, and few state parties, have "bosses," in the sense of being headed by leaders or groups of leaders enjoying the power to "command" and "be obeyed" by all the lesser party leaders and workers within their respective organizations. The incidence of command power appears to be higher in city and county party organizations than on the higher levels. But even the local "bosses" are for the most part independent of each other and of the state and national leaders, so that the "informal" organization of the parties is hardly less decentralized than the "formal."

Decentralization in Nominations and Elections. In the United States all elective officers except the president and vice-president are elected by *sub-national* constituencies—states, congressional districts, legislative districts, municipalities, wards, etc. Primary responsibility for and control over the processes by which each is selected tends, accordingly, to reside in the subnational party organizations operating in each constituency. The local organization, not the national, decides who gets the party's nomination (as witness what happens when national party leaders attempt to control local nominations by any means other than that of enlisting the help of the local organizations); even presidential and vice-presidential nominations, moreover, are made by coalitions of state and local party leaders, not by all-powerful groups of national leaders. The state and local organizations also have the last say about campaign strategy and tactics, and about the conduct of election organization and machinery within their particular bailiwicks. In a given presidential campaign they may well decide to follow the national organization's plan of battle; but no one can *make* them do so.

Decentralization in Their Conduct of Government. The various party agencies operating in Congress and in the state legislatures—caucuses, steering committees, floor leaders, etc.—do not constitute a chain of command and obedience any more than the extragovernmental party agencies. Presidential and gubernatorial *party*—as opposed to executive—leadership is, moreover, most of the time and in both the national and most state governments, a matter of cajolery and persuasion rather than of power to issue commands, apply sanctions, and exact obedience.

HETEROGENEITY AND REPRESENTATIVENESS

Each major party draws at least some of its leaders, workers, "members," and electoral support from *each* major group in the population—rich and poor, Negro and white, Catholic and Protestant, business, farm, labor, etc.—though neither party, of course, draws on each *in the same proportion* as the other party. Neither party, that is to say, is all-Negro or all-Catholic or all-poor; nor does either receive the support of all the Negroes, all the Catholics, or all the poor. Both, like the general population itself, are *heterogeneous,* and one of them is in as good a position as the other to regard itself as "representative" of the general population—in the sense that it attempts, with some degree of success, to attract persons of all types to its membership and leadership.

MODERATION AND INCONSISTENCY

Each major party directs its appeals in most areas to *all* the community's major groups and interests, being careful to leave none out. This fact, as we would expect, is reflected in its program, that is, its public stands on issues. The programs of both are always, for one thing, *moderate,* and clearly based on the strategic principle of offering *no* group *everything* it wants, and yet offering *every* group *something* of what it wants (this "something" being, the party hopes, at least enough to attract a considerable number of the group's members, and bring them to its support). The programs of both, for another thing, always tend to a certain amount of inconsistency and equivocation, ignoring altogether issues that seem to be so divisive that any kind of "middle" position will alienate more voters than it will attract. Unreconstructed extremists who insist on their party's taking an extreme stand on any issue soon find themselves obligated to choose between moderating their views, or at least keeping quiet about them, and ceasing to exercise influence on the party's deliberations and decisions.

Almost invariably there is considerable logical inconsistency among the various appeals and proposals in the programs and platforms of each major party. The explanation is simple. Each major voting group has goals and demands that differ to some extent from the goals and demands of all the other groups. If a party's program clearly promised to satisfy the demands of voting group A, groups B and C would be dissatisfied, and perhaps flock to the support of the opposition party. So the former party promises to satisfy the demands of groups B and C as well, even though such promises are logically inconsistent with what it has already promised group A. Neither party, in other words, hesitates to put forward such pairs of appeals as "a national fair-employment-practices law" and "states' rights," "more social security" and "lower taxes," "parity prices for the farmer" and "lower food prices for the consumer"; and neither party can be greatly embarrassed—especially since both do it—by someone's directing attention to such inconsistencies in its program.

SIMILARITIES AND DIFFERENCES

The Republican and Democratic parties are alike in yet other respects. Both are committed to maintaining America's present form of government; neither advocates any root-and-branch changes in our economic system; and both hold the general American belief system that we described in Chapter 20. Each party's program and candidates, accordingly, always closely resemble the other's, and no contest between them ever presents the voter with un-equivocal, black-and-white choices—that is, choices that force him to put his bets on, say, capitalism as opposed to socialism, centralization as opposed to decentralization, or racial equality as opposed to the status quo in race rela-tions. The parties' very names symbolize their *similarities,* not their differences. As D. W. Brogan points out:

> The fact that all Republicans claim to be democrats and all Democrats to be republicans, makes the confusion of party names nearly complete. There may be significance, too, in the fact that parties with more meaningful names, negative or positive, the Anti-Masonic party, the Free Soil party . . . have never, except in the case of the Progressives in 1912, looked like having any chance of national success and, for the most part, died within an election or two of their birth.[1]

We must not, however, leap to the conclusion, as observers sometimes do, that the parties are *identical* and present the voters with no meaningful choices whatever—that they are, in Lord Bryce's phrase, "two bottles, each having a label denoting the kind of liquor it contains, but each being empty." [2] American *voters,* certainly, seem to shy away from this conclusion, since, as we noted in Chapter 9, a high proportion of them regard the parties as *differ-ent enough* to warrant a greater or lesser feeling of "identification" with the one or the other. No major stratum of the population, to be sure, regularly and unanimously supports either party. But the Republican party, according to recent empirical studies, usually carries with it most persons with high in-comes, most persons with a high level of formal education, most persons liv-ing in rural and suburban areas, most Protestants, and most persons in the older age groups; and the Democratic party carries with it most persons with low incomes, most persons with a low level of formal education, most persons

---

[1] D. W. Brogan, *Politics in America* (New York: Harper and Brothers, 1954), p. 47. See also pp. 451-52 in this book.

[2] James Bryce, *The American Commonwealth,* rev. ed. (New York: The Macmillan Company, 1911), Vol. II, p. 29.

living in metropolitan areas, most Negroes, most Catholics, and most persons in the younger age groups.[3]

If most voters feel that there *are* differences between the Republicans and the Democrats, the next question to ask is, What, concretely, do these voters say when asked what the differences are? The most complete answer we have to this question comes from the Survey Research Center of the University of Michigan, which in 1952 interviewed a national sample of 1,614 citizens about the good and bad points of each major party. On the basis of their respondents' answers, the SRC researchers offered the following conclusions regarding "the voters' perceptions of the parties": More respondents offered comments, favorable *and* unfavorable, on the Democrats than on the Republicans, which suggests that the former have made a deeper impression *as a party* than the latter. The comments indicated that voters tend to regard the Democrats as the party of economic prosperity, the party that bids for and wins the support of certain specific groups (the "comman man," workers, farmers), and the party of maximum involvement in foreign affairs. And they tend to regard the Republicans as less dependent than the Democrats on the support of specific groups (only a few described the GOP as the party of the rich and privileged), and more committed than the Democrats to certain general principles (economy in government, lower taxes, deflation, and a reduction of our commitments abroad). Few respondents answered that the parties are completely unlike, or that they are identical.[4]

VARIATIONS IN COHESION FROM SITUATION TO SITUATION

Some students of the American party system are much concerned about the so-called "low degree of cohesion" displayed by the major parties, particularly at the national level, and the consequent fact that they cannot be held responsible *as parties* for what the government does or does not do. There is evidence, however, which points to a somewhat different—and more complex—conclusion, which is that the parties show different degrees of cohesion from situation to situation, and that a correct picture of them is to be had only by identifying the situations in which they show a high degree of cohesion, those in which they show a lesser degree, and those in which they show little or

[3] Cf. Paul F. Lazarsfeld, Bernard Berelson, and Hazel Gaudet, *The People's Choice*, 2nd ed. (New York: Columbia University Press, 1948), Ch. III; Bernard Berelson, Paul F. Lazarsfeld, and William N. McPhee, *Voting* (Chicago: University of Chicago Press, 1954), Chs. III and IV; and Angus Campbell, Gerald Gurin, and Warren E. Miller, *The Voter Decides* (Evanston, Ill.: Row, Peterson and Company, 1954), pp. 70-73. See also Heinz Eulau, "Perceptions of Class and Party in Voting Behavior: 1952," *American Political Science Review*, Vol. XLIX (June, 1955), pp. 364-84.
[4] Campbell, Gurin, and Miller, *op. cit.*, pp. 42-52. In 1944, the *Fortune* poll asked its respondents, "Do you feel that the Republican and Democratic parties mainly stand for the same thing, or that they stand for quite different things?" The answers were as follow: "mainly the same," 46.2 per cent; "quite different," 41.7 per cent; "don't know," 12.1 per cent: Reprinted in Hadley Cantril, ed., *Public Opinion, 1935-1946* (Princeton: Princeton University Press, 1951), No. 51 on p. 581.

none. Let us briefly review the available facts which point to this interpretation.

Both parties at all levels, national, state, and local, are normally far more cohesive in activities related to the *selection of governmental personnel* than in those related to the *formulation of public policy*. During most election campaigns most party leaders and workers set aside their differences, close ranks, and work together loyally and cooperatively to elect the party's ticket from top to bottom. ("Bolting the ticket," as we have seen above, is *the* unforgivable sin for a party leader or worker to commit; and they are careful to avoid even the appearance of it.) And in Congress and many state legislatures all the members of the party are always lined up against all the members of the other party on such matters as the selection of presiding officers and the allocation of committee posts and chairmanships.

On matters of public policy, however, we find markedly different degrees of cohesion from one governmental area to another, and from issue to issue within each governmental area—in other words, according to where we look. On certain issues, for instance, the parties in Congress usually adopt sharply different positions, and usually show a high degree of cohesion with respect to them. On other issues party lines are normally weaker, though still detectable. And on still other issues, party lines usually break down altogether. In some states—Connecticut and New York, for example—party cohesion in the legislature is very high on almost all issues; in others—such as Illinois and Pennsylvania—it is much weaker; and in still others—notably most of the modified one-party and one-party states—party lines usually mean little or nothing in legislative votes on policy matters. Both parties at most levels of government, to be sure, are markedly less cohesive on *all* matters of public policy than are the parties of the other democracies (Great Britain and France) for which we have comparable data. And certainly our major parties at most levels are less cohesive than the advocates of "responsible party government" wish them to be. The fact remains, however, that to speak of them as having a low degree of cohesion, and let it go at that, is highly inaccurate.

Why American Parties Are as They Are

The following pages will present, and attempt to explain and document, this main thesis: American political parties are as they are—and unlike, say, British parties or French parties or South African parties—because they originated and developed in *American* rather than British or French or South African conditions, and because they operate today in the *American* rather than the British or the French or the South African political environment. In Chapter 5 we examined the conditions in which American parties originated and evolved, and in Chapter 20 we observed the political environment within which they operate at the present time. Let us now look more closely at some ways in which this environment has shaped, and continues to shape, the parties.

THE INFLUENCE OF THE FORMAL-GOVERNMENTAL SYSTEM [5]

Federalism. The United States possesses not one but forty-nine governments, each of which, constitutionally and actually, possesses an area of power and activity in which the other forty-eight observably do not interfere. This situation affects the nature of our party system in at least the following ways:

First, *it makes for decentralized parties.* Most of the laws that regulate party membership, organization, nominating machinery, electoral machinery, campaigning activities, and finance are *state,* not federal, enactments. The first concern of any party organization, therefore, must be with the government of the state within which it operates; for what that state's governor, legislature, and courts do can be literally a life-and-death matter for the state's parties. All elections, moreover, are conducted within statewide constituencies or smaller ones (even the president is elected by a series of statewide constituencies rather than by one great national constituency). The states, therefore, have for some purposes a far more direct impact on and interest for the parties than does the national government; and each state party has to assign top priority to the problems it faces in its state, and can direct its energies into the problems it faces nationally only when, and to the extent that, everything is under control at home. Federalism, in short, is the *main* reason why each national party is a loose confederation of state and local parties rather than a unitary national organization with state and local subdivisions.

Secondly, *federalism encourages the parties to concentrate on winning elections rather than on making policy.* The fact that we have not one government but forty-nine, each with its elected executive and legislature, and each with its many local governments and local elected officials, gives us as a matter of course a vast number of elective offices to fill in the nation and in each state. The parties' nomination-making and election-contesting activities, accordingly, call for coordinated effort by what amounts to vast armies, which never have enough officers and soldiers to perform all the tasks these activities call for and have, therefore, good reason to leave alone matters—such as internal quarrels over questions of public policy—that might divide them and so make these tasks more difficult to get done. Suppose, moreover, that a national party *did* decide that more than anything else it wanted the nation to adopt a certain *policy*—equal rights for all races, public ownership of the railroads, abolition of the income tax, or whatever—and suppose it won control of the presidency, the Congress, and the national Supreme Court. It still could not enforce that policy uniformly throughout the land, for each of these policies

---

[5] Some general discussions of the influence of the formal-governmental system on the nature of American parties are: J. Allen Smith, *The Spirit of American Government* (New York: The Macmillan Company, 1907), pp. 208-14, 226-27; Peter H. Odegard and E. Allen Helms, *American Politics,* 2nd ed. (New York: Harper and Brothers, 1947), pp. 124-30; Dayton D. McKean, *Party and Pressure Politics* (Boston: Houghton Mifflin Company, 1949), pp. 29-46; Norton E. Long, "Party and Constitution," *Journal of Politics,* Vol. III (May, 1941), pp. 198-209; and E. Allen Helms, "The Presidency and Party Politics," in Robert S. Rankin, ed., *The Presidency in Transition* (Gainesville, Fla.: The Journal of Politics, 1949), pp. 46-64.

relates to a sphere in which the states have considerable power. The party would, therefore, have either to capture control of all forty-eight state governments, or, one way or another, take away from the states their powers over the matter in question, thus moving us away from federalism. For the present, at least, neither of these alternatives is realistic, and the national parties always settle for something considerably short of a uniform national policy on matters over which there are strong differences of opinion among the various states and sections.

Separation of Powers. Not only is governmental power in the United States divided among forty-nine governments, but within each of these governments it is further divided among the executive, the two houses of the legislature (except in Nebraska, where there is only one house), the courts, and (actually if not formally) the bureaucracy. Within most houses of most legislatures, moreover, power is further divided among the various standing and special committees. In short, no American government has what all the *parliamentary* democracies have, namely, a *single* locus of power, the possession of which gives a party with a majority full control over the entire government. Thus separation of powers, like federalism, makes it difficult for the majority party to ram through its program regardless of opposition even if it tries to. The parties, accordingly, have here a further sound reason for concentrating on controlling the personnel rather than on making the policies of government.

Separation of powers also results, from time to time, in a situation unknown to the parliamentary democracies, that is, a situation where control of the different branches of the government is over a considerable period divided between the parties. In Chapter 17 we noted the following facts in this connection. Divided control has obtained in the national government almost a third of the time since 1868. In many states—especially those in which party competition is keenest—divided party control has been even more common than in the national government. In such prominent states as California, Connecticut, Massachusetts, New Jersey, New York, and Wisconsin the Democratic party has *never* controlled the governorship and both houses of the legislature at the same time. And the ever-present possibility of such divided control tends to keep a party temporarily in control of both the executive and the legislature from relying solely on its own resources to force its program through regardless of the opposition's wishes and feelings. As Key and Silverman sum it up:

> The combination of party system, separated powers, and over-representation of the non-metropolitan estate often makes irrelevant any conception of party collaboration in the operation of government or any theory of party accountability for its conduct.[6]

[6] V. O. Key, Jr., and Corinne Silverman, "Party and Separation of Powers: A Panorama of Practice in the States," in Carl J. Friedrich and J. Kenneth Galbraith, eds., *Public Policy* (Cambridge, Mass.: Graduate School of Public Administration, Harvard University, 1954), p. 406.

Fixed Terms, Staggered Elections, and Frequent Elections. The timing of elections in the United States is determined, in Herring's words, "by the movement of celestial bodies . . . rather than in accordance with the demands of current issues." [7] In other words, if an election is by law scheduled for such-and-such a date, it is held on that date regardless of whether there happens to be at the moment great public interest in governmental affairs; and, by the same token, if the voters are up in arms about a particular issue or set of issues but no election is scheduled at the time, they have to bide their time until the calendar gives them a chance to "throw the rascals out." Fixed terms of office mean that there is no necessary relationship between the holding of an election and a high level of current popular interest in governmental affairs. And if a low level of interest happens to coincide with an election, the parties—which, remember, have to get out their voters one way or another if they hope to win—must somehow drum up some interest. This not only affects the nature of our campaigns, but also the nature of our parties. As Professor Ewing puts it:

If the country is not in political crisis and there are no really pressing issues, apparent differences must be manufactured. Political blockbusters are rained upon the public. The people must be awakened! The country must be saved from purely imaginary perils. . . . Generally, there is an atmosphere of artificiality, which no doubt contributes to lack of voter interest and to an increase in the influence of traditionalism in the voter support of party candidates. . . . To conduct campaigns which ignore issues, or present merely fictitious ones, means, therefore, that the controversies and differences occur in the legislative halls rather than in the constituencies and renders indistinctive the party label as a criterion of a legislator's views upon political subjects.[8]

Most American governments, moreover, have *staggered* elections—i.e., the terms of officers are, as a matter of deliberate constitutional policy, different from post to post, so that not all the officials are replaced at the same time; and elections for some are held at different times from elections for others. The national government is the extreme instance here, but each of the state constitutions phases elections to a greater or lesser degree.[9] In very few American elections, then, can the voters turn *all* the rascals out, since in any given election only part of them can be got at. And this of course has the effect of reducing still further a party's chances of capturing the *whole* power of a government in any single election, and thus further limits the "responsibility" it can be expected to assume for how the *whole* government is run.

The American calendar of elections is such that the longest period be-

<hr>

[7] E. Pendleton Herring, *The Politics of Democracy* (New York: Rinehart & Company, Inc., 1940), p. 290.

[8] Cortez A. M. Ewing, *Congressional Elections, 1896-1944* (Norman: University of Oklahoma Press, 1947), pp. 28-29.

[9] Cf. E. Pendleton Herring, *Presidential Leadership* (New York: Rinehart & Company, Inc., 1940), pp. 23-24.

tween elections in any area is two years, and the parties in most areas are confronted with *some* kind of election—for state, local, or national officers—*every* year and sometimes several in a single year. Thus the parties hardly have time to finish all their post-election chores following one campaign (contesting recounts, paying off campaign bills, etc.) before they have to start making nominations, gathering funds, and lining up their organizations for the next. To sum up, the sheer *frequency* of American elections and the great *volume* of offices to be contested for encourage the parties to devote their attention and energies largely if not exclusively to making nominations and contesting elections, rather than to formulating public policy.

The Direct Primary. In Chapter 12 we noted that most nominations for most offices—local, state, *and* national—are made by direct primary. This means that the last word as to who gets the nominations and thus bears the parties' labels rests, legally at least, *with the party voters in each state and local constituency.* This affects the American party system in a number of ways, of which we now take special notice:

(1) A party's *national* leaders can affect the kind of representatives and senators who come to Washington bearing the party's label only by enlisting the support of the state and local party organizations concerned; and they cannot be sure of doing so even then. Assume, for example, that the local leaders have decided to support the national leaders in an attempt to block the renomination of a maverick congressman, and are doing all they can. There is still nothing to prevent the rank and file, who may admire the incumbent's "independence," from ignoring the leaders' wishes and renominating him. The direct primary, in other words, is *par excellence* a system for maintaining *local* control of nominations; and as long as American localities continue to be so different from one another in economic interests, culture, and political attitudes, the national parties are likely to retain their present ideological heterogeneity and their tendency to show differing degrees of cohesion from issue to issue.[10]

(2) D. W. Brogan suggests, indeed, that the general adoption of the direct primary in the first two decades of the twentieth century may well have prevented the kind of party realignment that some observers regard as desirable. As he puts it:

The direct primary turned the flank of the historically inexpungeable party system. Voters in South Carolina, voters in Wisconsin still cast their ballots for the nominee of the sacred Democratic (or Republican) party. But the real election became the primary. In the contest for the nomination, the formal unity of the party was disregarded; live issues, local and national, were fought over. Reality was restored to local and national politics and, in very different parts of the country, very similar programmes of legislation and administration were put into effect. Mere appeals to the memory of Lincoln or Lee did not work in the decisive election, the primary. The victor, of course, was sound on Lincoln (or on Lee) but he might

[10] Herring, *Presidential Leadership,* pp. 24-25.

be very unsound on other more recent personalities and problems than those made classical during and after "the war." [11]

The direct primary, in other words, enables voters who share a common loyalty to a particular party but differ sharply on other matters to test their relative strength at the polls without compromising their party loyalty; and it does this by providing them machinery for conducting their fights *within* the party. Without the direct primary they would have either to ignore and repress their differences or bring about a situation where respective strength could be tested in a fight *between* the parties.

(3) There is some reason to believe, as we noted in Chapter 12, that the direct primary, by permitting voters to fight out disagreements *within* each party, has encouraged a trend toward one-partyism in certain parts of the United States. In the absence of the direct primary, contending blocs of voters within a dominant party might well be tempted to transfer their allegiance from it to the second party, and the latter would see to it that they did not lack inducements for doing so. With the direct primary, however, the dominant party is often able to hold its members, and, increasingly, to attract most able young men who are thinking of going into politics, and thus progressively weaken the leadership and lessen the attractiveness of the second party. A modified one-party area, as a result of this process, can little by little transform itself into a one-party area.

The Electoral-College System. The national presidency, the greatest single electoral prize in American politics, is captured, strictly speaking, not by winning a majority of the popular votes in the whole nation but by winning popular *pluralities* in enough *states* to build up a total of 266 or more votes in the electoral college. "Carrying the nation," in other words, means carrying a sufficient number of states. Consequently, the national parties to a considerable extent plan their campaign strategies and set up their campaign organizations on a state-by-state basis rather than on an across-the-board national basis. Their appeals for votes, moreover, are always combinations of general national appeals and appeals aimed at particular states or sections. In 1952, for example, the Republicans talked everywhere about "communism, corruption, and Korea," but they made it their business to talk also about offshore oil in the Gulf states, states' rights in the South, civil rights in the industrial states, parity in Minnesota, and social security in southern California; and the Democrats, while they talked everywhere about "prosperity" and the "gains of the New Deal and Fair Deal," rang the changes on civil rights in New York, public power in Oregon and Washington, and the TVA in Tennessee. Any programmatic "mandate" the winning party may have had when the election was over, therefore, was neither entirely national nor entirely sectional.

Each major party, moreover, normally launches its drive for votes from a "home base," that is, certain states and sections in which it traditionally has

---

[11] *Op. cit.,* p. 66; see also pp. 67-68.

the upper hand—the South and the big cities for the Democrats, and the predominantly rural states and sections for the Republicans. And both parties tend to neglect these traditionally "solid" states and sections, choosing instead to direct their appeals to and concentrate their campaigning activities and expenditures in the "critical" or "marginal" states and sections that may go either way. This not only causes the *amount* of campaigning to vary from state to state and from section to section, and helps to keep the two-party areas two-party and the one-party areas one-party; it also encourages decentralization of party organizations and discourages any move in the direction of programs without internal inconsistencies.[12]

The Influence of the Formal-Governmental System: A Summary. The basic organizing principle of the American formal-governmental system, as we observed in Chapter 20, is the *fragmentation, dispersion, and counterbalancing of power.* It reflects an intention on the part of the framers of the Constitution to make it impossible for any single interest group—particularly one representing a popular majority—to seize the whole power of government over the whole nation and work its will at the expense of all other interests and groups. The formal government is therefore *decentralized,* both as among the national government and the state governments and as among the various formal agencies within each of these governments; and nowhere in the governmental system is there a single locus of power to issue commands and receive obedience from all governmental officials everywhere.

This is the system our political parties work with and within. To a considerable extent it determines the character and dimensions of their tasks, defines the conditions under which those tasks must be performed, and places limits upon what they can do. It is not surprising, then, that the national parties are, like the formal-governmental system, decentralized as among their national and state and local organizations and as among the various party agencies within any constituency; or that, again like the formal government, the parties lack leaders or groups of leaders who have the power to issue commands and exact obedience over the entire nation. The formal-governmental system, though only one of several aspects of the political environment that shape American parties, undoubtedly accounts for many of their most prominent characteristics.[13]

THE INFLUENCE OF THE COMMUNITY AND ITS BELIEF SYSTEM

Professor E. E. Schattschneider takes sharp issue with the idea put forward in the preceding paragraph; and so does the Committee on Political Parties of the American Political Science Association. Schattschneider writes:

[12] Cf. Alexander Heard, *A Two-Party South?* (Chapel Hill: University of North Carolina Press, 1952), pp. 174-75.

[13] Cf. Arthur N. Holcombe, *Our More Perfect Union* (Cambridge, Mass.: Harvard University Press, 1950), p. 189; Brogan, *op. cit.,* p. 33; and Herring, *Presidential Leadership,* pp. 25-26.

Nor are there grounds for excessive pessimism about the possibilities of inte-grating party government with the constitutional system. The greatest difficulties in the way of the development of party government in the United States have been intellectual, not legal. It is not unreasonable to suppose that once a respectable sec-tion of the public understands the issue, ways of promoting party government through the Constitution can be found.[14]

Professor Schattschneider, as the passage just quoted makes clear, as-sumes the desirability of "party government," which he believes we have not yet adopted because not enough Americans understand the issue between it and what we now have. He and the members of the committee think poorly, in other words, of the kind of parties we have described in the foregoing chapters, and believe that other Americans would think poorly of them too if they were better informed. In short, these writers contend that the parties (and the formal-governmental system)—*as they are now*—are *not* appropriate to the governing system the American people really want. And they are con-vinced that our present parties are a serious obstacle in the path of our achiev-ing that governing system.

Others—including Pendleton Herring, Herbert Agar, Ernest S. Griffith, and the present writers—contend, however, that the present nature of the American party system is determined not only by the decentralized formal-governmental system within which it must operate, but, even more, by the nature of the American community and the American belief system. And they are convinced that our present parties *are* appropriate to the governing system the American people really want.

Let us look now at some of the ways in which the nature of the party system is influenced by the nature of the American community and belief system.

Heterogeneity of the Population. In Chapter 20 we noted that the American people are—ethnically, occupationally, religiously, educationally, economically, and in many other ways—perhaps the most heterogeneous national population in the world. This means, for one thing, that when the parties plan their slates of candidates and their appeals to the voters, they do not confront a few large, definite, homogeneous, and ideologically consistent voting groups whose prefer-ences, habits, and prejudices are well understood and whose behavior is readily predictable, but rather a multitude of disparate, shifting groups that crisscross, none of them big enough to account for any considerable proportion of the votes. Out of these groups they must, jigsaw-puzzle fashion, piece together

[14] E. E. Schattschneider, *Party Government* (New York: Rinehart & Company, Inc., 1942), pp. 209-10. The APSA Committee comes to this somewhat more cautious conclusion: "The parties have not carefully explored the opportunities they have for more responsible operation under existing constitutional arrangements. It is logical first to find out what can be done under present conditions to invigorate the parties before accepting the conclusion that action has to begin with changing a constitutional system that did not contemplate the growing need for party responsi-bility when it was set up": "Toward a More Responsible Two-Party System," *American Political Science Review*, Vol. XLIV (September, 1950), Supplement, p. 36.

majorities as best they can. Not only does this militate against the writing of crystal-clear, logically consistent, and unequivocal platforms; it also—when taken together with the absence of any permanent "ruling class" of the traditional British Oxford-Cambridge type—helps explain the heterogeneity and "representativeness" of party leaders and workers that we noted at the beginning of the present chapter. And while such groups, despite differing backgrounds and attitudes, can be brought together for purposes of winning elections and distributing public offices, it is far more difficult to bring them together for purposes of writing and forcing through unequivocal programs of public policy.[15]

Diffusion of and Inconsistencies in the Belief System. In Chapter 20 we attempted to describe the American belief system and called attention to its two most prominent characteristics: (a) the wide diffusion of common beliefs and values through American society's numerous strata and groupings; and (b) the large number of inconsistencies and contradictions contained in those common beliefs and values. The American community, in consequence, is not made up of homogeneous sociopolitical groupings that confront one another each with its own distinct, internally consistent corpus of ideas; and, this being the case, it does not offer the human and ideological raw material for building national—or, for that matter, state and local—parties that would be consistent in ideology and united on detailed programs of public policy.

The American Attitude Toward Politics. We also noted in Chapter 20 that the predominant American attitude toward politics is, increasingly, the "inside dopester's" special kind of apathy—an apathy that is characterized by greater popular interest in the question, "Who's going to win?" than in the question, "Whose winning would be in the community's interest?" and that makes politics, for most Americans, a kind of spectator sport rather than an arena for making decisions about matters of life-and-death importance. Many Americans, moreover, deem politics as played by the "pros" a rather disreputable game,[16] and in any case are little disposed to believe that the ills of man and society can be cured solely or even mainly by politics and legislation. Perhaps it is their low opinion of "politicians" and "party wheelhorses" that makes most Americans admire—and vote for—the "independent" public official, who "refuses to be dictated to" by the "party bosses." As Professor Schattschneider puts it:

> In the folklore of [American] politics the greatest virtue of public officials is "independence." Thus, independent candidates are better than party candidates. Thus also, a member of Congress who refuses to work with the members of his

[15] Cf. V. O. Key, Jr., *Techniques of Political Graft in the United States* (Chicago: private edition, distributed by the University of Chicago Libraries, 1936), pp. 68, 85-86, 397-98.

[16] Perhaps this is another example of a contradiction in the American belief system; for "patronage" and "graft" are at least as common in American business and in American life in general as they are in American politics; but few Americans regard business—or American life in general—as disreputable: Cf. Key, *op. cit.,* p. 67; and John T. Flynn, *Graft in Business* (New York: The Vanguard Press, 1931).

party is more moral than a member who does work with his party. Independence *per se* is a virtue, and party loyalty *per se* is an evil.[17]

Certainly our belief system has not yet reached the point where it would be common and unremarkable for the primary voters of a party to rise up and, in righteous wrath and as a matter of course, strip the party label from a man who had dared to rebel against the national party "line."

   The American Attitudes Toward the Party System, Pluralistic Politics, and Majority Rule and Minority Rights. Our decentralized, office-oriented, and programmatically vague parties are, as we have said, both influenced by and appropriate to our formal-governmental system, which was designed to prevent the formation and seizure of the whole power of government by any homogeneous, programmatically precise, and highly cohesive popular majority. Perhaps, however, most Americans are sick and tired of pluralistic politics, a "horse-and-buggy" Constitution, and a party system the like of which no other country has ever seen. Perhaps they would prefer a more majoritarian and action-producing governmental structure, and a more "rational" party system. And perhaps they remain without these things because no one has yet shown them the correct moves to make.

   Perhaps—but there are a number of reasons for believing quite the contrary, namely, that the formal-governmental system and the party system, *as they now are,* are substantially as most Americans wish them to be. Among those reasons the following seem too urgent to be left out of even this brief treatment of the problem.

   First, for at least the past half-century a number of able and prominent writers have been urging the general position that our governmental system and our party system should be made more like their British counterparts;[18] and we might fairly expect, if the idea is ever to gain a strong foothold in public opinion, some evidence of some shift in its direction by this time. In point of fact, however, the changes that have been made in our governmental system during the period mentioned—for example, the growth of presidential power, the Twenty-Second Amendment, and the growth of the independent regulatory commissions—have clearly been moves away from, not toward, par-

---

[17] E. E. Schattschneider, *The Struggle for Party Government* (College Park, Md.: Program in American Civilization, University of Maryland, 1948), p. 6. See also Ernest S. Griffith, *Congress: Its Contemporary Role* (New York: New York University Press, 1951), pp. 155-56.

[18] Among the writers who have emphasized reform of the Constitution may be mentioned at least the following: William MacDonald, *A New Constitution for a New America* (New York: B. W. Huebsch, Inc., 1921); William K. Wallace, *Our Obsolete Constitution* (New York: The John Day Company, 1932); William Y. Elliott, *The Need for Constitutional Reform* (New York: McGraw-Hill Book Company, Inc., 1935); Henry Hazlitt, *A New Constitution Now* (New York: McGraw-Hill Book Company, Inc., 1942); and Alexander F. Heymeyer, *Time for a Change* (New York: Farrar and Rinehart, Inc., 1943). Writers who have emphasized reform of the parties are Woodrow Wilson. A. Lawrence Lowell, Henry Jones Ford, Frank J. Goodnow, E. E. Schattschneider, James M. Burns, and the members of the Committee on Political Parties of the American Political Science Association. For a general summary of these writers' views, see Austin Ranney, *The Doctrine of Responsible Party Government* (Urbana: University of Illinois Press, 1954); and pp. 151-52 above.

liamentary government. There is reason to think, moreover, that the parties in Congress today are much *less* cohesive than during, say, the McKinley administration. In a word, the proposals and supporting arguments of the writers mentioned simply have not caught on.

Second, the available evidence appears to point to a positive attachment to certain aspects of the present system that the writers mentioned object to most, so that it cannot be argued that Americans in general have no strong opinions on these matters one way or the other. The public-opinion polls, for example, have consistently found substantial majorities of the population in favor of such anti-majoritarian aspects of our constitutional system as federalism, separation of powers, and judicial review. The polls have also found substantial majorities opposed to any realignment of the parties along more "rational" lines. On five different occasions between 1937 and 1947, for instance, the Gallup organization asked its respondents this question: "It has been suggested that we give up the present Republican and Democratic parties and have two new parties—one for the Liberals and one for the Conservatives. Would you favor this idea?" The answers are summarized in Table 33. Again for

TABLE 33   Popular Attitudes Toward Realignment of the Parties[19]

Date	Yes	No	No Opinion
August, 1937	22%	52%	26%
April, 1938	24	55	21
September, 1938	15	65	20
January, 1946	12	67	21
April, 1947	13	72	15

instance, in October, 1944, the *Fortune* poll asked, "On the whole . . . do you find that you are usually satisfied with the stands taken by one or the other of the present big parties, or would you like to see a strong new party entirely different from either of the present parties?" Seventy-eight per cent replied "usually satisfied," 14 per cent replied "new party," and 8 per cent had no opinion.[20] And, for a final instance, in January, 1950, the Gallup poll asked, "Would you like to have the Republican party officially join with the Southern conservative Democrats in a new political party . . . ?" The Republican respondents answered as follows: yes, 33 per cent; no, 33 per cent; no opinion, 34 per cent. Southern voters answered in these proportions: yes, 29 per cent; no, 42 per cent; no opinion, 29 per cent. Nonsouthern Democrats opposed the idea by a two-to-one margin.[21] In short, none of the polls have shown any

[19] These data are taken from George H. Smith and Richard P. Davis, "Do the Voters Want the Parties Changed?" *Public Opinion Quarterly*, Vol. XI (Summer, 1947), pp. 236-43.

[20] Reprinted in Cantril, *op. cit.*, No. 50 on p. 581.

[21] Published in the *Public Opinion Quarterly*, Vol. XIV (Spring, 1950), pp. 183-84.

strong and widely held desire among Americans to make basic changes either in our party system or in our formal-governmental system.

Third, we noted in Chapter 1 and again in Chapter 20 that most Americans believe in majority rule *and* minority rights, in popular sovereignty *and* checks and balances. It is no great intellectual feat to demonstrate, as we attempted to do in Chapter 2, that these ideas are *logically* contradictory; but most Americans seem to find no difficulty in clinging to both pairs. Accordingly, they are, as we have just seen, unreceptive to proposals intended to make our politics more "rational," i.e., transform them into a struggle between two homogeneous, programmatically precise, clearly differentiated, and highly cohesive parties, so that the whole power of government will be employed by the winning party to carry out every last item of its program. This is not to say that Americans are never dissatisfied with the log-rolling, inertia, and turgidity characteristic of our pluralistic politics; for recent history teaches us that in times of national crisis, such as during great depressions and wars, the people seem to be willing enough to have the normal procedures set aside. At such times, however, they have in the past turned, not to stronger parties and parliamentary government, but to "presidential dictatorship." And when the crises have passed, the power of the president has settled back to its normal level, and we have resumed our customary political pluralism.[22]

In short, the most powerful reason why American parties and the formal-governmental system that has helped to shape them are as they are is that most Americans prefer them that way. It may be, of course, that they are mistaken in clinging to these traditional arrangements. It may be that the nation would have more sense-making politics, enjoy more efficient government, and become a finer community if our politico-governmental system were drastically reformed. We cannot profitably canvass this question, however, until we have clearly in mind a picture of the role the party system, as it now exists, plays in American life, and some notion of how the parties' role might change if they themselves changed. That is our final problem for the present chapter.

The Role of the American Party System

ORGANIZING ELECTIONS

Most of the "classical" theorists of democracy assumed that if a community but writes its laws so as to provide for representative government, election of all key public officials, and enfranchisement of all the members of the community, then popular consultation—and democratic government in all its other aspects—will follow as a matter of course. But the experience of the past hundred and seventy-five years, during which certain Western nations have actually attempted to realize democracy in their governing institutions,

---

[22] Cf. Clinton L. Rossiter, *Presidential Dictatorship* (Princeton: Princeton University Press, 1948); and Long, *op. cit.*, p. 208.

has taught us that popular consultation and democracy are less easy to achieve than the classical theorists thought. A community, we have learned, needs *some* agency or agencies (a) to define the alternatives open to it, (b) to make clear to the voters what actually is involved in the choice among those alternatives, and (c) to encourage them to use their sovereign power to make the choice for themselves. The more heavily populated the community, moreover, the more acute is the need for such agencies—and in the United States, with its population of over 160,000,000 persons, the need is urgent indeed.

In the United States, as in the other democracies, the *parties* have taken on these tasks. They make nominations and write platforms, and so "boil down" the number of alternatives to a manageable number; they organize, finance, and conduct campaigns, and so acquaint the voters with what is involved in the choice among them; and they staff the election machinery, oversee its operation, and get out the vote, thereby assisting the voters to use their powers. During the first half of our national history, indeed, the parties performed these tasks almost completely unaided by the formal government (the parties even printed the ballots!);[23] and even today they are the main suppliers of the fuel and energy that animates and operates the legal election machinery.[24]

The parties do not, of course, present the voters with black-versus-white choices; but, as we observed in the early pages of the present chapter, they present *sufficiently* distinct choices—between parties, between candidates, and even between programs—to satisfy most Americans. In a word, the parties make the electoral process *work*. Perhaps an agency of some other kind would make it work better; we cannot say—nor can anyone else except on the level of pure speculation. For no other type of agency has ever been tried out in this country on a scale sufficiently large to cast much light on the problem.

ORGANIZING GOVERNMENT

The Founding Fathers, as we have seen, intended a formal-governmental system that would permit purposeful governmental action only when near-unanimity prevailed among all its many agencies and levels. And they designed their system of "mutual antagonisms" so well that, left to itself and allowed to operate in its "pure" form, it might well result most of the time in deadlock after deadlock—that is, in virtual inactivity. The parties, however, have managed to inject into the system just enough elements of coherence and cooperation to let it produce, regularly and without excessive delay, the pluralistic compromise decisions and cautious action that are normal in present-day American government (and by the same token oceans apart from the reso-

[23] Andrew C. McLaughlin, *The Courts, the Constitution, and the Parties* (Chicago: University of Chicago Press, 1912), pp. 172-73.

[24] Cf. Alfred H. Kelly and Winfred A. Harbison, *The American Constitution, Its Origins and Development* (New York: W. W. Norton and Company, Inc., 1948), pp. 327-29; Henry Jones Ford, *The Rise and Growth of American Politics* (New York: The Macmillan Company, 1898), pp. 305-06; and Holcombe, *op. cit.*, pp. 403-04.

lute decisions and swift action called for by the advocates of parliamentary government and disciplined parties). The parties have done this mainly by "organizing" the formal governments—that is, by providing an unofficial agency for filling key posts in legislative committees and controlling the allocation of legislative time, plus an unofficial meeting ground on which the legislators and the executive can meet together, talk over governmental problems, and work out a measure of cooperation. In short, American governments in normal circumstances still do not have the kind and degree of coherence and mutual cooperation among their various agencies that characterize the parliamentary democracies; but what coherence and cooperation they do have is for the most part provided by the parties.[25]

DEMOCRATIZING THE CONSTITUTIONAL SYSTEM

In Chapter 20 we noted the Founding Fathers' fear of democracy and popular majorities and listed the devices they wrote into the Constitution to prevent democracy from gaining any further foothold in the nation. In general, however, these devices have not produced the desired results, and the American formal-governmental system is today far more democratic than the Founding Fathers would have believed it could become without scrapping the Constitution. And the parties have undoubtedly been in large part responsible for this miscarriage of the Fathers' intentions. Concretely, they have democratized the constitutional system particularly in the following two respects.

Electing the President. The framers of the Constitution, knowing that the president would be a powerful figure, determined to reduce popular influence over his selection as much as possible without removing it altogether. The means they chose to this end was the electoral college, whose members, the electors, they intended to sit as a sort of nominating body, with the final selection being made by the House of Representatives. Almost from the beginning, however, the parties kept the system from working as planned, first by taking over the nominating process (in only two elections, that of 1800 and that of 1824, was the final decision made by the House), and next, after the Jacksonian Democrats had successfully urged that the electors be popularly chosen, by making candidates for the college publicly announce their presidential preferences—so that the electors in each state shortly became mere rubber stamps for registering the presidential preference of a plurality of the state's voters. In only two elections after the Jacksonian era (that of 1876 and that of 1888) was the winning presidential candidate's national total of popular votes smaller than the loser's, and even those instances resulted from the federal principle,[26] not from electors "violating" their instructions. The electoral college today is

---

[25] Cf. Griffith, *op. cit.,* p. 169; Herring, *The Politics of Democracy,* pp. 123-24; and McLaughlin, *op. cit.,* p. 126.

[26] In other words, from the fact that each state, regardless of its population, has at least three votes, plus such further votes as its population warrants.

still far from being an ideally democratic election system; but most of the time it produces a winner directly supported by a national plurality of the voters. And for this radical change from what the framers intended the parties are largely responsible.[27]

Staffing the Bureaucracy. Until the early years of the nineteenth century, most civil servants in America were recruited from selected strata of the population, held office for life, and both constituted and thought of themselves as a sort of self-perpetuating "ruling class." To most Americans, therefore, government seemed remote and unfriendly, something acting *on* them, a matter of "them" against "us." The Jeffersonians and the Jacksonians smashed the whole bureaucratic-ruling-class system by introducing the spoils system, under which loyal party workers from *all* ranks of life got public jobs, and because of which the bureaucracy became more representative of the *whole* population.[28] Although merit-system civil-service laws now put many bureaucratic posts, particularly in the national government, beyond the parties' reach, numerous patronage appointments continue to be made at all levels. Here again, therefore, we find the parties acting, from an early date and right down to the present day, as a force making for democratization.

In addition to democratizing the election of the president and the staffing of the bureaucracy, the parties, by organizing elections and organizing government in the manner described above, have added still further impetus to the nation's progress toward democracy since 1789. They were not responsible, even indirectly, for certain other democratic reforms (the extension of the suffrage, for example, and the direct election of senators). But, these exceptions apart, they have played a major role in the achievement of the more democratic features of our present formal-governmental system.

NURTURING CONSENSUS

The Task and How the Parties Do It. In Chapter 20 we spoke of the high "civil-war potential" in American society, and commented upon some of the social forces that tend to maximize it. We observed, on the other hand, that our society is one that manages to keep its civil-war potential from being realized. Violent conflict among hostile and uncompromising social groups is the exception, not the rule. American society, in other words, has its own peculiar kind of consensus—consensus, certainly, of a lower degree than we find in certain other countries (England, for example, or Norway or Denmark). The belief system of American society, to be sure, contains so many contradictory values and beliefs that the nation is seldom if ever able to take vigorous, ideologically inspired, programmatically consistent governmental action. The moment such action is suggested, large numbers of Americans speak out

[27] Kelly and Harbison, *op. cit.,* pp. 213-16; Ford, *op. cit.,* Ch. VII; and Holcombe, *op. cit.,* pp. 107-08, 401.

[28] Cf. Ford, *op. cit.,* pp. 133-40, 169-72.

in protest, because they do not agree with the ideology and program in question. But for that reason, such action is seldom suggested, so that while we clearly have a low degree of consensus on the ideological level, we have a high degree of consensus on another level, namely, that of keeping ideology out of politics. In short, we disagree too much, both about fundamentals and about trivialities, to be rallied easily—even a majority of us—behind any program, whether it be a program of rapid change or a program of stand-pat conservatism; but we agree to disagree that much, and that enables us to live together peaceably *as one society*.

Although many American social forces and social characteristics operate to minimize our civil-war potential, it is the party system, more than any other American institution, that consciously, actively, and directly nurtures consensus. And it performs this function in the following ways.[29]

First, the parties draw their leaders, workers, and candidates from all strata of American society, and so give everyone the feeling that *his* stratum is "represented" in the mainstream of the nation's life and politics and has a "friend at court." [30]

Second, the parties direct their appeals for votes at—and nurse the feelings, prejudices, and sensibilities of—all the strata, and so give everyone the feeling that the rest of the society is concerned about the welfare and prestige of people in his stratum, which, therefore, has its "place" in American society.

Third, the parties promise (and, on pain of not winning elections, deliver) to each group *some* but never all of what it wants, and so give each group a concrete reason for believing that what it regards as its legitimate needs and aspirations *are* getting a hearing, and that it has a real chance of achieving all or most of its goals. No group, in other words, has reason to feel that the rest of the society is a kind of giant conspiracy to keep it out of its legitimate "place in the sun." No group feels that it may at any moment have to drop everything else and defend itself against an onslaught by some other group. And the available evidence suggests that the major elements of the population feel safe vis-à-vis both parties as well as vis-à-vis each other; for none lines up unanimously behind one party or the other. The Survey Research Center's study of voting behavior in the 1952 election, for example, showed that some of the principal demographic groups divided as shown in Table 34. Similarly, studies of voting behavior in

---

[29] For general discussions of the party system's role in nurturing American consensus, see Robin M. Williams, Jr., *American Society* (New York: Alfred A. Knopf, 1951), pp. 243, 530-31; Allen Johnson, "The Nationalizing Influence of Party," *Yale Review*, Vol. XV (November, 1906), pp. 283-92; Herbert Agar, *The Price of Union* (Boston: Houghton Mifflin Company, 1950), *passim;* and Herring, *The Politics of Democracy, passim.*

[30] See, for example, Samuel Lubell's account of how both parties have been careful to draw some of their leaders and candidates from such groups as the Italo-Americans, the Irish Catholics, the Polish-Americans, and the German-Americans: *The Future of American Politics* (New York: Harper and Brothers, 1951), pp. 52, 66-75, 133-34, 159-60, 222-25.

TABLE 34 *Voting Behavior of Major Demographic Groups in the 1952 Election* [31]

Demographic Group	Voted Republican	Voted Democratic	Voted Other	Did Not Vote
Protestants	45%	26%	1%	28%
Catholics	41	43	1	15
White	47	31	1	21
Negro	6	26	1	67
English descent	55	25	1	19
Irish descent	38	55	2	5
Italian descent	38	49	2	11
German descent	58	20	2	20
Trade-union affiliation	33	48	1	23
No trade-union affiliation	46	26	1	27
Income under $2,000	30	23	—	47
Income $2,000 to $5,000	39	36	3	22
Income over $5,000	59	28	1	12

the 1940 and 1948 elections show each of the major demographic groups divided in its party preferences.[32] The importance of this fact, from the standpoint of containing the civil-war potential in American society, cannot be over-emphasized. The day some major element completely deserts one party in favor of the other, the stage will have been set for the kind of conflict that leads to actual civil war, and our parties will have failed to maintain our kind of consensus. But there is no evidence that such a day is at hand.

Fourth, the parties combine conflicting ideas and ideologies in their platforms, slogans, and campaign appeals, and so—at whatever sacrifice of neat logic—minimize the likelihood of ideological strife triggering our civil-war potential. Both parties provide an ideological home, and apparently a satisfactory one, for Catholics and Protestants, "liberals" and "conservatives," "isolationists" and "interventionists"; each, in the Biblical phrase, is a house of many mansions, where people can, ideologically speaking, keep out of each other's way. As John Fischer puts it, "The purpose of European parties is, of course, to *divide* men of different ideologies into coherent and disciplined organizations. The historic role of the American party, on the other hand, is not to divide but to unite." [33]

Fifth, the "stuff" of our formal-governmental system is a set of abstract and inexorable rules, stated in complex technical legal jargon; and the system

[31] These data are taken from Angus Campbell, Gerald Gurin, and Warren E. Miller, *The Voter Decides* (Evanston, Ill.: Row, Peterson and Company, 1954), Table 5.1 on pp. 70-73, and Table 5.3 on p. 77. Reprinted by permission of Row, Peterson and Company.

[32] Lazarsfeld, Berelson, and Gaudet, *op. cit.*, Ch. III; and Berelson, Lazarsfeld, and McPhee, *op. cit.*, Chs. III and IV.

[33] John Fischer, "Unwritten Rules of American Politics," *Harper's*, Vol. CXCVII (November, 1948), p. 32. Italics added. See also Herring, *The Politics of Democracy*, p. 105.

is dedicated to the lofty but grim principle of the rule of law—which not only sounds cold and impersonal when it is set down in black and white, but tends to *be* cold and impersonal in its actual operation. The parties have, however, created a sphere of politico-governmental activity *outside* the formal structure, where the watchword is not the rule book and where great emphasis is put on human warmth, friendliness, flexibility, and common sense. As D. W. Brogan puts it:

[Party leaders and workers] must be the bridge between the strange, unfriendly, or remote and meaningless, formal organization of society, and the poor and ignorant who [have] greater trust in the realities of luck and favour than in the empty formulas of justice that [please, satisfy, and usually serve] the more prosperous. It was put in final and classical form by Martin Lomasney of Boston: "I think . . . that there's got to be in every ward somebody that any bloke can come to—no matter what he's done—and get help. Help, you understand; none of your law and justice, but help." [34]

Sixth, the history of political society teaches us that when a group or combination of groups forces a policy or law or way of life on others, there is always the danger that the latter will find it intolerable and opt for civil war— actual, shooting civil war. Whatever else there is to be said about our pluralistic political system, it makes things extremely difficult for any group or combination of groups that wants to work its will on the rest of society; and when it does fail to keep A, B, and C from forcing something intolerable on D, it at least sets in motion forces likely to keep A, B, and C from becoming entrenched in power, and so lessens their temptation to go too far. It gives each major group in the community a virtual "veto power" for self-protection; and it produces majorities that are themselves bundles of compromises rather than homogeneous, ideologically uniform, and dedicated political armies. And the party system is certainly the main agency that operates to keep the system pluralistic. Not only are the parties the principal arenas in which the "concurrent-majority" compromise programs are worked out; they are also the place in which each group in the community can most effectively make known its intention to veto all or part of any proposed program. As Peter F. Drucker puts it, "As soon as it cannot appeal to at least a minority in every major group (as soon, in other words, as it provokes the veto of one section, interest or class), a party is in danger of disintegration." [35] The parties, whose leaders know this, do their level best to avoid such group vetoes, and, in the process

[34] *Op. cit.,* p. 132. Cf. Sebastian de Grazia's contention that the parties, by their social activities and by the very fact that so many Americans feel they "belong" to one or the other party, help to break down the impersonality of American life and the isolation of the individual American from his fellows: *The Political Community* (Chicago: University of Chicago Press, 1948), pp. 149-53.

[35] Peter F. Drucker, "A Key to American Politics: Calhoun's Pluralism," *Review of Politics,* Vol. X (October, 1948), p. 417. See also Henry Steele Commager, *Majority Rule and Minority Rights* (New York: Peter Smith, 1950), pp. 58-60; Agar, *op. cit.,* pp. 686-87; and Herring, *The Politics of Democracy,* pp. 131-33.

of trying to avoid them, see to it that no group or combination of groups shall rock the boat—or, if not that, that they shall not rock it too hard or too long.

Seventh, we observed in Chapter 19 that some groups in American history have come to regard any substantial compromise with other groups as complete surrender, not partial victory, and have founded minor parties whose programs were open protests against the pluralistic politics we have just described. No such group, however, has ever launched or tried to launch a violent revolution; each of them, having become a minor party, has lived out its more or less brief existence bidding for votes in the normal American manner. The number and strength of such minor parties at any given moment is, nevertheless, a measure of how well or how badly the major parties are succeeding in making everybody feel that he is getting enough of his way about things to think it worth while not to leave the political mainstream. And the absence of any strongly supported *and* long-lasting minor parties in twentieth-century America suggests that our party system, and the pluralistic politico-governmental system it animates, are succeeding more than ever in the past in making people feel just that.

The Parties, the Breakdown of Consensus, and the Civil War. The role of the party system in nurturing consensus can perhaps be most clearly seen by examining the only occasion in our national history when consensus broke down completely: the Civil War. The story, as most historians tell it, runs as follows. In the 1840's two extremely hot and divisive issues arose to plague the nation—whether slavery was to be extended into the territories with resultant disturbance of the balance of power between the South and the North in national affairs; and whether a state was free to secede. The population split, along sectional lines moreover, over these questions, and each side became increasingly hostile and bitter toward the other. The Whig and Democratic parties, however, officially ignored the new issues and continued to talk about the old ones, while behind the scenes leaders of both parties frantically sought for some kind of compromise that would satisfy both southern and northern voters.

After the 1852 election, the Whig party collapsed mainly because of its leaders' inability to find an acceptable compromise between its pro-slavery and anti-slavery elements; and it was replaced by the frankly sectional, highly unified, and unambiguously and uncompromisingly anti-slavery Republican party, which in its first national election (1856), finished a strong second to the Democrats. From 1856 to 1860 the fissure between the two halves of the nation deepened and widened, so that by 1860 the Democratic party, primarily through the efforts of the faction led by Stephen A. Douglas of Illinois, was the only major social institution still trying to find some kind of compromise. The party's motive, of course, was that of maintaining the North-South electoral combination that had served it well through a long period; it was, in any case, the last national institution to give up trying to prevent a civil war. At the 1860 Democratic national convention in Charleston, South Carolina, however, the Douglas Democrats, while willing to write a platform that was neither completely pro-slavery nor completely anti-slavery, refused to accept the clear and uncompromising pro-slavery stand demanded by the southerners; and they carried the convention. Immediately thereafter, the Alabama, Mississippi, Louisiana, South Carolina, Florida, and Texas delegations walked out of the convention, which subsequently broke up without nominating any candidates. The northern Democrats later nominated Douglas, and the southern Democrats John C. Breckenridge. The Republicans, running on a straight anti-slavery platform, won the election. South Carolina seceded from the Union, ten other southern states followed her, Fort Sumter was fired upon, and the Civil War began. The normal party system, in short, broke down, and it did so precisely when there was no party left that could put itself forward as a truly *national* party, combining all sections and all points of view, and so capable of effectuating the compromises and counseling the moderation needed to prevent disruption. And once this breakdown had occurred, the Civil War came as a matter of course.[36]

Just as it had been the last social institution to give up on preventing the war, the Democratic party was one of the very first to try to reunite the nation after 1865. Its leaders, North and South, knew that each section needed the other if the party was to challenge the Republicans' supremacy; and they early developed a compromise program on which both sections could unite. The "deal" of 1877 (the Democrats agreed not to challenge Rutherford B. Hayes' highly debatable legal claim to the presidency, in return for the Republicans' promise to withdraw all occupation troops from the South) was, though no doubt "reprehensible" from some points of view, a step toward reunion. It was also an important turning point in the history of our party system; for the parties' record in nurturing consensus and so preventing even the whisper of civil war has ever since been well-nigh impeccable.[37]

The lesson of the Civil War for understanding the nature and general role of the American party system is well summed up by D. W. Brogan in the following passage:

It can hardly be doubted that the immediate cause of the greatest breakdown of the American political system was the breakdown of the party system, the failure of the party machinery and the party leaders to remember their national function, which, if carried out, was the justification of the varied weaknesses and absurdities of the party organizations and policies. Not until the party system broke

---

[36] The best account of the coming of the Civil War and of the efforts of the Democratic party to prevent it is Roy F. Nichols, *The Disruption of American Democracy* (New York: The Macmillan Company, 1948). See also Allan Nevins, *Ordeal of the Union,* two volumes (New York: Charles Scribner's Sons, 1942); Wilfred E. Binkley, *American Political Parties: Their Natural History* (New York: Alfred A. Knopf, 1944), Chs. VIII-IX; and Avery O. Craven, *The Coming of the Civil War* (New York: Charles Scribner's Sons, 1942).

[37] For the story of the reuniting of the nation and the party system's role therein, see Paul H. Buck, *The Road to Reunion, 1865-1900* (Boston: Little, Brown and Company, 1937); and C. Vann Woodward, *Reunion and Reaction* (Boston: Little, Brown and Company, 1951).

down, in the dissolution of the Whigs, in the schism of the Democrats, was war possible. . . . Although it may be rash to suggest a belief in a national memory, it is at any rate possible that the American shrinking from doctrinaire parties, from people who knew their own minds, who would not compromise, who had a social theory to defend or attack, owed something to the recollection of the time when America *had* such parties, when, to the astonishment of each side, North and South found themselves at war.[38]

[38] *Op. cit.*, p. 54.

Chapter 22

DEMOCRACY AND THE AMERICAN PARTY SYSTEM

Appraising the American Party System

DEMOCRACY AS A CRITERION

The task of appraising any political or social institution, as we argued in Chapter 2, is essentially a matter of comparing it with an agreed-upon "model" or "ideal type," and reaching a conclusion as to the degree of correspondence between them.

In Chapter 1 we stated our intention of appraising the American party system solely in terms of the single criterion of *democracy*. We then noted that the term "democracy" today means different things to different Americans; but we added that during most of its history the word has had a generally agreed-upon meaning, and that the present confusion about its referent dates only from World War I. In Chapter 2 we conceded the point that *no* conception of democracy has any claim, either a priori or "scientific," to be regarded as the *only* legitimate one; but we also suggested that the purposes of clarity and consistency in our present analysis would be served best by a straightforward exposition of what "democracy" means wherever it appears in the present book. We therefore stated that for purposes of our present analysis, "democracy" means a form of government based upon the principles of popular sovereignty, political equality, popular consultation, and majority rule; and we noted that this particular conception is derived partly from the historic meaning of "democracy" and partly from our analysis of what is involved in the present-day areas of *agreement* about its meaning. Finally, in Chapter 3 we presented our conception of the structure and operation of a "model" democracy, derived from our attempt to adapt the principles of the New England town meeting to the conditions of the modern nation-state.

DEMOCRACY AND POPULAR CONSULTATION

The particular principle of democracy most relevant for our appraisal of the American party system is that of popular consultation. This principle, as we observed in Chapters 2 and 3, requires some kind of institutional machinery capable of performing the following three tasks:

(1) Encouraging at all levels of government a maximum amount of *creative* popular discussion of public issues—that is, not just any kind of talk about such issues, but the kind of discussion in which each of the participants seeks an answer to the question, Which governmental policies are *best for the community?* It therefore differs sharply from the "war of competing propagandas" type of debate, in which each segment of the community attempts only to sweep out of the way all the arguments put forward by other segments, with a view to imposing its will upon them and realizing its particular goals, regardless of what they may think or feel about it.

(2) Fostering the kind of consensus among the community's members that provides a context congenial to such creative discussion.

(3) Channeling the results of this discussion into the lawmaking and law-enforcing apparatus of government, in such fashion that public policy can accurately reflect the "sense of the community"—or, if no fully articulated "sense of the community" has had time to emerge on some problem that requires immediate governmental action, in such fashion that the holders of public office will know what action is desired by *at least a majority* of the members of the community.

In the remainder of this final chapter we shall attempt to evaluate the American party system as an instrument for accomplishing these three tasks in our total governing system.

The American Party System and Popular Consultation

ENCOURAGING CREATIVE DISCUSSION

Discussion Between *the Parties.* The kind of discussion that normally takes place between the major parties in electoral campaigns and in the agencies of government resembles only remotely the model of creative democratic discussion we described in Chapter 3. For one thing, most discussion between the parties takes the form of a *debate,* i.e., a forensic combat between two sides in which the object of each is to defeat the other at the polls; it bears little resemblance to a *discussion,* i.e., a process of group thinking in which the object of all the participants is to seek the answer to a particular question, namely, What public policies are best calculated to advance the *common* welfare and *shared* interests of all the members of the community?

For another thing, the discussion between the parties largely or completely bypasses the issues on which the people are most sharply divided. As we have noted repeatedly in the preceding chapters, the major parties tend to take clear and unequivocal stands only when such stands are likely to receive near-unanimous approval (e.g., "opposition to communist aggression," "preserving the American way of life," and "maintaining an adequate national defense"). On issues about which major segments of the community clearly and heatedly disagree (e.g., "McCarthyism," universal military training, and racial segregation in housing) the parties are usually either vague or silent.

Finally, as we pointed out in Chapter 21, American elections are held on legally designated dates, without regard to how much or how little public interest in governmental affairs there may be at the moment. The parties cannot hope to win unless their sympathizers actually go to the polls; and most party leaders feel that most voters simply will not take the trouble to vote unless the election is made to seem "important" to them. Party orators, therefore, insist in each and every election that a "great crisis" is at hand, and that in each and every one the nation (or state or city) "stands at the crossroads." On the other hand, few voters appear to take seriously all these repeated cries of havoc; as Professor Schattschneider observes, ". . . by a well-understood convention of American politics, the extravagant language of party orators, major and minor, deceives almost no one. . . . Elections are not followed by waves of suicide." [1] Nor do the party leaders—between campaigns, at least—appear to take them seriously.[2] Thus the discussion that normally takes place *between* the parties is an often-repeated, highly stylized *drama,* like a western movie in that it has conventional heroes, villains, and plots whom everyone understands to be fictional. It bears little resemblance, therefore, to the serious, creative discussion of genuine public issues called for by our model of democracy.

Discussion Outside *the Parties.* The fact that discussion does not normally take place *between* the parties, however, does not mean that no serious exchange of ideas, arguments, and facts takes place about issues on which the people are genuinely divided. Such exchange goes forward all the time at a number of points in our politico-governmental structure, including at least the following: (a) the negotiations among the various economic, occupational, ethnic, religious, sectional, and other interest groups outside the government, in the course of which these groups seek to arrive at a compromise program that they can collectively (and thus with extra force) urge upon the government; (b) the negotiations between pressure-group representatives on the one hand and legislative committees, executive and administrative agencies, and courts on the other; and (c) the negotiations among the governmental officials themselves, leading to the formulation and execution of actual public policy.

This peculiar brand of pluralistic, bargaining-compromising, bread-and-

---

[1] E. E. Schattschneider, *Party Government* (New York: Rinehart & Company, Inc., 1942), p. 91.

[2] Perhaps the best-known illustration of this point is the often-quoted remark by Wendell Willkie, made to the Senate Foreign Relations Committee in 1941, that his 1940 public prediction that Roosevelt's re-election would plunge the nation into war was "a bit of campaign oratory": quoted in Mary Earhart Dillon, *Wendell Willkie* (Philadelphia and New York: J. B. Lippincott Company, 1952), p. 243.

butter discussion (which we described in greater detail in Chapter 20) does not, to be sure, correspond exactly to our model of creative democratic discussion, mostly because the participants are far more eager to instruct than to learn. But it meets at least one of the tests for such discussion: its object is to arrive at a program that will satisfy *all* the participants *enough* to make sure that none of them will refuse to play the game altogether, *not* to determine the "winners" and "losers" so that the former may get all they are after and the latter nothing.

This kind of discussion may well be, indeed, the closest approximation to our model of creative democratic discussion that a community like the United States, with its large and heterogeneous population, its multiplicity of conflicting interest groups, and its widely diffused but self-contradictory belief system, can reasonably hope for. Certainly it is far closer to the model than, say, the bitter debate over *apartheid* between the two major parties in South Africa, or the often witty but governmentally sterile exchanges among the many and variegated "rationally differentiated" parties in the French National Assembly.

In short, the discussion *between* American parties must receive low marks when compared to our model; but not so the discussion *outside* the parties. And the party system contributes greatly to the latter by fostering the consensus which, as we saw in Chapter 21, provides a congenial context for it.

FOSTERING CONSENSUS

In Chapter 21 we argued that the United States has developed a certain kind and degree of consensus, that that kind and degree of consensus is sorely needed for the proper functioning of its politico-governmental system, and that our parties, more than any other institution, have highly refined techniques for generating and maintaining it. Fostering consensus, then, is the phase of popular consultation on which our parties make their best showing; and on the latter rests the party system's strongest claim to be regarded as a valuable agency for democratic government.

EXPRESSING MAJORITY WILLS

Circumstances, as noted above, sometimes make it necessary for the government to take action on a problem it has in hand before a "sense of the community" on it has taken shape. A democracy therefore needs institutional machinery to which the holders of public office can turn for guidance as to what action would meet the approval of at least a majority of the members of the community. Ideally, in other words, governmental officials should not act in the absence of a "popular mandate," i.e., a clear, unequivocal directive from not less than a majority of the people.

American elections usually result in clear and unequivocal popular mandates only on the question of *who* shall hold office, and rarely on the question of *what* the government shall do on this or that matter of public policy. The 1940 presidential election, for example, clearly indicated that a majority of the

American electorate wanted Franklin Roosevelt rather than Wendell Willkie to be president; but after the election as before it was anyone's guess whether a popular majority favored or opposed, say, lend-lease, a peacetime draft, and all-out aid to the Allies at the risk of American entry into the war. The 1952 presidential election, again for example, clearly showed that a majority of Americans wanted Dwight Eisenhower rather than Adlai Stevenson to be president; but it clearly provided no mandate either to end the Korean war on any terms we could get, or to prosecute the war more vigorously, or to pull out of the Far East altogether. And the 1954 congressional elections, for a final example, showed that a majority of voters in a majority of the nation's states and congressional districts preferred their particular Democratic candidates to their particular Republican candidates; but the elections left wide open the question whether a national popular majority approved or disapproved of President Eisenhower's leadership, or of the Republican program of more tax relief for businessmen, or of the new security program in the federal civil service. Political commentators and government officials must always tease out of the election results what is at best an *inference* as to how the majority views the issues of the day; almost never can they confidently tell themselves that there is a clear popular mandate to follow this or that line of governmental action.

Under present conditions, it could hardly be otherwise. In most campaigns the parties address themselves to many different issues, talk vaguely about some, not at all about others. After any given national election, accordingly, no one can say with assurance which particular issues a majority of the voters regarded as crucial, or which party they regarded as having the better position on this or that specific issue. Moreover, recent studies of how voters make up their minds suggest that concern with issues is only *one* of the factors that determine the vote of any individual (among the others are his "party identification" and his preference for one candidate's *personal* qualities over those of another), and is by no means the main factor for most voters in most elections.[3]

The party system, however, is not alone in this regard. In Chapter 4 we canvassed the principal institutions employed by the Western democratic nations in their attempts to solve the problem of translating the popular will into clear mandates, and concluded that the town meeting is the only really satisfactory solution men have yet devised (and that even it is not a satisfactory solution in a heavily populated or a "low-consensus" community). Each of the other traditional institutions, we found (representation in its various forms, direct legislation, and the recall), has shortcomings and limitations of its own as far as providing the popular mandates called for by our model of democracy is concerned. The parties, then, compare quite favorably in this regard with the other traditional agencies for popular consultation.

[3] Cf. Angus Campbell, Gerald Gurin, and Warren E. Miller, *The Voter Decides* (Evanston, Ill.: Row, Peterson and Company, 1954), *passim*.

The American Party System and Majority Rule

MAJORITY RULE AND THE FORMAL-GOVERNMENTAL SYSTEM

Extreme Majoritarian Criticism of the Constitution. In Chapter 20 we spoke of the so-called "anti-majoritarian" features of our formal-governmental system, and of the extent to which they reflect the avowed intentions of the Founding Fathers. There is, as we noted, an impressive array of them—so impressive that it has led at least some partisans of majoritarian democracy to conclude that the majority of the American people (by which these critics seem to mean the low-income strata of American society) are, in terms of both governmental procedures and public policy, permanently at the mercy of a small minority (by which they seem to mean the rich and prosperous), and that it will continue so until steps are taken to revise the system from top to bottom. The best-known of these critics is J. Allen Smith, whose work *The Spirit of American Government* (1907) has profoundly influenced a number of commentators on our Constitution writing since his time.[4]

What Smith appears to have wanted (he wrote as an unabashed majoritarian) was a series of constitutional reforms that would make the American constitutional system as much as possible like the British system. A large number of writers on American government after Smith have followed his lead in attacking particular anti-majoritarian features of our system—particularly the seniority principle in legislative committees, and the electoral college; but, curiously enough, few writers on American government after Smith have attacked (as Smith did) the *whole* array of anti-majoritarian features, or put themselves forward as out-and-out majoritarians. Smith's view as to the *facts* of the matter, on the other hand, has become the prevailing view among most present-day writers on American politics, who tend to assume that our system puts insurmountable barriers in the way of popular majorities. Thus no one in recent decades has reopened the *factual* question Smith raised, either to ask whether he was right about the situation as of fifty years ago, or to ask whether the situation has perhaps changed somewhat in the interim.

Considerations of space in the present chapter forbid an exhaustive inquiry into this problem, but there is reason to believe that Smith overstated his case, that the case has grown weaker as the years have passed, and that recognition of its weaknesses is essential to a correct understanding of our constitutional and political system. Let us, therefore, fix attention briefly on those weaknesses, and state what the present facts of the matter appear to be.

---

[4] J. Allen Smith, *The Spirit of American Government* (New York: The Macmillan Company, 1907). On Smith's showing, we might note in passing, revising the system from top to bottom would have been possible only through overthrow of the system by unlawful means, or as the result of the minority's backing down, despite its unassailable constitutional position, and giving a majority bent upon revision its way. Smith does not *say* this; but the more he pressed his point about the impotence of the majority in the face of the minority-veto machinery devised by the framers, the more foolish it became for him to expect revision by constitutional and legal means.

In order to do so, however, we must distinguish sharply between two aspects of the problem that have been confused over the years during which it has been neglected, namely, the position of popular majorities vis-à-vis the Constitution itself, and their position vis-à-vis the federal statute book.

Popular Majorities and the Amending Process. Those majoritarians who have adopted Smith's position direct their harshest criticisms at the arrangements the Founding Fathers provided for amending the Constitution. What the framers set out to do, they argue, was to make the Constitution impossible to amend save in response to overwhelming nationwide sentiment in favor of a proposed change, and yet keep it from having the look of an attempt on their part to subject the nation indefinitely to the dead hand of the past. Concretely, they point out, the arrangements the framers wrote into their draft gave to one-third-plus-one of the members of *either* house of Congress the power to prevent any proposal for constitutional change from even being initiated, and gave one-fourth-plus-one of the states the power to block ratification of any proposed amendment. Like Smith, they draw attention to two types of data: first, data regarding the number of proposed amendments that have been defeated, and second, data calculated to show how, because of alleged over-representation of certain states in Congress, and because of the veto power in one-fourth-plus-one of the states, it is logically possible for such-and-such a combination of thinly populated states, accounting for such-and-such a shockingly small percentage of the nation's population, to force its preferences about the Constitution upon the remainder. In both cases the arithmetic is scrupulously careful and sufficiently elaborate to distract attention from the following considerations: First, in order to prove that the Constitution is impossible or even very difficult to amend, it is necessary to show, not that a great many proposed amendments have failed, but that one or more amendments have failed despite such-and-such evidence that they enjoyed at least majority support. (The fact that Mary has turned down 1,873 suitors for her hand does *not* prove that Mary is unmarriageable, but merely that none of the 1,873 has met her requirements.) Second, the power of such-and-such combinations of states to prevent constitutional change against the wishes of a popular majority is just as great as, and no greater than, the realistic chances of the combination's actually being formed.

In short, the case against the amending process, which enables these critics to deny to the anti-majoritarian aspects of the legislative process the presumptive justification that they must be desired by the majority else they would have been set aside by amendments, not only fails; it is not, in view of the lack of attention to data relevant to the issue, even plausible. Or, to put it a little differently, it does not meet at any point this objection: Any bare numerical majority of the nation's citizens, *if fairly evenly distributed over the country,* ought to be able to account for two-thirds-plus-one of the members of the two houses, and ought to be able to put through ratification in three-quarters of the states. In order to prove their point, the critics must show that there is some good reason to expect bare numerical majorities *not* to be evenly distributed geographically. The framers, to be sure, put their bets, as far as the amending process was concerned, on the likelihood that proposed constitutional amendments would necessarily pit geographical section against geographical section, and that popular majorities on such issues could not be evenly distributed. But even by Smith's time this notion had, with the blurring of sectional differences, lost most of what plausibility it had ever had; and in our time the presumption against it appears overwhelming.[5]

The present writers' view is that there is little reason to expect future issues concerning the Constitution to divide the nation regionally in such a way as to give a smallish minority the kind of veto the framers intended it to have and the majoritarian critics believe that it does have. The amending process is therefore always at the disposal of any movement that can rally a numerical majority behind its proposal for constitutional change, and the anti-majoritarian features of our legislative process therefore do have the presumptive approval of at least a majority of the electorate.

Popular Majorities and the Legislative Process. The writers whose criticisms we are summarizing are also indignant about constitutional barriers which they think stand in the way of majority access to the statute book. Suppose, they say in effect, a majority out over the country wants such-and-such a new law passed, and organizes so as to get control of one-half-plus-one of the seats in both houses of Congress (which means keeping itself in being for two years, and so getting around the "barrier" of staggered election of senators). One barrier it may run up against at once is federalism: the power to make laws on the topic in hand may be one of the powers reserved to the states (in which case, on these writers' showing, the representatives must launch themselves upon the impossible venture of amending the Constitution). Another barrier is the seniority rule in congressional committees, which may enable a hostile committee chairman to bottle the bill up in committee for a long period. Still another is the veto power of the president, who may well have been elected before the majority came into being, or, because of the electoral college, may have become president against the wishes of the majority. Even if the majority hurdles all these barriers, however, it may find itself up against a judicial veto by having the Supreme Court declare its new law unconstitutional. Here again, then, what these critics see in our constitutional system is an unbeatable set of arrangements for frustrating majorities and placing in the hands of minorities an unlimited power to block legislative action they deem distasteful.

The first thing to notice about this argument is that it proves that the majority cannot control the statute book only if we accept two premises: first

---

[5] Smith himself makes the rather astonishing admission in the closing pages of his book that as a matter of history the American people seem always to have regarded their constitutional machinery with profound satisfaction. But he did not see how damaging the admission was to his case against the amending process.

(and one that is entirely unrelated to the constitutional system itself), that a popular majority cannot be kept in being for the four years it would need to exist in order to surmount all the barriers save that of judicial review; and second, that there is nothing a determined congressional majority backed up by a friendly president can do about a judicial veto. The latter premise is clearly false: Congress and the president can increase the size of the Supreme Court and pack it with appointees congenial to their point of view; or Congress can use its constitutional power over the appellate jurisdiction of the Court to see to it that no further case involving the statute comes before it. And once the majority has Congress, the president, *and* the Court on its side, the Constitution is no longer a barrier to whatever it desires. As Dean McBain put it:

> There is no limitation imposed upon the national government which Congress, the President, and the Supreme Court, acting in consecutive agreement, may not legally override. In this sense the government as a whole is clearly a government of unlimited powers; for by interpretation it stakes out its own boundaries.[6]

As for the barriers other than judicial review, Smith and his followers have undoubtedly overestimated them. A numerical majority of the population, more or less evenly spread over the entire nation, would overnight find itself in control not of a mere majority of the House, but very probably of the two-thirds majority required for overriding a presidential veto. Within two years it would have similar strength in the Senate. And once it had a two-thirds majority of both houses, the extent to which the president would dare frustrate the majority's wishes by vetoing its legislation would depend, for the most part, on the extent to which the majority was willing to use the separation-of-powers weapons that the Constitution clearly places in Congress's hands. It would have the power, for example, to bring the whole machinery of government to a standstill by withholding appropriations and refusing confirmation of presidential appointments.

It therefore appears that there is nothing in our *formal* constitutional machinery to prevent a movement that can mobilize a majority of the nation's citizens from either amending the Constitution or passing a law without amending the Constitution. At most one can say that our constitutional machinery prevents action by *temporary* majorities (that is, majorities that, by definition, cannot keep themselves in being for the two to four years that may be needed in order to get full control of Congress and the presidency). What prevents legislative action by longer-lived majorities is *not* our formal constitutional machinery, but the whole complex of the people's attitudes and the character that those attitudes impose on our politics. In other words, the *main* barrier that any movement bidding for majority support runs against is the sheer *unmobilizability* of average Americans for political purposes,

[6] Howard L. McBain, *The Living Constitution* (New York: The Macmillan Company, 1941), p. 38. Used with the permission of The Macmillan Company.

which we noted in Chapter 20. This unmobilizability, the present writers believe, is largely a matter of that fundamental unwillingness to use the unlimited power of the majority in an unlimited way that, in Chapter 3, we called *forbearance* on the part of the majority. In practical politics, that forbearance appears to work in the following fashion. The first hundred thousand supporters for a constitutional amendment calling for, say, the abolition of the states, or a statute providing for, say, the legalization of bullfights, may be easy to get; but the second hundred thousand will be more difficult than the first, the third still more difficult—and so it continues to at least that degree necessary for bringing political mobilization in America under the operation of what economists call the "law of diminishing returns."

In short, relatively persistent national popular majorities do have unlimited power under our present Constitution despite what the framers intended; and that unlimited power is always present as a necessary part of the context our politico-governmental system requires for its normal working. Such majorities arise relatively infrequently, to be sure; but the reason for that lies in the nature of the American community and its belief system, not in any insurmountable barriers set up by the formal constitutional system.

The Major Parties and Majority Rule. As we noted in Chapter 20, the typical popular majority in American politics—that is, one which votes a president into office, or switches control of Congress from one party to the other—is a "bundle of compromises," composed of a number of variegated interest groups, each of which holds many beliefs and values in common with the groups in the minority *and* many conflicting beliefs and values as among its own members and as between itself and the other groups who are temporarily cooperating with it to make up the majority. Its program is the product of pluralistic bargaining and compromise among its constituent groups, and is not, therefore, a clear, logically precise, and internally consistent body of doctrine to which all the individual persons making up the majority are deeply committed. But let us be quite clear as to the reason for this: *political majorities in America tend to be cross sections, not segments, of the community.*

As we noted in Chapter 21, the party system more than any other American institution sustains and perpetuates the pluralistic politico-governmental system that produces the kind of popular majorities just described. By doing so it enables the American people to have their governmental cake and eat it too—that is, it enables them to reconcile their logically self-contradictory beliefs in "majority rule *and* minority rights" and in "popular sovereignty *and* checks and balances" in the following manner. On the one hand, by organizing elections, organizing government, and staffing the bureaucracy, the party system is the principal agency in the American system that enables popular majorities of *whatever* nature and composition to make known their desires and to induce the government to act upon them despite such formal anti-majoritarian features of the constitutional system as federalism, separation of powers, and judicial review. On the other hand, the party system also does much to ensure that the actual popular majorities that arise *shall* be "bundles of compromises," and, accordingly, will seek such modest and limited goals that no minority is likely to regard them as intolerable.

The Party System and Democracy: A Summary

The American party system, when measured against the conception of popular consultation outlined in Chapter 3, gets very high marks indeed. By sustaining and refreshing the consensus on which our society and governmental system are based, it makes possible our characteristic brand of pluralistic bargaining-compromising discussion of public issues, which is probably about as close to the model of creative democratic discussion in the nation-state as a community like the United States can hope to get. Moreover, the party system usually produces clear popular mandates on the issue of *who* shall rule, although, like every other traditional institution for popular consultation except perhaps the town meeting, it rarely produces clear popular mandates on the issue of *what* the government shall do on this or that matter of public policy. Finally, the parties, more than any other aspect of our governing system, do see to it that law-making and law-enforcing go forward under a loose sort of majority control, the essence of which we do not understand unless we think of the relevant majority as usually cutting across party lines, and in such a way as to create no irreconcilable minorities that will divide the nation into warring camps.

For these reasons, therefore, few persons today would argue that American government would be more democratic with *no* party system at all than with the one it has; and few would quarrel with the proposition that the party system is one of the most powerful forces, if not *the* most powerful, operating to "democratize" our formal-governmental system, which, be it remembered, was not intended to be democratic and which, if permitted to operate in its "pure" form, would probably provide a far less democratic system of popular consultation and majority rule than that which we actually have.

In pondering the role and appraising the value of the present system, accordingly, the fruitful question is not whether it is more democratic than *no* party system at all, but where some *other* kind of party system would be more democratic than our present one. A number of eminent and thoughtful commentators, including Woodrow Wilson, Henry Jones Ford, Frank J. Goodnow, E. E. Schattschneider, James M. Burns, and the members of the Committee on Political Parties of the American Political Science Association, have answered the latter question in the affirmative by arguing that a more "responsible" party system would be more "democratic" than our present one. And other writers, including Pendleton Herring, Herbert Agar, Ernest S. Griffith, and the authors of this book, take the contrary position that a more "responsible" party system would probably be *less* "democratic" than our present system, given the nature of the American community.

We cannot hope to settle this controversy once and for all in the present chapter (or, for that matter, in the entire book). We can, however, conclude our appraisal of the American party system by summarizing in some detail the position of each group of writers, so that the areas of agreement and disagreement between them can be clearly understood by the reader as a basis for making up his own mind as to what kind of party system he wants. That task we propose to undertake in the following and final section of the present chapter.

Would a More "Responsible" Party System Be More "Democratic"?

THE DOCTRINE OF RESPONSIBLE PARTY GOVERNMENT [7]

The Need for Improved Governmental Action. The advocates of responsible party government argue that the government of the United States today faces domestic and foreign problems of such magnitude that they can be solved only by comprehensive, internally consistent, and expertly designed programs of public policy that are consistently supported both by a majority of federal officeholders and by a majority of the people throughout the nation. Anything less than such programs risks national disaster. We do not, however, want such programs *any* way we can get them; rather we want them to be developed, adopted, and executed *democratically*. In other words, we want not *action* alone, but *democratic* action as well.[8]

The Crucial Role of the Parties. The national political parties, according to these writers, are the only agencies that can conceivably provide us with the kind of governmental action just described. They are comprehensive and representative in their membership and leadership, while their only possible rivals, the pressure groups, are limited and narrow in both respects. The parties are concerned with the *national* interest, while each pressure group is concerned only with its particular *special* interest. The parties operate in the open and deal directly with the voters, while the pressure groups operate largely in se-

[7] For a general summary of this position, see Austin Ranney, *The Doctrine of Responsible Party Government* (Urbana: University of Illinois Press, 1954), Ch. II; and for summaries of the ideas of Wilson, Ford, and Goodnow, see Ranney, Chs. III, V, VI. The leading present-day expositions of the argument summarized in the text are: E. E. Schattschneider, *Party Government* and *The Struggle for Party Government* (College Park, Md.: Program in American Civilization, University of Maryland, 1948); the Committee on Political Parties of the American Political Science Association, "Toward a More Responsible Two-Party System," *American Political Science Review*, Vol. XLIV (September, 1950), Supplement; James M. Burns, *Congress on Trial* (New York: Harper and Brothers, 1949); and Fritz Morstein Marx, "Party Responsibility and Legislative Program," *Columbia Law Review*, Vol. L (March, 1950), pp. 281-99.

[8] Some of the writers associated with this school put a great deal more emphasis upon the necessity for *action* than upon the importance of such action's being taken *democratically*. Schattschneider and the Committee on Political Parties, however, emphasize each value about equally.

cret and deal for the most part only with governmental officials. If we are to have democratic and comprehensive programs for the national interest, then, only the national parties can provide them.

The Inadequacy of Our Present Party System. The responsible-party-government writers are convinced that our present national parties are incapable of furnishing the nation with the kind of governmental action described above. The argument runs as follows. The parties' lack of cohesion both inside and outside the government makes it impossible for them to draw up or execute sense-making programs of public policy. And this same lack of cohesion also prevents the voters from holding *either* party "responsible" in any meaningful sense for whatever the government does or does not do. Our present system of decentralized and loose parties and the pluralistic "concurrent-majority" kind of policy-making process they foster makes for *in*action rather than action; and it therefore simply cannot handle such problems as resisting Communist aggression without bringing on thermonuclear war, or stabilizing the economy without stagnating it—problems that by their very nature demand vigorous, coherent, and *national* action.[9] Consequently, the present party system breaks down in time of crisis and in the face of such problems, and policy is made by "presidential dictatorship." We therefore cannot escape the conclusion that the present parties are incapable of sustaining democratic government at such times.

Necessary Party Reforms. In order to get the kind of governmental action we need, these writers contend, we must make our party system more "responsible." In particular, they advocate at least the following types of party reforms.

CENTRALIZATION. The control of the parties must be taken out of the hands of the congeries of state and local leaders and organizations where it now resides, and put into the hands of the *national* leaders and organizations. The Committee on Political Parties has made the most specific proposal for accomplishing this reform. They propose that each major party create a party council of fifty members, composed of representatives from the national committee, the congressional party organizations, the state committees, the party's governors, organizations like the Young Republicans and Young Democrats, members-at-large chosen by the national convention, the presidential and vice-presidential incumbents and nominees, and the highest national party officials. The council should meet regularly and often, and propose a preliminary draft of the platform to the national convention, interpret the platform during the campaign and after, and generally act as the party's authoritative spokesman on policy matters.[10]

DISCIPLINE. The national party leaders must have the power to keep the party's members in public office in line behind the party's program. Although exactly *how* this power is to be exercised is not made clear, the implication

---

[9] Cf. Peter F. Drucker, "A Key to American Politics: Calhoun's Pluralism," *Review of Politics,* Vol. X (October, 1948), pp. 421-24.

[10] "Toward a More Responsible Two-Party System," pp. 43-44.

seems to be that our national party leaders should, like their counterparts in the British parties, have the power to control local party nominations and thus to grant or refuse permission for a congressional candidate to run for office under the party's label.[11]

INTRAPARTY DEMOCRACY? The Committee on Political Parties argues that "intraparty democracy" (i.e., "the responsibility of the party leaders to the party members, as enforced in primaries, caucuses, and conventions") must be maximized, since it is a good thing in itself and since it will induce party members to argue themselves into agreement and thus supplement discipline as a device for getting party cohesion.[12] On the other hand, Schattschneider, as we noted in Chapter 9, argues that such notions, if acted upon, are likely to keep the parties loose and decentralized and therefore "irresponsible." Democracy, he insists, can result only from a certain kind of relation *between* the parties, never from any kind of situation *within* the parties.[13] This, however, is the only major issue on which the advocates of more "responsible" parties are seriously divided among themselves.

The Prospects for Action. As we noted in Chapter 21, the advocates of more centralized and disciplined parties argue that the American people can have such parties any time they want them. Admittedly, the people have not as yet set up any great clamor for a reformed party system; but, as Schattschneider argues,

The revolution in communications, the dissolution of nationality blocs, the impact of the labor movement, urbanization, the revolution in public policy, the expansion of the practicing electorate in recent years, and the new world position of the United States are only a few of the influences likely to give an impetus to political reorganization in the present generation. It is obvious that the *purposes* of political organization are not what they once were. There was a time when it might have been said that the *purpose* of the party system, or of large parts of it, was *obstruction*. In an era of perpetual crisis political organization is reasonably certain to reflect the anxieties that now dominate all public life.[14]

THE DEFENSE OF THE PRESENT PARTY SYSTEM [15]

The case against making our parties more centralized and disciplined may be briefly summarized as follows.

Questions About the British Model. The advocates of more "responsible" parties regard the British party system—or rather an idealized version of it—as

---

[11] *Ibid.,* pp. 43-44, 48, 52-53, 61, 66-67.

[12] Cf. *ibid.,* pp. 23-24, 65-70.

[13] Cf. Schattschneider, *Party Government,* pp. 57-61.

[14] Schattschneider, *The Struggle for Party Government,* pp. 28-29. Italics in the original.

[15] The leading general defenses of our present party system are: Pendleton Herring, *The Politics of Democracy* (New York: Rinehart & Company, Inc., 1940); Herbert Agar, *The Price of Union* (Boston: Houghton Mifflin Company, 1950); and Ernest S. Griffith, *Congress: Its Contemporary Role* (New York: New York University Press, 1951). Some critical analyses of the Report of the Committee on Political Parties are: T. William Goodman, "How Much Political Party Centralization Do We Want?" *Journal of Politics,* Vol. XIII (November, 1951), pp. 536-61;

a working model of the kind of party system they want to see the United States adopt. British parties, they feel, actually do put forth internally consistent, sense-making, *and* clearly distinguishable programs arrived at in each party by a process of intraparty discussion and decision. Accordingly, British parties present the voters with a clear choice at each election. Moreover, the high party cohesion and discipline that result from the national party leaders' power to approve or disapprove local candidates for Parliament mean that the majority party is always clearly and unequivocally responsible for how the government is run. Hence, if someone objects, "But the kind of party system you advocate simply cannot work," these writers can (and often do) reply, "Of course it can: look at the British system!"

Some writers, however, have raised questions about the British model and its applicability to American conditions. For one thing, they say, the British party system does not in fact operate as its idealizers believe. And they have received impressive support for this argument from a recent article by David Butler, Fellow of Nuffield College, Oxford, and one of the leading British writers on the British party system, in which he explodes two "American myths about British parties." [16] The first of these "myths" is that British parties offer the voters distinct and sharply differentiated programs. The fact is, says Butler, that the Conservative and Labor parties have clearly disagreed with each other on only one issue since 1945, that of the nationalization of certain industries; and even that issue has become very minor, since Labor now makes few demands for more nationalization and the Tories are willing to accept what nationalization now exists. The main differences between the parties now are merely those between "ins" and the "outs." Butler even argues that "the fate of Britain ten years hence will be far less affected by whether the Conservatives or the Labour Party win the next election, than the fate of the United States will be affected by the decision it will have to take in 1956 between a Republican and a Democrat [for president]." [17] The second "myth" is that party policy is made by the rank and file via "intraparty democracy." Here, Butler says, Americans should not mistake the form for the reality; for the fact is that the parliamentary leadership of each party makes the party's policy, though with due regard for the forms and for the sensibilities of the rank and file, and sees that it gets adopted. For example, despite the fact that the Labor rank and file in many of the constituency organizations are enthusiastic followers of Aneurin Bevan, the party itself is unquestionably controlled by Bevan's right-wing opponents—so that in a considerable number of instances Bevanite con-

Austin Ranney, "Toward a More Responsible Two-party System: A Commentary," *American Political Science Review*, Vol. XLV (June, 1951), pp. 488-99; Murray S. Stedman, Jr., and Herbert Sonthoff, "Party Responsibility—A Critical Inquiry," *Western Political Quarterly*, Vol. IV (September, 1951), pp. 454-68; and Julius Turner, "Responsible Parties: A Dissent from the Floor," *American Political Science Review*, Vol. XLV (March, 1951), pp. 143-52.

[16] David Butler, "American Myths about British Parties," *Virginia Quarterly Review*, Vol. XXXI (Winter, 1955), pp. 46-56.

[17] *Ibid.*, pp. 51-52.

stituency organizations have to accept and campaign for *anti*-Bevanite Labor candidates.[18] Butler concludes: "Much may be wrong with American parties, but those who have looked to the British system for remedies have surely erred in their analysis of its excellencies." [19]

The "excellency" of the British system most admired by American advocates of more "responsible" American parties, however, is the high cohesion and strong discipline of the British parliamentary parties; and Butler does not deny that these phenomena exist. But British parties are cohesive and disciplined, according to our second group of writers, because of the special nature of the British community and its belief system, which, in certain crucial respects, differs sharply from the American community and *its* belief system. Concretely, the leaders of both British parties are for the most part drawn from the public-school–Oxford–Cambridge "ruling class"; and the parties operate within a highly centralized culture, in which most Britons read London newspapers, listen to the B.B.C., and have no commitment to anything resembling the American traditions of "federalism" and "states' rights." Until we develop American equivalents for the British traditions of the "gentleman in politics" and unitarism, argue these writers, we are not likely either to want or to be able to get British-type parties.[20]

Great Britain, moreover, pays a price for having the kind of parties it has. In Ernest Griffith's words, when the investigator goes behind the scenes in England, he finds such things as these:

A bureaucracy maturing almost all legislation and increasing by leaps and bounds; the two parties outbidding each other with promises of governmental largesse, so as to attract marginal groups; a division of the nation along class lines; the sacrifice of independence of thought and action on the part of the individual member; the pressing home of such a drastic measure as the nationalization of steel, though a majority of the voters supported candidates opposed to it at the last election.[21]

The British party system, furthermore, breaks down in a crisis every bit as much as does the American system. As Professor Arthur N. Holcombe points out, of the fourteen ministries that have held office since the Parliament Act of 1911, only six, holding office only about a third of the time, have been composed solely of representatives of a single party approved by a majority of all the voters. Of the others, which together have held office about two-thirds of the time, five have been coalition or "national" ministries composed of representatives from several parties, and three have been formed by a single

[18] *Ibid.*, pp. 54-55.

[19] *Ibid.*, p. 56.

[20] Cf. Herring, *op. cit.*, pp. 53-59; Norton E. Long, "Party Government and the United States," *Journal of Politics*, Vol. XIII (May, 1951), pp. 187-214; and Don K. Price, "The Parliamentary and Presidential Systems," *Public Administration Review*, Vol. III (Autumn, 1943), pp. 317-34.

[21] *Op. cit.*, pp. 156-57.

party having less than a majority in the House of Commons and in the nation, and have held office only by the temporary sufferance of the other parties.[22] In the British party system, therefore, the "national" or "all-party" ministry is the equivalent of "presidential dictatorship" in the American system —that is, what the governing system turns to when, in time of crisis, the party system ceases to function "normally." And the incidence of such deviations from the party-system "norm" are certainly at least as frequent in Great Britain as in the United States.

The Probable Price of Centralized and Disciplined Parties. In order to determine whether we want centralized and disciplined parties, say our second group of writers, Americans must understand the probable price of such parties and decide whether the probable benefits are worth it. The major items in the bill such parties would present the nation are as follows.

THE BREAKDOWN OF FEDERALISM. The primary purpose of centralizing and disciplining our parties is to enable them to formulate and execute *national* programs without regard to the demands of state and local interests and organizations. The technique for accomplishing it is to vest control of the state and local parties—and, through them, the state and local governments—in the hands of the national party leaders, so that state and local interference with national programs will be reduced to an absolute minimum. It may well be, therefore, that if such a party system were developed in the United States, it would mean the end of the reality if not of the form of federalism, and the states would become little more than administrative subdivisions of the national government. Perhaps the American people desire—or ought to desire— the demise of federalism and the installation of unitarism; but at least they should recognize that such a development would likely be a part of the price for centralized and disciplined national parties.[23]

A MULTIPLE-PARTY SYSTEM. The advocates of more "responsible" national parties seem to assume that the new party alignments would pit a party made up of all the nation's "liberals" against another made up of all its "conservatives," thus retaining at least the two-party feature of our present national party system. But political conflict in the United States is enormously more multifarious and complicated than a simple division between pro–New Dealers and anti–New Dealers; and a great many groups could find their home in neither party. Suppose, for example, that the "conservative" party firmly and unmistakably pledged itself to oppose any federal civil-rights legislation, to end or greatly reduce farm price-supports, to end or greatly reduce our economic and military commitments abroad, and to prevent any further federal development of electric power and water resources. Could such a party hope to carry the South, the rural and urban areas of the East and Middle West, and the Northwest? By the same token, could a "liberal" party taking the opposite

[22] Arthur N. Holcombe, *Our More Perfect Union* (Cambridge, Mass.: Harvard University Press, 1950), pp. 410-11.
[23] Cf. Griffith, *op. cit.*, p. 167; Goodman, *op. cit.;* and Stedman and Sonthoff, *op. cit.*

stand on each of these issues hope to carry all those sections? If the "liberals," for instance, pledged themselves to a national civil-rights program and meant business about it, the conservatives could hardly do less unless they were re-signed to being a permanent minority. In such a situation, what would the South do? Form a third party? Or, as now, simply defy the national platform of whatever party it operated within? In the former case, we would get a mul-tiple-party system; in the latter, there would be no essential change from our present system.[24]

It has often been remarked that the congeries of bipartisan and intraparty "blocs" in Congress is, in effect, a multiple-party system masquerading under the labels and formalities of a two-party system. To the extent that this is an accurate description of our present national party system, it results, not from any mere organizational deficiency in our national party machinery, but rather from the diversity and multiplicity of our interest groups and the heterogeneity and complexity of the political conflict they express.[25] So long as the basic na-ture of the American community remains the same, therefore, centralizing and disciplining our national parties would very likely result in a multiple-party rather than a two-party system.

But perhaps the new parties could change the nature of the community itself. What would be the likely result of that?

THE BREAKDOWN OF CONSENSUS. If each of our national parties were central-ized and disciplined, it would have to mobilize electoral support in a consid-erably different manner from that employed by our present parties. It would have to make specific promises to certain groups, and, accordingly, reject with equal specificity the demands of certain other groups. Moreover, the winning party would have to fulfill its promises pretty much to the limit, since the groups supporting it might well regard the party's failure to keep its promises as even worse than not making them at all or making them in vague and loose terms. The most likely result of such a situation would be the near-complete identification of particular groups with particular parties—labor and the lower-income groups with the "liberals," business and the higher-income groups with the "conservatives." And this, in turn, would clearly and unmis-takably pit one class against another class in such a way that conflicts between them would become cumulative rather than, as at present, blurred and dis-persed.[26]

Take, for example, the present bitter controversy over racial segregation in the southern public schools. On the one hand we have a group, spoken for by the NAACP, which regards the ending of all such segregation immediately as a matter of the most sacred rights of man and the most urgent necessity.

[24] Cf. Griffith, *op. cit.*, pp. 159-61; Stedman and Sonthoff, *op. cit.*

[25] Cf. Bertram M. Gross, *The Legislative Struggle* (New York: McGraw-Hill Book Company, Inc., 1953), p. 73; Robin M. Williams, Jr., *American Society* (New York: Alfred A. Knopf, 1951), p. 518.

[26] Cf. Herring, *op. cit.*, p. 102; Agar, *op. cit.*, p. 689; Griffith, *op. cit.*, pp. 157, 162-65; Price, *op. cit.*

On the other hand we have opposed to them another group, spoken for by the "Dixiecrat" element of the Democratic party, which regards the continuation of such segregation as absolutely essential to the whole southern way of life and its most cherished values. Clearly there is a high "civil-war potential" in this explosive situation. Our present politico-governmental system, as we noted in Chapter 20, is handling it as it handles all such matters: both major parties make vague platform declarations in favor of "equal rights for all races," but neither pledges itself to the federal enforcement of desegregation of southern schools come what may. The Supreme Court greatly pleases the anti-segregation group by declaring segregation unconstitutional—but federal troops are not ordered into South Carolina and Mississippi to make sure the Court's decision is carried out; and if the anti-segregationists were to make any such proposal, the southern senators would certainly filibuster it to death. The situation, however, is not entirely static: in Washington, D. C., and in the border states, segregation is being ended completely in some schools and modified in others. Thus the anti-segregationists and the pro-segregationists each get part—but not all—of what they want; no interracial or intersectional civil war breaks out; and a situation is preserved in which the gradual erosion of southern-white attitudes toward the Negroes that has been taking place during the past quarter-century or more—and in which, in the present writers' opinion, lies the best hope for the ultimate solution of this difficult problem— can continue its work. Certainly this is not the "swift, purposive, and vigorous" national governmental action demanded by the advocates of more "responsible" parties; but it *is* a kind of action which, whatever else can be said about it, preserves our consensus and yet does not permanently fix the status of Negro schoolchildren at its present level.

Suppose, however, we had centralized and disciplined parties. Both the Negroes and the southern whites are large and significant blocs of voters, and it seems unlikely that either would be content with parties which took clear positions on all other issues and acted upon them when in power but remained silent or vague on this particular issue. Either each group would form a third party, or one of the major parties would take up its cause. Suppose, again, that the "liberal" party pledged itself to end segregation and the "conservative" party to defend it. If, as now seems likely, the "liberals" won an election on this issue, they would either have to redeem their pledge, probably by sending federal troops into the South to enforce desegregation, or welsh on it in an "irresponsible" manner. Neither line of action would satisfy *both* groups to the extent that they are being satisfied under our present party system; and the consequences of the former for the American community are too obvious to be described, and should be taken into account in any attempt to calculate the social costs of centralized, disciplined, and programmatically precise national political parties in the United States.

Conclusion

As the reader should be well aware, the present writers, like the second group of commentators whose views we have just summarized, feel that the American party system as it now exists performs a role of great usefulness in our national politics and government; that, judged by the criterion of our conception of democracy, that role is of great value and deserving of high praise; and that the price America would probably have to pay for more centralized and disciplined national parties is, from the standpoint of democracy and in the light of the present nature of the American community, too high. We are, however, aware that other students of these matters have come to quite different conclusions. Our purpose in the present chapter as in the entire book, therefore, has been, not to persuade the reader to adopt our point of view and to accept uncritically our particular conclusions, but rather to help him understand the issues involved as they affect the prospects for realizing *his*— not our—values. And our hope is that, in this at least, we have had some success.

Index

Index